McFarlin Library
WITHDRAWN

WAR MEMOIRS OF
DAVID LLOYD GEORGE
1917–1918

M. CLEMENCEAU AND MR. LLOYD GEORGE

WAR MEMOIRS

of

DAVID LLOYD GEORGE

★ ★ ★ ★ ★

1917–1918

WITH ILLUSTRATIONS

LITTLE, BROWN, AND COMPANY

BOSTON 1936

Copyright, 1936,
BY DAVID LLOYD GEORGE

All rights reserved

Published December, 1936

PRINTED IN THE UNITED STATES OF AMERICA

CONTENTS

I	OUTLOOK FOR 1918	3
II	THE BELLIGERENTS STATE THEIR PEACE TERMS	19
III	BOLSHEVISM CONQUERS RUSSIA	74
IV	THE PROBLEM OF MAN POWER	133
V	CLEMENCEAU	194
VI	THE MILITARY POSITION	206
VII	EXTENSION OF THE BRITISH FRONT	265
VIII	THE FALL OF ROBERTSON	285
IX	BEFORE THE OFFENSIVE	325
X	THE MARCH RETREAT	363
XI	THE AMERICAN ARMIES IN FRANCE	394
	INDEX	455

ILLUSTRATIONS

M. Clemenceau and Mr. Lloyd George	*Frontispiece*
Lenin	76
Extension of the British Front January 1918	226
Field Marshal Sir Henry Wilson	312
The March Retreat	368
General John J. Pershing, Commander-in-Chief American Expeditionary Forces	408

WAR MEMOIRS OF
DAVID LLOYD GEORGE
1917–1918

CHAPTER I

OUTLOOK FOR 1918

Spreading war-weariness — Military situation — Cost of Allied offensives — British Army exhausted — Casualties exceed estimates — State of German Army — Italian Front — Successes at sea against Turkey — Military balance in favour of Central Powers — German estimates of outlook — Our last opportunity in Turkey — Advice of Versailles experts — Bulgarian weakness — Austrian food shortage — German Transport problem — Supplies from Russia — German estimate of American menace — Mutual miscalculations — British pacifists encourage Ludendorff.

THE federated nations were now facing their fifth campaign. They were all exhausted and all disillusioned. The war fever had burnt itself out long ago in all the warring countries. Enthusiasms had cooled down. There were no more patriotic demonstrations in the streets. Ours was the only country where anti-War organisations were allowed to pursue their activities and to organise public meetings. Even amongst the supporters of the War there was a deep and silent prayer that it would come to an end soon. But nowhere except in Russia was there any indication that the belligerent peoples were ready to give in. The struggle was kept going by that stubborn determination not to turn tail which keeps brave animals fighting as long as they can stand.

A superficial review of the appearance of the vast battlefield as a whole would lead to the conclusion that the Central Powers were winning. Serbia and Belgium were almost entirely in their hands. The greater part of Roumania was occupied by their troops. The Russian armies had ceased to exist as a fighting force and were rapidly disintegrating into a mutinous rabble. The heroic if unintelligent and ill-coordinated efforts put forth in 1917 by the armies of France and Britain to drive the Germans out of Belgium and the occupied territories of France had been sanguinary failures. So shattering had been the French repulse that it had temporarily destroyed the morale and undermined the discipline of their fine army, and, since the defeat of April, 1917, French troops could not be relied upon for any operation that involved sustained attack on a great scale. It was not certain that after a year's rest and recuperation French soldiers could be depended upon for a campaign which would involve the only kind of effort which could hope to break through the German defence. General Pétain was for concentrating on defence in 1918 and postponing the final offensive until 1919. He reckoned that by 1919 the Americans would be ready with an army that would give the Allies that overwhelming strength which would enable them to overcome the resistance of an enemy worn out by five campaigns. As to the British Army, it kept on fighting doggedly right into the December mists, but it was tired and without confidence in the wisdom of the leadership which was responsible for the stupid and squalid strategy of the last two months of Passchendaele, and for the egregious muddle which threw away the great opportunities of Cambrai.

The unsuccessful and costly offensives of 1915–1916–1917 had impaired the Allied strength and efficiency in two directions: —

1. They wasted the best man power of the Allied Nations without either attaining any strategic advantage or inflicting corresponding, let alone greater, losses on the enemy. In these battles, as a whole, the Allies lost three men for every two who fell on the German side. Every one of these futile offensives thus reduced substantially the superiority in effective man power which the Allies possessed at the commencement of the War. The irreparable losses amongst experienced officers and N.C.O.'s were much heavier in the

French and British Armies than on the side of the enemy. This increased the weight of the adverse balance of casualties.

2. The British Army, which in June was the most formidable force on the Allied side, had fought incessantly from March up to the first week in December a series of terrible battles without achieving any strategic results. These sanguinary attacks had succeeded, with excessive losses, in creating two fresh salients which were admitted by G.H.Q. to be untenable. That is, the ghastly sacrifices of our fine Army had increased the strategic advantages of the enemy. The Expeditionary Force was weary in body and spirit. To quote the words of the French Official History of the War: —

"It was manifest now at the beginning of winter that the English Army was passing through a phase of weariness, a consequence of the substantial and sustained efforts put up throughout the summer; it was at length beginning to experience the gravest difficulty in reconstituting its forces; in mid-December, its infantry showed a deficit of 116,000 men." [1]

Haig talked about "the fatigue of his forces"; he alluded to them as his "weary and depleted units", pleaded that "having been engaged on the offensive since the spring" his army had been unable to devote either adequate men or time to the organisation of the British Front for the defensive.

Both the fatigue and the depletion due to these ceaseless offensives played a great part in the British unpreparedness for meeting the enemy assault in the spring. The pervading weariness prejudicially affected the physique, the training and the tone of the whole Army, from the High Command to the infantry in the trenches and the labour battalions who had been working incessantly behind the lines. Nervous and mental lassitude can alone explain the extraordinary inde-

[1] "Les armées français dans la grande guerra", Vol. VI.

cision and inactivity of our G.H.Q. which characterised the three months that followed the end of the 1917 campaign. It permeated mind as well as muscle.

The effect on our reserves of the slaughter that never for one hour stopped either day or night for four months was inevitable. When the Cabinet Committee were considering in June, 1917, the Commander-in-Chief's proposals for an advance in Flanders, Sir William Robertson calculated, on the basis of estimates furnished by G.H.Q., that 130,000 men would cover the losses sustained on the whole British Front during the period of the offensive. We actually sent to France during the progress of the battle a much larger number to make up losses. As Sir William Robertson told Field-Marshal Haig in his letter of November 3rd, 1917, the Government had done better in the matter of infantry drafts to France during 1917 than they had promised. Haig had been informed that the numbers which would be sent to France between March 1st and October 31st would amount to 356,-000. The drafts actually sent totalled 376,000 men. The ghastly massacres of the Flanders campaign completely falsified the estimates of the Chief of the Imperial General Staff; the total casualties on the whole British Front during the progress of the battle mounted up to the appalling figure of 399,000 men — three times the official military estimate. The infantry bore the brunt of these casualties. Had the original forecast been justified, there would have been an increase in the actual numbers of our combatant strength on the Western Front of 160,000 instead of a deficit of 100,000 men. For the massacre of brave men that won just four miles of indefensible mud the Government were not prepared by any warning or prediction given us by the military leaders. When we discovered what the actual deficit was, no conceivable measures taken by us then could have closed that bleeding gash before the end of March.

What about the German fatigue and losses in this campaign? They also were kept fighting until the first week in December, but their casualties were far less than ours. Their total losses on the British Front between July 1st and December 31st, 1917, amounted to 270,000. Had the casualties we inflicted on them been equal to those we sustained, the Germans could not have claimed any superiority in numbers for the spring offensive.

What about the tiredness of the German troops who had been engaged in these conflicts? Most of our soldiers had been flung into the battle of the morass between July and December; just over half of the German forces on the Western Front had fought in the Flanders campaign, and there was no exceptional strain placed upon the divisions which held the rest of the line. Moreover, the continuous stream of divisions that was brought over from Russia between December and March had already enjoyed a period of prolonged rest on that front. For months the fighting in Russia had been quite negligible. Their task was tedious but not tiring. These contrasts constituted the most serious disadvantage in which we were placed by the events of the last few months. There is some controversy as to whether we had more combatants on the Western Front than the Germans possessed on March 21st, 1918, or whether there was a small percentage in their favour. Even if the latter estimate were correct, a slight superiority, which would not appear till March, in the numbers of the German infantry would not have put in jeopardy an army defending prepared positions against an attack by troops who had all passed through the same exhausting experiences as themselves. The Germans had held the Western Front for two years against a combination which was 50 per cent. stronger than their own as far as numbers were concerned. The Allies, in spite of German reinforcements from the Eastern Front, had a considerable superiority in the West in the matter of guns, aeroplanes, tanks and machine-guns.

What was the position on the Austro-Italian Front? The Italian Army had been beaten and broken in one of the most disastrous defeats sustained by the Allied Powers since the early days of the War. It was being reformed and reconstituted, but that process would take time. Nothing much in the way of a serious offensive could be expected from the Italians during the campaign of 1918.

There were two areas in the vast battle where the Allies had done well. On the ocean the British Fleet were beating off the submarine attack, and in the East the British Armies had driven two Turkish Armies before them in headlong rout, captured some of the most famous cities in history, and reduced the Turkish Empire to such a state of exhaustion that one more resolute push would make it crumble to bits. The Turkish Army was utterly demoralised; its establishments were reduced by desertion to a half: so that in every regiment there was one deserter from the colours for every man that remained.

Nevertheless, taking East and West as a whole, on balance the *land* campaign had gone unmistakably in favour of the Central Powers. The less spectacular, but more decisive, fact of Britain's renewed command at sea was at the time not recorded and was ignored by the military advisers of the Allies. All they knew was that supplies of ammunition and food reached them regularly and in increasing quantities. The way to ultimate triumph was sought by great Generals on land. The life and death struggle on the great waters was never alluded to by the military chiefs of the Alliance, except insofar as it was used as an argument for withholding reinforcements of troops and munitions to remote battle areas. There is not a hint in any military appreciation by the British or French Staff of the events of 1917 or of the prospects for 1918, that the issue of the struggle with the submarines would ultimately decide the fate of the War.

The military situation at the end of the 1917 campaign thus gave a misleading impression of the relative position of the contending nations and of the actual progress of the War and of its prospects. The German leaders — both military and civilian — realised better the actual state of affairs. Documents revealed since the War display the great anxiety felt by both the German High Command and the political chiefs on two questions: food, and the weakening of Germany's allies. In these two respects the situation was becoming so critical that the German High Command agreed that a final decision must be forced early in 1918, as it was considered unlikely that the Central Powers could feed their populations or that the tottering allies of the Fatherland could or would stagger through into 1919. These allies were fast becoming liabilities, not assets. To use Herr Hitler's striking phrase, the fate of Germany was entangled in a "coalition of cripples." The military ardour of Germany's allies was evaporating for many causes. The Turkish and Bulgarian peasants realised that they were being sacrificed in a quarrel which was not their own. The Turkish officers were sulky with resentment at the imperious Germans who bullied and shouted about inefficiencies and ineptitudes which were part of the tradition of the Turkish Army. The Turk was made to feel more and more that this was a German War, and that his interests were made subservient to those of the arrogant Goth. He saw that he was not fighting for Islam. Two groups of infidel nations were struggling for mastery. Which of them won was no concern of his. The Anatolian peasants therefore deserted the army not only by the thousand, but by the hundred thousand.

These facts must have been known to the Intelligence Department of our War Office, or at least, they ought to have been known. They were however withheld from the War Cabinet. For the War Cabinet was predisposed to strike a blow there, to disintegrate the Turks still more, to eliminate them completely; so a bandage had to be kept on its eyes, lest the realities of the situation should unduly encourage it to take exceptional measures to exploit Turkish disintegration in order to eliminate that Empire from the War. One-fifth of the men uselessly sacrificed at Passchendaele could have achieved that end, and put the Turks out of business by the end of 1917. The large British forces engaged on the two Turkish Fronts would have been available partly to reinforce our Army in France, partly to strengthen our troops on the Vardar. Bulgaria, with her Turkish flank uncovered, could not have resisted an attack. Roumania would then have revived her effort and Austria would thus have been outflanked, and the effect on Russia would have been incalculable. Nothing but substantial help given by Germany in troops and equipment could have saved a break-up of the Central Alliance.

The first intimation given to us of the actual military situation in Turkey was in the famous paper prepared by the military advisers at Versailles which is known as Note 12.[1] But the Germans were fully aware of the deplorable state of the Turkish forces, and it was one of the circumstances that drove them to the inevitable conclusion that their Far Eastern ally might not be able to see them through 1918 — certainly not beyond that year. As to Bulgaria, her peasant soldiers were heartily tired of the War. Their traditional enemies, the Turks, were now their allies. Their Serbian foes were a broken and a fugitive remnant in a strange land. The Bulgarian people were never united on the wisdom of joining the Central Alliance, and now Bulgarian fields were neglected, the harvests were disappointing, the cultivators lived in

[1] The text of Note 12 is given on page 251.

trenches on the bleak slopes of the Balkans, far from their beloved plains. What for? The peasant is a slow thinker, but although his mind travels slowly, he plods unerringly to the end of his journey, and he ultimately realised that all his privations and perils were endured, not for the honour, the security or the enlargement of Bulgaria, which could have been better assured by a timely understanding with the Western Powers, but in order to achieve the domination of the Teuton in Eastern Europe. This growing conviction weakened the fine fighting mettle of the Bulgarian soldiers. They became less and less eager to incur the risks and discomforts of this endless, and for them purposeless, war.

The General Staffs of the Western Powers do not seem to have understood what was going on, for they anticipated a strong enemy offensive in the Balkans as part of the troubles for which they had to provide in 1918. It appeared to them probable that the Germans and Austrians might divert to the Balkans some of the divisions released from Russia and this contingency caused them much apprehension. Only towards the autumn of the year 1918 did they discover how completely the fighting spirit of the Bulgarian Army had evaporated. But the Germans knew it well by the end of 1917. This aggravated their worry about the issue of the War if it were prolonged into the autumn of 1918.

But there is something still worse. The War Cabinet was left in ignorance not only of the Balkan, but also of the Austrian situation. Facts that have come to our knowledge since the War demonstrated clearly that by the end of 1917 and the beginning of 1918 Austria was almost at the point of collapse, owing to the food situation in that country, and General von Arz made urgent representations from Vienna to the German G.H.Q., in December, 1917, that "a number of armies had not even a single day's ration of flour in their possession."[1] The Army rations had to be severely cut down early in January, and it was reported officially that "the conditions were in fact of such a kind that only the endurance of the severest deprivations made it possible for them [Austria] to hold out."[1] The plenipotentiary of the Imperial War Food Ministry in Vienna, Baron von Raberau, reported on January 20th, 1918: —

"Whether Austria will be in a position to last out through February is questionable. . . .

"Without any kind of reserves people will be living day by day from hand to mouth."[1]

He implies that help from Germany is essential even to postpone the collapse until February, and he adds: —

"How far Germany still has an interest in supporting Austria will have to be regarded, no longer merely from the standpoint of German food supply, but as a question of high policy."[1]

Seidler, President of the Austrian Ministry, and Landwehr, Austrian General of Supplies, reported: —

"The situation is as follows: Without help from outside, masses of the people will be dying in a few weeks. Germany and Hungary will contribute no more."[1]

The Germans were in no position to contribute. Their own population was already suffering from the food shortage. The vitality of the people at home was being lowered. Even the men in the trenches had to be rationed severely, in some important ingredients of food. But Herr Seidler's reference to Hungary has a meaning. It shows that both the Germans and the Austrians were convinced that Hungary had a surplus of corn and meat but that she selfishly appropriated it for her own needs. That conviction was ominous;

[1] Report of the Reichstag Commission, Vol. III.

it was another sign of the approaching disruption in the ramshackle Empire. The Allied Governments were not fully apprised of the real condition of things in Austria-Hungary. It was vital to decision on the plans for 1918 that these facts should be known. But if the Army Intelligence Departments were in possession of the truth they did not pass it on to their respective Governments. Ludendorff and his Staff, however, knew it, and so did the Kaiser and his Ministers, and they came to the conclusion that Germany must anticipate that the structure of her alliances would crumble away before the end of 1918. Her own food situation was becoming more and more precarious. Even a good harvest would leave her with a shortage of 300,000 tons of corn, and her meat and milk supplies were quite inadequate to meet the minimum requirements of her Army and her population. There was a crippling shortage of fodder for the horses at the front. This, coupled with the lack of sufficient rubber, lubricants and petrol, reduced seriously the mobility of the German Army. Not merely was there an inadequate supply of draught-horses, but the deficiency of grain to keep up their strength considerably impaired their value. These conditions, whether they were known or not to the Allied Staffs, never seemed to be taken into account in their comparisons of the relative capacity of the two armies for waging such a campaign as was anticipated in 1918. Rapidity of movement was essential on both sides for conducting an offensive on a great scale, now on one part and then on another part of the front. It is computed by competent military authorities that, owing to these shortages in the essentials of transport, no more than a third of the German Army could be regarded as mobile, the remaining two thirds not being equipped with the necessary means of removal from one sector to another.

When we come to the story of the campaign of 1918, this paramount consideration will account for the long intervals which supervened between one great German attack and another, even when the time left to them was short and fast running out. During these anxious weeks, when every day we anticipated a renewal of the attack before we were able to reorganise a new front, I was at a loss to understand why Ludendorff gave us so much time to reinforce and reform our broken divisions, and to dig and wire formidable new positions. On the other hand, when the fateful moment came for Foch to launch his offensive he gave the German Army no time for restoration or reformation. The difference in the temperament of these two great soldiers is not altogether responsible for the contrast in their methods. It was largely a question of the mobility of the rival armies. The Allies were abundantly supplied with the means of transport to and from railheads. I was given a striking illustration of the extent to which deficiences of transport hampered the movement of the German Army at a critical juncture by the late Hugo Stinnes. In the course of a conversation I had with him after the War, I asked him to explain why the victorious German Army did not capture Amiens in March, 1918. I informed him that they had already got through all our defences, and that we had no organised forces between the German advance guard and that city. He said it was entirely due to the breakdown in their transport, owing to the lack of rubber. There was a sharp snowstorm, the rubberless wheel rims became clogged, and it was impossible to bring up the necessary ammunition for the troops and for the guns. The soldiers could not even be fed.

The shortage of food in Central Europe indirectly diminished the number of German and Austrian troops that could be released for operations in the west owing to the Russian peace. The only hope which the Central Powers had of obtaining supplies of food and certain essential raw materials was in the exploitation of Russia. This could not be done without employing considerable forces in the occupation of the Russian cornfields and in pushing forward into the regions where oil was obtainable. These garrison and far-distant raiding columns absorbed a number of both German and Austrian divisions. Most of them, but not all, were of secondary quality, but even these, if brought to the west, could have occupied quiet sectors and could have released fighting divisions for the battle front. They would also have been helpful as labour battalions.

All these considerations drove the German General Staff to the conclusion that a decision must be forced at the earliest possible moment.

That is why the German High Command did not attach overwhelming importance to the American Army. They did not anticipate that its intervention would count for a great deal until late in the campaign of 1918. They were confident of destroying one or other or both of the Allied Armies in France before the Americans were in a position to render effective aid. Their information as to the progress of American recruitment, training and equipment was on the whole accurate. They knew that a vast number of men had been called to the colours in the United States of America, but they also knew that their training was very deficient and their equipment utterly inadequate. They were also fully persuaded that "the preoccupation of tonnage with the supplying of the Entente excluded any extensive transport of troops, especially so long as the U-boat warfare was being maintained." Their conclusion on this point was "We need not therefore bother about the question as to the extent to which the Entente is in a position to bring strong American forces to Europe."[1] It is true that by the beginning of 1918 the check received by the submarine owing to the establishment of the convoy system forced the German Intelligence Department to revise

[1] Reichstag Committee: General Von Kuhl's Report on the American troops.

their estimates. But even then they did not foresee what British shipping was capable of achieving under the pressure of a great emergency. They also underrated the fighting qualities of the American divisions that were brought over. They did not doubt the excellence of the material, but they did not think it possible to train it in time for use except in quiet sectors of the Western Front. The Germans calculated that only a comparatively small proportion of the American Army could be put into the fighting line during the critical months of 1918. In this respect both the French and British military authorities were of the same opinion. Pétain thought the American Army would not count until 1919; our G.H.Q. were just as contemptuous of the arrival of American reinforcements and even more of their utility when they landed.

A perusal of the documents written during the War, whether on the side of the Germans or the Allies, reveals that both were in the dark. The fog of war was everywhere: we can see how apt adversaries in any conflict are to miscalculate each other's strength and weaknesses, each other's opportunities and resources. Some difficulties are exaggerated, others are underestimated or altogether ignored. The strength of opponents is in some respects under-assessed and in others over-stated. These errors are by no means confined to military problems. They occur in politics, in law and in business. It is difficult to judge at any given moment whether these misconceptions constitute the basis of a given policy, or whether the policy has not inspired the miscalculation. Is an erroneous estimate of the facts responsible for the strategy, or is the strategy already determined upon responsible for the false manipulation of facts? As far as the Great War is concerned, time and reflection will ultimately provide the answer. As the years go by, and the realities stand out more clearly, and as personal prejudices fade or are eliminated, and more impartial conclusions can be derived from a calm survey of indisputable facts, it will be easier to reach a decision on these questions.

The Allied Staffs had not a monopoly in the realm of illusions. General Ludendorff was convinced that the pacifist movement in Britain was formidable and was growing in power day by day. He was of opinion that a reeling blow struck at the British Army would precipitate a political crisis in England, throw out of office what he conceived to be a bellicose and implacable War Ministry, and substitute for it a more pacific and amenable combination headed by Mr. Asquith and Lord Lansdowne. His Staff papers published by him since the War show what a part this estimate of the political possibilities in Britain played in his strategical schemes.

Did the necessity for finding arguments in favour of a great offensive tempt him to exaggerate the reports he received, or was the information which came to him the reason which prompted him to decide in favour of an offensive? On the other side Marshal Haig was persuaded that the German Army had exhausted its reserves early in October, that the terrible blows he was inflicting upon it at Passchendaele were destroying its morale, that one hundred and thirty-five divisions were already pulverised and that the Germans were therefore not in a condition to resist an offensive on the Passchendaele Front continued up till November and then resumed in the spring. Did his ardour for the offensive he had planned and prosecuted colour his information, or did his information determine his strategy? Events which it will now be my duty to set forth show clearly how both Ludendorff and Haig were misled as to the fundamental facts which ought to have shaped their strategic plans; partly by informants upon whom they relied, partly by their own predispositions; and in each case their war plans were necessarily faulty. In the case of the German Army it led to irretrievable disaster. Ultimately in the case of the British Army the projected renewal of the Flanders offensive in the spring, when the Germans were at their strongest and the Allies at the greatest disadvantage, was overruled and irreparable catastrophe was averted.

CHAPTER II

THE BELLIGERENTS STATE THEIR PEACE TERMS

The War-weariness of Austria — Smuts and Kerr to meet Mensdorff — Smuts' account of their discussion — No separate peace possible with Austria — Austria fears partition — Smuts urges a liberal autonomy — Essential conditions for a League of Nations — Problem of Poland — Serbia — Italy — The evening conversation: no discussion of general peace terms — Britain must break German militarism — Mensdorff pleads for compromise peace terms — German-British coöperation vital for world peace — A further interview — Austria anxious to mediate peace — Inferences from Smuts' report — Need to state Allied peace aims — Turkish approaches — An answer necessary to pacifist propaganda — Trade Union problems — I prepare an agreed statement of peace aims — Asquith and Grey approve — Caxton Hall Conference — My statement of War aims — British opinion united — Clynes' letter — Wilson announces his "Fourteen Points" — Germany plans a reply — Hindenburg's letter to the Kaiser — No peace without a German victory — Hertling's speech — No surrender of Alsace-Lorraine — Germany's free hand in Russia — No concession as to Belgium — Germany in no mood to make peace — Declaration of Supreme War Council — Fresh approach by Austria — Views of War Cabinet — Interchange of messages — Smuts and Kerr meet Skrzynski — Smuts states British attitude — Austrians cooling off — Hopes of German offensive — No peace moves from Germany — Appendix A: Report of Mr. Philip Kerr's Interview with Dr. Parodi, Head of the Mission Scolaire Egyptienne, on December 18th, 1917 — Appendix B: The Peace Declaration.

WERE no efforts made to stop all this horrible slaughter of brave men in many lands? There were tentative approaches and soundings. Towards the end of 1917 informal communications were received by us through Switzerland which indicated that Austria and Turkey were anxious to bring the War to an end by negotiation. They were both in a bad way. In spite of the overthrow of Russia and the signal defeat inflicted on Italy, the internal situation in Austria was extremely serious. Food supplies were so short that parts of the Empire were on the verge of starvation, and even in the Army it was difficult to feed the troops. The Slavonic populations were never enthusiastic about the War, and economic conditions produced discontent even in the Germanic areas of the Empire. The Emperor and his advisers were apprehensive of uprisings which might end in Revolution. The Cabinet, while naturally anxious to avoid futile *pourparlers* like those initiated by Prince Sixte's letters, which excited so much suspicion in the breasts of Italian statesmen, were alive to the importance of detaching Austria from the Central Alliance. They were convinced that the time had not come for entering into general peace negotiations. Germany was in no mood for conceding any terms which would be acceptable to the Allies or to America. She had humbled Russia to the dust. She had destroyed the Roumanian Army and was consuming Roumanian corn and drawing oil supplies from Roumanian wells. She had beaten off our attack on Flanders and had helped Austria to put the Italian Army to flight. She was far from being convinced that her submarine campaign had failed. She was still sinking our ships, and with her accession of fresh strength which came from the release of divisions from the Russian Front she was preparing a crashing attack on the exhausted French and British Armies in the west. A Peace Conference with such a Germany would give us none of our objectives and was only attainable on terms which would have left German militarism triumphant over all its foes. The point for the Cabinet to consider in all their Swiss feelers was whether there was any chance of effecting a separate peace with either Austria or Turkey, or with both.

When it was intimated to us that the Austrian Prime Minister, Count Czernin, was willing to send Count Mensdorff to Switzerland to meet a representative of the British Cabinet to discuss Peace, we felt that the dispatch of such a messenger constituted the best proof that the Austrian Government was in earnest in seeking a peaceable accommodation of the bloody quarrel. For us, Mensdorff was a highly acceptable emissary. Before the War he was one of the best liked and most trusted of the foreign Ambassadors in this country. We decided therefore to send General Smuts to meet him in Switzerland. General Smuts was to be accompanied by Mr. Philip Kerr (now Lord Lothian), who was on my staff. Their instructions were to confine themselves to the discussion of a separate peace with Austria and not to be drawn into any conversation as to the terms of a general peace. They were also to ascertain through our Minister there what value there was in the approaches which had been made to him ostensibly from Turkish sources.

I give General Smuts' account of the conversations that took place. His report is an historical document of the first importance. It is a remarkable contemporary record of a frank interchange of views which took place at a critical stage of the War between one of the most experienced, as well as one of the ablest and sanest diplomatists of the time on the one hand, and on the other, one of the most enlightened statesmen of the day. Apart from the fact that it puts clearly before us the opinion thus formed by men of high intelligence as to the problems of peace, it has also a special value as representing very fairly the conclusions formed by men of calm judgment on either side, not only as to the attitude but also as to the military position of the belligerents at the end of 1917.

"December 18–19, 1917.

"I reached Geneva on the morning of 18th December and had a short interview with Count Mensdorff in a quiet suburb in the outskirts of Geneva. I had another long conversation with him in the afternoon, and a third conversation in the evening of the same day. I proceed to summarise the principal points of interest which emerged from these conversations.

"Before leaving London I discussed separately with the Prime Minister and Mr. Balfour the line I should take in these conversations, and I conceived that the objects of my mission were twofold: first, to instil into the minds of the Austrians that in case they freed themselves from German domination and made a fresh start in sympathy with the British Empire they would have our full sympathy and support; and secondly, to gather as much information as possible while declining to enter into a general discussion of peace terms so far as the Germans were concerned.

"As will appear from the sequel the conversations have been fruitful in both these respects. A third object which I had in mind was, if possible, to induce the Austrians to conclude a separate peace; but the subject was from many points of view a risky one to open, as I was anxious to avoid laying ourselves open to the charge in future of having intrigued with the Austrians for a separate peace. Before I reached this point in our discussions, however, Mensdorff saved me from the difficulties of my task by taking the initiative himself in declaring that a separate peace was for Austria entirely out of the question, that it would be madness on her part even to entertain the idea, that her circumstances rendered it impossible for her to carry it out, and that bad as her plight was it was not so desperate that she would do anything so treacherous and dishonourable. He said that she was not going to follow the example of Italy, and at the close of the conversations he returned to the subject and pointed out once more in the strongest language that a separate peace was not to be thought of. Austria was prepared to do anything to secure an honourable peace short of deserting her ally during the War. I gathered the impression that Mensdorff thought that the principal object of my mission was to discuss a separate peace, and I am therefore glad that I did not raise the point, but left it to be raised by him, which he did in the strongest language possible, and with evident sincerity.

"I opened the conversations by saying that I had come in response to the numerous unofficial overtures from Austria which had reached us both through Holland and Switzerland in recent months. We thought it only courteous that some definite response should be made to these overtures and that an opportunity should be given to hear what Austria had to say. I pointed out to him that the friendly feeling towards Austria which had existed among the British people before the War had by no means disappeared, that a great deal of sympathy continued to be felt for Austria, especially as she was looked upon not so much as a principal antagonist, but valued as having been used by Germany both in the policy which led to the War, as well as during the course of the War. The downfall of Russia had created fresh anxiety for the political future of Europe, and it was feared in many influential quarters that unless some counterweight was established on the Continent to Germany in the place of Russia, the future peace of Europe might continue to be precarious. From this point of view it was a matter of grave concern that Austria should no longer continue her rôle of subordination to Germany, that she should be emancipated from German domination, and should, with the assistance of the Entente, and especially of the British Empire, make a fresh start of complete independence *vis-à-vis* the German Empire. If Austria was prepared to play that rôle and break with Germany she would have not only our sympathy but our active support, and we would do everything in our power to uphold and strengthen her and to assist her economic reconstruction.

"To this Mensdorff replied that he was most gratified to hear this, and all the more so because the last word which we had spoken officially in regard to this matter was in the Allied reply to President Wison's Note at the beginning of 1917, in which the practical break-up and partition of the Austro-Hungarian Empire was foreshadowed as one of our principal war aims. I assured him that that note never had had such an intention, and that its object, and still more our object now, was to assist Austria to give the greatest freedom and autonomy to her subject nationalities. The best way to strengthen the bonds of sympathy between the British and Austro-Hungarian people was to liberalise as much as possible the local institutions of Austria-Hungary. We had no intention of interfering in her internal affairs, but we recognised that if Austria could become a really liberal Empire in which her subject people would, as far as possible, be satisfied and content, she would become for Central Europe very much what the British Empire had become for the rest of the world. She would become a

League of Free Nations, very largely free from the taint of militarism, and she would have a mission in the future even greater than her mission in the past. Looking to the future of Europe, and the new orientation which it was necessary to give to the published policy of Europe, it seemed to thoughtful people in England that the above rôle was not only the nobler one for Austria-Hungary, but was also necessary in order to secure the full sympathy and coöperation of the Entente, and especially of the British Empire and America, and was still more necessary to prevent any future military dictatorship in Europe with its promise of fresh troubles for the world. For all this it seemed to me absolutely necessary that Austria should become entirely dissociated from the German Empire and should establish the friendliest relations with those Entente Powers that were actuated by fundamental pacific tendencies. I continued to labour this point with him and to point out what a success the British Empire had made of the government of divers races and peoples, and that Austria, by following the same liberal policy — a policy directed to the peaceful self-development of its peoples through the widest local autonomy — could probably achieve a no less striking success in Central Europe, and that peoples not now directly within her orbit might be drawn to her in future by the attractions of her new policy. For her, peace and liberty were as essential as for the British Empire, and now that Russia had disappeared as the principal military danger upon her flank there was no reason why she should not adopt this policy and lean more and more towards the British Empire and dissociate herself from German militarism.

"Mensdorff replied that these views would find the heartiest response in the most influential quarters in Austria-Hungary. Austrian statesmen were determined to make a fresh start after the War, but he emphasised once more that nothing could be done to break away from Germany or to begin the new policy while the War lasted. The views which I had expressed with regard to the political future of Austria-Hungary would appeal very deeply to its rulers. He knew that both the Emperor and Count Czernin were actuated very much by sentiments similar to those which I had expressed. Czernin, he said, was not a diplomat of the old school, but a young statesman descended from the ancient Royal House of Bohemia, full of lofty political idealism, and determined to see an end to all this military régime which has been the undoing of Europe. The views which he had so strongly and repeatedly expressed in favour of general disarmament and a League of Nations to safeguard the public order of Europe after this war, represented his deepest political convictions, and had incurred the wrath of influential sections of the German people. Mensdorff regretted that no word of sympathy had come from England for the policy stated by Czernin. Instead they in Austria had met only either with cold disdainful silence or the sneers of the Press. He hoped that it would still be possible for British statesmen publicly to extend their sympathy to Czernin's views, and in that way to create a better atmosphere for solving the problems of the future.

"I pointed out in reply to this that the views of the British Government were perfectly well known to be favourable to a League of Nations, and that our leading statesmen had repeatedly expressed their agreement with President Wilson in that regard. But we felt very strongly that the mere machinery of a League of Nations would not only be useless, but would be positively dangerous unless it was established on the basis of a satisfactory peace, a peace which would not leave Germany in military predominance on the Continent, and which, in its territorial aspects, would as far as possible satisfy the principle of nationality. The German Empire had developed unsuspected military strength and predominance during this war, and the British people felt that whether Germany was inside or outside a League of Nations, it would, through the military power which it had developed, be able, at any time, to wreck the good work of the League. The danger and fear which have overhung Europe and led to this war would continue to exist, and anxiety among the other nations for their future would continue to stimulate them to fresh military preparations. It was therefore essential for a League of Nations that the German military domination should be broken in this war, and that the political dispositions of Central Europe after the War should afford some safeguard against its reëstablishment.

"He said in reply to this that we were evidently underrating the new developments in Germany which were making for a new order. The Parliamentarisation of Germany had already proceeded much further than was commonly appreciated, and the effect of the repeated Chancellor crises was that it had now become impossible to have a government in Germany without a majority in the Reichstag. That was the real inwardness of all the obscure crises which had recently taken place. If we expected more at present and looked forward to a revolution in Germany during the War we were much mistaken. The German working-classes were highly educated, and had developed great political capacity (*Regierungsfähigkeit*), and even before the War the Socialist Party in Germany was the most powerful in Europe. But they certainly were not going to follow the example of the Russians, nor would they betray their country while it was in danger; and it was generally anticipated that as soon as the War was over and the armies returned from the fronts, and the German people settled down again there would be the most far-reaching political changes. To my observation that the German civil government seems rather to have lost ground in comparison with the General Staff, whose efficiency had more and more established its predominance in Germany during the War, he replied with a contemptuous gesture that the whole military régime would be blown away as soon as the War was over and the German people could speak.

"He then tried to get on to general peace terms and said that in his opinion the time had come to open informal discussions between Great Britain and Germany, and if Austria as a friendly party could be used as an intermediary she would be highly gratified. I thanked him, but said that the time for discussing peace terms with the Germans had certainly not come, that neither the British public nor the British Government were in a temper to discuss peace with the German Government, and that our conversations should be confined entirely to questions affecting Austria-Hungary. To this he agreed, but with evident regret, and

THE BELLIGERENTS STATE PEACE TERMS 27

several times thereafter he made attempts to open a general discussion of German terms of peace, but was constantly met by a blank refusal by me to enter into a discussion of this topic.

"The conversation then drifted on to territorial questions in connection with the peace, which might affect Austria-Hungary. Mensdorff himself raised the question of Poland, which, he said, from its superior culture had rather a Western than an Eastern orientation. I said it was essential from the point of view which we had been discussing that the future Polish Kingdom should not have a German orientation. He replied that there was little fear of that; that owing to the liberal policy that Austria had followed the future Polish State was much more likely to coöperate with Austria than with Germany. I said that we were pledged to an independent Kingdom or State of Poland, but that if Austria really broke away from Germany and realised the mission sketched out above, the possibility of some link of a personal or a loose nature between Austria and Poland was not excluded, and that the addition of Galicia to Poland might be a desirable move from that point of view. He said that a solution of the Polish question on those lines would commend itself to Austria-Hungary and might even appeal to the Poles themselves. There were constitutional difficulties, but he thought that it was possible to bring the future larger Poland within the orbit of the Austrian Empire of the future.

"I asked him next if some such solution was found of the Polish question and Austrian influence was thereby greatly increased that means should be found to satisfy the reasonable claims of those States to whom we were pledged by various promises made during the War, such as Serbia, Roumania, and Italy. He said that he thought the case of Serbia did not present much difficulty so far as Austria was concerned. Austria disliked the Karageorgevitch dynasty, which was founded on assassination, and would welcome guarantees which would prevent Serbia from becoming once more a centre of anti-Austrian intrigue. He also thought that Bulgaria would hold on to the Bulgarian parts of Serbia and that it would be a wise policy to acquiesce in her doing so. I replied that Serbia might in that case legitimately claim compensation, and that it was worthy of consideration whether the best policy even from the Austrian point of view was not to follow the principle of nationality and add Bosnia-Herzegovina to Serbia and bring Serbia into the Dalmatian coast, and to bring the greater Serbia thus constituted into a more friendly relation with Austria-Hungary. He asked what relation I meant, whether it was a loose political union or some economic union. I replied that I could not say, and that it was a question in which Serbia would have to be consulted, but that it seemed to me essential if the foundations of a future peaceful Europe were to be laid that rearrangements on a national basis should as far as possible be effected, and that a far-sighted policy followed by Austria now might conciliate the Southern Slav peoples and assist her to realise the great mission and position which might be in store for her. I pointed out that Russia would no longer be there to foment anti-Austrian feeling among the Southern Slavs and that was the best guarantee which Austria could have for the future. The rest must be left to wise statesmanship, and sound territorial arrangement. Mensdorff appeared to me to be not unfavourable to this point of view which I was urging, although he did not openly commit himself. When, however, I came to Roumania he became somewhat excited and said that Roumania was finished and that they would do nothing for that treacherous State, and Hungary would refuse to surrender an inch of territory to Roumania, and that his brother-in-law, Count Apponyi, who was really a pacifist, had assured him only a few days ago that Hungary would fight to the last ditch rather than surrender any territory to Roumania. Mensdorff added that it was only a fringe of Transylvania which was inhabited by Roumanians. I pointed out in reply that considerable parts of Bukovina and Bessarabia had a predominantly Roumanian population, and that as Bulgaria was also claiming the Bulgarian part of Dobrudja, the question of bringing together the Roumanian people into one State was one well worthy of consideration and that it was in the interest of Austria-Hungary to have a friendly and satisfied Roumania on her flank. He said that Bukovina was on a different footing from Transylvania, and that he hoped that no proposals would be made which meant any partition of Hungarian territory as this would be most fiercely resisted by the Hungarians. Bessarabia was, of course, a question in which Austria was not concerned, and I did not gather that he was opposed to my suggestion so far as Bukovina was concerned.

"This brought us on to Italy. Mensdorff asked how we could defend the national principle in connection with the promises which we had made to Italy in the Balkans, where we had promised to Italy territories which contained few Italians and a predominantly Slav and Slovene population. He also asked how it was possible if we were favourably disposed towards the future Austria-Hungary that we could think of practically cutting her off from outlets to the sea and planting the Italians on both shores of the Adriatic. Apart from Dalmatia, Trieste had never belonged to Italy, had voluntarily decided centuries ago to come under Austria and had been under Austria ever since. Austria would never agree to Trieste being wrenched from her or to be deprived of proper access to the Adriatic. Italy had no right to be at Valona either.

"I did not want to discuss these questions with him as I was not fully conversant with them but it seemed to me indisputable from every point of view that the Trentino should be ceded to Italy. The strategic frontier of Italy in the north was impossible, and Trentino was an almost entirely Italian population. To his observation that after the treachery of Italy there was no disposition to make any concessions to her, I replied that Italy would never have been induced to desert Austria if the latter did not sit on territory which Italy could legitimately claim to be hers, and that from the point of view of future peace and security it seemed to me desirable in the highest interests of Austria to suppress all feelings of resentment towards Italy, to deal with her on high statesmanlike lines, and by the surrender to her of the Trentino to secure a friend and ally in Italy. To this he made no further objection, and I did not press him any further on the point. My own feeling was that Austria would be prepared for a deal, although he did not expressly say so.

"In all this discussion of territorial questions I purposely abstained from going too deeply into details at this stage, as I intended merely to have a preliminary canter over the ground in order to satisfy myself in my capacity as a scout of the general attitude of the Austrians on the question of territorial concessions. The impression I formed was that the Austrian mind was in an accommodating mood, and that moderate and reasonable proposals from us would meet with serious and favourable consideration. Further I did not think it wise to go at this stage, as not only are we not in possession of the revised views of our Allies, but I am also doubtful whether the War Cabinet has come to even provisional conclusions on the difficult matters touched upon in these conversations.

"This finished the conversation in the afternoon.

"In the evening we had another conversation, in which Mensdorff made repeated efforts to induce me to discuss general peace terms. I, however, firmly declined to do so, but allowed him to make several statements of great interest which I shall mention later. He seemed to have been under the impression that I was merely manœuvring in refusing to discuss general peace terms, and when finally he realised that he was wrong he seemed deeply disappointed. He exclaimed that in that case there was no peace in sight and that this horrible War must go on. Europe, he said, was dying at the centre, America was becoming the financial and economic centre of the world, while Japan at the other end was gathering to herself immense power and resources and the whole trade of Asia. Why were we going on fighting? The British Prime Minister had said that we must have victory, Asquith had said that Prussian militarism must be crushed. If another year of this destruction had to pass the position of Europe and civilisation, already so pitiable, would indeed be beyond repair. What was the sort of victory we had in view? How would we know it and when would we consider it to be achieved? Did we want the Hohenzollerns to go? Surely, that was not likely to happen during the War, and would in any case not justify the practical destruction of European civilisation. Any political revolution in Germany would follow, not precede, the peace. Or did we intend the break-up of the German Army, or the occupation of Belgium? Surely that was no reasonable expectation either.

"I explained to him how deeply impressed the British people were with the dangers to the future political system of Europe, if Germany survived as a sort of military dictator, and that we meant to continue the War until either victory had been achieved or the dark forces of revolution had done their work in Germany as they had already done in Russia. We were in a good position to go on. America was coming in with resources far greater and more real than any we had lost through the defection of Russia. France had suffered but little this year, and her Army had a very high morale and quite sufficient reserves for next year; while our full resources in mechanical and man-power were only now being mobilised for the decisive phases of the War. I explained to him how the submarine and shipping situation had altered since last spring, and that we were now in a position, if necessary, to go on indefinitely as we had done during the Nalopeonic Wars. The menace of Germany was no less grave than the menace of Napoleon, and was meeting with an even more determined temper on the part of the British people.

"He replied that that would indeed be the end of Europe. Was it really worth while? He again asked what this vague victory was for which all these immeasurable sacrifices had to be made. What was the definition of it, or what was the measure of proof of it? Surely the German Army was not going to put up the white flag and openly abase itself and acknowledge defeat. It would continue the defence as brave men knew how to do. To his mind it was necessary to define clearly what we meant by victory. He could see only one test of our victory, and that was that we should define our aims closely, and place our terms before the enemy, and that the enemy should either accept or reject them. Otherwise the War would continue in misunderstanding, in darkness and fog, so to say. If the enemy accepted our terms we would have won; if not, we could go on until he was forced to accept them. He pleaded for reasonable terms. He urged that the way should be prepared for their acceptance by Germany by means of preliminary conversations with Austria, in which the Germans were or were not to take part, according as we wished. He did not anticipate that the German attitude would be unreasonable. Belgium, he thought, would be evacuated, provided German economic and industrial interests, which before the War were very great in Belgium, were not injured or hampered. He did not believe there was any intention to annex any of the occupied parts of Russia. He could not say this for certain, but would be most surprised if the Germans made any such claim. About Alsace-Lorraine he knew that there were great difficulties, but incidentally he here asked the significant question, whether France wanted the whole of Alsace-Lorraine back. He continued that the Germans were very keen to get their colonies or some of them back, and he thought they would claim heavy compensation if we declined to return them. Above all, they would resist to the utmost a post-War economic war, as that would mean their practical boycott from the markets of the world. Such an economic war would be inconsistent with the new international system which we wished to promote after the War, and Austria, no less than Germany, would resist it to the utmost. He hoped that the objects which we had in view would be fair, reasonable and moderate; if they were, the time had come for their achievement, and for that purpose it would be highly desirable to clear up the situation by further discussions of an informal character, in which the Germans need not necessarily take a part to begin with.

"I did not enter into a discussion of these general questions, and the Count went on to say with obvious sincerity that the two greatest peoples on earth, the two greatest peoples that had ever existed, were the British and the Germans, that the future of the world depended on both of them and on their coöperation, that it was not in the interests of the world that either of them should be utterly defeated, even if that were possible, and that such a defeat would become the source of fresh calamities for the future of mankind. He hoped most earnestly that reason would prevail. I replied that it was only because of our solicitude for the future that we did not wish to leave the root of the evil to survive and to grow afresh in the future. It was not from any warlike spirit but because of our horror of war that we were prepared to endure its evils longer for the present in order to end them for the future — to which he retorted, in lighter vein, that the Entente did certainly seem more warlike at present than the Central Powers.

"This brought our conversations to an end, and we said goodbye to each other.

"The following morning, 19th December, the Count, who had ascertained that I was stopping another day in Geneva, sent a message to ask whether he could have another interview with me. I therefore saw him again in the afternoon of the same day, and he said to me that he was anxious that both of us should be clear on certain points. In the first place, Austria would be prepared to go any length with us in pressing on Germany a policy of disarmament, including the submarine and similar developments, and the policy of conferences and arbitration against war in future. In the second place, he was profoundly thankful for the sympathy which I had expressed for the Austro-Hungarian Empire, and when in future they took a line of their own independent of Germany they would count on our support. In the third place he trusted that at the peace we would use our influence with our friends to moderate their demands, and in that case Austria would do her best to meet us fairly.

"In reply I repeated some of the views already expressed in the preceding conversations. I added that Austria had now a great opportunity to show the highest statesmanship and thereby to help the world towards an early, satisfactory and lasting settlement. She would have to free herself from German influence and make a fresh independent start of her own. She would also have to give up some small things in order to realise the greater destiny that might be in store for her. He replied that it was very hard to give way after the shocking behaviour especially of Roumania and Italy, but Austria would be prepared to meet us reasonably if we stood by her and made no unfair claims.

"I soon saw, however, that something else was really on his

mind. He then came out with it. He said that the War must be ended, and that it was the fervent ambition of Austria to be the instrument for bringing this about. A separate peace would be impossible, but Austria, whose sympathies were really with Great Britain, wished in future to work with her. Austria could stand between the great enemies and help towards peace if use was made of her. She was ready and anxious to do anything. Especially must we not separate now that conversations had started. He hoped we would meet again to pursue our discussions, if possible into greater details. Next time, or the time after next, he felt sure that Count Czernin would come to the discussion if we wanted one who could speak with more authority. He hoped it would be possible in such a case to fix a meeting-place nearer the Austrian frontier. If we did not wish to speak to the Germans the discussion might again be confined to the Austrian aspect of peace. If again we wished to have a more general discussion but still not with the Germans, we could make use of Czernin, who was in sympathy with British ideals and could usefully smooth away preliminary difficulties with the Germans.

"He hoped that the agencies which we had used to get into touch on this occasion would be used again for the same purpose, and that we would meet again soon. He returned once more to the subject of victory and *said it was misleading to talk of victory, for while the Germans had been successful in Central Europe, the British Empire had gained far more lasting and far-reaching victories over the whole world, and was now in complete control of everything outside Central Europe.* The victory was already ours in a very important sense, and it was useless to continue to shed the blood of tens and hundreds of thousands of the youth of Europe for a greater measure of military success, which might or might not be achieved in future.

"I repeated to him what I had previously said, that I did not think we were prepared to talk to Germany, but we appreciated his suggestion to keep the present conversations on foot, and would bear in mind what he had said about Czernin. If, on their part, the Austrians wished to speak to us again, the same channels

would avail unless secrecy demanded resort to other channels.
"We then parted.

"In conclusion I wish to say that I have not the least doubt that the line we have taken with Austria on this occasion will prove most useful and fruitful. It evidently made a deep impression on Count Mensdorff. From the very depths of her abasement and despair, Austria has been made to see daylight, and I expect that she will strain every nerve to induce Germany to accept moderate terms, and that she will thereafter strive, with our assistance, to recover and assert her political independence of Germany. Whether the vision of a truly liberal Austria will really appeal to her statesmen, the future alone will show.

"In all these conversations I deliberately refrained from a word of reference to Turkey."

It will be observed that at that date we did not contemplate a complete break-up of the Austrian Empire, but rather that within its bounds there should be set up a number of free autonomous and practically independent States on the model of the British Empire. There are a few outstanding inferences to be drawn from this remarkable document: —

1. At that date the negotiation of a separate peace with Austria was out of the question. Mensdorff, representing as he did the Austrian Prime Minister's views, would regard such a peace as dishonouring to the Empire. That was in itself conclusive as to the impracticability of further negotiation. Even had we agreed to a general Conference, France would treat it as an abandonment and a betrayal.

2. No concessions were to be made to Italy and Roumania. Their entry into the War on the side of the Allies was regarded as an act of unutterable treachery. In fact, Mensdorff said that if Austria were to make a separate peace with the Allies she would be "as base as Italy." There was the additional objection to conceding any territory to either Italy

or Roumania, that at that moment they were both in the position of beaten foes. We could not take that view without betraying Italy, who was still fighting on our side.

3. Germany was, in the estimation of Mensdorff, militarily triumphant. He evidently believed she could not be beaten. The worst that could befall her would be a stalemate. She could not, therefore, contemplate a peace based on the assumption that she was already defeated or was likely to be beaten in the end.

The Cabinet considered this report a complete justification of their view that the time had not yet arrived for a general Peace Conference in which Germany would be included.

On the other hand, Mensdorff made a fruitful suggestion which we felt might be acted upon without delay. He urged us to state our peace terms in a way which would be so clear and definite that our enemies could not fail to understand what were our aims. If they felt they were reasonable they would be accepted. On the other hand, if they did not form a basis for discussion they would be rejected. We would all then know exactly where we stood.

A similar suggestion came from Dr. Parodi, an agent of the opposition party in Turkey, who had come to Switzerland with the intention of establishing contact with the Allies, and was interviewed there by Mr. Kerr. He admitted that for the time being the Germanophile section of the Committee of Union and Progress which governed Turkey was uppermost, but he thought that the proclamation of moderate terms might reverse the proportions. Enver Pasha, the strongest man in the Government, was a pure militarist Germanophile, and was still confident that Germany would win the War. His principal colleague, Talat Pasha, thought Germany would be neither victorious nor beaten and that there would be a *paix blanche* more or less on the basis of the *status quo*. Philip Kerr's informant thought if we made it clear that one of our objects was to establish Arab autonomy it would hearten the Arabs and further the antagonism which existed between the Arab and Turkish officers.

Mr. Kerr's interview with Dr. Parodi was not satisfactory. Parodi did not profess to represent the Turkish Government and it was clear from this conversation that the governing party in the Turkish Empire was not yet ready to enter into any negotiations with the Allies on any terms which we could entertain — or even discover. Mr. Kerr's Report is given in full in Appendix A to this Chapter.

The net result of this visit to Switzerland was to leave the impression that a separate peace with Austria and Turkey was not attainable just yet, but that the time had arrived when it was desirable that the Government should re-state the terms upon which it was prepared to make peace.

There was another reason why a re-statement of our war aims was necessary at this juncture. We were coming to the last, and in so many ways the most critical stage of the War. There was a great deal of pacifist propaganda at home which, operating on a natural weariness, might develop into a dangerous anti-war sentiment that would undermine the morale of the nation at a time when the event depended on the staying power of the nations. All the belligerent nations were confronted with this situation. In Germany, Austria and Russia the Peace sentiment was fostered amongst the population by hardship and privation and even actual hunger. It was one of the reasons why I attached so much importance to the question of maintaining our food supplies. The desire for peace was spreading amongst men and women who, although they were convinced of the righteousness of the War, felt that the time had come for putting an end to its horrors in the name of humanity, if it could be done on any terms that were honourable and safe. Lord Lansdowne constituted himself the spokesman of this sentiment. He represented a powerful and growing section of the people not only in social, but also in industrial circles. The suffering was not confined to one class. All classes alike shared the tortures of sorrow for the fallen, and the anxieties of incessant apprehension for those who were in the zone of death. Amongst the workmen there was an unrest that was disturbing and might at any moment become dangerous. The efforts we were making to comb out more men for the Army were meeting with resistance amongst the Trade Unions, whose loyalty and patriotism had throughout been above reproach. I attached great importance to retaining their continued support in the prosecution of the War. Had they been driven into hostility, a dangerous rift in the home front would have been inevitable. Germany was to find out how fatal to success was the alienation of organised labour. The influence of the MacDonald section of the Labour movement was becoming greater, and their agitation was intensifying and gaining fresh adherents. One of their number informed me that he never attended more packed and enthusiastic meetings than those which he addressed on peace during the last year or two of the War. It was essential to convince the nation that we were not continuing the War merely to gain a vindictive or looting triumph, but that we had definite peace aims and that these were both just and attainable.

The difficulties with our man power had almost produced a deadlock with the Trade Unions. Without their goodwill and coöperation, we could not have secured further recruits from amongst the exempted — certainly not without a resistance which might have alienated organised labour throughout the land. It therefore became necessary to open negotiations with them. I decided, first of all, to invite the Trade Unions to a Conference on the subject of our war aims. In order to ensure their coöperation it was necessary to place before them with complete frankness the purpose with which we were prosecuting the War. The Parliamentary Committee of the Trade Union Congress and of the Labour Party had already formulated their peace proposals on December 16th. They did not differ in any material respect from those which we were putting forward. That rendered my task very much easier, for there had been mischievous statements circulated in the Press and at meetings and in private that our aims were of an "imperialistic" and predatory character, and that we were only continuing the cruelties and sufferings of war in order to secure these nefarious objects.

I therefore had a detailed and a careful statement prepared of our peace objectives. They were considered in the greatest detail by the Cabinet and approved by them. As I had been informed by an eminent American, who was in touch with the Asquith section of the Liberals, that they thought "opinion in favour of continuing the War was weakening in this country", I thought it desirable to secure their assent to the peace proposals we intended to put forward, so that the peace terms we proclaimed should be national in the true sense of the word. I arranged a private meeting with Mr. Asquith and Sir Edward Grey to discuss our peace declaration.

We met at breakfast at Mr. Asquith's house. I read to them the document which I had prepared. I had already obtained the Cabinet assent to its terms. With some slight alterations, entirely in the wording, they approved its terms. The suggested amendments were duly incorporated. The Cabinet took the necessary steps to inform the Dominions of the nature of the statement I proposed to make. Their approval was secured before we committed ourselves.

The Conference with the Trade Unions took place at the Caxton Hall on January 5th. It was a crowded gathering of delegates and thoroughly representative. I gave to them in full the declaration of our war aims. Although no resolution was passed, at the end of the meeting there was every indication of a general acceptance by the delegates of the proposals submitted to them. Inasmuch as the terms of peace outlined on this occasion represented not merely the views of Ministers and their supporters, but of Labour, the Independent Liberals and the Dominions, and were subsequently embodied in the Treaty of Versailles, the statement I made to the Trade Unions is an essential part of my narrative of the War. I accordingly include the full text of my speech in Appendix B to this Chapter. As will be seen by a reference to it, I made it clear that our one object in the War was to defend the violated public law of Europe, to vindicate Treaty obligations and to secure the restoration of Belgium. We intended to stand by French democracy in its demand for the restitution of its lost provinces and to secure national freedom for those parts of the Austrian Empire which were at present held in unwilling bondage to an alien race. As to the ultimate peace settlement, I concluded my speech by saying: —

". . . whatever settlement is made will be suitable only to the circumstances under which it is made, and, as those circumstances change, changes in the settlement will be called for.

"So long as the possibility of dispute between nations continues, that is to say, so long as men and women are dominated by passioned ambition, and war is the only means of settling a dispute, all nations must live under the burden not only of having from time to time to engage in it, but of being compelled to prepare for its possible outbreak. The crushing weight of modern armaments, the increasing evil of compulsory military service, the vast waste of wealth and effort involved in warlike preparation, these are blots on our civilisation of which every thinking individual must be ashamed.

"For these and other similar reasons, we are confident that a great attempt must be made to establish by some international organisation an alternative to war as a means of settling international disputes. After all, war is a relic of barbarism, and just as law has succeeded violence as the means of settling disputes between individuals, so we believe that it is destined ultimately to take the place of war in the settlement of controversies between nations.

"If, then, we are asked what are we fighting for, we reply, as we have often replied — we are fighting for a just and lasting peace — and we believe that before permanent peace can be hoped for three conditions must be fulfilled.

"First, the sanctity of treaties must be reëstablished; secondly, a territorial settlement must be secured based on the right of self-determination or the consent of the governed; and, lastly, we must seek by the creation of some international organisation to limit the burden of armaments and diminish the probability of war.

"On those conditions the British Empire would welcome peace; to secure those conditions its peoples are prepared to make even greater sacrifices than those they have yet endured."

Prince Max of Baden in referring to my speech in his Memoirs says: —

"Immediately after this speech, the rift in the British home front closed."

Henceforth, those who were seeking disunion for political or personal motives were forced into another tack in which Labour had no interest.

Shortly after the meeting I received the following letter from Mr. Clynes, who was Minister of Food at that time: —

"DEAR PRIME MINISTER,

"I have had the opportunity within the past few days while on work for the above Ministry of meeting representative men in Conferences and in other ways, and I would like to send you this line to say what a splendid effect your speech to the Labour Delegates has had on the minds of men who were getting rather unsettled because of the length of the War and the effects of a form of propaganda which has been freely continued.

"Most of what was said of course was not new, but the occasion and the form of the speech have been of the greatest value.

Yours faithfully,
J. R. CLYNES."

A few days later, President Wilson gave utterance to his famous Fourteen Points. This declaration, which subsequently played such an important part at the Armistice and the Peace Conference, was not regarded by any of the Allies as being at variance on vital matters, except in respect of Freedom of the Seas, with their own declarations — although we never formally accepted them, and they constituted no part of the official policy of the Alliance.

In an allusion to my speech President Wilson said: —

"Within the last week Mr. Lloyd George has spoken with admirable candour and in admirable spirit for the people and government of Great Britain."

M. Pichon also made a declaration on behalf of France which corresponded with that of the British Government.

Meanwhile, the Germans felt that it was essential that some response should be made by them to the peace declarations of Allied statesmen. They knew that not only the world but their own people were waiting for their answer. The prolongation of the War or its end depended not on the voice of Austria, but of her powerful ally, Germany. Long communications on the subject passed between the Kaiser, Hindenburg, Ludendorff and the German Chancellor. These messages or their purport were not of course known to the Allies at that time, but they have since seen the light, and as an indication of the German attitude towards peace at the beginning of 1918, the letter written by Hindenburg to the Kaiser on January 7th is significant. The underlining of passages was made by the Kaiser at the time and indicates his attitude.

"General Headquarters,
7th January, 1918.

"YOUR MAJESTY,

has been pleased to command that General Ludendorff and I should take a responsible part in the peace negotiations. Your Majesty, in doing so, made it our right and duty to see to it that the result of the peace corresponds to the sacrifices and achievements of the German people and army, and that the peace strengthens us materially and brings us such strong frontiers, that our opponents will not be so ready to venture to let loose a fresh war.

"In all discussions under the presidency of Your Majesty and with the Chancellor we have pointed to the importance of protected frontiers as a vital question for Germany. It is doubtful whether such frontiers will obtained, and this troubles me considerably."

Then follows lengthy complaints of the way the Army Staff's views regarding Austria, Lithuania and Poland had been overlooked. He was especially angry about the cession of Poland to Austria. He points to the criticism of the Army outside and adds the ominous sentence which is underlined by the Kaiser: "I cannot suppress the fear that the manner in which the negotiations were conducted and the result in Brest will unfavourably influence the temper of the Army."

But the most significant paragraphs of all are the following: —

"The latter is now being put to a great test. In order to secure for ourselves the political and economic world position, which we need, we must beat the Western Powers. For this reason Your

Majesty ordered the attack in the West. This involves by far the greatest effort we have made during the whole war; the greatest sacrifices will be asked for. After the incidents at Brest I doubt whether at the conclusion of peace we shall obtain the rewards which our predominance demands and which are *worthy of our sacrifices*. *The unavoidable effect* would be a *terrible disappointment* for the home-coming army and for the nation which would have to bear prohibitive taxes. . . .

"I am definitely convinced that the policy advocated by us leads to a strengthening of the monarchy and an extended predominance of Germany, whilst the opposite policy can only bring Germany down from the height to which Your Majesty and the ancestors of Your All-Highest led her."

On the publication of the speeches of President Wilson and myself, Count Hertling, the German Imperial Chancellor, and Count Czernin were charged with the enemy replies. On January 24th, Count Hertling spoke in the Reichstag and, after referring to the Brest-Litovsk negotiations, proceeded: —

"Two announcements have, as we all know, been made in the meantime by enemy statesmen — the speech by the English Minister, Mr. Lloyd George, of 5th January, and the message of President Wilson of the day after. I freely admit that Mr. Lloyd George has changed his tone. He no longer uses abuse, and thus appears to wish to establish again his claim to negotiating abilities, of which I had previously despaired. All the same I cannot go so far as the many opinions from neutral countries which claim to read in the speech of Mr. Lloyd George a sincere desire for peace, and even a friendly spirit. It is true that he declares that he does not wish to destroy Germany, and that he has never wanted to destroy her. He even finds expressions of respect for our economic, political and cultural position, but amongst them there is no lack of other utterances, and between the lines there is always present that it is his duty to sit in judgment on guilty Germany for all sorts of crimes.

"This is the spirit, gentlemen, with which naturally we can have nothing to do, and in which as yet we can observe no trace of a sincere desire for peace. We are supposed to be culprits over whom the Entente is now sitting in judgment."

He then entered into an elaborate defence of Germany's action in waging war and holding on to Alsace-Lorraine. His announcement that Germany would not part with it was received in the Reichstag with "Loud cheers." He then made a very significant and sinister allusion to German designs on the invaded provinces of France.

"The occupied parts of France are a valuable pawn in our hands. Here also forcible annexation forms no part of the official Germany policy. *The conditions and mode of the evacuation,* which must take into consideration the vital interests of Germany, must be agreed between Germany and France. I can only once again expressly emphasise that there can never be any question of the separation of the Imperial Provinces. We will never permit ourselves to be robbed of Alsace-Lorraine by our enemies under the pretext of any fine phrases — of Alsace-Lorraine, which in the meantime, has become more and more closely allied internally with German life, which is developing more and more economically in a highly satisfactory manner, and where more than 87 per cent. of the people speak the German mother tongue. [Loud cheers.]"

Not much hope there. Even the provinces of France occupied in this war were only to be returned "on conditions."

As to Russia and Poland, we were brusquely told to mind our own business: —

"The Entente States having refused to join in the negotiations within the period agreed upon by Russia and the four Allied Powers, I must decline, in the name of the latter, any subsequent interference. The question here involved is one which alone concerns Russia and the four Allied Powers.

"It was not the Entente — who found nothing but meaningless words for Poland and before the War never mediated on her behalf with Russia — but the German Empire and Austria-Hungary who freed Poland from the Tsaristic régime which was oppressing her national individuality. Therefore, it must be left to Germany and Austria-Hungary and Poland to come to an agreement about the future organisation of that country. We are, as has been proved by the negotiations and declarations of the last year, well under way with the task."

But his treatment of Belgium was a final blow to any hope of peace: —

"As far as the Belgian question is concerned it has been declared repeatedly by my predecessors in office that at no time during the War has the forcible annexation of Belgium by the German Empire formed a point in the programme of German politics. The Belgian question belongs to a complicity of questions, the details of which will have to be regulated during the peace negotiations. As long as our enemies unreservedly adopt the attitude that the integrity of the territory of the Allies offers the only possible foundation for peace negotiations, I must adhere to the standpoint which, up to the present, has always been taken, and must decline any discussion of the Belgian question until the general discussion takes place."

Italian claims he treated as a question entirely for Austria. We shall see later on what Austria had to say about them. The fate of Arabs in Mesopotamia and Arabs and Jews in Palestine was a matter entirely for the Turks. The Turks said nothing on the subject.

It is evident both from Hindenburg's letter and Hertling's speech that the Germans were in no mind to discuss any tolerable peace. They were full of the assurance of victory. Hertling's real attitude is revealed towards the end of his speech: —

"May they believe me when I state that our military situation was never so favourable as it is now. Our highly gifted Army

Leaders face the future with undiminished confidence in victory. Throughout the whole army, in the officers, and in the men, lives the unbroken joy of battle."

The Supreme War Council held at Versailles on February 2nd reviewed the whole of these Peace Declarations. As a result of the discussion it was decided to issue a joint declaration embodying the results of the session of the Council. This was published in the Press of the Allied countries on February 4th and included the following paragraph: —

"The Supreme War Council gave the most careful consideration to the recent utterances of the German Chancellor and of the Austro-Hungarian Minister for Foreign Affairs, but was unable to find in them any real approximation to the moderate conditions laid down by all the Allied Governments. This conviction was only deepened by the impression made by the contrast between the professed idealistic aims with which the Central Powers entered upon the present negotiations at Brest-Litovsk, and the now openly disclosed plans of conquest and spoliation. Under the circumstances, the Supreme War Council decided that the only immediate task before them lay in the prosecution with the utmost vigour, and in the closest and most effective coöperation, of the military efforts of the Allies, until such time as the pressure of that effort shall have brought about in the enemy Governments and peoples a change of temper which would justify the hope of the conclusion of peace on terms which would not involve the abandonment, in face of an aggressive and unrepentant militarism, of all the principles of freedom, justice and the respect for the Law of Nations which the Allies are resolved to vindicate."

But if the statement of our peace aims set out in my speech of January 5th had brought forth no favourable public response from the Central Powers, one of their most important Ministers — Count Czernin, the Austrian Foreign Minister — secretly harboured and expressed more kindly thoughts of our proposals. Very soon after the delivery of my speech there was a renewal of the approaches to us from Austria.

Our Minister at Berne received a message that Count Czernin wished to meet me in Switzerland. The Minister had indirectly received a communication from a highly-placed Austrian who had paid a visit to Switzerland in order to convey the message to Sir Horace Rumbold. This Austrian official's diagnosis of the position has an interest of its own. It was set out in a telegram from Sir Horace Rumbold, dated January 11th, 1918, of which the following is a paraphrase: —

M. de Skrzynski yesterday visited Geneva for an interview with Dr. Parodi. According to his statement, there were in the addresses recently delivered by Mr. Lloyd George and by President Wilson a number of points about which there was agreement between the Government of His Majesty and that of Austria-Hungary. There were various other matters in addition referred to, apart from these points, where it seemed that further discussion might well lead to a satisfactory understanding. The comments of a section of the Vienna Press upon the views of Mr. Lloyd George must not be taken by H. M. Government as representative of the views of Count Czernin or of the mass of the people. A part of the Press of Austria-Hungary, and nearly all the Press of Germany, is controlled by munitions manufacturers, and these raise an outcry the moment they observe a glint of peace beginning to dawn. Count Czernin, so M. de Skrzynski proceeded to say, has been compelled to maintain a titanic struggle at Berlin in order to secure the adoption of his 'no annexations' formula. Count Hertling, on the day when a declaration to this effect was made by Kuhlmann, had hardly dared to leave his dwelling, fearing that the mob in the Berlin streets would hiss him.

"A section of the German public is utterly fanatical in supporting militaristic projects of annexation, but there is also a powerful body of Pacifist opinion, which is bound to exert considerable influence.

"As a price for securing the adherence of Germany to his

THE BELLIGERENTS STATE PEACE TERMS 49

formula, Count Czernin was compelled to agree to dispatch certain Austro-Hungarian regiments to the Western Front in order to display the solidarity of Austria with Germany. The military aid thus promised was two or three regiments, and these are already in Belgium or about to proceed thither. It is suggested as desirable by M. de Skrzynski that in commenting upon this the Entente Press should not attach much importance to the military assistance thus rendered, since Germany is really getting it as a sort of blackmail. As regards Turkey, the Austro-Hungarian Government thinks that a formula might be devised which would assure a considerable degree of autonomy to Mesopotamia, Syria and Palestine without ostensibly depriving Turkey of any territory. In any event M. de Skrzynski stated that if Mr. Lloyd George was willing to have an interview with Count Czernin, the latter would come to Switzerland to meet him."

The Cabinet was doubtful as to the wisdom of my accepting the invitation. A meeting of two Prime Ministers from the opposing Powers to discuss Peace was necessarily a more formal occasion and would attract much more attention than private conversations between a Minister and an ex-Ambassador. Besides, Czernin had not answered the question put to Mensdorff as to whether Austria was prepared to negotiate a separate peace. Personally I was strongly in favour of keeping up these communications with Austria. If they came to anything we should have one foe the less to fight. If they did not, even then it would have the effect of making the Austrians less inclined to antagonise the Western Powers by sending troops to fight them in France. So I urged the Cabinet that we should take advantage of every overture which might lead to a separate peace with Austria and might reduce the Austrian Army to the same state of impotent inactivity as the Russian Army had been in during 1917.

It was decided that the opportunity for any serious request for peace *pourparlers* ought not to be ignored, and it was resolved to send a member of the War Cabinet to meet Count Czernin. Messages passed to and fro for weeks, but no meeting could be arranged until late in February. The negotiations made no headway. Czernin was tricky, and our Foreign Office very sticky. The reluctance of the latter to press matters to a conclusion was due to their suspicions of the genuineness of Czernin. They thought he was playing a deep game for Germany. It was clear that he was deceiving one side or the other. If his messages to us were sincere then he was deceiving Germany. If his speeches represented his real intentions then he was playing with us. The truth of the matter probably was that the Austrian Government were pulled in both directions and that they were thoroughly distracted. On the one hand, there was the dread of approaching doom from which they wanted to escape; on the other hand, was the fear of a powerful Germany which enchained them with infrangible steel. It was finally agreed that General Smuts should once more go on his errand of peace and proceed to Switzerland to ascertain the exact meaning and scope of these overtures, whether Count Czernin was actually behind them and, if so, the general line of his proposals.

General Smuts again took with him Mr. Philip Kerr, and they reached Berne on March 9th. At first it appeared as if there had been a complete change in the Austrian attitude and that at last they were prepared to confine the discussions strictly to the problems of an Austro-Hungarian peace. It seemed as if this time the Austrians meant to get out of the War with or without their allies. They were convinced that the War was being prolonged owing to Prussian annexationist ambitions, and they were prepared, once they had negotiated a separate peace, to leave the orbit of Prussian influence, and remodel their institutions on federal lines. Mr. Kerr, being of a naturally hopeful disposition, and being also young and therefore with his belief in human nature not yet vitiated by experience, at first took a sanguine view of the proposals and in a telegram to me from Berne on the situation, said: —

". . . I think that, subject to what Skrzynski may say, very great results might follow from a conversation between Czernin and a British negotiator as to a possible settlement between Austria-Hungary and the Entente, provided that it were absolutely clear that we were not prepared to discuss terms with Germany at all. It is possible that it might end in the three Southern Allies of Germany coming out together. Nor do I see any real danger can follow unless discussion leads to discord with our own Allies, or unless it fails because an agreement cannot be reached because our terms are unreasonable. In latter event Czernin would go back and re-unite his people on the ground that the Entente were impossibly greedy. It therefore seems to me essential that if the Czernin meeting is to take place we should discuss basis of a separate Austro-Hungarian peace with our Allies including Serbia as soon as possible because if anything is to come of a meeting with Czernin he ought to be in a position to reach a preliminary understanding on the spot if he himself is reasonable. . . ."

General Smuts was instructed that he could go ahead on these lines. He had a long conversation with M. de Skrzynski in the course of which the Austrian emissary expressed the fear on Czernin's part that the Entente were simply endeavouring to detach Austria-Hungary in order to isolate and defeat Germany. General Smuts assured him that what the Entente were after was a settlement on terms which would bring about a just and lasting peace everywhere, with a prospect of general disarmament. He added that unfortunately the treaties of Brest-Litovsk and with Roumania were not, in the eyes of the Entente, in keeping with these principles.

The position at which the exchange of views was left on March 14th, 1918, was that if any conversation was to take place it would be for the purpose of arriving at a settlement of all questions outstanding between Austria-Hungary and the Allies, the *principle of settlement being not the bargaining of territory against territory but that justice must be done to all peoples*. On no other basis was it possible to construct a lasting peace. It was understood that the meetings would proceed to discuss the practical application of this agreed principle to the matters in dispute between Italy, Serbia, Roumania and Austria-Hungary, and that inasmuch as certain internal racial questions vitally affected international relations and therefore the possibility of lasting peace, these questions could not be excluded from discussion. It was also clearly understood that the Allied Governments would refuse to be drawn into a discussion of peace terms with Germany.

General Smuts, however, drew one other inference from his meeting with Skrzynski, that between the time when the meeting was first suggested and his actual arrival in Switzerland, a change had once more taken place in the attitude of Count Czernin, and that his eagerness for *pourparlers* with the Entente had diminished in that space of time. This is explained in the conclusions which were set out after the interview in a memorandum by Mr. Kerr: —

". . . In the first place it may be due to the effect of the collapse of Russia before the German advance, coupled with the improved military situation of Germany in the West. Count Czernin may have decided that his best policy was to abandon separate negotiations and see what terms military necessity or a new peace offensive against the civilian populations of the Allies might force us to give him. In the second place the change of attitude may be explained by the opening of the negotiations with America. Czernin may have made up his mind that it would be easier to do business via America because U.S.A. was not tied to Italy by Treaty, and would therefore be more likely to stand out for moderate terms, and also because the U.S.A. was the

Power from which Austria-Hungary could probably get most financial assistance. In the third place, Count Czernin may have begun to realise that once he entered into a conversation with a British plenipotentiary he would be unable to draw back owing to the pressure in favour of peace from popular opinion inside the monarchy, and that once begun the negotiations would inevitably lead on either to a separate peace or to the break-up of the monarchy owing to internal divisions in regard to peace. If so, especially in view of the extreme obscurity of the political situation of the moment, and possibility of a growing realisation of the difficulties which confronted him as he got near the brink of negotiation, Count Czernin may have been merely concerned to gain time, and to avoid committing himself to a meeting which was bound to have fateful consequences. On this hypothesis, which is consistent with M. de Skrzynski's explanation of the change in Count Czernin's attitude, my arrival must have put him in great difficulties. He had indeed no alternative but to temporise."

The proximity of the March offensive, and no doubt the confidence expressed by the German Staff in its success, had damped the Austrian ardour for peace. In this temper no business was possible, and when in a few days the great attack was made and prospered, all question of the continuation of peace conversations was ruled out. All that came of these *pourparlers* was the hesitancy of Austria to throw her army into the deadly struggle in the west. It may be of some interest, not untinged with regret, to conjecture what might have been the effect on the settlement of Europe if peace had been concluded with Austria in the spring of 1918. The Austrian Empire would have remained; instead of breaking up into a number of independent States, not always friendly to the Central authority, there would have been perhaps half a dozen autonomous dominions all owing allegiance to the Austrian Crown and working harmoniously together for their common interests. As for Germany, we received no direct or indirect intimation of her desire for peace except on terms that were not even debatable. The Germans meant to fight it out unless they got terms that would leave them better off territorially and economically at the end of the War than they were at the beginning. The militarists dared not march back to Berlin after signing a peace which was an admission that they were beaten. It was their war and they meant to end it with banners flying. They meant to try one big gamble for such a victory as would enable them to ensure their own terms. Ludendorff urged the politicians at home to support the offensive of his army by an elaborate peace offensive that would undermine the morale of the English nation and make it less eager to put all its strength into the fight. He complained that these politicians were not helping him as they ought to do by a peace propaganda which would weaken and divide the enemy peoples. That was his sole motive for our peace talk.

APPENDIX A

REPORT OF MR. PHILIP KERR'S INTERVIEW WITH DR. PARODI,
HEAD OF THE MISSION SCOLAIRE EGYPTIENNE, ON
DECEMBER 18TH, 1917

Prefatory Note by General Smuts

The Prime Minister asked me before leaving London to look into the Turkish position so far as material was available in Switzerland. Dr. Parodi of Geneva had had several conversations with members of the Turkish Red Cross Mission now in Switzerland and had gathered very interesting information in regard to divergent views in the Committee of Union and Progress. He had also had numerous conversations with many other Turks recently. As I was very busy with the Mensdorff conversations I asked Mr. Philip Kerr, who accompanied me from London, to go into the whole matter with Dr. Parodi, and Mr. Kerr has prepared a note summarising Dr. Parodi's information and views hereto annexed (*a*) which discloses the line of cleavage in the C.U.P. and suggests a line of diplomatic action for us in order to get Turkey out of the War.

I also sent Mr. Kerr to Berne to discuss the whole matter with Sir Horace Rumbold, as I could not myself go there without grave risk of my presence in Switzerland being detected. Mr. Kerr discussed the matter with Sir Horace Rumbold and thereafter again with me, and in consequence a memorandum has been drafted annexed (*b*) of which a copy has been left with Sir Horace Rumbold and in which a line of action is suggested for our endeavours to induce the Turks to make a separate peace. If the War Cabinet approves of this document a telegram sent to Sir Horace Rumbold will enable him to set the whole business going without further delay. Or in the alternative, action may be taken on the document with such modifications as the Cabinet may consider advisable. The whole matter has been carefully discussed with Dr. Parodi, who strikes me as a man of considerable ability and discretion, and I have no doubt that he will prove very useful to Sir Horace Rumbold in the preliminary and informal stages of the business. Sir Horace Rumbold awaits Foreign Office instructions in order to take action. Action should not be delayed as Mouktar Bey, who is at the head of the Turkish Red Cross Mission now in Switzerland, is expected to return to Turkey at the end of the year. He is said to be a friend of Talaat's with leanings towards a settlement with the Entente and may be a useful man with whom to have a preliminary informal conversation.

20th December, 1917.   J.C.S.

Mr. Philip Kerr's Report

Dr. Parodi says that the Committee of Union and Progress is divided into two parts — the larger and the Germanophile, the smaller more disposed towards the Entente and especially Great Britain. The most active leader of the Germanophile section is Enver Pasha. Enver is a pure militarist Germanophile, having no ideas for the future save that Germany will win the War and recover the Turkish Empire, of which he then will be Dictator or Sultan. Talaat also belongs to this section, but is now in an uncertain frame of mind and ready to go with the winning side. He thinks that Germany will neither be victorious nor beaten and that there will be a *paix blanche* more or less on the basis of the *status quo*. On this assumption there is no sufficient reason why Turkey should break with Germany. He listens to what the smaller section of the Committee — the Ententophile — says, does not oppose them but does not act on their opinion.

Turkey is in a very bad way economically but except

for the Committee of Union and Progress, there is nobody capable of taking the initiative at all. The opposition in Europe is powerless because it has no connections or friends inside Turkey. Any movement must, therefore, come from the opposition within the Committee itself. There is no other organised force in Turkey save the Committee, and its force rests on the officers of the Army.

The views of the opposition within the Committee are something as follows: They are getting more and more afraid of Turkey becoming a German province, and are more and more embittered by the arrogant manners and despotic methods of the Germans. To save Turkey from falling completely under German control, they would like to cut free from Germany and lean on England, which they say has always been a friend to Turkey, if they could get moderate terms. The greatest obstacle in their way is the fact that the Germanophile section is able to point out persistently that whereas Germany is pledged to the restoration of the Turkish Empire, the Entente is committed to dismembering it. A number of well-known Turks, *e.g.*, Djemal Pasha, surgeon of the Sultan, Lufti Bey Fikri, député d'Adana, Kamal Bey, and others have all within the last month or two told Dr. Parodi that while they dislike intensely the German connection and can hardly endure to live in Turkey because of it, and that while they greatly fear for the future of Turkey under German control, and are entirely sympathetic to the Entente and especially Great Britain, it is useless and impossible for them to oppose the existing régime because they have no answer to the Germanophile propaganda that whereas the Germans are pledged to recover the Empire, the Allies are pledged to destroy it.

According to Dr. Parodi the Ententophile section is prepared to consider a settlement on something like the following lines: —

(a) ARABIA. That Turkey should acknowledge the complete political independence of the Kingdom of Hedjaz and of the rest of Arabia. The Ententophile section of the Committee recognise that they have failed to govern Arabia properly, and that even if it were possible for them to keep it, it would prove an intolerably burdensome and expensive possession. They are willing, therefore, to concede its complete independence. It could be formed either into the Kingdom of Hedjaz, and a number of independent Sheikdoms, or the latter could be federated. As to the Caliphate the Party is divided. Some would let the King of the Hedjaz have it, others want it for the Sultan. The division apparently follows the line of cleavage between the Pan-Turanian and the Pan-Islamic schools. They would want tribute, however, from Arabia in order to enable the Turkish treasury to make both ends meet.

(b) SYRIA, MESOPOTAMIA, PALESTINE. The Ententophile section of the Committee would be prepared to see these established as autonomous provinces either as separate entities or federated together under the Turkish flag. The autonomy to be real; either a form of Government chosen by the people themselves, or a system of Administration, through European advisers, as in Egypt before the War. The flag, however, must be preserved as the symbol of the unity of the Turkish Empire, and a tribute to be paid to the Ottoman Treasury as in the case of Hedjaz.

(c) ARMENIA. The Ententophile section of the Committee recognise the utter failure of the Turkish Government in Armenia, are ashamed of its record of assassination and atrocity and are willing to leave the fate of Armenia to be entirely decided by the European Powers. In order to facilitate this they are willing to transfer the Kurds from Armenian villayets into a separate Kurdish villayet.

(d) CONSTANTINOPLE. As to Constantinople it must remain Turk. On this they lay the utmost stress, and it would have the most enormous moral effect in Turkey, if it became known that the Allies would be willing that Constantinople should remain Turkish. The Allied declarations which still hold the field are those of Miliukoff. These have never yet been amended. They also wish for a strategic rectification of their frontier towards Bulgaria. They are extremely bitter about the part they surrendered to Bulgaria as the price of getting her into the War and fiercely demand it back. As to the Straits, Bosphorus and Dardanelles, they would agree that they should be neutralised — a special International Commission to be appointed to control the waterways, quays, etc. They would dismantle the forts and make no new ones within a certain radius.

In order to enable the opposition to make any headway it is essential, according to Dr. Parodi, that the Allies should let the C.U.P. (the whole Committee including Talaat and Enver and not merely the opposition) know the Allied views in regard to Turkey. If the Allied views are moderate and anything like those outlined above it will give the moderate section the arguments they require for propaganda in the C.U.P., the Army and elsewhere, and thereby enable them to get control over the Organisation.

A communication of the views of the Allies could be made through a suitable source to Mouktar Bey, who is now in Switzerland as President of the Commission about the exchange of prisoners, and who will remain here till about January 1st, and who could probably be induced to stay longer if necessary. The communication should be made in this form; a suitable agent who could speak as one friendly to Turkey should inform Mouktar Bey that the views of the Allies in regard to Turkey are not extreme, that he has the best of reasons in fact for believing that the sort of terms they would be prepared to consider are so and so, and that if Talaat and the Committee wish to know what the views of the Entente are in regard to the future of Turkey they should make a request for information through an official channel when an official reply would be sent.

The effects of a moderate declaration by the Allies — which would be immediately known through the branches of the C.U.P. — would be (*a*) to stimulate and give sound arguments to the Ententophile propaganda within the Committee; (*b*) to hearten the Arabs in Arabia, Syria, Mesopotamia and Palestine by showing that the aim of the Entente was to secure them autonomy; (*c*) to further the antagonism between the Arab officers and troops within the Army and the Turkish officers and troops and so lower the morale of the army itself.

If the Ententophile section gained the ascendancy (probably through the murder of Enver) they believe they could deal with the German troops and officers in Turkey themselves. The C.U.P. is strong enough for that. But they fear a Bulgarian attack, and if there was any chance of the Revolution against German control taking place it would be necessary for the Entente to have ships and troops ready to rush through to Constantinople *via* Dardanelles or Smyrna.

There is one further point. The Ententophile section is much concerned over the financial problem. They owe about £300,000,000 to the Germans. So long as they owe this they cannot live as an independent power. They will simply be concession-ridden and in German hands. They want the Allies to help them in this matter, and also to give them a loan to enable them to reorganise Turkish finances. They also want agricultural machinery, etc., so as to raise food. Not the least of the inducements to the Turks to make a separate peace is the prospect of having the economic support of the

THE BELLIGERENTS STATE PEACE TERMS

Entente powers. They can only recover with outside assistance. German assistance means German control. If they could see their way to making a fresh start in close relations with the Entente it would be a great inducement to them to make an immediate peace.

I arranged with Sir Horace Rumbold that subject to confirmation by telegram from London, Dr. Parodi should cause a communication in the following sense to be made unofficially and verbally to Mouktar Bey. The communication to take the form of a conversation between Mouktar Bey and a friend to Turkey who had exceptional means of knowing the views of the Allies. The exact method to be left to the discretion of Dr. Parodi.

1. That in view of the military reverses which had been already sustained by Turkey and of the tremendously strong position held by the Allies *vis-à-vis* the Central Powers, not merely militarily, but owing to their command of the economic resources of the world, a position which was bound to become steadily stronger, the Allies were by no means inspired by the hostile intentions attributed to them by the German propagandists, but were on the contrary moderate in their views and were quite prepared that Turkey should occupy an adequate place among the peoples of the world, provided she was willing to break immediately with Germany and make peace with the Allies.

2. That in the event of an immediate peace the Allies would be prepared, provided the Dardanelles, Sea of Marmora and the Bosphorus were neutralised, that Constantinople should remain the capital of Turkey. Neutralisation to consist of the dismantlement of all forts and the withdrawal of troops within a certain distance of the waterway, and the handing over of the control of the waterway between the Mediterranean and the Black Sea and of any quays

and docks which might be necessary to an International Commission, as in the case of the Suez Canal.

3. That the Allies were determined that the Administrative Authority of the Turks must be entirely withdrawn from Armenia, Syria, Mesopotamia, Palestine and Arabia, so that the inhabitants of these territories might conduct autonomous governments of their own, or be governed by a mixed system of local and European officials under the protection of one or more of the Allied Powers, as has been the case in Egypt. As to the international status of these territories, Armenia and Arabia would have to be entirely separated from the Turkish dominions. In the case of Syria, Palestine and Mesopotamia, however, the Allies might be willing in the event of an immediate peace, to consider the retention of the Turkish flag as the symbol of Turkish suzerainty, provided it carried with it no executive authority.

4. That the Allies would be willing to free Turkey of the debt incurred in respect of the above-mentioned territories, to give liberal financial and other economic assistance to Turkey to enable her to make a fresh start, and to free herself from the German economic incubus, and so go forward as one of the states in friendly relations with the Entente group of powers, which is bound to be the strongest in the world.

NOTE. — Negotiations in regard to peace between Turkey and the Allies to be inaugurated upon the receipt of a private official enquiry from the Turkish Government, or any highly placed Turkish statesman or official of authority, which would be made *via* the British Legation, Berne, to the effect that the Turkish Government or such statesman or official was anxious to know the conditions which the Allies would propose for an immediate peace with Turkey. A method of communication could then be arranged.

19th December, 1917.   P.H.K.

APPENDIX B

THE PEACE DECLARATION

*Mr. Lloyd George's Speech to the Trade Unions,
January 5, 1918*

When the Government invite organised labour in this country to assist them to maintain the might of their armies in the field, its representatives are entitled to ask that any misgivings and doubts which any of them may have about the purpose to which this precious strength is to be applied should be definitely cleared, and what is true of organised labour is equally true of all citizens in this country without regard to grade or avocation.

When men by the million are being called upon to suffer and face death and vast populations are being subjected to the sufferings and privations of war on a scale unprecedented in the history of the world, they are entitled to know for what cause or causes they are making the sacrifice. It is only the clearest, greatest and justest of causes that can justify the continuance even for one day of this unspeakable agony of the nations. And we ought to be able to state clearly and definitely not only the principles for which we are fighting, but also their definite and concrete application to the war map of the world.

We have arrived at the most critical hour in this terrible conflict, and before any Government takes the fateful decision as to the conditions under which it ought either to terminate or continue the struggle, it ought to be satisfied that the conscience of the nation is behind these conditions, for nothing else can sustain the effort which is necessary to achieve a righteous end to this war. I have, therefore, during the last few days taken special pains to ascertain the view and the attitude of representative men of all sections of thought and opinion in the country. Last week I had the privilege not merely of perusing the declared war aims of the Labour Party, but also of discussing in detail with the Labour leaders the meaning and intention of that declaration. I have also had an opportunity of discussing this same momentous question with Mr. Asquith and Viscount Grey. Had it not been that the Nationalist leaders are in Ireland engaged in endeavouring to solve the tangled problem of Irish self-government, I should have been happy to exchange views with them, but Mr. Redmond, speaking on their behalf, has, with his usual lucidity and force, in many of his speeches, made clear what his ideas are as to the object and purpose of the War. I have also had the opportunity of consulting certain representatives of the great Dominions overseas.

I am glad to be able to say as a result of all these discussions that although the Government are alone responsible for the actual language I propose using, there is national agreement as to the character and purpose of our war aims and peace conditions, and in what I say to you to-day, and through you to the world, I can venture to claim that I am speaking not merely the mind of the Government but of the nation and of the Empire as a whole.

We may begin by clearing away some misunderstandings and stating what we are *not* fighting for. We are not fighting a war of aggression against the German people. Their leaders have persuaded them that they are fighting a war of self-defence against a league of rival nations bent on the destruction of Germany. That is not so. The destruction or disruption of Germany or the German people has never been a war aim with us from the first day of this war to this hour. Most reluctantly and, indeed quite unprepared for the dreadful ordeal, we were forced to join in this war in self-defence, in defence of the violated public law of Europe, and in vindication of the most solemn treaty obligations on which the public system of Europe rested, and on which Germany had ruthlessly trampled in her invasion of Belgium. We had to join in the struggle or stand aside and see Europe go under and brute force triumph over public right and international justice. It was only the realisation of that dreadful alternative that forced the British people into the War. And from that original attitude they have never swerved. They have never aimed at the break-up of the German peoples or the disintegration of their country or Empire. Germany has occupied a great position in the world. It is not our wish or intention to question or destroy that position for the future, but rather to turn her aside from hopes and schemes of military domination and to see her devote all her strength to the great beneficent tasks of humanity. Nor are we fighting to destroy Austria-Hungary or to deprive Turkey of its capital, or of the rich and renowned lands of Asia Minor and Thrace, which are predominantly Turkish in race.

Nor did we enter this war merely to alter or destroy the Imperial constitution of Germany, much as we consider that military autocratic constitution a dangerous anachronism in the twentieth century. Our point of view is that the adoption of a really democratic constitution by Germany would be the most convincing evidence that in her the old spirit of military domination had indeed died in this war, and would make it much easier for us to conclude a broad democratic peace with her. But, after all, that is a question for the German people to decide.

It is now more than a year since the President of the United States, then neutral, addressed to the belligerents a suggestion that each side should state clearly the aims for which they were fighting. We and our Allies responded by the Note of the Tenth of January, 1917.

To the President's appeal the Central Empire made no

reply, and in spite of many adjurations, both from their opponents and from neutrals, they have maintained a complete silence as to the objects for which they are fighting. Even on so crucial a matter as their intention with regard to Belgium they have uniformly declined to give any trustworthy indication.

On December 25th last, however, Count Czernin, speaking on behalf of Austria-Hungary and her allies, did make a pronouncement of a kind. It is indeed deplorably vague. We are told that "it is not the intention" of the Central Powers "to appropriate forcibly" any occupied territories or "to rob of its independence" any nation which has lost its "political independence" during the War. It is obvious that almost any scheme of conquest and annexation could be perpetrated within the literal interpretation of such a pledge.

Does it mean that Belgium, Serbia, Montenegro and Roumania will be as independent and as free to direct their own destinies as the Germans or any other nation? Or does it mean that all manner of interferences and restrictions, political and economic, incompatible with the status and dignity of a free and self-respecting people, are to be imposed? If this is the intention then there will be one kind of independence for a great nation and an inferior kind of independence for a small nation. We must know what is meant, for equality of right among nations, small as well as great, is one of the fundamental issues this country and her Allies are fighting to establish in this war. Reparation for the wanton damage inflicted on Belgian towns and villages and their inhabitants is emphatically repudiated. The rest of the so-called "offer" of the Central Powers is almost entirely a refusal of all concessions. All suggestions about the autonomy of subject nationalities are ruled out of the peace terms altogether. The question whether any form of self-government is to be given to Arabs, Armenians, or Syrians is declared to be entirely a matter for the Sublime Porte. A pious wish for the protection of minorities "in so far as it is practically realisable" is the nearest approach to liberty which the Central statesmen venture to make.

On one point only are they perfectly clear and definite. Under no circumstances will the "German demand" for the restoration of the whole of Germany's colonies be departed from. All principles of self-determination, or, as our earlier phrase goes, government by consent of the governed, here vanish into thin air.

It is impossible to believe that any edifice of permanent peace could be erected on such a foundation as this. Mere lip service to the formula of no annexations and no indemnities or the right of self-determination is useless. Before any negotiations can even be begun, the Central Powers must realise the essential facts of the situation.

The days of the Treaty of Vienna are long past. We can no longer submit the future of European civilisation to the arbitrary decisions of a few negotiators striving to secure by chicanery or persuasion the interests of this or that dynasty or nation. The settlement of the new Europe must be based on such grounds of reason and justice as will give some promise of stability. *Therefore it is that we feel that government with the consent of the governed must be the basis of any territorial settlement in this war.* For that reason also, unless treaties be upheld, unless every nation is prepared at whatever sacrifices to honour the national signature, it is obvious that no Treaty of Peace can be worth the paper on which it is written.

The first requirement, therefore, always put forward by the British Government and their Allies, has been the complete restoration, political, territorial and economic, of the independence of Belgium and such reparation as can be made for the devastation of its towns and provinces. This is no demand for a war indemnity such as that imposed on France by Germany in 1871. It is not an attempt to shift the cost of warlike operations from one belligerent to another, which may or may not be defensible. It is no more and no less than an insistence that before there can be any hope for a stable peace, this great breach of the public law of Europe must be repudiated, and, so far as possible, repaired. Reparation means recognition. Unless international right is recognised by insistence on payment for injury done in defiance of its canons it can never be a reality. Next comes the restoration of Serbia, Montenegro, and the occupied parts of France, Italy and Roumania. The complete withdrawal of the alien armies and the reparation for injustice done is a fundamental condition of permanent peace.

We mean to stand by the French democracy to the death in the demand they make for a reconsideration of the great wrong of 1871, when, without any regard to the wishes of the population, two French provinces were torn from the side of France and incorporated in the German Empire. This sore has poisoned the peace of Europe for half a century, and until it is cured healthy conditions will not have been restored. There can be no better illustration of the folly and wickedness of using a transient military success to violate national right.

I will not attempt to deal with the question of the Russian territories now in German occupation. The Russian policy since the Revolution has passed so rapidly through so many phases that it is difficult to speak without some suspension of judgment as to what the situation will be when the final terms of European peace come to be discussed. Russia accepted war with all its horrors because, true to her traditional guardianship of the weaker communities of her race, she stepped in to protect Serbia from a plot against her independence. It is this honourable sacrifice which not merely brought Russia into the War, but France as well. France, true to the conditions of her treaty with Russia, stood by her Ally in a quarrel which was not her own. Her chivalrous respect for her treaty led to the wanton invasion of Belgium; and the treaty obligations of Great Britain to that little land brought us into the War.

The present rulers of Russia are now engaged without any reference to the countries whom Russia brought into the War, in separate negotiations, with their common enemy. I am indulging in no reproaches; I am merely stating facts with a view to making it clear why Britain cannot be held accountable for decisions taken in her absence, and concerning which she has not been consulted or her aid invoked. No one who knows Prussia and her designs upon Russia can for a moment doubt her ultimate intention. Whatever phrases she may use to delude Russia, she does not mean to surrender one of the fair provinces or cities of Russia now occupied by her forces. Under one name or another — and the name hardly matters — these Russian provinces will henceforth be in reality part of the dominions of Prussia. They will be ruled by the Prussian sword in the interests of Prussian autocracy, and the rest of the people of Russia will be partly enticed by specious phrases and partly bullied by the threat of continued war against an impotent army into a condition of complete economic and ultimate political enslavement to Germany. We all deplore the prospect. *The democracy of this country means to stand to the last by the democracies of France and Italy and all our other Allies.* We shall be proud to fight to the end side by side with the new democracy of Russia, so will America and so will France and Italy. But if the present rulers of Russia take action which is independent of their Allies we have no means of intervening to arrest the catastrophe which is assuredly befalling their country. Russia can only be saved by her own people.

We believe, however, that an independent Poland, comprising all those genuinely Polish elements who desire to form part of it, is an urgent necessity for the stability of Western Europe.

Similarly, though we agree with President Wilson that the break-up of Austria-Hungary is no part of our war aims, we feel that, unless genuine self-government on true democratic principles is granted to those Austro-Hungarian nationalities who have long desired it, it is impossible to hope for the removal of those causes of unrest in that part of Europe which have so long threatened its general peace.

On the same grounds we regard as vital the satisfaction of the legitimate claims of the Italians for union with those of their own race and tongue. We also mean to press that justice be done to men of Roumanian blood and speech in their legitimate aspirations. If these conditions are fulfilled Austria-Hungary would become a Power whose strength would conduce to the permanent peace and freedom of Europe, instead of being merely an instrument for the pernicious military autocracy of Prussia that uses the resources of its allies for the furtherance of its own sinister purposes.

Outside Europe we believe that the same principles should be applied. While we do not challenge the maintenance of the Turkish Empire in the homelands of the Turkish race with its capital at Constantinople — the passage between the Mediterranean and the Black Sea being internationalised and neutralised — Arabia, Armenia, Mesopotamia, Syria and Palestine are in our judgment entitled to a recognition of their separate national conditions.

What the exact form of that recognition in each particular case should be need not here be discussed, beyond stating that it would be impossible to restore to their former sovereignty the territories to which I have already referred.

Much has been said about the arrangements we have entered into with our Allies on this and on other subjects. I can only say that as new circumstances, like the Russian collapse and the separate Russian negotiations, have changed the conditions under which those arrangements were made, we are, and always have been, perfectly ready to discuss them with our Allies.

With regard to the German colonies, I have repeatedly declared that they are held at the disposal of a Conference whose decision must have primary regard to the wishes and interests of the native inhabitants of such colonies. None of those territories are inhabited by Europeans. The governing consideration, therefore, in all these cases must be that the inhabitants should be placed under the control of an administration acceptable to themselves, one of whose main purposes will be to prevent their exploitation for the benefit of European capitalists or Governments. The natives live in their various tribal organisations under chiefs and councils who are competent to consult and speak for their tribes and members, and thus to represent their wishes and interests in regard to their disposal.

The general principle of national self-determination is therefore as applicable in their cases as in those of occupied European territories. The German declaration, that the natives of the German colonies have, through their military fidelity in the War, shown their attachment and resolve under all circumstances to remain with Germany, is applicable not to the German colonies generally, but only to one of them, and in that case (German East Africa) the German authorities secured the attachment, not of the native population as a whole, which is, and remains, profoundly anti-German, but only of a small warlike class from whom their Askaris, or soldiers, were selected. These they attached to themselves by conferring on them a highly privileged position as against the bulk of the native population, which enabled these Askaris to assume a lordly and oppressive superiority over the rest of the natives. By this and other means they secured the attachment of a very small and insignificant minority whose interests were directly opposed to those of the rest of the population, and for whom they have no right to speak. The German treatment of their native populations in their colonies has been such as amply to justify their fear of submitting the future of those colonies to the wishes of the natives themselves.

Finally, there must be reparation for injuries done in violation of international law. The Peace Conference must not forget our seamen and the services they have rendered to, and the outrages they have suffered for, the common cause of freedom.

One omission we notice in the proposal of the Central Powers, which seems to us especially regrettable. It is desirable, and indeed essential, that the settlement after this war shall be one which does not in itself bear the seed of future war. But that is not enough. However wisely and well we may make territorial and other arrangements, there will still be many subjects of international controversy. Some indeed are inevitable.

The economic conditions at the end of the War will be in the highest degree difficult. Owing to the diversion of human effort to warlike pursuits, there must follow a world-shortage of raw materials, which will increase the longer the War lasts, and it is inevitable that those countries which have control of the raw materials will desire to help themselves and their friends first.

Apart from this, whatever settlement is made will be suitable only to the circumstances under which it is made, and, as those circumstances change, changes in the settlement will be called for.

So long as the possibility of dispute between nations continues, that is to say, so long as men and women are dominated by passioned ambition, and war is the only means of settling a dispute, all nations must live under the burden not only of having from time to time to engage in it, but of being compelled to prepare for its possible outbreak. The crushing weight of modern armaments, the increasing evil of compulsory military service, the vast waste of wealth and effort involved in warlike preparation, these are blots on our civilisation of which every thinking individual must be ashamed.

For these and other similar reasons, we are confident that a great attempt must be made to establish by some international organisation an alternative to war as a means of settling international disputes. After all war is a relic of barbarism, and, just as law has succeeded violence as the means of settling disputes between individuals, so we believe that it is destined ultimately to take the place of war in the settlement of controversies between nations.

If, then, we are asked what are we fighting for, we reply, as we have often replied: We are fighting for a just and a lasting peace, and we believe that before permanent peace can be hoped for three conditions must be fulfilled.

First, the sanctity of treaties must be reëstablished; secondly, a territorial settlement must be secured based on the right of self-determination or the consent of the governed; and, lastly, we must seek by the creation of some international organisation to limit the burden of armaments and diminish the probability of war.

In these conditions the British Empire would welcome peace; to secure those conditions its peoples are prepared to make even greater sacrifices than those they have yet endured.

CHAPTER III

BOLSHEVISM CONQUERS RUSSIA

World Importance of Russian Revolution — Great men in revolutions — Strength of Lenin — Buchanan's account of Government confusion — The Czar's drugs — Nervousness of Kerensky — Growing power of Bolsheviks — Report of conditions at Cronstadt — Buchanan reports growing confusion — Confirmation from another source — Brusiloff's offensive — Knox's account of Russian retreat — Terrible position of officers — Peace or massacre — View of Inter-Allied Conference in July — Help for Russia proposed — Opinion of military chiefs — Bolshevik rising of 16th of July — Buchanan's account — Order temporarily restored — Squabbles in the Government — Korniloff reinstated — Robertson's hopes — Inter-Allied Conference sends congratulations — Position in September: Knox's views — Korniloff's rebellion and fall — Kerensky's complaint — Lenin and Trotsky overthrow Kerensky — Russia breaks with the Allies — Perils of Bolshevik Intrigues — Discussion in the Cabinet — Kaledin — Russian Armistice with Germany — Paris Conference discusses the position — Allied attitude to Russia — Mr. Balfour's memorandum — No breach with Russia — Cabinet decision — Terms of Russian Armistice — Problem of British in Russia — Trotsky's peace proposals — Vague reply of Central Powers — British memorandum submitted to French Government — British attitude in January, 1918 — Balfour's statement — Buchanan's view — Knox on military situation — Russian Armies disappearing — I do not fear Bolshevism — Despatch to Lockhart — Wilson's greeting to Bolsheviks — Our disgust at Peace Terms — Protest by Supreme War Council — Appendix A: Trotsky's statement of Bolshevik policy.

THERE are two of the direct consequences of the War which have already exerted a palpable influence on the course of human affairs and will continue to do so more and more as the years roll by. One is the establishment of the League of Nations — the other is the Russian Revolution. The question whether the Russian Revolution will have as great an effect on the lives of the people in all countries as had the French Revolution, or an even greater, will be determined by one eventuality: it will depend on whether its leaders can keep their movement in the paths of peaceable development or whether its energies will be wasted and its purpose deflected by war. If Russia remains at peace then the Revolution will become one of the greatest factors in fashioning the destiny of the masses in all lands which mankind has ever witnessed or experienced.

Those of us who had entertained the hope that the Russian Revolution would consolidate and reinvigorate the fighting strength of Russia in the last War came reluctantly to recognise as time went on how incalculable is the course of all revolutions. The rot in Russia had gone too far, and had eaten too deeply into the existing organisation of the Russian State to be cured by bandaging the sore at a clearing station under gun-fire. The Provisional Government, which had ruled Russia since the abdication of the Czar, thought temporary remedies could be applied to Russia's wounds in order to send her back to the fighting line. That Government fell at the end of May because it was so completely out of touch with realities.

It is no use saying now that if the Russian reformers had thrown up one strong man and placed him in command then events would have taken a different turn. Often the strong man in a revolution is not the person who initiates it, but the man who subsequently exploits it. Events precipitate a situation, personalities fashion its shape and direct its course.

There are those who contend that no personality, however powerful he may be, can ordain the course of events, or change them except transitionally. Their interpretation of great historical upheavals is that the times are ripe for certain happenings and that they would occur, even if a great man had not appeared on the scene and pulled the lever which precipitated them. This always seems to me to be a misreading of history. There have been occasions in which a man of power has postponed, if not averted, a catastrophe which seemed imminent and was ultimately inevitable. There have also been times when a strong man has accelerated changes which but for him would have been long postponed. Nations become static just as individuals sink into indolence. In that condition they both deteriorate. A strong influence may shake them up and thus save them. Lvoff and Miliukoff could not have directed the Russian Revolution. Neither could Kerensky. It might have ended in utter anarchy and the break-up of Russia into countless small and warring states fighting about undefined frontiers, or it might have culminated in another military dictatorship. Russia was accustomed to the sovereignty of brutal soldiers. Korniloff very nearly established such an autocracy. Lenin, with the aid of Trotsky, averted these calamities and directed Russia through chaos, bloodshed, and suffering into an amazing Reformation which, if it succeeds, may yet change the whole economic condition of the world.

The one really powerful personality thrown up by the Russian Revolution was more concerned about overthrowing the existing order of society than about defeating the Germans. Lenin was an exile from Russia when the Revolution broke out. The first reforming leaders were not anxious to welcome his presence. He owes his return to the facilities provided by the German military authorities who thought that he would be an element of discord in Russia and thus help to break up Russian unity. Their calculation was sound. But what a price Germany has paid and is still paying for a short-lived triumph! It is difficult to take long views in war. Victory is the only horizon. It is a lesson to the statesmanship which takes short-sighted views of a situation and seizes the chance of a temporary advantage without counting the certainty of future calamity.

Soon after the Revolution broke out the shadow of the tremendous figure of Lenin began to rise above the horizon. It fell on the green table of Downing Street for the first time

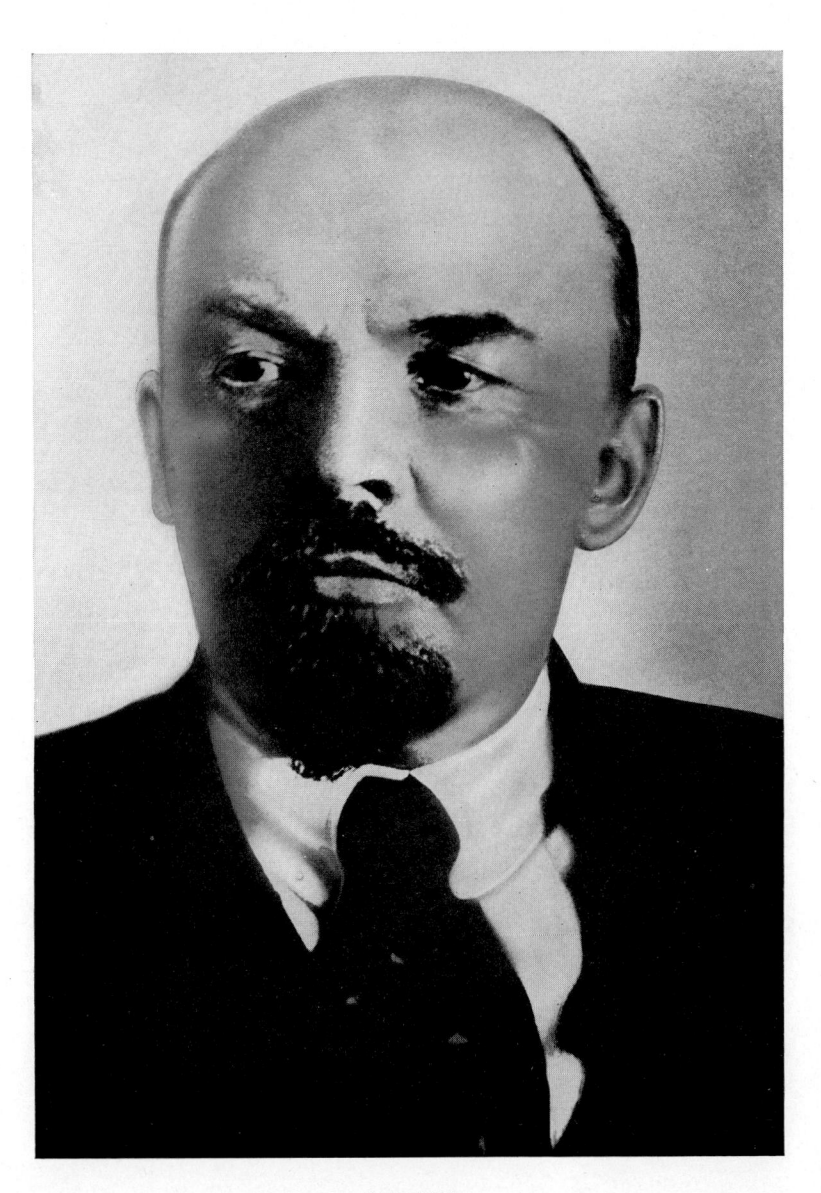

LENIN

in a despatch from Sir George Buchanan, who wrote as follows.

"Petrograd,
30th April, 1917.

"As you will have seen from my telegrams the situation here continues in much the same state of uncertainty as before and it is impossible to say what may happen from day to day. If one listens to Ministers one hears that all is going well and that the Government is gradually consolidating its position; while, if one takes the opinion of those who are in touch both with the Government and the Workmen's Council, one gets exactly the opposite impression. A battle royal seems to be proceeding between Kerensky and Miliukoff on the famous formula 'Peace without annexation', and, as the majority of Ministers are, according to all accounts, on Kerensky's side, I should not be surprised if Miliukoff has to go, as he remarked the other day that he would be a traitor were he to give in on the subject of Constantinople. He would be a loss in many ways as he represents the moderate element in the Cabinet and is sound on the subject of war; but he is not a strong man and has so little influence with his colleagues that one never knows whether he will be able to give effect to what he says. If he does go there is no saying who his successor will be, but I trust that it will in any case be someone who can speak with authority in the name of the Government.

"The Government is still playing a waiting game and prefers that the initiative in dealing with Lenin should come from the people, rather than that they themselves should give the order for his arrest. They are probably right, as the feeling against Lenin is growing stronger both among the soldiers and the people, I should not indeed be surprised if things came to a crisis during the May Day celebrations to-morrow. If there is to be a row, and perhaps more street fighting, I would sooner that the crisis came at once so that we may get it over and that the country may be able to give more attention to the War. The military situation is no doubt very unsatisfactory; but there are, I think, signs of improvement and the Russians have such a happy knack of getting out of scrapes, that I personally do not take such a pessimistic view of it as some of our experts who judge it more particularly from the deplorable lack of discipline reported from certain points on the front. I am afraid, however, that the Army will not be able to take the offensive so soon as some of the Ministers had led me to believe. This is to be regretted, as the sooner the fighting begins the better it will be for the internal situation.

"It is most difficult to express an opinion on the relative positions of the Provisional Government and the Council of Workmen and Soldiers' Deputies. The latter is being completely reorganised. Its numbers have been reduced to 600 and a new Executive Committee has been appointed. The effect of this reorganisation will be to render it a more moderate, but at the same time, a stronger body. It is not therefore likely to renounce its claim to control and direct the policy of the Government, but if it is really animated by a greater spirit of moderation it may perhaps work more harmoniously than before with the Provisional Government. On the other hand, the possibility of a conflict between the two rival bodies cannot altogether be excluded. It seems that the former Extremist Members, who are not included in the reorganised Council, are going to set up a Committee of their own and I trust that, as I remarked to Miliukoff yesterday, this does not mean that there will be three instead of two rival Governments. I do not think that the Council is likely to press for an early peace; but it will probably give us a good deal of trouble as to the terms on which the Allies ought to accept peace and as to the interpretation to be placed on the word 'annexation.' The chief danger that I foresee is the not improbable eventuality of Germany putting forward plausible conditions of peace, as such overtures might be seized on by the pacifists here and pressure be brought on the Government to induce the Allies to open peace negotiations. . . .

"They are now attacking our Labour Delegates as being the paid emissaries of the Government and not real representatives of British labour. It is very difficult to know what to do with people who stick to their preconceived ideas and will not listen to reason. . . ."

Here is some light thrown on the scandalmongering in high places which was a prelude to the poor Czar's downfall. It did much to bring about the Revolution: —

"Felix Yousoupoff, who came to see me the other day with a message from Empress Marie, told me that he knew as a fact that the Emperor had been treated by a Thibetan Doctor here with drugs that had seriously affected his mental powers. He had himself been taken by Rasputin to see this Doctor one day when he was feeling unwell, and, on the question as to the effect of these drugs being broached by Rasputin, the Thibetan had said that, if taken for any length of time, they produced in the patient a state of callousness and complete insensibility to anything that befell him. Yousoupoff said that he had afterwards extracted from Rasputin the admission that the Emperor had had a course of these drugs, and he believes that they are in a great measure responsible for the Emperor's abnormal conduct and almost childish indifference to the loss of his Crown. He could not say who it was that had induced the Emperor to take them; but the idea had evidently originated with someone who wished to render the Emperor incapable of having a will of his own. I have been told much the same story by the Grand Duke Nicolas Michailovitch and others and after what Yousoupoff said I think there must be some foundation for it."

The letter reads like a despatch from Paris after the fall of the Bastille, when gossip about the tragic Royalties of the day was becoming more and more calumnious and when Marat and Robespierre were profiting by it to challenge the Girondists with their respectable revolution.

Kerensky was a man of high ideals, but he had a highly strung and nervous temperament. Like the Girondists he was endowed with an unsurpassed gift of dynamic eloquence which moved vast audiences to any display of emotion he sought to arouse. But he relied too much on oratory and did not follow it by deeds. Rhetoric which does not lead to action is mere play-acting. This defect foredoomed him to failure when he was confronted with men whose first impulse was action. It marks the difference between the rhetorician and the revolutionary. The situation needed a man of a sterner make than Kerensky. One of the shrewdest observers we sent to Russia, General Knox, who was at the head of Russian affairs at this time, thought that "the heart of the people was sound, but that force was required, and force could have been assembled if the Government had contained a single man of will." As Lenin represented at that time only a minority of the workers and practically none of the peasants, General Knox's view is probably correct.

The Allies were anxious to give the Russian Government every help in their power to stabilise its position at home and to reconstitute its front towards the enemy. They believed that even now a whole-hearted and sympathetic effort on their part to give Russia practical support would rally and unite her people, and keep her in the War as an effective fighting force.

But the powerful forces that were at work against us were irresolutely grappled with by the Provisional Government. Lenin, Zinovieff and others had arrived at Petrograd in April via Germany, and throughout the early summer of 1917 their influence was gradually gaining in power, while the discipline in the Russian Army was as steadily diminishing.

Here is a picturesque but discerning account of the situation from a British officer who wrote from Cronstadt at this time of perplexity and confusion: —

". . . Just at the moment the industrial situation is grave. Skobeleff, the Minister of Labour, delivers himself of declarations which read like a nightmare of undigested terminology. Confiscation of bank surpluses, whatever that may mean, being the latest on Friday; the Minister of Commerce, Konovaloff, resigned in a demonstration against him, saying that it was impossible to maintain output or financial equilibrium in face of the unchecked demands of the workpeople. Under occidental conditions Skobeleff would be a State-control man and Konovaloff a Manchester Liberal, as far as I can make out. Unfortunately, just now there is in Russia no State to control anything. Men are striking for 100 per cent. rises retrospective to the beginning of the War, for six-hour days, for six months' payment in advance. One firm has been confronted with a demand for increases which amount to about 20 per cent. more than its capital. The same firm had been making a profit of 40 per cent.

"All our domestic troubles with labour are here seen magnified; prices four times the normal and profits accordingly. Wages two and a half times the normal and therefore forcing up prices without overtaking them. To this add fraud and corruption on one side and the complete absence of any organisation on the other. Two years of paper money (they are said to be issuing another 2,000 million roubles) and two months of revolution complete the tale, which is one of simple disintegration.

"As for politics, take this as an instance. Cronstadt has proclaimed itself as an independent republic. At the bottom of this remarkable act was apparently nothing more than a simple belief in the wisdom and beauty of decentralisation which happened to be the word in vogue. The Republicans were genuinely shocked when the Commandant said that being an officer of the Government he must go; they explained that they didn't want him to go, so why should he? All yesterday the humour was that they were going to bombard us; Socialist deputations trickled down all day to give them their first lessons in Political Science. To-day the current account is that the Government was going to attack Cronstadt with an army according to some, with destroyers according to others. There is to be a railway strike next week. I am trying hard to find out whether in all this welter there is anything like a Labour Executive in the Council; the Commercial Attaché thinks there is a kind of clearing house through which the demands of the workpeople are passed. If there is, then with Skobeleff vague but fervently determined to do something and a Labour group actually collating the workpeople's unrestrained desire for a good time, there may be something for Henderson to work on. Next to strike and Cronstadt, the great topic of discussion is peace *v.* offensive. I am inclined to think that the policy of the Government is to coax the people into a summer offensive in the hope that peace will then slip into the background. I am not hopeful. Everyone is clear that Russia is sick of the War. The only other thing they are clear on is that in Russia you never know what will happen next and several people have told me that Petrograd is even sicker of the existing state of affairs. Next time, they say, the Cossacks will shoot. . . ."

Contemporary letters written by experienced and observant men who were passing through the experiences of the first weeks of the Revolution threw a valuable light not merely on this particular convulsion, but on the process by which discontent develops into revolution through unwise and ineffective handling.

On June 15th, just before Kerensky's assumption of office, our Ambassador wrote: —

". . . The situation in Petrograd is as bad as ever, which is hardly to be wondered at seeing that there is no proper police force to maintain order; and the uncertain attitude of the troops causes the Government considerable anxiety. There are, however, signs of a reaction, not in favour of a monarchy, but of a stable Government capable of maintaining order and putting an end to the existing anarchy that is steadily spreading over the country. The Government has, I am convinced, only to act with firmness and it will have the mass of the people behind it. From what Terestchenko tells me, they consider that the psychological moment has arrived for action and, if he really represents their views, they are going to get rid of the Petrograd garrison and employ the Cossacks, who can be thoroughly relied on, should the occasion arise. The result of the recent municipal elections shows that the Extremists are but a small minority and their position is likely to be seriously compromised if, as he hopes, Terestchenko is able to prove that many of their leaders are in German pay. The convocation of an all-Russian Conference of Delegates from all the Workmen's Councils in Russia, which is to meet in a day or two, will be a new and interesting factor in the situation. It will transform the local Council into a national one and invest it with greater authority and influence. It is generally expected that the admission of Workmen's and Soldiers' Deputies from the provinces will act in a moderating sense, and if this proves to be the case there will be closer coöperation between the Council and the Government. . . .

"As regards the Army the outlook is more hopeful, though the pessimists declare that it is quite incapable of taking an offensive. Ministers, on the other hand, speak with considerable confidence, and an offensive will, in my opinion, be certainly undertaken as soon as the difficulties of supplies, etc., have been surmounted, but with what measure of success it will be attended is a matter on which I will not venture to prophesy. . . .

"Since writing the above I have seen the Chief of the General Staff who told me that the latest information from the front was far more satisfactory, and that the offensive would be taken within the next fortnight. . . ."

Another letter, written from another source on June 24th, ran as follows: —

"We had another crisis on 22nd–23rd June which most people thought would not be surmounted without serious bloodshed. The 'Bolsheviki' called on all their followers to make an armed demonstration against the Government, who had allied themselves with the capitalists and were responsible for the War and all the misery entailed by it. Leaflets of an even more inflammatory kind were distributed inciting to open violence.

"Fortunately the Government had just been reinforced by votes of confidence from the All-Russian Council of Labour and Soldiers' Delegates and the All-Russian Peasants' Congress; and those two bodies, backed by the Executive Committee of the Petrograd Council and all the Socialist organisations, issued counter-proclamations requesting everyone to stay at home. The Government forbade all demonstrations for three days, and even the *Pravda* and the *Novaya Zhizm* supported them. The result was that yesterday was perfectly quiet and to-day, Sunday, looks as if it would be the same. . . .

"The possible result may be imagined. It seems to me that the longer bloodshed is put off the more chance there is of avoiding it and all its incalculable results. A few judicious arrests would be another matter when the Government feel that the time is ripe. . . .

"Terestchenko attaches the greatest importance to not weakening the Salonika Front at present, as you know, and wants the whole thing thrashed out at Paris. . . . At the moment of writing, it looks as if an offensive really would take place, but the results it is quite useless to try to foresee. Most people think that a failure will be a disaster. There is no doubt that the Army at the front is in a better state than it was; but the divisions vary terribly in their 'morale' and few have their heart in the business.

". . . Most people think it out of the question that the Russian troops will consent to pass another winter in the trenches, whatever the higher command may desire. It does not follow that this is correct and it won't, probably, be clear till September whether it is so or not; but the contingency must be considered. If it proves correct, the question arises whether it would not be desirable in the general interest that Russia should make peace before she is overwhelmed — especially if Austria were at the same time to drop out. I know the enormous difficulties in the way of this arrangement, and I do not think that, at the present moment, the Russian Government would listen to a proposal of the kind. Nevertheless, I draw your attention to it because I have for some time been trying to think of the best way out of our difficulties in the event of a general dissolution of the Russian Army under the influence of the first snows."

At the beginning of July, in spite of their internal difficulties, the Russian Army, under General Brusiloff, took the offensive against the Germans and in one place succeeded in breaking through the enemy lines to a depth of seven miles over a front of fourteen miles. In the course of the whole offensive they took 26,000 prisoners and 84 guns.

But the offensive was not sustained. The army did not want to fight. Discipline had disappeared. On July 10th, General Knox sent a despatch in which he described the offensive and indicated the extent to which indiscipline prevailed throughout the whole of the Russian Army and the general collapse of morale. The demoralisation and disintegration seems to have started in the lower ranks of the Army — the result of dissatisfaction with conditions which had prevailed since the beginning of the War, and before.

Here is a description of the fight by General Knox: —

"There were evidences of indiscipline everywhere. Every bivouac of a mounted unit was full of horses galloping backwards and forwards untied, every village full of horses tied up without food in the sun for hours while their owners slept or attended meetings. No one seemed to do a full day's work except the company cooks. The roads near the front were in a disgraceful state and no one made an attempt to repair them, while the men spent the day in bathing and in lying drying in the sun. No observation post that I saw was properly defended and many of them were not even properly concealed. Most of the mechanical transport was handed over to 'delegates,' who seem now to have priority over the staff and the service of supply.

"Most of the staffs were changed a short time before the action. All the corps commanders and most of the divisional commanders had been changed in the past three months.

"However, all the regular officers that have survived the War and Revolution worked heroically to stem the tide of socialistic cowardice and to restore order out of chaos. . . .

"The operations were postponed two days to allow of the arrival of the Minister of War, who brought with him the proclamation of the All-Russia Council or Workers' and Soldiers' Deputies calling on the troops to take the offensive. Kerensky spent his first day in the 11th Army and had a bad reception in the 2nd Guard Infantry Division, half of the men of which refused to give him a hearing. No one really knew whether the infantry would attack, few of the units were actively mutinous, but almost every division had one bad regiment. The cavalry and artillery were sound. . . .

"The infantry, with the exception of some few regiments, commenced well. . . .

"Progress, however, was much interfered with by the indiscipline and stupidity of the men. The left regiment of the 16th Division had been allotted a passive task. . . .

"The observation posts were crowded by correspondents, army delegates and idle soldier spectators who hampered the officers at work. . . .

"At 2 P.M. I went to the headquarters of the 7th Army, where I sat in the General Quartermaster's room and got a general idea of progress. All were then in good spirits, but from 3 P.M. the picture began to change.

"The 74th Division was making no progress and complained of heavy gun-fire from its left. The Commander-in-Chief, who was with Kerensky, telephoned that many men of this Division were streaming to the rear, and ordered that all available delegates be dispatched at once to hearten them. The 'delegate' is now looked upon as the universal panacea, but he is not half so effective as were the subaltern's boot and fist in former times. . . .

"The retirement can only be explained by the miserable morale of the infantry. The men were impressed by an artillery fire to which they had been little accustomed and they went as far as the enemy's trenches had been destroyed. They had lost many of their officers and had no incentive to further effort; in fact, they knew that further progress would be attended by risk, while they could retire without fear of being punished. To dig themselves in was too much trouble, so they went back to their old ready-made defences. . . .

"The 81st Czech Regiment surrendered *en bloc* to the VIth Corps and the next day marched to the rear through Tarnopol headed by its band.

"The Russian losses were given officially two days later — 17,339 killed, wounded and missing.

". . . The Chief of Military Communications of the South-West Front superintended the evacuation of the wounded from Kozova on the 1st July. He states that in a train of 850 cases he considers that only some 15 men were really wounded; the remainder were wounded in the hands, and he suspected that many of the wounds were self-inflicted.

"On the night of the 1st July, the 19th Siberian and 23rd Division of the XXXIVth Corps and the Corps Staff were withdrawn on relief by the IInd Guard Corps. The units of the XLIst Corps gave it to be understood that they would not attack again. The 7th Army has not moved since.

"Now simply on account of the disaffection in this Corps the whole advance of the 11th Army had to stop on the 3rd, 4th, and 5th.

"Morale and discipline — Kerensky has appointed 'commissaries' to each army to assist in the maintenance of discipline. These men are all hall-marked revolutionaries. Most of them have spent several years in penal servitude. The commissary of the 11th Army was six years in Siberia; the one in the 7th Army, Savinkov, was the chief organiser of the murder of the Grand Duke Serge Alexandrovich, since which he has lived in Switzerland. They are both working with courage, and in complete agreement with the command to reëstablish orders.

"I was struck by the terrible position of the officers in one of the Finland Regiments visited. They were mere boys who had just joined from the military schools. They were all anxious to do their best, but found themselves at once the object of wholly unmerited suspicion.

"During some trench negotiations on the Northern Front recently some German officers came over, and there was an informal discussion regarding the causes of the War. The Russian and German officers, of course, disagreed, but a Russian soldier said that he preferred the word of a German officer to that of a Russian one. In taking leave the German officers told the Russians that they were 'really sorry' for them, for their 'position was dreadful.'

"The Polish Division has been hastily filled by Catholic recruits from Volhinya and Podolya. Its discipline is bad, and it refused for some weeks to go near the front. Its commander, General Simon, though a Pole, asked to be transferred to serve with Russian troops, as he could 'do nothing with the Poles.' The Division has now been weeded out. Company commanders pointed out to the Commissary the men they wished to get rid of. For instance, one company leader said, pointing out one of his men: 'One night on the march I mistook the road and led the company 40 yards out of its way. I overheard this man say to the company: "Gentlemen, I suggest we throw this son of a pig into the river." '

"The Commander of the 1st Division of the Guard told me that his officers were martyrs suffering daily tortures. Some nights ago a company commander of the Yegerski Regiment was riding along with his command when his men called to him through the darkness to get off, as they did not see why a 'bourgeois' should ride when they walked. When he dismounted the men at once began to consider whether he had not better ride so as to be able the quicker to get them billets when they arrived at their destination. He mounted again, and they again required him to dismount. This officer cannot have been much good, but after all he was only following the example set by his superiors in yielding to the men in everything.

"It is impossible to avoid the uncomfortable conclusion that the war in Russia is coming more and more to be regarded as a secondary matter. . . .

"General Klembovski, the Commander-in-Chief of the Northern Front, is reported by several papers to have said in a recent speech at Riga, that the present offensive was all-important because a winter campaign was impossible, and all the combatants would soon begin negotiations for peace.

"Kerensky works hard as Minister of War, but his speciality is revolution, and he does not yet altogether grasp that the only way to cause revolution in Germany is to defeat her army in the field. Even at the front, half his attention is directed to Stockholm. On the 1st July three German prisoners, the first taken, were led past his observation post. He sent to ask them — not what troops were on their right and left and rear — what political party they belonged to and whether there would soon be a revolution in Germany. They replied they did not belong to any political party. They did not know anything about the interior of Germany, but at the front where they had been all the War there was no sign of a revolution.

"I was sitting with the General Quartermaster of the 7th Army at Buchach the day before we moved up to the front for the offensive, when two members of the Petrograd Council of Working Men and Soldier Deputies were announced. They had come to lecture on two things, War and Peace and the Constituent Assembly.

"Ensign Krilenko, an anti-war socialist, stated in a speech delivered to the Committee of the 11th Army that he had organised a plebiscite in the 13th Finland Regiment regarding the course of action to be followed by Russia in three eventualities: —

1. If the Allies abandoned all claim to annexations, but Germany did not.
2. If both the Allies and Germany refused to abandon the idea of annexations.
3. If the Allies refused to abandon the claim to annexations but Germany agreed to do so.

"The reply, he stated, was in each case 'war,' but in the third case 'war against the Allies.'

"This man calmly contemplates war against the world and maintains that the worst that could befall Russia would be the loss of the Caucasus, Finland, Siberia and Poland. He professed to believe in the existence of secret treaties between England and Germany.

"Most officers shudder at the idea of a fourth winter of war. They often quote Hindenburg's remark about nerves and confess that Russian nerves have been the first to give way.

"Korniloff told me that he considered the offensive the last chance, and that the economic condition of Russia and the breakdown of the railways will make the continuation of the War through a fourth winter impossible. The Report of the American Railway Commission on these matters will be of interest.

"The opinion of Ignatiev, who now commands the 1st Division of the Infantry of the Guard, is worth quoting, for he is capable and generally a cheery optimist. He is a younger brother of the Count Ignatiev, late Minister of Education, and their father was the Ambassador at Constantinople.

"He considers that peace is essential for Russia, for if there is not peace soon there will be a general massacre. The prolongation of the War is driving the country to economic ruin. From the very beginning the peasants had hated the War, which was only at first popular with the educated classes. He said, 'If you were to go out into the square now, and to announce that the War will end at once on the one condition that Nikolai Romanov return to power, everyone would at once agree, and there would be no more talk of a democratic republic.' (I believe this is true. The Revolution has been a revolt against the burden of the War, and not a protest, as the English Press at first tried to pretend, against the half-hearted way in which the late Government prosecuted the War.)

"I asked Ignatiev whether the reconsideration of the terms of peace would have any effect on Russian public opinion. He said it would on conscientious people, but the mass of the soldiery only wanted an excuse for saving their skin. They belonged neither to the party of the Bolsheviki nor to that of the Mensheviki, but were 'Skurniki'[1] pure and simple, *i.e.* 'fearers for their own skin.'

"I pointed out that if by any chance Germany were not beaten as she deserved it would be entirely Russia's fault. He agreed and said he fully expected that no foreigner would speak to a Russian for the next twenty years. In England's place he would get out of the War as soon as possible while there was yet time. . . ."

At the Inter-Allied Conference in Paris on July 25th and 26th we took stock of the Russian position, in view of the disturbing news from that front. It was quite clear that the situation had got completely out of hand as far as Kerensky and his Government were concerned. The abolition of the death penalty, and to a great extent the impotence of the officers to inflict any other punishment for indiscipline, had made it impossible to deal with desertion and even with insubordination. But it is doubtful whether any penalties would have reëstablished discipline. The probability is that their infliction would have precipitated open mutiny. The position of Kerensky was indeed desperate. He had to stimulate and organise the Armies in the field, which were rapidly disintegrating into an incoherent rabble, whilst simultaneously he had to confront seditious risings and rebellions in and around his own capital. All the time, the Bolsheviks were plotting to undermine his authority as soon as he thought he had reestablished it. Was ever man more precariously situated? It needed a leader of dominating power and decision to control and direct such a situation. Kerensky was a man of genius, but it was not the genius of action.

At the Paris Conference, the British representative put forward a memorandum containing suggestions for giving help to Russia which were as follows: —

[1] Skura — A Skin.

". . . The Allied Governments should make every sacrifice in order to retain Russia in the Alliance, and, by affording her constant support in every department, to infuse into her Government the energy necessary to hold out at all costs. . . .

"To carry out this programme, France, Great Britain and the United States, the only powers in a position to act in Russia, should come to an agreement without delay to determine the part to be assigned to each of them.

"Questions of propaganda in the interior of the country, and of financial and economic help are matters for the Government concerned, and are not treated in the present Memoranda.

"From the point of view of military and economic help it would seem that the activities of the Allies might be distributed as follows: —

"England will attend to the Navy.
"France to the Army.
"United States to the reorganisation of transport.

"In this task of reorganisation, Japan could, perhaps, co-operate by furnishing material or technical labour."

The Military Conference which met on July 26th was attended by Generals Cadorna, Robertson, Pershing, Pétain and Foch. Their statement was an indication of the grave consequences which they apprehended would ensue from the desertion of the Allied cause by Russia: —

"The fall of Russia would entail the following consequences: —

"*Political.* It would modify the political aims of the Entente. It is, therefore, suggested that the Governments should at once consider and decide what would be the new political aims to be pursued.

"*Economic.* It would place at the disposal of the Central Powers the vast resources of Russia, especially grain, and thereby greatly minimise the efficiency of the blockade.

"*Morale.* It might result, especially in the case of the smaller Allies in the Balkans, in a profound depression which might cause them to seek a separate peace. It is practically certain that Roumania would be compelled to share the fate of Russia and that, in consequence, the Bulgarian forces, and even a certain number of Turkish divisions, might be free to augment the forces at the enemy's disposal."

Events were marching very fast in Russia — too fast for control by a divided and flaccid Ministry. Most of the Ministers were able men but there was no agreement amongst them and there was no compelling personality to direct and unite them in a coherent effort. A crisis arose in Petrograd over the recognition of autonomy for the Ukraine, and four Ministers of the Cadet Party resigned. There were disorders and fighting in Petrograd. The effect of the news from the capital upon the troops at the front was devastating. They practically abandoned trenches, guns and ammunition to the Germans without striking a blow.

Whilst the Paris Conference was in session, a despatch was on its way to us from our Ambassador in Petrograd which gave a vivid account of the chaos reigning there, and of the outbreak of disorders and rebellion that, although for the moment suppressed, were destined to recur and increase until the last remnants of order and government melted away in a sea of anarchy.

Sir George Buchanan's message, dated July 23rd, 1917, describes how, on hearing of the resignation of the four Cadet members of the Government on the 16th, he had gone to visit Terestchenko, one of the leading Ministers, whom he found laid up with internal trouble. Terestchenko was querulously indignant at the desertion of the Cadets, instigated by Miliukoff, over the Ukrainian question, which broke up the Coalition Government, but he evidently had no inkling of the storm of riot and civil conflict that was imminent in the capital. Indeed, the story told in this graphic letter illumines once more the historic truth that successful revolutions are generally due to the obtuseness of able but unimaginative men in authority, who quarrel amongst themselves about trivial repairs, improvements and decorations to the building while the whole fabric is tottering to a complete crash. Terestchenko here was worrying about Constantinople, and Miliukoff about Ukrainian autonomy, when the whole structure of Russia was collapsing into flaming fissures.

Buchanan's letter goes on to relate how that very evening motor lorries and cars filled with armed soldiers and machine-guns began to pour into the streets of Petrograd. Presently a long procession formed: —

"It was composed of a large number of workmen and three regiments — all fully armed — with banners bearing the usual inscriptions — 'Down with the Ten Capitalistic Ministers'; 'Down with War'; 'Give us Bread', etc. The majority marched across the Champ de Mars into the town. We soon afterwards heard shots at the back of the Embassy and many of the crowd bolted for safety down the quay. There was rifle and machine-gun firing in many quarters of the town during the greater part of the night. A number of motor cars filled with soldiers went to the Warsaw station to arrest Kerensky, but fortunately only got there a quarter of an hour after he had left. Others went to Prince Lvoff's official residence to arrest him and some of his colleagues, who were holding a council there. Their courage, however, failed them, and though there were no troops on guard there, the disloyal troops, on being invited to enter and talk to the Ministers, feared that a trap was being laid for them and contented themselves with requisitioning the Ministers' motor cars. . . ."

Cossacks were held in readiness by the Government, but were not actually used to restore order and the streets were full of crowds and troops engaged in faction fighting. On the following day, things looked blacker, for several thousand sailors arrived from Cronstadt, now a hotbed of Bolshevism — indeed, Trotsky describes the Cronstadt sailors as the "fighting crusaders of the Revolution." There was another monster procession, and more street fighting. And Buchanan wrote thus: —

"On this Tuesday afternoon I really was afraid that the Government would have to capitulate, as they were really at the mercy of the disloyal troops, had the latter had an ounce of courage and been properly led. The Cossacks and a few loyal regiments who came out to protect the Government saved the situation. As it was, Tchernoff, the Socialist Minister of Agriculture, was roughly handled by the disloyal troops and temporarily arrested. While we were at dinner the Cossacks charged the Cronstadt sailors, who had gathered in the square by the Embassy, and sent them flying for their lives. The Cossacks then marched up the quay, but a little later got caught in a cross-fire and suffered heavy losses. We saw several riderless horses returning at full gallop, and a little later two Cossacks who were bringing back a prisoner were attacked by some soldiers under our windows and nearly murdered."

The despatch describes the further course of the disorders and how they were gradually overcome. The next day, Wednesday, was comparatively quiet, and on Thursday the main bodies of mutinous troops were rounded up. Friday saw fresh sporadic outbreaks, and then a temporary calm supervened. Buchanan notes the close connection of this rebellion with the progress of the German campaign. He says: —

"There can be no doubt that this so-called counter-revolution — a term which everybody interprets in his own sense — was engineered by the Germans to synchronise with their offensive. The news of what was passing in Petrograd was circulated among the troops at the front by German aeroplanes and by Bolshevik agitators, and the collapse of the Russian Army would never have been so complete but for this. On the other hand, the Russian reverse — serious as it is, more especially from the point of view of the abandonment of heavy artillery, guns and military supplies

— has secured for the Government the full support of the Soviet and of the Socialists, who have now given them full power to put down indiscipline in the army and anarchy at home. . . ."

Buchanan was optimistic — unduly so, as events were to prove. He thought that this rebuff to the Bolsheviks would be permanent.

"It is always difficult in this country to look far ahead; but in spite of the disastrous news from the front I take a more hopeful view of the situation as a whole than I have for some time past. Though the industrial, economic and financial situations are all serious, there is at last some prospect of orderly Government, even if a little time must elapse before we feel its effects. So long as anarchy reigned supreme one could not expect any real or lasting improvement, but the restoration of order ought to react favourably on all branches of the national life. . . ."

Unhappily, the restoration of order was far from being achieved. There was no stable foundation upon which it could be built. That scene of wild chaos on July 16th and 17th which Buchanan has so graphically described — leaderless mobs that seethed to and fro, insurgent troops marching to arrest members of the Government, street fighting and irresponsible murder — illustrated the state of Russia at the time. Except for the Cossacks, there was no force available that could be relied on to obey orders; and on the side of the Government there was no one with the authority, vision and firm grasp needed for suppressing revolt and compelling unity and order. The only man in Russia strong enough for that task was on the other side.

Buchanan clearly recognised how much depended in this crisis upon the quality of leadership which might be forthcoming. He goes on in his despatch to outline the form the reconstituted Government will take, and to comment on its prospective members: —

"Tseretelli is apparently to be Minister of the Interior, but Terestchenko tells me that he is too much of an idealist for the post, and that he is not likely to retain it for long. Nekrassoff, who is to act as President of the Council when Kerensky is away, does not inspire confidence, as he is too much of an opportunist and has changed parties more than once in order to advance his own interests. His ambition is to become Prime Minister. He is, however, a capable and strong man. Of the other Socialist Ministers, Skobeleff and Tchernoff are the most influential. From all I hear the former is too flighty and not very intelligent, while the latter is said to be very able but quite untrustworthy. Prince Lvoff told a friend of mine yesterday that he regarded him as the most dangerous man in the revolutionary movement."

Jealousies, rivalries and squabblings on the rim of the crater! No wonder they fell in and dragged with them the cause they all cherished. How little these Girondists, all suspicious of each other, knew of the really dangerous men who were lying in wait for all of them! They were under the impression that they had now disposed of Lenin and his mob of fanatics, and they only feared reformers in their own ranks — and the abler these were, the greater their distrust. They were jealous of the ambitions of Nekrassoff, alarmed at the socialist projects of Tchernoff. Soon they were broken by the ruthless directness of Lenin, the ruthless methods of Trotsky. The conclusion of our Ambassador's despatch tells of the movements that were being started in Russia to establish its future Government on the English model. He repeats a remark of Prince Lvoff to the effect that Russia would have a Constitutional Monarchy before the year was out. This struck Buchanan as symptomatic of that change of heart and revulsion against extreme Socialism which he hoped to see. He concluded that: —

"We should have a monarchy again in a very few months if only there was any eligible candidate to the throne, and I do not know of anyone likely to command the suffrages of the nation."

There was, in fact, such a man in Russia, and before long he was wielding a power more terrible than that of any Czar. But he was not a Romanoff. Neither Lvoff nor Buchanan had looked for a monarch among the Bolsheviks. Our Ambassador soon realised that Russia was not being swung in the direction of Constitutionalism.

On August 4th our Military Attaché wrote: —

". . . The country is moving straight to ruin as things stand at present. During past fortnight no real steps have been taken to re-establish the prestige of the officers and discipline amongst troops in rear. Till discipline is established in rear and troops are made to fight it is impossible to look for any improvement in the army at the front. Till discipline is established in the army, it is impossible to force the men in the railway repair shops and the mines to work, and if they continue as at present, a general breakdown of railway transport in the winter and a famine at Petrograd and in the army will occur. Kerensky is at present the only man with any magnetic influence amongst the Ministry who has not yet understood the necessity of discipline.

"None of his immediate military advisers are men of character. Socialists want to run a class war in preference to the race war, and this appeals to the mass of the soldiers as being less dangerous.

"Tseretelli and others think they can run both wars simultaneously. We have to tell Russian Government plainly that this is impossible."

And on the 6th came another telegram from him: —

"General Staff Officer complained apparently of coldness of England's attitude. He said that our opinion carries more weight than that of any other Ally. He suggested statement in Parliament of sympathy with Russia in her difficulties, with a delicate hint that, while we were ready to make any sacrifice to help Russia with a strong Government, our duty to ourselves and our other Allies might make us question the advisability of helping a Government that delayed to take necessary steps to restore discipline."

On August 5th, General Korniloff, an excellent soldier who for some months had been in disgrace as a result of his criticisms of the Government for being, as he thought, guilty of weakness in dealing with the Army, was reinstated as Commander-in-Chief of the Russian Armies in the place of General Brusiloff. He was not *persona grata* in the eyes of the Soviet Government, who regarded him rather in the light of a counter-revolutionary, but upon his appointment as Commander-in-Chief the attacks on him were modified. Kerensky agreed to give Korniloff a free hand.

Sir William Robertson said that he had great hopes that this appointment would lead to the restoration of discipline and the regeneration of the Russian Army. In spite of this, however, pessimistic reports continued to come from Petrograd, and we were told that it would be useless to expect any further military assistance from Russia in 1917. The Allies were attempting, with the aid of a technical Railway Mission from the United States, to reorganize the Russian railways, as the difficulties of transport in Russia seemed to be one of the chief causes of the trouble. But the Russian temperament is not, or at least was not in those days, helpful in putting things on a business basis. It turned out that the Mission, through no fault of its own, was utterly unable to cope with the situation. The pre-War Russian at his best never shone as an organiser. When he became inebriated with revolutionary sentiment he was useless for the common tasks of an ordered society. Intoxication is no corrective for inefficiency.

At the Inter-Allied Conference on August 8th the Russian situation came up for discussion, and the following telegram was sent to the Russian Government: —

"The Representatives of the Allied Governments met in London on 7th August greet with heartiest sympathy the bold effort of reorgansation which the Provisional Government and its leader are carrying on in Russia.

"They note with satisfaction that in this tragic hour all forces of Russia are consolidated around the Government to reinforce its power and that the popular will expressed from day to day in more definite forms and through a more complete representation, proclaims loudly the necessity of national defence.

"They send their heartiest greeting to M. Kerensky and his colleagues and express firm confidence in their controlling authority and in the reëstablishment of a strict discipline which is clearly indispensable to all armies, but above all to the armies of free nations. It is by discipline that the Russian Army will secure alike popular liberty, national honour and the realisation of the war aims which are common to all the Allies."

On September 7th, however, the War Cabinet again reviewed the position, and considered an appeal for more guns for Russia. They decided that "the supply of guns was part of the general question as to whether we were to continue to support Russia in view of the lack of discipline that prevailed in the Army of that country and the serious economic situation there." At this same Cabinet meeting General Knox, who had just returned from Russia, gave an account of the position in that distracted country. He said that: —

". . . There were three powerful forces tending to drive the Russians to make a separate peace.

"The great mass of the soldiers did not want to fight. They had not wanted to fight before the Revolution, but had been forced on by their officers. There had been frequent cases of indiscipline before the Revolution; now they were quite general.

"In the second place, workmen were making huge economic demands on their employers, and British manufacturers were closing factories and moving away. It was expected that there would shortly be a general lock-out. The workmen had probably enough money to last them for a month; after that time, there would be a state of anarchy. The Government had repeatedly promised to organise a militia or police force in Petrograd and Moscow, but nothing had been done.

"The third force was the confusion on the railways. There was an enormous surplus of grain in the Caucasus, but the level at which the price of bread had been fixed was not such as to tempt the peasants to part with their grain. Nor would cash purchases at high prices attract them. They preferred to barter grain for goods which they actually wanted, such as agricultural implements and calico.

"Force would have to be applied if the grain was to be forthcoming. The harvest in the Volga governments had been a failure, and to bring the grain from the Northern Caucasus and Western Siberia was very difficult owing to the condition of rolling stock. In June, 1916, 18 per cent. of the engines were under repair; in June, 1917, 24 per cent.; and the number was increasing at the rate of 2 per cent. per week. The average number of days per month worked in some of the repairing shops was only 13. . . .

"In reply to questions as to the likelihood of a *coup d'état*, headed by General Korniloff, General Knox said that he did not know what preparations were being made. When he left Russia, on the 18th of August, Korniloff and Savinkoff were in agreement. Korniloff was a strong character, an honest patriot, and the best man in sight. He had the support of the Cossacks. They numbered 1,000 squadrons of 150 each. He (General Knox) had no faith in Kerensky. . . . Kerensky was afraid of shedding blood and was allowing matters to drift towards anarchy. A force of 10,000 loyalists would be enough to subdue Petrograd — the main source of disorder. . . . If Kerensky were to suggest a separate peace he would certainly have the great majority of the country with him. As to some of the prominent generals in Russia, Alexieff was a student of war and not suited to a crisis; Brusiloff was a politician, Kaledin, the commander of the 8th Army, was one of the best generals, and had been chosen by the Cossacks of the Don as their Chief. . . .

"In concluding his statement, General Knox strongly urged

on the War Cabinet the importance of a joint representation from the Allied Governments, recommending to the Russian Government that in view of Russia's desperate situation and the peril of putting back democracy, General Korniloff should be fully supported in the measures which he wished to take to restore discipline at the front, on the railways, and in Petrograd."

While these deliberations were going on, however, an open quarrel had broken out between Kerensky and Korniloff. The latter had been roused to anger by Kerensky's procrastination in giving him powers, including the reimposition of the death penalty for disobeying orders, and had been persuaded to agree to an attempt to get himself proclaimed Military Dictator. Kerensky called upon him to resign, and Korniloff, assured of the support of the Commanders of all the Groups on the Western Frontier, raised the standard of revolt and appealed to the people in an order which ended thus: —

"I pledge you my word of honour as an officer and a soldier, and assure you once more that I, General Korniloff, the son of a simple Cossack peasant, have by my whole life, and not by words only, shown my unfailing devotion to my country and to freedom, that I am opposed to all counter-revolutionary schemes, and stand on guard over the liberties we have won, desiring only that the great Russian nation should continue independent."

The rebellion of Korniloff failed. Had he been successful in establishing a military dictatorship it is more than doubtful, in view of the complete disintegration of the army, whether it would have been helpful to the Allies. The stubborn qualities of the Russian peasant soldier, which gave him that endurance which made him formidable even in defeat, had now been converted into a sulky and immutable resolve not to do any more fighting at anyone's bidding. Moreover, Korniloff's defiance of the Government was essentially an anti-Kerensky movement and for this reason the Allied Governments found themselves in an awkward position. The position was debated in the Cabinet on September 12th: —

". . . It was felt that, difficult though it was for the British Government to interfere in the present situation without appearing to take sides with General Korniloff, it was essential, in the interests of the Allies and of democracy generally, to make an effort to improve the situation, although it was realised that any steps in that direction would have to be taken through M. Kerensky, as he was the representative of the existing Government. It was suggested that he should be informed that the British Government viewed with the greatest alarm the probabilities of civil war, and urged him to come to terms with General Korniloff not only in the interest of Russia herself, but in that of the Allies."

Events, however, delivered us from the dilemma of choosing between Kerensky and Korniloff, for Korniloff was denounced as a traitor and arrested. But Kerensky himself says that though the Korniloff rebellion was crushed, it shook the authority of the Government, and weakened it sufficiently to give the Bolsheviks, who had suffered a temporary check in the summer, their chance. "Without the Korniloff affairs," says Kerensky, "the crucifixion of Russian liberty on the Golgotha of Lenin's dictatorship would have been impossible." I cannot help thinking that he is taking too sanguine a view of the efficacy of his own leadership. Men of his temperament are doomed to failure in revolutionary times. They cannot reconcile idealism with action. Statesmen who hesitate in quiet times often gain thereby a reputation for moderation and sagacity. But in a tumult they are a national calamity.

It was clear that Russia as a fighting force was falling to pieces. Austrian prisoners were being allowed to escape and return to their own lines; Russian roads were blocked with deserters. We had news in October that fifty-nine third-line Russian divisions were being disbanded.

The situation was now rapidly getting worse. By November, anarchy prevailed in Petrograd and severe fighting was taking place in Moscow. News came that "Kerensky was endeavouring himself to command three weak divisions of Cossacks, in the vicinity of Tsarskoe Selo, which place had been occupied by the Bolsheviks." The telegram adds: "The behaviour of M. Kerensky appeared to be lamentable and to give little hope of any success on his part." Lenin and Trotsky, both resolute men, marched on Petrograd and on November 7th overthrew the Kerensky Government with the greatest ease. Kerensky put up no fight. The Bolsheviks were in power.[1]

On November 22nd the War Cabinet discussed the question of their recognition: —

". . . The difficulty was that any overt official step taken against the Bolsheviks might only strengthen their determination to make peace, and might be used to inflame anti-Allied feeling in Russia, and so defeat the very object we were aiming at. Nor was anything known of the actual position which would justify us, at this juncture, in backing either Kaledin or any other leader of the party of law and order."

On November 26th a telegram came from General Knox to say that, apart from anything the Russian authorities might do, the Russian troops at the front were now insisting upon an armistice. "It appears quite clear," said Knox, "that whatever happens politically in Russia, the bulk of the Russian Army refuses to continue the War."

Coöperation between Russia and the rest of the Allies had gone by the board with the Bolshevik refusal to imple-

[1] For Trotsky's statement of Bolshevik Policy, see Appendix to this chapter.

ment the London agreement of 1914. Trotsky demanded the release of Chicherin and Petroff, who were interned in England, and threatened reprisals against British subjects in Russia should these demands not be satisfied. A situation of the utmost complication was developing in our relations with Russia. Had the whole of Russia been under Bolshevik rule our course would have been clear. We should have treated with them as the *de facto* Russian Government. Had the Bolshevik leaders been the *de facto* Government, we could not have made war on them, or supported rebellion against their authority merely because they had made peace with Germany. But outside the towns — and they were not all Bolshevik — they had no authority. Vast portions of Russia were anti-Bolshevik, and Lenin's writ did not run over a third of the vast Empire built up by the Romanoffs. The peasants, who constituted 80 per cent. of the population, were hostile or unconcerned. It was a revolution of the industrial workers in an agricultural country. The Cossacks of the Don were opposed to them. The Ukraine wished a Government of its own. The Caucasus was by no means Bolshevik. Neither was Siberia. These were facts of great moment to us. The parts of Russia which were not yet Bolshevised were its granaries and its oilfields and it was vital to us that these resources should not fall into the hands of the Germans either through conquest or by arrangement with Lenin and Trotsky. The difficulties Mr. Balfour and I experienced in persuading certain members of the Government to have any dealings with Petrograd which would involve recognition of the Bolsheviks were considerably enhanced by Trotsky's revolutionary appeal to all nations to rise against the rule of the *"Bourgeoisie."* That term became the standing phrase for anyone who possessed private property of any sort or description. There was a genuine fear that recognition would involve admitting into Allied countries a swarm of Bolshevik intriguers to foment revolution. The Home Office drew our attention to an article in the *Woolwich Pioneer* by M. Litvinoff, given under his official seal, inviting the munition workers of Woolwich to start a revolution. The War Office reported that he had also been endeavouring to tamper with the discipline of British troops, notably Russian Canadians. These were some of the difficulties confronting us when we came to consider the problem of recognition.

The Cabinet considered the situation on November 29th. M. Trotsky had issued to the Military Attachés of Allied Powers, on November 27th, a note stating that he and his supporters were endeavouring to bring about a general and not a separate armistice, but that they might be driven to a separate armistice by the Allies if they refused to negotiate. If the Allied Governments would not recognise the Bolsheviks the latter would appeal to the peoples as against their Governments. Sir George Buchanan urged that a reply should be issued immediately to this "insolent communication", pointing out that Trotsky's proposal for a general armistice reached the British Embassy nineteen hours after the Commander-in-Chief had opened *pourparlers* with the enemy, and that the Allies were determined to continue the War until a permanent peace had been obtained. Sir George Buchanan further urged the Government that, as the situation was now desperate, it was advisable to set Russia free from her agreement with the Allies, so that she could act as she chose, and decide to purchase peace on Germany's terms or fight on with the Allies. In his opinion the policy of the Bolsheviks was to divide Russia and Britain, and so pave the way for what would virtually be a German protectorate over the former. The course he recommended, if adopted, would make it impossible for the Bolsheviks to reproach the Allies with driving Russian soldiers to slaughter for their Imperialist aims. In the telegram sent to the Chief of the Imperial General Staff the Military Attaché at Jassy proposed that, if it were found that Kaledin, a great Cossack Chief, was well-disposed to the Allies, a French and a British Mission, fully accredited, should be sent to his headquarters; that financial support up to £10,000,000 should be guaranteed to Kaledin; and, generally, that the British Mission should have full power to act without awaiting instructions from England.

The War Cabinet were informed that a message from Trotsky, addressed to the Ambassadors of Norway, Holland, Spain, Sweden, Switzerland, and Denmark, had been stopped by the Press Bureau. It asked that pressure should be brought to bear by the Socialist and working-class organisations in these countries in favour of peace.

Some members of the War Cabinet were impressed with the objections to the policy of entering into active coöperation with Kaledin without further information. Steps had been taken to obtain such information, but it had not yet been received. Little was definitely known of Kaledin's personality, and there were signs that the Cossacks were not prepared to fight. The scheme, on General Ballard's admission, was not one which could be regarded as hopeful, and its only result might be to drive the Russian Government definitely into the arms of Germany.

Alternative courses open were to follow Sir George Buchanan's advice or to wait a little longer in the hope that the situation would subsequently become clearer. In any case, we could not act alone; the subject was one which should be referred to the conference now meeting in Paris.

But on the very day the Cabinet was discussing those communications Germany had accepted Lenin's offer of an armistice and Russian delegates crossed the German lines.

This Armistice altered fundamentally, to the detriment of the Allies, the whole military position in the West. Until it was signed the Germans and Austrians could not withdraw any substantial portion of their army from the Eastern Front. Some of their best officers and men had been taken away to the West to fill up gaps in divisions depleted by the heavy fighting and inferior material had been sent to take their place on the Russian Front, but not many complete divisions had been withdrawn. There was still an element of doubt as to what the Russian Army might or might not do. It was known that the Kerensky Government was making great efforts to revive its fighting spirit and no one can forecast with certainty what direction a revolution may take. The Germans could not gamble on what would emerge out of chaos. Kerensky's efforts kept them guessing for months. That was a real service he rendered to the Allies. But as soon as he was swept out of power and his place taken by more resolute men, there could be no doubt that Russia meant to desert her Allies. France, Britain and Italy had to face a new and exceedingly dangerous situation. A power which had for three years absorbed millions of the best soldiers and thousands of the guns of the Central Powers had finally withdrawn from the fighting line. By the end of November the German strength on the Western Front had risen from 150 to 160 divisions. Other divisions were only awaiting transport.

At the Inter-Allied Conference in Paris which began on November 30th, I communicated to the representatives of the other Allies the proposal which had been put forward by Sir George Buchanan, that in view of the conditions in Russia, the Allies: —

"should release Russia from the engagement entered into in the Pact of London not to make a separate peace, and that they should tell the Russian people that, realising the extent to which they are worn by war, and the effects of the disorganisation resulting from a great revolution, they would leave them to decide for themselves whether to obtain peace on Germany's terms, or fight on with their Allies who were determined not to lay down their arms until they had obtained guarantees for the world's peace."

After long discussions, in the course of which M. Clemenceau said that if Russia made a separate peace she would thereby betray us, and that "if M. Maklakoff and all the celestial powers asked him to give Russia back her word, he would refuse", several draft messages were produced. In reference to Sir George Buchanan's suggestion of a joint declaration freeing Russia to make her own Peace, I suggested that each nation should tell its own Ambassador to let it be known in Russia that we were ready to discuss war aims. It should be left to the discretion of each Ambassador to let this be known in the way which he considered best. I pointed out that in view of the Russian retirement there was some case for discussing war aims. Consider Russia's war aims, for example. She had aspired to the control of Constantinople, the Bosphorus and the Dardanelles. What was the use of talking of that now? Much less was it possible to talk of the annexation of the Bukowina as a Russian war aim. It was, therefore, not for us to refuse reconsideration of our avowed war aims. At present the Russian war aims stood in the way of any separate peace with Turkey. It was decided that the representatives of the Great Powers who were signatories of the Treaty of London, dated September 4th, 1914, and those who have since adhered to this treaty, should declare that they were ready to proceed to the examination of the war aims and of the possible conditions of a just and durable peace in concert with Russia, as soon as a regular Government, having the right to speak in the name of the nation, should be established in Russia.

We had now to consider what our attitude should be in regard to the new Russian Government, which at its very best, would in future be in the position of a neutral towards the Allies.

The problem with which the British Government and indeed the Allies as a whole were faced, was a purely military one. We were not concerned with the internal political troubles of Russia as such. What we had to consider as a war problem was how best to prevent Germany from revictualling herself afresh from the cornlands and the oilfields which would be laid open to her if she succeeded in penetrating to the Don and the rich provinces of the Caucasus. It was for this reason, and not from any anti-Communist motives, that we decided to give support to the loyalist Russians who were in control of these fertile areas, and who were not prepared to desert the others. If the Central Powers should suceeed in obtaining possession of the vast stores of Russian wheat and oil, so essential to their continued prosecution of the War not only for themselves but also their allies, it would mean the prolongation of the struggle, perhaps by years. We realised how vital a matter it was to Germany and Austria — in fact a matter indeed of life and death to their population — and we had a conviction that every effort must be put to cut off the enemy from those supplies. The War Cabinet, therefore, discussed the need of organising the forces of resistance inside Russia. We examined the measures to be adopted to assist the anti-German formations which still existed in certain parts of Russia. The difficulty was to do so without appearing to wage war on the Bolshevik Government now established at Petrograd.

I had several discussions on the matter with the Foreign Secretary and we found ourselves in agreement as to the line to be taken. As there were members of the Government who were inclined to take up a strong anti-Bolshevik attitude, and Mr. Balfour was unable to attend the next meeting where our policy would be decided, I was anxious that his personal views should be communicated to his colleagues. I therefore asked him to embody the conclusions we had reached in a

Memorandum for circulation to the Cabinet. It is one of Mr. Balfour's most notable State documents.

NOTES ON THE PRESENT RUSSIAN SITUATION

As I may not be able to be present at Cabinet to-morrow, I desire to make these notes.

The following points have to be specially kept in view: —

1. The safety of our Embassy in Petrograd and of British subjects in Russia.
2. The interests of Roumania and her Army.
3. The best course to adopt in order to diminish as much as possible the advantage which Germany will be able to extract from the dissolution of the Russian Army as a fighting force.

These subjects are all interconnected, though so far as possible I will deal with them separately.

(1) The greatest danger to Sir George Buchanan and the British colony arises probably out of the possibility of mob-violence, excited by the anti-British propaganda fomented by German money in Petrograd and elsewhere. The only real security against this is to be found either by the establishment of a strong and order-loving Government in Russia, or by the removal of the British, official and unofficial, to some safer country.

The first we can do nothing to secure. The second cannot be obtained unless we are able (*a*) to provide the necessary transport either through Sweden or through some northern port of Russia, and (*b*) to win the goodwill (in however qualified a form) of the present rulers of Petrograd.

The question of transport is hardly a Foreign Office matter, but the policy of avoiding the active malevolence of the Bolshevik Party raises most important diplomatic issues.

It was suggested at the Cabinet on Friday that, after their recent proclamations, the Bolsheviks could only be regarded as avowed enemies, and to treat them as anything else showed a lamentable incapacity to see facts as they are, and to handle them with decision.

I entirely dissent from this view and believe it to be founded on a misconception. If, for the moment, the Bolsheviks show peculiar virulence in dealing with the British Empire, it is probably because they think that the British Empire is the great obstacle to immediate peace; but they are fanatics to whom the constitution of every State, whether monarchical or republican, is equally odious. Their appeal is to every revolutionary force, economic, social, racial, or religious, which can be used to upset the existing political organisations of mankind. If they summon the Mohammedans of India to revolt, they are still more desirous of engineering a revolution in Germany. They are dangerous dreamers, whose power, be it great or small, transitory or permanent, depends partly on German gold, partly on the determination of the Russian Army to fight no more; but who would genuinely like to put into practice the wild theories which have so long been germinating in the shadow of the Russian autocracy.

Now, contrary to the opinion of some of my colleagues, I am clearly of opinion that it is to our advantage to avoid, as long as possible, an open breach with this crazy system. If this be drifting, then I am a drifter by deliberate policy. On the broader reasons for my view, I will say a word directly, but its bearing on the narrower issue of the safety of Sir George Buchanan and the British colony is evident. I am personally of opinion that the Cabinet should reverse the decision it came to some little time ago and should deport to Russia the two interned Russian subjects [1] in whose fate the Russian rulers appear to be so greatly interested. I was not in England when the decision to retain them was come to, and I am imperfectly acquainted with the reasons for it. Doubtless they were sufficient. But I certainly think that we may now with advantage send these two Russians back to their own country, where, judged by local standards, their opinions will probably appear sane and moderate.

I have already instructed Sir George Buchanan to abstain completely from any action which can be interpreted as an undue interference with the internal affairs of the country to which

[1] Chicherin and Petroff.

he is accredited, and I am unable to think of any other step which would help to secure his safety.

(2) As regards the Roumanian Army, events have marched rapidly. Everything that could be done, even as a forlorn hope, has been done to enable the Army to join with other forces in Russia prepared to continue the struggle, but for the moment no such forces appear to exist, and the Roumanian Army is under the strictest military necessity of acquiescing in the Armistice, or rather the cessation of hostilities, on its part of the line. . . .

(3) I have already indicated my view that we ought, if possible, not to come to an open breach with the Bolsheviks or drive them into the enemy's camp. But there are wider reasons for this policy than the safety of the British colony in Russia. These wider reasons are as follows: —

It is certain, I take it, that, for the remainder of this war, the Bolsheviks are going to fight neither Germany nor anyone else. But, if we can prevent their aiding Germany we do a great deal, and to this we should devote our efforts.

There are two possible advantages which Germany may extract from Russia's going out of the War: (i) She may increase her man-power in other theatres of operation by moving troops from Russian Fronts, or by getting back German prisoners. There is little hope of stopping this, and I say no more about it. (ii) She may obtain the power of using the large potential resources of Russia to break the Allied Blockade. I am not sure that this is not the more important of the two advantages, and it has so far been very imperfectly examined. As regards oil, we want to know what means of transport there is in the Black Sea available to the Germans, and how far the anti-Bolshevik elements in the Caucasian regions can be utilised to interfere with the supply on land. As regards cereals, the difficulties the Germans are likely to have arise mainly, I suppose, from the chaotic condition of the country, the disorganisation of all means of transport, and the determination of the Russians to use their own produce for their own purposes.

If we drive Russia into the hands of Germany, we shall hasten the organisation of the country by German officials on German lines. Nothing could be more fatal, it seems to me, both to the immediate conduct of the War and to our post-War relations.

Russia, however incapable of fighting, is not easily overrun. Except with the active goodwill of the Russians themselves, German troops (even if there were German troops to spare) are not going to penetrate many hundreds of miles into that vast country. A mere Armistice between Russia and Germany may not for very many months promote in any important fashion the supply of German needs from Russian sources. It must be our business to make that period as long as possible by every means in our power, and no policy would be more fatal than to give the Russians a motive for welcoming into their midst German officials and German soldiers as friends and deliverers.

A. J. BALFOUR.

9th December, 1917.

I strongly supported the sagacious counsel given in this document. Mr. Balfour's views were not acceptable to several members of the Government, but ultimately the Cabinet decided that His Majesty's Government was not primarily concerned with the composition of the Russian Government or with the local aspirations of the Bolsheviks or other political parties, except insofar as they bore on their attitude to our conflict with the Central Powers. This was the line we had taken during the Czar's reign, and there was no reason to depart from it. Our dominant purpose throughout the revolution should be: —

(*a*) If possible, to keep Russia in the War until our joint war aims were realised; or

(*b*) If this could not be secured, then to ensure that Russia was as helpful to us and as harmful to the enemy as possible. For this purpose we should seek to influence Russia to give to any terms of peace that might be concluded with the enemy a bias in our favour.

This attitude, if successful, would have averted the worst disasters of Russian defection. It was difficult to foretell how strong the Bolsheviks might become, or how long their power might endure; but if, as seemed likely, they maintained an ascendancy for the next few months only, these months were critical, and to antagonise them needlessly would be to throw them into the arms of Germany. There were at the moment signs that within a few days, when the elections of the Constituent Assembly had been completed, the Bolsheviks would be installed in power not only in a *de facto*, but also in a constitutional sense, for a considerable part but by no means for the whole of Russia.

In this connection messages had been received from the British Embassy at Petrograd. The terms were given of a six months' Armistice proposed by the Bolsheviks, and it was stated that there was a remarkable change in the official Press, the Allies not being attacked for the first time for several weeks.

In the *Times* of that day there appeared a report that the Germans were making the following conditions: —

(*a*) Germany to obtain, for fifteen years, a control of the Russian wheat market.

(*b*) Importation into Russia of all German goods duty free.

(*c*) No territory now occupied by German troops to be surrendered.

Attention was also drawn to a telegram to the Chief of the Imperial General Staff, dated December 5th, 1917, recounting a private and unofficial interview with Krilenko, the Bolshevik Commander-in-Chief of the Russian Army, during which he said that he had issued an order that all Armistice agreements should contain a clause forbidding transfer of troops from one front to another. He appeared most anxious to make a favourable impression on Allied officers and had carried out all suggestions made to him for safeguarding the lives of officers and their families. In a telegram dated December 6th, 1917, Sir George Buchanan reported an interview between Captain Smith and Trotsky, at which the prohibition of British subjects leaving Russia was discussed in connection with the detention in this country of Messrs. Chicherin and Petroff. Trotsky denied that the prohibition was intended as a threat. His object had been to emphasise the difference between the treatment accorded to Russian subjects in the United Kingdom and British subjects in Russia. On publication in the local Press of a *communiqué* to the effect that the British Government would reconsider the cases of all Russian subjects interned in Great Britain and would give facilities for return to their country of all Russians innocent of any offence punishable by the laws of Great Britain, he (Trotsky) would the same day restore full liberty of movement to all British subjects in Russia. Sir George Buchanan urged His Majesty's Government to agree to accept the compromise proposed by Trotsky; otherwise he feared that British subjects would be held up indefinitely.

The Cabinet accepted the Ambassador's advice and released the two Russians.

The making of peace between Russia and Germany was a somewhat protracted affair. Trotsky had on December 22nd, 1917, put forward terms for a general peace which were plausible. They were as follows: —

1. No forcible annexations of territory taken during the War.
2. Complete restoration of independence to the nationalities who had lost it during the War.
3. Nationalities not hitherto enjoying independence to

have the right to decide by plebiscite whether they would be united to other States or acquire independence.

4. Safeguarding of the rights of minorities in territories inhabited by several nationalities.

5. No war indemnities, but war requisitions to be returned.

6. Colonial acquisitions to be decided on the same principles. Economic war was condemned by the Russians.

Count Czernin, the Austrian Premier, in his reply to the Russian overtures on December 25th, delivered a speech which accepted the suggestion of a general peace and as far as phraseology was concerned seemed to concede all that we were fighting for. On closer examination of its terms its language was nebulous and ambiguous. None of our specific demands were conceded, although they appeared all to be covered. It was essential that we should ascertain what his utterance meant when we came to practical details. To enter into negotiations on the basis of vague formulæ embodied in a speech delivered by a statesman from a country that was not in a position to settle the issue of peace or war, would be to walk into an unknown territory in a mist. Germany had said nothing. We must therefore come to grips with the realities of the problem. We could only do that by stating in the frankest and clearest language what were our war aims. I came to the conclusion that the time had arrived when that should be done. The interpretation placed upon Czernin's vague expressions in subsequent speeches by German statesmen and the military chiefs and also the practical application given to them in the Brest-Litovsk Treaty amply justified our caution.

On the 21st we again discussed the situation. It was decided to send Lord Milner and Lord Robert Cecil to Paris to confer with the French Government as to the attitude we should adopt in view of the Bolshevik peace overtures with Russia. After a full consideration by the Cabinet of the line they ought to take, they proposed the following Memorandum for submission to the French: —

"At Petrograd we should at once get into relations with the Bolsheviks through unofficial agents, each country as seems best to it.

"We propose to send Sir George Buchanan on leave for reasons of health, but we shall keep a Chargé d'Affaires there. We do not suggest that our Allies should follow our example. Sir George Buchanan's long residence in Petrograd has indelibly associated him, in the minds of the Bolsheviks, with the policy of the Cadets, and he stands to them for much the same as, say, M. Miliukoff.

"We should represent to the Bolsheviks that we have no desire to take part in any way in the internal politics of Russia, and that any idea that we favour a counter-revolution is a profound mistake. Such a policy might be attractive to the autocratic Governments of Germany and Austria, but not to the Western democracies or America. But we feel it necessary to keep in touch as far as we can with the Ukraine, the Cossacks, Finland, Siberia, the Caucasus, etc., because these various semi-autonomous provinces represent a very large proportion of the strength of Russia. In particular, we feel bound to befriend the Ukraine, since upon the Ukraine depends the feeding of the Roumanians, to whom we are bound by every obligation of honour.

"As for the War, we should carefully refrain from any word or act condoning the treachery of the Russians in opening peace negotiations with our enemies. But we should continually repeat our readiness to accept the principles of self-determination, and subject to that, of no annexation or indemnities. We should press on the Bolsheviks the importance of not being satisfied with empty phrases from the Germans, and point out that unless they get specific undertakings from them as to such questions as Poland, Bohemia, the Roumanian parts of Transylvania, not to speak of Alsace-Lorraine and the Trentino, they will get nothing. Meanwhile their powers of resistance are melting away, and they will soon be, if they are not now, at the mercy of the German Kaiser, who will then snap his fingers at all their fine phrases and impose on them any terms he pleases. They should be told that it is now probably too late to do anything to save the personnel of the Army. But the material of the artillery can still be preserved, and at the very least it should not be transferred to our enemies to be used against the Western democracies. Most important of all, the Bolsheviks should prevent, if they can, the wheat districts of Russia, such as the Ukraine, falling into the control of or being made available for the Central Powers. This makes another reason why we are anxious to support and strengthen the Ukraine and why we urge on the Bolsheviks that, so far from trying to coerce the Ukrainians, they should enter into close coöperation with them.

"In Southern Russia our principal object must be, if we can, to save Roumania. Next we must aim at preventing Russian supplies from reaching Germany.

"Finally, we are bound to protect, if possible, the remnant of the Armenians, not only in order to safeguard the flank of our Mesopotamian forces in Persia and the Caucasus, but also because an Armenian, united, if possible, with a Georgian, autonomous, or independent State, is the only barrier against the development of a Turanian movement that will extend from Constantinople to China, and will provide Germany with a weapon of even greater danger to the peace of the world than the control of the Baghdad Railway.

"If we could induce the Southern Russian armies to resume the fight, that would be very desirable, but it is probably impossible. To secure these objects the first thing is money to reorganise the Ukraine, to pay the Cossacks and Caucasian forces, and to subsidise the Persians. The sums required are not, as things go, very enormous, but the exchange presents great difficulties. If the French could undertake the finance of the Ukraine, we might find the money for the others. It is understood that the United States will assist. Besides finance, it is important to have agents and officers to advise and support the provincial Governments and their armies. It is essential that this should be done as quietly as possible so as to avoid the imputation — as far as we can — that we are preparing to make war on the Bolsheviks.

"We would suggest that the Ukraine should be again, in this matter, dealt with by the French, while we would take the other south-east provinces. A general officer from each country would be appointed to take charge of our respective activities, but they would, of course, keep in the closest touch with one another through carefully selected liaison officers in order to ensure the utmost unity of action.

"It is for consideration whether we should facilitate the return to Southern Russia of the numerous Russian officers at present in France and England."

This Memorandum was accepted by M. Clemenceau and M. Pichon on December 23rd. Difficulties subsequently arose, however, between the Bolsheviks and the Germans, and the Brest-Litovsk negotiations were interrupted.

Our own attitude towards the Bolshevik Government at this time was not easy of definition. On January 17th, 1918, Mr. Balfour expressed to the War Cabinet the opinion that from a purely Foreign Office point of view there would be great advantages in cutting off all relations with the Bolsheviks. The latter had broken their treaty with the Allies, had repudiated their debts to us, and were openly trying to raise revolutions in all countries. The Italian Government were anxious that this course should be taken. On the other hand, we still had great interests in Northern Russia, and a number of British subjects there whose position had to be considered. It was, therefore, necessary that communications of a practical kind should take place through agents. He was quite clear that we could not give full recognition to the Bolsheviks until they could show that they were representative of the Russian people.

Mr. Balfour then read a reply given on the previous day

in the House of Commons to questions put by Mr. Ramsay MacDonald and others, which was as follows: —

". . . We have not recognised that Administration as being *de facto* or *de jure* the Government of the Russian people, but we carry on necessary business in an unofficial manner through an agent acting under the direction of our Embassy at Petrograd.

"The Bolshevik Administration have appointed M. Litvinoff as their representative in London, and we are about to establish similar unofficial relations with him.

"M. Nabokoff, who was the Chargé d'Affaires under the late Republican Russian Government, will presumably remain in London until he is either confirmed or superseded in his post by a Government recognised as representing the Russian people.

"The present arrangement is obviously both irregular and transitory. Though it cannot be fitted into any customary diplomatic framework, it is, in our opinion, the best that can be devised to meet the necessities of the moment."

Subsequently, on January 22nd, in setting forth his views on our Russian relations, he made a statement which showed that he, as well as the rest of us, was torn between conflicting considerations. He said that: —

"In view of recent events in Petrograd, it was necessary for the War Cabinet to consider very seriously what our relations were to be with the Bolshevik Government. We were the only Allied nation that had admitted a Bolshevik representative; in fact, he gathered that we were the only nation to whom the Bolsheviks had appointed a representative. No formal recognition had been given, but the necessary business was transacted through an agent, namely, Mr. Leeper. The main difficulty was that the Bolsheviks would not in the least mind quarrelling with us; they think that they have nothing to gain by keeping on good terms with England. It was a question, therefore, whether the Bolsheviks would commit some act which would provoke a rupture. He, personally, was inclined to the view that we should postpone a rupture as long as possible, as it was quite clear that the Bolsheviks provided the Germans with more difficulties than would be presented by the Social Revolutionaries. From the point of view of postponing a separate peace between Russia and Germany, and stopping the Germans getting supplies out of Russia, it would appear that the Bolsheviks were more likely to effect such a policy than any other party in Russia. The Bolsheviks, however, appeared determined to spread what he described as 'passionate propaganda' in this country, and also in Germany. He had been informed by Mr. Leeper that the Bolsheviks are convinced that social and political conditions in Germany are very bad, and that internal trouble is inevitable in the near future. This information is given them by one Radek, an international Jew of the same type as Trotsky, who is in close touch with the German Socialist Parties. Two views were current regarding Trotsky; one view was that he was in the pay of the Germans, and was playing the German game; the other view, which seemed the more probable, was that he was a genuine fanatic bent on spreading the doctrines of revolution throughout the world, but particularly in the two countries which he regarded as Imperialistic, *viz.* England and Germany."

Sir George Buchanan stated that he had always advocated a policy which would prevent an open breach with the Bolsheviks. On the other hand, it was clear that we should, sooner or later, have to choose between a rupture and complete reciprocity in everything. For instance, if we did not allow M. Litvinoff to send cypher telegrams, Trotsky would stop our representatives in Petrograd from sending cypher telegrams. Sir George said he would sooner see a rupture than allow Bolshevist propaganda on a large scale in this country, as such propaganda was dangerous, and attractive to those who had nothing to lose. He thought it was clear that the Germans would like to see a rupture between us and the Bolsheviks, and would like our representatives at Petrograd to be withdrawn, in order to give them a clear field. Any steps towards recognition by us would be exploited by the

Bolsheviks in their own interests. Regarding the Social Revolutionaries, he thought that, although more correct in their methods, they were less of a nuisance to the Germans. The Social Revolutionaries had no backbone, and were, if anything, more anxious than the Bolsheviks to make a separate peace with Germany. Two things tended to cause him to modify his view that we should, if possible, avoid a rupture with the Bolsheviks, namely, the recent maltreatment of the Constituent Assembly by the Bolsheviks, and secondly, the possibility of the Japanese or Americans, or both, giving effective military assistance to those elements in Southern Russia who were inclined to resist the Bolsheviks. In any event, he thought that the Bolsheviks would not ask us for assistance.

I sought the opinion of General Knox regarding the military situation in Russia, and the possibility of preventing the Germans from obtaining food and other supplies from Southern Russia. He thought that, even assuming a separate peace, it would be fully six months before the Germans could obtain anything important from Southern Russia. However, after six months they could obtain practically all their requirements, which would in effect break down the blockade. The only way to prevent this eventuality was the creation in Southern Russia of some effective force to resist German force. As regards the land, very little sowing had been done on landlords' property in South Russia, which meant that, unless the Germans could organise and get possession of this land before April, very little surplus corn would be available for export from Russia. The district of real importance was the Donetz coal basin, and whoever had effective possession of this was in a position to hold up the transport and resources of practically the whole of Russia, but the high prices which the Germans would offer would draw grain to enemy countries rather than to North Russia. A number of

Russian officers had spoken to him in Petrograd with regard to the possibility of joining General Kaledin. As long, however, as we appeared to be giving any form of recognition or support to the Bolsheviks, it was not likely that they would take this step. Our dealings with the Bolsheviks undoubtedly decreased the effectiveness of the moral and material support we were giving to the Cossacks.

The information which we received from the Intelligence Department of the War Office was that it would appear that the Russian Armies were rapidly melting away. The Germans were advancing towards Pskoff, without meeting any form of resistance. Sixty per cent. of the Baltic Fleet had deserted, and even on the Roumanian Front the Russian troops were being evacuated at the rate of twelve full trains a day, leaving material and guns behind. As to the available resources in Southern Russia, a man who had been in the Ukraine as recently as last October had informed him that there were large quantities of cattle in that part of Russia.

Mr. Bruce Lockhart, our representative in Petrograd, kept us in touch with the situation, and on February 7th there was a discussion in the Cabinet as to our attitude towards the Bolsheviks.

Mr. Balfour adhered to the view he had already expressed in his Memorandum.

I expressed the opinion that it was no concern of the British Government what Socialist experiment or what form of government the Bolsheviks were trying to establish in Russia. In regard to the particular question before us, it was necessary to bear in mind that the Bolsheviks were a formidable menace to Austria and Germany, and that our information regarding the internal conditions in Austria was such as to encourage the view that the internal political conditions of that Empire were seriously embarrassed by the spread of Bolshevism. I had no fear that Bolshevism was a formidable menace to the internal peace of this country. The recent by-election at Prestwich in Lancashire showed that, even in an industrial constituency, the vast majority of the nation were opposed to revolutionary ideas and in favour of carrying on the national war to a successful issue. I therefore thought that the grant of fuller authority to Mr. Lockhart might prove a useful opportunity for getting certain conditions agreed to by the Bolshevik Government in regard to their non-interference in the internal politics of Allied countries. I was also most anxious that the War Cabinet should not refuse the advice tendered to them by the British representatives in Russia, and I instanced several cases in the past where I thought errors had been made in refusing to accept such advice. The opinion I had formed of Mr. Lockhart was such as to cause me to hesitate before rejecting any advice he offered.

Some members of the Government viewed with considerable misgiving any dealings with the Bolshevik Government which would enhance its prestige and thus increase its propagandist influence.

The War Cabinet requested the Secretary of State for Foreign Affairs to prepare a draft reply to Mr. Lockhart's telegram, for their further consideration. Mr. Balfour's draft, as approved by the Cabinet and dispatched to Petrograd, was in the following terms: —

"It would appear that there is some degree of misunderstanding in regard to our policy *vis-à-vis* the Petrograd Government. It is a mistake for you to suppose that we are 'disinclined to take the line of a qualified recognition of the Bolshevik', and no less a mistake to fancy that our decision in this matter is influenced by 'anxiety as to the injury that might be inflicted on the Bourgeois elements in Russia by such a course.' I must state clearly and emphatically in regard to this second point that we are in no way concerned with the internal affairs of Russia as such; our sole interest in them is how they affect the War. Should it be the case that extensive areas of the country at present favour the Bolshevik form of Socialism, that is the concern not of Britain but of Russia, and it does not seem to us to have anything to do with the issue of whether we recognize the Russian Government diplomatically.

"My opinion in regard to this matter is that there is no material difference, as regards the form of recognition to be accorded, between the view you have cabled and that which His Majesty's Government holds. We both agree that at the moment it is impossible to accord full and complete recognition, and most undesirable to make a complete rupture. The precise nature of the intermediate course to be adopted is the only problem. Provided it is understood that our diplomatic relations are no more than informal and semi-official, there appears to be no reason why you should not function as the British Embassy's acknowledged representative. With the *de facto* Bolshevik Government at Petrograd we are prepared to enter into relations in just the same way as we have done with the *de facto* Governments of the Ukraine, Finland and elsewhere.

"But greater difficulties arise as regards the lines on which you should conduct your conversation with Mr. Trotsky. Naturally we do not want at the present time to spend time discussing past grievances such as the broken treaties, the debts repudiated, the military stores abandoned, the outbreak of war with Roumania, etc., but dealing merely with the present and the future, we note certain basic issues in regard to which we cannot meet the wishes of the Bolsheviks nor they ours. We desire that they should refrain from Bolshevik propaganda in the territories of the Allies. And they wish us to refuse aid or encouragement to any military or political movement in Russia of which they disapprove. The former demand would involve the abandonment by the Bolsheviks of their loudly advertised principles, while the latter would compel us to leave in the lurch our Allies and friends in those parts of Russia where the *de facto* government is not Bolshevik.

"Apart from these, however, there are numerous important

matters in regard to which there would be valuable scope for judicious diplomacy. For the moment the first of these is to persuade the Petrograd Government against making a separate peace with Germany, and to get them to cease their hostility to Roumania. Direct efforts to stop peace with Germany would very likely defeat the end in view, but it would help matters to point out that the Germans will be more stubborn on questions of the freedom of Esthonia and Lithuania while they are without anxiety about the Roumanian border. It is our earnest wish to postpone as long as we can a break with the Petrograd Government — even if in the end a break cannot be avoided — and to make our semi-official dealings with them in the meantime pleasant and businesslike. So we agree to your suggestion that from now on you shall have the status of a recognised intermediary acting for us. We lay down no conditions for authorising this, because we shall reach a hopeless *impasse* the moment we start discussing conditions. As far as we can, we shall check Bolshevik propaganda in this country; and if agents of the Bolsheviks are guilty of outrageous conduct we shall deport them, in the same way as we should treat representatives of any other Government that started interfering with our internal affairs. Trotsky will no doubt adopt the same attitude; but if he wants us to terminate our relations with the Cossacks and the Caucasus, he will first have to prove that the *de facto* Government in those regions is Bolshevik.

"I am certain, in the last place, that there is one matter on which we agree, whatever our differences. Both the Bolsheviks and ourselves want to bring about the end of militarism in Central Europe. That being so, there will doubtless be questions of policy on which it will be possible for us to coöperate, and on which invaluable aid can be diplomatically rendered by you. For example, Trotsky might refuse Germany any supplies that would help her to prolong the War, or strengthen the efforts of the militarists to suppress any movements for a democratic peace on the part of the people at large.

"We will for our part wait for suggestions from him as to what is the best we can do in such circumstances to help, with necessary supplies and in other directions."

But after many vicissitudes, peace was signed between Russia and Germany on March 3rd, 1918. A treaty had already been signed between the Central Powers and the Ukraine on February 9th. Roumania, pitifully situated, had no other alternative but to make peace, which she did on February 27th.

On March 12th, however, President Wilson thought fit to send a message expressing sympathy with the people of Russia on the occasion of the opening of the Congress of Soviets at Moscow.

It was pointed out (in the Cabinet) that this document did on behalf of the United States exactly what Mr. Lockhart had urged the British Government to do. The American public, however, had not the same cause for resentment against Russia as the European Allies, who had made great investments in Russia, and who had been deserted in the midst of the struggle.

But when the full text of the Peace Terms became known to us, the attitude of the Allies took a more definite and homogeneous form, and the question of this final betrayal by Russia of her Allies was the subject of a political conference of the Allies in London on March 16th. It was decided to issue a declaration expressing their indignation and M. Clemenceau prepared and read to the conference a draft. After substituting the word "Entente" for "Supreme War Council" — since it was pointed out, much to M. Clemenceau's disgust, that President Wilson objected to intervention by the Supreme War Council in political matters — the draft was substantially adopted.

On March 18th, the statement drafted by the most mordant pen in Europe was issued on behalf of the Allies, protesting against the Russo-German Treaty. It did not lack vigour. It ended by a repudiation of the Treaty itself.

". . . Peace treaties such as these we do not, and cannot, acknowledge. Our own ends are very different; we are fighting, and mean to continue fighting, in order to finish once for all with this policy of plunder, and to establish in its place the peaceful reign of organised justice.

"As the incidents of this long War unroll themselves before our eyes, more and more clearly do we perceive that the battles for freedom are everywhere interdependent; that no separate enumeration of them is needed; that in every case the single but all-sufficient appeal is to justice and right.

"Are justice and right going to win? In so far as the issue depends on battles yet to come, the nations whose fate is in the balance may surely put their trust in armies which, even under conditions more difficult than the present, showed themselves more than equal to the great cause entrusted to their valour."

APPENDIX A

TROTSKY'S STATEMENT OF BOLSHEVIK POLICY

The power of the Soviet is the power of the workers and peasants and soldiers; and remember that the soldiers are simply the self-same workers and peasants. This is the first really large-scale trial of Government by the labouring masses. Till now the Government of a country was simply an instrument of power wielded by a small section which possessed everything over a large part which possessed nothing. Our plan is to form a Government based on the power of the larger mass of the people, which larger mass is now freeing itself from the oppression of the small mass. Government by the small mass has so far generally caused poverty and misery to the larger mass. The Soviet is the main organ of this new power in the centre and provinces of Russia.

Our programme is dictated by the interests of workers and peasants. Peace is essential to them. The power of our Soviet is an instrument for fighting for peace. In this fight for peace we are not reckoning on the goodwill of the bourgeois and its diplomacy, but on the pressure of the people. No official or semi-official patriotic lie can screen the fact that the labouring masses in all the warring countries are revolutionised to the very depths by this disgraceful slaughter, which does no more than show up the criminal character of capitalistic rule. The masses in all the countries hate the War and those who caused the War.

Revolution broke out first in Russia only for the reason that the machinery of Government was weaker in Russia than in other countries. But the War has in all countries caused an accumulation of revolutionary yearnings in the very depths of mankind, and revolution will break out earlier than is expected by the ruling parties of Europe. The plan of our universal policy is to give a push to the revolution in the centre and on the west of Europe. This is the real road to a democratic peace.

What about Belgium? Alsace-Lorraine? We did not at the commencement of the War believe, and we do not believe now, that the War is carried on by the ruling class for the sake of guarding the rights of weak nations. No! The bourgeois of all countries are fighting for property. If it could be imagined that the War will pass without punishment to the ruling classes, and that imperialism will remain the guiding hand in politics of so-called civilised people, it would be naïve to think of the defending of weak and backward nations. Imperialism took everything and made slaves of everybody. Only the undefeated revolution of the working classes against imperialism can free Belgium, Alsace-Lorraine, and all weaker countries.

We are convinced that the German peoples, who are now shedding their own blood, will not allow the German ruling-class officers to attack revolutionary Russia. We are sure there will be a temporary peace on all fronts. But if (though we find it impossible to imagine this) against our straight and open proposition of immediate democratic peace, the German people remain passive and the German Kaiser moves his armies against us, our Army will defend itself to the last drop of blood, because it is not now a question of an imperialistic war, but it is the question of guarding the revolution, which offers peace to everybody.

We have given over the land of Russia from the landowner to the peasant, and the peasant will not pay anything for it.

We are placing a workers' control over production, with the object of gradually changing over the basis of production from capitalistic on to socialistic lines.

We are nationalising all banks, with the object of making

one national bank. In these matters we shall act fearlessly and without pity, overcoming the resistance of landowners and capitalists who do not wish to give up their privileges without a fight.

Our plans are colossal, difficult, grandiose, but the strength of the people, opened up by the revolution, will overcome all difficulties and fulfill its ideals.

L. TROTSKY,
Smolny Institute.

3rd November, 1917.

CHAPTER IV

THE PROBLEM OF MAN POWER

1. THE OUTLOOK FOR 1918

British recruiting achievements in the War — Full strength put forth — Supply nearing exhaustion by end of 1917 — Military attitude to man-power problem — Complex task of Government — Military Squandermania — Non-military demands on British man power — Importance of sea-power — Foch's limited comprehension — Munitions — Agriculture — Finance — Organisation of national effort — Combing-out process — A far-reaching system — Short-sighted demands of the military — Complaints of shortage unwarranted — Need to maintain morale of home front — Confusion of military estimates — Varying and contradictory demands — Estimates of wastage — Obsession with rifle strength — Importance of new mechanised arms — Growth of mechanical services — Importance of military transport — Statistics of growth of special arms — Man-power Committee set up — Smuts "No Soldier"! — Allied and enemy strength — Prolonged Allied superiority — Allied forces adequate for defence — German troops from Russia — Allied troops from Italy and the East — American troops — Reserves — Other factors — Committee's verdict — Demand and supply — For the Navy — For the Army — Infantry not the only combatants — Reduction of size of divisions — Haig's opposition — Reduction recommended — Reduction carried out — Rate of wastage — Cost of attack *v.* defence — Overestimates for minor theatres — War office underestimate supply of men — No obsession with invasion peril — Committee's recommendations for economising man power — Scanty residue of man power still available — Statistics — Limits of dilution — Psychological factors — Keeping peace on the home front — Committee's order of priority — Numbers to be combed out — Recruits available for the Army — Unwarranted charges of withholding men — Government's recruiting success; statistics — V.K. Forces — Expeditionary Forces — Imperial forces: grand total.

AT the beginning of the War there were in round figures about nine million men of military age (between nineteen and fifty) in Great Britain, and roundly a further million reached military age in the course of the War. Meantime, of course, several hundred thousand passed beyond the military age limit; but altogether there were about ten million men who at one time or another during the War were of military age. Of these ten million, it may be estimated that approximately six million were fit for general service.

Before conscription came into force, at the end of May, 1916, there were serving with our naval and military forces, apart from those of the Dominions and India, just over four million of these men. Between then and the end of the War a further two million men joined the armed forces of the country. This included men who had already attested before conscription was enforced but had not been called up, and it also included some men who were not qualified for the "A" category and were used for service behind the lines. It is worth noting that fully two out of three of the men who joined our forces from the population of this island during the Great War, to fight for their country, were volunteers, not conscripts. Altogether, upwards of six million men from Great Britain served at one time or other with the forces of the Crown in the Great War, a total roughly corresponding with the number of fit men of military age in the Kingdom. While there were some fit men retained throughout the period of the War in civilian occupations, because they were judged to be of greater value to the nation's war effort there than they would have been in the Army or Navy, numbers of men not fit for general service were drawn into the forces for auxiliary work, thus redressing the balance.

These figures show that in the course of the War the nation put forth its full strength, and made the most thorough use of its available man power. Nearly every fit man of military age served with our Forces, while the remainder of the male population, and a large part of the female population, undertook some form of work designed to aid the war effort.

When the man-power Committee of the Cabinet made its investigation of our remaining man-power resources in December, 1917, this process had been very nearly carried out to the full during 1917 under the auspices of the special department instituted for that purpose, and the margin which they then found available for further exploitation was meagre in the extreme. They prefaced their report with the statement that the drain on the robust manhood of the country which it had been foreseen the War would impose was now no longer prospective but actual. We were not the only belligerent country that found itself in that predicament. All had used up their man power to the last limit of exhaustion. I maintain that we made a more prudent distribution of our resources than any of our partners or foes. We acted on the assumption that staying power was what mattered most. Had we not taken that view the Allies would have collapsed before America had time to come to the rescue.

Viewed through the eyes of military historians and controversialists the problem of man power seems to have been a very simple one. Here were so many millions of young men in Britain fit for soldiering. There were too many to send simultaneously to the War, but all who were at first left behind would be reserved for the inevitable wastage. Our behind-the-line warriors could not understand the parsimony with which a niggardly and unsympathetic civilian Government doled out recruits when there was still a remnant of unspent manhood left at home to pursue their ordinary vocations. Their minds were bogged in the ideas and traditions of a bygone age when war conditions were so essentially different from those of this mechanical era. There was a time in the past when a nation's total wartime man power was reckoned by counting all men of any age who could carry a spear or wield a sword and endure the hardships of a campaign. Most of the arms and munitions used in battle were carried by the men who employed them. A few carts would bring along all the reserve of javelins that were needed. Much of the siege artillery was improvised from material available in the forests and the army lived on the country through which it passed. The latest examples of such an army were the Boer Commandoes in the South African War. The farmer took up his rifle, filled and put on his bandolier, packed his saddle bag with biltong, had a few Cape carts for a reserve of cartridges and food, and thus equipped he and his followers became an army that held up the British Empire for over two years. In ancient wars the requirements of the population at home were very simple. Old men, with the help of women and children, could plough the land, harvest the crops and mind the cattle. At sea one has only to compare the requirements of the fleet of small wooden ships that fought the Armada with our monster steel ships and the thousands of craft, great and small, that guarded our communications. Even in 1918 there were responsible military leaders whose ideas about man power were unconsciously governed by this primitive conception of warfare.

But to any Government responsible to the nation for the successful prosecution of a protracted and exhausting war under modern conditions, the problem of how to make the best disposition of our national man power was much more complex. We had not only to provide and keep supplied the immense equipment of modern armies and navies, but to administer and conserve our highly developed national life and activities at home. We were responsible for maintaining the whole war effort of the nation, military, naval, commercial, industrial, financial, diplomatic, and to a large extent for sustaining the effort of our Allies. To carry out that wide range of tasks, our dwindling man power had to be husbanded and carefully allotted among these conflicting claims. All had to go short of the supply they desired, and to carry on as well as they could with such resources as could be spared to them. Every nation was profligate of its man power in the early stages of the war and conducted its war activities as if there were no limit to the number of young men of military age who were fit to be thrown into the furnace to feed the flames of war. The Allies, who had an enormous superiority in the number of fit young men available, nearly threw away their advantage by the reckless prodigality of their military leaders. The German tactics had a more constant regard than the Allied military methods to the importance of winning without wasting valuable lives. Had they emulated Allied heedlessness in this respect they would have been broken by sheer exhaustion before the end of 1916. The British and French casualties on the Western Front were twice as heavy as the German losses. Russia lost three times as heavily as did her German assailants. The idea of a war of attrition was the refuge of stupidity and it was stupidly operated, with the consequence that the overwhelming superiority in man power which the Allies enjoyed at the beginning of the War had by the fourth year been melted down to the dimensions of a dubious equality. For this reason, had America not come in at the last moment of exhaustion, the event of the War would have been different. We might not have been beaten, but we should have had to accept a deadlock solution.

The British man-power problem differed in some essential respects from that of our Allies. In a special measure we had to carry the burden of maintaining, not ourselves alone, but our Allies as well. The command of the seas, without which Allied victory would have been impossible, was preponderatingly our charge, and our Navy had the supreme task of keeping the seas clear, hunting down the German submarines, holding the enemy warships pinned to their harbours, and convoying the merchant shipping which bore supplies not only for ourselves but for our Allies. The French and Italian Fleets made their contribution to this work, but compared with ours it was insignificant, and involved no serious drain on the man power of those two countries. Men were needed not only for the manning of our immense Navy and

Mercantile Marine, but for the building of new ships and swarms of new craft to patrol the sea, and to keep these constantly repaired and refitted. There was a difference equivalent to several army corps between the numbers absorbed by the manning and equipment of our naval and mercantile marine and those employed by France, Italy, Russia or Germany in the same tasks. The occupation of the corn-growing and cattle-rearing plains of Northern France by the Germans deprived Frenchmen of a large proportion of their wheat and meat resources. Without our ships, neither Italy nor France could have carried on for a single year. They would have been starved into surrender. Nor could we have conveyed our troops and theirs — including American troops — to the various theatres of war and maintained them there. But the manning of our naval and mercantile fleets, the provision of men for their docks, their building and repairing yards, their arming and munitioning, the maintenance of minelayers and minesweepers and of the endless contrivances invented to fight the deadly submarine — all these demands in the aggregate absorbed well over a million of our man power. If the men of military age and fitness amongst these were counted, it would be the equivalent of at least thirty divisions. There is no greater proof of the exclusiveness of a profession than the fact that great soldiers of exceptional intelligence like General Foch could never understand how essential sea power was to the very existence of the alliance. Nelson taught Napoleon his first lesson in the importance of sea power at the Battle of Aboukir. The isolation of Napoleon's Army from its sources of reinforcement and supply brought home to him the sinister possibilities which lurked in the sea for the schemes of a captain of land forces. And in the years which followed he was given many more warnings of the difficulty of overcoming a foe that ruled the waves. But it was never impressed on the mind of Foch by any drawback or deficiency. He never understood that the unlimited ammunition with which his armies were supplied and the fact that not only his men but their families were well fed were attributable to the might of the British Navy and the enterprise of our great Mercantile Marine. He thought the allocation to the sea services of so many fit men who could have been sent to the Army was sheer waste, and the traditional obsession of a great sea power. He once flew into a temper over this criminal lavishment of good men on ships and Clemenceau had to pull him up. He always asked: "What have the Navy done? Have they done any fighting?" Our own generals, too, in their various memoranda, almost completely ignored the call of the sea on our manhood. And yet they would have had no armies on any battlefield, had it not been for the complete command of the sea which our sailors and their auxiliary helpers on shore succeeded in maintaining, and the British people would have been driven to make peace in order to avert famine.

But sea power and shipping services were by no means the only rival claimants with the Army for men. Our coal mines needed them. We had not only to supply fuel for our forges, rolling mills, arsenals and munition works, but also to supply France, whose best coal mines were in German hands, and Italy, who had no coal of her own. As it was we could supply Italy with only a meagre proportion of her needs; and not only were her population suffering severely from lack of fuel, but her war effort was being crippled through lack of coal for her workshops. Our munition workers were straining to keep pace with the fabulous demands of the Army for munitions of every kind, traditional and new. These demands increased from battle to battle. During the first six months of the War the total expenditure of artillary ammunition was approximately one million rounds, including only a very trivial amount of heavy shell. In September, 1918, we were expending nearly a million rounds in a single day, including over 160,000 rounds of heavy and very heavy shell (six-inch to fifteen-inch). The factories in this country were also turning out considerable quantities of armaments of various kinds for our Allies. We provided a good deal of equipment for the American forces, including heavy artillery and ammunition.

The vital part played by the exploitation of British soil during the last two years of the War to aid in feeding the nation has been described elsewhere by me.[1] But for that achievement, Britain would have suffered the fate which ultimately overtook Germany and her allies, of being starved first into discontent and then into surrender. As it was, our home-grown food supplies not only enabled us to divert cargoes of imported wheat to France and Italy, but to take the grave risk with our food which was involved in turning the shipping engaged on its transport to the task of bringing over the American troops. All this meant the retention of more men on the land.

Throughout the War we had to maintain our financial position for the benefit of ourselves and our Allies; and this meant keeping up a certain measure of industry to provide goods to sell abroad in exchange for the supplies we were purchasing. Indeed, when the American Mission, headed by Colonel House, met us in London in November, 1917, one of its members, Mr. Colby, Assistant Secretary to the United States Treasury, expressed regret that we had gone as far as we had in scrapping our export industries to use our man power for our military effort. He declared that for many reasons the United States Government, especially the Treasury, would have preferred that these trades, for economic and financial reasons, had not been killed.

For all these vitally important tasks, as indispensable

[1] Vol. III, Chap. VII.

to our war effort as service in the trenches, men were needed, and the Government had to take care that at least a minimum supply of labour was reserved for each. I have previously described how, as the War progressed, legislation was adopted and administrative measures were taken for the purpose of rallying the whole available man power of the nation and distributing it as economically as possible where it was required.[1] In course of time the reservoir of population engaged in ordinary civil avocations, which could be drawn on to supply additional man power for one or other of the various tasks essential to our national effort, dwindled and shrank until it was practically dry. The whole manhood of the country had been surveyed and directed, either into the defence forces of the realm, or into work of vital national importance for supplying our Army and Navy, feeding the nation and our Allies, maintaining what were recognised as essential trades and industries, public utilities and administration. Some of our indispensable services had at one stage been allowed to become so depleted of workers that it was found necessary to bring back men to them out of the trenches.

In this process of organisation of our man power the ranks of men within the military age limits had been combed and recombed with meticulous care. Every one of them who could be regarded as fit for military service (and the standard grew progressively lower and more elastic as this destructive war went on) was promptly claimed for the Army unless compelling reasons were forthcoming to warrant his retention in civil life — that is to say, that his services to the national effort would be more valuable there than in the Army. If he was not indispensable, or if a substitute could be found for him among men not of military age and fitness, he was put into khaki. The military tribunals were constantly

[1] Vol. I, Chap. IX, "Ministry of Munitions", 3, "The Problem of Labour"; Vol. II, Chap. VI, "The Coming of Conscription"; Vol. III, Chap. VIII, "A System of National Service"; Vol. IV, Chap. V, "Problems of Labour Unrest."

busy all over the country, and the military representatives upon them were always calling insistently for the enlistment of each man brought before them. Every able-bodied man was fought for. No doubt a number passed through the net who ought to have been caught; but the Government could not override the decisions of tribunals set up by Parliament.

Complete national service, in the sense of conscripting the whole population and requiring every citizen, whatever his age or condition, to place himself under orders and take up such work as was prescribed for him by officials, was never finally enforced. Even Germany shrank from that drastic expedient, in spite of constant pressure from powerful military leaders. Nevertheless, as the War progressed, social pressure and the economic measures taken by the Government combined to bring about a state of affairs more and more nearly approximating what could have been ordained under such a system. But so far as men of military age were concerned, the working of the Conscriptions Acts brought it about that every one of them was marked down, registered, and either taken into the Army or allocated to some job where his service would be of still greater value to the national effort. Doubtless there were some shirkers, or "skrimshankers" and "khaki dodgers", as they were contemptuously designated, who managed to evade the Army when they should rightly have been in it. But they were not a high percentage; had all such been ruthlessly picked out, the total reinforcement they would have provided would have been trivial in numbers and poor in fighting quality. Before the end of 1917 it might safely be asserted that there was no source of potential recruits left uncombed, no reservoir of man power undrained. Apart from the annual increment of youths reaching military age, the only way to secure further reinforcements for the Army was to divert to it men already serving the country in other ways, in munition works, coal mines, shipyards, transport, food production, public utilities, essential trades and industries, where their services had hitherto been judged indispensable.

Whether any considerable body of these men should be thus diverted to the Army was a problem for statesmanship. It could not just be settled by the requisitions of the Army authorities. The generals could not be expected to judge the issue dispassionately. Their reckless wastage of the man power so lavishly placed at their disposal also vitiated their judgment. Apart from that consideration, they were not responsible for ensuring the maintenance of our naval services, our shipping, our dockyards, our railways, our agriculture, our arrangements for feeding and clothing the nation, nor even our munition supply. Neither were they concerned with the preservation of national unity by avoiding the irritation and exasperation which threatened to impair the national spirit. They were solely concerned with military operations. They desired bigger and bigger armies with an insistent and almost querulous appetite. In the constant demands made upon the Government for more and more men to fill up gaps and equip the new services in the Army, there was no indication that our great Generals realised that there could be any other demands for man power entitled to recognition. They were not to be persuaded that we could not carry on these essential non-military services entirely with the rejects of medical examiners. Every fit person diverted from their armies to any other purpose represented a betrayal of trust by pusillanimous and undiscerning politicians. Were there not hundreds of thousands of men in Britain still allowed to skulk at home? If sent to Flanders, they would pave the highway to a glorious triumph! It was a war of attrition; as Sir William Robertson had written: "We should follow the principle of the gambler who has the heaviest purse and force our adversary's hand and make him go on spending until he is a pauper." [1]

The Official History of the Military Operations in France and Flanders laments that the reinforcements called for by the generals were not always provided in full and promptly. Yet we sent more men to reinforce our armies on the Western Front in 1917 than we had promised to provide, because the casualties exceeded the worst anticipations. Our military critics would have been in a better position to complain, had they given the Government the aid of their influence in stopping the criminal wastage of so many hundreds of thousands of our picked young men on enterprises which they must have known had no chance of success. Had they done so, the German success in the spring offensive of 1918 would have been anticipated and averted. Further, it must be remembered that the big reinforcements originally demanded by Sir Douglas Haig in the late autumn of 1917 were not just to defend his line until the arrival of the American Army should make a great offensive all along the front a feasible operation, but in order that he himself should be able to continue in the spring his Passchendaele attack, and thus throw away another 200,000 or 300,000 men before our Allies were ready to coöperate. To these plans the French Generals and many of our own were opposed, and we had no intention of disorganising our national arrangements in order to provide them. On the other hand, it seemed clear from the figures available to us — including those furnished by Sir Douglas Haig himself — that the forces at his disposal, with such reinforcements as we could supply, were adequate to repel any attack provided the defences were put in good order, the troops wisely distributed along the line in suitable proportions, and the reserves properly adjusted in readiness to support any threatened sector.

[1] Vol. IV, Chap. IX, p. 374.

Nor was the problem purely material. The morale of the home front was fully as vital to success as the defence of the line in France. Ruthless expedients for reinforcing the Army which precipitated civil disturbances, strikes and possibly revolution in Britain would have been a poor way of seeking victory. Some of the emergency measures which in the crisis of the spring of 1918 were taken to reinforce our hard-pressed Army were not only measures so detrimental to the nation's war activities in other vital directions that nothing less than such a crisis would have justified them on material grounds; they were measures which only that crisis rendered psychologically possible. Had any attempt been made to enforce them previously, it would have provoked civil disturbance and domestic collapse. As it was, they produced a violent national protest in Ireland and we got no recruits there.

It is with these considerations in mind that the man-power demands of the Army at the end of 1917, and the Government's attitude to those demands, must be studied.

One of the greatest difficulties experienced by the Government in allocating man power was attributable to the constantly shifting figures of War Office requirements. An official who had been working at what was for him a purely statistical problem at the War Office once informed me that it was the most hopeless task he had ever undertaken. No one seemed to understand the simplest principles of arithmetic. It was not that they could not add or subtract, but he could not find anyone who was certain what ought to be added and what subtracted. Categories shifted about from day to day. The result depended on the view taken at the time by the individual officer who performed the operation or his superior. That view was a changeable one and according to the exigencies of opinion the figures fluctuated. Amidst all the shuffling and transmutations no one could answer with certainty a simple question as to the numbers of our fighting men. One distinguished General who had been deputed to investigate the actual position told me that when he started his inquiry he found 40,000 men had vanished altogether; and although they were on the pay-roll no one could explain where they were. I can understand the unreliability of guesses made at enemy casualties. These are always exaggerated on both sides. One estimate given to me, of 1,000,000 Germans killed and wounded on the Somme opposite the British line alone and of almost a similar number put *hors de combat* in the Battle of Flanders, did seem a particularly wild guess. When, however, you come to add up the numbers on the pay-roll of your own army, it seems to be a simple sum for unbiased mathematicians. But the fact remains that military Staff figures had no relation to actual conditions or facts; they varied according to the case which the High Command had to make for the time being. When G.H.Q. were bent upon either launching a new offensive or continuing or renewing an old one, then the men at their disposal indicated an overwhelming superiority over those which the enemy could put into the fighting line.

In the discussions of the War Committee of the Cabinet in June, 1917, when the Passchendaele offensive was under consideration,[1] Sir William Robertson said that regarding man power he anticipated no difficulty. He hoped to have 150,000 men to send out, with which to supply the 20,000 or 30,000 wanted to complete the establishment of the Army in France and replace the casualties suffered in the attack. He would also send out the 67th Division.

The drafts sent out to the Army in France in the summer of 1917 were in fact in excess of the amounts promised. According to a War Office letter to Sir Douglas Haig of February 15th, 1917, and subsequent letters, he was promised

[1] *Cf.* Vol. IV, p. 362.

356,000 men between March 1st and October 31st, 1917. The number actually sent was 376,000 — an excess of 20,000.

The German strength on the Western Front in 1917 was considerably below that of the Franco-British forces, and in pleading for his Flanders offensive in June, Haig insisted that much of it was of inferior quality.

On October 8th, in response to a request from me, Haig wrote to the C.I.G.S. giving his appreciation of what rôle the British Armies should adopt if Russia were forced out of the War. He then declared that our forces were in good fettle, that the Germans were badly broken, that their reserves of man power would be exhausted by May or June, 1918, and that by April 1st, 1918, the Allies would outnumber the Germans in actual numbers by 30 per cent. even after allowing for the number of divisions which the Germans might be able to bring across from their Eastern Front.

It is true that this estimate was based on the assumption that the gaps in the British Army would be filled by reinforcements from home; but the total deficiency reported to the Government only amounted to 75,000 men — a number well within our capacity to supply — and even if it were not filled, our superiority according to Haig's October estimate would still be well over 20 per cent. These were the figures submitted to us when it was necessary to exaggerate our strength in order to justify a costly offensive.

But when the policy changed, and it was decided to postpone offensives until the American troops arrived, and Haig was invited meanwhile to take over more line, then the alleged superiority disappeared and was transformed into an alarming deficiency. During the whole time the Cabinet Committee was investigating the question of man power, the figures supplied through the War Office were being constantly altered, and the Cabinet were quite unable to get any stable and reliable estimates as to the actual position.

The estimates supplied in the War Office letter of November 3rd, 1917, showed that by October 31st, 1918, allowing for men recovering in France from wounds and returning to the forces, there would be a net infantry deficit of 259,000 men, most of which would be offset by a considerable increase in the numbers of men attached to mechanised arms at the disposal of our Army.

A fresh estimate, contained in a Memorandum by the C.I.G.S. dated November 19th, 1917, stated that the Army was then nearly 100,000 men below strength. There was no clear indication of the basis of this estimate, which appeared to make no allowance for the increase in arms other than infantry. "To provide for the normal winter wastage, and bring the Armies up to strength by April, 1918, we require 500,000 men," it continued. "Towards this we have now in sight 225,000 men. By the end of October next it is calculated that, if no further measures are sanctioned, the Armies will be 300,000 men below strength."

Five days later, another and yet more gloomy estimate was furnished in a letter from Sir Douglas Haig. Writing on November 24th, 1917, to the War Office, he declared that "it is evident from calculations based on previous experience that the British Infantry in France will be approximately 250,000 or about 40 per cent. below establishment on the 31st March next."

According to another G.H.Q. calculation made at about this time, quoted in the Official History,[1] the shortage by October 31st in the infantry on the Western Front would be 460,000. All these changing figures proved to be purely fanciful. They were not estimates carefully prepared by officials who understood the elements of accountancy but merely a succession of grouses from generals who had failed to achieve what they had hoped for and had promised and were

[1] "Military Operations in France and Belgium, 1918", Vol. I, p. 27.

THE PROBLEM OF MAN POWER 149

anxious to put the blame for their discomfiture on the politicians who had dared to predict the failure.

The figures supplied by the Adjutant-General in the latter part of December to the Cabinet Committee on Man Power provide yet a further variant of the rate of wastage and the need for reinforcements. It is suggested by these figures that up to March 31st, the wastage of troops in France will amount to 260,100 men — equivalent to 86,7000 men a month. These figures were a ludicrous exaggeration, and it is difficult not to regard them as a deliberate miscalculation.[1] These were the computed losses involved in holding the trenches during the winter. They obviously do not include estimated losses during some great battle. Pétain estimated his losses for the same period for a longer line at 40,000 a month. The total estimate of the number of men needed for the Army up to the end of September, 1918, was put at 1,304,-000; and after reckoning the men already in khaki who could be drafted out from the forces in Britain, and recovered wounded and sick, it was stated that 600,000 new recruits would be needed.

On reviewing all these different estimates, it can be noted, first, that they each contradict the other, and secondly, that they become progressively more alarmist and rapacious.

Another curious feature in the calculations of our military strength by the War Office was the way they concentrated on rifle strength, and ignored the man power allocated to other combatant services. As the War went on the mechanical power at the disposal of the Armies increased rapidly. In artillery, machine-guns, aviation, tanks and transport, machinery was playing a more and more important part in the struggle and was consequently absorbing more and more men. The mechanical superiority of the Allies in 1918

[1] The total casualties actually incurred in France, between January 1st and March 31st, 1918, were 196,567. These included the heavy losses of the Battle of St. Quentin.

was largely responsible for the acceleration and the completeness of the victory. Infantry comparisons are therefore misleading, and when used in controversial attacks on Governments deliberately confuse the issue for those who are ignorant of the make-up of modern armies. It has been suggested for instance, that the Government had only provided for the British Army in France for the whole of 1918 a reinforcement of 100,000. This is, of course, flagrantly untrue.

The letter from the War Office to Sir Douglas Haig on November 3rd, 1917, dealing with the man-power outlook, explained that the total man power in sight to meet his needs for the next twelve months including new recruits and recovered sick and wounded would be 688,000. But while this number of 688,000 was anticipated as available to make up his man power, it would not all be used up by the infantry. There were other imperative calls, of which the most formidable was 110,000 to be used to form entirely new units for the flying corps, the artillery, the machine-gun corps, tanks and military railways, while a further 80,000 were set aside for maintaining the strength of existing formations of these mechanical arms. Obviously, such arms as tanks and machine-guns were worth, in effect, many times the number of their personnel, compared with infantry. So that if a proportion of men was deducted from potential infantry reinforcements and sent, instead, as new units of these mechanical arms that were coming to play a rapidly growing part in the conflict, the net result was to multiply, not to diminish, the value of the man power supplied for the line. But the rigid traditionalism of the military authorities never fully appreciated this lesson, which was the most conspicuous discovery and development of the War. When the War Office gave us its estimates of man-power requirements, the men set aside for these formidable engines of war were not counted. The figures given to the Government were those of "rifle strength." It mattered not that a single tank with its crew might be capable of forcing a break in an enemy line more efficiently and cheaply than a whole company of infantry; that half a dozen machine-guns, well placed, could hold up a battalion. That was no consolation for the fact that potential reinforcements for the infantry had been withheld. If these new-fangled weapons, which had played no part in the lessons taught them at the Staff College, must be used — and it was gradually acknowledged that they had a subsidiary value — then they must be manned without detriment to the numbers of the infantry.

Up to this hour, when a case has to be made against the Government of the day for neglect of its duty to the Army, or an excuse manufactured for generals who have failed, the figures quoted are always confined to the infantry. The drain on man power involved in providing the vast increases in the mechanical powers of the Army, in artillery, machine-guns, tanks, aeroplanes and railways behind the lines, is completely ignored, although these appliances multiply the power of the Army a hundredfold. Since the early days of the War the mechanical weapons of offence on the British side had multiplied enormously. The heavy artillery once numbered in tens could now be counted in thousands, and in weight, calibre and range they were vastly more powerful. The machine-guns, of which there were a few scanty hundreds in 1914, by 1918 had mounted up to scores of thousands. Tanks were not even thought of in those early days. Now they played an essential part in any great offensive. As for the increase in aircraft, it was immeasurable, in numbers and in power. Infantry were still essential to hold the line, and to exploit the activities of the mechanical arms, but every infantryman to-day counted for many times more than he did in those gloomy days when he could be bombarded with impunity in his trenches, and when the feeble artillery with which he was supported could not even tear gaps in the barbed wire against which he was called upon to advance, let alone destroy the trenches which sheltered the enemy riflemen or the machine-gun emplacements which mowed down our advancing troops. Mechanical appliances of all kinds rendered the deadly duties of the infantry easier and less costly. But increasing appliances implied the need of more and more men to handle them, and less and less pure riflemen to support them. The artillery tore up barbed wire, smashed the trenches and emplacements that provided cover for enemy riflemen and machine-gunners, protected advancing troops with a barrage of shell; the tanks crashed through all obstacles and thus gave facility and support for the attacking infantrymen. The aeroplanes not only helped by observation, but they took part in the fight. In the battle of the spring where our infantry were hard pressed by the enemy our aeroplanes attacked from the air with bomb and machine-gun and helped to relieve the pressure and to check the speed of the German advance. It is only those who survived Neuve Chapelle, Festubert and Loos, where our infantrymen were shot down at leisure in front of unbroken barbed wire, who knew what the enormous improvement in mechanisation meant to the British infantry. No infantryman would ever complain if these machines were rendered more powerful, even if the size of his division was thereby reduced.

The enormous improvement in our communications behind the line also constituted a source of new strength to our armies. Hundreds of miles of new roads and railways were constructed by us to facilitate transport of men and material directly to the line and laterally from one part of the line to another. The facility and speed with which troops could be moved from one part of the front to the other made it unnecessary to mass such large numbers of troops on any one sector. This fact is noted by the famous German Staff officer, Colonel Wetzell, in the advice he gave to Ludendorff prior to the March offensive: —

"We are in a position very quickly to transfer extraordinarily large forces by rail, but our enemy on the Western Front can do so in a still higher degree, thanks to the excellent railway communications behind his front. Besides, both hostile armies possess a very large number of motor vehicles, which have already often contributed decisive services (Verdun) by the rapid bringing up of reinforcements. . . . In view of the favourable and numerous railway communications the possibility of very rapid counter-measures from the north by the British, and from the south by the French, must be regarded as on the cards. We must reckon with certainty that, should we have a striking initial success, we shall soon be involved in a wearisome struggle with the main forces of both our opponents."

Colonel Wetzell was right in his apprehension that the German offensive would be wrecked by the excellent communications developed behind the Allied lines. These railways and roads saved our Third and Fifth Armies from being overwhelmed by numbers in the spring offensive, and had they been used sooner, would have checked the German advance at an earlier date. They also enabled us to check the German break-through on the Lys by the timely transport of reinforcements. Roads and railways are a fundamental part of the equipment of a modern army. They are formidable weapons of war. It is interesting to note that this improvement in our communications was achieved by a civilian reorganisation of the transport arrangements in France, which was forced upon the War Office in September, 1916. It led to a conflict between myself and the Army Council at the time. Nevertheless, it turned out to be one of the outstanding successes of the War.[1] These communications not only

[1] *Cf.* Vol. II, Chap. XI, p. 225 *et seq.*

saved us from disaster in March and April, they also contributed materially to that rapid concentration of troops and guns which broke up the German Armies in the autumn of 1918.

But all these mechanical improvements which constituted such a feature of this war involved the diversion on a great scale of man power from infantry and cavalry to other and newer services. Every other army in the field recognised that fact at a fairly early stage, and consequently reduced the traditional standard of numbers in their brigades and divisions. The Germans were the first to recognise that machine-guns automatically multiplied the numbers of their riflemen. The French soon followed suit. We were the last to perceive the shift of values, and adapt our divisional formations to it.

Nothing will enable us better to understand how thoroughly the developments of the War changed the distribution of man power in the Army than a comparison of the figures of 1914 with those in the last year of the War. These are set out in the following table, showing the total strength of the British Army, Regular and Territorial Forces (excluding Colonial and Indian troops) at home and abroad in August, 1914, and March, 1918. In connection with the figures for August, 1914, it should be pointed out that more than half the total nominal strength consisted of Territorial troops, who were only very partially trained, and were unready for full active service for months. Their number is given alongside the grand total of the 1914 forces in which they are included.

ARM OR BRANCH.	TOTAL	AUGUST, 1914. Territorial (included in previous column)	MARCH, 1918.
Cavalry	46,496	(25,418)	89,074
Artillery: Light	58,766 ⎫	(39,977)	339,135
Heavy	27,275 ⎭		194,540
Royal Engineers	24,035	(13,808)	304,241
Foot Guards and Infantry	306,654	(166,701)	1,750,202
Cyclist Corps	—	—	20,430
Machine-Gun Corps	—	—	100,879
Tank Corps	—	—	20,173
Royal Flying Corps	1,200	—	144,078
Royal Army Service Corps	14,491	(8,184)	318,700
Royal Army Medical Corps	17,840	(13,770)	141,740
R.A.O.C., R.A.V.C., A.P.C.	3,588	(153)	78,966
Labour Corps	—	—	348,555
Non-Combatant Corps	—	—	3,277
TOTAL	500,345	(268,011)	3,889,990

From this table it will be seen that the infantry strength of the Army was multiplied nearly sixfold, but the other branches (excluding cavalry which just doubled) increased fourteenfold. The augmentation of the mechanical power of our forces 14 times represents a much higher multiple in the striking-power of the Army as a whole. Another feature of this increase which had a direct bearing on the criticisms directed against the War Cabinet is the fact that the army commanded by Marshal Haig had a much higher percentage of this mechanical reinforcement in proportion to the total numbers of the men in a given theatre of war than any of our armies on any other front. The "side-shows" were very skimpily treated in the matter of artillery — especially heavy artillery and aeroplanes. Tanks were a luxury almost completely denied to these abominations.

In view of these striking figures it is simply dishonest to dwell on the numbers of riflemen in the infantry as if that represented fairly the efforts made by the Government in the supply of man power for our forces at the various fronts.

There is only one explanation for it. The enormous increase in mechanical power — artillery, ammunition, machine-guns, aeroplanes, tanks and transport — was due to the initiative, vision and enterprise of civilians.

It was not easy for the Cabinet, in face of the medley of discrepant figures and estimates presented to it, to decide what the real needs of the Army were. And that knowledge was an essential preliminary to any prudent apportionment of our dwindling man power to the best advantage amongst the competing claims of vital services for a share in it.

As we had been advised that the War would probably continue until 1919 and that we must contemplate the probability of having to provide for the requirements of two more campaigns, we decided in December, 1917, to set up a special Committee of the Cabinet to examine the whole question of man power and submit proposals as to the action it would be desirable to take to deal with this problem. The Committee consisted of Lord Curzon, Mr. G. N. Barnes, Sir Edward Carson and General Smuts, with myself in the chair. The figures were obtained by the Ministry of National Service from the Departments concerned including the War Office.

The problems reviewed were: the comparative strength of the Allies and the enemy on the Western Front; the existing reserves available on both sides; the civilian man power in Britain; the purposes it was needed to serve; and the amount of it which could be made available for military use. Here the general principle adopted by the Committee was that the chief aim must be to safeguard the staying power of all the Allies until the Americans could come into the fray with their great resources and turn the scale in our favour. And that safeguarding must involve the maintenance not only of the armies, but of the nations as a whole.

The Official History declares, in a tone of censure,

THE PROBLEM OF MAN POWER

that not one of the members of this Committee was a soldier. That General Smuts should be classed as "no soldier" is surely a consummate example of the workings of the professional military mind. True, he had not devoted all his life to soldiering; neither had Sir Douglas Haig's Chief of the Staff, Sir Herbert Lawrence. Those who had campaigned against Smuts in the South African War could hardly deny his remarkable military quality. And in the Great War, after a brilliant campaign in German South-West Africa, he commanded during 1916 our forces in East Africa in the fight with von Lettow-Vorbeck. In any case, this was a Committee of the Cabinet, composed of Ministers of the Crown, responsible not only for governing the country and guarding all the interests of its citizens, but also for the direction of the War as a whole on sea and land. The Army had no such wide responsibility, and army officers as such obviously could have neither the knowledge nor the authority to settle matters involving the whole economic life of the nation and its whole war effort, diplomatic, naval, industrial, commercial and financial. The Army had no special knowledge of these problems, and could claim no more right than the Navy, the Ministry of Munitions, the Treasury, the Board of Trade, the Ministries of Labour and of Agriculture, the Shipping, Coal or Food Controllers to a representative on the Committee. But the man-power Committee were supplied with all figures possessed by the General Staff of the War Office, bearing upon their investigation, and the Director of Military Intelligence and the Adjutant-General attended on behalf of the War Office to give such further explanations as the Committee might require on these matters. Every draft of the Report was submitted to the War Office for its observations. Thus the insinuation of the Official History that the military view was not represented at the Committee's session is disingenuous.

Among the main features of the Report noted above, the first was that of the comparative strength of the Allies and the enemy on the Western Front. After the Report was first drafted, the General Staff came to the conclusion that the figures under this head which it had supplied were too favourable, and submitted revised figures. Yet even these could hardly be regarded as seriously alarming.

According to the General Staff's amended tables, the position in the West in December, 1917, was that the Allies had 169½ divisions on the French Front against 151 German divisions; and a combatant strength of 3,420,000 (exclusive of 11,800 Indian troops) compared with 2,536,000 for the Germans — *i.e.*, an Allied superiority of 18½ divisions, and of 884,000 combatant troops. On the Italian Front the Allies had a superiority to the combined Austrian and German forces of 409,000 combatants.

Despite this considerable superiority, we had been unable to break the German Front. As a matter of fact, ever since 1915 the Allies had held on the Western Front a marked advantage in numbers. In 1917 this amounted to more than seven Allied to four German soldiers. At the end of 1917 the combined total combatant strength (not ration strength) of the French and British forces in all theatres of war was 3,700,000, while that of the Germans on all fronts, East and West, was 3,400,000. If the total forces of the Allies on all fronts (including Italians, Belgians, Portuguese, etc.) be compared with the total forces of the Central Powers and their Turk and Bulgar allies, then the Allies, without including any Russians or Roumanians, had a combatant strength of 5,400,000 against a combatant strength of 5,200,000 for the Central Powers.

Russians and Roumanians were excluded from this calculation; but even if they concluded a separate peace with Germany, she would still have to maintain a considerable force on her Eastern Front, for reasons I give in another chapter. She could transfer a number of divisions to the West; enough to exceed the Allied Armies in the number of divisional formations, and approximately to equal them in rifle strength, though not in artillery, tanks and aeroplanes. But if the Allies, with a seven to four superiority, had been unable to break through the German lines in 1917, was there any reason to suppose that the Germans, with approximately equal rifle strength, with troops whose quality was poor and whose fighting value was low (according to Haig's memorandum of October 8th, 1917), would be able to break through the Allied lines in the spring of 1918, especially as the mechanical strength and mobility of the enemy was definitely inferior to that possessed by the Allies?

We had to take full cognisance of the fact that the superiority we still held in December, 1917, was rapidly diminishing owing to the transference of German troops from Russia, and that by the following spring there might be proximate equality until the Americans arrived. The Committee was bound to consider what the position would be in May, 1918, assuming that the Germans were able to withdraw from the Russian Front all the divisions they could afford to take away, having regard to the disturbed condition of that country and the need for organising its resources to supply German deficiencies in food and raw materials. The revised estimate of the Staff was that 41 divisions might be thus transferred, including 824,000 combatant troops. The possibility was also envisaged of Austrian divisions being brought to the front, but this, quite correctly, as it turned out, was reckoned to be improbable in any appreciable numbers.

On the Allied side, the possibility was noted that troops might be transferred to France from other fronts. We were of opinion, as were the Versailles Council, that British and French divisions ought to be withdrawn from Italy or in the alternative that Italian divisions should be brought to France. For the delays that occurred in bringing troops from Italy the General Staffs were entirely responsible. It was their business and not that of the Governments concerned to make arrangements for the transfer once they had secured the assent of the Government to the removal. The Governments concerned not only approved that course but actually suggested and urged it. It was also contemplated that in the event of an emergency, troops should be withdrawn from Egypt and Palestine, as we were ridiculously over-insured in our Turkish campaigns. It had been decided to fill three white divisions with Indian troops in order to bring the British units to France. Here also there were unaccountable and reprehensible delays on the part of the military authorities. But, apart from these reinforcements drawn from other theatres, the main hope of additional formations lay with the advent of American troops. How soon these would materialise was uncertain, but General Bliss at that time hoped to have ten fighting and two replacement divisions in France by May, and as many more by December, 1918. It will be remembered that an American division had three times as many men as a British, French or German division.

Passing from the question of additional reinforcing formations to that of reserves, the Committee set out the estimates of the numbers of men on each side that would be available for maintaining the strength of these formations and making good the casualties during 1918. On the German side, assuming that some 76,000 men could be drawn from defence divisions left on the Eastern Front, after the 41 active divisions, above mentioned, had been transferred to the West, the total reserves that would be available in

THE PROBLEM OF MAN POWER

the course of the year would be 926,000. On the Allied side, the estimated reserves in sight during the year — British, French and American — were put at 1,356,400. This included an estimated 202,400 American reserves, in addition to the twenty fighting divisions it was hoped they would supply before the end of 1918. Actually the American contribution vastly exceeded this estimate before the conclusion of hostilities in November, 1918, owing to the special arrangements we made for carrying American troops across the Atlantic in British ships.

There were, the Committee pointed out, other non-statistical considerations, such as generalship, organisation, national morale, fighting quality. The Allies had, as an ultimate resource, the vast potentialities of the United States, and there were fewer boys and elderly men in their forces than in the enemy ranks. They also had more artillery, tanks, aeroplanes and available lorries on the Western Front. The German defenders of the March offensive before the Reichstag Committee claimed that they had a *slight* superiority in numbers, but admitted that they were inferior in guns and other mechanical equipment. All our experience of offensives on the Western Front justified us in believing that under these conditions the Germans would not possess the necessary superiority to break through the Allied lines and defeat our armies — always provided these armies were reasonably well handled. No mathematical superiority can save unintelligent leadership from disaster. After reckoning all these factors, the man-power Committee of the Cabinet concluded that they: —

"do not appear to modify the general conclusion to be drawn from the man power figures, that the Allies ought to be able to hold their own on the Western Front until the period when the increase of American strength begins to alter the balance of advantage in their favour."

Despite an unusual display of strategical and tactical ineptitude in the Allied conduct of the spring operations, this forecast was justified by the event.

From this branch of the survey, the Committee proceeded to an examination of the remaining man power of Britain, the uses to which it was being put, the nature of the demands for it, and the number that could be taken from other services for our armed forces — naval as well as military. They considered the requests for further recruits made by all the Services, the calculations upon which those requests were based; the numbers and occupations of men of military age still in civilian life, and the degree of urgency of demand for their work; and recommended a number of further measures, administrative and legislative, to secure the best distribution of our man power and the maximum contribution to the Army.

The demands laid before the Committee by the Services, for additional able-bodied recruits to be withdrawn from civilian work and handed over to them, amounted to 90,000 new men for the Navy and R.N.A.S. and 600,000 for the Army. These demands were additional to those for lower-category men for non-combatant work with the Army and Air Force, and for the recruitment of all youths fit for service as they reached the age of eighteen.

The representatives of the Navy could give the Committee no figures analysing the basis of their demand for 90,000 new men; so that the Committee could not scrutinise this estimate. However, in their recommendations, the Committee made an allowance of 50,000 for the Navy out of the number of "A" men they thought it possible to withdraw from civilian work.

The demand of the Army for an additional 600,000 recruits from the civilian population was based upon a long and elaborate series of calculations. Several of the items of this series were by no means convincing.

THE PROBLEM OF MAN POWER 163

The Army authorities placed their gross demand for an additional supply of men during 1918 at 1,304,000. This figure represented: —

165,300 men wanted for expanding the flying corps and artillery, and creating new units in such growing services as machine-gun corps, tanks, etc.

95,000 to make up the Army in France to establishment.

671,700 to replace wastage in the Army in France up to September 30th, 1918.

192,000 to replace wastage in other theatres to October 31st.

160,000 to be in training to meet wastages in all theatres between October and the end of January, 1919.

20,000 to replace skilled shipwrights which the Army was being asked to release to aid the shipbuilding programme.

To meet this gross demand for 1,304,000 men, the Army authorities reckoned they would be able to draft 449,000 "A" men from the forces at home, up to October 31st, 1918, while of the sick and wounded becoming fit for general service they reckoned there would be 240,000. Together these totalled 689,000, leaving 615,000 deficit on their estimated requirements.

Now in the argument presented by these figures there were obvious gaps, to some of which the Committee drew attention.

To begin with, the 165,000 men to expand the mechanical strength of the army could not be treated as a deficit to be made up. Quite the reverse. It would obviously not entail any reduction in the total number of our combatant forces, if the men required for expanding the artillery and flying corps and creating fresh units for tanks and machine-gun corps were drawn from the ranks of existing recruits. True, such a process would deplete the infantry establishment, but all these new formations gave redoubled support and strength to the infantry. As our supplies of cannon grew more lavish, we could economise more on "cannon-fodder."

Since there was not the man power available to expand these new units to the extent desired and at the same time keep all our infantry divisions reinforced up to the full traditional establishment, it became a question of either cutting down the number of divisional formations, or of reducing the establishment of ordinary infantry in each division. The second course was that recommended and already adopted by all the other leading belligerent armies. It had been urged upon us by the French for some time. In order to secure the fullest advantage from the new weapons now available — machine-guns, trench mortars, etc. — and the greatly increased artillery strength, it was clearly necessary to attach full complements of these to as many infantry formations as possible. To achieve this end, a reduction of the number of battalions in a division from twelve to nine had already been carried out by both the French and the German Armies, and the numbers constituting each battalion had also been reduced. This reduction did not mean that the resources of these two belligerent countries had become exhausted. Indeed, Germany had a larger number of men in the various battlefields in 1918 than she had in 1914. But the enormous increase in the mechanical power at the disposal of her armies had rendered it necessary that she should allocate a considerable proportion of her men to the new units thus created. The net result was that with diminished numbers of infantry her divisions were three times as powerful as they were at the commencement of the War.

Sir Douglas Haig, however, was opposed to such a reconstruction. He held that if through shortage of man power it were impossible to keep the divisions up to the existing

THE PROBLEM OF MAN POWER 165

infantry establishment, it would be preferable to break up some of them, rather than to reduce them to nine battalions each. Foch, on the other hand, was always specially insistent on the importance of keeping up the number of divisional formations, even although it were found impossible to maintain the standard number of troops in each division. The German Staff took the same line, until their divisions were so reduced that they consisted of only 2,000 or 3,000 men. It could hardly be suggested that the military authorities of France and Germany were inferior to the British in expert knowledge and sound judgment on problems of military organisation. Yet alike our Army Council and our Commander-in-Chief protested bitterly against such a reorganisation and as usual blamed the politicians. They were accustomed to twelve-battalion divisions, and they could not understand that methods of warfare had been revolutionised since the days of the Expeditionary Force of 1914 when we depended on the firing efficiency of our riflemen and their skill in bayonet practice, and when our artillery was almost entirely light; when we had few aeroplanes, still fewer heavy guns, not many machine-guns and no tanks.

The Cabinet Committee on Man Power strongly urged that we should follow the example of the French and Germans by reducing the number of infantrymen in a division. The Army objections to it were obviously ill-founded. Indeed, the Official History, while it feels in duty bound to support the Army Council and the Commander-in-Chief in their protests, cannot pretend to accept their reasons, and fumbles for a different ground. The Official Historian writes: —

"It was not so much the nature of the change — which would indeed increase the proportion of guns per thousand infantry, *which was eminently desirable* — but the time selected for it which was open to objection."

It would be interesting to know what better time than January and February — a quiet time at the front — could have been chosen for an "eminently desirable" change. The diary of the War shows that there was a complete cessation of all serious military operations on the Western Front from the end of December, 1917, to the middle of March, 1918. It was the longest quiet spell we had known for two years.

The reduction of the divisional establishments advised by the Committee was finally ordered by the War Office on January 10th, 1918. It was anticipated that the change-over would be complete by February 15th. Actually, it was carried through more slowly. Only three of the four armies in France completed their divisional reorganisation before the end of February, the Fourth Army finishing it on March 4th. The infantry holding Passchendaele must not be reduced until the last possible moment whatever happened elsewhere! The whole affair, including the wrath of the Army Council and the Commander-in-Chief at the proposal, the dilatoriness with which it was finally carried through, and the lingering resentment at it displayed by the Official History, furnishes a melancholy illustration of that rigidity and reluctance to adopt new methods to fit new conditions, which so constantly handicapped our efforts in the War and cost us needlessly heavy casualties. It was left for civilians to force on the Army the use and development of tanks, machine-guns and machine-gun corps, heavy guns, high explosives, improved transport and all other means of economising man power and heightening its efficiency. It is perhaps worth noting in this connection that on January 15th, 1918, the War Cabinet decided to send a telegram to the Military Representatives on the Supreme War Council at Versailles, saying that: —

"In order to secure the advantage of the experience of other Allied Armies, the Military Representatives at Versailles are requested to report as soon as possible on the economising of manpower, casualties and tonnage, which might be effected by the fullest and most scientific employment of machine-guns, automatic rifles, tanks, and other mechanical devices."

The second matter queried by the Cabinet Committee was the estimated rate of wastage. It was at a higher rate than that experienced in 1917, when we had been continually on the offensive in the most sanguinary fighting. Further, French experience showed that the *net* wastage (total casualties less the number of wounded and sick that returned to the forces) represented only 25 per cent. of the combatant strength; whereas the War Office was calculating a 55 per cent. rate. The British Army had of course been fighting hard on the offensive all through 1917; but as it was to stand on the defensive for the early part of 1918, the Committee considered that the military estimate was likely to prove unduly large.

In their reply to the Committee, the Army Council were indignant at the suggestion that the defence cost less than the attack. They wrote: —

"There is nothing in the experience of this war or in any other to support the argument that a defensive policy necessarily entails fewer losses than an offensive policy, once fighting begins, and therefore in the opinion of the Military Members the adoption of a defensive policy does not justify making provision for a lower rate of wastage than that estimated by the War Office. . . ."

The actual experience of the War as a whole, as since ascertained, disproves this contention of the Army Council. The casualty figures in the War, secured as the result of very careful inquiry by the Historical Section of the Committee of Imperial Defence, in 1922, show conclusively that in the course of our offensives — and except for the spring of 1918, our forces in France were almost continually acting on the offensive — our total casualties were as three to two of the Germans opposite our front. On the Somme, in Flanders and elsewhere, we habitually suffered at least 50 per cent. more casualties than we inflicted. On the other hand, in the big German offensives of March and April, the proportion was reversed. Between March 21st and April 30th, 1918, the total losses in killed and wounded along the British Front were: British, 209,466; German 308,825. It is true that on account of the big sweep forward achieved by the Germans, our losses during this period in prisoners and missing were heavier than theirs. But when these further losses on both sides are added, the balance is still against the Germans, the total figures being respectively: British, 302,869; German, 348,769. The Germans were often accused by our military authorities of understating their casualties, especially in the latter part of the War. If there is substance in this charge then the German casualties during their offensive must have been still more heavy than ours.

The killed are of course the final casualties, for a considerable proportion of wounded recover and return to active service. In the British Army the proportion that recovered and returned to the forces was five out of nine, while of the remainder, the larger part recovered sufficiently to return to civil life and take up work which released other men for the Army. In the number of *killed* during the German offensives of March and April, the respective losses were: British, 28,128; German, 56,639. Thus in killed alone, the Germans lost more than twice as many as the British.

When, later in the summer, we resumed the offensive, our casualties again became three to two of the Germans.

In the estimates submitted by the Military Authorities to the man-power Committee, the figure of wastage in other theatres appeared to be particularly excessive. The actual total casualties in all theatres other than France during 1917 were 48,000. The Army Council put the figure for 1918 at 192,000. Even after making a generous allowance for contingencies, the Ministry of National Service thought that 120,000 would be ample under this head. Whether the number wanted would prove to be 120,000 or 192,000, it was clear that comparatively few of them would be required in these other theatres till well on in the year, so that if an emergency arose in France in the spring, the drafts for our Eastern Armies would still be available for the French Front.

While the War Office estimates of the number of additional recruits they would need in 1918 were thus magnified by every artifice, their reckoning of the numbers they could dispose of to supply their needs, apart from further recruits from the adult civil population, were cut down to the lowest point. Even the Official History seems to be somewhat surprised at their assumption that they would be able to furnish only 449,000 men to the Overseas forces out of the troops they had available in Britain. According to the War Office returns, there were on January 1st, 1918, in the United Kingdom, 74,403 officers and 1,486,459 other ranks of the British Army, of whom 38,225 officers were fit for general service; while of the "other ranks", 607,403 were then "available", 78,886 belonged to permanent cadres, and the remainder, some 800,170, were recruits in training, men engaged in administrative services, and "indispensables." A large proportion of these 800,000 recruits under training would before long become fit to send overseas if wanted. Upwards of 100,000 of them were lads under nineteen years old. A pledge had been given in Parliament regarding these that only in the event of a grave national emergency should they be sent out of the country before they had completed their nineteenth year. After the March offensive nineteen years was reduced to eighteen years and six months. Here we followed the example of Germany and France. Altogether it seemed reasonable to assume that if a crisis arose, a far larger number than 449,000 in all could be supplied from the Home Army to the Expeditionary forces, especially since the military bogy of a German invasion of Britain had now been definitely laid.

In addition to these large forces of British troops retained on British soil there were also in Britain, belonging to the Overseas contingents, 8,324 officers, of whom 4,493 were fit for general service, and 187,491 other ranks (excluding permanent cadres), of whom 41,065 were recorded as "available."

It has been suggested that I was responsible for keeping these great masses of men at home because of my "obsession" as to the danger of a German invasion. I have never entertained such a fear. In fact I always regarded it as a bogy invented by those who wanted to reëstablish permanent conscription. I agreed with the decision of the Asquith Government that the Germans could not possibly accomplish more than a rush and a raid without artillery support.

Thus apart from any further contribution which might still be squeezed from the numbers of "A" men still in civilian occupations, it is evident that the Army authorities had under their hand, already in khaki, a quite considerable body of troops on which to draw for reinforcing their Overseas Armies, and all they had to do was to make the best use of them. On the whole, therefore, the Committee were justified in coming to the conclusion that, with the enormous reserves of men trained or in training at home and with arrangements the Ministry of National Service had made and was still making to increase these numbers, our forces ought to be able to hold out in 1918 until the Americans turned equality into decisive superiority, provided meanwhile certain measures were taken to economise losses and make the fullest and most skilful use of the men available. Among the measures proposed by the man-power Committee were that every effort should be made to avoid the appalling waste of man power hitherto sustained, by the adoption of suitable strategy and tactics, and by the improvement of the defences; that the divisions should be cut down from four battalions per brigade to three; that the bulk of the cavalry should be broken up and used to reinforce the tank corps and flying corps; and that the Home Army should be drawn on much more heavily to reinforce the Overseas Armies, and also to provide the "B" category men required for auxiliary work. The French and Germans put this class in the trenches to hold the quieter parts of the line. The Germans had fourteen divisions of Landsturm troops in the line. Both Haig and the War Office declined to follow this course. They would have nothing but "A" men for the war zones. In the course of the summer of 1918 on the advice of Foch this objection was dropped by our Generals with excellent results. The "B" men did well.

There was comfort in knowing that the needs of the Army, if serious, were not so desperate as some of the figures submitted were intended to convey, and that a good deal could be done to improve the prospects by a verification of War Office statistics, and the rest achieved by a more efficient utilisation of the existing supply of man power in the Army itself. When the Committee turned to examine the residue of man power still left in civilian work in this country, they found that it was very nearly exhausted, and certainly could not be expected to furnish that 600,000 "A" recruits, additional to lads reaching eighteen, and lower-category men, for which the Army was asking.

There were still 3,500,000 men of military age in civilian occupations in Great Britain; but of these only 950,000 were fit for general service. Of these 950,000, some 355,000 were in munition works and shipyards, 330,000 were in coal-mining or agriculture, 187,000 were in railways, transport and public utility occupations, and the balance of 78,000 men were a carefully combed remnant in a variety of positions where hitherto they had been considered by the tribunals indispensable. From the practical point of view it would have been impossible to remove all these men from their jobs. On the one hand, much of the work was of a heavy nature, for which men physically fit were essential. Fit men were needed for the mercantile marine, for shipbuilding and ship-repairing yards, for coal-mining, forges, rolling mills, heavy armament manufacture, for hewing timber, agriculture, railways and other industries and utilities. Further, numbers of men fit for general service had been retained perforce in their positions because they were highly skilled and irreplaceable — skilled engineers, key men in industry, commerce, finance, public administration — and were more valuable to the nation where they were than in shouldering a rifle. Not a few had been brought back from the Army to the factories by the Government for that reason. Indeed, at this very time we were scouring the Army for another 20,000 skilled shipwrights, urgently required for our shipbuilding programme, to make good the losses inflicted by the German submarines. Our shipping, always vital to the nation for its very existence, was about to play in 1918 an even more spectacular part in the promotion of the Allied victory by bringing over American troops to France. By making that feat of transport possible, the men retained in the shipyards or brought back to them from the Army contributed a reinforcement of many times their number to the forces in France.

Thus although dilution, the substitution of women workers and of men medically rejected by the Army examiners for those who could be recruited for general service, was being steadily pressed forward, there were numbers of tasks and of men to which it could not be successfully applied. The Army authorities became ruffled and red with impatience at the sight of any fit man not in khaki. But the Army authorities had not to shoulder the responsibility for governing the country and maintaining all its manifold essential activities — a fact which neither they nor some of their historians and apologists seem to have realised.

Further, in considering this question of dilution of skilled occupations, and the removal of "A" men, whose well-paid jobs would be taken by others less fit for military service, it has to be borne in mind, as I pointed out in a previous chapter,[1] that Britain had not the same background of social training as Continental nations for the acceptance of universal compulsory military service. On the Continent, lads grew up from early childhood with the knowledge that in due time they must unquestioningly take their place in the Army and serve their time there, and that if a national emergency arose, they would be recalled to the Army as a matter of course, whatever work they might be doing. But in Britain the Army had always been a voluntary service. The notion that men should be forced to throw up well-paid work to engage in this riskiest, worst paid and most tethered of all professions, however unwillingly, was quite a new principle, with no backing of social tradition, while the labour dilution which was its corollary was equally a menace to the slowly built fabric of trade unionist regulations designed to protect the worker against inroads on his craft. The Unions had accepted such measures, I will not say grudgingly, but with misgivings and only because they were forced by the extremity of the war emergency. Patriotism is the last stand of every creed and these Union leaders conceded to the needs of the country what they would not sur-

[1] *Cf.* Vol. II, Chap. VI: "The Coming of Conscription."

render to any other appeal. We had to apply these concessions carefully, with tact not tyranny. Entire nations are not yet — not even in war — on the parade ground where Ministers can bellow at them orders which must be implicitly and promptly obeyed on peril of the guard-room. There are countries moving in that direction. But in the days of Imperial autocracy even the docile Russian rebelled in the end against such a disciplinary exaction.

Thus in reckoning the maximum limit of further levies which might be made upon the "A" men still in civilian callings we had to take care not only to avoid crippling essential services, but also to preserve peace on the home front. The residue of fit men in the ranks of labour consisted in large part of those who either had not felt called upon to volunteer for the Army, or had been deterred from doing so by pressure from the management of the concerns which could not have been kept going without their help. To these must be added those who had actually volunteered, and even in some cases had gone out to France, but had been sent back to mine or factory or dockyard because their services there were judged indispensable. These latter men did not want to be played about with. They were mainly volunteers. Had they been left in the Army, they would have done their duty there. Being released from it without their own effort, and told they could best serve their country at home, they would have felt naturally aggrieved if they had again been dragged out and thrust into khaki, labelled as conscripts and flung into unhealthy salients to spend their winter. The squeezing process in Germany of the last few months of the War was driving tens of thousands into desertion and ere many months passed it drove hundreds of thousands into rebellion which overthrew the throne. Some of the more powerful Trade Unions were showing signs of becoming resistant to the pressure for combing out more of their men for the front.

Thus in weighing up the question of what further fit men we could withdraw from civilian services for the Army and Navy we had on the one hand to examine what number could be taken without causing a material disorganisation or breakdown of essential industries, and on the other, how far we could revive press gang tactics by pouncing on eligible individuals here and there without provoking a psychological reaction that would create more disastrous trouble than the number of men obtained would be worth. Government is in part a science but it is more of an art. To be a success there must be not only regulation but understanding.

The Cabinet Committee on Man Power came to the conclusion that as regards the relative urgency of demand between the different essential services, first place must be given to the Navy. As I have already noted, its maintenance was clearly of supreme importance to the nation and to the Allies. If it failed, overwhelming disaster to the Allied cause was inevitable. With it was bracketed the Air Force. The development of aviation since the War had given this branch of the Service an importance beyond the conjecture of any military teacher before the War. Supremacy in the air had become one of the essentials of victory. This arm had also an importance of its own for the defence of our cities against hostile attack. Shipping, which included shipbuilding and repairing as well as manning, came next. For feeding and supplying the nation, for carrying troops, munitions and rations to the different theatres of war, for assisting our Allies, for bringing over American troops, it was vital to make good the shipping shortage which the submarine war had created. Of hardly less importance was to be reckoned the manufacture of the mechanism and munitions of war. This included coal production for ourselves and the Allies. After these in order of merit were placed food production and timber felling.

While in this list the requirements of the fighting personnel of the Navy and Air Force were given absolute priority over all other services, the supply of man power to the other essential services was made subject to the charge that the Minister of National Service should economise it with the utmost care, in order to make all the provision possible for release of men for the Army. After careful examination of the labour schedules, the Committee on Man Power came to the conclusion that by carrying out some sort of general post with the available labour force in Britain, tending to bring about further dilution of the supply with women and with men of low medical categories, it would be possible to secure in 1918 for the forces from the ranks of men of military age then in civilian life, a further 150,000 men of category "A" and 100,000 men of lower categories.

Of these, they proposed to allot 50,000 category "A" men to the Navy, leaving 100,000 category "A" men and 100,000 men of lower categories for the Army. While these second hundred thousand were not up to the medical standard of fitness for general service, there were a number of tasks to be done in the Army which they could perform, thus releasing from those sources fit men to be taken into the line and increase our combatant strength.

Thus, while the Army was asking for 600,000 recruits of "A" category from the civilian population during 1918, the conclusion of the Committee was that it could only see the possibility by the most drastic combing of securing 100,000 "A" men and another 100,000 men of lower categories in addition to 120,000 youths reaching military age during the year. Reviewing their problem in retrospect, it seems quite clear that they could not at that stage in the War have promised more. The 600,000 demanded by the Army was, for reasons I have given, in any case a figure which could not be justified on the most superficial examination. When the German attack in March, 1918, broke our front, and it became a life and death issue to send abroad every man capable of bearing arms, we slashed desperately at some of our vital war industries, and made encroachments upon the scanty man power left at home, which nothing but the need for restoring confidence in a momentary panic created by a great defeat could have justified. We got few more recruits for the War, though the effort did help to calm excited nerves. Cuts were then carried out that would have been psychologically impossible previously — cuts to which organised labour would have refused to submit but for the spectacular urgency of the situation. The last available men were thrust into the Army. But even when these desperate expedients were resorted to, it was not found possible to secure any really considerable additional numbers. As I have stated, the man-power Committee had proposed a total recruitment of "A" category men in 1918 for Navy and Army (other than boys to be conscripted on reaching the age of eighteen) of 150,000. The actual number of adult "A" men recruited in 1918 was 284,649 — an increase of less than 135,000 over the original estimate, after using the maximum pressure and taking the maximum risks.

A great deal of nonsense had been talked, and many foolish charges brought against the Government of failing to provide a larger number of recruits in the early part of 1918. A somewhat flagrant example of this is a comment contained in the Official History [1] in a footnote giving the numbers of troops sent out to France in January–August, 1918. The writer points out that a total of 548,327 "A" men were sent to France during those eight months, and draws the following curious conclusion: —

[1] "Military Operations, France and Belgium, 1918," Vol. I, p. 52.

"It is obvious that the British Armies in France could have been brought up to full establishment before 21st March without unduly weakening forces elsewhere had the Government so willed."

This is an amazing statement to be made by a writer with access to the Official Statistics of the Military Effort of the British Empire. In the first place, he must be aware that those 548,327 "A" men were not obtainable by recruitment, however much the Government might will it. The great bulk of them had to be, and were, provided by the Army authorities from the troops already in khaki by the beginning of 1918; troops that were under their hand in this country, ready trained or in course of training, or recovering from wounds or sickness. So it would seem that if the Army historian is entitled to make any criticism in this connection, he should direct it against the Army authorities.

But in the second place, it is a grotesque *gaffe* on the part of a military writer to suggest that because men were actually sent out in August, they could equally well have been sent out in March. Of the total troops in this country in March, 1918, including Regular Army, Territorial Force and Overseas contingents from the Dominions, upwards of 700,000 were "A" category officers and men; but of these, only 227,-545 officers and men were shown by the War Office returns to be trained and available for dispatch overseas, including all the youths of under nineteen who had finished their necessary training. The remainder of the "A" men here at that time were recruits not yet trained, and sick and wounded not yet fully recovered or not "hardened" after recovery in preparation for sending out again. Each month saw a further batch ready for dispatch overseas. But the Official Statistics place it beyond dispute that the men drafted overseas between April and August were not available for that purpose in March. The writer of the Official History must have been aware of these facts or he must have been too busy writing about events to examine the facts — in which case writers are apt to fall back on gossip. He must have known that there was no spectacular expansion of belated recruiting by the Government to bear witness to an earlier neglect; and that the fact of drafts being sent out in August could not be taken as evidence that they were available in March.

The accusation, often made, that at this period the British Government was starving the Army of men will not bear a moment's examination if the official figures published by the War Office are studied. Let us consider those figures in regard to: —

(a) The total strength of the British Army recruited from the United Kingdom.

(b) The total strength of the Expeditionary Forces in all war theatres.

(c) The grand total of British forces of all kinds throughout the Empire.

(a) In March, 1918, the total strength of the British Army, Regular and Territorial, raised in this country — excluding all Dominion, Colonial, Indian and native troops — was 3,889,990.[1] This was the colossal giant which the War Cabinet are accused of having reduced to a skeleton army. *It was the highest total strength which the British Army ever reached. At no time in the whole course of the War were there so many men from this country in the ranks of the Army at home and overseas as at the date of the German offensive in March, 1918.* It was the supreme moment of the War, the supreme moment of British history, so far as the massing of our sons into the Army was concerned. Despite all the terrible slaughter of the Somme, and the awful massacres of Passchendaele, our military authorities had under their command in March, 1918, more men than

[1] "Statistics of the Military Effort of the British Empire, 1914–1920", p. 231.

ever before, drawn entirely from the population of this little island.

(b) Similarly, the total British strength in all the theatres of war — our total Expeditionary forces, including Dominion and other Overseas contingents, but excluding coloured labour units, *reached in March, 1918, its high-water mark*, with a total of 2,834,690.[1] *This, too, was the record figure for the military effort of the British Empire at any moment during the War.* It included some 253,000 Indian and African troops.

The Expeditionary forces on the Western Front had been sorely depleted by the casualties of the Flanders campaign, which had calamitously exceeded the forecast of probable losses for which we had provided. On the eve of that campaign, on August 1st, 1917, the total strength of the B.E.F., France, was 2,044,627 [1] (exclusive of coloured labour units) — the highest figure it reached. You cannot quickly train men and draft them across to replace casualties totalling nearly 400,000. But by March 1st, 1918, the total strength of the B.E.F., France, together with the troops sent along from France to the Italian Front (which the Italians offered to make up by an equal number of their troops) amounted to 2,019,773 [1] — within 25,000 of the pre-Passchendaele total.

(c) The grand total of all the forces of the Empire, at home, in the various war theatres, in India and garrisoning ports, *reached its maximum in March, 1918, with 5,559,573.*[2] This included 4,982,254 troops, British, Dominions, India, etc., and 577,319 coloured labour. *Each* of these totals was the highest ever attained in the whole course of the War. It was an immense effort for a commonwealth where universal

[1] "Statistics of the Military Effort of the British Empire, 1914–1920", Table facing p. 64.
[2] *Ibid.*, p. 34.

military service was an unknown tradition in the lives of the people and where this supreme sacrifice of liberty for millions and of home and life for multitudes was incurred in a war waged for the independence of another nation. There was no invader on our soil devastating our towns and villages as in France. We had not, as Italy had, territory and a population which belonged to our race and spoke our language, to be redeemed from a foreign yoke. We fought to vindicate international right which had been outraged by a wrong inflicted on a small country which we were covenanted to protect.

In face of these facts and figures, all of them given in the Official Statistics issued by the War Office, the charge that in the spring of 1918 the Army was being starved of men can be seen to be not only false but silly.

2. Negotiations with Labour and Ireland

Conferences with Labour — My speech to the T.U.C. — Our terms refused by Germany — Necessity of fighting for our rights — Questions — No sectional negotiations — Armament nationalisation — Alsace-Lorraine — Conscription of wealth — Man-power Bill — Irish problem — March emergency proposals — General Mahon's memorandum — Views of Campbell and Carson — Complexities of the issue — Irish conscription and Home Rule to be simultaneous — Confused reactions of opinion — Attempt to revise voluntary recruiting — Arrest of rebel leaders — Conscription never enforced.

It was by no means an easy matter to carry out the proposal of the man-power Committee for recruiting a further 150,000 "A" men and 100,000 men of lower categories from the remaining industrial population. The men of military age were an often-sifted residue, all of them holding pledges of absolute or conditional exemption from military service; and to call up a large, fresh batch of them meant anxious diplomacy and frank consultation with the leaders of the Trade Unions. Sir Auckland Geddes, the Minister of National

Service, had a general conference with the leaders of Labour, which he had to adjourn early in January, in order to see how far he could reach agreement with each trade union group about the measures it would be necessary to take in their particular industry to carry through this recruiting programme. The General Conference was resumed on January 18th, 1918, when about 350 delegates attended at the Central Hall, Westminster, from all parts of the country.

The chair at this gathering was taken by Mr. George Barnes, the representative of Labour in the Cabinet, and two other Labour holders of Ministerial office, Mr. G. H. Roberts and Mr. Clynes, were also present. At the previous meeting of this Conference on January 5th I had attended and delivered the speech outlining the peace aims of the Allies which is reproduced in Chapter II, Appendix B. I also addressed this second meeting of delegates about the situation, and gave the reasons which made it necessary to take further steps to extract men for the Army and Navy from amongst those in their ranks who had been hitherto exempted.

I began by urging the fullest frankness between the Government and the representatives of Labour, and promised to answer, at the end of my speech, any questions on general policy. I then proceeded: —

"With regard to the proposals of the Government, let me say this at the outset as to the method. There are no other alternatives for raising men except either raising the military age, as they have done in Austria, where it is 55, or sending wounded men back and back again into the battle line. . . . As to the urgency of the need, no man standing like my colleagues and myself on the watch-tower can deny it. Unless the need had been urgent, we should not have brought forward this demand now. . . . The Government view is this: It would be folly to withdraw men from industries one hour sooner than the need arose. On the other hand, it would be treason to the State, treason to our country, treason to democracy, treason to the cause of freedom, if when the need did arise we did not make the demand."

I pointed out that unless we succeeded in resisting the military power of Prussia we could never hope to obtain from the Kaiser and Ludendorff even the most moderate terms that the most pacific of us could dream of accepting. It was not a question of fighting on to gain some big imperialist aim. I had already indicated our peace terms in my speech to them a fortnight before, and President Wilson had almost at the same time put forward substantially the same demand. They had been received in all the Allied countries with acclaim, except perhaps by extremists who thought they should have been stiffer.

"What has been their reception in Germany? I beg you to consider this, especially those who think that we are responsible for perpetuating this horror. I would not have this war for a second on my soul if I could stop it honourably. . . . There has been no response from any man in any position in Germany that indicates a desire on the part of the ruling powers in that land to approach the problem in a spirit of equity.

"We demanded the restoration of Belgium. Is there one man here who would make peace without the complete restoration of Belgium and reparation for its wrongs? [Cries of "No!"] Is there one man? ["No!"] I would like to see him stand up. Is there one man who would do it? What is the answer from Germany? There has been but one answer, and it came from von Tirpitz's soul — 'Never!' "

The same answer, I pointed out, was given to the suggestion of the restoration of Alsace-Lorraine, and to the demand that Mesopotamia and Palestine should not be handed back to Turkish tyranny. To the peace aims formulated by the British Trade Unions themselves, there had not been a single favourable response from anyone in Germany with authority to speak. In fact, there had been no civilian statement from Germany at all. Von Kuhlmann had been kept silent by the War Lords, whose only answer to civilisation would be given from the cannon's mouth.

"Do not let us harbour any delusions. . . . You might as well stop fighting unless you are going to do it well. If you are not going to do it with all your might, it is real murder of gallant fellows who have stood there for three years [Hear, hear]. . . . If there are men who say that they will not go into the trenches, then the men who are in the trenches have a right to say, 'Neither will we remain here!' Supposing they did it, would that bring the War to an end? Yes, it would. But what sort of an end?"

The Russian soldiers, I reminded them, had done that; and the Germans had proceeded to take Riga and the Russian islands. If we stopped now, we should leave Britain as well as France at the mercy of the most relentless military autocracy the world had ever seen. We could not turn Hindenburg out of Belgium with trade union resolutions, but we could with trade union guns and trade unionists behind them. Only by such means could we carry to triumph those great aims which had been put forward alike by the Trade Unionists, the Government and President Wilson as the objects for which we were committed to fight.

"Let us harbour no delusions. We must take the world as it is, and the story of democracy is this: no democracy has ever long survived the failure of its adherents to be ready to die for it. . . . If one profession, one trade, one section, or one class in a community claims to be immune from obligations which are imposed upon the rest, that is a fundamental travesty of the principles of democracy. . . . We are fighting now against the privilege claimed by a military caste. Democracy must mean that the people of all classes . . . must merge their privileges and their rights in the common stock. . . . My own conviction is this, the people must either go on or go under."

At the end of my speech I invited questions, and a number were put, the majority of them bearing upon the issue of whether peace negotiations were possible at this stage, and whether any good end could be served by a meeting of British and German Socialist and Labour representatives at Stockholm or elsewhere. In reply to this question which recurred in several guises, I pointed out that ultimately a peace could only be negotiated by the accredited representatives of a country's Government. The great democracies, America and France, as well as Italy and British, all took that view.

". . . It is a fundamental misconception of democracy that any section, however powerful, really represents the whole of the people. Whoever goes there to speak and to negotiate must represent the whole of the country, and not merely a part of it."

I said that I had examined this question very carefully, with an original prejudice in favour of encouraging such sectional conferences; but had been driven to conclude that it would be a very dangerous experiment. If you let the Socialist sections meet to confer on peace terms, you would have to let other sections do the same — the financiers of Britain and of Germany, the industrialists, merchants and so on. It would all end in confusion. The only effective way was for the people of each country to see that their Government represented their views, and then leave it to negotiate the peace.

A delegate inquired whether I would give an undertaking that the production of armaments here should be nationalised, and private profiteering in these engines of destruction brought to an end. My reply was: —

"All I can say is that, speaking for myself, I am entirely in sympathy with that proposition. I do not think there ought to be any pecuniary incentive to encourage armaments in the world, and I am entirely in sympathy with the spirit of that question."

Another question raised the issue of our policy in regard to Alsace-Lorraine. To this I replied: —

"I stated the view of the Government, I think, quite clearly last time. My view is that the people of this country will stand by the people of France. It is a question for them to decide. You must remember this is not really a question of territory to them. It has been a question of vital principle. It has been like an open sore in their side for nearly 50 years. They have never been able to live in peace during the whole of that time, and their view undoubtedly is that you cannot have peace in France until you have settled this question once and for ever; and if you cannot have peace in France, you won't have peace in Europe. You must settle this question unless you are going to have a series of wars in Europe."

Another point which clearly preoccupied the minds of the Labour delegates was the contribution which wealth ought to make to our war effort. Was I going to conscript it?

I answered that "in no country and in no war has wealth been as heavily taxed for war purposes as in this country. Even at this moment the taxation of wealth is higher here than in any other belligerent country, not even excluding Germany, and if my questioner will just look at all the budgets of the world, past and present, he will find we have gone farther on that road than any other country. I do not say that we have come to the end of the path yet." In another reply to a question about taxation as opposed to borrowing, I pointed out that we had maintained a higher percentage of taxation to borrowing than any other government.

Finally, I assured my hearers that we were at pains to ensure that the war aims of America and the Allies should be consolidated as fully as possible, and that it was our purpose so to settle the peace of the world that it should be possible to do away with conscription, not only here, but in every other country. But unless the strength of militarism was really broken, that would be impossible.

This frank discussion ended in a really good understanding between the Government and the representatives of Labour, and enabled us to secure their agreement for the further measures of recruitment which were necessary to provide the additional numbers of men for the Navy and Army proposed by the man-power Committee.

A Bill to enact the legislation requisite for enabling us to cancel exemptions and conduct a further comb-out of our man power had already been introduced by Sir Auckland Geddes, the Minister of National Service, on January 14th. After this understanding had been reached with the representatives of Labour we were able to press the measure rapidly through its further stages, and on February 6th, 1918, it received the Royal Assent. The principal objection raised to it in Parliament came from the Ulster Members, who wanted to include conscription for Ireland in its terms. Sir Auckland Geddes explained that: —

"The reason why the Government excluded any reference to Ireland from this Bill was that in their considered opinion, after fully investigating the matter, they considered that to have included a proposal to apply compulsory military service to Ireland would not have helped on the War. . . . It is not at this time possible to risk delay for weeks and months in getting the measures which we propose into force if we are to obtain the men the Army requires."[1]

This was, however, a question which was to cause us a great deal of trouble during the remainder of the year.

When the great German offensive of March, 1918, drove in our front, we at once made plans for still more drastic measures to raise recruits. At the War Cabinet of March 25th,

[1] Official Report, January 17th, 1918, Vol. 101, Col. 579.

Sir Auckland Geddes was asked to prepare at the earliest moment a short Bill which would give us powers to raise the age limit for military service to fifty or fifty-five, to conscript the clergy and ministers of religion, to send conscientious objectors abroad for labour services, and to extend conscription to Ireland. This last question gave rise to serious differences of opinion in the Cabinet, as it subsequently did in and out of Parliament. The divisions did not altogether follow Party lines. Bonar Law was just as doubtful as I was about the wisdom of the project. But other Unionist members of the War Cabinet were insistent upon it, and we learned that Labour would be restive at the further drastic extensions we proposed if the manhood of Ireland were left untouched. Mr. Duke, the Chief Secretary, was strongly opposed to it as a method of recruiting the Army, and on March 27th he laid before us a Memorandum from General Mahon, the G.O.C., Irish Command, with additions inserted in italics by General Byrne, the head of the Royal Irish Constabulary. This ran: —

"Conscription can be enforced, but with *the greatest* difficulty. It will be *bitterly* opposed by the *united* Nationalists and the clergy. The present time is the worst for it since I have been in Ireland, because the cry will be: 'England down, Ireland's opportunity.' Some of the difficulties would be *organised* strikes *dislocating the life of the country,* railway, post office and telegraph communications cut. There are fewer troops in Ireland than there have been for some time. More have to be taken. We would have to have additional troops for the time, at least two brigades (*? I think considerably more*). These I do not anticipate would be required for more than three months.

"Ireland would have to be divided into several districts. It would be a question that will have to be considered if compulsion is put into force in the whole simultaneously, or district by district. But to render it feasible either way, the country must be put under some kind of military control. Law would have to be dropped, because ordinarily, for the first fortnight at least, there would be bloodshed and a great deal of suffering to the civil population in every way, and hardships.

"The number of men we would get I cannot estimate. Ten months ago I estimated 160,000, with very liberal exemptions. It ought to be more now with increased age. I am of opinion that *some of the men when got would make good and reliable soldiers (a considerable number might be likely to give trouble). The police would have to be concentrated into larger parties, thus curtailing their usefulness. Coast watching would be interfered with, also tillage.*

"I would suggest that the first thing is to get all known leaders out of the way at once; *extra troops should be on the spot simultaneously,* and everyone, irrespective of who he is, arrested on the first sign of giving trouble.

"These measures would be drastic, but the situation is serious, or it would not be considered necessary to have conscription at this inopportune time."

This document showed how grave were the objections felt by those in touch with the Irish situation to the introduction of conscription. We held a second Cabinet meeting that afternoon to discuss it further, and on the following morning, March 28th, I summoned Sir James Campbell, the Irish Lord Chief Justice, to the Cabinet, to give us his views. Sir Edward Carson, who had left the War Cabinet because of our decision to negotiate once more with the Irish Nationalist leaders for measures of Home Rule which would be acceptable to the Irish people as a whole, was also invited to be present to express his opinion.

Sir James Campbell was clear that conscription could now be enforced in Ireland only at the cost of tremendous bloodshed, and the number of men worth getting whom it would yield would be very small. This verdict was of special interest, because Campbell had been a strong advocate of conscription for Ireland. Somewhat to our surprise, Sir Edward Carson agreed with him. He said he was forced to the conclusion, with much regret, that the result of conscription in Ireland would be such that its introduction was not worth contemplating, in view of the disturbances that would be caused. If, however, the British Government found themselves unable to get men from Great Britain without enforcing conscription in Ireland, the question became a very different one.

It is almost impossible to depict the complexities in which this issue of Irish conscription was wrapped. At that time the Irish Convention was still sitting, and we were hoping that it would yield us some measure of agreement upon which we could proceed to frame and carry a Home Rule measure. For such a measure we could not hope for support from the Unionists unless they at least secured the *quid pro quo* of Irish conscription; yet we were warned that if we announced our intention of proposing such conscription, the Convention would break up at once. Some of our advisers thought the conscripts we got would be useless — Mr. Duke thought we might as well enlist Germans! The Army authorities, on the other hand, had few misgivings, and Haig thought there would be no trouble with the conscripts once he had them in France. Against the view that conscription would set Ireland ablaze was set the alternative view that removal of the young men there into the Army would cut the claws of the Sinn Fein movement. Irish conscription, especially if unaccompanied by Home Rule, would have a very damaging effect on public opinion in America. But if nothing was proposed in regard to it, I could see clearly that we could not hope to carry our Bill for raising the age limit to fifty or fifty-five, and still further cutting down exemptions. Organised labour had intimated that it would bitterly resent the pressing through of a measure which combed out scores of thousands more of the members of Unions which had already contributed millions to the fighting forces, whilst we exempted the Irish peasantry which had done well out of the War and had given us nothing but trouble in return. After all, we were fighting for the redemption of a small Catholic country whose independence had been crushed; and the Irish who were demanding self-government ought in return to be ready to make their contribution to this effort.

After carefully reviewing these conflicting views and considerations, we ultimately decided that we would not immediately enact Irish conscription, but we would insert in the Bill a provision authorising the Government to impose it by Order in Council. We would also, but independently, press forward with a Home Rule measure for Ireland. We felt that if such a measure could reach the Statute Book by the time we had completed our arrangements for imposing Irish conscription, the worst difficulties confronting this step would be removed.

The new Military Service Bill was introduced on April 9th. It made all men under fifty-one liable to compulsory military service, with power to raise that limit by Order in Council to all men under fifty-six. And it made further provisions for cancelling exemptions and limiting the power of tribunals to grant them. As regards Ireland, it provided that: —

"His Majesty may by Order in Council extend this Act to Ireland, and this Act if so extended shall, subject to such modifications and adaptations as may be made by the Order for the purpose of making it applicable to Ireland, have effect accordingly."

The reactions to this measure were as confused in Parliament and the country as they had been in the Cabinet. The Southern Irish members, as had been expected, violently opposed the clause, though in the Committee stage Mr. Devlin promised he would join up himself if we would bring the Irish Parliament into existence. Mr. Asquith also opposed it, though on account of the national emergency he said he would not carry his opposition into the lobby. The National Liberal Federation Executive passed a resolution urging that a Home Rule measure should be passed through both Houses of Parliament at once and come into operation simultaneously with the application of the Military Service Act to Ireland. In the Committee stage, Mr. Bonar Law promised that the Government would do their best to achieve this. In the House of Lords, both Lord Lansdowne and Lord Londonderry opposed the application of conscription to Ireland. The Bill, however, passed safely through both Houses and received the Royal Assent on April 18th.

Before attempting to apply conscription to Ireland, we decided to make one more effort to secure recruits thence on a voluntary basis. Mr. Duke put forward a scheme for inviting each district, on the model of the old Militia ballot, to furnish a quota of recruits for the Irish regiments. And we proceeded forthwith with the drafting of a Home Rule Bill. But while this was being prepared, we received information pointing to a German conspiracy to raise a fresh rebellion in Ireland, in which the Sinn Fein leaders were implicated. Evidence of this accumulated to a point which compelled us to take the action of having those leaders arrested and interned. Therewith all hope of carrying an agreed measure of Home Rule passed for the time; and the projected introduction of conscription into Ireland was also suspended. We carried on with the scheme for regional recruiting campaigns, but without much success. From time to time we were pestered to go ahead with conscription; as near the end as October 21st, 1918, Sir Henry Wilson spent the greater part of an evening vehemently urging it upon me. But I stood firmly by the arrangement we had agreed on, that conscription and Home Rule must be introduced together. If we could not carry the second, I would not impose the first.

It is idle to speculate what would have been the result had we seriously attempted to force conscription on Ireland in 1918. That we should have had bloodshed and violent resistance there can be no doubt, nor that American opinion would have been gravely exasperated. Whether we should have secured any adequate compensation for these evils in the form of recruits is harder to say. Happily, we succeeded in winning through without being forced to resort to so desperate an expedient. As I have already indicated, our final Military Service Act did not in fact achieve any very striking increase in the numbers of recruits; apart from Ireland, no such increase was possible, for in spite of its critics the Government was already doing all that wisely could be done to supply our military effort with man power. And the supply proved equal to the necessities of the situation. When the "Cease Fire" sounded in November, there were still more than three-and-a-half million of the manhood of this island under arms; our Navy held the mastery on water and our Mercantile Marine sailed the seven seas; our factories were turning out munitions on a scale greater than ever before, and our granaries were filled with the biggest harvest which the soil of this country had yielded for many a year. In every one of the spheres where British man power had been called upon to make its indispensable contributions to the victory of the Allied cause, it had proved equal to its task.

CHAPTER V

CLEMENCEAU

Character of Painlevé — Bouillon's assurance — Painlevé falls — Clemenceau unpopular — His contempt for his contemporaries — A man of action — An old growler — The lobbies call for him — His Germanophobia — Its cause — A successful War Minister — His courage — His cynicism — His last defeat — Duel with Deschanel — Greatness as a statesman — Failure to understand sea-power — Our friendly relations — An opening quarrel.

CLEMENCEAU'S predecessor, Painlevé, was a man of high intelligence and of considerable charm. He was a mixture of simplicity and astuteness which was attractive but perplexing. He was something of the academician in politics, and war is the most cunning of all pursuits. But if he was childlike in his ways, he was penetrating and shrewd in his judgments. He had a real insight into the heart of the problem. What he lacked was the manœuvring skill and the force necessary to convert his ideas into the action which sweeps aside obstacles, cuts through entanglements and bears down the intrigues of parliamentary and military cliques. He was too sensitive and too excitable for the position of a national leader in a bad crisis of a nation's destiny. He shrank from personal criticism with the dislike of the man who could not retort in kind. He could not have borne the shivering height of isolation in the most exalted and therefore the most exposed parliamentary position, had it not been shared, however irregularly, by a politician of a totally different type. His friend, Franklin Bouillon, became virtually his partner in the Premiership. He had none of the sensitiveness and the timidities of Painlevé. He was confident, ebullient, flamboyant. They both had courage of a high order. But Painlevé lacked assurance. Franklin Bouillon had enough and to spare for both. But it is fair to say that he was not merely aggressive — he was also dauntless and within limits, effective. He ran Painlevé. He spoke for him and over him and instead of him at interviews and consultations and conferences. At the Rapallo Conference Painlevé hardly had a look in. He managed to interject a few rapid observations, but the torrential Bouillon, under the guise of interpreting Painlevé, swept his Chief on one side and declaimed a series of speeches of his own on every topic that arose.

But a time came when Painlevé had to stand alone and speak for himself. When the murmurs of the couloirs rose into a growl and he knew he would soon have to face an assembly angry with events for which he was not responsible, but which he had failed to control, he literally cowered at the prospect. He knew that he could not dominate a gathering which great orators like Viviani and Briand had often failed to quell. When the discussion that sealed his fate was impending he literally fled to England, ostensibly on a mission to me as British Prime Minister, but in reality to enjoy a few days' shelter from the rising storm. He spent a weekend with me at Chequers. He was uneasy, distrait and unhappy. I was sorry for him, because he was a good fellow. He knew he had done his best for his country. He was convinced that he was on the right line to save it. But he also understood that nothing would save him from the humiliation of being trampled upon as a failure by an infuriated assembly that found France preparing to face another year of war with no better prospect of victory than at the end of any other campaign. He fell, and with him, France seemed to have exhausted its waiting list of possible and seasoned Premiers. Viviani, Briand, Millerand, Ribot, Painlevé — they had all been tried and found wanting. Then came a dramatic change which had a decisive effect on the conduct of the War.

There was only one man left, and it is not too much to say that no one wanted him. The President, Poincaré, disliked him. He had insulted every prominent politician in France and conciliated none. He had no party or group attached to him. He was the Ishmael of French politics. I once said of him that he loved France but hated all Frenchmen. That is a substantially fair account of his personal attitude throughout his career. He was nevertheless much the most arresting and powerful personality in the arena of French politics during the Third Republic. He was a deadly controversialist who had brought down one Minister after another, with his piercing and pertinacious sword. The men out of whom Ministries were composed he held in the utmost contempt. His scorn for them was all the more withering because it was partly justifiable and entirely genuine. He counted even Gambetta a theatrical sham, and he stripped him of the trappings of his greatness. Briand he despised as a mellifluous ranter of turgid commonplaces. Poincaré he could not abide. I never heard him speak with respect of any French politician except Jaurès, the great Socialist leader, and he was dead. Once upon a time he had crossed swords with Jaurès in a memorable debate and he had learnt to admire his intellectual quality. As for the rest, he held them all in unmitigated derision. When you asked his opinion, as I often did, of some one or other of them, he concentrated his reply either into a contemptuous ejaculation (not always publishable) or into a fierce snort. In his estimation they were just flabby and flashy Parliamentarians and nothing more. That meant he considered they were merely adepts at all the arts and crafts of the political game, either in or out of Parliament. They talked the jargon that won or held votes or *applaudissements*. They could manœuvre themselves or their groups into Ministerial offices. But they were not doers. When they got into office, the most hard-working amongst them only toiled at Minutes or despatches submitted to them by bureaucrats whose main purpose was not so much to solve a problem finally as to get it disposed of for the time being. When they attended Conferences, these parliamentary leaders regarded it as a triumph if at the end they were able to say there was an *accord complet*, and could get an agreed *communiqué* to the Press which implied a great deal to the general public but meant nothing to the initiated. Clemenceau knew them all well — too well — and held them in utter disdain. He made no allowance for the fact that they all served to the utmost of their capacity, and even Clemenceau could do no more than that.

Clemenceau was a master of words. No orator of his day had a more perfect command and choice of word and phrase. But he was preëminently a man of action. His scorn was for the men who thought words a substitute for deeds and not a stimulus to deeds. He was not always fair even to the doers whom he personally disliked. I always thought him unjust to Albert Thomas, who was an organiser and worker of the first rank.

During the whole of the War, he had criticised and condemned everybody and everything. His newspaper had been suppressed. He started another. It had no circulation — except in the quarters that mattered to him. Deputies and Senators read every word of it. He made few speeches, but in parliamentary Committees he was a terror not so much to evildoers as to those who, in my opinion, are worse in an emergency — the nondoers. For three years no one thought of him as a possible War Premier. He was a growler, and an old growler at that. He was seventy-eight years of age. He had only just recovered from a bad operation when the War started. Shortly before he was called upon to form a Ministry, I ventured to suggest to a prominent French Deputy that Clemenceau ought to be given his chance. He scoffed at the idea. The Tiger was in his opinion, and in that of every trotter through the couloirs of the Chamber of Deputies, clean out of the reckoning. I pointed out that shortly before the War he had held office, and turned out to be one of the strongest Prime Ministers of the Republic. My informant replied that he was no longer the man he used to be. He was now only a petulant and querulous old fellow. Then all of a sudden there came a cry from the lobbies of the Chamber of Deputies. "Why not give the Tiger a turn? If he fails, as he probably will, it will stop his snarling, and we can then try someone else, and we can silence him by an allusion to his own failure." His success was attributable to a desire for his discomfiture. These whisperings reached the ears of Poincaré and he listened to them. Hence the greatest War Ministry in the whole long succession of French Cabinets during this conflict. At seventy-eight Clemenceau began the most notable episode in his strenuous and stormy career.

As he exerted such an influence on the course of events I should like here to give my personal impression of this remarkable man.

The first time I ever met Mr. Clemenceau was at Carlsbad in 1910. I was having tea with Mr. T. P. O'Connor in his rooms. M. Clemenceau was known to be taking his annual cure, and I was anxious to meet him. T. P. arranged a meeting. Soon after I arrived there bustled into the room a short, broad-shouldered and full-chested man, with an aggressive and rather truculent countenance, illuminated by a pair of brilliant and fierce eyes set deeply under overhanging eyebrows. The size and hardness of his great head struck me. It seemed enormous, but there was no dome of benevolence, reverence, or kindliness. It was an abnormally large head with all the sympathetic qualities flattened out. I am not now analysing the man, but giving my first impressions of his appearance. He looked the part of the Tiger — the man-eating Tiger who had hunted down Ministry after Ministry, and rent them with his terrible claws. He came into the room with short, quick steps. He was then seventy years of age, and his greatest days were to come seven or eight years later.

We were introduced and he greeted me none too genially. I was then Chancellor of the Exchequer, and was doing my utmost to urge an understanding with Germany on the question of naval construction. I feared war was inevitable, unless such an understanding could be reached. M. Clemenceau referred to my efforts with scornful disapproval. His hatred of Germany had a concentrated ferocity which I had never seen before, not even among the most violent of our British Germanophobes. Their hostility to Germany always seemed to be calculated and histrionic — his was of the blood. Later on I understood it better.

My first interview with M. Clemenceau was not a success. He made it clear that he thoroughly disapproved of me. Had I never seen him again, I should have recalled him as a powerful but a disagreeable and rather bad-tempered old savage. It was years — eventful years — after this meeting that I discovered his real fascination: his wit, his playfulness, the hypnotic interest of his arresting and compelling personality. And a day was to come — sooner than any one of us had anticipated — when events occurred that explained to me his apprehension of the menace as well as his detestation of the arrogance of German imperialism.

I remember driving with him back to Paris from the historic meeting at the Trianon Palace Hotel, Versailles, after he had handed to M. Brockdorff-Rantzau and the German delegates the draft of the Peace Treaty. As we passed the ruins of the palace of St. Cloud, which had been burned by the Germans in 1871, he told me how he remembered seeing the blaze. He was Mayor of Montmartre during the siege of Paris, and from the heights of his mayoral domain he witnessed the destruction of the famous château. That event seemed to have burned itself into his memory even more than the scenes of hunger and privation to which he so effectively ministered.

On this occasion he spoke with unwonted placidity about the events of 1870, rather like a man in whom the internal fires of revenge had at last been quenched by the cooling draught of victory. There is only one incident of 1871 of which he spoke to me with emotion, and that was of the poignant scene in the French Assembly when Jules Favre came straight from an interview with Bismarck to report to the deputies the nature of the terms demanded, and the ruthlessness with which the triumphant Chancellor had treated the supplication of the French delegates for some amelioration in the demands. Tears came into M. Clemenceau's eyes — for the first and only time in my intercourse with him — as he described how "the old man [Favre]", in attempting to describe the harshness of the conqueror, broke down in the tribune and wept. I then understood something of M. Clemenceau's hatred of the Germans. They had not only invaded France, defeated her armies, occupied her capital, humbled her pride, but in the hour of victory had treated her with an insolence which for fifty years had rankled in the heart of this fierce old patriot. When I met him at Carlsbad the sore was still stinging him into anger. He was essentially an angry man. Those who read his relentless words on the death of Herr Stresemann will know that not even victory had completely stamped out the embers of vengeance in the bosom of this terrible volcano of rumbling and surging hatreds — personal, national, political and religious.

That he should have succeeded as War Minister is not a matter of surprise. He possessed restless energy, indomitable courage and a gift of infecting others with his own combativeness and confidence. I know nothing of his qualities as an administrator or organiser. The greatest tasks of organisation were over before he took office at the end of 1917. A combination of energy, courage and common sense was needed at that hour, and he possessed these three attributes in an exceptional degree.

As for his courage, there is no better illustration of it than the characteristic story which is told of him when it was proposed that the French Chamber of Deputies should move to Bordeaux at the beginning of the War. The Germans were within a few miles of Paris, and President, senators and deputies thought it better to get out of range of the German guns ere it was too late. M. Clemenceau refused to go, and when he was asked whether he did not think they ought to leave Paris his answer was "Yes, we are too far from the front."

His courage was never questioned by even his bitterest foes, but they were not as ready to acknowledge his wisdom. When he was not in a passion, or when his personal or political prejudices were not engaged — and he had his lucid intervals of composure — he took as sane, sensible, and penetrating a view of a situation as any man I ever met.

By conviction and temperament he was an inexorable cynic. He had no belief in the ultimate victory of right. His essential creed — if he had any — was that history demonstrated clearly that in the end might invariably triumphed over abstract justice. In fact, as he once put it bluntly in the course of a conversation, "Might is right." His faith was in organised and well-directed force. It was in the interest of humanity that strength should prevail over weakness. One of the most piquant passages of arms between himself and President Wilson was one in which he reminded the American idealist that the United States of America would never have come into existence without force, and that but for force it would have fallen to pieces half a century ago.

The last time I saw him as Prime Minister was after the defeat of his candidature for the Presidency of the Republic. It was for him defeat accompanied by every circumstance of humiliation, and he felt it deeply. It was the first and only occasion on which I ever saw this brave old man betray any feeling over a personal hurt to himself. He had not sought nomination. On the contrary, he had resisted up to the last moment pressure brought to bear upon him to allow his name to go forward. He did not want it. He only gave in because he was assured by many who afterwards betrayed him that it was in the interests of France that he should remain at the helm until the peace was firmly established and France had recovered from her wounds.

It was represented to him that the unique and commanding influence he had won, not only in France but throughout the world, was indispensable for some years to come. He listened to their urgings, and very reluctantly complied. He allowed his name to go forward. An intrigue largely personal but partly religious engineered a rebuff for him in the face of the whole world. A man whom he despised (and whom did he not despise?) was chosen in his place.

When I left Paris the following morning he came to the station to see me off. He did not attempt to conceal his chagrin that Frenchmen should so soon forget his services. When I said to him, "The public soon forget; it is the ultimate fate of all who serve it faithfully," he replied, "They will not do it quite like this in England."

Apropos of his defeat by M. Deschanel in the contest for the Presidency, there is a very good story told of a duel he had once fought with his successful rival. It is related that the fight took place in a garden somewhere in the suburbs of Paris. They fought with swords. M. Clemenceau was a very formidable swordsman, and as he pressed his opponent the latter retreated farther and farther from the threatening weapon. At last M. Clemenceau got tired of this continuous retreat, and, putting his sword under his arm he waved his hand, and with a bow towards M. Deschanel, he said, "Monsieur is leaving us." Twenty-seven years later, in a different duel, it was M. Deschanel who drove the expert fencer off the ground.

M. Clemenceau was the greatest French statesman — if not the greatest Frenchman — of his day. He was in every fibre of his being a Frenchman. He had no real interest in humanity as a whole. His sole concern was for France. As long as France was humbled he cared not what other people were exalted. As long as France was victorious he did not worry in the least about the tribulations of any other country. To him France was all in all. When he began public life he found his beloved country humiliated to the dust. When he ended his career he left France the most powerful State on the Continent of Europe — largely through his exertions.

In criticism he was virulent and ferocious. He was by nature a killer. But in action he was calm, restrained and practical. He was always ready to concede or to compromise in order to get a move on. My first experience of this quality was over the Versailles Council. When he came into office his first impulse was to sweep away all the decisions arrived at by his predecessors. Amongst them was the effort to organise an Inter-Allied General Staff at Versailles to coordinate the war effort of the Allies on sea and land. His notion was to run the War from his office in Paris. He soon discovered that Britain, Italy and America were not disposed to take orders from the French War Office. Like all Frenchmen in the War — Generals and Ministers — he concentrated his mind exclusively on the land campaign and was inclined to say with the rest of his distinguished compatriots, "there shall be no more sea." He gradually realised the decisive importance of command of the sea. Here he saw that the British Fleet and British shipping were predominant, and that he was quite incompetent to undertake the direction of operations on the waves. Even on land, the contribution of the Allies in the aggregate out-numbered that of the French. When he came into power he had not made a real study of the war problems as a whole. His eyes were on Noyon where the Germans were entrenched not so many leagues from Paris. But he was not above learning his job. Like all great men, he was not too proud to perceive his mistakes or to alter his plans to conform with that perception. At first he was difficult and dictatorial, but he soon understood that this would not do, and after his first meeting at Versailles he realised that a new organisation which surveyed and kept itself informed, and took cognisance of all the Allied activities in every quarter and element, would be helpful to him in the discharge of his onerous duties. It was the first time he had come into contact with certain aspects of the struggle — notably those that finally decided the issue of the War, the blockade by the Allies and the efforts made to thwart the desperate but dangerous counter-blockade initiated by the enemy. He realised for the first time how completely the Allies depended not only for their war resources but for their daily bread on our shipping, and how necessary it was to protect it and to repair its losses. It was here also that he was given the information which demonstrated how those flank attacks made elsewhere than in France were threatening the cohesion of the Central Powers, and gradually disintegrating those forces which safeguarded the Eastern and Southern frontiers of Germany whilst they menaced the British Empire on its more vulnerable but important routes.

I have many a time been asked how I personally got on

with Clemenceau. There is always an expectation that the answer will reveal a cat-and-dog life led by us during our two years of close coöperation. Much of this belief is due to silly or malicious gossip. Sometimes a playful and harmless arrow sent across the table either in conversation or discussion is picked up by one man, the next passes it on with a barb attached, the third dips it in poison. Often it is the pure invention of the kind of person who likes to pass a new story or a phrase supposed to be characteristic of a prominent public man like Clemenceau when the old ones are getting rather stale. Sometimes, alas, these supposed unpleasantnesses were the creation of the spiteful fancy of men who disliked one or other or both of us. What is the real truth? I have never transacted more important business with any man than with Georges Clemenceau, and I have never met any man during the whole course of my public life with whom I more enjoyed doing business. The many opportunities I had of interchanging views with him are amongst the most delightful and treasured memories of my life. There is not an episode or a word that rankles. I came to the conclusion, at the very start of our official contact, that it was necessary to impress upon this strong-willed and overbearing old political warrior that any attempt to hector or to bully would not be tolerated, that he must treat all representations coming from the spokesmen of the British Empire with respect and that he must apply to them the best thought of his powerful mind. At an early date I chose a topic upon which there was some difference of opinion, but as to which I felt assured that we were entirely in the right. When he rather curtly and in his roughest manner tried to sweep me aside, I protested with an emphasis — perhaps a deliberate overemphasis — which completely astonished him. He very adroitly gave in. After that his temper, which could be savage, never ruffled our intercourse.

CHAPTER VI

THE MILITARY POSITION

1. Sir Douglas Haig's Views

Haig's memorandum of October, 1917 — Contempt for German Army — Allied superiority — Haig's miscalculations — Effect of Russian collapse — Divergent views of Pétain and Haig — French official account — Haig's letter to Pétain — Clemenceau becomes Premier.

I HAVE already related in a previous volume how, on the occasion of one of my visits to H.Q. in France, I requested the Commander-in-Chief to submit his views on the military position which would result from the probable event of Russia being unable to maintain an active part in the War for another campaign. It was quite clear from the elaborate answers which he gave to my question, that he had only one idea in his mind, and that he had given no real consideration to any alternative plans or projects. He only considered the question of "the feasibility of overcoming the resistance of the German Armies by direct attack." That attack was to be prosecuted in the Passchendaele salient for a few more weeks, and the offensive was to be resumed in the same promising bog as soon as possible in the spring. When Gough's Army was defeated in the following spring, there was a controversy about man power; so it is instructive to take note of the conclusion to which Sir Douglas Haig had come in October as to the probable strength of the German Army in 1918. Even if Russia "failed us to the extent of making a separate peace" his view was that it would not make such a difference to the German strength as to justify the British Army in postponing its offensive. The Germans, according to him, had already brought most of their best divisions from Russia to the West. Most of those that were left on the Russian, Danubian and Balkan Fronts were "of low fighting value, and only 32 divisions are estimated as fit to take part in severe fighting on the Western Front." The remaining 59 divisions would probably be fully employed in watching Russia and in maintaining German influence over the armies of our Allies as at present. He calculated that the addition of the 32 more efficient divisions would give Germany a total of 179 divisions on the Western Front. But when he comes to examine the composition of all these divisions he expresses a low opinion of their quality.

"Nineteen of the German divisions now on this front are of poor quality; only fit for defensive on quiet Fronts; 135 of the remainder have already suffered heavy defeats this year, and that number will be increased in the next few weeks. Of the 170 German divisions therefore, the value of *at least* 154 (135 + 19) must be written down considerably."

He takes a still more contemptuous view of the reserves upon which the Germans had to rely for filling up their depleted divisions. He estimates that the wastage which he had inflicted and was still inflicting on the enemy would leave at the end of the year but a small balance, *if any*, of the 500,000 men in the German reserves then available, and they were likely to commence the new year with only 500,000 to 600,000 reserves at their disposal, including the whole of the youths of eighteen, which, judging by his experience of the preceding class, would be of low fighting value. Haig constantly reverts to this question of the growing inferiority of the German troops.

"The German losses are being replaced now in large proportions by quite inferior material, and the proportion of such material in the German ranks will increase rapidly in the future, while by May or June, the German reserves will be exhausted."

When Haig comes to a review of the comparative equipment of the two forces he is still more hopeful and confident.

"In artillery, still more in munitions supply, and in aircraft, the Allies will have a marked superiority, and the power of increasing that superiority very greatly. In reserves of man-power the Allies, including America, have a still greater superiority."

As to the French Army, he estimates that the 100 French Divisions might be reckoned as fully equal to a corresponding number of German divisions "under the conditions explained above." Those conditions put a very low valuation on the quality of the German troops; so this assessment of the fighting value of the French Army was, to say the least, not very flattering.

The War Cabinet have been criticised because in their distribution of our man power between the various war services which made competitive claims upon our dwindling reserves, they did not estimate the German strength at its real power; if that criticism is justifiable there was no one who was more responsible for the miscalculation of the strength of the Army the Germans could muster on the French Front in 1918 than Sir Douglas Haig himself. His considered review of the comparison of the Germans and the Allies, not only in numbers but in quality and equipment, came at a time when the Cabinet were giving a good deal of consideration to the demands for additional men made by the Fleet, by our transport services on sea and land, and by the production of coal and food supplies.

When Haig discovered his mistake it was too late for any rearrangement. The Government had by then apportioned the national man power. Not a single battalion could be added to the trained men available for the Western Front in the spring. We know now that even if we had been in a position to comply with every requisition which Sir Douglas

Haig had made in his October paper, by withdrawing men from essential services in England, by starving the forces in other theatres, and by refusing to comply with the insistent requests of the French to take up more line, we could not have furnished him with such a superiority of numbers as would have enabled him to conduct a successful spring offensive in Flanders. He underestimated the German reserves that were available, the number of divisions that could be withdrawn from Russia, and the fighting quality of most of the German human material. He ludicrously overestimated the losses which he had succeeded in inflicting upon the German Army. Even with a great preponderance in numbers and guns he was unable to break through the German lines during the long fighting at Passchendaele. His strategic conception for 1918 was therefore based on demonstrably false premises.

The final overthrow of Russia and Roumania had now completely changed the military prospect for some months to come. The best part of the immense Army which Germany and Austria had been compelled to maintain on their Eastern Front was now free to take part in operations on the West; in France and in Italy. Until the American Army had been trained and equipped to appear on the scene of action in sufficient numbers to counterbalance the enemy reinforcement, the situation would, as far as numbers were concerned, be more or less that with which the Allies were confronted in the first year of the War before the British Army had rolled up in sufficient numbers to alter the comparative strength of the rival hosts. By mid-October, 1917, it was quite evident that the Russian Army could no longer be relied upon to do any more fighting. In these circumstances, Pétain was for maintaining a strictly defensive attitude until the Americans were ready. In his judgment they could not help in our offensives until 1919. Haig was for renewing the offensive in the spring of 1918 without waiting for them.

Thus Haig and Pétain could not agree on the appropriate strategy for the Allied forces on the Western Front, while the preparations were being made for the spring campaign of 1918. Repeated conferences took place; but they could not fix on any plan — defensive or offensive. In the summer and autumn fighting of 1917 each had gone his own way according to his own strategical notions. There was no cohesion and not much concert in their plans. One hammered at the Germans and the other pecked. The hammer was buried in the sludge. The pecking succeeded in the little it was designed to achieve. On the whole this arrangement suited the Germans.

Here is the French official story of the divergencies of opinion between the two Commanders: —

"Marshal Haig, deep in the battle of Flanders, was absorbed in his task of the hour; at a time when neither public opinion, nor even his own army expected any further important result from the operations in progress, he continued to hope for events so decisive as to alter profoundly the same year the situation on the Western Front. In these circumstances, he was far from sharing the anxiety of the French Command over the attitude adopted by Russia. At all events he thought that the best method of remedying the collapse of this Ally was to assume a strenuous offensive on the Anglo-French Front as soon as possible." [1]

This was emphatically not Pétain's view, nor was it Foch's opinion as to the most suitable strategy for the first part of the year.

On October 18th, 1917, an interview took place between Haig and Pétain at Amiens, at which the latter laid before the British Commander-in-Chief his ideas as to the military situation and the best method of dealing with it. He adhered to the opinion he had repeatedly expressed that we could not take the risk of a definite offensive in the early part of

[1] "Les armées françaises dans la grande guerre", VI.

1918 unless Russia remained in the War and the Russian Army recovered her fighting efficiency. If that condition were not fulfilled, our efforts would have to be concentrated upon securing the best distribution for defence of the forces available on the Western Front, and on arranging that the reserves of both forces should be capable of being concentrated in support of whatever part of the front the Germans decided to attack.

But Haig still clung to his view that the offensive must be renewed by the British Army next year, and confirmed his attitude in a note he handed to Pétain at the time and in a long letter with which he followed up the interview two days later. In this letter he developed his plan and his arguments for sticking to it: —

"G.H.Q. of the British
Armies in the Field,
19th October, 1917.

"My dear General,

"Since our interview yesterday, I have given most careful consideration to the arguments you developed and I beg leave to state my views on the question.

"The fact of drafting your relief over a front of six divisions would not only diminish the importance of the troops which it would be possible for me to muster for the offensive operations to be undertaken next spring, but, in addition, their fitness would be impaired on account of the reduction entailed in the rest and training indispensable.

"As, in addition, I am called upon to lose the valuable aid of General Anthoine's Army, my forces for the offensive would be so considerably diminished that, unless the resources at my disposal could be increased by reinforcements from other theatres of operations, an appreciable reduction in the scale of my Flanders offensive, if not its complete suspension, would result from my compliance with your request.

"In my opinion, such grave consequences would result for the

Allies' cause that I would call your attention to the following points: —

"(a) As you are aware, due to my offensive operations this year, *the German expenditure of divisions has more than doubled our own total.*[1] Six of my divisions on the defensive will only have to hold a similar number of German divisions, even less perhaps.

"*Employed offensively, on the contrary, these same divisions can exhaust a much greater number of the enemy's divisions of infantry — judging by this year's results, the total might amount to twelve.*[1] Consequently, from the point of view of the security of our defensive front, I am rendering it safer by increasing the strength of my offensive than by relieving a section of your defensive front.

"*This holds good whether or not the Germans bring back a certain number of divisions from the Russia Front.*[1]

"(b) As to the importance of maintaining the morale of your troops by the aid of offensive operations, local raids at frequent intervals, in the same way as operations of limited range, seem to me to yield excellent results from this point of view. I myself have tested this.

"(c) From what you told me yesterday, you are not contemplating a large-scale offensive before the month of August, and until that date you will only carry out operations of limited scope with, consequently, only local repercussions. These operations would play a useful part in the offensive I am intending to continue in Flanders, but alone they cannot achieve any decision.

"The question to which I draw your particular attention is that of knowing whether the Allies are in a position to run the risk of waiting for the month of August to try and obtain a decision. Your attention, moreover, will most certainly have been directed to the problem as to whether your reserves of available troops in the rear of your armies will be adequate for a decisive effort at this moment.

"I assure you that I understand and share your difficulties. I am extremely anxious to come to your assistance. Like you, I

[1] The italics are mine.

think that it is desirable for us both to reach agreement on a plan of action which we can propose to our respective Governments.

"But it is incumbent upon both of us to see that the plan upon which we are agreed affords every guarantee of our being enabled to reckon on the best results. I regret I cannot share your opinion that the best use to be made of the British troops would be to extend them over defensive fronts at the expense of the offensive to which they have proved they are equal, and from the success of which such great results can in all likelihood be expected in the future.

"Given the forces which will probably be at my disposal next year (from information in my possession at the moment) all that I can hope to do, with regard to the relief of your troops, would be to utilise my four divisions now on the coast, at the moment when you will take this sector, to prolong my front southwards. This relief might begin, for instance, during the last week in November.

"And that, in my opinion, is not even the best strategical use which can be made of these divisions, and I believe it would be a sounder military conception if you were to relieve them again in the spring.

"I consider that a prolongation of my front, carried out to the extent indicated above, would be possible next spring without compelling me to renounce my offensive in Flanders, although such an extension would still have a harmful effect. However, in order to come to your assistance and to facilitate agreement between us, I agree to this concession.

"I trust that you will see fit to consent to this solution. I am simultaneously communicating with General Robertson to learn whether next spring I can hope to receive divisions issuing from other theatres of operations.[1]

Yours very sincerely,

D. HAIG,
Marshal."

---

[1] Attempts were made to fill up three British divisions in Egypt with native troops in order to release the white troops for France.

Once more to quote the French official narrative of the events of the autumn: —

"Marshal Haig laid down as a fundamental principle that, even if Russia made peace, the best decision would still be to pass on to the offensive with all the coalition forces. The principal attack, the important effort of the Entente, would take place in Flanders; the English Army would assume responsibility, merely asking the Allies for their help, either directly by participating in the battle, or in carrying out operations on other parts of the front. Imbued with these ideas, the Commander-in-Chief of the British Army obviously could not look with favour on the obligation to relieve a section of the French troops; however, he promised, though with manifest regret, to devote four divisions to extending his front towards the Oise, beginning from the end of November.

"General Pétain sought in vain to convince Marshal Haig in the days after the Amiens Conference that existing circumstances necessitated drawing up, above all, a defensive plan; his efforts met with no success."[1]

The winter was near and the time was approaching when it was indispensable that the Allies, especially on the French and Flemish Front, should come to a definite agreement as to their joint plan of campaign under entirely new conditions — the withdrawal of Russia and the growing contribution of America. The absence of the Russians would only have its full effect in the spring; the presence of the Americans could not substantially influence the military situation before the summer of 1918. By the beginning of November, 1917, Russia was practically out of the War, and the Germans acted on that assumption and concentrated their reserves on the Western Front. On the other hand, an important event had occurred which reinvigorated the indomitable spirit of France drooping from its wounds, and weary with the strain of many disappointments.

[1] *Ibid.*

Clemenceau had become President of the Council. I have related in the previous chapter how he came to be appointed. His rise to power was of critical importance for the further conduct of the War.[1]

2. PLANNING THE 1918 CAMPAIGN

Paris Conference of November 29th–December 2d, 1917 — Clemenceau's opening address — Our agreement on policy — Support for "Side-Shows" — Italians unwilling for offensive — Salonika forces to be strengthened — Situation referred to military experts.

Towards the end of November, 1917, I went over to Paris to attend a series of Allied Conferences, called to review the whole situation. I was accompanied by Mr. Balfour and Sir William Robertson. Italy was represented by the Prime Minister, Signor Orlando, and the Foreign Minister, Baron Sonnino. America was represented by Colonel House, General Bliss and General Pershing. Mr. Venizelos had come over from Greece. There was a large attendance of generals and state officials from the Allied countries at the opening meeting on November 29th, and the big room at the Quai d'Orsay was more of a General Assembly than a Council of War. M. Clemenceau presided. It was his first appearance at any War Conference and it was evident from the start that he had made up his mind to use different methods from those of his predecessors and also to let us know his intentions. He disdained to follow the stately rhetoric of Ribot or the resonant oratory of Briand. He uttered two or three short snappy sentences, delivered rapidly in a high-pitched voice with an imperative accent, calling upon those present to get to work at once.

So large and promiscuous a gathering could evidently not transact business. It therefore appointed a number of Committees to consider different questions that called for de-

[1] Chapter V: "Clemenceau."

tailed attention. A good deal of time was taken up with discussion of the position in Russia: that I relate in another chapter. But the real examination of the military problems confronting the Allies was reserved for a meeting of the Supreme War Council held at the Trianon Palace Hotel, Versailles, on December 1st, over which M. Clemenceau presided. He was supported by General Foch and General Weygand. I was accompanied by Lord Milner, Sir William Robertson, and Sir Henry Wilson. General Cadorna was the military adviser of the Italian delegation and General Bliss was associated with Colonel House.

Knowing how important this meeting would be, and how it must give a direction to the whole course of military policy, I saw M. Clemenceau at the War Office in Paris, and spent much time in conferring with him as to the lead he should give as President in his opening address. I felt that his presidential address at the first meeting at Versailles of the Supreme War Council must strike the keynote of our policy. It was a source of great satisfaction to me to find that the relentless critic of past War Ministries in France and I were in accord on general principles and agreed as to our policy for the prosecution of the War on sea as well as on land, in the East as well as in the West. What he said about the best use to which we could put our resources of man power should be noted. British writers who praise all that Clemenceau did whilst condemning all my ideas and endeavours will be disconcerted to find that in his first official deliverance as the War Leader of France the policy he advocated was the same as that I had been consistently urging upon the Allies. I need hardly say that he was not one of those affable and pliable folk who can be persuaded into any declaration against his will because he prefers harmony to argument. Throughout the whole of his contentious career he never went out of his way either to seek concord or to shun disagreement.

In opening the proceedings he said that "the substance of his address had been agreed upon in consultation between himself and Mr. Lloyd George." The full text of this declaration of policy, which covers the whole ground of the War, is given in Appendix B to this Chapter. It is worth perusing as a broad and comprehensive statement of the view then taken by the Allied leaders as to the course of the War and the action which ought to be taken to bring it to a victorious conclusion.

It had always been suggested that M. Clemenceau had been resolutely opposed to diverting any forces from the Western Front to any other flank of the enemy line. The discussions which occurred on this occasion both at Versailles and at the Paris Conferences show how thoroughly misinformed were those who claimed the new French Prime Minister as an opponent of the so-called "side-shows." M. Clemenceau in his opening speech declared that the question of the situation in Italy should be the first and the most serious consideration: —

Of the questions to be considered, one was whether our attitude in Italy was to be purely defensive, or were we to assume the offensive. He did not consider the question of conducting an offensive should be simply left to the enemy. He proposed to circulate to the members of the Supreme War Council and the Military Advisers a Memorandum on the subject prepared by General Micheler, who had made a special study of it and who was convinced that an offensive could be effectively carried out with 28 divisions.

I have already regretted that M. Clemenceau had not been at the head of affairs during 1917. As I pointed out in the course of this discussion, I had made a similar proposal at the Rome Conference in January, 1917. I failed then even to interest the Italian Commander, and the Italian Ministers were equally indifferent to the project. As I related in previous volumes, the proposal was revived after the failure of the Nivelle offensive by Pétain, and subsequently by Foch. Haig had, however, already committed himself to an attack in Flanders. The idea of a great offensive in Italy was consequently put off until either he had succeeded or had assured himself that no real progress was possible in that direction. When the Passchendaele offensive stuck in August, the matter was again raised at a conference in Paris. The Italian military representative declared that it was then too late to attempt anything because of the weather. Ten weeks later the Germans launched their Caporetto offensive with calamitous results.

The way Signor Orlando received M. Clemenceau's proposal on this occasion was, to say the least, lukewarm and discouraging. The chiefs of the Italian Army and the heads of the Italian Government during the War not only never pressed for an Inter-Allied offensive on their front, but gave a chilling and a killing reception to every suggestion made by either British or French statesmen or by French generals that a joint attack should be made in Italy on the Austrian Armies by a force strengthened by British and French contingents and with the help of the heavy artillery with which Britain and France alone could equip such an offensive. This is not easy to understand. Perhaps they remembered the last occasion on which French troops had come to their assistance in 1859 and the price — Nice and Savoy — they had ultimately had to pay. In any event the failure to anticipate the disastrous Italian defeat at Caporetto by a combined Allied offensive against the Austrians must be put down to this strange refusal of the Italian General Staff. It was the second time they had shrunk from seizing the helping hand so opportunely tendered to them by their Allies.

The reason for this reluctance must be left to conjecture. The idea of an Italian offensive, even if it emanated from

THE MILITARY POSITION

amateur strategists, had the support of some of the ablest soldiers on the whole battlefield. Foch, Pétain and Micheler were amongst them.

Clemenceau's proposal was referred to the Permanent Military Advisers. They were directed to study the immediate situation on the Italian Front from the standpoint not only of the defensive but of the offensive also, and to report within the next fortnight on the military possibilities of the Italian Front.

Amongst other questions to be considered was that of transport of troops and material to Italy in case of such a campaign. Personally, I felt that the proposal came too late. These measures if adopted in the previous year would have changed the whole course of events. There would have been no Chemin des Dames or Passchendaele horrors to record or repair. Neither would there have been a Caporetto nor a Russian and Roumanian collapse. The Germans would have been forced to strain their resources to the utmost to keep the half-starved and half-mutinous Austrian Armies from falling to pieces. It might be urged that in Austrian defiles we should have had to meet the same Germans as we encountered in Flemish slime. But here the Italian Army with its overwhelming superiority in numbers would have been enabled by our superior equipment to pull its full weight. On the other hand the armies of the Central Powers, weakened by the half-hearted and discontented troops of the Slavonic Provinces of Austria, would have presented more vulnerable fronts to the persistent attacks of the Allied infantry, artillery and tanks than the homogeneous German Armies that repelled these fierce and ceaseless onslaughts in France and Flanders. One of the reasons why the Germans were not anxious to seek the help of Austrian divisions in France in 1918 was that they did not think them reliable. Although I favoured the plan strongly in 1917 I felt that now in 1918, when both Russia and Roumania were for every practical purpose out of the way and the Germans were preparing to hurl the troops released from the Eastern Front against the Allied Armies in France, it was too late to divert our forces to Italy.

Clemenceau again demonstrated his breadth of view by his attitude towards the Salonika expedition. He not only stated categorically that it could not be abandoned, he actively supported proposals for strengthening our forces on that front. The Salonika expedition was detested by the Army authorities both in France and in Britain; this hatred was displayed in a revelation which took the political leaders at the Conference completely by surprise. M. Venizelos came to Paris to place before the Conference the food position in Greece. It was extremely serious and he appealed that supplies should be instantly sent to that country in order to avert starvation. He stated that the food shortage was interfering with recruitment for the divisions of the Army which he was endeavouring to raise for the Salonika Front. He reminded us of the fact that in July he had communicated to the military authorities of the West a project for raising twelve divisions of Greek troops for Salonika, if the necessary finance were provided as well as the requisite equipment. It was a plan which would constitute a real relief to the strained manpower of France and Britain. The Allied Military Chiefs, by failing to supply the equipment required for these divisions, neglected a remarkable opportunity. They might in this fashion have increased the pressure on the southern flank of the Central Powers without diverting a single man from the reinforcement of the armies in France and Flanders. The Greek troops, when thrown into the battle line later on, had fought with great courage and skill and made even greater progress in their attack than the British and French contingents. It was the kind of country that suited them, and the climate, to which they were accustomed, did not have such injurious effects upon their physique as it unfortunately had upon men drawn from the more temperate climate of the North. The addition of such a powerful contingent would have enabled the French and ourselves either to withdraw divisions from Salonika long before the March offensive, or to make such an attack upon the tired and disillusioned Bulgarians as would have compelled the Germans and Austrians to come to their rescue. Many of the enemy divisions which found their way to France would have thus been diverted to the Balkans. The average military mind is fearfully and wonderfully made, and where its prejudices are engaged it is not always responsible for its actions.

The conferences concluded with a general direction to the military experts of the Supreme War Council. They were directed to survey the whole position in view of the new conditions which had arisen through the collapse of Russia, and to prepare plans for submission to the Governments and to the Staffs of the Allied Armies for their consideration. It was decided to hold another meeting of the Supreme Council as soon as these proposals were made.

In order to assist the military representatives on the Council to formulate their plans, the Council passed a series of resolutions as to the furnishing of full and up-to-date information to the Council by the military authorities and by the other departments of the respective Governments.

3. The Allied Strategy for 1918

Continued disagreement of Pétain and Haig — Foch's memorandum: plans for 1918 — Pétain's comments — No hope of success in 1918 — Military disagreement in plans — Conference at Compiègne — Foch disagrees with Haig and Pétain — Commanders oppose General Reserve — Difficulty of appointing a Generalissimo — Plans recommended by Versailles military chiefs — Need for strategic unity — Victory in the West unlikely in 1918 — Haig suggests abandoning Salonika — Offensive recommended against Turkey.

Meanwhile, the question of the extension of the British Front was becoming acute.

The two Commanders-in-Chief were in contact during the month of December on the question of the plans for 1918. But the defection of the Russian Army and the steady and alarming stream of fresh German divisions towards the West do not seem to have made any impression on the stubborn and sticky mind of the British Commander. He would still attack them at Passchendaele, and attack alone without French help, and the greater their numbers the more complete their destruction. According to the French Official History: —

"during December the Commanders-in-Chief of the British and French Armies did not succeed in reaching that close and comprehensive agreement which, however, was more than ever indispensable. . . . Thus, from the outset of the initial efforts at deciding on the plan of campaign for 1918, the two Commanders-in-Chief were obliged to state that their points of view were at variance; they had been able to reach a relative agreement on a question of secondary importance — the draft of relief; they remained, on the contrary, as throughout the summer, in disagreement on the essential ideas which each judged indispensable as fundamental to the conduct of our forthcoming operations. From that time on, amid the perils threatening the immediate future of the Allied Powers, and even before the issue of the gravest difficulties which were to surge up inevitably at the moment of the enemy attack, the drawbacks for the dispersion of the command in the coalition were once more revealed."

On December 17th, Haig visited Pétain at the French Headquarters and discussed the relief of the French line, but — to quote again the French Official History: —

"the most essential [question] remained unsolved. At this juncture every day added to the danger of procrastination; the Allies should have hurried for fear of being surprised before being able to reach agreement."

In conformity with the resolutions adopted by the Supreme War Council at its meeting on December 1st, 1917, and with a view to assisting the deliberations of its Permanent Military Advisers at Versailles, General Foch prepared a memorandum setting out the plan of campaign for 1918 which he recommended. As it contains in essence the strategical plan which he pursued with such success after he was made Commander-in-Chief of the Allied Forces in 1918, it will be interesting to set it out in full at this stage of the narrative. Had he been placed in full command of the Allied Reserves before March 21st, the disasters of March and April would have been avoided and his plans for a counter-offensive would have fructified sooner than they did.

"From the beginning of 1918 we must expect a heavy German offensive. . . .

"We shall counter it by defensive preparations, now in process of execution on both the English and French Fronts; these give grounds for optimism that the enemy offensive will be checked without having registered any decisive successes.

"We shall also confront it by an attitude which, far from being passive, will involve, on the contrary, for the Entente Armies, the necessity of seizing every opportunity of imposing their will on the enemy and of resuming the offensive as soon as possible, which is the sole method of leading to victory.

"With this aim in view, the Allied Armies must: —

"(a) *In the event of an enemy attack,* not merely arrest and counter-attack the enemy on the very ground of their attacks, but also undertake heavy counter-offensives as a diversion on ground selected and prepared beforehand for as rapid an operation as possible;

"(b) *If the enemy does not attack,* be prepared to take the initiative in operations with a limited objective, with the object of overcoming the enemy, wearing him down, and preserving the fighting spirit of the troops;

"(c) *In both cases,* be capable of amplifying this action

in the form of a *concerted offensive with decisive aims* if the wearing-down of the enemy or any other favourable circumstance in the situation as a whole brings such a result within reach.

"These are the necessary motives underlying the action of all the Allied Armies on their several fronts.

"But, in addition, in certain quarters of the front which are particularly advantageous for the enemy, their attack may assume important proportions, extend over a long period by making fresh strides from time to time, may seek to wear down the material or moral forces of an Ally, may reopen another Battle of Verdun, a fierce long-drawn-out effort, destined to smash the nerves of a nation.

"If the enemy is bent on this action, the danger of which is beyond discussion in the fourth year of war, there is only one method of compelling them to let go, of terminating this venture to undermine morale: this is for us to attack on another point of their front.

. . . .

"It is accordingly in action of a parallel nature, *i.e.,* by a *counter-offensive to create a diversion* on the part of the Allied Armies, that it should be sought to *check the wearing-down offensive* engaged in by the enemy.

"Yet, to be launched in time, it is imperative for such a type of counter-offensive for *diverting* purposes to have been *prepared some months ahead.*

"For such a battle to offer adequate scope and significance, without remaining merely the conflict of a single Allied Army, a battle exclusively French — to free Verdun, for instance, which would not suffice — for it to occupy, in this carefully prepared action, the whole of the available Allied troops and for it to ensure concentrated, simultaneous efforts making them strive together to attain a common goal, it is essential: that it should have been *devised* at the Inter-Allied Supreme War Council, the sole body competent to ensure common action, subsequently *prepared* in both British and French Armies.

"This counter-offensive seeking to create a diversion, and prepared to reply to a persistent offensive on the part of the enemy would, at the same time, correspond to paragraph (*c*).

"I beg you, therefore, to request the Supreme War Council: —

"1. To have a plan of action, corresponding to the views I have set forth, drawn up by both British and French Generals, Commanders-in-Chief.

"2. To draw up, in agreement with the same general officers, the scheme for a concerted offensive which will have to be decided with their consent, each being responsible for his relevant preparation, subject, however, to the reserve that the preparation indispensable for this counter-offensive is only to be undertaken after the fronts assigned to the several armies have been allotted in proportion to their respective troops."

This Memorandum was forwarded to the two Commanders-in-Chief as well as to the Supreme Council.

The advice given in it was by no means accepted by General Pétain, the French Commander-in-Chief. After studying the Foch Memorandum for a week, Pétain sent to the military advisers his comments upon it, which were as follows: —

"The letter dated 1st January, 1918, addressed to the Supreme War Council, considers as eminently desirable that the offensive should be taken by the Entente Armies: —

"1. Either, should the enemy attack, in the form of heavy counter-offensives for the purpose of diversion; or

"2. If the enemy fails to attack, in the form of operations having limited objectives, with intent to dominate and wear out the enemy;

"3. In both cases these actions ought to lead to a concerted offensive aiming at a decision.

"The principle is beyond dispute.

"Yet, however anxious we may be to recover the initiative for operations, we must bow to facts and draw up our forecasts, not on the basis of hypothetical data but on reality. *The American contribution is unlikely to carry weight in the battle before 1919, and until that date the Franco-British troops must be handled with such prudence as to leave the slightest possible rôle to be played by chance. . . ."*

He enters into an elaborate survey of alternatives and contingencies in order to demonstrate his theme. One of his assumptions is that the Austrians, relieved of the Russian pressure, will throw twenty-five of their divisions on to the French Front.[1] He ends his Memorandum on a note of pessimism as to the opportunities of 1918: —

"These prospects and the precarious situation of our troops compel great prudence on our part in the use of our resources, if we want to *hold out* in 1918, without being excessively and incurably worn down, until the juncture when our American Allies are in a position to afford us substantial aid in the battle.

"Undoubtedly, the nature of the German offensive may probably differ from that contemplated in the present letter. It is possible that for various reasons the enemy may attack on more confined fronts which will cost us less initially. With this assumption, several counter-offensives of retaliation or diversion are anticipated and the work of preparing the ground has been begun some time ago. But it is very important to bear in mind that these counter-offensives cannot be powerful, their performance is bound to be local and temporary for we must look to the outcome of the operations.

. . . .

"Finally, if our front is attacked over an area exceeding 50 km., we shall lack even the bare minimum for resisting the attack and it will be absolutely imperative for the English to come to our aid.

"In sum, the 1918 battle will be defensive from the Franco-British side, not by the express desire of the Command but by

[1] The Austrians never sent more than five divisions to the French Front. The Germans had lost faith in Austrian troops.

**EXTENSION OF THE BRITISH FRONT
JANUARY 1918.**

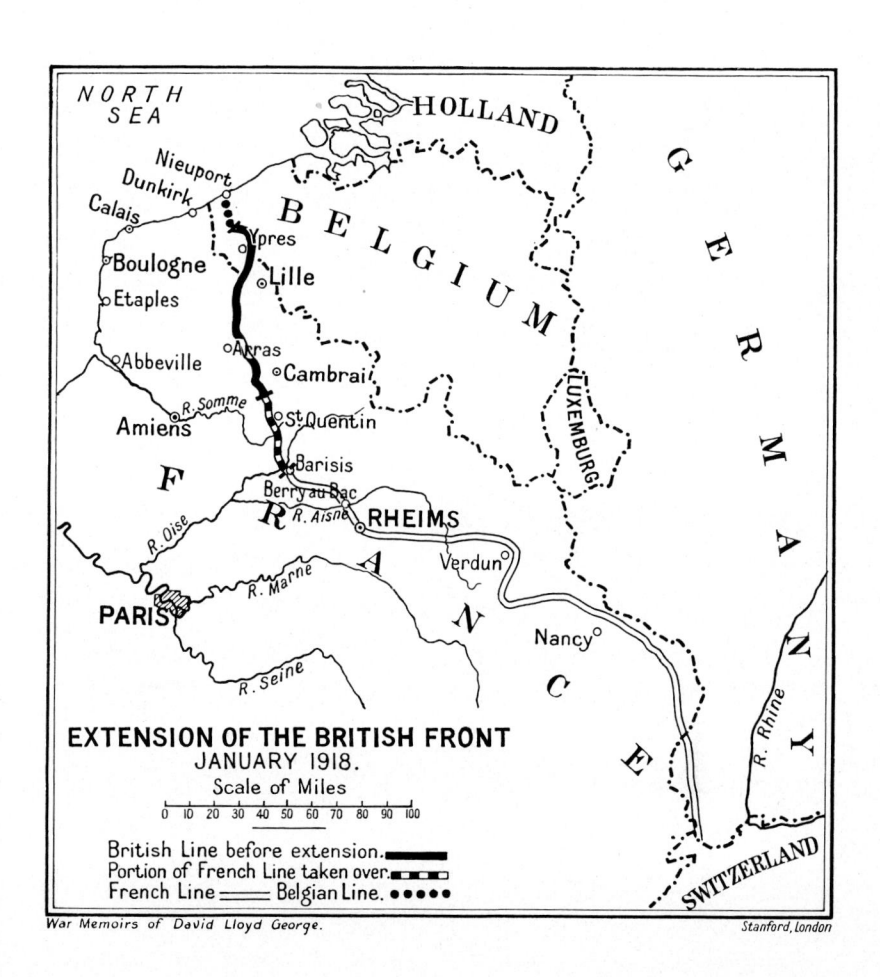

Scale of Miles

British Line before extension.
Portion of French Line taken over.
French Line ——— Belgian Line. •••••

War Memoirs of David Lloyd George.   Stanford, London

the exigency of the situation. Lack of resources also imposes it upon us. It is better to realise it at once and to organise in consequence. . . ."

As will be seen later on, Marshal Haig was now disposed to take General Pétain's view as to the impracticability of any offensive on a great scale in 1918. Up till now he had been confident that a British offensive alone might force a victorious decision. He now felt doubt as to whether even a combined Allied attack was advisable or possible.

The Foch document and Pétain's reply revealed the fact that there were serious differences not only between the Commanders-in-Chief of the two armies but between the two principal French Generals. The conflict here disclosed between the views of Pétain and Foch is fundamental. Foch insists on a single plan of action for the two armies, a simultaneous effort, and a counter-offensive in which both armies coöperate. Pétain's idea was that, if he was attacked, the English must come to his aid. Pétain also demanded that nothing should be left to chance; yet he was in fact doing so. For he could not reckon how the English, or when the English, or in what strength the English would come to his aid. He could not be sure, and was therefore leaving everything to chance — the chance that the British Commander whose primary responsibility was the safety of his own Army would, when the battle commenced, take exactly the same view as to the direction and development of the German attacks as he, with his anxieties for his own Army, would take. In the event it was Haig who found himself in this situation, "a single Allied army in conflict" (to use Foch's prophetic words) not knowing how the French, or when the French, or in what strength the French would come to his aid. Furthermore, mutual aid was too vague a system. A battle is a terrible drama moving with the swiftness and confusion of a whirlpool to a climax and a decision: it leaves no time to improvise methods of help. In this deeply erroneous strategic conception lies the origin of the impending disaster. Pétain must be blamed for originating it, Haig for adopting it.

These differences rendered the task of the Versailles Military Representatives one of exceptional difficulty and delicacy. All the rival plans were reviewed and discussed by them at Versailles when preparing their recommendations for the Supreme War Council. Their Report represented a compromise between the conflicting views, to such an extent that General Weygand on January 22nd, in a note to the Versailles Military Representatives, says: —

"To-day under the menace and on the eve perhaps of the sternest effort which the enemy has yet attempted against us, no general plan for the 1918 coalition operations is in existence. . . ."

So perturbed was General Foch at the absence of any plan of campaign for 1918, that he felt it essential, in agreement with General Robertson, Chief of the Imperial General Staff, to call a conference of the three Commanders-in-Chief, Pétain, Haig and Pershing, in order to evolve an agreed scheme of operations to deal with a situation which was charged with danger. Foch contemplated that they should discuss all the very important problems which would shortly be submitted to the Supreme War Council: the adoption of a General Inter-Allied Reserve, the expediency of recalling troops from Italy and the transport of American troops to France. The Conference met on January 24th at Compiègne, the French Headquarters.

General Pétain opened the discussion with a restatement of the opinions he was known to hold. The French Commander-in-Chief —

... did not conceal the fact that he believed it hardly possible for the situation of our effectives to permit us to take the offensive in 1918; in his judgment, the means of attack indispensable for its execution would be lacking as long as the coöperation of the American Army had not made itself significantly felt.[1]

Marshal Haig then expounded his views: —

... It was more than ever essential to reinforce our defensive organisations, train our reserves, prepare the process of transporting them, endeavour to be acquainted in good time with the enemy plans. Was it possible that we, in our turn, would be able to resume in 1918 the initiative for operations? *Marshal Haig refrained from expressing any very definite opinion on this point;* he contented himself with pointing out that our successful resistance might leave us so weakened as to compel us to await the expansion of the American Army before we should find ourselves in a position to obtain the decision. ... He upheld the point of view he had formulated on 19th January: he declared his agreement with General Pétain on the need for observing a defensive attitude, as on the use of the troops and the action of the reserves; like the French Army, the English Army held in readiness three fields of action for the offensive with the power to engage five divisions on each.

This last offensive contemplated a number of small offensives with limited aims.

The case developed by General Foch during the sitting was to a considerable extent at variance with the views of the two Commanders-in-Chief. The French Chief of General Staff in fact vigorously upheld the ideas which he had established as fundamental to the draft plan of campaign addressed in January to our Permanent Military Representative: he accordingly insisted on the necessity for executing a strenuous counter-offensive in order to check the German offensive; he said: —

[1] "Les armées françaises dans la grande guerre", VI.

"... *Our need is not for two separate plans, but a general plan, anticipating and preparing for the offensive action at the appropriate juncture and upon a joint scene of action of all the available Allied forces.*

"... In our plans, nothing is provided for the final battle, utilising all the remaining available French, British and American Allied forces."

He accordingly demanded "not that more offensive battlefields be organised but that preparation be made for the utilisation of the Allied troops which at a given moment will remain available. . . ."

The two Commanders-in-Chief replied to General Foch's arguments by again describing the poverty of their effectives *which left very feeble hope of the Anglo-French Armies being in a position to take a vigorous offensive during the forthcoming battle.*

Here again are two schools of thought. As Foch said, what was required was one plan for the two armies, not each army with its own plan. Haig and Pétain kept up their lamentations about the poverty of their effectives. All is relative. The effectives of each army standing alone might seem poor next to the German. The united effectives of the two Allied Armies were still richer, and at the climax of the German strength were equal in numbers and more powerful in machinery than the German. But Pétain and Haig were determined to fight the Germans with separate armies, operating separately, as the Allies had so obligingly done for three years. Motives can only be conjectured: but probably the objection of each to a single plan lay in this — it would have diminished his authority over his army. Hence their obstinacy, which only a catastrophe broke down.

Pershing's chief contribution to the discussion was his insistence on the proposition that: —

". . . on the day when an offensive action is required of the American troops, the American Army will have to be autonomous."

At the Conference of Compiègne the high military authorities had again failed to reach an agreement on the important questions of the Allied campaign for 1918. True, the two Commanders-in-Chief professed that they were now agreed on their plan of campaign. They claimed that they had even begun to prepare to execute it; the emergence of the Supreme Council's plan of an Inter-Allied Reserve under independent direction had forced Pétain and Haig on to a common front — not against the Germans, but in opposition to the Versaillais. In effect, however, their views were at variance not only with the proposals made by General Foch with regard to the Western Front, and with the suggestions submitted by the Permanent Military Representatives to the Allied Governments, but also in some important respects with each other. It was still more significant that the Conference had not broached the question, capital as it was, of the single command, even in such an attenuated form as the constitution of a General Inter-Allied Reserve.

In the days following the Conference of Compiègne Marshal Haig and General Pétain did not conceal the repugnance they felt for the scheme for an Inter-Allied Reserve forwarded to them for consideration. On January 27th, General Pétain declared to General Foch that he regarded the reserves now stationed behind the Franco-British Front as barely adequate "to safeguard the liberty of manœuvre of the Franco-British High Command in the initial stages of the defensive battle." In his opinion, the General Reserve could only be levied from the Allied forces in Italy; in such case, it seemed advisable that it should include four Italian divisions retained on the plain of the Po and four French and English divisions respectively which would be recalled from Italy to France.

The result of the Compiègne Conference was eminently unsatisfactory in that it revealed a fundamental difference of opinion between Generals who had within a few weeks to face the most formidable attack launched on their front since the first German attack in 1914. General Weygand's solution was the appointment of a Generalissimo of the Allied forces. Complete unity of command under one general would no doubt have been the simplest, most direct, and much the most effective method of establishing strategic unity. It was obviously the appropriate remedy for the weaknesses of a divided command from which the Allies had suffered such damage. Why then was not the proposal of the French Military Representatives agreed to by the other Military Representatives? Neither Henry Wilson nor General Cadorna accepted the suggestion. Not only was it not adopted — it had not the slightest chance of being adopted at that moment. There were national prejudices, political susceptibilities and personal jealousies to overcome. One can understand the dislike which one great nation would have of placing its finest army under the command of another — and not a greater — nation. It was easier for the French to advance and support the idea than for British Generals or Ministers. But even they had political susceptibilities which hindered that desirable solution of Allied difficulties. Foch was never an acceptable military chieftain for the ardent Republicans who have governed France for at least a generation. And the personal rivalries which intervened were just as intense on the French side as on ours. Haig was convinced that he was a better practical soldier than Foch, and Pétain thought himself a safer general with an equal, if not superior, record of success. A worse element was the rivalry of the various staffs. If Foch were made Generalissimo, the whole status of the two G.H.Q.'s was lowered to second place. It is sad to think that these little human frailties should influence men in great issues. But no profession is free from them and experience makes me think that members of the military profession are no more immune from propensities that disturb the balance of judgment than those who are engaged in other honourable avocations. Clemenceau at that date would not have placed Foch above Pétain for reasons I give elsewhere. Neither Orlando nor I could at that time have agreed to making Foch Generalissimo without encountering formidable opposition in the Senate and the Services, and without facing a risk of repudiation at home which would have had a chilling effect on our relations with the French Army and the French people. The next best thing was to unify the general reserves and place them under a single direction. This was a subtle solution of the difficulty. We avoided the drawbacks and obtained the advantages of a Generalissimo. Each Commander-in-Chief would retain his full authority unimpaired: thus the objection to a Generalissimo was avoided. When an offensive on a great scale is anticipated the preparations made by the enemy behind their lines give a general indication of the quarter where the blow is likely to fall. But it is not possible to define its limits or the point where the enemy is likely to concentrate his greatest strength. The result is that it is not easy to determine the exact spot where the reserves should be placed in order to reach the battlefield in the shortest time. That is why in every attack, whether made by the Allies or by the Germans, the assaults have generally had overwhelming numbers for the first day or two. At Neuve Chapelle the British had a superiority of ten to one. On the first day of the Somme we had six to one. When the Vimy Ridge was carried, we had at least three to one. In the battle of March 21st the Germans had three to one on the Fifth Army Front and two to one against the Third Army. That is why the first assault generally succeeds. The best a defending General can do is to arrange his reserves behind the threatened area in such a way as to be available to be thrown in at the weakest point with the least possible delay. That was the reason that compelled Foch and the Versailles representatives to recommend the formation of a large General Reserve which could be placed in the vicinity of the threatened sector as soon as it became clear where the Germans were massing their forces. Upon this eminently practical and sensible project the Versailles Staff concentrated, and they embodied it in the recommendations they submitted to the Council in two remarkable memoranda known as Notes 12 and 14. (As Joint Note No. 12 contains a comprehensive but compendious review of the whole position, and formed the basis of discussions which had momentous results, I have thought it desirable that this document should be given textually in Appendix A to this chapter.)

The proposals contained in these two Notes were governed by the consideration that: —

"The Allies were confronted with a fundamental, if not permanent change in the conditions upon which their strategy had to be based, as compared with the conditions, existing or anticipated, as long as the Russian Armies kept the field."

They contemplated a heavy attack by the Germans on the Allied positions in France in the early spring, an attack which might possibly, in their opinion, attain a strength of 96 Divisions, exclusive of *roulement*. They considered that the first and foremost task of the Allies was to organise their resources to resist this impending German attack. In order to make the position secure in France it was necessary that the Allied forces should be continuously maintained at the strength which they possessed at that date, and that they should also receive "the expected reinforcement of not less than two American divisions a month." That meant that France and Britain should make an effort to maintain during the struggle their numbers at the figure they amounted to at that moment. They also regarded it as a necessary condition of security that there should be a substantial progressive increase in the mechanical strength of the Allied Armies; in guns, in machine-guns, in aeroplanes, and in tanks. They attached importance to strengthening and coördinating the Allies' system of defences, *"more particularly in the sectors most liable to heavy attack."* Their last and most important recommendation is one which they developed in a separate paper: —

"That the whole Allied forces in France should be treated as a single strategic field of action, and that the disposition of the reserves, the periodic rearrangement of the point of junction between the various Allied forces, and the actual front, and all other arrangements, should be dominated by this consideration."

To those of us who had been labouring hard to secure strategic unity, this last recommendation seemed to be far and away the most fruitful suggestion in the whole document. That the Allies failed for three years to break through the German line, in spite of a 50 per cent. superiority, was largely if not mainly due to the fact that the Germans possessed the incalculable advantage of a United Command, and could, without negotiations between Commanders and Governments representing completely independent armies on the same front, distribute and redistribute the forces according to the exigencies of the situation. That was worth more to them than a mere numerical equality which a large contingent of Austrians on the same front would have given them.

It was for this reason that I attached more importance to the recommendation as to the General Reserve than to any other part of the Versailles Staff document. No possible withdrawal of troops from Russia could give the German Army even a temporary and evanescent numerical superiority on the Western Front in 1918 of more than 5 per cent. That slight advantage, if it were attained, would disappear in the late spring when the Americans had rolled up, and from the start it would be far more than countered by the unquestionable superiority of the Allies in guns, ammunitions, machine-guns, tanks, aeroplanes, and above all, in transport. When they came to consider whether there would be any opportunity in the course of 1918 of securing in the main Western theatres a final or even a far-reaching decision against the enemy, they accepted the prognosis of Pétain: —

". . . If the enemy cannot gain a final decision against the Allies the question arises whether there is any opportunity in the course of 1918 for the Allies to secure, in the main Western theatres, a final, or even a far-reaching decision, against the enemy? The Military Representatives are of the opinion that, *apart from such measure of success as is implied in the failure of the enemy's offensive, or may be* attained by local counter-strokes, *and leaving out of account such improbable and unforeseeable contingencies as the internal collapse of the Enemy Powers,* or the revival of Russia as a serious military factor, no such decision is likely to be secured during the fighting period of 1918. Neither the addition of the American troops in view during this period, nor such reinforcements as could be secured for any one of the main theatres by withdrawing from the secondary theatres any margin of troops that may be available above the necessities of local defence, would make a sufficient difference in the relative position of the opposing forces to justify the hope of attaining such a decision."

In the following concluding sentences they seemed to veer to the Foch thesis of the possibility of a general offensive with a view to reaching a decision: —

"This should not prevent the Allied General Staffs closely watching the situation in case an unexpected favourable development should furnish an opportunity for vigorous offensive actions

THE MILITARY POSITION 237

for which they should always be prepared. In any case the defensive on the Western Front should not be of merely a passive character, but be worked out definitely and scientifically, with the intention of gaining the maximum advantage from any opportunities offered in this theatre."

The consideration of the nature of the measures that should be envisaged for defence, as well as for taking advantage of any opportunity that might offer, was dealt with in another paper. This outlined a proposal of a General Reserve under a central authority to meet any emergency or take advantage of any opportunity that might arise. To form this Reserve the French, British and Italian Armies were each to make their contribution.

These measures excluded the possibility of achieving any far-reaching decision in the Balkans. Owing to "the strength and comparative homogeneity of the numerous forces against them," the experts thought it possible that in this theatre the Allied forces might find themselves heavily attacked and might be compelled to give ground. To provide against this eventuality, they suggested that adequate preparations should be made in time for the occupation of shorter and stronger lines, covering the mainland of Greece, and if possible, Salonika.

It is stated by the British Official History, that at the Compiègne Conference, Sir Douglas Haig proposed that the whole of the British and French troops should be withdrawn from Salonika and brought to France. He may have done so in the course of the interchange of ideas. It fits in with his obsession that all the men and all the guns and all the ships must be given to him for his front. The proposal, if adopted, would have laid open the whole of Greece, with its convenient ports for submarines, to the unresisted occupation of the Central Powers. Without a struggle they would have secured a number of submarine bases at the most vulnerable points of the pathway to Egypt and our Eastern Empire. The Mediterranean would have been practically closed to our shipping. Constantine was an instrument ready to their hand to be used for any purpose for which he could have pleaded the slightest appearance of duress. He had already voluntarily handed over two Greek divisions to the Germans. Had we taken away all our troops from the Balkans, he would have placed the whole Greek Army at the disposal of the Powers with whom lay his real sympathies. The Bulgarian Army, released from the presence of a formidable enemy force south of the Balkans, could have spared a few divisions to help one or other of their Northern allies or to support the hard-driven Turkish Army, to check the British advance in Palestine. This acknowledged and accepted defeat in the Balkans would have adversely changed the whole situation in the East without giving us a greater superiority of numbers in the West than the British Army possessed in its Flanders campaign. Haig's suggestion was so patently fatuous that it received no encouragement from any other soldier, British, French or Italian, and consequently never appeared at the Conference table. Neither Sir Douglas Haig nor Sir William Robertson ever hinted to the Cabinet that they harboured such a thought. I would never have heard of it had it not appeared in the Official History.

The Military Members at Versailles, after dealing with the Western Front and Salonika, urged strongly that an effort be made to: —

". . . inflict such a crushing series of defeats upon the Turkish Armies as would lead to the final collapse of Turkey and her elimination from the War would not only have the most far-reaching results upon the general military situation, but might also, if not too long deferred, be in time to enable the Allies to get into direct touch with, and give effective help to, such elements of resistance to German domination as may still exist in Roumania and Southern Russia."

THE MILITARY POSITION

In order to achieve this end they did not contemplate the withdrawal of any units or reinforcements from the West. They considered: —

". . . that the existing Allied Forces in Palestine and Mesopotamia are already sufficiently superior to the enemy in numbers, equipment and morale to justify the hope that successful operations can be carried out with these forces providing they are maintained at full strength. They would also strongly urge that any additional minor reinforcements such as could be provided by the *termination* of the East African operations, by the raising of new units in India or in the French possessions, by the transfer of superfluous mounted troops from the Western theatre, or possibly at a later date, by the transfer of one or two Divisions from Salonika, if the enemy make no serious offensive in the Balkans, and the organisation of the Greek Army makes sufficient progress to enable it to be relied upon to replace the Divisions sent away, should be concentrated in the Turkish theatre."

As to the Italian Front, the main recommendations were directed towards the reorganisation of the Italian Army. The proposal put forward by M. Clemenceau at the first meeting of the Supreme Council for a joint Allied offensive on a great scale on the Italian Front was not encouraged. It was generally felt to be too late to consider such a project when the German clans were gathering from east and south for an immense onslaught on the Allies in France. Actually, Note 12 was signed by the Allied Military Representatives on the day that Ludendorff finally decided that his first great attack should be made on the British Front at the earliest moment at which it was possible to stage so gigantic an operation.

4. The Meeting of the Allied Supreme Council

War plans laid before Supreme Council — Discussion on outlook — Haig's pessimism — General Reserve — Robertson's approval — Clemenceau's definition of the scheme — Unanimous agreement — I propose Foch — Principles of the policy — Appendix A: Note 12 — Appendix B: Clemenceau's first address to the Supreme Allied Council.

The meeting of the Supreme Council to consider the military situation and to examine the recommendations of the military advisers was held on January 30th and lasted for four days. Its principal business was to come to a decision on the measures already proposed and thus to secure a united front for this critical year. The foremost of these measures was the scheme worked out for setting up an independent General Reserve. Rumours had reached me that both Commanders-in-Chief were angrily opposed to the proposal. They disliked the idea itself, they disliked even more the notion of having their strategic plans subordinated to the arbitrament of General Foch. When Milner and I reached Versailles and heard the gossip of the G.H.Q.'s we expected a rough passage for the General Reserve propositions.

The assembly at the Trianon Palace Hotel was a notable one not merely for the importance of its theme, but for the representative character of those who attended it and took part in its discussions. Clemenceau, in the chair, was surrounded by an array of important Ministers from all the Allied countries. The Commanders-in-Chief (Marshal Haig and General Pétain) and the Chiefs of the Staff of France and Britain, General Foch and Sir William Robertson, were present. The Italian and Belgian Armies were also represented, as were the Allied Navies. The Military Representatives of the Supreme Council were present. America was represented by General Bliss. No one could challenge the authoritative character of the gathering. It was thoroughly representative not only of the Allied Governments, but of the military and naval services of the Allies.

Before we came to an examination of the proposal for setting up a General Reserve, there was a general discussion on the position in the West. There is nothing that strikes one more in perusing the notes taken of that discussion, and the memoranda furnished by the Allied General Staff, than the extent to which all our military advisers overestimated the strength of the enemy and thus understated the possibilities of the 1918 campaign. General Foch was the only exception to the general pessimism of the rest, probably because he took a general view and did not exclude from his mind everything but his own particular front. There were decisive factors of which either they were completely ignorant or which they chose to ignore. They either were not informed about, or did not appreciate the effect of the serious food and fuel shortage on the enemy side. It ultimately precipitated the collapse of the Central Powers by destroying the morale and mobility of their armies, by weakening the spirit and the will of the nations behind the army, and it also deprived both the Austrians and the Germans of the full benefit of the Russian Peace, for it compelled them to maintain large forces in Russia in order to exploit its food reserves. There was also an incomprehensible agreement amongst all the military chiefs that the American contribution would have no appreciable effect upon the campaign of 1918. Sir Douglas Haig was doubtful whether they could allow in 1918 "for the addition of American units of a total strength equivalent to eight divisions." And he added: —

"As regards the American forces, our own experience had been that our new divisions required nine months' home training and six months' training in France, before they were fit for hard fighting, though they could be put into quiet sections of the line before that. Nor could we expect that the American divisions could be placed in the line together in any number without inviting a heavy German attack. He *consequently did not consider the Allies could expect the American force, as a force, to be of effective support this year.*"

He therefore stated that he had come to the conclusion that: —

"A large offensive such as had been indicated by General Foch, was not, in his opinion, practicable."

In fact, he took such a depressing view of the prospects that: —

"he considered that if the enemy attacked in force the situation would be very serious by the autumn."

This indeed was a come-down from the exalted altitudes in which he dwelt in October, 1917. He then thought that the German Army was so demoralised, that its fighting value was so deteriorated, and that its reserves had been so completely destroyed, that if we furnished the British Army with reinforcements (which we did not fail to do, for we created mechanically powerful new units), his army alone could conduct a triumphant offensive against them so long as the French just held their line with an occasional disquieting push to prove that they were still alive and present. There is no way of explaining why this second and contrary idea should displace his first and previous idea, except by supposing that in neither case was there any clear or accurate thinking. There was no change in circumstances. For in his first plan he had fully reckoned on the withdrawal of the picked German divisions from the Russian Front and discounted its effect.

Sir William Robertson was of the same opinion as to the impracticability of a great offensive operation in 1918 and said that General Foch "had proposed an offensive on a bigger scale than he thought possible." General Pétain was of the same opinion, and said: —

"As regards the American Army, he agreed entirely with the conclusions arrived at by Sir Douglas Haig. In fact, in his opinion, the American Army, if it wished to retain its autonomy, would be of no use to the Allies in 1918, except perhaps along some quiet section of the front."

We all know how completely these pessimistic estimates of the American contribution were falsified by the event.

Then we arrived at our decision as to the General Reserve. Let this be noted carefully at this stage: for a few weeks later the fact is going to become important. Sir William Robertson, Sir Douglas Haig and General Pétain were present during the whole of the proceedings and took part in the discussions, and accepted the resolutions which were ultimately agreed to. There was no dissentient voice from any quarter when the final proposals were put to the meeting. M. Clemenceau opened the proceedings by propounding four questions: —

" 'Shall we constitute a General Reserve?'
" 'Will it be a Reserve for the whole front from the North Sea to the Adriatic?'
" 'How shall it be disposed?'
" 'Who will command it?' "

"GENERAL FOCH said that, in the existing condition of our front, we had to defend a line from Nieuport to Venice without knowing where the enemy was concentrating or where or when the attacks would be made. In this situation it was difficult to envisage completely the question of reserves. Nevertheless, the necessity of having a Reserve was absolutely indisputable. Moreover, there was no doubt that the reserves should be constituted for the whole front from the North Sea to the Adriatic, and consequently it should be drawn from the British, French and Italian Armies. This Reserve must be additional to the divisions which each army has behind its own front. It was also necessary to have some authority to conserve the reserves and to decide when the time had come to use them, to arrange for their transport to the north or south, and to decide all details in conjunction with the commanders of the armies to whom they might be sent,

To summarise, there must be one authority, able to constitute, conserve, and prepare for the employment of the General Reserve by the various armies, in agreement with the commanders. When the moment arrives to make use of the Reserve the same authority must decide on their use, must arrange for their transport, and feed the battleline in which the Reserve might be utilised. As the Reserve might be utilised to support any of the Allies, the central authority must be Inter-Allied in character. *It must be able and entitled to make all the necessary preparations.* Moreover, this Inter-Allied organ must be required to take decisions if the Governments were not in session at Versailles. *In fact, it must be an Inter-Allied organ of execution.* The only question that arises is as to how this central authority should be constituted. If he were asked for a concrete proposal he would suggest to bring together the Chiefs of the Staff who advise their Governments on the different questions, in order that they might carry out their duties in agreement. To these principal members of the central organ there should be added representatives of the American Army and of the Belgian Army."

Serious discussions were to arise later when the time came for the execution of the resolutions. The Reply made by Sir William Robertson to General Foch's speech should therefore be read with the greatest attention.

"GENERAL ROBERTSON said that he *was in general agreement with General Foch in regard to the necessity of creating a General Reserve.* The fundamental question, however, was the command of the Reserves. If this were settled, the composition of the Reserves would settle itself. *He himself doubted the need of the General Reserve at the moment,* because most of the Allied troops were needed where they were, except in Italy. *Any day, however, it might be necessary to form the proposed Reserve, and therefore the question of the organisation should be studied in detail.* He agreed with General Foch that the best persons to control the Reserve would be the Chiefs of the Staff. This arrangement would perfectly well suit Great Britain and France, but it would not suit Italy as well, as the Italians had no Chief of the Staff, except with the Commander-in-Chief of the army. He also understood that General Pershing commanded all the American troops in France. The questions of the Italian and American representation would want working out in detail, but these minor difficulties could be surmounted. *Whoever commands the Reserve must be in a position to issue orders immediately the emergency arises.*"

This sentence emphatically expresses Sir William Robertson's opinion. He insists on the importance of confining authority over the disposal of the Reserves to men on the spot. This should be noted because there was subsequently a great controversy on this point.

"The central controlling body, however, should interfere as little as possible with the Commanders-in-Chief, who were responsible to their respective Governments. What the central body had to do was to perform those duties which could not be undertaken by the Commander-in-Chief of any one of the fronts."

What Sir William Robertson states must be remarked. He says he is in general agreement with Foch on the necessity of creating a General Reserve for an emergency. He also approves the idea of a composite reserve with an independent controlling board and his only doubt is as to the time when it ought to be brought into existence. As to the composition of the controlling authority, he is insistent that so far as France and Britain are concerned, the Chiefs of the Staff would be the best choice.

Throughout the discussion it was made quite clear that this General Reserve, whilst acting in consultation with the Commanders-in-Chief, should be independent of them as far as the allocation of the troops constituting the forces of the General Reserve was concerned. There was therefore no question of principle raised either by Robertson, Pétain or Haig in opposition to the idea of an independent General Reserve. M. Clemenceau put it with his usual clarity and force when he said: —

". . . At the moment he did not want to discuss the question, but merely to know what was intended. . . . He understood that each General would have a reserve of his own; for example, there would be French, British, Italian and American reserves. In this scheme he did not see how the great army of reserves which he wanted was to be created. He did not want to discuss the question for the moment from a military point of view, but merely from one of common sense. If each General had the free disposition of his own reserves what would happen? When one General was attacked he would gradually use up his reserves until there was none left. In the meanwhile, the General commanding the adjacent army might have the whole of his reserves in hand. Hence a situation of great danger might arise. When the question of creating an Inter-Allied Reserve had been raised it had been with the idea that, as we could not have a single Commander-in-Chief, such as a Hannibal or a Charlemagne, we might at least have a Commander of Reserves. *He considered it very desirable that we should build up an Army Reserve which could be sent to any point where it would be useful.*"

Generals Cadorna, Pétain and Bliss showed clearly that they were thoroughly cognisant of the nature of the transaction. An answer given by General Pétain to a question put by Signor Orlando makes this clear: —

"SIGNOR ORLANDO suggested that when General Pétain talked of the reserves being disposed of by the new central body he understood that this did not apply to the reserves at the disposal of particular armies. He understood that each army would continue to have its own reserves in addition to those under the Inter-Allied central body.

"GENERAL PÉTAIN replied in the affirmative. The idea was to

constitute an Inter-Allied Reserve in addition to the local reserves of the armies."

The principle of a separated and independent General Reserve having been generally accepted, and it having been made abundantly clear that it should not be under the control of the Commanders-in-Chief, but of a central body to be constituted, the Council then proceeded to consider its composition and the constitution of the body which should control it.

Ultimately the following resolution was adopted unanimously: —

1. The Supreme War Council decided on the creation of a General Reserve for the whole of the armies on the Western, Italian and Balkan Fronts.

2. The Supreme War Council delegates to an Executive composed of the Permanent Military Representatives of Great Britain, Italy and the United States of America, with General Foch for France, the following powers to be exercised in consultation with the Commanders-in-Chief of the armies concerned: —

(*a*) To determine the strength in all arms and composition of the General Reserve, and the contribution of each national army thereto.

(*b*) To select the localities in which the General Reserve is normally to be stationed.

(*c*) To make arrangements for the transportation and concentration of the General Reserve in the different areas.

(*d*) To decide and issue orders as to the time, place and period of employment of the General Reserve; the orders of the Executive Committee for the movement of the General Reserve shall be transmitted in the manner and by the persons who shall be designated by the Supreme War Council for that purpose in each particular case.

(*e*) To determine the time, place and strength of the counter-offensive, and then to hand over to one or more of the Commanders-in-Chief the necessary troops for the operation. The moment this movement of the General Reserve, or any part of it, shall have begun, it will come under the orders of the Commander-in-Chief to whose assistance it is consigned.

(*f*) Until the movement of the General Reserve begins, it will, for all purposes of discipline, instruction and administration, be under the orders of the respective Commanders-in-Chief, but no movement can be ordered except by the Executive Committee.

3. In case of irreconcilable differences of opinion on a point of importance connected with the General Reserve, any Military Representative has the right to appeal to the Supreme War Council.

4. In order to facilitate its decisions the Executive Committee has the right to visit any theatre of war.

5. The Supreme War Council will nominate the President of the Executive Committee from among the members of the Committee.

I proposed that the new body should have a President and that that President should be General Foch. I stated my reason thus: —

"He (MR. LLOYD GEORGE) thought it very desirable that as the proposed Committee was to have executive powers it should have a President. Some members of the Supreme War Council desired to insert the name of the President in the text which constitutes the body, but his own view was that it was best not to insert the name. It was preferable that the Supreme War Council should nominate the President. The President of the Committee must necessarily have special qualifications, and the members of the Supreme War Council had agreed — that is to say, the three heads of Governments attending that meeting had agreed, and in the absence of the President of the United States had ventured to assume the latter's concurrence — that the right man to be President was General Foch, on account of his experience, his record and his energy, his military gifts and his reputation.

"GENERAL BLISS said he was sure that the three Prime Ministers were right in assuming that President Wilson would acquiesce in this suggestion.

"MR. LLOYD GEORGE went on to give the reasons why he and his colleagues had come to this decision. General Foch was loyal not only to France, but also to the Allies. When the British Army in Flanders was in difficulties he threw all his weight into rendering it assistance. So prompt and generous was that assistance that General Foch might almost have been an Englishman himself. Again when Italy was in trouble General Foch, without any hesitation and on his own responsibility, decided to send troops to her aid. General Foch therefore commanded the confidence not only of the French but also of the British and Italians, and he was glad to hear, the Americans. They could be quite sure that as President of the Committee, General Foch would be quite unbiased. He had, therefore, great pleasure in announcing this decision of the Supreme War Council."

I had already put the suggestion before M. Clemenceau and Signor Orlando at a private conference, and made the proposal with their concurrence.

The military policy formulated by the Versailles Inter-Allied Staff was thus the one ultimately adopted by the Council and accepted by the Allies. Its principles were: —

1. The organisation of the whole of the forces of the Allies for defence against the German attack on the basis of a united front. To achieve this aim, power to be given to a Central Authority to form and direct a General Reserve available for use at any part of the front where that Authority deemed it advisable to throw them in for defence or counter-attack. The Council appointed General Foch President of an Inter-Allied body of Generals who constituted the authority in control of the General Reserve. In the West, Foch was ultimately given the sole command of the Allied Armies. That was undoubtedly an improvement on the original plan. But he was so easily the dominant personality on the Board that in effect the scheme would have given him supreme direction of the Allied strategy in the West.

2. To watch the situation in case an unexpectedly favourable development should furnish an opportunity for vigorous offensive action. The defensive was "not to be of a merely passive character, but to be worked out definitely and scientifically, with the intention of gaining the maximum advantage from any opportunities offered in the Western theatre." Foch was the only General who was confident that opportunities of this kind might arise in 1918.

The Versailles discussion ended in complete accord between all the statesmen and Generals of the Allies as to the plan of campaign to be pursued by the Allied Armies on all fronts during the years 1918.

I have no recollection of any dissent being expressed by anyone when the resolutions, ultimately adopted, were put to the meeting, and there is no record of any protest from any quarter.

There was a very free discussion, and statesmen and Generals expressed their minds very fully. But neither at the time that the resolution was put to the meeting, nor after it dispersed, did the Government receive any notification from any of the Generals that they disapproved of the conclusions at which the Council had arrived.

APPENDIX A

NOTE 12

The Military Representatives have the honour to inform you that at their Meeting held on 21st January, 1918, they passed the following Resolutions: —

1. In submitting to the Supreme War Council their advice on the military action to be undertaken during 1918, the Military Representatives think it necessary to place before the Supreme War Council in the briefest possible manner the grounds on which their advice is based.

2. Looking out over all the theatres of war they examined the state of affairs both in the main theatres and in the secondary theatres, first of all from the point of view of the security of the fronts in those theatres, and then from the point of view of the opportunity which may present themselves for gaining a decisive or, at any rate, far-reaching success in any of those theatres.

3. It was assumed that the United Kingdom was safe from all serious invasion and that the necessary measures, both naval, military and air, for its defence against the contingency of an attack, involved no interference with the operations of the British force overseas.

4. It was agreed, after the most careful and exhaustive examination, that the safety of France could also be assured. But in view of the weight of attack which the enemy can bring to bear upon this front, an attack *which may possibly, in the opinion of the Military Representatives, attain a strength of 96 Divisions, exclusive of "roulement"*, they feel obliged to add that France will be safe during 1918 *only* under certain conditions, *viz.:* —

(*a*) That the French and British forces in France are

continuously maintained at their present total aggregate strength, and receive the expected reinforcement of not less than two American Divisions a month.

(*b*) That there shall be a substantial progressive increase in the total Allied equipment in guns of all calibres, in machine-guns, in aeroplanes and in tanks, with the personnel necessary to man them, and the most effective coordinated employment of those and all other mechanical devices.

(*c*) That every possible measure shall be taken for strengthening and coördinating the Allied system of defences, more particularly in the sectors most liable to a heavy attack.

(*d*) That the rail transportation be improved and coordinated.

(*e*) That the whole Allied Front in France be treated as a single strategic field of action, and that the disposition of the reserves, the periodic rearrangement of the point of junction between the various Allied forces on the actual front, and all other arrangements should be dominated by this consideration.

5. It was agreed that Italy was safe, but again under certain conditions, *viz.:* —

(i) That the Italian Army be reformed, trained and re-equipped with artillery before 1st May, and that several positions in rear of the present line be constructed on modern principles.

(ii) That the power of rapid rail transport be increased both in the interior of Italy itself, and between Italy and France in order to secure strategic unity of action over the two theatres.

(iii) That, in addition to the necessary measures taken against pacifism by the Italian Government itself, the

Allies should assist Italy by the provision of coal, wheat and other necessaries, as well as financially, in order to prevent the creation of economic conditions which would diminish the strength of the interior resistance of the country.

6. If the assumptions in paragraphs 3, 4 and 5 are accepted then we have got this far in our examination of the problem, *viz.:* that the enemy cannot in 1918 gain a definite military decision in the main theatres which would enable him to break finally the resistance of any of the Allied Powers.

7. If the enemy cannot gain a final decision against the Allies the question arises whether there is any opportunity in the course of 1918 for the Allies to secure, in the main Western theatres, a final, or even a far-reaching, decision against the enemy? The Military Representatives are of the opinion that, apart from such measure of success as is implied in the failure of the enemy's offensive, or may be attained by local counter-strokes, and leaving out of account such improbable and unforeseeable contingencies as the internal collapse of the Enemy Powers, or the revival of Russia as a serious military factor, no such decision is likely to be secured during the fighting period of 1918. Neither the addition of the American troops in view during this period, nor such reinforcements as could be secured for any one of the main theatres by withdrawing from the secondary theatres any margin of troops that may be available above the necessities of local defence, would make a sufficient difference in the relative position of the opposing forces to justify the hope of attaining such a decision. This should not prevent the Allied General Staffs closely watching the situation in case an unexpected favourable development should furnish an opportunity for vigorous offensive actions

for which they should always be prepared. In any case the defensive on the Western Front should not be of merely a passive character, but be worked out definitely and scientifically, with the intention of gaining the maximum advantage from any opportunities offered in this theatre. A detailed consideration of the nature of the measures that should be envisaged is given in a paper which is appended as an annex to this Note.

8. The Allies are therefore confronted with a fundamental, though not permanent, change in the conditions upon which their strategy has to be based, as compared with the conditions, existing or anticipated, as long as the Russian Armies kept the field. They are accordingly obliged to consider how that strategy must be modified in order to take the fullest advantage out of such opportunities as remain open to them during the phase of deadlock on the Western Fronts. In other words, pending such a change in the balance of forces as we hope to reach in 1919 by the steady influx of American troops, guns, aeroplanes, tanks, etc., and by the progressive exhaustion of the enemy's staying power, it remains to consider what action can meanwhile be taken against the enemy, elsewhere than in the main Western theatres, which may enable us to secure a decision far-reaching in its effect upon the political situation in the Near East and in Russia, both during and after the War, and valuable in paving the way towards a subsequent definitive decision against the enemy's main armies. To allow the year to pass without an attempt to secure a decision in any theatre of war, and to leave the initiative entirely to the enemy would, in the opinion of the Military Representatives, be a grave error in strategy apart from the moral effect such a policy might produce upon the Allied nations.

9. The possibility of achieving any far-reaching decision in the Balkan theatre is clearly excluded, for the present at

any rate, by the strength and comparative homogeneity of the enemy forces, and by the great superiority of the enemy's system of communications. It is, indeed, possible that in this theatre the Allied forces may find themselves heavily attacked, and may be compelled to give ground. Such a contingency, though undesirable in itself, need give rise to no serious apprehensions provided always that adequate preparations are made in good time for the occupation of shorter and stronger lines covering the mainland of Greece and, if possible, Salonika.

10. There remains the Turkish theatre. To inflict such a crushing series of defeats upon the Turkish Armies as would lead to the final collapse of Turkey and her elimination from the War would not only have the most far-reaching results upon the general military situation, but might also if not too long deferred, be in time to enable the Allies to get into direct touch with, and give effective help to, such elements of resistance to German domination as may still exist in Roumania and Southern Russia. Even a lesser measure of success such as would definitely liberate the Arab regions of the Ottoman Empire from the Turkish yoke and compel the Germans to divert considerable forces to the East in order to save Turkey from destruction, would, both from the point of view of the military situation and from that of eventual peace negotiations, greatly strengthen the Allied position, and be worth any effort that can be made compatibly with the security of our defence in the Western theatres.

11. The present condition of Turkey is one of almost complete material and moral exhaustion. The Turkish forces have progressively dwindled, till they now amount to 250,000 men at the utmost, and will dwindle even more rapidly if seriously attacked, owing to the entire lack of reserves. Such as they are these forces are dispersed, and are neces-

sarily dispersed over enormous areas. The communications between the different fronts are so defective that any transfers of troops can only be carried out extremely slowly and with heavy wastage through sickness and desertion. The main railway communication with Constantinople and the Central Powers is itself of very limited capacity, and vulnerable to air attacks. Reinforcement of troops or munitions from Germany could only be accumulated very gradually, and the sending of them would involve a heavy strain on the enemy's transport resources.

12. The Military Representatives realise that in view of the potential menace to the Western Front, as well as in view of difficulties of tonnage, there can be no question of a transfer of troops on any considerable scale from the Western to the Eastern theatre of operations under present circumstances. They consider, however, that the existing Allied forces in Palestine and Mesopotamia are already sufficiently superior to the enemy in numbers, equipment and morale to justify the hope that successful operations can be carried out with these forces providing they are maintained at full strength. They would also strongly urge that any additional minor reinforcements, such as could be provided by the termination of the East African operations, by the raising of new units in India or in the French possessions, by the transfer of superfluous mounted troops from the Western theatre, or possibly at a later date by the transfer of one or two divisions from Salonika, if the enemy make no serious offensive in the Balkans, and the organisation of the Greek Army makes sufficient progress to enable it to be relied upon to replace the Divisions sent away, should be concentrated in the Turkish theatre.

13. The problem of securing a decisive result in this theatre is, however, not so much one of numbers as of means of communication. The difficulty is not so much that of

dislodging the Turkish troops from a particular position as of being able to follow them up, prevent them rallying, receiving reinforcements and reorganising and so convert their retreat into rout and final annihilation. This is a question partly of the mobility of the Allied forces themselves, *i.e.*, of their power to advance rapidly and at a considerable distance from their nearest railhead or port, and partly of the rapidity and energy with which the Allies can construct new railways — normal gauge, narrow light or aerial, as the case may be — repair existing ones and reëquip them with rolling stock and open up and improve successive new supplementary bases in the coast ports. The effort required in this respect is a great one. But upon it depends the whole prospect of achieving any decisive result for the Allied cause in 1918, and looking upon the resources in material and in technical skill possessed by the Allies, not only in Europe, but in Egypt, India, the British Dominions, and the United States, the effort should not be beyond the compass of our powers.

14. The question of tonnage and escort is a serious limiting factor both as regards the actual supply of provisions and munitions for the troops and of railway material, and as regards the possibility of strategic operations depending on the movement of troops by sea. Everything that would facilitate the development of sources of supply east of the Suez Canal or locally — such as, for instance, the occupation of the Hauran — would ease the tonnage and escort situation in the Mediterranean and to that extent also help to liberate tonnage and escort for military movements by sea, if such movements were desirable for strategical reasons.

15. Aviation is of particular importance in this theatre of war, both because of the opportunities for strategical air offensives against the Turkish communications, and because of the general advantages which superiority in the air gives in regions where communications are limited, concealment

difficult and anti-aircraft arrangements defective. This superiority is enjoyed by the Allied forces in the Turkish theatre at present and the necessary measures should be taken to maintain and, if possible, increase it. The creation of independent strategic aviation bases in Cyprus and in the Aegean, and the organisation of the naval air services in the Eastern Mediterranean for concentrated strategic offensives, are essential elements in any scheme of serious operations against Turkey.

16. In considering both the Turkish situation in itself and the political objects which the Allies have in view in this quarter of the world, the Military Representatives are convinced of the necessity that strategy and policy should go absolutely hand in hand. While the success of the military operations may of itself bring about profound changes in the political situation in Turkey and the Near East generally, it is certain that these changes can be stimulated, and this success hastened on, by a definite, coördinated and vigorous political offensive both among the non-Turkish races of the Ottoman Empire and among the Turks themselves. Any lack of coherence on the part of the Foreign Offices in dealing with the political problems directly or indirectly connected with the Near Eastern situation, any evidence of mutual jealousy or of individual self-seeking, will be bound to prejudice not only the future settlement but the actual military operations.

17. The aspects upon which stress has been laid in the preceding paragraphs emphasize the need for the most energetic coöperation and the closest coördination not only of the Allied Military forces in Palestine, Mesopotamia and Armenia, but also of the Allied Naval and Air Forces along the whole coast of Asiatic Turkey, of the local Governments in Egypt, India, Cyprus, or from whatever country materials, supplies or labour can be furnished, and not least, of

the Allied Foreign Offices. It is essential to the success of the offensive against Turkey that it should be envisaged not as a series of disconnected operations, but as a single coordinated scheme whose object is to eliminate one of the Enemy Powers from the War.

18. The Military Representatives do not consider it part of their function to prescribe the particular series of operations on the different fronts by which an offensive against Turkey can best be carried out. That can only be done by the Commander-in-Chief to whom the task of coordinating and executing these operations is entrusted. There are certain more immediate objectives, indeed, such as Haifa, the friendly grain-producing region of the Hauran, Damascus and Beirut, which seem clearly indicated not only by their military, economic and political importance, but also by the prospect of striking effective blows at the Turkish forces which are not likely to abandon them without a contest. But the object of the Military Representatives is not to suggest specific geographical objectives, but to lay down a general line of policy which, to whatever extent it succeeds, will materially strengthen the position of the Allies, whether from the point of view of the further prosecution of the struggle in 1919, or from that of the willingness of the enemy to concede reasonable terms of peace.

19. From this point of view the Military Representatives, having examined with the greatest care the whole problem of the War of 1918, having laid down that *if certain conditions are fulfilled* it will not be within the power of the enemy to reach a decision adverse to the Allies in the main Western theatres, having also come to the conclusion that the Allies cannot, apart from certain at present unforeseeable contingencies, in those theatres obtain a real decision against the enemy, and having considered all the factors bearing upon the military and political situation in the

Turkish theatre, are of the opinion that the Allies should undertake a decisive offensive against Turkey with a view to the annihilation of the Turkish Armies and the collapse of Turkish resistance.

| WEYGAND, | HENRY WILSON, | L. CADORNA, |
| Military Representative, French Section Supreme War Council. | General Military Representative, British Section Supreme War Council. | Military Representative, Italian Section Supreme War Council. |

Versailles,
21st January, 1918.

APPENDIX B

CLEMENCEAU'S FIRST ADDRESS TO THE SUPREME ALLIED COUNCIL

I suggest that the first task of the Supreme War Council is to consider the nature of the military campaigns to be undertaken in 1918. In order to enable us to reach a decision I suggest to my colleagues that we should invite our Permanent Military Advisers to study the whole situation in detail and to advise us as to the operations which they recommend.

The first step to be taken is for each Government to call for the views of its own General Staff, and these views should at once be transmitted to the Permanent Military Advisers of the Supreme War Council, and I would invite my colleagues to give instructions in this sense without delay.

There are certain recent changes in the situation to which I think we should particularly direct the attention of our Permanent Military Advisers in making their report to us.

The first of these is the situation in Russia. I propose that we should instruct our Permanent Military Advisers to assume as a basis of their studies that, in 1918, Russia cannot be counted on to render any effective military assistance. It will be for them to estimate, on the basis of the intelligence they will obtain from the General Staffs of the Allies, the amount of the forces which Russia's impotence will set free for operations on other fronts.

The second new factor is the situation in Italy. After a grave reverse, which came near to disaster, equilibrium has been reëstablished for the time being on the Italian Front.

For the first time in the War, substantial British and French forces are engaged on that front. It is undeniable that the detachment of these forces makes a considerable drain on the strength of the Anglo-French forces on the Western Front, and correspondingly weakens their power of offence and defence. The fact that such large forces are concentrated on the Italian Front necessarily raises the question whether offensive operations are not indicated.

A third new factor introduced into the situation of 1918 is the gradual maturing of the forces of our new Ally, the United States of America, on the Western Front. To what extent can we count on the coöperation of the United States Army at different dates in 1918? This depends, to a large extent, upon the shipping situation, which itself constitutes one of the most vital factors in the investigations of the Permanent Military Advisers. During the last few days the shipping experts of the nations concerned have been examining this question, and they have been invited to prepare data as to the number of American divisions which it should be assumed for the purposes of calculation, can be transported to and maintained in France during 1918. The results of their investigations will be placed before you.

The restoration of the shipping situation itself has an important bearing on the intensity of the Allied effort in 1918. In order to avert the risk that any of the Allies may sink from exhaustion, a calamity which, at all costs, must be avoided, the restoration of the shipping situation is essential. Apart from naval measures for reducing our losses, two means are available for this. The first is to reduce our dependence upon imports by stimulating home production as much as circumstances permit, and by cutting down the needs of the population as far as possible; and the second is to increase the number of ships. Both these essentials make some demand upon our available man power, and to that extent limit the number of men available for the armies. The Permanent Military Advisers must obtain from their respective Governments an estimate of the man power available for 1918, after providing the bare necessities for ensuring the staying power of the nations concerned. I would ask that the conservation of man power shall not be overlooked.

If the amount of shipping available affects the intensity of the military operations, the Permanent Military Advisers must also bear in mind that, conversely, the character of the military operations decided on and prepared for in 1918 reacts no less on the amount of shipping available for the accumulation of reinforcements in the future. For example, a prolonged operation of the character attempted on the Somme in 1916, and in Flanders in 1917, involved an expenditure of material far greater than defensive operations or than offensive operations of the type of the recent attacks on the Chemin des Dames or in the region of Cambrai. The accumulation of the vast supplies of warlike stores required for the former type of attack, and the transport of the raw materials for their manufacture, involve the use of tonnage which would otherwise be available for the transport of American troops.

I would propose to invite our Permanent Military Advisers in their examination of the problem, not to forget that the War has become largely one of exhaustion. It may be that victory will be achieved by endurance rather than by a military decision. Russia has already collapsed, at any rate, for the present, but it must be remembered that Turkey and Austria are neither of them very far from collapse. The final objective now, as formerly, is the overthrow of Prussian militarism, but I would ask the Permanent Military Advisers to weigh carefully whether possibly that object may not be brought nearer final achievement by the overthrow, first of all, of Germany's allies, and the isolation of Germany:

whether in fact the final overthrow of Germany may not best be reserved until the forces of the Allies, greatly augmented by a fully matured American Army, can be focused and concentrated as a climax to the War on this final objective.

In conclusion, I suggest that each Government represented here to-day should give its definite undertaking to furnish to our Permanent Military Advisers all the information that they require for the examination of these grave problems.

Apart from the question of primary importance which I have just referred to, there is a point of great immediate importance to which the attention of the Permanent Military Advisers should be directed. I refer to the military situation in the Balkans. I suggest that it is a proper subject for present inquiry by our Military Advisers whether the Allied forces in the Balkans are so disposed, and in such strength, that they may be expected to hold their own against any force which can reasonably be brought against them.

There is one point which I would ask our Permanent Military Representatives to bear carefully in mind, namely, that their function is to advise the Supreme War Council as a whole and not merely as the representatives of their respective nations on the Council. They are required to view the problems confronting them not from a national standpoint, but from that of the Allies as a whole. I trust that, as far as possible, their advice will be unanimous, and that it will be submitted to the Supreme War Council in a collective form carrying with it the signature of each of the Permanent Military Representatives.

Paris,
   28th November, 1917.

CHAPTER VII

EXTENSION OF THE BRITISH FRONT

Constant bickerings over relative length of fronts — Strength of British Expeditionary Forces — Repington on French losses — Growth of French demand for extension of British Front — The Boulogne Conference — Haig and Pétain left to settle adjustment — Haig's attitude — Wants to renew Flanders offensive — Continued bickering — Agreement reached between Haig and Pétain — Haig's delays — Clemenceau puts his foot down — Proposals of the Versailles representatives — I suggest Italian reinforcement of French Front — Clemenceau urges further extension — My support for Haig — Nominal approval given for further extension — Further extension not carried out — Misleading account in Official History — Actual extension justified.

ONE of the most tiresome questions which British and French Governments had to adjust from time to time was the extension of the line to be held by the British Army on the Western Front. The French were compelled to put forth their utmost effort in the first years of the War when we were not ready. As our Army grew and grew with amazing rapidity, the French, who had borne the brunt of the fighting during the first two years of the War and had sustained immense losses, naturally pressed us to take over more and still more of the line which they had held so gallantly, but at such cost, whilst we were preparing. Our Generals sometimes treated these demands with consideration. Now and again, when they were incompatible with ambitious plans they were cherishing, they were inclined to be sticky or almost stingy. The delays caused by disputes over extension of the line were responsible for some serious setbacks in the War. I have already dealt with the postponement of the Nivelle offensive, due partly to Haig's reluctance to take over more line. Nivelle could not constitute the army of manœuvre that was an essential part of his scheme until Haig had released some of the French divisions by taking over part of the line. Decisive weeks were wasted over this somewhat selfish feud.

The consequent postponement of the operation enabled the Germans to bring up reserves from the East. I shall in a later chapter show how the delays and the temper aroused by taking over more line on the Somme in the winter of 1917–1918 were fatal to the effective organisation of defences in that sector which was attacked so successfully by the Germans, and equally disastrous in its influence on the distribution of forces and particularly of reserves. In the absence of a united front, taking human nature as it is, these unfortunate clashes were inevitable. Great generals, even in the exercise of their profession, are not above the pettiness in motive and temper which has marred many a promising enterprise in other spheres.

At the end of 1917 the British Expeditionary Forces of all ranks and services in all the theatres of war numbered 2,759,419, excluding coloured labour corps. We had 1,978,393 men in France and Flanders. Our great new army had fought its first battle on the Somme in the summer of 1916. Up to that date the brunt of the fighting and therefore of the casualties had fallen on the French. The French resisted the German invading army in September, 1914, in a succession of great battles fought on a front of hundreds of miles. The French losses were enormous. The great offensives of 1915 in Artois and Champagne were in the main conducted with French troops. And the sanguinary Battle of Verdun, which lasted for several months and cost the defending army hundreds of thousands, was fought exclusively between the French and the Germans. Our losses on that scale began at the Battle of the Somme in the third campaign of the War. France was now coming to an end of her resources in young men fit for battle. Sir Douglas Haig called attention to this exhaustion when he stated his case for the Passchendaele offensive. On the other hand, the contribution of men we sent overseas to our armies from Britain and the Dominions had grown each year and in 1918 we reached the climax. It was inevitable, therefore, that the French should constantly press us to take over more line.

Colonel Repington, one of the most brilliant of our military critics, and one who was accorded the special confidence of the Army leaders at home and was chosen by them as their special champion and spokesman in the Press against meddlesome politicians, put the French case for the taking over of more line by the British Army in poignant language. Needless to say, he was not stating the facts in order to support that plea. He was using them in another conjunction and for a totally different purpose. They are nevertheless so relevant to an examination of the merits of this particular controversy that I quote them. Motive cannot alter facts. Writing on January 24th, 1918, after pointing out that the French Army was seriously reduced in numerical strength, he adds: —

"I want to tell the people of England, and particularly those ministerial poltroons who bleat about our losses, that our total casualties killed, wounded, and missing — since the War began — are but little higher than the number of the French dead. The only suitable recognition that we can make of French heroism is to help them in their hour of need."

In view of the subsequent history of the French sector so reluctantly and tardily taken over by the British G.H.Q., and of the animadversions surrounding the transaction, a full statement of the facts regarding it are of considerable historic importance. Fortunately, there exists abundant official record of all the proceedings, and I propose to leave these to speak for themselves.

In the summer of 1917, the feeling steadily gained ground among the French that the British ought to be willing to take over a larger proportion of the line. They would have much preferred our helping them in this way than our setting out on the "duck's march through Flanders", to quote Foch's apt phrase. In July, a French Deputy who was chairman of a Parliamentary Committee appointed to examine the question of French man power, approached our Ambassador in Paris with the plea that we should relieve the strain on the depleted resources of French manhood by extending our front. They were facing the problem of war-weariness among their people, the mutinies in their Army, the casualties incurred in a struggle where they had hitherto borne by far the largest part of the fighting and the loss. The density of troops on our front was double or treble that of the French. Besides, the French, with a smaller total population than we, had put nearly all their able-bodied manhood in uniform, and without the help of some of these, their lands could not be tilled nor their harvests gathered, and the nation would be threatened with food shortage. We had (so it was contended) far too many troops in England.

There existed contrary arguments. Considerable sectors of the French Front were "quiet"; there was little military activity on them and no great likelihood of major offensives; and the French had considerable room for manœuvre behind their part of the line, if they should be dislodged from their positions, without being perilously driven away from contact with their bases. The British, on the other hand, cramped in the northern part of the line, had little room for manœuvre, and a serious loss of ground would drive them into the sea or away from their bases at the channel ports; and hardly any part of their front could be called "quiet": it was the scene of constant military activity, and opposite to it there were large German forces. Yet after allowing for these arguments, there was still a marked disproportion between the forces behind the respective fronts; and the actual facts of gigantic losses sustained by the French, the temporarily weakened morale of their troops, and the desperate shortage of workers for their essential agriculture, could not be gainsaid.

Accordingly, when at the Boulogne Conference of September 25th, 1917, M. Painlevé, the French Prime Minister, accompanied by General Foch, his Chief of Staff, met Sir William Robertson and myself, and reported the strong pressure of the demand in the French Chamber for the British to take over a larger part of the front, we could not refuse to consider this request. At this discussion Sir William Robertson sympathised with the French demand and considered that it ought to be met. He said that: —

the question must be regulated on the basis of next year's plans of operations. The matter should, therefore, be left for arrangement between Field-Marshal Haig and General Pétain as soon as the offensive operations now in progress come to an end. So far as the Governments were concerned, the principle of taking over more of the line was already admitted.

On the other hand, it was clear that the military considerations involved in such a step must in the first instance be a matter for examination and, if possible, adjustment by and between the Commanders-in-Chief of the two armies concerned. We eventually reached agreement in the following terms: —

"The British Government, having accepted in principle the extension of the line held by the British Army on the Western Front, the two Governments are agreed that the question of the amount of the extension and the time at which it should take place should be left for arrangement between the two Commanders-in-Chief."

This agreement I communicated on the following day to Sir Douglas Haig, whom I visited at G.H.Q.

The Commander-in-Chief did not give a direct refusal to the French demand. But he certainly did not entertain it with cordiality.

That very morning he had captured a few kilometres of Flemish mire, and General Charteris came into the room whilst we were discussing the French appeal to inform his Chief that he had received the most reliable reports showing that three more German divisions had been completely shattered. He added to these the fifty or more enemy divisions which had already been destroyed. Haig naturally felt at such a moment that to send the troops to occupy quiet trenches was a poor use to make of a victorious army. Pétain's tried and demoralised troops were good enough for that. It was evident to me that the fundamental conflict of views between the British and French commands as to the strategy to be pursued once more complicated the issue as it had already done when a similar proposal was made in the early spring. In the case of Nivelle the clash of plans involved an element of personal rivalry between two Commanders who each sought for his own army the leading part in a great operation which promised decisive results. In this case the French Generals considered Haig's idea of an offensive enterprise to be premature. Foch and Pétain were strongly of the opinion that the new situation created by the collapse of Russia, the deep repugnance felt by all ranks of fighting men in the French Army to mass attacks on the German entrenchments, and the accession of an unprepared America to the Allied side, could be best met by a suspension of great offensives, until the American Army was ready to throw in its full weight; and meanwhile that a defensive attitude should be maintained, varied by limited offensives whenever and wherever the opportunity was favourable for striking a blow at the enemy. They also advocated pressure on other and weaker flanks of the enemy line on other battle fronts. Haig on the other hand urged a concentrated offensive on a great scale with a view to driving the enemy out of Flanders and outflanking him in that direction. The disastrous and costly failure of that plan only stimulated him to justify his project by a resumption of his attacks in the spring of 1918. He did not desist from his intention until it became clear to him that the reinforcements available could not furnish a number of men sufficient to overcome an army which was reinforced by picked divisions withdrawn from Russia. A man reluctantly forced to abandon plans which seem to him to present hopes of glorious achievement never throws himself whole-heartedly into the working of alternative schemes which he has consistently set aside as inferior to his own. It looks to him too much like an admission of a fundamental error of judgment in his original conception. This mood working on an obstinate mind accounts for what happened in the rearrangement of forces rendered necessary when a great German offensive in the spring of 1918 grew certain. It was this mood which I encountered in my conversation with Marshal Haig. I found him stubbornly opposed to the proposal. He was never articulate in the expression of his views at an interview. He however promised to send me a Memorandum as to his views on the military outlook in the event of Russia being forced out of the War. That I received about October 10th. In it he expressed his opinion about the question of extending his front. Here is an extract: —

"The armies have undergone almost superhuman exertion and hardships during the last few months, and unless the demands made on them during the winter are reduced to a minimum they cannot be expected to respond fully to the further heavy calls entailed by a renewal of the offensive next year."

Haig by this time realised that his break through could not be achieved, as he had confidently anticipated, in the course of this year. He therefore contemplated renewing his attacks in the same sector early in the spring of 1918.

"I urge this point very strongly and it entails resistance to any French demands on us to take over more line. A refusal by us to do so will undoubtedly be both justifiable and wise."

Pointing out that the French Army was not in a mood for offensives, and that the British would therefore be the only attacking force, and that the French soldiers got more leave than the British, he proceeded: —

"This aspect of the case must not be overlooked any more than the purely military arguments, and it is on popular feeling amongst the French people rather than on military argument that the French demand on us to take over more line is based. The actual extent of front measured by miles is no test of what we should hold. The true test is the relative number of enemy divisions engaged by us, and still more the rôle to be allotted to us in next year's campaign (*i.e.* the renewal of the offensive). For all these reasons it is necessary in my opinion to refuse to take over more line and to adhere resolutely to that refusal, even to the point of answering threats by threats if necessary."

Haig wanted all his forces to repeat his Flanders blunder. He could not, therefore, spare a man for any other part of the front.

The discussions between the soldiers passed into that phase, all too familiar among the Franco-British forces throughout the War until we eventually achieved unity of command, of pleas and protests and counter-protests, of appeals by the respective Commanders-in-Chief to their Governments for support, and of reproaches, consultations and official representations, leading to nothing but misunderstanding. These constituted the usual dreary preliminaries to every compromise agreement. Valuable time was wasted, and essential defensive preparations in the contested area were completely neglected.

The French Government continued to urge upon me the necessity of an extension of the British line. But in accordance with the decision of the Boulogne Conference, I left the matter at this stage for the soldiers to discuss between themselves. The Cabinet thought the French had a case for an extension of our front, and that opinion was imparted to Haig, but the details were left to be settled between the Commanders. I therefore urged the C.I.G.S. to arrange an early meeting between Haig and Pétain. That took place about mid-October at Amiens and resulted in an agreement about extension, but not about strategy.

The nature of the agreement is stated by Marshal Pétain in a letter by him on October 23rd to the British Commander-in-Chief: —

"In accordance with my expressed request you have fixed the date for the extension of your front for the last week in November. The relief operations will thus have no repercussion upon the development of the battle in Flanders. The number of divisions which you are intending to put into the line will easily bring your right as far as the Oise."

He had pressed Haig to extend his line a little farther to the south. He gives his reasons for that request in this letter. Haig in his reply on November 2nd writes: —

"As I have already told you, I am prepared to prolong my right up to the Oise; I can even fall in with your wishes by relieving a sector, insignificant in extent, south of the river."

The limit of this further extension was fixed by the two Commanders-in-Chief at Barisis.

The taking-over by the British of the French line up to

Barisis had thus been agreed to between Haig and Pétain by the beginning of November. It is important to note that no extension of the British line further than this took place before the great German offensive in March.

The agreement between the Generals was only the beginning of trouble. Haig thoroughly disliked the idea of parting with divisions which he had depended upon for his mass of manœuvre in the spring renewal of his Flemish campaign. He went back on the arrangement both in substance and in time. He pleaded that he could not spare the necessary divisions to carry out the full extensions he had promised. Even the restricted relief to the French which he undertook was indefinitely postponed.

The French grew impatient at this attitude. M. Clemenceau demanded to know when the promised relief was to take place. The C.I.G.S. telegraphed this query to Haig on December 1st, and got the reply that since the arrangement had been made with General Pétain he had been compelled to send divisions to Italy and to use at Cambrai those detailed to begin the relief on the French Front. As active operations were still in progress, he did not feel justified then in carrying out any extension at all.

This was naturally a very unsatisfactory reply for the French. If we had promised five divisions to Italy, they had undertaken to send six.

Pétain wrote on December 14th to press that the relief should be begun, and told his Government that if it were not carried out he would refuse to continue to accept responsibility for the safety of the French Front. Clemenceau, who strongly supported Pétain, thereupon sent us word that he would himself resign unless the British took over the front as far as Berry-au-bac, an extension thirty-seven miles longer than the one originally requested. We agreed that the arrangement already entered into between the two Commanders-in-

Chief for extension to Barisis must be honourably fulfilled, but we could not assent to the further demand. We succeeded in persuading Clemenceau to allow the matter of the further extension to Berry-au-bac to be referred to the Supreme War Council; and pending its discussion there, the Military Representatives at Versailles were asked to examine the question. Information to this effect was wired to Sir Douglas Haig on December 15th.

The news decided Sir Douglas Haig. Without waiting to see what would be the verdict of Versailles, he met Pétain on December 17th and after giving a number of reasons for delay, agreed to relieve two French divisions by January 10th, and complete the relief to the River Oise before the end of January. This arrangement Pétain accepted, and it was in due course carried out.

Early in January I received an urgent communication from M. Clemenceau pressing us to exercise our authority as a Government to order Haig to agree as to the further extension requested by Pétain. As we were anxious as a Cabinet to obtain Haig's opinions on the military position as a whole, I appealed to him to come over to confer with us on the subject. Haig informed us, when the matter of the extension of the front was raised, that he was on the point of taking over the line up to the River Oise, and that General Pétain seemed to be quite satisfied with this arrangement.

As to the demand made by M. Clemenceau for a further extension, the Permanent Military Representatives at Versailles went carefully into the whole question — the relative strength of the fronts, the opposing enemy forces, the respective needs for relief and training; and reached the conclusion that the logically right point for the juncture of the respective fronts was neither Barisis nor Berry-au-bac, but the left bank of the Ailette on the Laon–Soissons road, a point which was 14 miles beyond Barisis.

The Joint Note of the Military Representatives in which this recommendation was recorded (Joint Note No. 10), was issued on January 10th, 1918. Although Haig and Pétain had reached an agreement with regard to the extension to Barisis, Pétain, backed by Clemenceau, was at this time still pressing for more — in fact, for the extension to Berry-au-bac.

At the Meeting of the Supreme War Council which was held on February 1st, I anticipated to some extent the discussion about extension of the line by proposing that in view of the fact that the French and ourselves had no less than eleven divisions in Italy, we should bring a contingent of Italian troops to France. The minutes record that I said: —

"Before coming to the question of the extension of the British line, or the creation of the reserves, I suggest, if my Italian colleague would consent, that we ought to discuss the question of bringing Italian troops to the Western Front. The alternative is to bring the British and French troops from the Italian to the Western Front. This, however, is undesirable from the point of view of morale. Hence it would be better to bring Italian troops here."

I then called attention to the figures in tables prepared by the Allied Staffs, for the information of the Supreme War Council, and I pointed out that on the Italian Front according to these tables, "there were 1,440,000 Allied compared with 860,000 enemy combatants, a superiority of 580,000 combatants; whereas on the French Front, the Allied superiority was only 160,000 combatants." I further pointed out that the movements of enemy troops was towards the French rather than towards the Italian Front.

Signor Orlando, the Italian Prime Minister, said he was "in principle in entire agreement with Mr. Lloyd George", and he proceeded to support my proposal with emotional warmth. M. Clemenceau summed up the remarks of Signor Orlando and Baron Sonnino in the sense that the Italian Government would leave the decision as to such a movement to the new War Board which it was proposed to set up to take charge of the General Reserve. It is significant of the general attitude of the British and French Staffs that although they knew at that time that German reinforcements for the West were pouring in from Russia, they took no steps to implement this valuable Italian promise until after March 21st. This indifference or slackness was partly due to their lack of appreciation of the fighting value of the Italian infantry, who, it is only fair to say, fought well when they ultimately came to France. But so far as the French were concerned the slackness was partly attributable to their suspicion that the proposal, if adopted, would be used by the British as a further excuse for not taking up more line.

The prospect of a possible reinforcement of the French Front by Italian troops did not therefore avail to appease the urgency of the French demand for a further extension of the British line to Berry-au-bac. When Note No. 10 came up for review on February 2nd, M. Clemenceau proposed that since the point on the left bank of the Ailette was that fixed by the joint advice of the military experts it should be accepted, and the Commanders-in-Chief be asked to agree to arrangements for the carrying out of the recommendation. But Haig promptly protested.

With the effectives at present at his disposal, it was impossible for him to extend his front beyond the point that he had agreed upon with General Pétain. . . . With the utmost desire to comply in every way possible with the French demands, he felt bound to point out to the Supreme War Council that with the troops now at his disposal it was quite out of the question for him to take over any more front.

I then intervened to ask General Pétain whether he had agreed with Sir Douglas Haig that the British Front should extend to Barisis only. Pétain replied that —

It was true that there had been an agreement between himself and Sir Douglas Haig to the effect that the British Front should be extended to Barisis. Later, however, he had been compelled to ask for a further considerable extension. . . .

Inasmuch as it has been suggested that the British Government, and particularly myself, were responsible for forcing Sir Douglas Haig, against his better judgment, to accept this further extension, I will now quote fully the statement which I made upon the recommendation of the Supreme Council: —

"Mr. Lloyd George asked that before the Joint Note was adopted he might be allowed to put before the Supreme War Council certain very serious considerations. The Field-Marshal had said that he could hardly be held responsible for the security of his front if he had to extend his line. He had pointed out that the most vital parts of the Allied Fronts were held by the British. The British lines of communication ran parallel to their front, and the enemy were only ten miles off; this constituted a very dangerous situation. Further, an advance of a few kilometres by the Germans on the French Front would not be a very grave matter. If, however, the Germans advanced only six miles in Flanders they would deprive us of certain valuable coal mines which at present provide no less than ten million tons of coal a year. If they were deprived of this supply of coal it would have to be made up by Great Britain. This would mean a large diversion of labour to the coal mines, and of tonnage for the transportation of coal across the Channel. The second point was partly military and partly political in character. The French soldier by the law of his country — and he would remind the Council that the French were fighting on their own soil — got leave every four months; the

British soldier on the other hand, got leave only once a year. The British Army had come to be aware of this fact, which was causing the gravest dissatisfaction. No doubt this disparity in regard to the granting of leave was in part due to the shortage of tonnage, but it was a serious consideration which could not be ignored. He would remind the Supreme War Council that the British Commander-in-Chief had said that if he had to extend his front he could not be responsible for the security of his line. If, therefore, the Council decided to accept the recommendation of the Military Representatives, a very grave responsibility would rest upon them. There were then three considerations which he wished to put before his colleagues: —

"1. That the British hold a line which covered indispensable ports and valuable coal mines, neither of which was it possible for us to relinquish.

"2. The question of leave.

"3. The British had borne the brunt of the fighting during the past year, and as they had advanced their line in many places it was impossible to give the men the rest they badly needed, as it was necessary to prepare new lines of defence. Further, these lines had to be constructed in the abominable climate of Flanders, which was very different from the climate of Italy, for instance.

"If in addition to the dissatisfaction caused by the disparity in regard to leave, by the necessity of having to forgo their well-earned rest in order to construct new lines of defence, the British Army were told that they had to take over a new portion of the French Front they would be seriously disheartened to say the least of it. He therefore would again press that a solution of the difficulty might be found by transferring Italian divisions to France. A large contribution of Italian troops to the Western Front would, in his opinion, best solve the most difficult problem which M. Clemenceau and he had to consider. Mr. Lloyd George thought that the question of the extension of the line and that of the transference of Italian troops to Flanders should be considered together."

Signor Orlando then gave general support to my plea, and he referred to the proposal which I had made at the preceding meeting, that the difficulties should be solved by inviting the Italian Government to send divisions to France to take over this part of the line. He concluded by saying: —

He agreed with Mr. Lloyd George that the question of the extension of the line and of Italian troops being sent to France must be considered together, and that they were questions for the deliberation of their military experts.

After a reply from General Pétain, a note was passed to me — as far as I can recollect, from Sir Maurice Hankey — stating to my great surprise that Field-Marshal Haig had changed his mind and did not now view the proposed extension as altogether unacceptable. I then intervened further to say (I will now quote the Minute): —

"Mr. Lloyd George said he understood that the Field-Marshal would now be prepared to accept the recommendations in Joint Note No. 10 [*i.e.*, the recommendation for further extension] in principle subject to an agreement between himself and General Pétain as to the method of giving effect to it. The resolution therefore that was about to be moved must not be regarded as an order requiring immediate execution."

The actual Resolution that was passed in reference to this respect is recorded in the following terms: —

"Resolution in regard to the extension of the British Front. The Supreme War Council adopt Note 10; subject to the time and method of the extension of the British Line being left for arrangement between General Pétain and the Field-Marshal Sir Douglas Haig."

Haig and Pétain subsequently met and came to an understanding to take no further action for the time being on this troubled question.

These, therefore, are the actual facts as to what took place. I proposed that the difficulties which had arisen on the question of the extension of the British line should be solved by the sending of eleven Italian divisions to France in substitution for the British and French divisions on the Italian Front. The Italian Prime Minister warmly accepted the proposition and was prepared to recommend it to his military authorities. When the actual discussion of the proposals of the Supreme Council for extension came up for discussion I strongly supported Sir Douglas Haig's protest, and again urged the alternative of Italian troops. The Italian Prime Minister supported my protest, and again urged the idea of Italian troops. Sir Douglas Haig then, without any previous consultation with me, withdrew his objection and agreed with Pétain to take over further line in accordance with the recommendations of the Council. In actual fact, this extension which Haig agreed to in principle, even after my strong protest at his request and on his behalf, was not carried out, and the only result of his untimely intervention was that the proposal for making arrangements to bring eleven Italian divisions to France was dropped, and not revived until after the March offensive. The actual extension which took place was the one that Haig had himself agreed to with Pétain at Conferences where no member of the Government was present.

In view of these facts, of which there is official record in contemporary documents, it is rather hard that the whole of the responsibility should be placed on my shoulders and that it should be suggested that Haig was compelled by me to take over a line which he had not sufficient troops to defend.

I would specially draw attention here to the very misleading account of what took place as the result of the Versailles meeting which is given in the Official History of the War: —

"At the meeting which took place between Sir Douglas Haig and General Pétain on the 17th December the latter urged as reasons for the extension, that the British offensive operations had come to an end, and that there were fears of a German attack on his troops near Châlons and through Switzerland. Sir Douglas Haig represented that the British troops after the recent severe fighting required a period of rest, and that the strength of units, depleted by casualties, was not being replenished by drafts from England; but nevertheless, he would relieve two divisions on the 10th January and endeavour to take over as far as the Oise by the end of the month; but the precise date for the later relief could only be settled when the situation became clearer. This arrangement General Pétain accepted. However favourable the situation might become, he had no intention of making any 'main attack' before August, thus confirming his earlier statement to Sir Douglas Haig.

"It was not until the 10th January, after an interval of over three weeks, that the Military Representatives at Versailles made their formal recommendation, without giving reasons, that the point of junction of the French and British Armies should be on the left bank of the Ailette, between that river and the Soissons–Laon road, about 17 miles from the Oise, but left the exact point to be decided by the two Commanders-in-Chief, who eventually fixed it as 5½ miles eastwards of the Oise."

This omits every reference to the objections I raised to any further extension of the line, and it creates an impression that as a result of what took place at Versailles, Haig had to make a further extension of his line, and that on a recommendation which was never formulated before January 10th. As a matter of fact, Haig never extended his line a single yard beyond the limit fixed in an agreement which he had entered into with Pétain on October 18th, 1917.

This paragraph is probably due to one of those oversights to which all historians are liable. Whoever wrote this misrepresentation must have had in front of him the actual

Minutes of the Meeting.[1] The least I can say about the writer who, with such information at his disposal, penned such a distortion, is that he made a slovenly use of the documents at his disposal.

Was the extension of our line which took place in January justified? It is clear that the grounds for it were both military and political. On the political side it must be remembered that feeling in France had reached a state of irritation at what appeared to be a flagrantly unequal proportion of the front held by the British: this feeling, for which there was much warrant, was a fact that could not be ignored or argued away. In order to maintain good relations with our Ally, and ease the tension of French public opinion, worn down by the long and bitter sufferings of the War, it was essential that we should make some concession of this sort, unless it could be shown beyond peradventure that such action would inevitably entail disaster for the Allied Armies. The military considerations were just as strong. Prior to the extension, the British held less than 100 miles of front, the French more than 350 miles, although the British forces were two-thirds the size of the French. Even after the British had added these 28 miles to their front, they held about 125 miles to the French 325 miles of front. In view of the far greater density of the British forces, it would be ludicrous to suggest that this comparatively small addition to the line they held was from a military standpoint unsound, taking into consideration the requirements of the Allied Front in France as a whole. After all due weight has been given to other grounds alleged by Sir Douglas Haig for objecting to taking over this sector, the fact stands out that his main objection was because using part of his forces for this would render him less capable of resuming his Flanders offensive in the spring. He urged in this connec-

---

[1] He rectifies it in a later page (p. 79) without calling attention to the previous misstatement.

tion that the alternative to continuing the offensive was to let the initiative pass to the enemy. But since in any event he could not have resumed a Flanders offensive as early as March, because the state of the ground there would have rendered it impossible, the Germans still would have been free to take the initiative as they did, further south, in March, if Haig had kept a larger force at Passchendaele, and the St. Quentin sector had been still held by the attenuated French Army.

The extremely able Staff officers working at Versailles — and they included both Italian and American experts — were in fact satisfied that on military grounds the British Army should have taken over, not less, but 12 miles more than they actually did. That was military advice. There was no politician on the body of experts who examined the question. This operation of taking over has often been alleged as one of the various causes which contributed to the German breakthrough on this front in March, 1918. That allegation cannot be justified on military grounds.

The British had far more ample resources for holding this sector strongly than the French. The trouble was that they did not distribute them wisely. This is a matter into which I shall have to enter more fully when I come to the dispositions made for the great battle which all knew was coming.

CHAPTER VIII

THE FALL OF ROBERTSON

Manipulation of reserves essential for victory — Anti-Government intrigues of military clique — Robertson's anger at being left off Versailles Committee — First hints of the storm — *Morning Post* telegram — Repington's position — Comments of the *Globe* — Milner's protest — My interview with Haig — *Morning Post* article — Allied plans betrayed — A call to revolt — Derby refuses to join rebels — Cabinet discusses *Morning Post* article — Culprits condemned and fined — Debate in Parliament — Asquith's attack — My reply — Danger of betraying valuable information — Appeal for confidence — Problem of Robertson's attitude — Choice between Versailles and C.I.G.S. offered him — Balfour's interview with Robertson — Threat of military dictation — Choosing Robertson's successor: character of Sir H. Wilson — Wilson's friends in the Cabinet — Discussion with Derby and Haig — Derby's resignation withdrawn — My statement in Parliament — Reasons for Versailles arrangements — Offers to Robertson — Parliament does not challenge decision — Wilson appointed — Waste of time aids wreck of scheme for reserves — Threat to national unity: Haig's patriotic attitude.

THE decisions of Versailles on the formation of a General Reserve were designed to give the Allies for the first time the benefit conferred by a united front, first in defence and then in attack. The Germans had enjoyed that advantage on the Western Front right through the War and it had enabled them to hold long lines against armies which had a numerical superiority of 50 per cent. When they saw that the Nivelle offensive was impending and that they were to be attacked on a great scale by preponderant numbers, they constituted a strong reserve behind their lines, of divisions drawn partly from the sectors of the Western line from which they could be best spared, and partly from Roumania. Hence a defence which was so successful that it put the French Army out of action as a seriously offensive force for the rest of the year.

Had the Versailles project been put into operation a

similar stunning rebuff would have been given to the German spring offensive after perhaps a slight preliminary success, and the German collapse would have come sooner and the British losses would not have been nearly so heavy. British and French divisions would have been drawn in time from parts of the line where they were too thick on the ground, and as it became increasingly evident at what point the German attack was coming, the reserves would have moved into positions where they would have been readily available when the German attack developed. Divisions would also have been brought from Italy — either French, British or Italian. Arrangements might have been made for conveying British divisions from Palestine and substituting Indian divisions from Mesopotamia, where the Allies had a superiority of six to one. All this was done later on. But it was after the worst defeat that had befallen the British Army during the whole of the War.

After the Versailles meeting there began to ferment on our home front events which rapidly developed into a serious political crisis and for a few days threatened the life of the Ministry, and paralysed our efforts to deal firmly with the hesitancies of the Commander-in-Chief on the question of the General Reserve. The trouble arose from the machinations of that military clique which had thwarted every effort I had made during the War either to equip the Army, or to prevent a wasteful use being made of the enormous resources in men and material placed at their disposal, or to achieve that effective unity of front which alone could enable us to make a decisive use of the advantages we possessed in men, material, and command of the sea.

That the German General Staff depended upon the activities of this junta is demonstrated by one of the documents published by General Ludendorff after the War. In a memorandum which is marked "Very Secret" attention is called to the weaknesses of the Alliance with which the Central Powers are confronted. One of them is thus described: —

"Another disruptive element will be the *English Military Party* [the italics are theirs, not mine] which will come forward and try at last to get rid of the Lloyd George they loathe so heartily."

We were about to witness a very determined effort — not the first nor the last — made by this party to form a cabal which would overthrow the existing War Cabinet and especially its Chief, and enthrone a Government which would be practically the nominee and menial of this military party. Exactly the same situation had arisen in Germany in July, 1916. The German Chancellor, Bethmann-Hollweg, determined to end the War, if he could, by a negotiated peace; so Hindenburg, Ludendorff, and their military clique overthrew him, and from that point onwards took over the political direction of Germany. The causes of the German defeat were investigated by the Reichstag after the War, and many statesmen of the Central Powers have written on the subject. No one can doubt that the cause of Germany's defeat lay in the usurpation of political powers by the military leaders. Bismarck had had almost exactly the same trouble in 1870 and 1866, but, with a great effort, had checked this attempted usurpation. Bethmann-Hollweg could not: in fact, it was their political system that failed the Germans. The same attempt was made by a military clique here, but did not succeed. Our political system did not fail us.

General Pétain and Marshal Haig did not relish the idea of having their reserves commanded by Foch. Not only did it pass the control of the forthcoming campaign into Foch's hands, but it removed divisions from their direct control in order to create such a Reserve. The hostility of the two Commanders-in-Chief, however, did not show itself immediately. Sir William Robertson, on the other hand, lost no time in taking action of a hostile character. When Sir Henry Wilson had first sketched out the project of the General Reserve to him he seemed quite enamoured of the idea, but in its original form the plan provided that the Controlling Board should consist of the three Chiefs of the General Staff, of whom Sir William Robertson would be one. That provision was dropped in the course of the discussions at Versailles because there were obvious practical objections to it. The General Reserve was intended to be brought into action in the event of a sudden emergency. Even before the emergency arose the intelligence received in the course of the coming weeks would involve a rearrangement in the location of the reserves. It is evident that neither the Italian nor the British Chiefs of the Staff could be present to take part in a decision until a great many fateful hours had passed. That is why it was imperative that the members of the Board should always be on the spot, ready for continuous consultation and decision without a moment's delay. As soon as the Supreme Council came to that conclusion, Sir William Robertson altered his attitude towards the whole scheme. A brilliant witness of the proceedings at Versailles writes: —

"Robertson, not unnaturally, was furious. This was quite visible. Long after the Supreme War Council had risen, after passing this resolution, and only a few secretaries being left in the room, Robertson still remained sitting alone in his place, motionless, his head resting on his hand, glaring silently in front of him." [1]

The first intimation the Cabinet received of brewing trouble was at a meeting of the War Cabinet held immediately on my return from Versailles, at which I reported the decisions arrived at by the Supreme War Council, dwelling particularly upon the proposals in reference to the formation of the General Reserve. Lord Derby, who was accompanied to the meeting by Sir William Robertson, stated that he had

[1] Peter E. Wright: "At the Supreme War Council", p. 61.

not yet had sufficient time to study the reports submitted in regard to this question, and therefore must reserve judgment thereon. In reply I pointed out that as the matter had been decided unanimously by the Allied Representatives, and by myself and Lord Milner, who had been endowed by the War Cabinet with full authority to deal with this question on their behalf, I trusted that the matter would be considered by the Army Council in a most helpful spirit, and that there would be no delay in preparing the necessary Order in Council, if such were required, to give effect to their decision.

The first open shot was fired by the *Morning Post* in a telegram which it printed on February 8th from its "Military Correspondent in Paris", and which ran as follows: —

"Paris, 5th February.

"The decisions of the recent Inter-Allied War Council regarding the control of British troops in the field are reported to be of such a strange character that Parliament should demand the fullest details and a Parliamentary Committee should examine them at once and take the opinions of our General Staff and of our Commanders in the field concerning the new arrangements."

There is no secret about the origin and the inspiration of this message. It was sent by Colonel Repington, who afterwards admitted his authorship and came out into the open under his own name with communications in the same vein. He was on intimate terms with Sir William Robertson, the C.I.G.S., and an active collaborator with the military clique which, as I have previously related, was intriguing with all the discontented elements in politics to overthrow the Government. Repington was the favoured confidant of the General Staff, whenever there were any criticisms that they wished to see directed against the War Cabinet and its policy. They supplied him with all the necessary material in the form of tit-bits of information, carefully selected, of course, and of a tendencious character. His diaries, where he records the interviews he had from time to time with Sir William Robertson and his principal coadjutor, the Director of Military Operations, Sir Frederick Maurice, and some mysterious person in the confidence of the War Office, who is referred to by Repington as "X", show how complete was his collaboration with the General Staff.

The communication from their Military Correspondent appeared in the *Morning Post* on February 8th, and the same evening the *Globe* reprinted what they called the "disquieting telegram" published by their contemporary. They further proceeded to pass upon it comments which are full of significance having regard to what happened subsequently: —

". . . It may be hoped that, as Mr. Asquith was responsible for entrusting the Higher Command to Sir Douglas Haig, as Commander-in-Chief in the field, and Sir William Robertson as Chief of the Imperial General Staff in London — who both to a peculiar degree enjoy the confidence of the British Army and the British nation — he will not stand by and allow this arrangement to be broken up to gratify the whim of any individuals, however important. It may also be hoped that the House of Commons, which claims to be the seat of power, will refuse to allow itself to be elbowed out of its proper functions, and that at least we may be allowed to know what is going on behind the scenes, as no arrangement can make for military efficiency that precipitates a crisis in our Higher Command on the eve of a new campaign. Is there or is there not a Generalissimo?"

This article was sent to me by Lord Milner with the following covering letter: —

"17 Great College Street, S.W.,
8/2/18.

"My dear Prime Minister,
"You have no doubt seen the enclosed from the *Globe*.
"I think the sooner we make a move the better. This kind of thing cannot be allowed to go on.

"About Haig, I greatly doubt whether he would make common cause with only W.O. people against the Government. I think he is too loyal to lend himself to such proceedings.

"On the other hand, I do think that he is likely to offer a resistance of his own to the proposal that he should allow any of his divisions to be placed in a General Reserve. He will use all the arguments with which we are so familiar, and he will never be convinced — as he is incapable of seeing any point of view but his own — that the creation of a General Reserve may end in giving him a much larger army than he has at present.

"Now the creation of the General Reserve is the key to the whole business. It is not only clearly right in strategy, but it is the basis of our quite good understanding with the French.

"It is no use having a great rumpus and getting rid of Robertson, if the policy is to be side-tracked, for quite different reasons, by Haig.

"But Haig will, I believe, obey orders, if he once clearly understands that your mind is made up. And if he were to stick his toes in the ground, which I do not anticipate, it would be better to lose both Haig and Robertson than to continue at the mercy of both or either of them. The situation is much too critical for that and no time should be lost. The Army would be quite happy, if the worst came to the worst, with Plumer and Harrington vice Haig and Bertie Lawrence, and would not then so much care who was the C.I.G.S. Du Cane, in fact, would fill the bill.

" 'Plumer as C.-in-C.,' a brigadier fresh from the field said to me the other day, 'would be worth ten extra divisions.' Extravagant, of course. I merely quote as showing that any change which brought Plumer more to the front would be popular.

"I don't *want* this, I like the plan you sketched this morning. My only point is that, *if* Haig were intractable, I believe we could still deal with the situation. The one vital thing is, since there must be a change, that we should be able once for all to get free to do what we know to be right.

Yours very sincerely,

MILNER."

As it turned out, the letter underestimated the formidable difficulties to be encountered here and in France when it came to overruling the opposition of the military chiefs. In order to ease matters I proposed that Robertson should be our representative on the Board of Control. This involved his vacating the position of C.I.G.S. In that event it was proposed that Sir Henry Wilson should be appointed to that post.

Sir Douglas Haig came over on the 9th and I had an interview with him and the Secretary of State for War on the situation. I wrote Milner the following letter which gives my impressions of that interview at the time: —

"9th February, 1918.

"My dear Milner,

"I have had an afternoon of it with Haig and Derby. Haig was quite reasonable. He did not quite like H. W. coming here, and thought the Army might be very shocked; but he said that was a matter for the Government. In fact, his attitude was perfectly correct. Derby, Haig and Macpherson thought that to make Robertson Deputy would be to humiliate him, and they thought it quite unnecessary in view of the fact that Wilson was made the Chief Adviser of the Government. Subject to that, the document was signed by Derby, and he is to see the King later on about it.

"Wully is to be told to-morrow by Macpherson, who is motoring over to Eastbourne to communicate the news to him. Derby is delighted with our change of plans; and as we had only the choice of three or four doubtful second bests, I am firmly convinced that this is the best of them.

Ever sincerely,

D. LLOYD GEORGE."

But although at that date Haig seems to have professed his readiness to stand honourably by the Versailles agreement to which he was a party, Robertson was not in the least propitiated. The *Globe* article was a clear indication that a formidable conspiracy was being worked up and that forces had already been gathered with a view to making a serious political attack on the Government in Parliament. Robertson and his friends meant this time to fight to a finish, and they had every hope of being able to build up a Parliamentary combination drawn from all parties which would reverse the Versailles decision, supplant the Government, and substitute for it one which would make Robertson virtual dictator for the rest of the War, as Hindenburg was in Germany and by the same means.

The next step of this clique, in its reckless disregard of the interests of the nation in a Great War, transcends anything for which — fortunately — there is any precedent in any war ever waged by this country. The conspirators decided to publish the war plans of the Allies for the coming German offensive. Let it be borne in mind that these war plans were not amateur schemes sketched out by presumptuous politicians and forced on unwilling and horrified soldiers. They were prepared by a body of able and experienced Generals — one of them acknowledged to be far and away the greatest military brain and leader thrown up by the Allies. There was no politician present at the meetings of the military members of the Supreme War Council which initiated and worked out these plans. They were then further considered and discussed at a gathering where the two Commanders-in-Chief and Sir William Robertson were present, and there they were adopted unanimously. Haig and Pétain were there and never dissented. On February 11th there appeared in the *Morning Post* a long article signed by Colonel Repington in which the proposal to set up a General Reserve under the command of General Foch was completely revealed to friend and foe alike. The article was headed: —

THE WAR COUNCIL.
PARIS DISCUSSIONS.
REMARKABLE REPORTS.

It began by asseverating that: —

". . . Prime Ministers and others have recently resolved themselves into a Council of War, have rivalled it in strategy, and have exclusively occupied themselves in teaching soldiers how and where to make war."

As I have already pointed out, I was not present at the meetings of the Military Representatives of the Supreme War Council where these plans in the first instance were formulated, nor was any civilian representative there. Foch would be the last man to submit to any dictation on questions of strategy from anyone, and certainly not from any civilian. He stood up to the redoubtable Clemenceau, who was his civilian chief, and that needed some courage.

But the essence of the article comes when under the heading of "A New Decision" Colonel Repington disclosed the military plan for countering the impending German attack. This is how he defends his treachery: —

". . . Newspapers have been strictly enjoined not to refer to one of the chief results of the Council. In this way it is hoped that criticism will be burked. But there are times when we must take our courage in both hands and risk consequences. One of the decisions taken is against all sound principles and can only breed confusion in a defensive campaign such as that to which we are restricted at present. . . ."

He then proceeds to give away the whole scheme: the reserve of manœuvre — its functions — the body set up to control it — the name of the President; and he emphasises the salient feature of the project, that it is to be independent of the two Commanders-in-Chief. There is a passage which shows that the inspiring motive of this malignant and treasonable article was not so much hatred of any particular politician — although Milner and I came in for special denunciation — but jealousy of authority conferred upon another set of Generals held up to contempt as "the Versailles soldiers."

". . . At present it is the duty of the Commander of the General Staff to issue the orders of the War Cabinet to the Armies. But now there interposes the Versailles soldiers, under the Presidency of General Foch, and the British General on this body is not apparently under the War Office, nor was he appointed by them. He owes his elevation to Mr. Lloyd George's favour alone. . . ."

The head and front of the "Versailles soldiers" was Foch, the greatest soldier of the War, and General Weygand, one of the ablest Staff officers produced by the War. With all respect for Sir William Robertson's admirable qualifications, he had not commanded in any of the battles fought in the War. In fact he had never been in action. His right-hand man and the architect of his downfall, Sir Frederick Maurice, was as comfortably placed as any politician in a Department at the War Office when the worst fighting of the War by the British Army began, and there he remained up to the hour of his dismissal. This invaluable piece of information as to the Allied plan of campaign was passed on to the Germans by partisans in a quarrel between rival Generals.

Repington, having exposed his real aim and motive, then incited the Army Council to an act of insubordination against the Government: —

". . . The Army Council will, I hope, make a firm and united stand in the interests of the rest of the Army, and will make the position perfectly clear. Everybody has to go 'over the top' sooner or later in this War, and it may now be the Army Council's turn."

Which of the men on the Army Council had even been "over the top" in this War? The article ends by saying that "this is the situation which Parliament must clear up in such a manner as it thinks best." The Army having given the cue by rebelling against authority, Parliament was then "to do its bit."

Repington did not only disclose to the enemy the existence of the General Reserve and its mechanism, but the entire plans of the Allies for the year. They were embodied in Resolutions which provided that the Allies would stand on the defensive in France, and resist the German attack with the scheme of the General Reserve, and that Allenby should take the offensive in Palestine. Repington's article does not disclose in a general way the discussions of the Supreme War Council and its decisions; he speaks with minute precision. He quotes from the very English text of the Minutes of the proceedings: he uses my own words as recorded then, "the delivery of a knock-out blow to Turkey." We had discussed Allenby's difficulty, and this discussion is in the Minutes. The words of the Minutes reappear in the *Morning Post* article: "How long will it take for our broad-gauge railway" to advance? No one could doubt that Repington had seen the text of the Minutes of the proceedings of the Supreme War Council, and (it will be noted) the English text. In fact, Repington admits it: on February 4th, 1918, being in Paris, he wrote in his diary: —

"This morning there is published an official and completely fantastic *compte rendu* of the proceedings of the War Council. . . . It tells absolutely nothing of the decisions taken."

He could not know this (which was, of course, true) unless he had seen the text of the Minutes and of the Resolutions.

I know nothing comparable to this betrayal in the whole

of our history. It was immediately appreciated in Germany. The *Morning Post* article appeared on February 11th; Professor Delbrück, the famous German authority on military and strategic questions, expressed his thanks for it in the issue of his magazine [1] of February 24th. He worked in close connection with the General Staff, and the information was evidently conveyed to him by their Intelligence Section.

Repington's betrayal might, and ought to, have decided the War. Professor Delbrück was one of the chief witnesses before the Commission of the Reichstag which later was to investigate the causes of the catastrophe of 1918 and his views, set out in writing, were virtually adopted by the Commission. These views are to be found at rather greater length in a book of his.[2] He pays me the compliment of saying that my plan for the Allies — a defensive in France and an offensive side-show elsewhere — would also have been the best plan for Germany to pursue, and, in terms, states that "Lloyd George, the civilian, appreciated the military experiences of the first four years better than Ludendorff." [3] Repington's disclosures, as he points out, enabled the German High Command to execute such a plan in perfect security. For it informed the German High Command that the Allies were not to take the offensive in France, and so enabled German divisions to be moved elsewhere from France without any risk. Delbrück was a Nationalist in politics and highly patriotic: great as were Repington's services to Germany, yet Delbrück is shocked by the perfidy, and applies the word "treason" (*Landesverrat*) to it.[4]

This extraordinary effusion was given prominence in the columns of the *Morning Post* and the benediction of a leading article. Had it appeared in the *Daily Herald* or the *For-*

[1] The *Preussiche Jahrbuch*.
[2] "Ludendorff's Selbstporträt."
[3] *Ibid.*, p. 52.
[4] *Ibid.*, p. 55.

ward or any other Socialist journal, we should have been constantly reminded in every political conflict waged since, how the Socialists betrayed secret information of great military value to the enemy at the most critical stage of the War.

Entries in the Repington Diaries show that this was not an indiscretion due to the impulse of an individual but that it was the first move in a concerted attack on a very wide front.

Here is an extract: —

"Saturday, 9th February. Met Gwynne at the Bath Club. We compared notes and experiences. After I had told him what I had learned, he told me that there was a big row on here, and that he hoped the Army Council were all going to stand firm. Asquith has stated that he will speak on the debate on the Address next Tuesday, and Gwynne and I agreed that I should write and expose the Paris proceedings either Monday or Tuesday. Gwynne is going to see Derby and try to hearten him up, and is all for fighting this matter out."

Great pressure from many quarters was brought to bear on Lord Derby to join the conspirators. They were under the impression that they had captured his sympathies and they were profoundly disappointed when subsequently he failed to follow their fortunes. I am convinced that they were not justified in relying upon his coöperation. There was soon evidence that the ramifications were not confined to one party. A body calling itself the Unionist War Committee in the Commons "passed strong resolutions warmly condemning the attacks on the Generals." These resolutions were brought to me by Lord Salisbury. I challenged him to point to one attack which I had made or encouraged on the Generals. Whatever I might think of them personally, I knew the importance of not undermining public confidence in them as long as they held their positions. The moment the Army lost their belief in their leaders they could not be expected any longer to face the horrors of the battlefield or to endure the chronic discomfort of the trenches. The mutiny in the French Army had taught us what might be expected from troops that had ceased to trust their Generals. At home I knew that such a feeling would spread the unrest. I therefore went so far as to take no steps to correct the impression of resounding victories created by false or incomplete reports from the front and in all my public utterances I referred in eulogistic terms to Haig personally. My only public criticism was directed to the lack of co-ordination between the Allied Armies. It is one of the greatest difficulties encountered by statesmen who have the supreme responsibility of directing the resources of a country in a war and are held accountable to public opinion for failure, that they cannot always openly state the facts as they know them until the conflict is over. And the necessity of pouring glowing panegyrics on Generals who did not merit the praise lavished on them, made it less easy — indeed almost impossible — to correct their calamitous errors. All this I pointed out to my critics at this time. But nothing availed. The train had been laid and I knew that when Parliament met it would be fired. The powder for the assailants was supplied from the War Office.

The treachery of the *Morning Post* was considered at a meeting of the Cabinet held on the day of the publication. The War Cabinet recognised that: —

"The article appeared to give valuable military information to the enemy, and constituted a definite breach of Regulation 18 of the Defence of the Realm Regulations, and also a defiance of the decision of the War Cabinet, as to the undesirability of any reference being made in British newspapers regarding the formation or command of a General Inter-Allied Reserve."

As a proof that Lord Derby was not implicated in these intrigues, I have a note taken at the time which showed that he denounced the article in question as clearly of a most mischievous character. He believed that it had been written from Paris, and said that it was clear that Colonel Repington had become acquainted with information of a secret and confidential character which had now been made public by the Editor of the *Morning Post*. Whether the plans were improperly revealed to Repington in London or Paris, they ought never to have been made public.

The Director of Military Intelligence stated that he had understood the article in question had been submitted to the Press Bureau on the previous evening. The Press Bureau had communicated with him, and Sir Edward Cook had informed him that he had told the Editor that the article infringed Regulation 18 under the Defence of the Realm Act, and ignored the special request issued to the Press on February 4th.[1]

Sir Edward Cook read to the War Cabinet portions of the article in its original form as first submitted to the Press Bureau. He said he had endeavoured to censor it, but its whole character was such that amendment was practically impossible. He had accordingly returned it to Mr. Gwynne with a letter conveying the warning above described. In spite of this fact, the article had appeared in a slightly amended form.

I pointed out that this was not the first occasion on which Colonel Repington had written articles for publication which were of the utmost value to the enemy. Further, in connection with the Cabinet inquiries regarding the man-power situation, Colonel Repington had written articles, published by the *Morning Post*, containing figures regarding our strength and reserves. In fact Repington in his diaries boasts

[1] Press Bureau, Serial D.621.

of these feats: he writes on January 24th, 1918: "My article exposing the failure of the War Cabinet to maintain the Army came out in the *Morning Post* to-day without going to the Press Bureau and caused much excitement." Also an article damaging to British interests had been sent by him for publication in America.

It was decided to consult the Solicitor-General and the Director of Public Prosecutions. In the subsequent discussion, the Solicitor-General called attention to the fact that the Supreme Council at Versailles had on February 6th passed a Resolution on the subject of the danger of Press revelations of the plans adopted at the recent Meeting. This Resolution said: —

"The Military Representatives wish respectfully to draw the attention of the Governments represented on the Supreme War Council to the undesirability for military reasons, of any public discussion in the Press or otherwise of the arrangements now being taken in hand for the creation and employment of an Inter-Allied General Reserve."

It was urged that unless action was taken in a case such as this against a wealthy and prominent London newspaper, it would be quite impossible to take proceedings if necessary against smaller Labour newspapers in future.

The difficulty we experienced was in framing the charge in such a way as to make it impossible to give further publicity to the actual plans agreed upon at Versailles. Any implication that the article contained a disclosure of the real character of the Versailles scheme would in itself aggravate the mischief. The charge had therefore to be confined to a breach of one of the Regulations of the Defence of the Realm. The culprits thus escaped with a fine.

Repington published with pride a letter he received after his conviction from Sir William Robertson, in the course of which this General Officer, who but recently held the most exalted office in the British Army, writes to a person who has been convicted of publishing the secret plans of the Allied Armies, condoling with him on the greatness of his sacrifice, and assures him that they had both done what was best for the country. No wonder he adds, "I am heartily sick of the whole sordid business of the past month" — Sordid indeed!

It did not end with the publication of the details of the Allied military plans in the Press. A concerted effort was made to secure even more details and fuller and more authentic publicity in Parliament. No prosecution would lie against a Minister who was forced by Parliamentary pressure to furnish information.

Parliament met on February 12th. It had been conveyed to me that Asquith as Leader of the Opposition would interrogate me as to recent events. But I was unable to ascertain through the recognised channels of communication what questions were to be put to me, although I endeavoured to do so. I was told that Asquith was out of town and would not be back before the meeting of the House. I mention this fact because something turns on it. I informed his Deputy, Mr. Reginald M'Kenna, that I was prepared to give Mr. Asquith personally and privately the information he sought as to the Versailles decisions but that I could not do so in public for obvious reasons. I received no reply to this communication. Mr. Asquith made no allusion to it in his speech and proceeded to demand a public revelation of what had occurred in reference to the Reserves. I had therefore to inform the House of the offer I had made.

Asquith, with the skill of the practised debater, opened the attack with a glowing eulogy on the "two great soldiers", Sir Douglas Haig and Sir William Robertson. "There are no two men in the whole of Europe whose military judgment I would more unhesitatingly accept." The fight against the Government was to be presented in the form of an issue between Sir Douglas Haig and Sir William Robertson on the one hand and myself on the other. It was a dexterous move. He meant to use the popularity of these two distinguished soldiers as a weapon with which to slay the Government. He then proceeded to cross-examine me as to the Versailles decision. He disclaimed any desire to seek information as to the result of the deliberations of the Conference so far as they related to military and strategic operations. But he wanted to know in what respect the Allied Governments had departed from their promise not to confer any executive authority on the Supreme Council, and what were the new functions and new duties undertaken by the Council. This is exactly what I proposed to give him in private had he responded to my invitation. But it must have been obvious to him — for he must have been fully informed on the subject by the General Staff with whom he was in touch — that I could not reveal the executive functions given to the Board without also disclosing the strategic purpose we had in view of the creation of a General Reserve and the way in which it would work in the battle. And I could not give information to the House as to the extent to which our decision affected the powers either of the Chief of the General Staff or the Commander-in-Chief without entering fully into details as to the working of our plan and the constitution of the Board that would exercise the control.

At the time I was suffering from a severe cold with a temperature, but I felt that only one who had attended the deliberations of the Allied statesmen and Generals could deal with the situation. I replied to Asquith: —

"My Rt. Hon. friend asked me a question with regard to the Versailles Conference, and he seemed to think that it was possible to answer without giving away any information as to the conduct of our actual military operations. There is no use giving partial information, and I think that if he reflects — even from the indications which he has seen as to the character of the decisions there — he will find that it is impossible to make any statement to the House as to the decisions which were taken without giving information as to the plans of the Allies. . . ."

I pointed out how the situation had changed since November owing to the certainty that Russia had withdrawn from the War and that, in spite of pledges given by her to the contrary to the Russians, Germany was withdrawing troops from that frontier in order to attack us in the West: —

"That was the situation with which we were confronted at Versailles. Up to this year, there was no attack which the Germans could bring to bear upon either our Army or the French Army which could not, in the main, be dealt with by the reserves of each individual Army. The situation is completely changed by the enormous reinforcements brought from the East to the West; and the Allied representatives at Versailles had to consider the best method of dealing with the situation, which was a completely different one from any situation with which they had been previously confronted. They had to deal with a situation where it may be necessary — where it is absolutely essential — that the whole strength of the Allied Armies — France, Great Britain, Italy and America — should be made available for the point at which the attack comes. Where will the blow come? Will it come here or there? Who can tell? All you know is that it is preparing. They have got a gigantic railway system behind which they may swing troops here or there. It is essential that arrangements should be made by which the Allies shall treat their Armies as one, to meet the danger and menace wherever it comes.

"That was the problem with which we were confronted at Versailles. If we had not dealt with it, we should have been guilty of a gross dereliction of duty. What happened there? In the old Conferences to which I have been accustomed military members met together, and when the civilian members met, the military members came with a written document saying what they had decided. I do not mind saying that at such a Conference, to discuss strategy was a pure farce. But here you had, for purposes of decisions, civilian members and military members sitting together for four or five days. The Commanders-in-Chief were there, the Chiefs of the Staffs, the military representatives of the Supreme Council and the Prime Ministers of the three countries, and other Ministers as well. The military members took part just as freely as the civilian members in the discussions, and there was an interchange of views during the whole of the time. And let me say that, as the result, complete unanimity was reached. There was not a division of opinion upon any resolution that was ultimately come to."

I then referred to the Repington disclosures: —

"With regard to this critical action which is involved in the extension of the Versailles powers, I must speak with caution, because I am talking about military decisions in the War Council. I wish there had been someone in Germany, or in Austria, whose ears were glued to the keyhole, when the War Council of Austria and Germany sat, and that he had published their decisions in the newspapers! The man who had done that and could tell us what arrangements the Austrians and the Germans had together come to, in order to co-ordinate most effectually their plans to attack our forces, would be worth many army corps to the Allies.

"When I talk about the War Council and its decisions I have to do so with caution, because if information is given to the enemy, I had rather the responsibility were on other shoulders than mine. . . . There are millions of gallant lives depending upon it, the honour of the State, the safety of our native land depends upon it — these great war aims, upon which the future of the world depends, turn upon it. To give away information which would imperil these is treason beyond description, and I decline to participate in it. It is enough for me to say that the decisions come to there were come to unanimously. We have to consider the best methods of carrying them out."

I begged Asquith: —

". . . not to press the Government to give information which any intelligence officer on the other side would gladly pay large sums of money to get, as to the arrangements which this country and the Allies have made for countering that great blow."

Mr. Asquith resented the implication that he was asking for information of that kind. I replied that I felt certain he had no wish to do so, but that I wanted him to realise that if I were to give the information to the House it would also be giving it to the enemy. I reminded him that I had offered to convey to him personally in confidence the whole of the Versailles decisions. I continued: —

". . . When you are conducting a war, there are questions which a Government must decide. The House of Commons, if it is not satisfied, has in my judgment but one way of dealing with the situation; it can change that Government. But to try and discuss military decisions ——

"Mr. Asquith: I made no such request.

"The Prime Minister: Believe me, this is a military decision. Does my right hon. friend know what it means? I say it is a military decision — a military decision of the first magnitude — and a military decision where some of the greatest soldiers of the Allies were present and to which they contributed.

"Mr. G. Lambert: Did Sir Douglas Haig and Sir William Robertson approve these decisions?

"The Prime Minister: Certainly; they were present there, and all those representatives approved. I could carry it further with regard to that. (Hon. Members: No, No! and an Hon. Member: 'Do not be drawn!') It is very difficult under these circumstances, because the House must realise that I am anxious not to give information which would be of the slightest help to the enemy. There is only one way when we go to councils of war — you must leave it to those who are there to decide, and if you have no confidence in them, whether they be military or whether they be civil, there is only one way, and that is to change them. But to go on and discuss these matters in the newspapers, whether on one side or the other — and if you begin discussing them on one side you are bound to have discussion on the other — makes war direction impossible — absolutely impossible!"

In conclusion I made an appeal to the House and to the Press: —

". . . I have been fighting hard against these paragraphs appearing in the Press. There is nothing that makes the work of government more difficult than discussions of strategical questions going on in the Press, and I appeal to the House of Commons, and I appeal outside the House of Commons to those who are interested in seeing this War conducted efficiently, to prevent discussions of this kind going on. If the House of Commons and the country are not satisfied with the conduct of the War, and if they think there is any Government which can conduct it better, then it is their business, in God's name, to put that other Government in! But as long as the House of Commons retains its confidence in the Government, then I say it ought to allow the Government a full and free hand in the direction of the War."

For all practical purposes this concluded the debate. The House was clearly satisfied with the explanation given.

I was hopeful that after the full discussion in the House and the failure of the opposition to make any case that stirred sentiment either in or out of the House against the Versailles decisions, Sir William Robertson would see the wisdom of reconciling himself to the situation. I was anxious not to complicate matters by dismissing Generals. Robertson had won confidence as an administrator which was fully justified both by his organisation as Quartermaster-General in France and by the way he pulled things together at the War Office. But he also had built up for himself a reputation as a great strategist which was not justified by any achievement in the studies of peace-time or in the active planning of war-time.

He had thus acquired a fame in the popular estimation far beyond anything his record would warrant. There had been much praise but no criticism. In war open detraction of Generals is deprecated — on the other hand, laudation, however extravagant, is encouraged. This method gives confidence to the Army at the front and to the public at home. Any public suggestion that the Army leaders are unfit or untrustworthy would demoralise the troops. This necessity places statesmen at a considerable disadvantage in their dealings with the military chiefs. I could not have published my memorandum on Passchendaele or pointed out how its predictions had been fulfilled. Had I overridden him without publishing my full reasons I should have been told I was interfering in matters for which I was not qualified by experience or training to express an opinion, and that I was setting aside the judgment of men to whom I and others had induced millions to entrust their lives. In France, in Germany, in Italy, in Russia, as well as in our own country, it had been a source of almost insuperable difficulty in securing the best leadership for the Army. In Germany, where Generals could point to a dazzling array of great victories in every battlefield, they acquired such authority that they dominated the Government in matters exclusively within the sphere of Ministers. In France, Joffre almost achieved that influence during the first years of the War. No doubt Robertson had been persuaded by the sycophants, whom great power without criticism always breeds, that he could establish a similar dictatorship in this country, and that this was his opportunity. He made up his mind to challenge a definite conclusion with the War Cabinet. He was convinced that the Government had lost whatever popularity it had ever acquired — that the nation would welcome a change — that there were forces in Parliament, drawn from every Party, strong enough to effect a coup — and that the issue between generals and politicians was well chosen. Robertson therefore dug in his stubborn toes. He refused the offer of a position on the Board of Control if it involved his surrender of the position of C.I.G.S. He insisted that the Chief of the Staff should be *ex officio* member with power to appoint a deputy when he was unable to attend.

I was determined that the military representative at Versailles should not be a mere mouthpiece or instrument of the Chief of the Staff, just a deputy who could not go beyond limited instructions sent him from England by a chief who had not heard the argument or even the proposals to be debated. That would have been a farce. Robertson would have probably sent there the subservient and rather unbalanced Frederick Maurice, one of those foolish devotees who bring the idols they worship to their downfall. This intention is recorded in Wilson's Diaries.[1] Maurice would have done just what he was told and no more. He did not possess the independence or the judgment which would have given to his chief the impartial information and good counsel which would have enabled him to form a sound opinion. From any point of view there could not have been a poorer choice. The Cabinet therefore presented Robertson with the alternative of either going there himself or remaining as C.I.G.S. at the War Office. In either case we made it clear that the Versailles nominee must meet his Allied coadjutors on equal terms and therefore must be free and unfettered. Robertson refused the nomination and challenged the whole Versailles decision.

During these critical days the chill I had contracted laid me up and I was unable to attend the Cabinet. I saw my colleagues in my room, especially Mr. Bonar Law, Lord Milner and Mr. Balfour. The last was reluctant to let Robertson go, and felt certain that a good deal of his attitude was due to

[1] Major-General Caldwell: "Field-Marshal Sir Henry Wilson", Vol. II, p. 22.

pique and a thorough dislike of Sir Henry Wilson, whom he suspected to be the alternative nomination. I told Balfour that if he could persuade Robertson to be reasonable I had no desire to have a rupture with him. He promised to interview him. Here is his account of the conversation, which he sent me at the time: —

"Foreign Office,
15th February, 1918.

"NOTES OF A CONVERSATION WHICH I HAD WITH THE C.I.G.S. ON THURSDAY, 14TH FEBRUARY, 1918, AT 3.30 P.M.

"By request of the Cabinet, I went to see General Robertson yesterday afternoon, in order if possible to persuade him either to retain the position of Chief of the Staff on its traditional lines; or, if he preferred it, to take the post of Military Member of the Allied War Council at Versailles.

"I pointed out to him that the Government gave him the alternative of accepting either of the two great Staff appointments connected with the conduct of the War on the Western Front. It seemed to me that they could do no more, and that, on public grounds, he ought to accept.

"General Robertson observed, repeatedly and with great insistence, that the fact of his having been offered whichever of the two posts he preferred had, in his view, nothing to do with the question. If his objection had merely been that the powers now given to the Council at Versailles, and therefore to the British Member of it, overshadowed the position of the C.I.G.S., it might have conceivably been worth while to transfer his activities from London to Versailles. But this was not his point of view at all. He objected to the new system,[1] and he equally objected to it whether he was expected to take a share in working it as C.I.G.S. or to take a share in working it as Military Member of the Supreme War Council. An objectionable object in the middle of a table (to use

[1] He had approved of it in his speech at Versailles, *vide* p. 293.

his own metaphor) was equally objectionable from whichever end of the table you looked at it.

"I did my best to persuade him that the responsibility of refusing a great position at the most critical moment of the War was one which he was hardly justified in taking. Extreme cases might be conceived, in which the machine to be worked was so obviously fated to break down that no man could be required to undertake the duty of working it. But it seemed to me impossible to say this of the present plan. Doubtless every scheme for introducing some measure of unity into the working of four different armies, under four different Commanders-in-Chief and four different General Staffs, belonging to four different nations, was open to objection, and holes could easily be picked in it. The Germans had, and must continue to have, an advantage over the Allies in the matter of unity of command. But it seemed to me, though I had nothing to do with the contrivance of the Versailles plan, that, with a little goodwill, it could be made to work smoothly and efficiently; and that, if this were so, I thought he should consider it his duty to work the plan.

"We discussed the matter on these lines for over half an hour; I regret to say with no result at all.

"General Robertson was very anxious that the scheme should be so modified that the Military Member at Versailles should be the subordinate and representative of the C.I.G.S. In that case he would be quite ready either to retain the position of Chief of the Staff or go to Versailles.

"I had, however, no commission from the Cabinet to discuss a scheme which had, I gathered, already been rejected at the late Conference, nor indeed was I qualified to do so.

A. J. B."

On that Memorandum it was evident to the Cabinet that they were up against a graver issue even than the one raised by the Versailles decision. It was now a question whether the Government of the day should submit to military dictation on a matter where they were by every constitutional precedent the supreme authority. The Inter-Allied Governments, including ours, were all represented at Versailles: their principal military advisers were also present. The decision taken there received the unanimous assent of both the civilian and military representatives of all the Allied nations. Even if the British Government had desired to alter the decision, they could not have done so without reopening the question with their Allies. A debate had taken place in Parliament on this very issue and the action of the Government was not challenged in the Division Lobby. Now an eminent and highly placed soldier, who was present at the Versailles Conference and acquiesced in the plan, took upon himself the responsibility of brushing it on one side. If the Government surrendered, then a military dictatorship would have been an accomplished fact. The Government of the day would have been as impotent in the face of protests or vetoes or orders issued by Robertson here as the German Chancellor and his Ministers had become after July, 1916, when confronted by the peremptory messages of Hindenburg and Ludendorff. We were bound to take a stand at the risk of much misunderstanding and the chance of a Parliamentary defeat. The War Cabinet were unanimous. There were, however, influential Ministers outside the Cabinet who gave trouble, and at least two threatened to resign. One of them — and he was by no means the least influential — actually placed his resignation in my hands. The situation for the moment seemed precarious. Nevertheless, we determined to stand or fall by the Versailles decision.

When Robertson refused to continue as C.I.G.S. on the terms we offered, he in effect resigned. The Cabinet therefore took steps to find a successor. It was not an easy matter. The obvious person for the post was Sir Henry Wilson. But like all men of brilliant gifts and marked personality he had not only fervent admirers but implacable opponents — in

FIELD MARSHAL SIR HENRY WILSON

the Army. Professional officers were sharply divided into these two schools. The men at the top were strongly anti-Wilson. Some actively disliked him: most of them distrusted him. Both schools were right. He possessed intellectual gifts which justified admiration. But he also had attributes which explained and, to a large extent, gave warrant for the suspicion and lack of confidence so widely felt about him. He was whimsical almost to the point of buffoonery. He answered a serious question or expounded a grave problem in a vein of facetious and droll frivolity which was undignified in a man of his grave responsibilities. Habitually he jested over questions of life and death. This habit detracted from the weight and authority which his position and capacity ought to have given to his counsel. He had undoubtedly the nimblest intelligence amongst the soldiers of high degree. He had also a lucidity of mind and therefore of expression which was given to none of his professional rivals. It was a delight to hear him unravel and expound a military problem. For that reason he was specially helpful in a council of civilians. But he had no power of decision. That is why he failed in the field. For the same reason he was not a complete success in council. He shrank from the responsibility of the final word, even in advice. I was always perplexed to know what to think of him. His friends had an extravagant opinion of his ability. They credited him with genius of a high order. I had been taught to suspect him, but only for political reasons. I was conscious of these prejudices and of their origin and was thus on guard against them. For that reason I discounted too much all my instinctive doubts about him. I always felt that the views of politicians about his merits or demerits had no reference to his military qualifications. They were formed from motives of political association and were therefore not impartial. Asquith hated him for his implication in the Curragh mutiny. For the same reason he was an undoubted favourite with Bonar Law, Milner and Carson. But neither Asquith nor the Unionist leaders judged him fairly as a soldier. They were too much prejudiced either for him or against him on partisan grounds. I did my best always during the War to discard political bias in my choice of men for service in any capacity. I did not think Wilson the ideal man for post, but he was much the best brain I had met in the upper ranks of our professional army and he did this country a memorable service: from the beginning he appreciated the genius of Foch, which was by no means perceived even by the French General Staff. His was the only military mind — French or English — subtle enough to understand the super-subtlety of Foch's genius.

However, I realised that the fact of this highly controverted and controverting personality being in the background of the discussion complicated the issue. Wilson was the living embodiment of the Versailles idea. He was partly responsible for it. This was generally known. For that reason a large number of Liberals whom in ordinary circumstances I could have relied upon to fight against military dictatorship in any shape or form swung right behind the military clique. And so did the Irish. What an ironical situation! The Liberals, who in 1914 fought an attempt at a military overlordship engineered by Wilson, now, because of their hatred of his intrigue, backed up a more dangerous conspiracy to establish a military dictator. On the other hand, the instigator and organiser of the effort of the soldiers in 1914 to override Parliament had become, only four years later, the champion and the standard bearer of the resistance of the Government of the day to a similar conspiracy. But I have seen these paradoxical situations so often in politics that they have long ago ceased to surprise me.

I am bound, however, to acknowledge that the friendship, amounting to affection, with which Wilson was regarded by

THE FALL OF ROBERTSON

powerful members of the War Cabinet helped to win their adhesion to the change at the War Office. Balfour, Derby and Robert Cecil were not of the number. They inclined the other way. But with Balfour, his interview with Robertson settled him. The other two were still recalcitrant, or rather one was hesitant and the other definitely captious. In the circumstances I thought it desirable to offer the post of C.I.G.S. to a soldier who commanded the respect and confidence of the whole Army without distinction of rank and of the nation without reference to party. I therefore first of all offered it to Plumer, who was then in command of the British Army on the Italian Front. I had consulted Haldane, who knew the Army well, and he had warned me against Plumer. He was fully alive to his fighting qualities, but thought little of his intelligence. He considered him quite unfitted for the duties of Chief of the Staff. Plumer, however, settled the matter by declining the post. He made it clear that his sympathies were with Robertson. I am not sure whether he decided on merits or out of personal loyalty. The Cabinet, therefore, fell back on Wilson. There was no other obvious alternative.

Haig and Derby came over on Sunday, February 17th, to see me at my cottage at Walton Heath. We discussed the whole position for hours. Haig put up no fight for Robertson. He clearly did not approve of his defiance of a decision come to by the Government. I thought it right to inform him that Derby had placed his resignation in my hands. I was under the impression that he had a great regard and respect for his civilian chief. I was anxious to find out at once whether that would affect his attitude. I was surprised to discover that, so far from the news disturbing him, he sniffed it aside with an expression of contempt. He had a poor opinion of Derby's stalwartness, and did not hesitate to show it. Haig himself had no intention of resigning and gave no indication that he was not prepared to accept the Versailles decision. He pointed out that as it was now becoming evident that the German attack would be on the British Front it would not be possible to take any of his reserves away from that front. I assured him that I felt confident Foch was fully aware of that fact and would not contemplate the folly of sending away troops to a sector which was not threatened. He expressed himself as being quite satisfied with that assurance. He never then objected to the plan by which the General Reserve would be placed under the command of Foch. Wilson saw Haig that evening at his house at Kingston and Haig told him that "all these quarrels had nothing to do with him, and that he was prepared to accept whatever was decided by the Cabinet, and then play up all he could."

When Haig left me, Derby remained behind to place his resignation in my hands for the third time during the past twenty-four hours. This time he insisted that it was irrevocable. He explained that he did not do so because of any disagreement with the line taken by the Cabinet, but out of loyalty to the men with whom he had worked at the War Office. And he told me his decision was final. As soon, therefore, as he left I got on the telephone to Bonar Law and we agreed that the vacant Secretaryship of State should be offered — subject to the King's consent — to Austen Chamberlain. He was out of town at the time, but he motored to London at Bonar Law's request. Before, however, he reached Downing Street, Ian Macpherson, the Under-Secretary for the War Office, called at 11 Downing Street to inform Bonar Law that he had succeeded in persuading Derby to withdraw his resignation! The following day Bonar Law reported the appointment of Henry Wilson to the Cabinet and it was approved by them without a single protest. But the struggle was by no means over.

Letters appeared in the Press which showed that the issue was to be fought out in Parliament, and the line upon which it was to be fought was indicated very definitely in the critical journals. As one of them put it: —

"The House of Commons, as representing the nation, has got to choose between the two men, Mr. Lloyd George and Sir William Robertson, and to choose between them with regard to a military question. That is the true issue. No one can be at one and the same time on the side of the Prime Minister and the Chief of the Imperial General Staff. (Sir William Robertson has told us that he has not resigned.)"

I decided to make a statement in the House of Commons on the 19th. I quote two or three extracts from that statement: —

"The Government were extremely anxious to retain the services of Sir William Robertson as Chief of Staff as long as that was compatible with the policy on which they had decided, in common with the Allied Governments, after prolonged consultation at Versailles. It is a matter of the deepest regret to the Government that it was found to be incompatible with that policy to retain the services of so distinguished a soldier. If the policy be right, no personalities should stand in the way of its execution, however valuable, however important, however distinguished. If the policy be wrong, no personalities and no Government ought to stand in the way of its being instantly defeated.

"What is the policy? I have already explained to the House. . . . It is not merely the policy of this Government. It is the policy of the great Allied Governments in council. There is absolutely no difference between our policy and the policy of France, Italy and America in this respect. In fact, some of the conclusions to which we came at Versailles were the result of very powerful representations made by the representatives of other Governments, notably the American Government. That policy is a policy which is based on the assumption that the Allies hitherto have suffered through lack of concerted and coördinated effort. There was a very remarkable quotation in yesterday's *Manchester Guardian* which, if the House will permit me, I will read, because I think it gives the pith of the whole controversy: —

"'Some great soldier once said that to find the real effective strength of an alliance you must halve its nominal resources to allow for the effect of divided counsels and dispersed effort.'

"Our purpose and our policy has been to get rid of that halving of the resources of the Allies, so that, instead of dispersion of effort, there should be concentration and unity of effort. There is a saying attributed to a very distinguished living French statesman, which is rather cynical, that —

"'The more he knows of this War, the less convinced he is that Napoleon was a great soldier, for the simple reason that Napoleon had only to fight coalitions all his life.'"

I then recapitulated the effect of the Versailles proposals, and I gave my reason for the final decision of the Versailles Supreme War Council not to appoint the Chiefs of the Staff as members of the Board controlling the Reserves and for according to them an independent position: —

". . . Nobody could tell where a decision would have to be taken. The men who take the decision ought to be within half an hour's reach. Eight hours, ten hours might be fatal. We felt it was essential that whatever body you set up should be a body of men who were there at least within half an hour of the time when the Council would have to sit, in order to take a decision. Nobody knows what movement the Germans may make. There may be a sudden move here or there, and preconceived plans may be completely shattered by some movement taken by the enemy. Therefore, it was essential that the body to decide should be a body sitting continuously in session.

"The third reason was this: Not merely have they to take decision instantly, but they ought to be there continually sitting together, comparing notes, and discussing developments from day to day, because a situation which appears like this to-day may be absolutely changed to-morrow. You may have a decision in London, and telegraph it over to Versailles, but by the time it reaches there you may have a complete change in the whole situation. Therefore, we felt it was essential that these men should be sitting together, so that whatever change in the situation took place they could compare notes, discuss the thing together, and be able to come to a decision, each helping the other to arrive at that decision. . . .

"If the Chiefs of the Staff sat in Paris, it meant that the Governments would be deprived for long periods of their principal military advisers, at a critical time, and at a time when action on other vital matters on other fronts might be required. Therefore, I have no hesitation in saying that the moment it comes to be examined — although we examined it with the greatest predisposition in its favour — it was found to be absolutely unworkable, for the simple reason that the moment the Chief of the Staff went to Paris, he would cease to be the chief military adviser of the Government, and either Versailles would have to be satisfied with a deputy who could not act without instructions, or the Government would have to be satisfied with a deputy who was not their full military adviser. For that reason, the Supreme Council rejected that proposal with complete unanimity. I think I am right in saying that the proposals were withdrawn. It was felt even by those who put them forward that, at any rate, without very complete changes, those proposals were not workable.

"Then it was suggested by the French Prime Minister that it would be desirable for each national delegation to think out some other plan for itself, and to bring it there to the next meeting, and that was done. It is very remarkable that, meeting separately, and considering the matter quite independently, we each came there with exactly the same proposal the following morning, and that proposal is the one which now holds the field. I hesitated for some time as to whether I should not read to the House the very cogent document submitted by the American delegation, which put the case for the present proposal. It is one of the most powerful documents — I think my right hon. friends who have had the advantage of reading it will agree with me — one of the ablest documents ever submitted to a military conference, in which they urged the present course, and gave grounds for it. . . ."

I also once more emphasised the fact that the Generals were present and took part in the discussion: —

"Sir William Robertson was present, and nothing was then said or indicated to me that Sir William Robertson regarded the plan as either unworkable or dangerous."

(This statement was never challenged by Sir William Robertson or his friends.)

I then informed the House of the interview I had with Sir Douglas Haig: —

"I was specially anxious that the Commander-in-Chief, who is more directly concerned in the matter than even the Chief of Staff, because it affected operations, perhaps, primarily in France, should be satisfied that the arrangements that were made would be workable as far as he was concerned. Therefore, before I arrived at this arrangement, I invited him to come over here. I had a talk with him, and he said that he was prepared to work under this arrangement."

I then recapitulated the alternative offers made to Sir William Robertson and his refusal of both the Versailles post and the position of C.I.G.S. under the new arrangement.

"We had to take the decision, and it was a very painful decision, of having to choose between the policy deliberately arrived at unanimously by the representatives of the Allied Powers, in the presence of their military advisers, and of retaining the services of a very distinguished and a very valued public servant."

I paid a warm tribute to his capacity, his character and his attractive personality.

I added that: —

THE FALL OF ROBERTSON

During the whole of the two to three years I had been associated with him, our personal relations had been not merely friendly, but cordial, and that even at the final interview, where I did my best to urge Sir William Robertson to take one or other of the alternatives offered to him, we parted with expressions of great kindliness.

I then dwelt upon the difficulties, not merely practical difficulties, but difficulties due to national sentiment and historical traditions, in the way of securing coöperation between Allies. I ended on a personal note: —

". . . I ask the House to consider this: We are faced with terrible realities. Let us see what is the position. The enemy have rejected, in language which was quoted here the other day from the Kaiser, the most moderate terms ever put forward, terms couched in such moderate language that the whole of civilisation accepted them as reasonable. Why has he done it? It is obvious. He is clearly convinced that the Russian collapse puts it within his power to achieve a military victory, and to impose Prussian dominance by force upon Europe. That is what we are confronted with, and I do beg this House, when you are confronted with that, to close down all controversy and to close our ranks.

"If this policy, deliberately adopted by the representatives of the great Allied countries in Paris, does not commend itself to the House, turn it down quickly and put in a Government who will go and say they will not accept it. But it must be another Government. But do not let us keep the controversy alive. The Government are entitled to know, and I say so respectfully, to know to-night whether the House of Commons and the nation wish that the Government should proceed upon a policy deliberately arrived at, with a view to organising our forces to meet the onset of the foe. For my part — and I should only like to say one personal word — during the time I have held this position, I have endeavoured to discharge its terrible functions to the utmost limits of my capacity and strength. If the House of Commons to-night repudiates the policy for which I am responsible, and on which I believe the saving of this country depends, I shall quit office with but one regret — that is, that I have not had greater strength and greater ability to place at the disposal of my native land in the gravest hour of its danger."

In reply, Asquith was unexpectedly mild, and it was evident that the advertised parliamentary challenge to our action would not materialise on this occasion. He was still distrustful of arrangements which would subordinate the British Army to Allied control, but he said: —

"I do not ask the House — for though I have every respect for it, I do not think we are an adequate tribunal to determine matters of this kind — I do not ask the House to pronounce its opinion one way or the other on this question; but I am sure the Government realise that they are taking upon themselves a great responsibility in discarding, on a question of that kind, a system which has been devised with the greatest strategical and technical authority."

Sir William Robertson left the War Office and took up the Eastern Command. His place was taken by Sir Henry Wilson. It is characteristic of Wilson's selfishness and ingratitude that the only comment he makes in his diary on the night of his appointment by me to the chief position in the Army was that it had been delayed for 11 days owing to my indecision. Eleven days spent in anxious conferences, in fighting through his policy and his promotion amongst Ministers and on the floor of the House of Commons! Invariably to me personally he was effusive. Behind my back he was abusive. One can understand the imputation of treachery which was associated with his name, and which, by the entries of his diary, he has done his best to justify.

After these Parliamentary and Cabinet discussions, the interviews with Haig and the change in the War Office, the crisis was over. The Versailles decisions had been accepted by Parliament and by public opinion and we were prepared to go forward with their execution. Why then were they not carried out? One reason was the time lost in these distracting controversies. The other was the change in the attitude of the French Government.

Priceless weeks had been wasted. A great deal of the energy and nerve of the Government had been consumed in an internecine struggle, which did not contribute in the least to the effective prosecution of the campaign. On the contrary, it took our attention away from matters of vital importance which required constant vigilance and supervision. The consequent delay and distraction had a great deal to do with the failure of the project to organise a General Reserve in time for the German offensive. There is nothing more absorbing or wearing than a prolonged parliamentary or Ministerial crisis. In peace it is the inevitable price of democratic government. Even then it hinders progress. In war, it engenders calamity. It is no use underrating the gravity of the crisis and treating it as if it were only a question of whether one set or another of politicians should sit in Downing Street. It was above all an issue as to whether the Government of the day as the sole representative of the national authority vested in King and Parliament should still be supreme in the exercise of its legitimate functions or whether the power should pass into the hands of the War Office. Had the conspirators won, the next Government would have been practically their creation and the Ministers their creatures. No Ministry, having our fate before their eyes, would have dared to challenge any decree issued by the General Staff. Least of all could you expect independence of judgment in a Ministry composed of the men who had got into power on the cry of "Trust the Two Generals" in preference to trusting a Council representing the statesmen and soldiers of all the Allies.

But that was not the only peril with which we were confronted in this unpleasant conflict. It looked at one time as if the national unity might be put in jeopardy on the worst issue that could be debated during the War — the merits or demerits of rival Generals and of competitive strategical plans. The discussion actually began in the Press — it continued in Parliament — on those lines. In the course of such a discussion much was revealed which helped the enemy. If it had continued much longer, more and more intelligence would have leaked out. I declined to enter into that discussion, but if the Government had fallen and a War Office Cabinet had been substituted for the War Cabinet, then bitter controversy would have developed, and it would have been difficult to restrain one set of partisans in defending their decisions against attack, from inadvertently following the example already set by the others. From this danger Haig's refusal to join the intrigue helped to save the nation by the correct and patriotic attitude he assumed. He took his stand on the constitutional position that it was for the War Cabinet to decide and that it was the business of the soldiers to accept their decision and to act upon it. Had he stood by this position to the end what a difference it would have made to the course of events in the spring offensive!

Robertson alone, without the glamour of Haig's prestige, was not powerful enough to overturn Ministers. Had we been faced with the resignation of both, the struggle would have been harder and the issue more doubtful. It was a misfortune to the British Army that Haig did not in the ensuing week continue to follow the fine example of constitutional loyalty he himself had set on this occasion. His failure to do so on the question of the General Reserve was disastrous in the event. But the main responsibility for his subsequent conduct is attributable to the encouragement he received from the departure of Pétain and Clemenceau from the decisions of Versailles.

CHAPTER IX

BEFORE THE OFFENSIVE

Haig's theory of German menace — Main attack to be against French — Pétain holds same view — Ludendorff's programme — Weakness of Germany's allies — Wetzell's view of British quality — British tied to Flanders — Forecast of Versailles experts — Allies strong enough for defence — Conditions for successful defence — How they were fulfilled — Bad state of Fifth Army trenches — Labour withheld — Evidence of General Edmonds — Area of attack known in advance — Unwise distribution of reserves — Germans attribute blunder to our ignorance — Mystery of Haig's action — Neglect of Fifth Army — Responsibility of G.H.Q. for defeat of Fifth Army — Lack of Allied coöperation — Good generalship is common sense — Haig satisfied with his arrangements — Pièrrefeu's condemnation — General Reserve scrapped by C.-in-C.'s — Original plan for General Reserve — Wilson muddles despatch of note to Haig — Haig determined to oppose plan — His reply to note — Wilson's warning — Versailles announces Haig's refusal — Attitude of War Cabinet — Foch's reputation — Clemenceau's prejudice against Foch — Clemenceau wants to be Generalissimo — Pétain refuses to supply divisions — General Reserve scheme killed: Foch's protest — Disaster for spring campaign.

BEFORE I tell the story of the doom of the General Reserve I propose to give a sketch of the military situation in France at the date of the distracting and futile discussions which I have already related. A great enemy offensive on the Western Front was now an assured prospect. Division after division was hurried up from Russia to the West, and there was every indication of great preparations for an attack. The Germans, by every artifice in the disposition of their reserves and material, managed for some time to conceal the direction and point of their onslaught. Haig did not believe in an offensive on a large scale. His view, expressed to the War Cabinet on January 7th, was that the Germans would "attempt to destroy the morale of the enemy peoples by attacks of limited scope, such as against Châlons, Arras or some salient." The latter seemed to him to be the more probable course for the enemy to adopt, because an offensive on a large scale made with the object of piercing the front and reaching Calais or Paris, for instance, would be very costly. Another reason assigned by him for doubting an attack on a grand scale with the object of breaking our line has a considerable bearing on the discussion about the disposition of British man power. He said: —

"Moreover the German man-power situation did not seem very satisfactory."

Although Haig subsequently altered his opinion as to the purpose of the German attack and came to the conclusion that the Germans would attempt to force a decision, he still held to his original idea that the attack would not be on a wide front, but that there would be limited offensives, a punch here, and a blow there on both the French as well as the British Fronts. Even on February 16th, when Haig held a conference of his Generals at Doullens, and gave to them his appreciation of the situation, "he thought the main effort would be against the French, and that the indications from the British Front showed no signs of an imminent attack." [1] I agree with General Gough that "it is not easy to understand how the Commander-in-Chief arrived at some of his conclusions, because at that very conference Brigadier-General Cox, the new Chief of the Intelligence Section of G.H.Q., estimated that out of the 68 German Divisions in reserve, 50 were on the British Front. He expected an attack in or before March." In spite of this information from his own Intelligence Section, Haig adhered to his own prediction. He only changed his mind on the subject three or four weeks before the attack, when it became abundantly clear from the immensity of the German preparations opposite our lines that the attack was coming there and on a scale

[1] Gough, p. 236.

unparalleled by any offensive on either side during the War. Even up to the last, G.H.Q. refused to believe that the attack would cover the Fifth Army Front.

Pétain, like Haig, had also come to the conclusion that the German attack would be on both fronts simultaneously: two on the French and one on the British; and he, misled as the Germans hoped he would be by the preparations staged on his front, held to that opinion even after the attack of March 21st. He distributed his reserves on that assumption, many of them at the remote southern end of his front; and his subsequent reluctance to part with his reserve divisions was due to the conviction that the German attack on the French Front would come as soon as he had thrown his reserves into the Somme battle. The French High Command was haunted by the fear of an offensive through Switzerland, like the offensive through Belgium of 1914. This operated to our disadvantage, for the French were piled up at the end of the line farthest from us.

Ludendorff had decided that his first attack must be on the British Front and that it must be on a colossal scale with a view to shattering the Third and Fifth Armies and turning the whole British line. The weather is too uncertain in Flanders for any operations in the early spring. The farther south the area of the offensive, the earlier could it be launched. Hindenburg said the idea of an attack in the Flanders and Lys area was set aside because up to the middle of April the country in that quarter was an unparalleled swamp. When the Germans were induced by the exceptional dryness of the spring to begin their attack on the plain of the Lys in the second week of April, their progress was retarded by the morassy condition of the ground. Now the submarines were failing to prevent the steady arrival of American troops; thus the German High Command realised the importance of forcing a decision at the earliest possible date, and they could not postpone their first blow beyond March. If they succeeded in their aim of smashing the British Army in the spring, the American troops arriving in the summer would be too late to retrieve the Allied position. It was a shrewd effort to make the best of a situation which was growing increasingly precarious for the Central Powers. Their man power was at the point of exhaustion, and there was no reservoir upon which they could draw. For them there was no America providing an untapped source of millions of virile young men of the best fighting qualities. Their food situation was becoming increasingly serious. Their allies were sagging, and every German statesman and soldier knew that neither Austria, nor Turkey, nor Bulgaria could be relied upon if the strain continued much longer. It is not creditable to our Intelligence organisation that we did not appreciate how the allies of Germany were gradually disintegrating. If the War Office had any secret information on the point they carefully withheld it from the War Cabinet and it played no part in the strategical plans of the High Command. They did not wish to give us any encouragement to direct any part of our forces to the task of finishing off the tottering confederates of our greatest foe. For that reason they always exaggerated grossly the numbers of the Turks and the prowess of the Bulgarians, and they certainly gave us no idea of the dejection and demoralisation that prevailed in Austria. But the Germans were under no delusion as to the real position. Their allies might be kept up leaning in their trenches with a rifle on the parapet for another year, but no longer. Hindenburg in his biographical notes shows how much these considerations were responsible for the March offensive: —

"Even though at the end of 1917 I considered that there was nothing to make me doubt the ability of us Germans to continue

BEFORE THE OFFENSIVE

our resistance through the coming year, I could not conceal from myself the regrettable decay of the powers of resistance of our allies. We must devote all our resources to secure a victorious conclusion of the War. That was the more or less expressed demand of all our allies." [1]

An early decision — and the earlier the better — was imperative if the Entente were to be forced into a satisfactory peace. That decided Ludendorff in favour of an attack on the only part of the British line where owing to weather conditions operations in March were practicable. A further inducement was the fact that at this point the defences were in an unsatisfactory condition and the line was weakly held. Ludendorff's final decisions were arrived at on January 21st. He then definitely settled on the plan which was put into operation on March 21st. All preparations were to be ready by March 10th.

It is interesting now to know that Ludendorff's ablest Staff officer, Colonel Wetzell, advised an attack on the French in preference to the British Front. His reasons are flattering to the British soldiers, although not complimentary to their leaders.

His first reason was that —

"we have a strategically clumsy, tactically rigid, but tough enemy in front of us."

He went on: —

"The French have shown us what they can do. They are just as skilful in the tactical use of their artillery as of their infantry. Their use of ground in the attack is just as good as in the defence. The French are better in the attack and more skilful in the defence, but are not such good stayers as the British."

He also said that on this part of the front —

[1] Marshal von Hindenburg: "Out of My Life", p. 340.

"the British infantry is very fully equipped with machine-guns, etc."

I hope my military critics may one day find not only the space but also the grace to give one line of acknowledgment to the fact that the plenitude of machine-guns, etc., was due to action taken by a civilian against the advice of Generals.

The Germans evidently thought little of our military leaders but they had a wholesome respect for the tenacious valour of the officers and men who held the British lines in front of them. And although Colonel Wetzell thought the French more skilful strategically and tactically, they were not considered to be as good stickers as the men whom he alludes to further on as "the obstinate British." Wetzell was very right when he thought it a mistake to rely on breaking through a line held by British soldiers! They do not retreat with sufficient celerity to guarantee that an attack will reach its objective before the reserves arrive, even when those reserves are delayed by misunderstanding and muddle. The battle of March 21st completely vindicated Wetzell's insight and foresight. He counselled an attack to pinch out Verdun because if it succeeded it would strike a deadly blow against the French. He did not preclude the possibility of a complete military collapse of the French Army.

He makes a point which has a decided bearing on the difficulties we subsequently experienced in extricating reserves from the north. He points out that we were "strategically tied in Flanders." How true that was will become more and more apparent as the story develops. Wetzell was doubtless thinking partly of the Channel Ports. But in addition, we were far too much committed to the Passchendaele salient. We could not spare the necessary troops from the defence of an unthreatened sector to save from destruction the very

Fifth Army that won it, for what it was worth, at an appalling cost.

The "Versailles soldiers" were of opinion that the first attack would be on the British Front and that the Germans would mass an enormous striking force with a view to breaking through on a wide front in the Arras area. But wherever the attack ultimately came there was no difference of opinion that a great German offensive was contemplated and that the Allies had to make every preparation within the limit of their resources to meet it. It was generally agreed that everything must be done to repel the attack and hold the line until the Americans arrived in sufficient numbers to give the Allies that superiority in men which would enable them to take the offensive.

At this stage I do not propose to discuss the comparative strength of the rival armies. I deal with it in another chapter. It was at one time a subject of hot controversy, and so much heat remains in the cinders of that dispute that it is not easy to handle the subject. The evidence placed before the German Reichstag Committee that inquired into the responsibility for the March 1918 offensive stated the position as being "a slight superiority in numbers" for the Germans, but inferiority in guns; that meant, if you accept Haig's estimate as to the lost morale of the Germans, a definite German inferiority in fighting strength. This fact may account for the complete absence of panic or even acute apprehension in Allied military circles before the battle. All were confident of the result or at least complacent about it. The only thing necessary to repel an attack on a fortified position defended by an army as strong as the assailants was that the defenders should make the best use of their positions and of their forces.

What were the requisites of defensive preparation?

Firstly, to put our defences in order: not merely the front line, but the battle zone, which had to be held at all costs if we were driven out of our front trenches — and then a further defensive system in the rear of the battle zone where we could fall back if the enemy succeeded in penetrating our second line of entrenchments.

Secondly, that the best use should be made of all the troops available by a rearrangement of the whole of our forces from Ypres to the Somme. The troops ought to have been so distributed that the part of the line which was known to be threatened should have an adequate defensive force both as to the numbers in the line and reserves behind. It was imperative that our strength should be economised and fully utilised by withdrawing divisions from indefensible salients, the holding of which was not essential to the defence of the line as a whole. It was very difficult to find enough men for all the war services of the Empire: this judicious rearrangement was a paramount consideration.

Thirdly, we were bound to secure the advantage of a single united front by means of the creation of a Central Inter-Allied Reserve disposed under a central direction and in suitable areas. Thus the Allied Reserves would be available to aid a hard-pressed sector wherever it was.

Fourthly, also to send from England every man that was needed to strengthen the line in France and to raise and train every available man that could be spared from our depleted resources of man power, but without regarding the demands of other equally essential services.

Fifthly, to make arrangements for bringing to France from Egypt without delay all the British troops in the three divisions which were to be filled with Indian troops and to bring either British or Italian divisions from the Italian Front.

I propose now to examine how those responsible for directing the defensive preparations discharged their responsibilities. Take first of all the putting in order of the defensive positions on our front. Between June, 1916, and early December, 1917, the British Army had been engaged in offensive operations on a great scale. In the course of these battles, all the available labour in the British Army was concentrated on preparations for an advance.

This involved the employment of an enormous number of men in the making and repairing of roads, railways, new aerodromes, hutments and structures of all kinds. One can judge the additional strain which these demands put upon our man power by quoting one figure — the labour forces in our army in France increased from 80,524 in January, 1917, to 302,904 in December, 1917. Of these, only 98,574 were coloured. As a consequence partly of the fighting, and partly of the baffling German withdrawal which Hindenburg so skilfully executed in March, 1917, in order to shorten the line and thereby increase his reserves, our front line had to be brought forward and our battle zone defences had to be reorganised. On the Somme and the Scarpe, at Vimy, Messines and Passchendaele, the close of 1917 saw us with a new front line. The thoughts of Headquarters were, however, so completely concentrated on the Flemish offensive that the preparation of new defensive lines was to a very large extent neglected on our front. In the area handed over to us by the French, the French front line was in fairly good condition, but behind that line the defences were negligible. General Gough says that the French had handed over part of their defences to the owners of the soil, who had filled in the trenches and ploughed them over. At the time, the British Army was engaged in offensive operations which demanded the energies practically of the whole of its available engineering and labour strength. Haig had hardly at his disposal a sufficient number of men to strengthen his new positions in the Passchendaele and Flesquières salients and at the same time to reorganise the defences of the line taken over from the French. He had therefore to choose the sectors on which he would concentrate most of his engineers and his labour battalions. He clearly ought to have devoted his first attention to the sector which was the most likely to be first attacked. For climatic reasons an offensive in upper Flanders was unlikely and well-nigh impossible until April whilst an attack on the Somme was a feasible operation a month earlier. That consideration never seems to have occurred to him. He pressed on with his Passchendaele defences with all his available resources as if an attack were imminent, whilst he attended in a leisurely fashion to the sector doomed to an early assault on an overwhelming scale. The Army occupying the sector to the south of Amiens, that was to be attacked with such overwhelming force in March, was made up of survivors of the tired and exhausted troops. Their strength and their spirit had been worn out in the muddy battlefields of Flanders. Even in numbers they were weaker than those which he allocated to the defence of any other part of his line. Both in engineers and in labour his greatest activity was directed to the strengthening of the defences of the Passchendaele salient. A month after he took over the French line, there were only 626 labourers allocated to the preparation of the defences of the Fifth Army. At the end of another month there were only 3,120. A report which had reached me on the subject caused a communication to G.H.Q. in France from the Cabinet on the labour deficiency in the area of Fifth Army. This had the effect of inducing them to send a stronger contingent; but by March 16th there were only 8,830 labourers actually working on trenches and machine-gun positions and wiring in the battle zone.

A comparison of the number of engineering companies in the Passchendaele sector and that defended by the Third and Fifth Armies, just before the battle, will give an idea of the attention which our Headquarters gave to the defences of the two sectors respectively.

Sixty-eight R.E. Companies and Units were allocated to the Second Army for a front of 23 miles. The First Army was given 56 for its 33 miles; the Third Army, 54 companies for its 28 miles; and the Fifth Army, where the defences stood most in need of restoration and improvement, 56 companies for its 42 miles. That meant 3 companies to every mile in the Passchendaele area; 1¾ companies to the adjoining Army. The threatened Third Army was given 2 companies per mile, but the Fifth Army had only 1⅓ companies per mile of its menaced line. That is, the Fifth Army, whose defences were in the worst state of all, was given to repair its deficiencies, even when it was evident that a great attack was coming on that part of the front, less than a half of the assistance allotted to the Passchendaele Army where there was no great concentration of German troops to indicate an imminent attack. The result was that when the attack came, the defences were found to be utterly inadequate either to offer resistance or to delay the German masses. This will be evident from an extract from a report sent by G.H.Q. to the War Office on March 12th, 1918, which states that: —

"the forward and battle zones were partially wired, and a beginning had been made towards preparing certain localities for defence, but the rest of the main line of defences, in the rear zone, was only spit-locked.[1]"[2]

General Edmonds, the compiler of the Official History, who was sent by the Engineer-in-Chief on March 14th, a week before the great battle, with Brigadier-General H. Biddulph, R.E., to report on the Fifth Army defences, "found that the front line only of the rear zone was marked out by a continuous ribbon of trench, seven feet wide and a foot deep, with occasional small belts of wire (tactical wire sited for

[1] Marked out on the surface with a pickaxe.
[2] "Official History, France and Belgium, 1918", Vol. I, p. 123.

sweeping by machine-guns; protective wire was to follow later). The sites for machine-guns and strong points were marked by notice-boards."[1] These were the defences which had been prepared in the event of a break-through of the forward line for defending a retreating army against overwhelming numbers.

This description of the lamentable condition of the line which the shattered and now neglected Fifth Army were doomed to defend is corroborated by General Gough in his story of what happened before and during the battle. So much for the first requisite.

Now for the second requisite. What about the disposition made of the British troops to meet the impending blow? Whatever Haig's anticipations might have been in January and the first fortnight or three weeks of February as to the direction and strength of the German offensive, by the end of February there ought to have been no doubt even in his obdurate mind either as to the part of the front against which the attack would be launched or as to the scale upon which it would be made. By the end of February and the first week in March the evidence of German preparations opposite the Third and Fifth Armies had accumulated to such an extent as to make it certain that the thrust was to be aimed at that sector of the line and that it would come soon and suddenly. Immense masses of troops, guns and material were gathered in that area. New aerodromes had been erected. Huge dumps of ammunition could be seen. New roads and railways were being constructed to feed the attack with the necessary supplies for a costly offensive. Hospitals were put up. Where the Germans had had one army in front of the Arras–St. Quentin line there were now three. All these obvious preparations for an offensive on an immense scale were made opposite the Third and Fifth Armies. Strong corroboration was supplied

[1] *Ibid.*

by our discovery through our Intelligence Service that Von Hutier, the conqueror of Riga, had been brought over from Russia to command the troops opposite the Fifth Army. He had been Ludendorff's favoured choice for command whenever one of his great offensives in the East had to be carried out. All this was known four weeks before the attack began.

Haig in his despatches writes: —

". . . By the end of February, 1918, these preparations had become very marked opposite the front held by the Third and Fifth British Armies, and I considered it probable that the enemy would make his initial effort from the Sensée River southwards. As the 21st March approached it became certain that an attack on this sector was imminent, and counter-preparation was carried out nightly by our artillery on the threatened front."[1]

In view of this fact the distribution of our troops at that date is incomprehensible. Including reserve divisions, there were on the Passchendaele sector — at the extreme left of the British Front where no attack was anticipated — 14 divisions with 34 brigades of artillery and 25 siege batteries, not brigaded, allocated to defend an unthreatened line of 23 miles. The First Army immediately to the right of Passchendaele was not then menaced. Nevertheless it had 16 divisions with 29 brigades of artillery and 15 siege batteries not brigaded for a front of 33 miles. The tired and threatened Fifth Army had 14 divisions (plus three cavalry divisions, equal to one of infantry) with 46 brigades of artillery and 15 siege batteries not brigaded for a front of 42 miles illsupplied as it was with defensive positions. The Third Army was a little better off in men and artillery but not as favoured as the Flanders Army. The Passchendaele sector had nearly one division for every one and a half miles of front it held: the Fifth Army, which G.H.Q. knew were about to bear the

[1] "Sir Douglas Haig's Despatches", p. 182.

brunt of an attack more formidable than any yet staged in this War, were allowed one division for every three miles of front. In addition the Passchendaele sector had two or three times as much heavy artillery per mile in its support as the neglected Fifth Army. This is the treatment Haig accorded to the army that had at his bidding fought so valiantly for his impossible enterprise in Flanders. Eight divisions were holding the Passchendaele salient alone and another five divisions the Flesquières salient. Haig had in his December memorandum intimated to his subordinate Commanders that both these salients were indefensible and were to be abandoned in the event of a heavy attack. Yet when an attack of a magnitude such as he had never seen or contemplated was about to be hurled on the weakest part of his line and he was short of reserves to meet it, he practically immobilised 13 divisions of his best troops in these worthless and indefensible salients. Ultimately, as the battle developed, first the Flesquières and then the Passchendaele salients had to abandoned, but only after great confusion had been caused and much damage had been inflicted on the British Army by the reckless and foolish decision to weaken our front at the point of danger, in order to hold these trophies of a blundering and blundered campaign.

Ludendorff, when trying to explain the weakness of our line at the point of attack — the faulty distribution of our troops — attributed it to the skill and care with which the attacking army had concealed their movements by night marches and other expedients. He boasts that the enemy had not discovered any of his vast preparations. He could not believe that our Commander knew what was coming "otherwise his defensive measures would have been more effective and his reserves would have arrived more quickly." He was very much mistaken. Captain Wright writes [1]: "General Cox,

[1] Peter E. Wright: "At the Supreme War Council", p. 125.

of G.H.Q. Intelligence, not only gave the exact area of the attack (a portion of the German line which was lying hushed and motionless while the whole of the rest of it flared up with artillery raids and preparations) but tipped the exact date on 20th or 21st March." In fact, as usual, everything worked to perfection in our Army except the minds of the Commanders. Hindenburg also, in his book, dwells on the way the British had distributed their forces, massing troops in Flanders and leaving the St. Quentin sector to be held weakly, also holding a salient at Flesquières which could be pinched out. He gives these dispositions as one of the reasons why the attack was made at the southern end of our line. He adds, "of course, it was always doubtful whether the English would keep their forces distributed in that way until our attack began." He, like Ludendorff, can find no explanation for their doing so, except the skill displayed by the Germans in concealing their intentions. Had he known that Haig had been fully informed by the end of February of these intentions, he would have had to fall back on another explanation which he gives earlier in his book — that the "English methods were too rigid." The English tacticians "did not understand how to meet rapid changes in the situation." G.H.Q. had made their dispositions on another assumption. They required more than four weeks and several hard knocks on the head in order to change their minds.

Ludendorff was responsible for the withdrawal of the Germans from the Somme salient in 1917 in order to save troops. A great attack was coming on his front and he wanted to build up his reserves for the battle. He could not comprehend Generals wasting their troops in holding worthless ground whilst they were short of defenders for another part of the line threatened by a huge force.

Haig's action is unaccountable. History can recall many cases of men in great positions who have been known to do inexplicable things in a great emergency. It is true that he was very much annoyed with the French for depriving him of his last chance of continuing his cherished Flanders plan by forcing him to extend his line. He felt he had sufficiently done his duty by sending the Fifth Army to occupy their trenches. If these were attacked it was for Pétain and not for him to dispatch adequate reinforcements. What happened after the first day of the battle gives a certain colour to this explanation. After much searching and questioning I can find no other. But the underlying motive which dominated Haig's dispositions for the great battle was the fetter of Passchendaele. It is not surprising that Wetzell in his famous diagnosis of the situation in December, 1917, said repeatedly that the British Army was "strategically tied to Flanders" and that the French were more dangerous because they had no such strategic chain. One of the legs of the Army was stuck in the great quagmire and it could not march to its greatest need. The evil wrought by Passchendaele was not at an end. It was responsible for the loss, running to hundreds of thousands, of trained officers and men at a time when both were badly needed. It wore out a splendid army to such an extent that they were too exhausted either to train for the coming battle or to prepare the necessary defences to fight it under conditions that would give them any chance of holding their own. It robbed them of the engineering and labour assistance which was necessary to enable them to put their defences in order. It left them without a sufficiency of troops to hold so long a line and it deprived them of the reserves which alone would have enabled them to check and counter-attack the enemy. Passchendaele was a festering sore which weakened the strength of the Army and diverted the attention urgently required for other weaknesses and defects in its system.

It is difficult to find any favourable explanation for Haig's extraordinary behaviour towards the Fifth Army. It was the remnant of the fine army which had served him with such inexhaustible courage in the greatest trial of endurance and valour to which any army had ever been subjected. It was led by a gallant officer who was an old friend of Sir Douglas Haig, and who had given to his chief an example of loyal and devoted obedience in the carrying out of plans in which he had ceased to have faith. In explanation of Haig's conduct it might be argued that no man carries out instructions of which he disapproves with the alacrity and zeal he displays when the orders commend themselves to his judgment. And constitutionally stubborn men such as Haig are apt to carry resentment so far into the realm of reluctance as to thwart and defeat the odious command and to punish with failure those who have issued it. We had already suffered from this temper in the early spring when every kind of tiresome question was raised to delay the Nivelle offensive. These delays were largely responsible for its defeat. Had the Government fallen in with Haig's plans for a resumption of the offensive in the spring of 1918, backed him through and through in his refusal to take up more line, sent him all the reinforcements he asked for, withdrawn divisions from the East and thus gathered together another immense army to be thrown into the Passchendaele salient for another great push, there would have been in his preparations on the Flanders Front none of the fatal dawdling and tardiness which characterized his treatment of the problem of improving the defences of the poor abandoned Fifth Army in the Somme area. He would have found all the labour that was necessary to make the preparations, all the reserves required to support the attack. But this St. Quentin Front was not his concern. He had another and a better plan and the French and the British Governments had between them thrown it over, and substituted this arrangement which deprived him of the great part he had mapped out for himself. The responsibility was theirs and it was their business to see it through. He would just obey orders. The Fifth Army could take over that line and those who had declined to accept sound advice would see what happened when it was neglected! The obstinate mind with a grievance is an ill-balanced mind and finds it difficult to conform to conditions which have been forced upon it by others. There are plenty of historical illustrations in every sphere of responsibility, of greater men than Haig who failed to engage their full powers in enterprises of which they disapproved. In those cases resignation, or direct refusal, is the only reputable course and to that extent Sir William Robertson, when he had no faith in a scheme, played a more honourable part than Sir Douglas Haig.

In brief, the Fifth Army was not beaten through any deficiency of skill or courage on the part of its own officers or men, or through any lack of provision or proficiency in its own Commander, but through causes for which the General Headquarters of the Army were mainly responsible. When it was settled that the British Army had to take over that sector of the line it is not clear that G.H.Q. made any preliminary inspection of the state of its defences and communications; certainly they imposed no terms on the French that they should remedy the defects before the British took over. When it was taken over they did not furnish General Gough with the necessary means to undertake the task. They only supplied him with labour under pressure from the Government weeks after he had occupied the neglected area. Even then it was quite unequal to the minimum requirements. They gave him no reserves in the least adequate to the menace, and even when it was certain that an overwhelming blow was directed at that point, they moved no adequate reserves to his support. When the battle was joined and the Fifth Army was fighting a desperate rearguard action against forces which were three times as strong as its own, assistance was sent slowly and grudgingly. It was only late at night on the second day of the battle that G.H.Q. invited aid from the French. When it is also borne in mind that the British Commander-in-Chief declined to join in the formation of a General Reserve that would have averted the whole disaster, it is not difficult to affix the responsibility for what occurred in the March offensive. This brings me to the third requisite I have mentioned.

It was not only essential that the British Army should have its troops distributed in such a way as to make the most effective use of its entire strength in the coming battle, but that the Allied Army as a whole should do so. This was not a limited offensive affecting one sector of the line; it was the beginning of a great battle in which the Germans aimed at destroying both the British and the French Armies in succession before the Americans started to count as a formidable force. First the British were to be attacked and crumpled up, then the French were to be broken and scattered. It was to be one vast battle lasting for weeks and fought from the coast to the Swiss borders. But whether the British or the French were to be dealt with first, it was essential that the reserves of both armies should be ready to be thrown in at any crisis of the battle. The Germans had not the necessary numbers to attack both armies simultaneously on that scale. They must therefore be assailed in turn. The German reserves were drawn from all parts of their line but they were concentrated mainly behind the sector of the next offensive and were thrown in under the direction of the Commander-in-Chief of the whole front. Prudence dictated that a similar course should be adopted by the Allies. That is why the War Cabinet gave their strong support to the idea of a General Reserve under a central authority not dependent on the apprehensions or sectional interests of the Commander of either army. It seemed to us to be the only practical and sensible arrangement short of the appointment of a Generalissimo, which no country and no army on either side was prepared at that date to accept. Strategy is not mumbo-jumbo, as second-rate soldiers would wish us to believe, but the application of common sense and experience to military conditions and illuminated by a flash of imagination. As the latest (1935) edition of the Field Service Regulations rightly points out, *"Tactics on the battlefield are governed by certain simple, common-sense precepts, which are in the main very similar to those which govern everyday life. The ordinary citizen who is planning a business transaction goes through much the same steps as the Commander who is planning an operation."* Haig rejected the plan of the General Reserve: perhaps it would be more correct to say he never even considered it. Once at Versailles the members of the British Staff played out for him, as a war game on a map, and very accurately, what they thought the forthcoming battle would be and also the way the General Reserve would operate. Haig disdained to accord to the exposition the courtesy of listening to it and sat ostentatiously reading his paper. Eminent soldiers had placed their training and experience at our disposal, and one of them at least, with a mind lit up with the lamp of genius, gave advice which seemed to us to be sound and recommended the General Reserve scheme. Once the battle commenced there was no time for conference between the two Commanders-in-Chief to decide first of all whether the occasion had arisen to throw in fresh divisions, and if so, which should do it. Should Haig, for instance, move his last G.H.Q. reserve into the fight before Pétain drew on his? Haig and Pétain were both convinced that there would be a triple attack almost simultaneously — one on the British Front and two on the French. Haig reluctantly and tardily changed his mind a few days before the battle. Nevertheless, he did not move one of his reserve divisions from the unthreatened area nearer the battle areas. Pétain still held the opinion that the biggest effort of the Germans would come on his front and that the March offensive was launched in order to induce him to shift his reserves to the British Front and entangle them in that struggle. Haig in his despatch describing the battle and the preparations made for fighting it says: —

". . . In addition to our own defensive schemes, completion of arrangements for the closest possible coöperation with the French was recognised to be a matter of great importance and urgency. A comprehensive investigation was undertaken into the various problems connected with the coöperation of the two Allied forces. Plans were drawn up in combination with the French military authorities, *and were worked out in great detail to meet the different situations,* which might arise on different parts of the Allied Front. *Measures were taken to ensure the smooth and rapid execution of these plans.*[1]

"Among the many problems studied by the Allied Staffs, those involved by a hostile offensive on the line of the Somme River and the passage of that river by the enemy had been worked out. The plans were applicable to such a situation, had been drawn up and were ready to be put into execution when required."[2]

It is conceivable, although not intelligible, that Haig and Pétain may have been under the impression that they had established a workable understanding for mutual assistance; but how anyone with an actual knowledge of the facts could, after the event, have penned this amazing paragraph about plans for coöperation "worked out in great detail to meet the different situations", and "ready to be put into execution when required", passes my comprehension. Had Pétain failed to carry out his agreement? Haig pays him "a personal tribute for the ready and effective assistance he gave him in the battle." In fact, Pétain sent more divisions than were stipu-

[1] My italics.
[2] "Sir Douglas Haig's Despatches", p. 180.

lated in the agreement, and sent them sooner. That fact, in the light of what happened, forms a grim comment on the efficiency of the agreement by which Haig set such store.

Both Pètain and Haig, when they were seeking to evade contributing to a General Reserve under Foch, assured their respective Governments that they had made the most complete arrangements for coming to each other's aid, whichever was attacked. Pierrefeu, the brilliant French writer who was at Pétain's Headquarters during the battle and when preparations for it were being made, categorically denies this statement. He was a strong Pétainist and what he writes is, therefore, not dictated by animus against the French Commander-in-Chief. This is his account of the so-called complete and detailed plans for coöperation between the two armies: —

". . . Unity of front not having been realised, it had not been possible to conclude the precise agreement which, automatically, would have effected the collaboration of forces. In spite of the excellent and friendly relations which united us to the English, there was a wall between the two battle fronts." [1]

When we come to what occurred during the fight it will be seen how accurate this description is of the looseness of the understanding reached by Haig and Pétain before a great battle which might have decided the fate of France. The agreement of February 22nd between the two Commanders-in-Chief did pass through the hands of Captain Wright, the Secretary of the Controlling Board. The following is an abstract by him of the agreement made before the battle between Haig and Pétain. He had an opportunity of perusing it at the time.

"The agreement provides that they are to assist each other, but in one way, and one way only; the extreme French left met

[1] Jean de Pierrefeu: "G. Q. G." Vol. II, p. 127.

the extreme British right at Barisis, the point of junction of the two lines. Whichever of the two was attacked, the other, in case of need, agreed to help his colleague by extending his own line, but by extension only. The helper would thus relieve a certain number of his colleague's divisions who would be released for use elsewhere. . . . The exact dimensions this extension of either the French left or the British right was to take had to be left unfixed, and depended on the judgment and goodwill of the helper. Further Pétain . . . stipulated that he was only bound to extend his extreme left if we were attacked at a portion of our line other than our extreme right." [1]

It was an arrangement the most vital details of which were left to be thrashed out and decided after the emergency had arisen.

What had become of the General Reserve which was to be placed under an independent Board as an Army of Manœuvre to meet this very emergency? It had been agreed to by the military as well as the political leaders of the Allies; the Commanders-in-Chief and the Chiefs of Staff of both the French and British Armies had accepted it. Pétain, Haig and Robertson had assented to it as well as Foch. No one would suggest that the great Generals simulated acquiescence in order to trick the political chiefs into a false belief that they had accepted the decisions and meant to abide by them. I would not dare to cast such an aspersion on their straightforwardness. They gave no indication at the Conference that they had any intention of acting upon its decisions. The statesmen left the details to be worked out by and between the Generals in the full confidence that they would honourably carry out a decision in which they had acquiesced. That trustfulness turned out to be a mistake. With our past experience of G.H.Q.'s we ought to have known that it was not enough to decide on the principle of a plan which, how-

[1] Peter E. Wright: "At the Supreme War Council", p. 87.

ever obviously wise, was objectionable to them on personal grounds: it was necessary to determine the actual details. We were anxious to secure the good will of the Commanders-in-Chief for the project and get their wholehearted coöperation in working it out. By that means we hoped to save time and ensure that the scheme would work smoothly and well. We ought either to have remained at Versailles until we had a watertight plan which the Generals could not refuse to operate without a direct challenge of the authority of their respective Governments, or to have adjourned for a week or ten days and held another session to determine any differences there might be between the Commander-in-Chief or between the Board and the Commanders-in-Chief. We realized when it was too late how little justified we were in trusting to the good faith and good will of men who hated an arrangement to which they had reluctantly agreed. They used every artifice of which the professional mind is capable to delay and by that means to defeat the project. They possessed the skill which is always attributed to a woman when she desires to frustrate an unpalatable wish expressed by her husband. She never commits the error of blunt refusal. She prefers to resort to procrastination. By that method she gets her way in nine cases out of ten. Repington attributes to his friend Sir William Robertson a saying which had reference to the Versailles decisions: "With these politicians the best thing to do is to gain time." All the Services understand the value of that advice when dealing with their political chiefs. One trouble makes you forget another and there are so many in a politician's life that the officials have ample opportunities for manœuvre. In this case the trouble which took our attention for some time from the execution of the Versailles decisions was caused by Robertson himself. Unfortunately for him, he was not only the source of the trouble, but its first victim. Still, the crisis he fomented incidentally served one of his main purposes — the postponement of the General Reserve until it was too late to act.

The Robertson episode had one unexpected repercussion which helped to kill the General Reserve. The Controlling Board, consisting of Generals Foch, Bliss, Cadorna and Wilson, agreed on February 6th as to the number of divisions that should compose the Reserve, and as to the numbers to be contributed by each army. It was estimated that for the moment a General Reserve of 30 Divisions would suffice. It was to consist of ten British, thirteen French and seven Italian divisions. A note embodying the decision of the Board was immediately sent to General Pétain and General Diaz. General Pétain's first reply, received on February 19th, stated that he could not allot more than eight divisions to the Reserve. Subsequently, when it was too late to act, he stated that he had none at all to spare for a General Reserve.

There was curious delay in the despatch of the note to Sir Douglas Haig. For some odd reason Sir Henry Wilson pocketed the document and said he would deliver it personally to Haig on the way to England. Wilson had been notified by his friends of the intention of Robertson to challenge the Government on the Versailles scheme, and he knew how it might end. Wilson was a shrewd politician. He also knew how it might affect his own career, and his ardent political supporters warned him to be on the spot to await the issue of the struggle. On it depended his chance of securing a glittering prize which he coveted above all others — the nearest position to that held by the Commander-in-Chief in his old Army days, but with the command of an army twenty times the size of the one he knew, and that in a world war. He was in too great a hurry to reach the scene of this fateful conflict to spend a night at G.H.Q. and he never thought of sending the note by another hand. He sent privately an unsigned copy of the letter to Sir Douglas Haig on February 8th, but either through policy or oversight held back the original. His mind was on something which excited him much more. In England he stayed watching with an avid but anxious heart the progress of the struggle between the C.I.G.S. and the War Cabinet. The official note was completely overlooked. When he remembered, or was reminded of it, he sent the official note on to Haig. During the time the Cabinet were fighting their way through the crisis Sir Henry Wilson never called their attention to the dangerous delays in the formation of the Reserve and to the intrigues that were going on to frustrate the plan.

Haig only received his Official Memorandum from Versailles on February 27th. Clemenceau paid a visit to Haig's Headquarters on February 26th and subsequently told Poincaré that the English Commander-in-Chief had informed him that "he did not want to carry out the Versailles decisions." Haig seems to have also told Clemenceau that "he had already informed Lloyd George that he would never give up his reserve divisions to form a reserve army — that he would rather resign." He made an exception of the two British divisions returning from Italy. I have no note of any such conversation. I had only seen Haig on the 9th and the 13th of February. The official Versailles Note on the reserves had not then reached him, although as I say he had been unofficially informed about its contents. Had I been aware of his attitude I should most certainly have laid so startling a fact before the Cabinet and I certainly would have imparted it to Milner, who was our civil representative on the Versailles Council. There is nothing in the War Cabinet Minutes on the point, and the letters I received from Milner at this date contain no reference to it. Wilson notes in his Diary that, on February 25th, Haig "flatly refused" to earmark any divisions for the General Reserve. But that refusal was not conveyed to me at the time. I have already recorded the only reference Haig made to the matter. That was in the conversation I had with him on the 14th. So far was he then from threatening to resign that Haig informed Wilson that his duty was to obey the orders of the Government, as it was for the Cabinet to decide. The conversation to which Clemenceau refers was never passed on to me.

Haig's reply was given on March 2nd. By that date there were unmistakable indications that the attack was coming on the British Front. The Cabinet received the official intimation of Haig's decision on March 6th. In it he said: —

". . . I have to make the following observations: An enemy offensive appears imminent on both the English and French Fronts. To meet this attack I have already disposed of all the troops at present under my command, and if I were to earmark six or seven divisions from these troops the whole of my plans and dispositions would have to be remodelled. This is clearly impossible, and I therefore regret that I am unable to comply with the suggestion conveyed in the Note."

(That is exactly what the course of the battle forced him to do.)

He then added: —

"To meet any emergency in the Franco-British Front I have arranged as a preliminary measure with the Commander-in-Chief of the French Armies for all preparations to be made for the rapid dispatch of a force of from six to eight British divisions with a proportionate amount of artillery and subsidiary services to his assistance. General Pétain has made similar arrangements for relief or intervention of French troops on the British Front. These arrangements, both French and British, are now being contemplated and zones of concentration opposite those fronts which are most vulnerable and likely to be attacked are being provided."

Subsequent events prove how vague, loose and dilatory these arrangements were when they were put to the test; and they had the fatal flaw that indefinite promises had to be interpreted, not by the terms of an agreement, but by decisions taken at the time by two men whose views of the military situation, and, to a certain extent, whose interests, were in conflict.

The C.I.G.S. himself realised the danger of Haig's decision, for he wrote on March 6th to the Secretary of State for War in the following terms: —

"S. of S.

"I much regret the attitude taken up by the Field-Marshal Commanding-in-Chief.

"He admits, indeed he claims, that an enemy offensive is imminent on both the British and French Fronts, and yet either because he 'foresees a wider employment, etc., of Allied Reserves than that foreshadowed in the Joint Note' — a remark which I confess I do not understand — or because he considers the General Reserve 'could not be earmarked or located, etc. . . .' which again I entirely fail to comprehend, seeing that every Reserve formation always is and always must be both earmarked and located — he declines to comply with the suggestion made to him by the Executive Committee at Versailles on the orders received from the Supreme Council.

"Field-Marshal Sir Douglas Haig is taking a grave responsibility in so acting, for both the other Commanders-in-Chief (Generals Pétain and Diaz) have agreed to allot divisions — General Pétain giving eight and General Diaz six divisions. But apart from this, the Field-Marshal is taking a grave responsibility, because if he is heavily engaged and unable single-handed to withstand the attack, he will find himself living on the charity of the French Commander-in-Chief who may be unwilling or unable to help.

"At the same time, I am strongly of opinion that no pressure should be put on the Field-Marshal Commanding-in-Chief at the present moment to make him conform to the action of our Allies.

HENRY WILSON,
C.I.G.S."

6th March, 1918.

This document was not communicated to the Cabinet at the time either by Sir Henry Wilson himself or by the Secretary of State to whom it was addressed. By writing to the Secretary of State, Wilson protected himself from the charge of condoning Haig's flagrant disobedience. By giving the advice to leave Haig alone, and omitting to communicate with the War Cabinet, he did in fact condone it: he thus retained the favour of Haig, which he always sought so zealously; at the same time he did not forfeit the favour of the War Cabinet, which he had gained so adroitly. In fact, he faced both ways, as usual. On March 6th I received from General Rawlinson, the head of the British Mission at Versailles, the following official intimation: —

". . . The Supreme War Council at its session of 2nd February, in presence of Commanders-in-Chief of French and British Armies and of Italian Minister of War decided upon creation of an Inter-Allied General Reserve and delegated to Executive War Board its powers in all that concerned the constitution, the positions, and use of its reserve.

"The Executive War Board in its sitting of 6th February drew up a joint letter to Commander-in-Chief making certain proposals with regard to constitution and position of the General Reserve.

"By a written and verbal communication between General Foch and General Pétain an agreement with French Commander-in-Chief was reached on 19th February.

"By a written communication between General Giardino and General Diaz an agreement with Italian Commander-in-Chief was reached on 2nd March.

"In his letter of 2nd March the Field-Marshal Commander-in-Chief of the British Army states that he regrets that he is unable to comply with the request contained in the joint note of the Executive War Board.

"Under the circumstance of the joint note the Executive finds itself unable to continue its work and therefore unable to organise the Inter-Allied General Reserve, as the Supreme War Council, at its sitting of 2nd February, had instructed it to do; and Joint Note of the Executive decides that each military representative shall so inform his own Government and ask for instructions."

It is evident from the terms of this resolution, that the Executive Board was still under the impression that Pétain stood by his offer of eight divisions. Sir Henry Wilson was also under the same impression. Foch and his colleagues had been kept as much in the dark as we were. They did not know Pétain's change of mind and how he was receiving not merely the acquiescence of Clemenceau, but a considerable measure of encouragement from him in his obduracy. The Resolution passed by the Board indicated that in their opinion the scheme of a General Reserve had been destroyed by Haig's refusal and that in the absence of further instructions from their respective Governments it was useless to proceed any further with it. Had the Cabinet only had to deal with their own Commander-in-Chief the difficulty would have been overcome. But we were soon to ascertain that we had also to deal with two very formidable persons who were not amenable to persuasion, and to whom we could issue no instructions: the French Prime Minister and his Commander-in-Chief, General Pétain. The whole scheme had to be recast and re-conferred and re-argued. There was no time for all this. We had to make the best of a bad job.

Haig's refusal was discussed in the War Cabinet from the point of view of Haig's special difficulties now that it was known that the first impact of the German offensive would be on his line. We felt, however, that this was all the more reason why the French and the Italians should contribute their quota. The Italians at Versailles had shown every readiness to send even eleven divisions to France. Since then they had reduced their offer to four. Haig, however, preferred to have two of his own divisions back. But the Italians, now that they knew the clouds were not gathering over the Julian Alps but above the fields of Picardy, would, we felt certain, release a few more divisions. We therefore suggested to Clemenceau that the Supreme Council should be summoned immediately to meet in London.

At this date we had not been informed that Pétain's attitude was equally recalcitrant and that he had threatened to resign rather than place his reserve under Foch. Nor had we been told that Clemenceau had also changed his mind and was no longer in favour of an army of manœuvre under Foch. The appointment of Foch seems to have been the reef on which the scheme was wrecked. Pétain would not submit to his command of the General Reserve. He felt it was a reflection on his own authority if arrangements were made practically for putting the general conduct of a great battle under another General. I was informed subsequently that our G.H.Q. had a poor opinion of Foch and his capacity for such an exalted and responsible position. They did not conceal their contempt for the old soldier. A man who could explain himself clearly must necessarily be shallow and garrulous. To be able to speak lucidly and fluently was bad enough; but he also spoke dramatically. Foch was a Gascon by birth and Latin exuberance seems as much a sign of folly to the Anglo-Saxon as insular reserve seems a sign of stupidity to the Latin. He was just a stage Frenchman to be mimicked and laughed over. He was referred to in high military quarters as that "old dotard Foch." How brilliant soever had been his past career, they were convinced that his best work was done and, judging by the comments made in Staff circles, he was treated as a has-been with nothing left but a blustering manner which they thought deluded politicians into the belief that he was a strong man. It was only those mad and muddling politicians who would ever dream of putting the reserves of the British Army in a great battle under such a commander. It may be thought that I am giving a burlesque account of what happened behind the scenes to destroy the scheme of a General Reserve; but those who heard the conversations in elevated military circles about Foch will not be in the least surprised.

But most fatal of all Foch's critics — I might say adversaries — was Clemenceau. Foch was a devout Catholic. There were many nominal Catholics in high command in the French Army. But they never obtruded their attachment to the Roman Church on the attention of their associates. They were not even practising Catholics. The governing party in France was and had for a long time been anti-clerical. The threat to the existence of the Republic in the days of Boulanger and of the Dreyfus affair had come from the clericalists in the Army, trained in clerical schools, received and petted in clericalist society. Clemenceau was the most inexorable of all the anti-clericals. His life had been spent in fighting the influence of the Church. He would never enter a church. His refusal when he paid a visit to Strasbourg after the Armistice to attend a celebration of the liberation of Alsace in that glorious cathedral lost him the presidentship of the Republic when he was the most popular and powerful man in France. Foch was not only himself an ardent Churchman, his brother was a bishop. Clemenceau had a deep distrust of all Catholic Generals. He disliked placing power in their hands. He never knew to what use they would turn their power. The spiritual antipathy between these two remarkable men developed in the course of the ensuing months into personal antagonism which was unpleasant to all those who took part in conferences with them. There is nothing more disagreeable in council than to witness the clashing hatreds of two strong personalities. The more Clemenceau pondered over the Versailles plan of a General Reserve under this clericalist soldier, the less he cared for it. There was another motive in explanation of Clemenceau's change of mind on the question of the General Reserve. Poincaré ascribes to Clemenceau the ambition of himself becoming the virtual Generalissimo of all the Allied Armies in every theatre of war.[1] Poincaré and Clemenceau were mutually antipathetic. I would have hesitated to accept Poincaré's suspicions as to Clemenceau's motives when Clemenceau threw over the scheme which placed Foch in the powerful position of Controller of the Allied Reserves and I would not have thought these suspicions worthy of quotation, had it not been that they are confirmed by another witness of undoubted authority. General René Tournès, in his able and on the whole well-documented book on the 1918 campaign, says, in commenting on another conflict between the ideas of Foch and Pétain when Clemenceau intervened, that he was "swayed by a vague whim to wield the military command of the Coalition which he revealed almost as soon as he was in power."[2] This may explain the somewhat ill-natured observation made by Clemenceau to Foch immediately after the signature of the Doullens Agreement: "Well, you've got the job you so much wanted!" There is a suspicion of pique in that comment, especially coming from the man who a few weeks before this incident

[1] *Cf.*, for example, Clemenceau's words during a visit to Poincaré on February 22nd, 1918: —
". . . We spoke of the difficulties which had arisen between Foch and Pétain. 'I shall settle that business,' he assured me. 'The organisation of the army of manœuvre is hardly defensible as it stands. *But I shall be there.* In the hour of attack I shall be on the spot. If there's a clash, I shall be the one to adjust it, provided I'm still in power.'"
—Raymond Poincaré: "Victoire et armistice 1918", p. 58; and again, Poincaré's account of Freycinet's opinion expressed on February 23rd, 1918: —
". . . In the afternoon Freycinet arrived, still much preoccupied with the relations between Foch and Pétain, as well as the command of the Reserve Army. I told him that Clemenceau was certainly banking on acting as arbitrator in emergency. 'But,' he replied, 'Clemenceau cannot ever be sure of being there at the decisive moment. And besides, it's doubtful whether our Allies will leave *the power of deciding the fate of an inter-Allied Army to a French politician.*'"
—*Ibid.*, p. 60. (My italics.)
[2] General René Tournès: "Foch et la victoire des Alliés" (Vol. IV of the "Histoire de la guerre mondiale"), p. 156.

had intimated his intention to get rid of Foch altogether. If Clemenceau ever harboured such an aspiration it would have inclined him towards Pétain rather than the dominating and dynamic Foch. Pétain shrank from bold decisions and would have been more disposed than Foch to leave the responsibility for taking them to the head of the Government. Whatever the motives that prompted Clemenceau's growing disinclination to confer supreme control on Foch, both Pétain and Haig soon realised its existence and took full advantage of it. Pétain was a cautious man — very cautious — so at first he confined his objection to an effort to cut down the contribution he had to make to the General Reserve. Why not eight Divisions, instead of thirteen? That was all he could spare. But he gradually grew bolder when he saw that Clemenceau did not strike him down with the lightnings of his wrath. At last he mustered enough courage to resist the whole idea of parting with any of his divisions in order to place them under Foch's direction. Poincaré states that he threatened to resign if the Government insisted on his doing so. Clemenceau was easily won over. He told Poincaré on February 22nd ("Memoirs") that "the organisation of a field army (*i.e.*, the army of manœuvre) was not at all defensible in itself." By that date Clemenceau's prejudices and prepossessions had been roused and rallied to the side of the Commanders-in-Chief who would not have Foch. When Clemenceau after his visit to Haig's G.H.Q. on the 26th repeated to the President what Haig had told him, he withheld from his Chief what he had told Haig. According to the Official History, Clemenceau told Haig that he gradually meant to *écarter* Foch. The two probably interchanged confidences about the distinguished but unwanted General and found that on this subject they were, from different motives, entirely in sympathy. At that interview the Reserve plan was finally put out of existence. Clemenceau called on Poincaré on the afternoon of his visit to Haig and told him that he had seen Pétain, who had again expressed his anxiety about the Reserve Army. Clemenceau said he had "reassured him." Then he added, "And for the rest events will arrange themselves. *The divisions of Versailles have ceased to be.*" It was after the "reassuring" talk with Pétain that Clemenceau visited Haig's Headquarters. When we bear that fact in mind we can understand better the character of the conversation that took place between Haig and Clemenceau. Haig knew then where he stood and that he could throw over the whole of the Versailles scheme without any fear of untoward happenings. Even the careful Pétain took a decision. On the 28th he reports to Poincaré that he is "very satisfied with his conversation with Clemenceau. The reserve army *a vécu.*" It was dead — but only for a short while, for a much shorter while than anyone then anticipated. These conversations were not four weeks distant from the day — a day of muddle and of disaster — when the despised Foch was called by the united voices of the men — Clemenceau, Haig and Pétain — who had thrown over him and his plans as things of no worth, to save the Allies from the calamity into which they had blundered.

Not one of these vital conversations which Clemenceau had with Haig, Pétain and Poincaré was ever communicated to me or to any other member of the War Cabinet. I knew that Haig was obdurate and that Pétain was difficult, but I knew nothing of the encouragement which had been given to them by Clemenceau.

Before the Supreme Council met in London on March 14th the fate of the General Reserve had already been settled. I ascertained enough about the position to understand that before our first sitting. General Bliss, who was an unswerving advocate of the policy of the army of manœuvre under Foch, was just as convinced as I was that it was impossible to revive it without provoking a controversy in which Britain, France and America would be at cross-purposes. The battle was a few days off. This was no time for another crisis. It had cost nearly three weeks to dispose of the Robertson controversy. This dispute would have involved a much more serious conflict, for Clemenceau, Haig and Pétain would all have been ranged against the British War Cabinet. We had to make the best of an unsatisfactory situation. Haig assured me before the meeting, as Pétain had already assured Clemenceau, that the most detailed arrangements had been perfected for the coöperation of the two armies in the coming battle. With that assurance I had to be satisfied. Bliss, Orlando and I expressed a hope that as the fight developed it might still be possible to organise a General Reserve on the lines of the Versailles scheme. Foch, however, knowing the magnitude of the risk that was being run, entered an angry protest. He complained that the experts of the Supreme Council had been completely ignored, and that they had not even been informed of the character of the arrangements which, it was alleged, had been made by the two Commanders-in-Chief, to throw their reserves into the battle line and to come to each other's aid. Clemenceau lost his temper and rudely told Foch to "shut up." Foch's only reply was, "I cannot hold myself responsible for what will happen." Clemenceau retorted by taunting the Versailles Board with their failure to carry out the Resolution of the Supreme Council which had been proposed by me and accepted by Orlando, to arrange for bringing eleven Italian divisions to France. Foch's answer was complete. He said that that was an essential part of the formation of a General Reserve. These divisions were to be Italy's contribution. When the General Reserve was shelved by France and Britain they could not ask Italy to be the sole contributors. The demand made by Versailles on the Italian Army had therefore to be dropped.

The attack on our lines by Germany's gigantic army had thus to be faced without putting the defences of the attacked front in order, because our labour was diverted to working on a salient admitted to be indefensible, and because numbers of divisions were put into the line and invaluable reserves were massed in support of favoured sectors which were not threatened with any immediate danger. We were also without any General Reserve to support the sector attacked by the enemy and deprived of the Italian reinforcements which would have been invaluable in filling up gaps on our weak Fifth Army Front. Haig, as we have seen, had a poor opinion of the Italian infantry. He had preferred two British to four Italian Divisions. But even assuming that he was right in his estimate of their quality — and here I venture respectfully to disagree with his estimate — they could have held the unassailed parts of our own or the French Front and thus released more seasoned troops for the battle line. It was soon to become evident that we had no sufficient working arrangement for coöperation between the British and French Armies. Had these matters been attended to, the German attacks could have been repelled with such devastating losses that any hope of their renewal would have been abandoned and a satisfactory peace might have been reached without having to wade through the terrible slaughter of another summer and autumn campaign. But the G.H.Q.'s decreed otherwise and at this stage there was neither the time nor the allied unity which was essential for any attempt on so formidable a resistance. Wrangles and recriminations between Foch and Clemenceau were futile to save the situation. I therefore refrained from prolonging this rasping quarrel between these two great Frenchmen. There was a suggestion that we should save our faces by setting up some simulacrum of a General Reserve. I dislike participating in shams. A reserve army without real divisions would have been nothing more. The soldiers had once more defeated the politicians and there were rejoicings amongst the Headquarter Generals, their Staffs and adherents. They had beaten off triumphantly all assaults on their positions. Both strategy and tactics in intrigue were masterly. Alas, that these gifts were so much less effective when directed against the foe they were engaged to fight! The nation and the poor fighting soldiers of the Fifth and Third Armies had to pay dearly for these brass-hat triumphs. It is one of the ironies of political warfare that the men subsequently attacked in Parliament for the inevitable results of these errors of judgment were not the real delinquents, but the men who strove hard to save the Army from the effects of their delinquency. The perpetrators of the calamitous mistakes which left the Fifth Army to be overwhelmed through sketchy defences and inadequate reserves were not only excused but lauded, and according to precedent ultimately rewarded.

CHAPTER X

THE MARCH RETREAT

Lethargy of military authorities — Haig's dubious Staff appointments — Lawrence becomes C.G.S.. — Butler's promotion — Enemy concentration — Conference at War Office — Fresh drafts for France: despatch of eighteen-year-olds — Reinforcements from Egypt — Price of political distractions — Cabinet discussions — Statistics of comparative strength — Further recruiting measures — Milner sent to France to secure Allied coöperation — Instructed to get Foch appointed — Progress of battle: Gough prevented from using reserves — Arrival of reinforcements — G.H.Q. slow to appreciate situation — Attitude in French G.H.Q. — French troops begin to arrive — Compiègne bombed — G.H.Q. neglect of Fifth Army — Stubborn stand of Third Army — Handicap of Flesquières salient — Position at end of four days — Milner learns the facts — Conference at French G.H.Q. — Foch's plucky attitude — Doullens Conference — Haig's defeatist memorandum — Haig and Pétain pessimistic — Haig agrees to appointment of Foch — Poincaré's verdict on Doullens agreement — Bliss's estimate of it.

As the battle approached, there was nothing that struck me more at the time, as even now when looking back upon it, than the kind of composure, amounting almost to supineness, which reigned amongst those who would have the most direct and terrible responsibility for the lives of myriads and the fate of nations when the struggle commenced. On the German side all leave had been stopped for some weeks before the battle. On ours it went on as usual. The strength of our divisions was substantially reduced by men home on leave. It is difficult to understand this confident demeanour in such circumstances. After the battles of the Somme, of the Scarpe, and more particularly of Flanders, the military nerve ceased to respond to the memory of past horror or the prospect of future ghastliness. The deadening effect of prolonged war upon the susceptibilities seemed to blunt the sense of responsibility in matters great and small. I have already shown how tardily the military leaders moved in the improvement of the defences, in the arrangements of the troops, in the disposition of the reserves. When danger was imminent, when it was known where it would fall, there was little quickening of movement at G.H.Q., not much hurry or hustle to see that no precautions had been omitted, or preparation overlooked, or contingency unthought of. There were two episodes, seemingly small in comparison with the immensity of the rapidly approaching portent, but significant of this attitude of irresponsibility.

It is the supreme duty of any man who is at the head of a concern, to choose his subordinates without reference to personal likes or dislikes, but entirely on their qualifications for the post. Many of the mistakes committed in war, in business and in politics, are due to a friendly desire to give a lift to men who are not qualified for a position to which they are elevated. It seemed to me that Haig was governed in his choice of men far too much by his desire to have around him those who were personally agreeable to himself, and who would not clash with his dictatorial temper by suggesting any difference of opinion.

There were two appointments made during the period of preparation for the conflict by the Commander-in-Chief which illustrate this cardinal defect. The first was the advancement of a divisional General, inconspicuous for achievement and not endowed with any exceptional ability, to the all-important post of Chief of the General Staff. The C.G.S. was the principal adviser of the Commander-in-Chief on all questions affecting strategy and tactics. With an army of over two million men holding a line of over 100 miles against the most formidable warriors in the world, it was essential that the Commander-in-Chief should have at his elbow the best strategist in the Army, in training, in experience and in intellect. There were men in the British Army who possessed these attributes in a high degree. Sir Douglas Haig overlooked them all, and appointed Sir Herbert Lawrence. He was a cavalry officer who held a very subordinate command in the Boer War but who had been in the same regiment as Haig. He there, no doubt, conducted himself with all the gallantry and dash one would expect from a British soldier in the task of chasing elusive Boers across the African veldt with indifferent horses and horsemen. As soon as the South African War was over he retired from the Army and threw himself into finance. After 15 years behind a city desk, he volunteered for the Great War. He acquired some experience of trench warfare in resisting sporadic Turkish attacks, supported by light artillery and inadequate ammunition, on the Gallipoli Peninsula. He came to France only in 1917. He was given a divisional command, and did his duty without distinction.

General Kiggell was retired from the post of C.G.S. in January, 1918, and suddenly Lawrence was promoted to the most important and responsible position in the Army, next to that of the Commander-in-Chief, and that at the most difficult and critical stage of the War. As far as the British Army was concerned he became the opposite number of Ludendorff, one of the two, or possibly three, most brilliant Staff officers on either side in the whole War. Nothing but genius of the highest order could merit or justify such dazzling promotion with such scant experience. Not the warmest, or the most charitable amongst Lawrence's friends — and as he possesses an amiable disposition and an attractive personality he must have attached to himself a great many friends — would claim that he possessed military genius of that or any other order. It is not the only action or omission of Haig's in this crisis which forces one to ask: Why did he do it?

Here is another episode. The Fifth Army was given the task of defending the part of the line where it became clear to all those who studied the symptoms that the attack was most likely to come. The defences were insufficient and the numbers of the defenders quite inadequate to such a task. Haig ought to have appointed his very best officers to command troops that were likely to be attacked under such conditions. A few weeks before the battle he removed a General who was in command of one of the army corps in that area. By every canon of prudent leadership he ought to have chosen the best man available as his successor. But he had at Headquarters a favourite officer, General Butler, who up to that time had not had an opportunity of commanding troops in the field at all. Haig thought this was Butler's opportunity. Surely this was the last choice he ought to have made. It was unfair to Butler himself. It was not fair to Gough. It was most unfair of all to the troops who were thus doomed to fight against enormous odds under a callow leader. Butler was a pleasant fellow with a forbidding frown, cultivated on the Robertson model of countenance. It was supposed to give an impression of calm and ruthless strength. It was not such a success as Robertson's and there was nothing like as much behind it. Butler was not devoid of intelligence but he had not that kind of brain that triumphs over inexperience in difficult situations.

I am not certain that the best commander of an army corps placed in Butler's unfortunate position would have altogether succeeded. But one never knows what a really tried and skilful leader will do in the worst conditions. As to Lawrence's appointment I have always had a feeling that an able soldier of exceptional intelligence equipped with a thorough knowledge of the problems of warfare on the Western Front, and possessing the adequate independence of character to give the best advice to his Chief without reference to his palate, would have averted some of the most serious blunders which landed us in the defeats of March and April.

And now after all these misunderstandings, mistakes and

negligences came the most stupendous battle ever fought on this earth. Three of the mightiest nations of the world were putting the last throb of their strength into a struggle which lasted without cease for months and into which they cast the millions which remained of their young manhood. Highly competent observers and students of this vast and deadly combat have written of its many fluctuations. I shall put down what I can recall with the aid of contemporary documents of how it appeared to one who witnessed its course from his seat at the head of the Government which had the supreme direction of the affairs of this country during these strenuous and anxious months.

On March 13th, the Director of Military Operations, Sir Frederick Maurice, reported to the Cabinet the appearance of the Brandenburg Corps in reserve south of Lille, but said that it made no difference in the total number of enemy divisions, which remained at 186. He informed us that this gave an approximate total of enemy rifle strength of 1,370,-000 men and an artillery strength of 15,700 guns, while the total Allied rifle strength on the Western Front numbered 1,500,000 infantry and 16,600 guns. The average strength of the British divisions was larger than that of the German divisions.[1] This report of March 13th was given to us the day before the meeting of the Supreme War Council to which I have already referred. The only further report as to numbers came on March 19th, when it was said that another 400 enemy guns had been located and two more German divisions. Even with this addition there was a definite superiority on the Allied side in both guns and men. But although slightly inferior in numbers, the Germans had managed to mass enormous forces behind the line of attack. That is why Foch was so anxious to build up a General Reserve of French and British divisions behind the threatened sectors.

When the War Cabinet met for its usual morning sitting

[1] The number of battalions in the Dominion troops had not been cut down.

on the 21st of March, it was informed by the C.I.G.S. that the Germans had commenced a heavy bombardment before dawn on a front of 80 kilometres, from the Scarpe to the Oise, and that this front of attack was in general accord with the one anticipated by the British Staff at Versailles. The news that arrived in the course of the day was very confused and gave us no clear idea of what had happened in the fighting. But there was nothing in the reports recorded to excite alarm. When we met the following morning, *i.e.*, the 22nd of March, the information conveyed to us by the C.I.G.S. on reports from G.H.Q. was not much more definite. There was the usual *communiqué* to which we had been accustomed, about "very heavy enemy casualties" but no particulars as to our own, and Sir Henry Wilson ended his statement by informing us that "the information received up to now gave no cause for anxiety." The Cabinet was anxious to have all the latest intelligence as to the comparative strength of the forces engaged on both sides together with the reserves. This he promised to have prepared. He was of the opinion that the attack would develop into a long-drawn-out battle, deliberately intended for a trial of strength, in order that a decisive result might be arrived at. Nothing reached the War Office during this second day of the battle to modify the reports which had been communicated to us in the morning.

By March 23rd the news from G.H.Q. was not as reassuring as that which we had received the previous two days. It was reported that on the Fifth Army Front the enemy had succeeded in penetrating our battle zone and reserve lines, and that a retirement had in consequence been made to the line of the Somme. A more serious indication of the state of affairs came with the report that our casualties were 40,000 and that not less than 600 guns had been lost. Even then there were reassuring items in the report. On the Third Army Front we were told that the enemy had

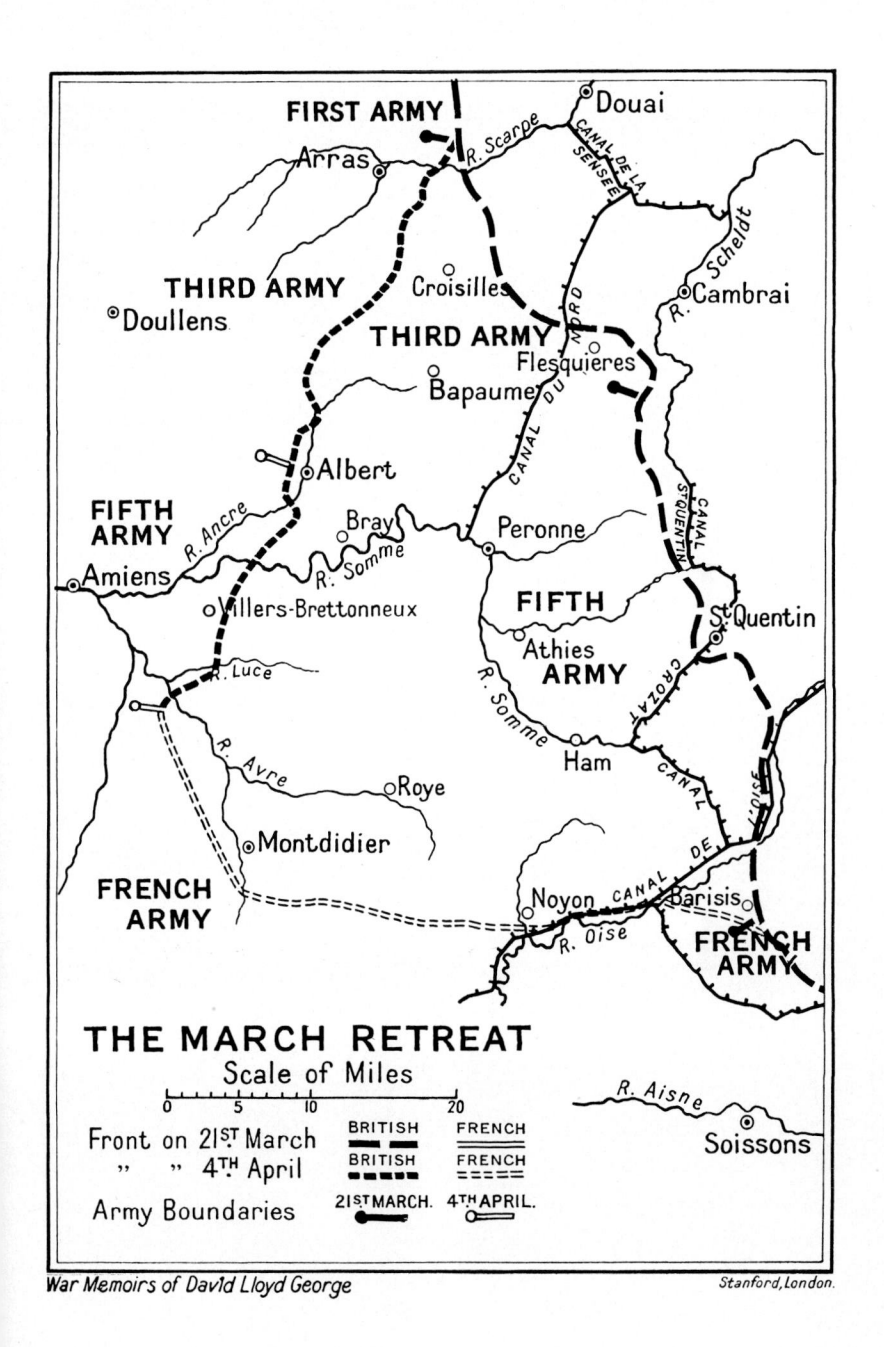

War Memoirs of David Lloyd George

Stanford, London.

in the main been held firmly in the battle zone except at Mory, and enormous slaughter had undoubtedly been inflicted on the enemy in places.

I had a feeling that the position was much graver than the G.H.Q. messages would imply. It looked as if Gough's tired army was giving way before the fierce onrush of the German hordes. It was evident that our line was broken and that we were relying upon patchwork defences hastily improvised to stop a victorious army. The news that all the reserves of the Fifth Army had been already thrown in was disconcerting. A report of Haig's visiting Pétain to persuade him to take over a part of the battle front was certainly disquieting. It showed that the vaunted arrangement between Haig and Pétain to help each other in the day of trouble had failed to function, and that even on the third day of the battle it was bringing no real reinforcement to troops which were fighting desperately against odds of three to one.

I always worked early in the morning and I received the battle news at the earliest available hour. I gathered on that Saturday morning that the War Office seemed to be either bewildered or stunned by the reports. I therefore decided to postpone the Cabinet and to take matters in hand at the War Office itself. I invited the Staff to meet me there in order to see what could be done to throw all available reinforcements into France with the greatest attainable celerity. The first thing to ascertain was what troops we had in this country, the next what we could spare and then how many per day we could send across the Channel. I instructed the Adjutant-General to have the figures ready as to troops in this country. To help us as to transport I asked the Shipping Controller to meet me before I went to the War Office, and explained to him the emergency and the importance of getting across as many men as he could carry in the shortest space of time. He promised to go into the question and find how many ships he could lay his hands on for that purpose.

At the conference I summoned at the War Office, Major-General Sir Robert Hutchison (now Lord Hutchison), the Director of Organisation, was prepared with figures as to trained men in the country who were immediately available for drafts. I found him prompt, efficient and reliable. We were informed by him that there were 170,000 who were ready to be moved at once to France as fast as there was transport capacity. This included 50,000 trained youths between eighteen-and-a-half and nineteen years of age. A pledge had been given in Parliament that youths under nineteen years old should not be sent overseas unless there was a national emergency. We decided that such an emergency had now arisen. The Germans had already incorporated a considerable number of their eighteen-year-olds in their divisions at the front. On further investigation the figure of the numbers of men available for drafting to France rose to over 212,000 by the 20th of April. We were astonished to ascertain that there were 88,000 men on the establishment in France who were on leave in this country.

The Germans had already stopped all leave some weeks before the attack. When an attack was expected any day on our front, it struck me that the absence of so many men from their battalions required some explanation. When an offensive was anticipated on our side leave was always postponed. Eighty-eight thousand men absent from their battalions would mean that each of the divisions in France would be short of its full strength, that is, by several hundreds per division. On that basis, the Fifth Army would have over ten thousand of their men on leave on the day of the battle. No wonder Gough complained that some of the battalions were not up to strength!

In addition to the above, there were 30,000 men in depots

in France and the Dominions had another 10,000 in this country and in France.

The next step was to take measures to transport the drafts to France. In practice it had been found possible to carry across 8,000 a day. After another conference with Sir Joseph Maclay I found he could scrape together the necessary shipping to take over to France 20,000, working up to 30,000 a day.

With the divisions it had already been arranged before the battle commenced to bring over from Italy, and divisions promised by the Italians, the present and prospective losses in the battle were thus more than made up. To give further confidence to our Army we decided to bring over at once from Egypt the men from the three divisions which it had already been arranged should be filled up by Indian troops.

Total Allied forces in the Turkish theatres (Palestine and Mesopotamia) were as six to five of the enemy forces, according to the War Office estimates given to the Man-power Committee. As a matter of fact our superiority was nearer two to one. Indian divisions could, at any time after the conquest of Baghdad and the overthrow of the Turkish Army in that country, have been brought to Palestine and thus released several divisions for France. But here again to do so would have meant telling the full tale of Turkish disintegration to these mischievous politicians at home. There was the real enemy upon which great soldiers had to concentrate their subtlest arts and wiles. In this emergency we decided to do at once what ought to have been done by the Staff months ago — bring British divisions from Egypt to France and replace them by Indian divisions that were not wanted in Mesopotamia. This reconstruction had in fact already been ordered weeks before the Battle of Amiens.

In going through all this process at the War Office I realised how the struggles between Versailles and the Chief of the Staff had diverted the minds of those who were directing the organisation and distribution of our forces from their primary and urgent duties. There is nothing half as absorbing of time, thought and energy as a quarrel between professional factions engaged in bitter rivalry. The Italian, Mesopotamian and Palestine arrangements ought to have been put through in time to reinforce our Army in France long before the German offensive was due.

I called a Cabinet Meeting in the afternoon of Saturday, March 23rd, at the War Office to consider the situation and to sanction the measures taken at the morning conference in view of the less favourable reports from the front. The Cabinet were given such information as to the course of the battle as had been received during the day from G.H.Q. There was some discussion about the French tardiness in helping us. It was stated that Field-Marshal Sir Douglas Haig had gone that day to meet General Pétain with a view to arranging that the French should take over more line. Wilson thought it better not to tell us that the telegram from Haig said that "the situation was serious." It was the first communication from G.H.Q. that displayed any real appreciation of the gravity of the position. Haig also informed Wilson that the arrangements for the French to come and take over the line of the Somme would not be completed till the 29th (the ninth day of the battle). Nor did Wilson repeat accurately what Haig had said about seeing Pétain. "I am going to meet Pétain to-night", was the actual phrase.

A question was raised as to whether it was necessary to put any political pressure on the French Government to render us the necessary assistance, and a suggestion was made that either Milner or myself should go immediately to Paris for that purpose. However, it was thought by the C.I.G.S. and his Staff undesirable for Ministers to interfere between the Generals unless and until it was found that Haig and Pétain could not adjust matters between themselves, so it was decided to wait until the result of Haig's conference with Pétain was known. In the course of the discussion which took place, I pointed out that if the Versailles scheme for the constitution and control of the Allied General Reserve had only been brought into full operation, it would not have been necessary to have this bargaining with the French in the middle of a battle, but that the Executive War Board would have decided immediately where the large reserves at their disposal could have been thrown in to the best advantage for checking the enemy advance. It so happens that we know exactly what would have taken place if the plan of the General Reserve had been persisted in. Great Commanders usually keep their plans to themselves, but on this occasion the great Commander was President of a Board, and was thus compelled to disclose his ideas. Two of the Controlling Board only understood English, and Foch's French had to be translated: the interpreter, who was also the Secretary, was thus compelled to learn Foch's plans. He has put them on record.

Foch in effect said to the Executive War Board: —

"Ludendorff must launch his mass of attack either eastward or southward, either towards the British side of the angle in the Cambrai region, or towards the French side of the angle in the Rheims region. But if he is successful, and drives one or other of these lines back, he himself presents an unguarded and open flank: and the more successful he is and the more he enlarges the angle, the longer and therefore the more open and unguarded his flank will be.

"I will, therefore, divide my General Reserves into three portions, of different sizes. The smallest portion I will place in Dauphiné, close to the best crossing into Italy; the largest I will concentrate round Paris; the third portion I will place round Amiens."

This is the disposition Foch intended to make of the General Reserve in February. As it became increasingly evident that the attack was to be made on the British Front, Foch would have moved more of his reserves into the Amiens area. It will be observed that Gough would thus have had twenty to twenty-five divisions ready to help him.

At the meeting of the War Cabinet held on Saturday afternoon — the third day of the battle — the Director of Military Intelligence, General Macdonogh, and the Director of Military Operations, Sir Frederick Maurice, supplied the latest figures of comparison between the enemy and Allied forces. They now increased the numbers of the German rifle strength to 1,402,800 and reduced the Allied numbers to 1,418,000; still a slight superiority, it will be observed, for the Allies. The comment of the C.I.G.S. upon this estimate was that he considered that for purposes of calculation, the present forces might be reckoned as approximately equal. This observation did not make any allowance for the mechanical superiority of the Allies.

Those who were on leave in England were counted in the estimate given two or three days before, as if they were in France. I believe the numbers actually in France at the date of the commencement of the battle were alone included in the second reckoning. If so, that may partially explain the disparity between the two estimates.

After disposing of the more pressing questions of sending immediate reinforcements to France, we turned our attention to searching out the ways and means of replenishing our reserves of men available for the front in the event of the War going on into the winter of 1918, and the spring of 1919. Here we were not so successful. There were only two sources available — the combing out of essential men in vital industries and the conscription of Ireland. The latter I agreed to much against my better judgment, by a pressure which came from many quarters at home and in France. But that part of the story I must postpone. On the whole we did an excellent morning's work and the machinery we set in motion for dealing with the immediate crisis worked without a hitch.

The same evening — the 23rd — the reports from France not improving, I decided that either Milner or myself must go over at once to see why and where the arrangements for mutual help had failed to operate and whether things could not be set right before possible disaster supervened. I sent for Milner and discussed the whole situation with him. We both felt that there was only one effective thing to do and that was to put Foch in control of both armies. We both agreed that if there had been in existence a General Reserve of thirty divisions under the independent control of a Commander with Foch's gift of lightning decision, enough reinforcements would already have been thrown in to restore the line. As soon as the news reached the Executive Board that the German concentration was taking place between Arras and the Oise, most of the reserves would have been moved into that area and a sufficient number would have been moved so close up to the line that they could have gone into action by the evening of the first day, certainly by the morning of the second. Instead of which we had all this manœuvring between Haig and Pétain as to which of them ought to rush in first with his reserves, and as to whether Pétain ought not to take over entirely part of the British line and if so when. We were informed that there was a question as to whether Haig's forces should not fall towards the north and Pétain's towards Paris, leaving a fatal gap between the British and French Armies. Had the General Reserve of thirty divisions been in existence there could have been no gap unless this formidable reserve were beaten. Pétain maintained that until the battle had fully developed he could not be certain that the Germans would not attack his front in the Champagne district where they had gathered considerable reserves. If they did so, Pétain said he might find his own reserves entangled in another battle. He was all for "Wait and See" before committing too many of his reserves to the Somme battle. On the other hand, Haig had most of the British troops which were available for reinforcement placed at the other extreme of his line. It would take a long time to move them. So the argument went on. They did not argue together face to face as they ought to have done. They conferred with their respective Staffs, each in his own Headquarters where they were all agreed that it was for the other wing to flutter first. Meanwhile the valiant soldiers of the Fifth Army were perishing for want of help from one or other of these exalted interpreters of a compact lacking precision. It was a deplorable outcome for the "complete and detailed arrangements" that were to "move quickly."

The news that had reached the War Office by the evening of the 23rd showed that this description was not mere conjecture on Milner's part or mine. And the facts, as we subsequently discovered, were an understatement of the muddle. It was therefore decided that nothing would put an end to this calamitous manœuvring but the direct intervention of the meddling politicians.

Accordingly we agreed that Milner should at once leave for Paris to see Clemenceau. We thought it better that I should remain in London to direct the plans I had made for the rapid despatch of reinforcements to France so that there should be no delay in that essential respect. I authorised Milner to do what he could to restore the broken Versailles Front by conferring upon Foch the necessary authority to organise a reserve and to control its disposition. How well Milner carried out this arrangement will appear when I tell the story of the Doullens Conference. It fell far short of the Versailles plan, but it was as far as he could obtain agreement and it was on the road to the establishment of final unity amongst the armies. Before I give an account of the Doullens decision I must first of all give a further account of what we ascertained was actually happening in the matter of reinforcing the broken front of the Third and Fifth Armies.

When the attack began on March 21st, G.H.Q. had two divisions — the 20th and the 39th — in reserve behind the Fifth Army. I have already reckoned these amongst the divisions holding that part of the front. As these two divisions were in Gough's opinion too far behind his army, he was anxious to move them closer up to the front. He moved the 39th Division a little closer to the front. The 20th Division was fifteen miles behind the front of the XVIII Corps, and he wanted to move up five to eight miles farther north of it. In addition he wished to move forward the 50th Division, which was a division just brought down from the Fourth Army and placed in Army Reserve. It was more than twenty-five miles behind his front, and he wished to bring it at least one day's march nearer. In his opinion, these steps were "most urgent, almost vital", and he asked the authority of G.H.Q. for these moves. He was refused permission to move a man. As he himself points out in his book, "no one had suffered more from the failure to recognise this principle than had Haig himself at the Battle of Loos, when Sir John French had denied him the use of his reserves until too late." In fact, French's dismissal and Haig's appointment as his successor were largely attributable to this action on French's part. There can be no doubt that G.H.Q.'s refusal to allow these two divisions to be shifted nearer to the front had injurious effects. Although when the battle started, Gough finally took the responsibility for ordering them up without permission from G.H.Q., the 20th Division did not come into action until the 22nd and the 50th Division not until the afternoon of the same day.

If these divisions had been thrown in during the first day of the battle, they might have helped to stay the German advance; but they were quite inadequate to restore a line which had been broken by a force where the assailants were in the proportion of three or four to one of the defenders and the best entrenchments had already fallen into enemy hands. There ought to have been many more divisions ready to be thrown in, at the latest on the second day of the battle. The first division sent by G.H.Q. to the broken front was the 8th. It reached Eterpigny, a few miles behind the line to which the army had retreated, by the 23rd — the third day of the battle, but only some of its units came into action on that day. On the morning of the 24th, the fourth day of the battle, its front line was six miles behind that held by the British Army on the previous morning, and fourteen miles behind the original front. The second division ordered to move in support of the Fifth Army was the 35th. Some incomplete battalions without artillery came into action on the fourth day, but it was only on the 25th — that is, the fifth day of the battle — that the division was complete. Its remaining battalions arrived that day, and its artillery came up in the course of the afternoon. As rail accommodation from the north was fully occupied in the movement of the 8th Division and of divisions which had been ordered to support the Third Army, the 35th had to march by road. Had these divisions been shifted nearer the threatened sectors as soon as it was discovered where the blow was to come, these tragic delays would not have occurred and these reinforcements might have exerted a decisive influence on the course of the battle. No other reinforcements were sent by G.H.Q. to that battle front during the week of incessant fighting.

On the night of the 24th the whole of the VII Corps, including the 35th Division, was transferred to the Third Army, and thus passed out of Gough's control. On the 28th the remainder of his army was placed under General Rawlinson's command. Gough's statement, therefore, that during the whole of the time he was in command in that battle he was only given one additional division (the 8th) from the reserves of G.H.Q. on other fronts is quite accurate.

This extraordinary tardiness in sending reinforcements may be explained by the slowness with which G.H.Q. came to comprehend the seriousness of the position. I have quoted the first telegram from Haig to C.I.G.S. which used the phrase "the situation is serious." That was received on the third day of the fight. Gough reports that he had a conversation with Haig's Chief of the Staff, Lawrence, late at night of the first day of the battle. To quote his words: —

"Lawrence did not seem to grasp the seriousness of the situation; he thought that 'the Germans would not come on again the next day'; 'after the severe losses they had suffered', he thought that they 'would be busy cleaning the battlefield', 'collecting the wounded, reorganising, and resting their tired troops.'

"I disagreed emphatically, but I failed to make much impression. It has always been my opinion that G.H.Q. did not fully grasp the magnitude of the assault on the Fifth Army, or the desperate odds which it had to contend with, and this may have accounted for the misconceptions that we allowed to circulate so freely, even in the Cabinet, during the following weeks."[1]

The telegrams from G.H.Q. passed on to the Cabinet by the C.I.G.S. show that if there were any misconceptions as to the condition of things in Cabinet circles, it was due to this lack of understanding on the part of G.H.Q. in France as to what had really taken place. As I pointed out, the first telegram from Haig which showed that he had at last woken

[1] Gough: "The Fifth Army", p. 271.

up to the gravity of the situation, came to the War Office on the morning of the third day of the battle.

What was happening in French Headquarters? The impression made on the mind of Pétain and his Staff by the first news was that this was not the real offensive — it was only a local attack in order to induce the French to take their reserves away from the Champagne Front where the real attack was to be made. During the whole of the first and second days of the battle, Pétain had no communication of any sort from Haig. During the first day nothing came to the French G.H.Q. at Compiègne except rumours and scraps of incoherent reports, not one of which came from the British G.H.Q. In the afternoon of the first day General Humbert, who had been appointed by Pétain to command the reserves which were to be sent to help the British in certain contingencies, visited Gough's Headquarters. Gough asked him whether he had brought reinforcements. Humbert answered that he had nothing except the little banneret fluttering on the bonnet of his car. Not a single battalion had been placed under his command. That was the "perfect arrangement worked out in every detail", which was to be the substitute for a General Reserve in the day of trial. It is only fair to Pétain to say that without waiting to be asked, he put arrangements in hand on the evening of the 21st for sending divisions of the French V Corps to assist the British. Haig sent a message thanking him for his prompt support, but saying he did not want the French to intervene yet.

On the second day, the 125th French Division began to arrive behind the British lines; but it was not complete and it was therefore not put into the line until the morning of the 23rd — that is, the third day of the battle. This was the first reinforcement of any kind Gough received.

On the evening of the second day, Pétain heard, probably from his own Intelligence Staff, that "the enemy had broken through a large portion of the British lines, and had driven back Gough's Army, which, beaten down by great masses of troops and overwhelmed by their numbers, was retreating precipitately. Behind the British right there was no reserve at all." But an event occurred that night which turned the attention of the French Headquarters to much more menacing things. German aeroplanes dropped a number of bombs on the Headquarters at Compiègne, killing two officers. This had never happened before in the whole course of the War. Headquarters on both sides were sacred and immune from the perils which befell the mere fighting soldier. But evidently there were depths of barbarism which the "Hun" had not yet plumbed. Headquarters were as excited as an ant's nest into which a stone had been dropped. Officers and archives were moved that night into the forest where they would be hidden from the German destroyer. Late at night, when Headquarters were made safe from bombers, they turned their attention once more to carrying out the arrangements made with Haig. A second division, and a cavalry division, were ordered to go to the British Front, and came into action in the afternoon of the third day of the battle, without their artillery or transport, and with only the ammunition they carried on their persons. The "arrangements" were beginning to work, but oh! how slowly and how timorously!

On the fourth day of the battle two more French divisions, but without their artillery or transport and with not much more ammunition than they carried in their bandoliers, arrived. This to help an army which had lost most of its guns!

On that day the French took over the southern end of the British line. After four days of desperate fighting, when the odds were so heavily against us, the entire reinforcements consisted of six divisions — three without their artillery. It transposed the odds from about three or four to one to a certain three to one; the three consisting of troops inspired by victory, the one made up mostly of the broken remnants of a defeated army and of divisions hurried along and arriving in the night panting and without their equipment of guns and ammunition.

That night Pétain and Haig met for the first time during the battle to discuss and decide arrangements. Gough saw Haig, for the first time since the battle began, on Sunday, the 24th, when he met him at Corps H.Q. and talked to him for about ten minutes. No General Officer from G.H.Q. had visited the Fifth Army to see what was going on, nor did any member of G.H.Q. (other than Lawrence) visit Gough from one end of the battle to the other. Haig's consolation to Gough for his defeat was "Well, Hubert, you cannot fight a battle without men." He never told him that but for the Passchendaele obsession his defences would have been better prepared and his line more strongly held, and that had it not been for Haig's refusal to work the Versailles scheme for a General Reserve, ample reinforcements would have reached him in time to counter-attack the enemy and fling them back. Three weeks before the battle he knew where it was coming. Had he then taken steps to rearrange his forces so as to hold the threatened sectors of the Third and Fifth as strongly as the two Northern (and unmenaced) sectors were then being held, there would have been 37½ divisions to face the enemy, instead of 30. What an enormous difference that would have made to the result, even without a General Reserve! And the fronts of the First and Second Armies could still have been held more strongly than that of the Fifth Army on the first day of the battle.

What was happening to the Third Army? This was much better cared for than the slighted and cast-out Fifth. Byng was given 16 divisions to hold 28 miles of line, to Gough's 14 to hold 42 miles. It had another advantage in that it was next-door neighbour to the privileged sectors where Haig had massed most of his troops. How great a pull that was the first few days of the battle demonstrated. The reserves were at least one day nearer. Between the 21st and 23rd of March, G.H.Q. issued orders for the bringing of eight divisions from the Northern Fronts to reinforce the Third Army — each division fully equipped and containing 50 per cent. more troops than the French divisions that came to Gough's aid. As these divisions came from contiguous sectors they also came into action several hours before the Fifth Army reinforcements. The Third Army might have held the ground without retreating at all had it not been for the complication of the Flesquières salient. The account of the battle given in the Official History shows how important and damaging a part that salient played in the fight. It completely disarranged and dislocated our defence. Three whole divisions had been set apart to defend it, although it had been admitted by G.H.Q. to be indefensible whenever seriously attacked. The Germans worked their way round it and Byng found it difficult to extricate his troops from toils he himself had woven and into which he had firmly tucked three unfortunate divisions. Instead of getting out whilst the going was fairly good he tried to hold half the salient. He was reluctant to give up the only bit of ground he had won in the bungled tank attack of Cambrai. The result was that right and left the whole defence of his line and part of Gough's were thrown out of gear. A great gap was opened between the Third and Fifth Armies. Tudor, with the 9th Division which had on March 21st conducted a gallant and successful fight on the left flank of the Fifth Army, was compelled by the Flesquières folly to retreat from a position his fine division had so skilfully and valiantly defended. The Fifth Army seemed to be doomed to bear the shortcomings and stupidities of all concerned both in the preparations for this battle and in its actual conduct. The Germans to the right of Flesquières and on the extreme right of Byng's Army were being held and their attacks repelled with appalling slaughter, but this serious tactical blunder gave them an opening. The Third Army was forced into a general and almost a headlong retreat and it was only the arrival of substantial reinforcements that enabled it to reform its front. Still on the front of the Third Army, taken as a whole, in spite of a considerable loss of ground by us, the Germans sustained much more damage than they inflicted. Their losses crippled them seriously at the time and still more in their future operations, and if the Third and Fifth Armies had even now been reinforced in time, the German advance could have been arrested and such a counter-blow delivered before they had consolidated their conquests as would have driven them back with severe losses. This check would have converted an enemy victory into a decisive defeat which would have put an end to any further hope of a German offensive. That is, the Allied victory of the 18th of July might have been anticipated. But would sufficient reinforcements reach the two Armies to avert disaster? What was the position on the whole battle front after four days of intense fighting? The Fifth Army was no longer an Army. It was broken up into fragments — still fighting as it drifted back. It is right to note that there was no running away. To quote one report: "There was no skedaddle." But the zig-zag where it rested on the night of the 24th was on an average over sixteen miles behind the line which it held at dawn on the 21st, and further retreats were inevitable. It was anticipated by British and French Headquarters that Amiens would be lost. The Third Army was also in full retreat. It had been driven miles behind the original line. Pétain on the fourth day was arranging to take over the southern portion of the Fifth Army area, but even on the sixth day of the battle he told Poincaré that he was afraid his divisions would not arrive in time to relieve the British Army. That was the prospect when Milner arrived in France on the afternoon of the 24th. From a member of our Staff at Versailles he learnt the actual situation. How little we had been told of the facts is made clear by one of the first sentences in the Memorandum he wrote on his visit for the benefit of the War Cabinet.

"The great mystery was the breakdown of the Fifth Army, which so far was not explained."

He was told that it was so much broken and its communications cut in all directions, that it was difficult to make out exactly what had happened. Apparently there was no one at G.H.Q. who was able to enlighten him. But he heard enough there, and on the road to Versailles, to come to the conclusion that "there was no doubt that this army was shattered and a breach effected in the Allied line between the right flank of the Third Army and the French." That meant that the Germans were within sight of attaining one of their great objectives — the separation of the French and the British Armies. The retreating troops were "still fighting at a number of points, and sometimes even counter-attacking, but were no longer anything like an organised barrier to the German advance."

The following day, Monday, March 25th, he attended a Conference held at Pétain's Headquarters, Clemenceau, Loucheur, Pétain and Foch being also present. Pétain took a very pessimistic view of the condition of the Fifth Army, which he said, as an army, had ceased to exist and would have to be completely reorganised. It had now been placed by Haig under his (Pétain's) orders. He was bringing up from the south and west — mostly from the south — "all the divisions he could possibly spare to support and replace the debris of the Fifth Army." But Pétain was still deluded by "the danger of the Germans pushing down the Oise from above Noyon, and a threatened attack in the region of Rheims."

Foch, who seems to have spoken with energy and determination, took a different view of the situation. He thought the danger of the German push to break in between the French and British in the direction of Amiens was so formidable that risks must be taken in other directions. In his opinion, even more divisions must, if possible, be thrown in, and, by a great effort, this might be done more quickly than Pétain thought possible. It is in an emergency that the real quality of a man comes out. In front of this grave crisis both Pétain and Haig were bewildered and incapable of the action which a desperate situation demanded, but Foch rose to the occasion with the might of a giant. That accounts for the complete change which Milner found in the attitude of both Commanders-in-Chief towards this great old General. They were now anxious to retrace the fatal steps they had conjointly taken on the Versailles decision and to secure the help of Foch to extricate them from the dilemma in which their repudiation of his supremacy had landed the Allied Armies. At the end of the Conference, Poincaré and Clemenceau urged that something should be done in order to reëstablish the complete coöperation of the two Armies. Although Milner had always been anxious for action on those lines, he could not take upon himself the responsibility of deciding until he had had an opportunity of consulting Haig. He might have pointed out that no one was more responsible than Clemenceau himself for the fact that the scheme agreed to by the Supreme Council seven weeks ago for securing such coöperation had been completely frustrated. After the Conference was over, Milner told Clemenceau that he had some misgivings "whether Pétain on his side was prepared to take sufficient risks in order to bring up all possible French reserves, on which, as it seemed to him, everything depended."

Clemenceau replied "that he agreed, but that Pétain was already doing *much more than he had originally contemplated,* and would, he believed, do more still." What an admission of the complete inadequacy of the arrangements made between Pétain and Haig as a substitution for the 30 Division Reserves under independent command!

The following day, March 26th, a Conference was held at Doullens at which Poincaré, Clemenceau, Pétain and Foch represented the French, and Milner, Haig and Wilson the British. When Milner arrived there, Clemenceau at once "seized him and startled him by the announcement that Haig had just declared that he would be obliged to uncover Amiens and fall back on the Channel ports." Milner immediately saw Haig, Plumer, Horne and Byng, and Haig assured him that he had been misunderstood. Haig did not inform them that he had only the day before handed to Weygand (Foch's Chief of the Staff) the following document: —

"SECRET.

"The intention of the enemy is evidently to push strong forces between the English and French Armies and having effected this purpose to detain the French Army while throwing his whole available strength on the English and force the latter back upon the sea.

"On the English Front from the sea to Ercheu the enemy have 65 divisions in line with 33 divisions in reserve of which latter 20 are fresh divisions. On the French Front from Ercheu to the Swiss frontier are 71 divisions in line with 24 divisions in reserve of which 21 are fresh divisions. But 15 divisions of the 71 in line are not fighting divisions.

"The battle, which has lasted since 21st on the English Front has probably exhausted a certain number of German divisions and they are now drawing on the divisions holding the line or in reserve elsewhere.

"But it is highly improbable that more than 21 reserve divisions are available for offensive on the French Front.

"*The progress made by the enemy on our right and along the valley of the Somme makes it evident that it can only be a question of time when the French and English Armies are driven apart.* It becomes necessary to take immediate steps to restore the situation, and this is only possible by concentrating immediately astride the Somme west of AMIENS at least 20 French divisions to operate on the flank of the German movement against the English Army, *which must fight its way slowly back covering the Channel ports.*

"Any delay in deciding upon this plan would make the situation critical.

"The two French divisions in Belgium should be concentrated immediately at DOULLENS.

"25th March, 1918.

"* Copy of above handed to General Weygand at Abbeville at 4 P.M.

* D. HAIG, F.M.
25th March, 1918."

(The asterisk signifies that this was written in Field-Marshal Sir Douglas Haig's own handwriting.)

Haig clearly took a desperate view of the position. It is difficult to comprehend in the face of this document why he should have told Milner that he had been misunderstood. Pétain expressed an identical opinion about the same time to Clemenceau, and according to Poincaré was actually ordering a retreat of the French Army to the south, and Clemenceau had agreed with Pétain. It would look, therefore, as if the two Commanders at this Conference on the evening of the 24th had come to the same conclusion. The supreme courage of Foch saved the situation. This was the greatest moment in his career. Here Poincaré's Diary on the subject is worth quoting, as, taken in conjunction with Haig's Memorandum, it shows the depth of dejection in which these eminent Commanders were floundering at this date.

"He [Clemenceau] broke off to confide in me sadly that General Pétain was contemplating the retreat of the French Army to the south while the British Army retired towards the north. Pétain, added Clemenceau, had given orders on this basis. Foch confirmed this last piece of information and told me of the order to retreat which Pétain had given. 'The President of the Council [Clemenceau],' added Foch, 'has only just lately begun to take part in military matters; he had accepted Pétain's point of view, but I declined to take any responsibility for it. I sent M. Clemenceau a note to tell him my views. Common sense indicates that when the enemy wishes to begin making a hole, you do not make it wider. You close it, or you try to close it. We have only got to try and to have the will; the rest will be easy. You stick to your ground, you defend it foot by foot. We did that at Ypres, we did it at Verdun.' And Foch stuck to his point with the same energy before Clemenceau, the senator and the deputy.

"Clemenceau, becoming more and more converted, took me aside and said: 'Pétain is annoying because of his pessimism. Just think of it, he said to me what I would tell no one but yourself. It was this: "The Germans will beat the British in open country; after that, they will beat us too." Ought a General to talk, or even think, like that?'"

Before entering into the Conference at Doullens, Milner had a few words with Haig alone about Foch, and "was delighted to find that, so far from resenting, as he had been led to believe he might do, the thought of Foch's interference, he rather welcomed the idea of working with the latter, about whom his tone was now altogether friendly." After some interchange of views, the Conference agreed to the following form of words: —

"General Foch is charged by the British and French Governments to coördinate the action of the Allied Armies on the Western Front. He will work to this end with the Commanders-in-Chief, who are asked to furnish him with all necessary information."

Haig "seemed not only quite willing but really pleased."

What had been accomplished by this decision? I will quote two opinions expressed, one by the President of the Republic, who was at the Conference, and another by a very competent military observer, General Bliss. In a conversation which Poincaré had with Milner immediately after the meeting, he said: —

"This coördination was not worth as much as unity of command. To which Milner replied that there was no knowing what the future held in store, and in any case, coördination itself represented a step forward and would offer great advantages."

Both Poincaré's statement and Milner's reply constitute a very fair appreciation of what had been accomplished. It was a long way off unity of command. That was for the future. Meanwhile it was, as Milner truly said, an improvement on existing conditions.

General Bliss, writing about the Doullens Conference, confirms Poincaré's and Milner's views about what took place. This is what he has written about the Doullens Resolution: —

"Many persons think that this action made General Foch the Allied Commander-in-Chief. It did not. His functions were limited to the British and French Armies. They did not extend to the American Army. No American was summoned to the conference at Doullens. No control was given over the Belgian or Italian Armies. *Moreover, there was given him no power of command. He could only consult and advise. The result was what might have been expected. He had to waste precious time in travelling to one headquarters and the other, persuading Commanders to do what he should have been empowered to order.*"

A day or two after the Doullens Conference, General Gough was superseded. After days of hard fighting with insufficient forces against unfair odds his army had been shattered. The French, very unfairly, threw the blame of the defeat on him. Haig practically adopted the same line by removing Gough from his command. In his Despatches on this battle Haig, explaining Gough's supersession, writes: —

"Our troops had been engaged for a full week with an almost overwhelming superiority of hostile forces."

He proceeds to say that this had "thrown an exceptional strain on General Gough and his Staff" and that "in order to avoid the loss of efficiency which a continuance of such a strain might have entailed", he decided to appoint General Rawlinson to the command of the Fifth Army. Gough was sent to the rear to look after the digging. Whose fault was it that there had been an overwhelming superiority against the Fifth Army for a whole week? It was certainly not Gough's. Taking the Western Front as a whole, I have quoted official figures to show that the rival armies were approximately equal in numbers with a slight superiority in favour of the Allies, but with a definite mechanical advantage to the British and the French. Haig acknowledges that he knew in time where the offensive was coming. Gough was not responsible for the disposition of the Allied forces in such a way as to give to the Germans overwhelming superiority at the point of attack, and he could not be blamed for the fact that at the end of a full week of hard fighting the Germans still possessed that overwhelming superiority on the battle front. It was not Gough who strangled the army of manœuvre which was designed for such an emergency as had arisen. Nevertheless, Gough's sacrifice has pointed the finger of censure at him. That was unfair — nay, it was shabby. Whatever may be said of this gallant officer, he was certainly unfortunate in the tasks which had been entrusted to him by his Commander-in-Chief in this War. In Flanders he had been put in charge of an enterprise in which the finest army in the world and the most brilliant general could not have won success. On the Somme he had been given a position to defend which no general could have held with so few troops and guns in the line and in reserve. With a little help on the first day he would probably have beaten off the Germans. A few divisions would have done it.

Contrary to what is frequently stated, the dismissal of Gough from command of the Fifth Army was ordered by Haig entirely on his own initiative, without any instruction from home.[1] The War Cabinet subsequently ordered Gough home, as this culminating dismissal of him by Haig, following the retreat of the Fifth Army, and the flood of rumours circulating in military circles against him made it *prima facie* appear that he was in some way culpable. Further inquiry did not support that case, and Lord Milner sent him a letter fully exonerating him and pronouncing him eligible for a fresh command.[2]

When Foch was given the rôle of coördinator the battle was going heavily in favour of the enemy. I recollect that on Good Friday morning the news filled us with anxiety and apprehension. The Germans were pressing British and French troops steadily back towards Amiens at a rate that made it seem inevitable that this important railway junction would fall into their hands. That would have been a catastrophe and we were not certain whether Foch's appointment had come in time to avert it. On the northern flank of the Third Army the Germans had launched another great attack which if it succeeded would have placed the whole of the Army in jeopardy. The only news received by Friday morning about the progress of this fresh development was not reassuring. We had been forced out of some of our positions and the battle was still raging. We were barely holding our own. Sir Maurice

---

[1] See "Haig's Diary", edited by Duff Cooper, Vol. II, p. 267.
[2] "Official History, France and Belgium, 1918", Vol. I, page viii.

Hankey and I sat for hours in the Cabinet Room waiting anxiously for further reports from the front. We decided at last to go to St. Anne's, Soho, to hear Bach's Passion music. As we took our seats we heard the clergyman intone that poignant supplication, "O God, make speed to save us." How fervently we joined in the response, "O Lord, make haste to help us!" When we returned to Downing Street we heard that the Germans had been beaten off by the Third Army with heavy losses and that their advance was slowing down opposite Amiens.

CHAPTER XI

THE AMERICAN ARMIES IN FRANCE

Wilson slow to start real preparations — Financial aid — Position after six months — Influence on Allied and enemy strategy — Anxiety over slow arrival of U.S. troops — America remote from the War — I invite House to bring a Mission to Europe — Composition of the Mission — Its arrival — Meeting at Downing Street — My speech — Need for man power — Shipping — Food — Naval and aircraft needs — Benson's reply — Troop transport — Pershing's complaint — Training deficiencies — Difficulty of transporting intact divisions — Proposal to brigade U.S. troops with British and French — Priority for combatant troops — Robertson's interview with Pershing — Robertson's gloomy view — My appeal to House — Pershing suspicious of his Allied colleagues — Report of situation on January 25th — Robertson sees Bliss and Pershing — Discussion at Versailles Conference — Pershing's Memorandum — Pershing carries his point — Pershing's admission of delay — Situation in March — We appeal for more American troops — Versailles recommendation — Pershing's alarm — Arrangements left in his hands — My message to Reading — His report of American conditions — Pershing offers troops to Pétain — My appeal to Wilson — Wilson agrees to our proposals — A further message to him — Pershing wrecks the arrangements — Problem of speed of transports — Pershing's fixed idea — My plea for immediate use of American troops — Compromise agreement reached — Pershing refuses to accept Wilson's ruling — Foch cannot move him — Discussion at Supreme War Council — Fresh compromise agreed — Military stubbornness not peculiar to America — Shortage of trained men — Another compromise on use of troops — Foch wants one hundred American divisions — An exaggerated demand — British success in shipping U.S. troops — Blunders over equipment — American contempt for European methods — Lack of drive at the top — Wilson's limitations — Contrast with Lincoln — Aeroplanes — Artillery tanks — Transport — Troops finer than their organisation.

On April 2nd, 1917, President Wilson declared that a state of war existed between America and Germany. I have already drawn attention to the fact that at the outset America was entirely unprepared for carrying on active military operations on an adequate scale. Wilson had consistently discouraged every appeal made to him in America to strengthen the forces of the republic in order to deal with the menacing contingencies in which the States might become involved. Even after the declaration, the preparations for a vigorous prosecution tarried and loitered in a manner which I find it difficult to explain when one looks at the dynamic energy and resourcefulness of this wonderful people. For almost a year after war had been declared, the contribution of the mighty republic to the struggle in France was on a comparatively insignificant scale. It was very much less than that which the far smaller British nation had succeeded in making in a similar period.

It will be understood that I am here speaking chiefly of the military effort of the United States. Her financial and economic assistance was from the outset invaluable, and had been developed on a considerable scale long before any large number of her troops were ready to take their place in the battle line. And her naval assistance became highly serviceable in helping us to counter the submarine menace. We were short of torpedo-craft for our convoys. Here the assistance of the American Fleet was eminently useful.

At the end of September, 1917, when America had been approximately six months at war, the total strength of the American Expeditionary Force in France was 61,531, and none of her divisions had as yet been placed in the line. America and Britain were alike in one respect. They had not trained their young manhood by conscript laws to the use of arms. They both relied on small professional armies and citizen organisations. But at the end of six months the British Expeditionary Force on the Western Front numbered 354,750. The 1st American Division was put into a quiet sector of the French Front on October 21st, 1917 — nearly seven months after the severance of diplomatic relations with Germany. No other American division went into the line until eleven months had elapsed since the entry of America into the War. A considerable period of training was needed to prepare recruits for the highly scientific methods of warfare which had been developed during the past three and a half years, involving the close coöperation of infantry with machine-guns, trench mortars, artillery barrages, tanks, etc.: the organisation of trench warfare, gas drill, and all the complexities of munitionment in this growingly elaborate and mechanised struggle. The tide of American forces in France, which was ultimately to swell to so large a flood, mounted only in a dribbling fashion during those early months. By the end of October it was 87,000; by the end of November, 126,000; and at the beginning of 1918, 175,000. That was nine months after the entry of America into the War. At that stage in our own war effort we had already thrown 659,104 into the various war theatres.

Yet this flow, so tardy for the time being, was watched with concentrated interest by friend and foe alike, and became the dominating strategical factor in the calculations of both sides. Hindenburg and Ludendorff on the one side, and Foch and Pétain on the other, framed their plans for 1918 with their eyes fixed on this gulf-stream of young manhood that was flowing from the shores of America towards Europe. It is clear, from a study of the accounts given of the struggle on the German side, that the prospect of that swelling flow of American troops was the consideration which finally determined the German High Command to risk all on a desperate thrust in March, 1918, in an effort to gain a decision before the arrival of the full flood of American fighting men in the battle area. Equally the prospect of the American reinforcement coming to their aid enabled the French, after the failure of the Nivelle offensive and the outbreak of mutiny in their ranks in the summer of 1917, to avert panic and resign themselves without undue despondency to standing quietly on the defensive for the remainder of the year and waiting until in the course of 1918 the American advent should turn the tide in their favour. In all the conferences and strategical discussions of the Allies during the autumn and winter of 1917, this prospective asset figures prominently. Before ever the Americans had fired a shot in battle, their coming turned the scale of confidence and hope in favour of the Allies.

In the autumn of 1917, however, this reinforcement was arriving with what seemed to be disconcerting and perplexing slowness. Both the French and ourselves were apprehensive lest, if it were not speeded up, it should arrive too late to save the Allied Front from collapse in face of the formidable German attack. The reservoir of French man power had almost run dry and ours was approaching exhaustion; and now that Russia was falling out, we knew only too well that the enemy would be able to bring masses of additional troops to the West, and that with this increased striking force he might achieve some decisive success before the Americans could turn the scale. Thus it became a matter of vital moment to press for a speeding-up in the transit of the American forces, and to coöperate with the United States as effectively as possible to this end.

As has been related elsewhere, one of the first steps taken by Britain and France after the entry of America into the War had been to send Missions to the States to ensure coöperation and good understanding with their new associate in the conflict. But before long it was evident that if America was to take her proper place in the councils of the Allies, and render the help of which she was capable, efforts would have to be made to bring prominent Americans into closer contact with the urgent day-to-day problems which the War brought forth.

I had a feeling that the remoteness of America in miles and still more in atmosphere from the scene of the conflict had much to do with the leisurely way in which her preparations for taking part in the actual fighting were being conducted. The enemy was on the soil of France and within a score of leagues of its capital. German ships occasionally bombarded our coast towns and German Zeppelins and aeroplanes raided our capital and killed hundreds of our women and children. City and village were everywhere darkened at night, so as to offer no guidance to the raiders as to where they could drop their shattering bombs with the deadliest effect. All our greatest town and country houses had been converted into hospitals which were crowded with the wounded from the ghastly battlefields of the Continent. And the prevalence of black in the costumes of our women testified to the numbers who were grieving over the most irreparable havoc of war. There was no need for speeches or exhortations in the Press to remind the nation that it was engaged in mortal grip with the most formidable enemy it had ever challenged. And yet even in Britain there were moments of slackness which impeded critical preparations. Men have been known to sleep amidst the greatest perils through sheer nervous exhaustion. And when our jeopardy was greatest we had to take special measures by visits from the King, by propaganda, and otherwise to stimulate workers of every grade to greater energy. We could, therefore, well understand why in a country which had none of these grim reminders that it was at war there was not the same constant urge to hurry and hustle. But I thought that, since we could not anchor the States within sound of the struggle, we might accomplish something if we could induce a few of their leading citizens to come over and see for themselves how pressing was the need.

I asked Lord Reading and Sir William Wiseman to propose to Colonel House that a United States Mission should be sent to Europe, composed of the heads of the more important departments concerned with the war effort, to study the problems at close range. Wiseman did so in a letter containing the following passage: —

"I believe the greatest asset Germany has to-day is the 3,000 miles that separate London from Washington, and the most urgent problem we have to solve is how our two Governments, set at opposite ends of the world, can effect the close coöperation which is undoubtedly necessary if the War is to be quickly and successfully ended. Would the President consider the advisability of sending plenipotentiary envoys to London and Paris, with the object of taking part in the next great Allied Council, bringing their fresh minds to bear on our problems, discussing and giving their judgment on some of the questions I have raised, and also to arrange — if that be possible — for some machinery to bridge over the distance between Washington and the theatre of war?"

This letter was dated September 26th, 1917. Colonel House, who knew European War conditions better than most of his countrymen, not excluding the President, acted promptly, and early in October President Wilson made up his mind that such a Mission was necessary, and decided to send one with Colonel House at its head.

On learning this, the Foreign Secretary, on behalf and at the request of the Cabinet, sent on October 14th, 1917, to Colonel House, a cable saying: —

"I am authorised by French and British Cabinets to extend to you a most cordial invitation to take part in conversations and conferences on all questions of war and peace. It is with the greatest gratification that they have learnt of the probability that this invitation may prove acceptable. I cannot speak officially of Italians and Russians, but you may safely assume that they share our interests. . . ."

President Wilson was saturated with the American suspicion and distrust of Europe, which would have been difficult to explain in a people whose ancestry was European, had it not been for the fact that the emigrants had fled from the privations and oppressions of Europe to seek a land whose economic opportunities were ampler and whose laws gave greater promise of freedom and equality. The President decided that this was to be a visiting, not a permanent Mission. The Mission was to be exploratory with a view to establishing liaison and to clear up outstanding issues. Apart from Colonel House, its principal members were: —

Rear-Admiral W. S. Benson, Chief of Naval Operations.
General Tasker H. Bliss, Chief of Staff of the Army.
Oscar T. Crosby, Assistant Secretary of the Treasury.
Paul Cravath, Legal Adviser to the Treasury.
Vance C. McCormick, Chairman of the War Trade Board.
Bainbridge Colby, representing the United States Shipping Board.
Dr. Alonzo R. Taylor, representing the United States Food Controller.
Thomas Nelson Perkins, Legal Adviser to the War Industries Board.

The Secretary to the Mission was Gordon Auchincloss, Assistant Counsellor of the State Department.

The Mission left the States on October 29, and arrived at Plymouth on November 7th, 1917. With their coming, the participation of the United States in the World War took on a new meaning and value. The representatives of economic and commercial interests were able, with their opposite numbers of France and Britain, to clear up difficult outstanding issues which had hitherto delayed progress. And General Bliss passed to the Supreme War Council at Versailles, which was set up shortly after his arrival here, as the American member of the body of Permanent Military Representatives. It was a happy choice, fortunate for America and specially fortunate for the cause of the Allies as a whole. He was level-headed, and endowed with an uncommon measure of common sense. He also possessed the valuable attribute of combining a complete independence of judgment with an exceptional gift of working harmoniously with others. He was one of the most valuable contributions America made to the successful prosecution of the War.

I invited this American Mission to 10 Downing Street, on November 20th, 1917, for a consultation on the immediate issues. On our side we had a very full assembly, numbering twenty-five in all. All the members of the War Cabinet were present. There were also the heads of the State Departments dealing with our war activities — the Foreign Office, Navy, Army, Blockade, Shipping, Food, etc. Admiral Jellicoe as First Sea Lord and Sir William Robertson as Chief of the Imperial General Staff were also present. One feature which lent an added interest to the gathering was that the room where we met was the same one in which, one hundred and thirty years previously, Lord North had decided and directed the policy which drove the Americans to revolt against the British Crown. I opened my speech to the Conference by referring to this fact.

I then proceeded to sketch briefly the ways in which it seemed to us, with three and a half years of war experience, that America could render most effectual service. This, I explained, was not altogether easy.

"All the things which are wanted for the efficient conduct of the campaign are urgent, because, naturally, the sooner you are ready, the sooner it will be over. But there are one or two things which are more urgent than others. After a good deal of consultation with my colleagues and our military and naval advisers, I should put man-power and shipping as the two first demands on your consideration. I am not quite sure which I will put first. I am not sure that you can put either of them before the other, because they are both of the most urgent importance; but if you will permit me, I should like to say a few words upon each."

With regard to man power, I pointed to the collapse of Russia and Italy, and to the fading man power of France.

The Russian collapse would enable Germany to bring thirty or forty of her best divisions from the Eastern Front and hurl them against us on the West. The Italian position was not nearly so bad as it had threatened to become a fortnight previously, but it meant that France and Britain had got to pour in very substantial assistance in the form of some of their best divisions, in order to save Italy from collapse. I further pointed out that France herself was very largely exhausted. For this reason there would be on the Allied side a considerably smaller number of troops available next year than there was this year. On the other hand, Germany, owing to the Russian collapse, would have six hundred thousand more men on the French and Flanders Fronts.

"That shows that it is a matter of the most urgent and immediate importance that you should send to Europe next year, and as early next year as possible, as many men as you can spare, to enable us to withstand any possible German attack. This is apart altogether from the possibility of inflicting any defeat upon them. It is better that I should put the facts quite frankly to you, *because there is a danger that you might think you can work your army up at leisure, and that it does not matter whether your troops are there in 1918 or 1919. But I want you to understand that it might make the most vital difference. . . ."*

I then called attention to the shipping position and the urgency of their taking immediate steps to increase their transport facilities for carrying troops and material to Europe.

"Sixty per cent. of our shipping is engaged on war service, on purely war service, for ourselves and our Allies. In order to show the extent to which we are helping our Allies, 2,600,000 tons of our shipping is devoted exclusively to helping the Allies — France, Russia and Italy — more especially France, and half the time another 2,300,000 tons of shipping as well is directed to the same purpose. Now, we are a country more dependent upon imports than probably any other great country in the world. It is a very small country as you have probably observed in crossing it — a very small country, and a very thickly populated country. We only grow about one-fifth of the wheat we consume. We are dependent on what we get from overseas for the rest. I am not sure if we cultivated every yard here that we could be self-supporting. . . . Taking the barest essentials not merely of life, but of war, we have also to import a good deal of our ore and other commodities, essential to our war equipment. Our exports have almost vanished, except war exports. I should like our American friends to realise what this means to us. The trade of this country is largely an international trade. We manufactured for the world, and we carried for the world, and we did a good deal of financing for the world; all that is practically gone. *We have stripped to the waist for war.* Such exports as there are we have only kept alive, because they are essential in order to enable us to finance certain essential imports in certain parts of the world. . . . There were ships of ours which never came home to this country. We were a people who lent ships and traded in ships. Now the Shipping Controller has brought them home from every part of the world. Why? We have had to get rid of our business, because we want it for war, and to help not merely ourselves, but to help our Allies. I am not sure it is sufficiently realised outside — the extent to which we have put our trade, as it were, into the War. We have risked it all on this great venture."

I proceeded to give figures to show the extent to which we were cutting down our imports, which by 1918 would have been reduced to less than half their pre-War bulk, not only because of the diversion of shipping to war services for ourselves and our Allies, but of the inroads made on our tonnage and on that of our Allies and neutral countries by the submarine.

"We shall have to ration, not so much for ourselves, but because the French production of food is down to 40 per cent. of what it was before the War, for the simple reason that the peasants who cultivated the soil are now shouldering the rifle instead of following the plough. They are defending their land, and that land is meanwhile getting weedy because the men are not there to cultivate it. The women are doing their best in France, even the old women and children are working, but the soil is getting impoverished, and therefore we have to pool our luck. . . . We have to divert our wheat to save the French and save the Italians — to save the Italians from actual privation.

"I met the correspondent of *The Times* in Paris the other day, and he said to me: 'I have just been through parts of France. I went to a village where they had had no bread for days.' If that had happened here, Lord Rhondda's head would have been put on a charger, and probably mine with it, too. The only remark that correspondent had heard was: 'Well, we are a very patient people.' As M. Clemenceau remarked to me, that is why we have revolutions in France — which is a very shrewd observation. . . . They are holding on with great fortitude, and there is not a single thought of giving in. The Government that proposed to give in would not last 24 hours. In spite of the gigantic losses they have sustained, and of the privations they are facing, France is resolute and as determined as ever she was. We feel it an honour to pool our luck with her, and we have agreed to do it."

These facts, I said, pointed to the need for a big shipping increase. I also asked for supplies of steel plates for Canada and ourselves for shipbuilding.

"To summarise what I have said as to the most important spheres in which the United States can help in the War. The first is that you should help France and the Allies in the battle line with as many men as you can possibly train and equip at the earliest possible moment, so as to be able to sustain the brunt of any German attack in the course of the next year; and the next point is that you should assist to make up the deficit in the shipbuilding tonnage of the year by extending your yards and increasing shipbuilding at an unexampled rate."

I passed on to pay a tribute to the great help which was being rendered by the United States Navy in combating the submarine menace, and to urge consultation with a view to developing our defences for this purpose. I dealt with the need for more aeroplanes. The command of the Air was as essential for victory as the command of the Sea. The Germans were now making a prodigious effort to secure it. In this direction I suggested that the Americans should be able to render very marked service, alike in the manufacture of planes and in the supply of efficient pilots. "Your people have got more than the usual share of enterprise and daring, which are essential qualities in a successful airman. I should have thought that an American naturally would make a first-class fighter in the air, because of those qualities of enterprise and dash and daring which are associated with your race, and which you have displayed on so many battlefields both in peace and in war." The climate too, and the expanse as well as the variety of their territory gave them ample opportunity for training.

I asked, too, for guns. The war was increasingly an artillery conflict, and only a great weight of artillery could make an advance possible without heavy loss. "The more guns the fewer casualties because they destroy the protection which the Germans have set up for their machine-gunners."

I further instanced the need for food supplies, especially now that the granaries of Russia were closed to us and Australian supplies were too far away to be brought over with our diminished shipping. In conclusion, I paid tribute to the value of the help they were rendering to the Allies in regard to finance and the tightening of the blockade upon Germany.

Admiral Benson replied on behalf of the delegation and opened the discussion upon the issues raised by me. He acknowledged the very full and frank way in which our Government departments had placed at the disposal of the Mission all information bearing on the matters in which they were interested. They had come to realise that they were unprepared with many forms of equipment. "But," he said, "the time has come when we feel that we must get closer together, and we must follow a definite line." He stressed the unity of the States behind the President and their readiness to bring all their resources to aid in securing victory.

As regards shipping, he said that the United States hoped within the next ten months to produce at least 267 destroyers. They were also building 103 submarines. They were not troubling about capital ships, but were devoting the rest of their shipbuilding capacity to construction of cargo ships. Food restrictions were being introduced in the States, to release as much food as possible for the needs of the European Allies. In regard to aircraft, it was hoped to be turning them out by hundreds a month in January, and by thousands in May or June. Their "Liberty" motor was yielding excellent results in trials.

In artillery production they were specially devoting themselves to manufacture of guns for use on ships, specially four-inch and five-inch guns for destroyers. Benson also spoke of the extent to which the United States Government was subsidising the erection of additional plant and foundries for the manufacture of arms and war material.

In reply to a question by Lord Derby, he said that when by June they were turning out 4,300 aeroplanes a month, they hoped also to be turning out trained pilots for that number of machines. (These optimistic forecasts never materialised. When the Armistice was signed in November there were no American field guns in France and very few aeroplanes.)

Discussion then passed to the question of tonnage for carrying men and materials to France. Here the figures for the present and near future were far from satisfactory. Mr. Colby said the tonnage at the disposal of the American Army at the moment amounted to 850,000 tons, and of the Navy to 150,000 tons. By January 15th, 1918, there would have been conveyed to France one army corps in addition to the American troops already there. But this army corps would not be completely equipped, and would not have all its transport animals. According to his estimate, the tonnage available would enable the United States to maintain 220,000 men in France.

It was obvious to us all that a force no larger than that would not suffice to turn the scale of victory for the Allies, and thus the tonnage problem became one of predominant importance. The conference proceeded to discuss for some time the possibilities of making fuller and better use of neutral tonnage, and eventually it was decided that a sub-committee should meet that afternoon to thrash out this issue. Lord Curzon, Lord Milner, Lord Robert Cecil and Sir Joseph Maclay were appointed to represent the British, and Messrs. McCormick, Colby, Perkins and Dr. Taylor the Americans. This Committee duly met and after considering various suggestions, decided on measures to secure mutual consultation between Britain and the United States of America on shipping matters, a full analysis of tonnage needs and assets of the Allied and Associated Powers, and a sharing round of the neutral tonnage which had been requisitioned. The United States Government were urged to requisition the 400,000 tons of Dutch shipping then sheltering in United States ports and use it to help in conveying troops and supplies to France.

It was clear that unless a serious effort were made to remedy the situation, the contribution of America would fall far behind what had been reasonably expected of her. Not only was the available tonnage insufficient, but the use being made of it was far from satisfactory. Bungling and delay occurred, of the kind which seems constantly to arise when military or naval officials try to take in hand what is essentially a commercial operation. General Pershing [1] complains

[1] "My Experiences in the World War", pp. 249–251.

that the situation as to numbers of troops and supplies at the close of the year was not what the Americans had every reason to expect after having been at war nine months. "We had not obtained full service from the limited amount of tonnage thus far made available for military use. . . . We had less than 175,000 men in France, including about 100,000 in four divisions in various stages of organisation and training, while there should have been at least ten divisions of combat troops and other forces in proportion. It was a very unsatisfactory state of affairs that confronted us, with little prospect of improvement."

Pershing voiced his alarm in a cable to the home Government in America, on December 20th, 1917, in which he pointed out that the programme supposed to be in operation for the despatch of American troops would not succeed in placing even three complete corps, with proper proportion of Army troops and auxiliaries, in France by the end of May: —

"The actual facts are that shipments are not even keeping up to that schedule. It is now the middle of December and the first Corps (six divisions) is still incomplete by over two entire divisions and many corps troops. It cannot be too emphatically declared that we should be prepared to take the field with at least four corps (24 divisions) by 30th June. In view of past performances with tonnage heretofore unavailable such a project is impossible of fulfilment, but only by most strenuous attempts to attain such a result will we be in a position to take a proper part in operations in 1918. . . ."

He pleaded for the allocation of more tonnage for the transport of troops. In his comments upon the situation he remarks: —

"It need hardly be recorded that we were occasioned much embarrassment in facing the Allies with such a poor showing of

GENERAL JOHN J. PERSHING, COMMANDER-IN-CHIEF
AMERICAN EXPEDITIONARY FORCES

accomplishment. Up to this time, we had been handicapped in our efforts by lack of aggressive direction of affairs at home. Whether this was due to inefficiency or failure to appreciate the urgency of the situation, the War Department General Staff, as the superior coördinating agency, must take the greater part of the blame."

All this sounds curiously like an echo of the kind of experience we in Britain had gone through with some of our War Departments in the earlier stages of the War, but almost incredibly worse.

Had there been available unlimited tonnage and ample port accommodation and clearing facilities at the European side, it would have been possible to bring over in a short space of time a number of complete American formations, and presently place on the French Front an intact American Army, which was the urgent wish of General Pershing. It is true that the troops and the Staff officers lacked experience of the intensive methods of warfare that had been developed in France, and stood in need of the training which a period of brigading with French or British formations could best supply; and the equipment was entirely inadequate. Pershing himself was alarmed at the serious training deficiencies of the units reaching him in France. These deficiencies could, however, have been corrected once the troops were on French soil and in direct contact with the great Armies of France and Britain, and with the enormous war supplies accumulated by the Allies the American shortage in essentials could have been made up. Here with our three years of experience of actual war we could have helped them to expedite their training. There would have been no language impediment.

The advent of the American troops, in fact, presented a series of problems. There was first the tonnage problem. Then there was the difficulty presented by the bottle-neck of the French ports, cramped, congested, a fertile source of intolerable delay. Then there was the question of whether the

American troops should be retained in intact American corps formation, or whether their battalions should be brigaded with French and British divisions, for a time at least, to gain better experience of the War, and to render help to our depleted forces earlier than it would be possible for them to do if they were kept waiting until the full personnel and equipment of entire divisions could be brought over and organised.

This last, in view of the tonnage shortage, was a burning issue. Time was of the essence of victory. A given amount of shipping could bring over a large body of infantry, capable of powerfully reinforcing the thinning lines of the Allies. But if the same amount of shipping had to bring over the full personnel and equipment of divisions intact, including their artillery, baggage trains, H.Q. Staffs and details, and all the paraphernalia with which a wealthy country could load up its forces, then the actual number of combatant troops which could be brought to France within a given period was drastically reduced. Throughout the winter and spring of 1917–1918 an incessant argument was going on between the Americans and the Allies as to which course should be followed. The French and British, painfully conscious of the exhaustion of their reserves by four costly campaigns, and of the imminence of a powerful attack by increased and rapidly increasing German forces, were anxious that the cramped flow of troops from across the Atlantic should consist in the largest possible measure of fighting units which could be used in emergency to stop the gaps and the thin patches in the line. That would involve these troops being incorporated for the time being in French and British divisions, since the personnel and material for making them up into intact American divisions would not be available for several more months. But here Pershing was stubbornly insistent that he wanted, at the earliest possible moment, to form an independent American Army, with its own bases and transport communications, its own part of the front, all under his separate command. The reason he gave for this was that national prestige and public sentiment in the United States required this, and that to merge the American forces with those of their Allies would be naturally and properly resented and would give a handle to pro-German agitation in the States. In this argument there was doubtless considerable force. He was afraid that if once he let his battalions be brigaded into French or British divisions he would never see them again. To withdraw them later might be a practical impossibility. Had war preparations been taken in hand promptly and effectively the question would not have arisen, for the United States might have raised, trained, equipped and sent to France in 1917 a force of at least a score of complete divisions ready to take part in the impending struggle. But we had to deal with a situation for which the delays of American war direction were largely responsible.

The matter was so urgent that on December 15th I had cabled to Colonel House as follows: —

"Having regard to Russian situation and the fact that both guns and troops are being rapidly transferred from the Eastern to the Western Front, the Cabinet are anxious that an immediate decision should be come to in regard to the inclusion with the British units of regiments or companies of American troops, an idea which was discussed with you at Paris. In the near future and throughout the earlier months of next year the situation on the Western Front may become exceedingly serious, and it may become of vital importance that the American man-power available in France should be immediately used, more especially as it would appear that the Germans are calculating on delivering a knock-out blow to the Allies before a fully trained American Army is fit to to take its part in the fighting.

LLOYD GEORGE."

The American Government naturally sympathised with Pershing's point of view. But they were unwilling to press their insistence upon the independent ordering of American troops to a point which might gravely handicap military operations. On December 20th, 1917, we received a copy of a cable which Newton D. Baker, the American Secretary of War, intended issuing to General Pershing, which said: —

"Both English and French are pressing upon the President their desires to have your forces amalgamated with theirs by regiments and companies, and both express the belief in impending heavy drive by Germans somewhere along the lines of the Western Front. We do not desire loss of identity of our forces *but regard that as secondary* to the meeting of any critical situation by the most helpful use possible of the troops at your command. . . . The President however desires you to have full authority to use the forces at your command as you deem wise in consultation with the French and British Commanders-in-Chief. . . ."

I found Mr. Baker able, broad-minded, and understanding in the dealings I had with him during the War. This cable is an illustration of his general attitude. He was not responsible for the delays which occurred in reaching even a half-satisfactory settlement of this troublesome question. Against the stickiness of the professional general officer standing for his rights, intelligence and common sense struggle in vain. Mr. Newton Baker discovered that stubborn fact during the War.

In the course of the discussions the suggestion had been mooted that if the Americans would consent to send over infantry formations in advance of full divisional staffs, for temporary brigading with British units, we might make an effort to allocate extra tonnage for their transport. This promise produced some effect. On January 2nd, 1918, Pershing had an interview with Haig, at which the latter explained how he would propose to use and train such American battalions with his divisions, and gradually, as the American element increased, turn them into American divisions forming the American Army.

Sir William Robertson, our C.I.G.S., had an interview ten days later with General Pershing, which he described as "not very satisfactory." In his note of this interview, he said that General Pershing apparently had never seriously considered the proposal I had sent to Colonel House, although the memorandum of the subject had been shown him by House.

"The fact is, he does not like the proposal because, (*a*) he is anxious to bring over his divisions, as such; (*b*) he naturally prefers to preserve national identity and argues, quite rightly, that American battalions cannot be expected to do as well in British as in American divisions. The result of the interview was that he will forward our proposal to his Government giving it a mild form of support and telegraphing me a copy of the communication he sends. . . ."

Robertson went on to describe the demand of General Pershing for more tonnage, in which he asked that it should be used, not to bring over infantry alone, but intact divisions.

"I had repeatedly to remind him that whereas the tonnage we can find will bring over some 150,000 to 200,000 infantry (say 150 battalions) who can be fighting in three or four months, it cannot bring over more than about three divisions (36 battalions) who will not be fighting for at least six months. Eventually he admitted the force of this argument. I added that the British Government could not, for the sake of these three divisions, run the great risks incurred in cutting down our stocks of food and war material in order to provide the special tonnage, though they would do so for the sake of the infantry reinforcements."

That passage from Robertson's memorandum sums up the problem with which we were confronted at this stage. I had correctly told the American Mission that we had no tonnage to spare to help them in bringing over their troops. We had not enough, in fact, to meet what had been regarded as the minimum needs for transport for our armies and Allies and our essential requirements at home. Yet if it became a life and death issue, where extra American troops promptly thrown in would turn the scale between victory and defeat, we came to the conclusion that it would be worth while to take the risk of even letting our own and Allied stocks of food and raw materials run down while we diverted tonnage to bring those extra troops to France. But it would not be worth our while to take that gravely hazardous step unless the tonnage so spared were utilised to its utmost capacity to bring over fighting troops. If it were merely going to carry across numbers of divisional H.Q. details and non-combatant personnel and equipment in order to minister to the pride and enhance the consequence of a single General, we could find a far more urgent use for it. Pershing demanded the ships, but would only bring over intact divisions in them. Germany brought over from the Russian Front hordes of fighting men to incorporate in their depleted divisions, and even the complete divisions they transported to the West did not carry with them their full quota of behind-the-line services.

General Robertson's Memorandum concluded with a pessimistic account of the prospects which, if perhaps rather exaggerated, was quite a characteristic grumble about foreigners of all sorts and kinds: —

"I have never been very sanguine as to American assistance in any form this year, and I must tell the War Cabinet that I have returned still less sanguine. The raising of new armies is a tremendous task for any country, and although one might expect that America, with her two previous experiences, and her supposed great business and hustling qualities, would do better than other countries, the fact is that she is doing very badly. . . . The French have lost all patience, and their relations with the Americans are the reverse of good. The French are always much too optimistic in such matters, but they may well be excused for being dissatisfied in the present case. The Americans are proceeding as if they had years in which to prepare. They have laid out cantonment areas for ten divisions, and are building the most luxurious huts to supplement billets; each man has a *bed* and three blankets. . . .

"My general impression is that America's power to help us to win the War — that is to help us to defeat the Germans in battle — is a very weak reed to lean upon at present, and will continue to be so for a very long time to come unless she follows up her words with actions much more practical and energetic than any she has yet taken."

It is almost amusing to compare this melancholy vaticination with the actual subsequent history of the American armies. Nevertheless there is no doubt that American effort at this stage sadly needed quickening. The fact that the principal military adviser of the British Government made such a report shows that at the time he was getting badly rattled at the alarming hang-back in the progress of America's military contribution to the Allied cause.

I promptly sent off a telegram to Colonel House on January 15th, 1918, informing him of the upshot of Robertson's interview with Pershing, and urging that Washington should authorise the proposed arrangement to provide the maximum man power for France by temporarily attaching American troops to British divisions. I stated the proposal as follows: —

". . . We have examined the question of sea transport carefully, and find that by making large temporary sacrifices in our food imports we could bring over about 150,000 American infantry, that is, 150 battalions, during the next three or four months, without in any way interfering with present arrangements for bringing over American divisions. We can arrange to feed these battalions, to supply all additional equipment, and to provide necessary training facilities. If these battalions were temporarily incorporated in British formations it would give us invaluable aid during the next critical six months. Later in the year they could, if desired, be withdrawn and incorporated in American divisions.

"If the above amount of shipping were allotted to bringing American divisions with full equipment over, not more than three could be brought, and further the time required to train divisions for the field is much longer than for companies or battalions. The Government does not feel justified in asking our people to bear the great additional sacrifices which diversion of shipping will entail for the sake of the assistance of three divisions at a distant date. . . ."

There can be little doubt that at this time there was a lack of hearty coöperation between the American General and his French and British colleagues. In his own comment upon his interview with Robertson (described in Robertson's Memorandum to which I have referred), Pershing declares that: —

"The arguments General Robertson advanced clearly indicated that the British were playing for advantage to themselves in offering to transport our troops. In other words, they had the shipping to transport American battalions on condition that they would serve in the British armies. Their purpose was to build up their own units instead of aiding the cause in general by augmenting the number of complete combat divisions on the Western Front." [1]

That suggestion shows a real lack of understanding of the desperate straits in which we were by that time for tonnage, and a somewhat unworthy suspicion that we were playing for a selfish advantage when as a matter of fact our one concern was to avoid a disastrous setback to the Allied Armies. As time went on, the Americans were persuaded by

[1] "My Experiences in the World War", p. 259.

the spectacle of disaster threatening the cause they had espoused, and as far as American statesmen were concerned this attitude of distrust gave way to a sounder understanding and franker coöperation. But for the time being it created a good deal of difficulty which hampered the adoption of wise arrangements.

At a meeting of the War Cabinet on January 25th, 1918, the Director of Military Operations read extracts from a French report concerning the state of the American Army. It was expected that there would be eight divisions in France in March, 14 in June, and 20 in September, 1918, and 28 in January, 1919, but these divisions would require six months' training in France before they would be fit to take an active part in operations. Hence at this rate by July only four trained divisions could be counted on, and by October only eight, with perhaps four half-trained divisions fit for a quiet sector. At the present moment there was one efficient division, and a second was now about to receive its first trench training.

It was asked whether these figures were independent of the 150,000 lately promised. The answer was in the affirmative.

It was also asked whether these 150,000 men would be as slow to become efficient as the divisions referred to in the French report.

The Director of Military Operations pointed out that battalions could be trained in one-sixth of the time required for the training of a division. If the transport of these troops began at once, we should have some of these battalions in the line in May.

The Secretary of State for War expressed a fear that the tonnage available for the transport of these troops was going to be cut down. He also adverted to the very backward state of the training of the American infantry.

On January 26th, 1918, General Robertson had long interviews in France with Pershing and Bliss about the issue. In a despatch of that date to the Secretary of State for War, he reported his interview, and complained that although Bliss and Pershing had been given authority by Washington to make arrangements for the 150-battalion project, they were afraid to take any responsibility for it. Bliss was taking his stand upon the American Military Programme which had laid down that 24 American divisions were to be in France by July — a programme which, in the absence of American shipping, there seemed at that time not the slightest prospect of realising — and was insisting that assent to our offer to bring over 150 battalions should be conditional upon our providing further shipping to enable the Americans to carry out their 24-division programme. Pershing gave Robertson a nasty jar by telling him he had not after all indicated to Washington that he was prepared to approve the 150-battalion proposal; he had gone no further than to say that it needed serious consideration. He stood still on the ground of national prestige, and would only consider letting us have temporary use of American battalions for training on condition that we brought over their full divisional personnel at the same time, a proposal which in Robertson's view was hardly worth accepting.

The issue was finally cleared up at a Conference held at Versailles on January 29th. General Pershing, General Bliss, and an A.D.C. represented America, while I had with me Lord Milner, Robertson, Haig, Wilson and Hankey.

As explained by Bliss, the position was that the original American programme had envisaged the transport of 12 American divisions to France by June, 1918. After the pressure brought to bear on them in November to increase their despatch of troops, they had put forward a programme to raise this number to 24. But while half the tonnage for this new programme was to be raised by Washington, the remainder would have to be provided by Britain, which had declared it could not do this. So they had fallen back on the original programme of 2 divisions a month. Now there was this further proposal for providing British tonnage to bring over additional American troops, in regard to which General Pershing demanded that it should take the form of bringing the fighting personnel of complete divisions, artillery as well as infantry.

In reply to a question from me, Pershing explained that he had not expressed approval of Robertson's proposal to bring 150 infantry battalions. He had merely referred it to Washington for serious consideration, and had subsequently cabled his Government on the importance of keeping the American troops under command of their own officers. We discussed at some length the pros and cons of Robertson's scheme, but it was clear that Pershing had a rooted objection to it. Eventually the meeting was adjourned until the following day, when Pershing produced a memorandum setting out in brief his objections to Robertson's scheme, and his counter-proposal, which we had no alternative but to adopt. This latter part of the Memorandum was as follows: —

"In order to meet the situation, as presented by General Sir William Robertson, and hasten the arrival and training of American troops, it is therefore proposed that the British Government use the available sea transportation in question for bringing over the personnel of entire American divisions under the following conditions: —

"1. That the infantry and auxiliary troops of these divisions be trained with British divisions by battalions, or under such plan as may be agreed upon;

"2. That the artillery be trained under American direction in the use of French *matériel* as at present;

"3. That the higher commanders and staff officers be assigned for training and experience with corresponding units for the British Army;

"4. That when sufficiently trained, these battalions be re-formed into regiments, and that when the artillery is fully trained, all the units comprising each division be united under their own officers for service;

"5. That the above plan be carried out without interference with the plans now in operation for bringing over American forces;

"6. That the question of supply be arranged by agreement between the British and American Commanders-in-Chief;

"7. That questions of arms and equipment be settled in similar manner.

We thus conceded the issue on which Pershing had taken his stand, as to the maintenance of the American divisional formations and the refusal to amalgamate for fighting purposes the American infantry, except temporarily, while training, with our forces. The decision went some way towards improving matters. In the event of a grave emergency it would ensure the presence on French soil of a considerable number of American troops who had received a certain amount of training by officers with a war experience. Haig declared two days later, at a meeting of the Supreme War Council on January 30th, that he did not consider the Allies could expect the American force to be of effective support this year.

At the time the American effort certainly appeared disappointing. The Director of Military Intelligence read to the War Cabinet, at their meeting on January 31st, 1918, extracts from a letter he had received from General Wagstaff at American General Headquarters. The letter stated that there was great enthusiasm among American divisions about to go into the line, and also that much satisfaction had been expressed by the American troops when they heard of the possibility of their battalions being incorporated in British formations. The letter also stated that the latter proposal had been well received by the American people. At the end of February, Pershing notes: —

"It was depressing to think that ten months had elapsed since our entry into the War and we were just barely ready with one division of 25,000 men. With all our wealth, our man-power and our ability, this was the net result of our efforts up to the moment. . . . Here we were likely to be confronted by the mightiest military offensive that the world had ever known and it looked as though we should be compelled to stand by almost helpless and see the Allies again suffer losses of hundreds of thousands of men in their struggle against defeat."

By that date, February 28th, 1918, the total strength of the American Expeditionary Force in France was just over a quarter of a million. But a high proportion were not combatants, but men occupied with the non-combatant services necessary for the maintenance of the force, and the bulk of the rest were imperfectly trained. Describing the nature of the American Army three weeks later, General Pershing writes: —

"The crisis had found us with less than 320,000 officers and men in France, of which about 100,000 were necessarily engaged in the Services of Supply."

Of the combatants only a minority were in divisional formations capable of engaging in battle operations at that time.

That was the position when we passed into the fateful month of March, 1918. General Pershing, fighting fiercely to ensure the corporate unity of the American forces in France, had been successful in defeating every proposition which seemed to him to entail a possible threat to that unity. His success had meant that there were far fewer fighting troops from the States in France than there would have been had the proposals of the French and British authorities been adopted. On the other hand, the ultimate formation of intact American divisions was facilitated as a result of his stand. This would have been poor compensation had we in the meantime lost the War; but he is entitled to point out that in fact we did not lose it, and that if we had made the distribution of our forces suggested by Foch and supported by the American Generals, we need not have lost a single battle.

When the German blow fell on the St. Quentin Front on March 21st, 1918, the American troops in France numbered about 300,000. They included one fully trained division, the 1st, and two more, the 2nd and 42nd, who were training on quiet sectors of the French Front south of Verdun, while the 26th was in reserve by the Chemin des Dames. Plans were on foot to set up the first American Army corps, bringing these divisions into line beside the 1st Division. But the sudden crisis postponed that move for the time, and also brought about a fresh development in the programme for shipping American troops.

By March 25th we were able to gauge in some measure the force of the German onslaught, and the gravity of the peril which was threatening the Allied Front. It was clear that to restore our broken line we should have need of every man the Allies could rally, and as I relate elsewhere, most drastic steps were taken to bring out from Britain all the troops that could be mustered, and by raising the age limit and combing over again the scanty remnant of fit men still retained in important civilian services, to squeeze into the Army everyone we could find. The urgency of getting as many combatant troops as possible from the United States grew more than ever apparent, and I felt certain that in this emergency the American authorities would see the force of our plea that while the crisis lasted the transport of fighting troops ought to have priority over that of divisional personnel of a non-combatant character.

Accordingly, on March 25th, Mr. Balfour and I had an interview with Mr. Baker, at which we pleaded for a modification of American policy in this direction. The nature of our suggestions is set out in a telegram which, after the interview, was sent by Mr. Balfour to Colonel House. It ran as follows: —

"Prime Minister and I saw Mr. Baker this morning and earnestly pressed upon him the urgency of obtaining from the proper authorities assent to the following suggestions: —

"First. That the four American divisions should be used at once to hold the line and relieve further French divisions.

"Second. We understand that transport is available for bringing six complete American divisions to this country. We strongly urge that, in the present crisis, this tonnage would be more usefully employed if it were not used to carry complete divisions with their full complement of artillery, etc., but if it were used in the main for the transport of infantry, of which, at this moment, we stand in most pressing need.

"Third. That, as a temporary expedient, American engineer units in France now engaged in preparing the bases and lines of communication of the future American Army and said to include many skilled engineers, should be diverted from present occupations and utilised as extemporised engineer units for construction of defences, etc., in rear of our armies.

"Fourth. That one of the American displacement divisions, which is reported to be complete with transport, should also be employed in the line, either as a separate division, or to increase the infantry in the combatant divisions.

"Mr. Baker seemed personally favourable to these suggestions."

Mr. Baker himself sent a telegram to General Pershing describing these proposals. His comment upon them to the General was: —

"No answer to the foregoing is necessary until I see you tomorrow when we can discuss the suggestions fully. If railroads in France are too fully occupied to make the Italian trip possible I should abandon it. At any rate we should not permit diversion of engines and cars if they can be used in present emergency. . . ."

Colonel House replied on the 26th to Mr. Balfour's cable, saying that he had passed it to the President with his urgent recommendation that orders should be issued on the lines suggested. He added an expression of confidence in the courage and tenacity of the British troops who were then undergoing the immense strain of the German attack. On the 27th we had a further telegram from him saying: —

"The President agrees with practically every suggestion that you make regarding the disposition of our Army. I am glad to inform you that Secretary Baker, after consulting with Generals Bliss and Pershing, has given orders making effective the recommendations set forth in your telegram."

On the same day a resolution recommending the same policy was unanimously adopted by the Military Representatives at Versailles, one of whom it will be remembered was General Bliss. Its text ran: —

"The Military Representatives are of opinion that it is highly desirable that the American Government should assist the Allied Armies as soon as possible by permitting, in principle, the temporary service of American units in Allied army corps and divisions, such reinforcements must however be obtained from other units than those American divisions which are now operating with the French, and the units so temporarily employed must eventually be returned to the American Army.

"The Military Representatives are of opinion that, for the present time, in execution of the foregoing, and until otherwise directed by the Supreme War Council, only American infantry and machine-gun units, organised as the Government may decide, be brought to France, and that all agreements or conventions hitherto made in conflict with this decision be modified accordingly."

All who have not experienced the vainglorious inflexibility of the professional mind where questions of status and authority are concerned would think that an order from the head of the Government countersigned by the Secretary of War would have settled this unfortunate dispute.

When General Pershing learnt of this resolution he was thoroughly upset, for it seemed to him that here was another attempt to rob him of his American Army. He got hold of Secretary Baker, and laid his misgivings before him. To meet them, Baker sent a covering note to President Wilson with the recommendations of the Military Representatives, in which he suggested that their proposals "ought to be conceded only in view of the present critical situation, and continued only so long as that situation necessarily demands it." He proposed that the President, in endorsing the recommendations, should lay it down specifically that: —

"Such units when transported will be under the direction of the Commander-in-Chief of the American Expeditionary Forces and will be assigned for training and use by him in his discretion. He will use these and all other military forces of the United States under his command in such manner as to render the greatest military assistance, keeping in mind always the determination of this Government to have its various military forces collected, as speedily as their training and the military situation will permit, into an independent American Army. . . ."

This specification of the conditions under which the proposals of the Military Representatives were to be applied was in due course approved by President Wilson. It practically left action entirely to the discretion of General Pershing. The one preoccupation of the French and British was to make the best use of all the forces available in order to bring this devastating war to a victorious end at the earliest possible date. Protracted negotiations with and between Generals to persuade the one or other of them to do what was to any sensible person obviously the best in the circumstances were wasting precious time and opportunity. And we had to secure the advent of the American troops at as early a date as possible. We did what we could to rouse public opinion in America with this in view. On March 27th I cabled a message to Lord Reading for communication to the President and the American public: —

"We are at the crisis of the War. Attacked by an immense superiority of German troops our Army has been forced to retire. The retirement has been carried out methodically before the pressure of a steady succession of fresh German reserves which are suffering enormous losses. The situation is being faced with splendid courage and resolution. The dogged pluck of our troops has for the moment checked the ceaseless onrush of the enemy and the French have now joined in the struggle. But this battle, the greatest and most momentous in the history of the world, is only just beginning. Throughout it French and British are buoyed up with the knowledge that the great Republic of the West will neglect no effort which can hasten its troops and its ships to Europe. In war, time is vital. It is impossible to exaggerate the importance of getting American reinforcements across the Atlantic in the shortest possible space of time."

On the same day, Lord Reading cabled an appreciation of the situation in the United States which ran as follows: —

"Effect of the great battle on American public opinion is wholly advantageous to the Allied cause. Nothing has occurred since America entered the War which has stirred more fully the national feeling or united the people so thoroughly against Germany. Display of German military power is a shock to America and the people at large realise for the first time that the Allies in general and England in particular have been standing between her and German militarism. It has produced feeling of admiration and sympathy for the British, quite contrary to the usual attitude. People of America are for the War and anxious to know how they can most effectively help. They have realised as it were in a flash their own military shortcomings and time they have lost since they entered the War. This has already produced outburst in the Press and Congress, which naturally enough takes form of attack on the Administration. . . . To the Administration the battle has been no less of a shock. They had hoped and believed that the effect of the President's speeches had been to strengthen Liberal party in Germany and sap morale of the Army and influence of the military party. To-day they are very conscious of their delusion and realise that there is no hope that speeches and propaganda will turn the German people against their military party or detach Austria from Germany. At last they face the fact that, if Germany is to be beaten, she must be beaten by force. . . ."

These last sentences account for the lack of energetic direction in organising the war resources of the States.

It seems amazing to those who did not appreciate President Wilson's psychology and his unbounded confidence in the crystallisation of ideals that after a year of participation in the War — in a war which had been going on for nearly four years — the Americans were only now waking up to a full realisation that they could not win unless they fought, and fought hard. The high-minded President persisted in believing that eloquent appeals to righteousness would arrest the march of victorious armies. Once blood is shed in a national quarrel reason and right are swept aside by the rage of angry men. Yet passages I have quoted from General Pershing's own statements show how difficult he had found it to rouse his Administration at home to real activity and energetic action; and similar attempts by the French and British had been viewed with considerable suspicion by the Americans, who seemed always afraid that they were being made the victims of some confidence trick by the designing diplomats of Europe. The grim reality of this big German smash-through in the West was needed to bring home to them that they were really participating in an elemental struggle with a system where force was a faith and the triumph of which was dependent on the unchallengeable supremacy of the sword.

On March 28th, I received through the American Ambassador a message from Baker telling me that Pershing had placed the four American divisions with trench experience at Pétain's disposal, and that they were being put into the line to relieve French divisions for service on the front of attack; and that for the moment British shipping could give precedence to bringing over the infantry of the six American divisions we had been about to convey to France. I replied to Mr. Page: —

"29th March, 1918.

"Dear Mr. Ambassador,

"Thank you very much for the message from Secretary Baker. Will you please convey to him my heartiest thanks for the prompt and efficient assistance which he and General Pershing have rendered in this critical time. The news has been greatly appreciated by the War Cabinet.

Yours sincerely,
D. LLOYD GEORGE."

About nine o'clock that morning, after thinking things over during a walk in the Park with my secretary, Mr. (now Sir) John Davies, I walked straight to the Adjutant-General's Department in the War Office to ascertain the exact numerical position of the Armies in France. I decided in order to expedite matters to make a personal appeal to President Wilson so as to secure his direct, urgent and authoritative intervention with the American military authorities in the States and in France.

I then sent a long cable to Lord Reading for communication to President Wilson, outlining the situation and the steps which seemed to me of first importance in order to deal with it. The message ran as follows: —

"We have now had time to consider the military problem in more detail. We have good hope of being able to check the enemy's present effort, but we may lose Amiens. The near future will show whether or not he will be able to reach that place. If he succeeds in doing this the military situation will be very grave. In any case, having undoubtedly proved his capacity to break through the Western Front on a wide front, *it is certain that his military command, if unable to obtain all they aimed at in this battle, will immediately begin to refit the army for another blow at the earliest possible moment.* Where he will deliver it will largely depend on the final result of the present operations. The whole military future will depend upon our being able to refit and maintain our armies in time to be able to counter his next blow. Looking past the immediate battle the fundamental problem before the Allies is that of man-power.

"Our losses up to the present in this battle which has only lasted a week amount to about 120,000 men. By drafting in all our resources in trained and partially trained men we can barely make this good, and in so doing we shall have used up all our trained reserves. We are, therefore, taking immediate action to raise troops by increasing the military age to 50, and taking boys of 18, and by making another large comb-out of industry, a proceeding which will cause the gravest dislocation and hardship to our industries. We are also prepared to face great trouble in Ireland, because we feel that it is vital that we should be able to prove ourselves stronger than the Germans this summer.

"Yet, though by these drastic measures we hope to obtain a reinforcement of between 400,000 and 500,000 men for our Army, they will not be sufficiently trained for use in France for at least four months. There will be a dangerous gap in the months of May, June and July — that is to say, about the time when we may expect the enemy to make his next great effort. If we are therefore to make sure of holding the enemy then, and preventing him from reaching a decision in the West, the deficiency during these months must be made good by American troops. In no other way can we make the Allied position secure.

"It is estimated by our shipping people here that if shipping is to be provided by Great Britain at a great sacrifice in other directions, we shall be able to embark in America in April some 60,000 men. Admiral Sims estimates that the carrying capacity of the American troop fleet is 52,000 men a month. In addition there is certain Dutch tonnage available for use by America, and we are obtaining the use of certain Italian tonnage. In all we believe that 120,000 American men can be embarked in April and rather more in the succeeding months.

"I want you, therefore, to formally urge upon the President on behalf of the British Government to give instructions for 120,000 infantry to be embarked and sent to Europe per month between now and the end of July — the battalions of these American regiments to be brigaded with British or French divisions on the same basis as arranged in the case of the six divisions plan. In accordance with the resolution of the Military Representatives at Versailles on March 27th and agreed to by General Pershing the troops transported should be infantry and machine-gun units only. As was agreed in the case of the six divisions, the battalions when trained can be reformed into regiments and sent to General Pershing as he may require them.

"Please see the President about this at once. In no other way can the hundreds of thousands of trained and half-trained men now in America be made available in this struggle; for they cannot be organised into separate units in time. Should it go against us in their absence the War might be over and the cause for which the President has so eloquently pleaded might be lost without America being given an opportunity to put in more than an insignificant fraction of her Army. I believe that the whole future of the War will depend on whether the Allies or the Germans are first in making good the losses of this great battle. The Germans will certainly not delay an instant. They have the man-power

THE AMERICAN ARMIES IN FRANCE 431

with which to replace their losses. There are also the Austrians of whom, according to the German papers to-day, there are already 250,000 on the Western Front.[1] Unless we can refit as fast as they can, we shall simply give Germany the chance to deliver that knock-out blow with which its leaders hope to win the War."

A very satisfactory reply was received from President Wilson to this request. Lord Reading cabled me on March 31st to inform me that the President had substantially agreed to my proposals; that he would issue directions for 120,000 infantry a month to be embarked during April, May, June and July, if the necessary shipping and equipment were available; and that only the limitations of shipping and port facilities hindered him from sending them faster. He also approved in principle the method of employment of troops suggested by me, but left the details of their disposal and use to be settled by General Pershing.

That was all to the good, but hitherto we had unfortunate evidence of the gap between programme and performance in the despatch of American troops. In a private message which I sent to Reading on April 1st, I asked him to give his personal attention to the measures to carry out the President's undertaking, pointing out that: —

"We have been let down badly once or twice before; in fact, we are largely suffering because the Americans have fallen egregiously short of their programme. They promised to have 17 divisions in France by March, they have actually only four, and these have only just gone into the line. . . ."

I followed this up by a longer cable next day, in which I reinforced my plea for every effort being made to ensure the actual despatch of the promised troops. I told Reading that

[1] This was a German bluff to create an atmosphere of terror on the Allied side. There were at this time no Austrian divisions on the Western Front. The first to come there arrived in July.

I thought he ought in particular to get Colonel House to give his whole time to this question, "as if it were an election campaign", until it was certain that the 120,000 American infantry were going, in fact and not merely on paper, in April and each succeeding month. I concluded by giving some particulars of the shipping arrangements we were making. Food supplies at home were running short and our wheat reserves were low. But I came to the conclusion that we should take even the grave risks of having to cut down our bread rations in order to provide ships for this pressing need in France. So in my further message for the President I said: —

"The estimates which follow relate to all troops other than those arriving under ordinary American War Office programmes. But they include the six divisions which it was arranged at last Supreme War Council should be sent over to be brigaded with us and the French. Of these I understand that only 1,700 men have so far started.

"It is estimated that 61,000 troops can be embarked in British tonnage in April in accommodation becoming available apart from unforeseen contingencies at the rate of 16,000 in each first and third weeks, 12,000 in second week, and 17,000 in the fourth week of the month. This does not include two Italian ships which will also be available. Practically all the men carried in British tonnage will be brought to England and transported to Northern French ports by us. This leaves Brest and the Bay ports free to deal with the men carried direct to France by American shipping. Please obtain from American authorities at once similar estimate of numbers which can be carried in tonnage provided by America during the four weeks, including such of the Dutch ships or other Allied tonnage as are suitable and available. It is vital that we should have this time-table as soon as possible in order that we may complete arrangements with Pershing in regard to reception, training and brigading with Allied forces.

"It is also very important that the vessels of the American line be fitted and used to carry the full number of men of which they are capable. Up to the present they have been carrying less than 1,000 men per voyage. If they were fitted up as our troopships they could carry 2,000 to 2,500. *Mongolia* and *Manchuria* could carry from 2,500 to 3,000."

Reading, with his usual tact and business aptitude, urged all these points on the President. In addition he kept in constant touch with the American military and transport departments. The Allies owed a good deal to his efficient activities. But a few days later this whole programme was threatened anew with disaster — and from the same quarter which had so far wrecked every arrangement. General Pershing rose up in angry protest against this last compact. He was quivering with suspicion that the French and British meant to rob him of his army and that once the American infantry got brigaded with European formations he would be unable to recover them. In a conference with Generals Whigham and Hutchison from the British War Office, on April 7th, he flatly refused to accept the 120,000 a month programme for transport of infantry and machine-gunners. He would agree to no more than the 60,000 infantry for which arrangements had already been made to be given priority.

On April 8th I talked the matter over with the Foreign Secretary and we decided to communicate with the President and once more seek his intervention. Mr. Balfour accordingly sent a long cable to Lord Reading, acquainting him with the grave difference of opinion which we had discovered in discussing the arrangements with General Pershing, and asked him to lay the issue before President Wilson.

"I am very unwilling," he cabled, "to embarrass the President, who has shown such a firm grasp of the situation, with criticisms of his officers. But it is evident that the difference of opinion between General Pershing on the one side and what we conceive to be the President's policy on the other is so fundamental and touches so nearly the issues of the whole War, that we are bound to have the matter cleared up."

The reply we received on April 10th from Lord Reading told us that he had seen President Wilson, who, while showing sympathy with our anxiety to secure an arrangement which would facilitate the best and promptest use of American forces, was evidently very unwilling to commit himself to a decision in regard to the dispute with General Pershing until he had consulted Baker, then on his way to the States. So despite the urgency of the issue, it had to stand over a few days, pending Baker's arrival in the United States.

The present position of the American Army was outlined by General Whigham to the War Cabinet at a meeting held on April 10th. He stated that General Pershing then had in France the 1st American Army Corps, consisting of four fighting and two replacement divisions, one of which was now being equipped to become a fighting division. The ration strength of the American Forces in France was 319,000, and the nominal combatant strength was 214,000, but this included up to the present only about 70,000 infantry for the fighting line. In the United Kingdom there were 10,000 American troops, including three-quarters of one battalion, and various portions of other units and details. The total striking force of this army, it thus appeared, was not for the moment very considerable. This was twelve months after the American declaration of war. I ascertained that at the corresponding period of our entry into the War we had 942,507 men (excluding Indian troops) in the various theatres, and our actual casualties were 312,075 (this also excludes the Indian troops).

We also learned at this Cabinet meeting the disquieting tidings that the American authorities were refusing to allow shipment of any of their troops in vessels with a speed of less than 12½ knots. We had scraped together every vessel that could possibly be spared for troop transport, and some of these were slower ships, with a speed of only 9½ knots. The refusal to allow the use of these would cut down by about 7,000 men per month the number we could transport. There was considerable cabling and consultation about this matter. Eventually a compromise was reached allowing American troops to be sent on vessels having a speed of not less than 11½ knots, and intensive work on the part of Graeme Thomson, whom I had sent to the States to assist the shipping programme, resulted in tonnage becoming available which would enable us to transport up to 200,000 men per month; considerably more, in fact, than our original programme.

But the problem remained as to whether arrangements could be agreed which would permit of these men being of any practical fighting value within the next few weeks — critical weeks for the issue of the War. The blunt truth was that in Pershing's view the building up of an American Army took precedence of the utilisation of these men to beat off the German offensive, while for us the defeat of the offensive and the consequent shortening of this destructive War was all-important. An American Army which could not be organised into an army until the late summer or autumn would be too late to intervene in this fateful conflict.

On April 18th, in anticipation of the next phase of the discussion between President Wilson, Mr. Baker and Lord Reading, I sent to the last-named a lengthy memorandum in which I set out the facts and arguments for allowing the American troops, brigaded in British and French divisions, to be used forthwith to aid in repelling the Germans, instead of waiting until Pershing could set up divisional formations and pass his troops through a period of training in them. I gave particulars of the German forces opposed to us, and their potential reserves; and of our forces and available reinforcements. I described the difficulties in the way of the French moving up any considerable body of troops into the imperilled northern area, because of the difficulty of maintaining their communication lines right across ours; and in any case the French had now a very long line of their own to guard. Our casualties in the recent fighting had been such that several of our divisions were reduced to their cadres, and since the Germans were still able to bring in further forces from the East, the disproportion of fighting strength was steadily increasing. My conclusion was that: —

"There can be little doubt that victory or defeat for the Allies depends upon the arrival of the American infantry. . . . For the moment infantry and machine-gunners are the only troops which matter, for the wastage of infantry is out of all proportion to that of the artillery and other services. Barring disaster it will not be impossible to keep the latter up to strength. The real fact is that the Allies have the necessary reserves of sufficiently trained infantry to make it impossible for the Germans to succeed. But these reserves are now largely in America. . . . It rests with America to win or lose the decisive battle of the War. But if it is to be won, America will have to move as she has never moved before, and the President must overrule at once the narrow obstinacy which would put obstacles in the way of using American infantry in the only way in which it can be used to save the situation. . . ."

Lord Reading had a series of conferences with Baker and President Wilson, the outcome of which was a compromise agreement, set forth in a memorandum of which, on April 21st, he cabled me the terms as follows: —

"Pursuant to direction of the President and in conformity with his approval of joint note of Permanent Military Representatives at Versailles, United States will continue throughout the months of April, May, June and July to supply for transportation, both in its own and controlled tonnage and in that made available by Great Britain, infantry and machine-gun personnel. It is hoped, and on the basis of study so far it is believed, that total number of troops transported will be 120,000 per month. These troops when transported will, under direction and at the discretion of General Pershing, be assigned for training and use with British, French or American divisions as exigencies of the situation from time to time require: it being understood that this programme to the extent that it is a departure from plan to transport and assemble in Europe complete American divisions, is made in view of exigencies of present military situation and is made in order to bring into useful coöperation at the earliest possible moment largest number of American personnel in the military armament needed by the Allies.

"It being also understood that this statement is not to be regarded as a commitment from which Government of United States is not free to depart when exigencies no longer require it, and also that preferential transportation of infantry and machine-gun units here set forth as a policy and principle is not to be regarded as so exclusive as to prevent Government of United States from including in troops carried by its own tonnage from time to time relatively small numbers of personnel of other arms as may be deemed wise by United States as replacements and either to make possible use of maximum capacity of ships or most efficient use of infantry and machine-gun units as such transported or maintenance of sources of supply already organised and in process of construction for American Army already in France.

"These suggestions are made in order that there may be a clear understanding of intention of United States and of mode of execution of that intention and they are not stipulated as indicating any intention on the part of the United States, until situation has in its judgment changed, to depart from as full compliance with recommendation of Permanent Military Representatives as nature of the case will permit."

On the whole, this was a satisfactory arrangement. We should naturally have preferred a definite guarantee of the

120,000 infantry and machine-gunners a month which the President had agreed to, and have liked discretion to have been given to Foch or the Supreme War Council to decide when the emergency was past, instead of it being retained in America. But Reading advised us that these were quite the most favourable terms we could hope to obtain, and strongly urged their frank acceptance. So at a meeting of the War Cabinet on April 23rd, 1918, it was resolved to authorise Lord Reading to accept the Memorandum, and to advise him that the War Office would take up the discussion of arrangements with General Pershing for carrying out its decisions.

But if we were satisfied, Pershing was raging with indignation. He crossed to London on April 21st, and on the 22nd had an interview with Lord Milner and Sir Henry Wilson, who had now succeeded General Robertson as C.I.G.S. At this meeting he was told of the Memorandum, which he had not yet seen, and at once declared that "it could not be possible that any such concession had been made, and that the classes of our troops to be shipped over and their disposition must be left to him." He did not receive his official copy of the document until his return to France, where he found it waiting for him. His verdict upon it was: —

"This concession went further than it was necessary to go, and much further than I had expected. Realising the complications that might arise from commitments so far in the future and the delay in forming an American Army that would follow, I did not agree in later discussions at the Supreme War Council with all that the Allies now felt justified in demanding. . . . It need not be further emphasised that such a concession, even though prompted by the most generous impulse, could only add to the difficulties of our task of building up an army of our own." [1]

[1] "My Experiences in the World War", p. 361.

Thus the decision of the President of the United States proved of insufficient value in face of the stubborn intransigence of the American Commander-in-Chief. He could see no further than the exaltation of his own command, the jealous maintenance of his own authority. It was President Wilson's first experience of just the same kind of professional egotism as we had frequently experienced in dealings with our own Army heads. Although he possessed autocratic powers on executive questions he could not secure obedience to his repeated behests from an officer who was his subordinate. Lincoln had encountered similar difficulties with McClellan. Where Presidents failed to control Generals it was not so easy for Prime Ministers, whose political position was precarious, to keep them in order. At the conference he held in London on April 22nd and 24th with Lord Milner, Pershing took upon himself the right to overrule the President's concession, and insisted on an arrangement whereby the shipments in May should not be confined to infantry and machine-gun units, but should also bring over the engineer and signal troops and various unit headquarters of six divisions — and, if there were shipping space available, the artillery of these divisions as well, and such personnel as might be required to build up corps organisations. Thereafter, instead of further combatant troops, Pershing required that shipments should convey such service of supply troops and other contingents as he might consider necessary. In fact, there was no assurance of concentration on the transport of combatant troops after the end of May.

On returning to France, Pershing was asked to go and meet Foch in Paris. Arriving there he found Foch, Weygand and Bliss. Foch took up the theme of the urgent necessity for the next three months of shipping over all the infantry and machine-gunners possible, leaving the other details of divisional formations to follow. But Pershing stood obstinately by his refusal to adopt this procedure. He would allow infantry to be brought over in May ahead of their divisional details, but the June shipments must be devoted to bringing across the corresponding artillery and auxiliary troops. All Foch's authority as Generalissimo of the Allied forces, and all his arguments based on the acute urgency of the crisis were powerless to stir Pershing from this position.

Needless to say, the change of plans caused bitter disappointment to our representatives in America, who had not only taken great pains to secure President Wilson's consent to the scheme for priority for infantry, but had proceeded to organise all the shipping arrangements for weeks ahead — as was of course essential — in accordance with this plan. By a ruthless cutting-down of other important shipping programmes, they had succeeded in rallying such a volume of tonnage that on April 30th they were able to put forward a programme for the conveyance of 700,000 American troops to Europe in May, June and July: 270,000 in American, and 430,000 in British ships.

At the meeting of the Supreme War Council, on May 1st and 2nd, 1918, the issue was again raised and discussed at considerable length. M. Clemenceau and General Foch were both very insistent that Pershing should agree to give priority to the bringing over of combatant troops. But he dug in his high heels and refused to make any concession. The most he would promise was to reconsider the matter later in the month. On the second day of the Council meeting I thrashed the matter out at length with him, and at last got him to agree to a resolution which set out that the arrangement he had already accepted in regard to May shipments — that priority should be given to the infantry and machine-gunners of six divisions, the rest of such shipping space as could be found being allocated to the transport of the other elements of their divisional formations — should be continued for June; and further, that if in addition to transporting the full personnel of six divisions (150,000 men) in June, we were able to find tonnage for any more, this should be used for infantry and machine-gunners. The whole situation was to be reviewed afresh, early in June.

The clause about additional shipping was inserted at my insistence, because although in our desperate need for reinforcements we were doing far more to aid the transport of American troops than we had previously undertaken, and were thereby incurring grave risks at home, we felt the crisis to be so serious that we were determined, if thereby we could get more men over, to slash at every other shipping commitment, however urgent it might be.

The agreement was the best we could conclude with him, but it was far from satisfactory. On May 4th I cabled an account of it to Lord Reading. In the course of my telegram I said: —

"I am just as disappointed about the Pershing agreement as you are. The whole difficulty arises from the fact that the American Government has issued no definite instructions to General Pershing. It has agreed to certain general principles, but has left the settlement of all the practical questions on which the value of the agreement really depends to Pershing. . . . Despite all our efforts and the strong appeal by General Foch, we could not move Pershing beyond the point of six divisions in May and June. I may add that Foch, who is much the greatest Allied General, was intensely depressed and disgusted . . . and Bliss, who was present throughout the discussions, sat absolutely silent and gave no support to Pershing. I hear privately that he has expressed to his colleagues complete disagreement with Pershing's attitude."

I went on to suggest that it would be very much better if some political authority from America were present who could deal with these issues, instead of leaving them to be settled by the General alone. If House had been present we should have got a better agreement. I described the actual situation regarding the fighting strength of the American Army, which was still persistently below the promised and expected level.

"It is maddening," I wrote, "to think that though the men are there the issue of the War may be endangered because of the shortsightedness of one General and the failure of his Government to order him to carry out their undertakings."

In my resentment at Pershing's refusal to carry out the arrangements made by his Government with their Allies or associates, I for the moment overlooked the fact that the American Government was not the only one that failed to induce Generals to obey definite orders and carry out specific undertakings — even when they had been given with their consent. Pershing wanted to fight his own battle and win his own victories with his own Army. Haig wanted his own offensive on his own front, ending in his own break-through. Pétain wanted to make certain of beating the enemy on that part of the front for which he was responsible.

In my telegram I also pointed out that from the point of view of the American combatant troops themselves it was desirable that they should get some experience of the new and very intense form of warfare now being waged, under the care of Staffs experienced in handling the necessary operations, before they were placed in formations entirely run by Generals who had as yet no such practical experience. And I concluded by urging Lord Reading to make it his business, whatever the agreement, to see that as many men as possible were shipped across without delay, and as many as possible called up in the States in readiness for the autumn battles. Once large masses of combatant troops were in Europe, I was convinced that Pershing would see to it that the War was not lost by his refusal to let them be used where reinforcements were vitally needed.

In his reply, Lord Reading told me that the attitude in Washington was much more sympathetic to our demands than that displayed by Pershing. He would continue to get as many infantry as possible sent out, though in view of the partial surrender to Pershing there would be also considerable shipments of other types of troops. As a matter of fact, it soon became apparent that there would be a difficulty in maintaining a full flow of infantry that had passed through the preliminary five months' training for which General Pershing was stipulating. This rule had not been strictly observed hitherto, with the result that the troops shipped were of a very miscellaneous order so far as training was concerned. I gathered from a conversation in the latter part of April with Captain Guest, who had seen and spoken to American troops embarking from this country for France, that men had been sent forward from the United States without any method, with the result that men with six months' training were to be found side by side with raw recruits. General Pershing confirmed this information, and expressed surprise at the occurrence, which, he supposed, was due to the haste with which the orders to push forward troops had been carried out. He told us he had found it necessary to sift and reorganise these troops before they could be employed.

For this reason Pershing was now insisting strictly on the five months' preliminary training before troops were sent out from America. But as the number of recruits who had been so long in training was limited, it soon transpired that unless there was some relaxation of this rule, the flow of shipments, at the rate we were now achieving, would exhaust the supply. In a telegram to me on May 24th, Lord Reading said that on the present basis, if June shipments were maintained, there would be only a smaller number available in July, and none thereafter until September. Congress had now given the President power to call up as many men as could be equipped, trained and used, until the War was ended. So the potential supply was almost unlimited, but the numbers ready trained were not. This was the result of the inexplicable delays of 1917 in raising, training and equipping troops. At the meeting of the Supreme War Council held on June 1st and 2nd, 1918, Pershing agreed to bring over troops which had completed three months' training, which enabled the rate of shipments to be maintained at full flow. Owing to the deterioration in the quality of the German troops, recruits with a few months' training were more valuable in the summer of 1918 than they would have been at any time from 1914 to that date.

At this Council meeting the vexed question of priority for infantry continued to be debated. The fresh German offensive against the French on the Soissons Front had just taken place, and the enemy had pressed up to Château-Thierry, seriously threatening Paris. The need for maintaining the strength of the Allies' combatant troops was more urgent than ever, and it was uncertain how long it would take to build up the American battalions now arriving into organised divisions capable of effective operation, whereas the empty cadres of British and French divisions, the infantry of which was exhausted, could take in these battalions immediately and utilise them while the crisis lasted. After long and heated argument, another compromise agreement was reached with the stubborn Pershing. This was set out in the following Memorandum: —

"The following recommendations are made on the assumption that at least 250,000 men can be transported in each of the months of June and July by the employment of combined British and American tonnage. We recommend: —

"*A*. For the month of June: 1st, absolute priority shall be given to the transportation of 170,000 combatant troops (*viz*. six divisions without artillery, ammunition trains or supply trains, amounting to 126,000 men and 44,000 replacements for combat troops); 2nd, 25,400 men for the service of railways, of which 13,400 have been asked for by the French Minister of Transportation; 3rd, the balance to be troops of categories to be determined by the Commander-in-Chief, American Expeditionary Forces.

"*B*. For the month of July: 1st, absolute priority for the shipment of 140,000 combatant troops of the nature defined above (four divisions minus artillery, etc., amounting to 84,000 men plus 56,000 replacements); 2nd, the balance of the 250,000 to consist of troops to be designated by the Commander-in-Chief, American Expeditionary Forces.

"*C*. It is agreed that if available tonnage in either month allows of the transportation of a larger number of men than 250,000 the excess tonnage will be employed in the transportation of combat troops as defined above.

"*D*. We recognise that the combatant troops to be dispatched in July may have to include troops which have had insufficient training, but we consider the present emergency is such as to justify a temporary and exceptional departure by the United States from sound principles of training, especially as a similar course is being followed by France and Great Britain.

FOCH, MILNER, PERSHING."

At the same meeting, MM. Clemenceau and Orlando and myself decided to send a telegram to President Wilson, expressing to him our warmest thanks for the great speeding-up of American reinforcements which he had authorised, and at the same time emphasising that the crisis still continued, and made even greater efforts necessary. We quoted the authority of General Foch for an estimate of the superiority at this stage of the German over the Allied forces on the Western Front, and his plea that the maximum possible number of infantry and machine-gunners should be shipped in

June and July to avert disaster. We added that General Foch —

"represents that it is impossible to foresee ultimate victory in the War unless America is able to provide such an army as will enable the Allies ultimately to establish numerical superiority. He places the total American force required for this at no less than 100 divisions, and urges the continuous raising of fresh American levies, which in his opinion should not be less than 300,000 a month, with a view to establishing a total American force of 100 divisions at as early a date as this can possibly be done."

It may be noted that this estimate by General Foch proved in the event to be exaggerated. It was due very largely to the panicky atmosphere created by the German victories. The enemy strength was overrated. Since an American division, numbering upwards of 25,000 troops, was nearly three times as big as the German divisions at their then strength, 100 American divisions would have given the Allies very nearly a 50 per cent. superiority over the Germans on the Western Front, without counting the French and British forces; and since the corresponding corps troops, supply services and other auxiliary units attached to an American Army overseas would add another 15,000 in respect of each complete division, the United States would have had to raise and maintain in France an army of four million to fulfil Foch's request. In the event, the Allies established a considerable numerical superiority over the Germans long before the total American forces in France were approaching a third of this proposed figure. Pershing states that in the final hostilities between September 26th and November 11th, 1918, some 22 American divisions were engaged. Including replacement and depot divisions or parts of divisions, there were in November 41 American divisions in all in France. But the importance of the American contribution was far from being bounded by the actual number of troops that participated in the battle. Not only did the presence of over a score of his American divisions give to the Allied Armies the numerical superiority needed to overpower the Germans; the fact that behind these there were another score of divisions in process of formation and training and yet other millions of men in America who could be brought over as need arose, enabled the French and British to fling their last reserves into the fight without hesitation or misgiving, and hammer ceaselessly at the German lines until they crumbled and broke. Most of the actual fighting throughout 1918 right up to the end, fell to the lot of the British and French troops and they sustained the heaviest casualties, but their sacrifices would have been in vain, had it not been for the part played by the American Army, notably in the last few months of this sanguinary campaign.

Conceivably the 100-division figure was put forward in the hope that by asking for 100 American divisions we might get at least 50. Hitherto the fulfilment had fallen far short of the promise where American troops were concerned. Pershing himself writes speaking of that big proposition: —

"We had fallen far short of the expectations of the preceding November, when I had asked Foch and Robertson to join me in an appeal for 24 trained American divisions by the following June. It is small wonder that the Allies were now so insistent in urging increased and continuous shipments of men, trained or untrained. . . ."[1]

With the drawing-up of this programme, the long series of discussions and disputes regarding the number and nature of the American troops to be brought over to France may be regarded as having substantially come to an end. Thereafter,

[1] "My Experiences in the World War", p. 446.

the steady flow of men across the Atlantic was based upon this schedule, and apart from temporary variations or difficulties, succeeded more or less in fulfilling it. The total ration strength of the American forces in France on November 1st was 1,868,000.

Of these forces, 51.25 per cent. were transported to France in British-owned or controlled vessels, 46.25 per cent. in American, and 2.5 per cent. in other vessels. Thus the principal share of the carrying and a large share in the convoying of the American Army was taken by the British Mercantile Marine and the British Navy.

When we come to the equipment of the American Army for the task, it is a lamentable story of indecision and bustling incompetency. The record of Britain's first ten months of blundering in the matter of equipment robs us of the right to point the finger of scorn at America's effort. But it must be remembered that when America entered into the struggle her industry was already largely organised for war by the immense Allied orders for war material of every kind which her industries had been executing for the Allies. In rifles, explosives, and artillery the work which had been turned out in American workshops ran into thousands of millions of dollars. In addition to that, they had at their disposal the experience acquired by the Allies in two and a half years of actual war. Allied officers were sent over to instruct the American War Office as to where the Allies had failed, and how they ultimately succeeded, what had been their difficulties and how they overcame them. Unfortunately, their advice was too often disregarded and somewhat discouraged.

It cannot be said that the Allied Commissions were altogether resented by the great industrial leaders who were charged with the duty of equipping the new American Army, but the impression was created of a sentiment that where mechanisation was concerned, America had nothing to learn from Europe. There was more than a lingering trace of the fixed idea that European methods were effete in industry as well as in government. "Europe" and "effete" were inseparable words in all popular American rhetoric at that date. As far as European workshops were concerned, certainly before the War, there was undoubtedly a great deal of justification for this conviction. So when we thought America might like to profit by the lessons we had learned in the trials of actual warfare, the American industrialists were inclined to regard our lectures as an invitation to them, who were masters of all the manufacturing arts, to take a post-graduate course at a dame's school. Hence they would have none of our aeroplanes nor of our cannon. They assumed on traditional principles the inferiority of these and they decided to have patterns of their own, which would demonstrate to antiquated European craftsmen what could be done by a nation which had demonstrated its supremacy in machinery. The world was to be impressed with the superiority of American workshops. No allowance was made for the practical consideration that finish and precision in every detail were essential to the weapons of war, and that for that reason, new patterns took a long time to evolve, to test and perfect. The serious delays that occurred in equipping the great army of men that America sent to Europe were largely attributable to this psychology.

All this would have been remedied, if there had been any real drive at the head of affairs. It is only the man at the top who can give direction, impulse and inspiration to those who labour at the multifarious tasks of Government. It is only the man who wields authority who can accept responsibility for decisions which may involve an overriding of national pride and susceptibilities. It is he alone who can supply the necessary push which saves valuable time and produces quick results. Languor at the top means flaccidity all round. Hesitancy at the top means vacillation and confusion of counsel and of action in every department of State. Procrastination at the top encourages sloth and slackness down below.

President Wilson was not cut out for a great War Minister. He knew nothing about war. Why should he? It was not his training, nor his temperament. He certainly had no delight in it. He shuddered at the thought of it. The turning-out of weapons for human slaughter not only did not interest him, it horrified him. When he was forced into declaring war, he could not adapt himself to the new conditions that were imposed upon him by this departure from pursuits and inclinations of a lifetime. He had a stubborn mind and walked reluctantly along paths he disliked, however necessary he had discovered it to be that he should tread them. No push or drive for war could be expected from a temperament so antipathetic to all its exigencies. To ask him to turn his mind on to the manufacture of cannon and bombing machines was just as if you expected him to oversee the output of electric chairs because the execution of criminals was an integral part of good government.

This attitude on the part of the President marked the essential difference between him and Lincoln; between a man brought up and dwelling in academic circles whose instinct was to lead the nation up to ideas of culture in an atmosphere of tranquillity, and the man who was reared and trained in hard surroundings where nature had to be fought at every step for every ounce of bread. Lincoln also detested war, and especially did he shrink from the fratricidal conflict which he had done his best to avert, but which circumstances he had failed to control had in the end forced him to wage. But here came the difference between him and his distinguished successor. Having reached the conclusion that the shedding of blood was the only alternative to the rupture of America, he threw the whole of his strong personality into the preparations for a successful termination of the struggle. With indomitable energy, he took steps to raise and train men to battle, and to manufacture adequate weapons to equip them for victory. It is one of the inexplicable paradoxes of history, that the greatest machine-producing nation on earth failed to turn out the mechanism of war after 18 months of sweating and toiling and hustling. The men placed in charge of the organisation of the resources of the country for this purpose all seemed to hustle each other — but never the job.

Let us take the aeroplanes as an example. When America entered the War, the British and French aeroplanes were as efficient as any that hovered over the battlefields of Europe. In their production the experiences of the War had taught designers what defects needed remedying, and by this time most of the snags had been overcome. For some time, the Germans had acquired a fortuitous superiority through the ingenuity of a great Dutch inventor, but owing to the lucky mistake which landed a German Fokker machine behind the Allied lines, we had achieved a design comparable with the best German machines. There were no better pilots in any army than the daring and skilful aviators of the French and British Air Forces. American manufacturers would have been wise to start their enterprise by manufacturing to French and British designs. They could have gone on improving and perfecting as experience taught them, wherever amendment and improvement were desirable or attainable, but unfortunately their untimely pride intervened. They considered that it would be a reflection on American inventiveness and ingenuity merely to keep to European patterns. They must have something original to send to Europe; something which would astonish the natives and drive the inferior German planes into the clouds to seek refuge from this new terror from the West. So the "Liberty" machine was projected, but refused to be invented. One machine after another was tried but each turned out to be as great a disappointment as its predecessor. When at last a new design had been achieved which seemed to be effective, and was ready for manufacture, General Pershing's Staff intervened with suggestions for further improvement. When these alterations had been made instructions came from General Pershing for fresh alterations.[1] The result was inevitable. No American aeroplanes were sent across the Atlantic during the whole of 1917. Even during the great battles of April, May and June, 1918, American aviators had to fly in French machines for they had none of their own. It was July, 1918, before the paragon was fully developed and then it turned out no better than, in fact not as good as, the thousands with which the British and French aviators had already won the command of the air before the "Liberty" machines had left the workshop or even the draughtsman's table.

When the Armistice was signed November 11th, half the aeroplanes used by the American Army were of French and British make.

The same tale of fussy muddle can be repeated in the matter of guns, light and heavy, for the new American Army. The light and medium artillery used up to the end of the War by the American Army was supplied by the French. The heaviest artillery was furnished by the British. No field guns

---

[1] "Reverting to the many changes recommended by General Pershing in his cables and reports from France, his custom was to appoint a board of officers to consider and determine for him the details concerning any foreign implement of war which he was told was necessary for the A.E.F. These boards were often a living exemplification of the old Army saying that 'a board is long, narrow, and wooden!' General Pershing himself knew nothing about airplanes, and so he approved and forwarded the report of a board which, from time to time, did not suggest a few changes in a standard type of airplane, previously recommended by it and him, for adoption and manufacture by the United States, but literally hundreds and hundreds of changes, including complete changes in the plane itself in favour of some other model. The wretched manufacturer at home would have to discard all his work and begin again on something else, only to find, later, that Pershing & Company had changed their collective mind again in favour of the first recommendation, since discarded, and the country and Congress were blaming the War Department for all these delays." (General Peyton C. March: "The Nation at War", p. 283.)

of American pattern or manufacture fired a shot in the War. The same thing applies to tanks. Here one would have thought that the nation who were the greatest manufacturers of automobiles in the world could have turned out tanks with the greatest facility and in the largest numbers, but not a single tank of American manufacture ever rolled into action in the War.

Transport was so defective that ships sometimes took a couple of months to turn round at the ports, and on land it was so badly organised that, in spite of help which was forthcoming from other armies, a large number of the American troops who fought so gallantly in the Argonne in the autumn of 1918 were without sufficient food to sustain them in their heroic struggle in a difficult terrain. The American soldiers were superb. That is a fact which is acknowledged, not only by their friends and British comrades, but by their enemies as well.

There were no braver or more fearless men in any army, but the organisation at home and behind the lines was not worthy of the reputation which American business men have deservedly won for smartness, promptitude and efficiency.

INDEX

AEROPLANES, efficiency of British and French, 451; failure of American, 451, 452.

Alexieff, Gen., a student of war, 101.

Allenby, Gen., to take offensive in Palestine, 296.

Allied Conference. *See* Inter-Allied Conference.

Allies, their strength impaired in two directions (1915–17), 4, 5; superiority on Western Front, 7, 8; successful on sea and against Turks, 8; ignorant of real conditions in Austria-Hungary (1918), 13; anxious to stabilise Russian government, 80, 91–93; attempt to reorganize Russian railways, 99; and Russo-German armistice, 107, 108, 110; protest Russo-German Treaty, 128, 129; prodigality of their military leaders, 137; their mechanical superiority, 148, 150; after overthrow of Russia and Roumania, 209, 210; confer in Paris (Nov. 1917), 215–221; and the question of a generalissimo, 232–234; and Versailles Staff proposals, 234–239; plan for setting up independent General Reserve, 240–250; the benefit of a united front, 285, 286; lose priceless time, 323, 324; total forces in Turkish theatres, 371; their forces composed with enemies', 374; progress of offensive on Western Front, 377–386, 392, 393; and problem of American troops, 410–420; gravity of peril to (March 1918), 422; after Soissons offensive, 444–447. *See also* Man-Power Committee.

Alsace-Lorraine, British policy regarding, 183, 186.

America. *See* United States.

American Mission, sent to London, 398–407.

Anthoine, Gen., 211.

Arz, Gen. von, asks Germany for army rations, 11, 12.

Asquith, Herbert, 17, 290; approves Lloyd George peace terms, 39; opposes Military Service Bill, 192; interrogates Lloyd George in Parliament, 302–307; his hatred for Henry Wilson, 313, 314; his reply to Lloyd George's speech, 322.

Auchincloss, Gordon, with American Mission in London, 400.

Austria, at point of collapse, 11–13; makes tentative peace offer to England, 19–37; renews approaches, 48–53. *See also* Central Powers.

BAKER, NEWTON D., American Secretary of War, his cable to Pershing, 412; and proposal to modify American policy, 423, 424; and Pershing's misgivings, 425; his message to Lloyd George, 428; and British complaints, 435–437.

Balfour, Rt. Hon. Arthur J., Foreign Secretary, and the Russian complications, 105; his Russian memorandum quoted, 111–114; and the Bolsheviks, 120–122, 124–128; at Allied Conferences (Nov. 1917), 215; reluctant to let Robertson go, 309–311; opposes Wilson, 315; his wire to Col. House, 423; House's reply to, 424; his cable to Reading, 433, 434.

Balkans, situation in (1918), 9–11.

Ballard, Gen., 107.

Barnes, G. N., on Man-Power Committee, 156; at Labour Conference, 182.

Belgium, in German hands, 3. *See also* Allies.

Benson, Rear Adm. W. S., with American Mission in London, 400, 405, 406.

Bethmann-Hollweg, Chancellor, overthrown by military clique, 287.

Biddulph, Brig.-Gen. H., R.E., reports on Fifth Army defences, 335, 336.

Bismarck, Chancellor, 200.

Bliss, Gen. Tasker H., his estimate of American troops, 160; at Allied Conferences (Nov. 1917), 215, 216; meets with Supreme Council at Versailles, 240, 246, 249; agrees on size of General Reserve, 349; accepts failure of

456 INDEX

Bliss, Gen. T. H. (*Continued*)
General Reserve, 359, 360; his opinion of Doullens Conference, 390; with American Mission in London, 400; appointed to Supreme War Council, 400, 401; explains American programme, 418, 419; and resolutions of Military Representatives, 424, 425; meets Pershing in Paris, 439; withholds support from Pershing, 441.

Bolsheviks, undermining authority of Kerensky, 91; in Cronstadt, 94, 95; at the helm, 104; British attitude toward, 120–129; policy of, 130–132.

Bouillon, Franklin, "partner" of Painlevé, 194, 195.

Boulogne Conference (Sept. 1917), 269, 273.

Brest-Litovsk negotiations, 117, 120.

Briand, Aristide, a great orator, 195, 215; despised by Clemenceau, 196.

British Fifth Army, neglected by Haig, 333–342; distribution of its troops, 336–338; Gough retired from, 366; giving way, 368, 369; depleted by leaves granted, 370; its broken front, 377–379, 382–384.

British Third Army, its broken front, 377–379, 382–385; makes a stand, 393.

Brockdorff-Rantzau, M., 199.

Brusiloff, Gen., his attempted offensive, 85; replaced by Korniloff, 99.

Buchanan, Sir George, 116; his despatch on Lenin, 77–79; on situation in Petrograd, 82–85, 93–98; advises freeing Russia to make own peace, 106–109; his view of Bolsheviks, 122.

Bulgaria, vulnerable to attack, 10; tired of war, 10, 11.

Butler, Gen., put in command of Fifth Army, 366.

Byng, Gen., fares better than Gough, 382, 383; Milner confers with, 387.

Byrne, Gen., head of Royal Irish Constabulary, and recruiting bill, 188, 189.

CADORNA, GEN., at Military Conference on Russian situation, 92, 93; at Allied Conferences (Nov. 1917), 216; rejects Weygand's suggestion of Generalissimo, 232; member of Versailles Staff, 260; agrees on size of General Reserve, 349.

Campbell, Sir James, confers with Lloyd George on Irish recruiting, 189, 190.

Carson, Sir Edward, on Man-Power Committee, 156; confers on problem of Irish recruiting, 189, 190; favors Henry Wilson, 314.

Cecil, Lord Robert, sent to confer with France, 117–120; opposes Wilson, 315; meets with American Mission, 407.

Central Powers, their control in Serbia and Belgium, 3, 4; their success in land compaigns, 8; after overthrow of Russia and Roumania, 209, 210; ultimately destroyed by food and fuel shortage, 241; prepare for great offensive on Western Front, 325–331; their situation precarious, 328, 329. *See also* Germany; Man-Power Committee.

Chamberlain, Austen, 316.

Charteris, Gen., reports to Haig, 270.

Chicherin, interned in England, 105, 112, 116.

Clemenceau, Georges, 294; on Russian situation, 109; accepts British memorandum on Russia, 120; and Russo-German Treaty, 128; restrains Foch, 139; "loves France and hates all Frenchmen," 196–198; meetings with Lloyd George, 198–200; his success as War Minister, 200, 201; his courage, 201; an inexorable cynic, 201; defeated for presidency by Deschanel, 202, 203; greatest French statesman of his day, 203; calm and practical in action, 203; comes to realise importance of sea power, 204; Lloyd George's estimate of, 205; importance of his rise to power, 215; presides at Allied Conferences (Nov. 1917), 215–221; would not place Foch above Pétain, 233; his proposal for Italian offensive not encouraged, 239; presides over Supreme Council at Versailles, 240, 243, 246, 249; his Council address quoted, 261–264; urges extension of British line, 275–277; at Council Meeting (Feb. 1918), 277; his visit to Haig, 350, 351; supports Pétain's policy, 354, 355; his antipathy to Foch, 356–361; Milner to confer with, 376; his conferences with Milner, 385–389; unable to budge Pershing, 440; his wire to Wilson, 445, 446.

Clynes, J. R., Minister of Food, writes to Lloyd George, 41, 42; at Labour Conference, 182.

Colby, Bainbridge, in London with American Mission, 140, 400, 406, 407.

Compiègne, Conference of, 228–232; the bombing of, 381.

Conscription. *See* Man-Power Committee.

INDEX

Cook, Sir Edward, and *Morning Post* article, 300.
Cox, Brig.-Gen., estimates German strength, 326; predicts German attack, 338, 339.
Cravath, Paul, with American Mission in London, 400.
Cronstadt, a hotbed of Bolshevism, 94, 95.
Crosby, Oscar T., with American Mission in London, 400.
Curzon, Lord, on Man-Power Committee, 156; meets with American Mission, 407.
Czernin, Count, Austrian Prime Minister, sends Mensdorff to confer with British, 20; his views on Allied peace terms, 44–53; replies to Russian overtures, 117.

DAVIES, JOHN (later Sir), secretary to Lloyd George, 428.
Delbrück, Prof., and Repington betrayal, 297.
Derby, Lord, reserves judgment on General Reserve plan, 288, 289; urged to join conspirators, 298; proof of his innocence, 300; resigns, 315, 316; meets with American Mission, 406.
Deschanel, M., defeats Clemenceau for presidency, 202, 203.
Devlin, Mr., and Military Service Bill, 192.
Diaz, Gen., informed regarding General Reserve, 349; divisions allotted to, 352, 353.
Djemal Pasha, 57.
Doullens Conference, 387–390.
Duke, Mr., Chief Secretary, opposes recruiting bill, 188, 190, 192.

EDMONDS, GEN., reports on Fifth Army defences, 335, 336.
England. *See* Great Britain.
English Military Party, its machinations to thwart progress of war plans, 286–307.
Enver Pasha, militarist Germanophile, 36, 56, 59.

FAVRE, JULES, 200.
Fifth Army. *See* British Fifth Army.
Flesquières, complication of salient at, 383, 384.
Foch, Gen. Ferdinand, 218; temperament of, 14; at Military Conference on Russian situation, 92, 93; fails to understand importance of sea power, 138, 139; at Allied Conferences (Nov. 1917), 216, 218; his Memorandum for 1918 campaign, 223–225; Pétain's disagreement with, 225–232; meets with Supreme Council at Versailles, 242, 245; disapproves of "duck's march through Flanders," 268; at Boulogne Conference, 269; and Repington's accusations, 294, 295; and General Reserve downfall, 347, 355–361; explains his plans to Executive War Board, 373, 374; Britain's desire to give him control, 375, 376; confers with Milner, 385–387, 389, 390; rises to the occasion, 386; watches America, 396; meets Pershing in Paris, 439, 440; unable to budge Pershing, 440, 441; estimates superiority of German forces, 445–447.
France, morale of its army weakened, 3, 4; and Russian situation, 117–120; lacks a seasoned Premier, 195; Haig's estimate of its army, 208; Versailles Staff recommendations for safety of, 251, 252; wishes British line extended on Western Front, 265–284; its enormous losses, 266; threatened by German attack on Western Front, 325–347; in the great offensive, 380–382; fears America will arrive too late, 397; its one preoccupation, 425, 426. *See also* Allies.
French, Sir John, and Haig, 377.

GEDDES, SIR AUCKLAND, confers with Labour on recruiting, 181, 182; his recruiting bills, 187, 188.
General Reserve Plan, formulated at Versailles, 235–250; British political crisis over, 285–324; reasons for War Cabinet support of, 343, 344; attitude of Haig and Pétain to, 344–359; its fate settled, 359–362; Foch's early scheme for, 373–375.
Germany, its 1917 losses, 7; causes for anxiety in, 9–11; food shortage in, 13–15; attaches little importance to American Army, 15, 16; in no mood to make concessions, 20, 54; replies to Allied peace declarations, 42–47; negotiates armistice with Russia, 107, 108, 115–117; peace with Russia, 128, 129; conserving of man power, 137; its offensive of March 1918, 187; strength of its army (1918) estimated by Haig, 206–208; the benefit of a united front, 285, 286; its political system fails, 287; appreciates Repington betrayal, 297;

458 INDEX

Germany (*Continued*)
skilfully withdrawn by Hindenburg, 333; masses enormous forces, 367; starts the offensive, 369; stops all leave, 370; attacks St. Quentin front, 422; quality of its troops deteriorates, 444; its strength overestimated by Foch, 445–447. *See also* Central Powers.

G. H. Q., British, contemptuous of American Army, 16; makes little preparation for defence, 363, 364; its news not reassuring, 368, 369; appreciates emergency, 372; its lack of understanding, 377–379. *See also* Great Britain.

Giardino, Gen., his agreement with Diaz, 353.

Globe, comments on *Morning Post* article, 290, 293.

Gough, Sir Hubert, 333; defeat of his army, 206; comments on Haig, 326; describes neglect of Fifth Army, 336; not given adequate reserves, 342; Haig's unfairness to, 366; complains Italians not up to strength, 370; his recommendations ignored, 377–381; his conversation with Lawrence, 379; Haig finally confers with, 382; superseded, 390, 391; unjust criticism of, 391, 392. *See also* British Fifth Army.

Great Britain, repulsed in Belgium, 4; weary in body and spirit, 5, 6; receives tentative overtures of peace from Austria and Turkey, 19–37; states peace terms, 36–41; complicated relations with Russia, 105–129; confers with France on Russian situation, 117–120; its attitude toward the Bolsheviks, 120–129; its man power early in war, 133–135; its special man-power problems, 137–151; its mechanical superiority, 151, 152; improved communications, 152–154; its policy toward Alsace-Lorraine, 183, 186; and Military Service Bill, 191, 192; urged to extend line on Western Front, 265–284; its strength on all fronts, 266; serious political crisis in, 286–312; fails to realise precarious position of Germany, 328; prepares to resist German offensive, 331–345; Fifth Army neglected by Haig, 333–342; distribution of its troops, 336–338; plans further drafts for France, 369–371; fears America will arrive too late, 397; and question of transport of American troops, 410–420; its one preoccupation, 425, 426; its severe criticism of American equipment, 448–453. *See also* Allies; Man-Power Committee.

Greece, food shortage in, 220, 221.

Grey, Sir Edward, approves Lloyd George peace terms, 39.

Guest, Capt., reports on American troops, 443.

Gwynne, Mr., warned regarding *Morning Post* article, 300.

HAIG, SIR DOUGLAS, 6, 218, 219; misinformed on conditions of German Army, 17; his demand for reinforcements, 144, 146–148, 150; opposes Man-Power Committee suggestions, 164, 165, 171; and Irish recruiting, 190; his faulty estimates of German and French power, 206–209; his disagreements with Pétain, 209–214, 222; his reaction to Foch's document, 227–232; his proposal to withdraw troops from Salonika, 237, 238; meets with Supreme Council at Versailles, 240–243; reluctant to extend British line, 265–284; opposes Foch's command of reserves, 287; comments on attitude of, 290–292; ready to stand by Versailles agreement, 292, 293; Asquith's eulogy of, 302, 303; at Walton Heath, 315, 316, 320; fails to maintain loyalty, 324; his theory of German menace, 325–327; his failure to protect Fifth Army, 333–342; his extraordinary conduct, 339–342; fails to carry out General Reserve plan, 344–359; his dubious staff appointments, 364–366; his disquieting visit to Pétain, 369, 372; reports situation serious, 372; constant manœuvring with Pétain, 375, 376, 380, 382; and Sir John French, 377; finally confers with Gough, 382; at Doullens, 387, 390; his memorandum to Weygand, 387, 388; displaces Gough, 390–392; his interview with Pershing, 412, 413; reports to War Council on American situation, 420; his desire for own offensive, 442.

Haldane, Viscount, opposes Plumer, 315.

Hankey, Sir Maurice, at War Council Meeting (Feb. 1918), 280; and Lloyd George, 392, 393; attends Versailles conference, 418.

Harrington, Gen., 291.

INDEX

Hertling, Count, German Chancellor, replies to Allied peace terms, 44–47.
Hindenburg, Field Marshal von, 184, 293, 327; writes to Kaiser regarding peace negotiations, 42–44; overthrows Bethmann-Hollweg, 287, 312; quoted regarding German weakness, 328, 329; skilfully withdraws Germany, 333; comments on distribution of British troops, 339; watches America, 396.
Hitler, Adolph, 9.
Horne, Gen., Milner confers with, 387.
House, Col. Edward M., heads American Mission to London (1917), 140, 398–400; at Allied Conferences (Nov. 1917), 215, 216; receives cable from Lloyd George, 411, 413; informed of Robertson-Pershing interview, 415, 416; exchange cables with Balfour, 423, 424.
Humbert, Gen., his visit to Gough, 380.
Hutchison, Maj. Gen. Sir Robert, Director of Organisation, efficient and reliable, 370; confers with Pershing, 433.
Hutier, Gen. von, to attack British Fifth Army, 337.

IGNATIEV, considers peace essential, 90, 91.
Inter-Allied Conference (July 1917), 91–93; (Aug. 1917), 99, 100; (Nov. 1917) and Russian situation, 108, 109.
Ireland, and the recruiting problem, 188–193.
Italy, its army broken (1917), 8; crippled by lack of supplies, 139; its representatives at Allied Conferences (Nov. 1917), 215; discussed at Allied Conferences, 217–221; Versailles Staff recommendations regarding, 252, 253. See also Allies.

JAURÈS, M., and Clemenceau, 196.
Jellicoe, Adm. Sir John, meets with American Mission, 401.

KALEDIN, GEN., one of best Russian generals, 101, 107, 124.
Kamal Bey, 57.
Kerensky, Alexander, not strong enough to direct Revolution, 76; his battle royal with Miliukoff, 77; his nervous temperament, 79, 80; as Minister of War, 86, 89; loses control of situation, 91; escapes arrest, 94; fails to understand necessity of discipline, 98; gives Korniloff free hand, 99; Knox's lack of faith in, 101; quarrels with Korniloff, 102, 103; overthrown, 104; keeps Germans guessing, 108.
Kerr, Philip (later Lord Lothian), accompanies Smuts to Switzerland, 21; interviews Parodi, 36, 37, 55; his Parodi report quoted, 56–62; meets Austrians at Berne, 50–53.
Kiggell, Gen. L. E., retired from post of C.G.S., 365.
Klembovski, Gen., on Northern Front, 89.
Knox, Gen., his view of Russian situation, 80; describes collapse of Brusiloff offensive, 85–91; reports to War Cabinet, 100–102, 104; his opinion of Russian military situation, 123, 124.
Konovaloff, resignation of, 81.
Korniloff, Gen., almost an autocrat, 76; considers Brusiloff offensive last chance, 90; made commander-in-chief, 99; Knox's opinion of, 101, 102; revolts, 102; his arrest, 103.
Krilenko, organises plebiscite, 89; favourable to Allies, 115, 116.
Kühlmann, Baron Richard von, kept silent by War Lords, 184.

LABOUR CONFERENCE. See Trade Unions.
Landwehr, Gen., reports on Austrian food shortage, 12.
Lansdowne, Lord, 17; spokesman of peace party, 38; opposes Irish conscription, 192.
Law, Rt. Hon. Andrew Bonar, 309, 316; doubtful of wisdom of recruiting bill, 188, 192; favours Henry Wilson, 314.
Lawrence, Sir Herbert, Haig's Chief of Staff, 157; appointed C.G.S., 364–366; his previous record, 365; ignores Gough's recommendations, 379.
League of Nations, its influence on human affairs, 74.
Lenin, Nikolai, his return to Russia, 76–80; his ruthless directness, 97; and downfall of Kerensky, 104, 105; offers armistice to Germany, 107.
Litvinoff, M., his article in *Woolwich Pioneer*, 106; representing Bolsheviks in London, 121, 122.
Lloyd George, David, fails to understand Ludendorff's policy (1918), 14, and Stinnes, 14; attaches great importance to maintenance of food supplies, 37, 38; prepares statement of peace objectives, 39; presents peace statement to Trade Unions (quoted), 39–41, 63–73; receives letter from Clynes,

INDEX

Lloyd George, David (*Continued*)
41, 42; and foreign comments on the peace terms, 42–48; anxious to keep up negotiations with Austria, 49; and the Russian complications, 105, 108–110; supports Balfour, 114; asks Knox's opinion of Russian military situation, 123; his view of Bolshevist government, 124, 125; requests Haig report, 147; chairman Committee on Man Power, 156; accused of fear of German invasion, 170; addresses Labour Conference on recruiting problems, 182–187; doubts wisdom of recruiting bill, 188; confers with Campbell on Irish recruiting, 189, 190; and Sir Henry Wilson, 192, 193; entertains Painlevé, 195; comments on Clemenceau, 196; his relations with Clemenceau, 197–200, 202–205; asks Haig's view of military position, 206; at Allied Conferences in Paris (Nov. 1917), 215–221; and question of a Generalissimo, 233; meets with Supreme Council at Versailles, 240–250; at Boulogne Conference, 269; visits Haig at G.H.Q., 270, 271; urges meeting between Haig and Pétain, 273; asks Haig to confer with Cabinet, 275; at War Council meeting (Feb. 1918), 276–282; efforts to thwart his plans, 286; reports General Reserve plan to War Cabinet, 288, 289; his correspondence with Milner, 290–292; denounced by Repington, 295; complimented by Delbrück, 297; and Unionist War Committee resolutions, 298, 299; questioned by Asquith in Parliament, 302–307; and question of Robertson's resignation, 309–322; his estimate of Henry Wilson, 312–315; offers C.I.G.S. post to Plumer, 315; and the Derby resignation, 315, 316; addresses House on Robertson resignation, 317–322; not aware of Haig's attitude on General Reserve, 350, 351; receives Rawlinson note, 353, 354; not informed of Clemenceau's attitude, 359; struck by British supineness before offensive, 363, 364; feels gravity of situation on Western Front, 369; summons emergency meeting at War Office, 369–371; calls Cabinet meeting to consider emergency, 372–374; sends for Milner, 375; sends Milner to France, 376; receives more encouraging news, 393; feels American remoteness, 397, 398; proposes American Mission, 398; confers with American Mission, 401–407; his cable to Col. House, 411, 413; informs Col. House of Robertson-Pershing interview, 415, 416; confers at Versailles on American programme, 418–420; urges Baker to modify American policy, 423; exchanges cables with Reading on American situation, 426, 427, 429–434; further communications with America, 435–438, 441–443; his resentment at Pershing, 440–442; wires thanks to Wilson, 445, 446.

Lockhart, Bruce, British representative in Petrograd, 124; Balfour's reply to, 125–128.

Londonderry, Lord, opposes Irish conscription, 192.

Loucheur, M., confers with Milner, 385.

Ludendorff, Gen. Erich, 183; aware of food shortage, 13, 14; misinformed on conditions in England, 17; and Allied peace declaration, 42, 43, 54; plans great attack on British Front, 239; comments on English Military Party, 286, 287; overthrows Bethmann-Hollweg, 287, 312; plans attack on British Front, 327–329; explains weakness of British line, 338, 339; watches America, 396.

Lufti Bey Fikri, 57.

Lvoff, Prince, not strong enough to direct Revolution, 76; in danger of arrest, 94; regards Tchernoff as dangerous, 97; expects constitutional monarchy, 97, 98.

McCORMICK, VANCE C., with American Mission in London, 400, 407.

MacDonald, Ramsay, strength of his Labour movement, 38; and the Bolsheviks, 121.

Macdonogh, Gen., Director of Military Intelligence, supplies figures to War Cabinet, 374.

M'Kenna, Reginald, Asquith's deputy, 302.

Maclay, Sir Joseph, prepares to transport drafts to France, 371; meets with American Mission, 407.

Macpherson, Ian, Under-Secretary for the War Office, 316.

Mahon, Gen., G.O.C., Irish Command, his memorandum on recruiting bill, 188, 189.

Man power, the problem of, 135–137; in Britain, 137–145; War Office figures and, 145–151; table showing distribution of, 154, 155. *See also* Man-Power Committee.

INDEX

Man-Power Committee, appointed, 156, 157; reports on comparative strength of Allies and enemy, 158–160; on available reserves, 160–162; on remaining British man power, 162–167; suggests reduction of divisional battalions, 164–167; on rate of wastage, 167–170; its conclusions, 170, 171, 175; on residue of civilian man power, 171–178; feels importance of Navy, 175; difficulty of carrying out its recruiting proposals, 181–187.

March, Gen. Peyton C., his "Nation at War" quoted, 452 n.

Marie, Empress, of Russia, 79.

Maurice, Sir Frederick, Robertson's right-hand man, 295, 309; reports to Cabinet appearance of Brandenburg Corps, 367; supplies figures to War Cabinet, 374.

Max, Prince, of Baden, refers to Lloyd George peace terms, 41.

Mensdorff, Count, confers with Smuts in Switzerland, 20–36; urges Britain to state peace terms, 36.

Michailovitch, Grand Duke Nicolas, 79.

Micheler, Gen., in favor of Italian offensive, 219.

Military Party. *See* English Military Party.

Military Representatives. *See* Versailles Staff.

Military Service Bill, 191, 192.

Miliukoff, Paul Kikolayevich, not strong enough to direct Revolution, 76; disagrees with Kerensky, 77, 78; instigates desertion of Cadets, 93, 94.

Millerand, Alexandre, found wanting, 195.

Milner, Lord, 309; sent to confer with France, 117–120; at Allied Conferences (Nov. 1917), 216; meets with Supreme Council at Versailles, 240, 289; his correspondence with Lloyd George on General Reserve plan criticisms, 289–292; denounced by Repington, 295; favours Henry Wilson, 314; not aware of Haig's attitude on General Reserve, 350, 351; to urge assistance of French government, 372, 375, 376; confers at Pétain's headquarters, 385–387; at the Doullens Conference, 387–390; exonerates Gough, 392; meets with American Mission, 407; attacks Versailles conference, 418; Pershing's interview with, 438, 439.

Morning Post, opens fire on General Reserve plan, 289, 290, 293, 294, 296, 297; War Cabinet considers treachery of, 299–301.

Mouktar Bey, 56, 59, 61.

NABOKOFF, M., replaced in London by Litvinoff, 121.

Nekrassoff, fails to inspire confidence, 97.

Nicholas, Czar, of Russia, a drug addict, 79.

Nivelle, Gen. Richard, failure of his offensive, 218; postponement of his offensive, 265, 266, 270.

O'CONNOR, T. P., introduces Lloyd George to Clemenceau, 198.

Orlando, Vittorio, at Allied Conferences (Nov. 1917), 215, 218; and question of a Generalissimo, 233; meets with Supreme Council at Versailles, 246, 247, 249; supports Lloyd George, 276, 280, 281; and failure of General Reserve, 360; wires to Wilson, 445, 446.

PAGE, WALTER HINES, American Ambassador at London, delivers Baker's message to Lloyd George, 428.

Painlevé, Paul, character of, 194, 195; fall of, 195; at Boulogne Conference, 269.

Palestine, Allenby to take offensive in, 296.

Parliament, British, Asquith questions Lloyd George in, 302–307. *See also* Great Britain.

Parodi, Dr., interviews Kerr in Switzerland, 36, 37, 55–62.

Passchendaele, the evil wrought by, 340.

Peace, tentative offers from Austria and Turkey, 19–37, 48–53; Great Britain states terms of, 36–41; between Germany and Russia, 115–117, 128, 129.

Perkins, Thomas N., with American Mission in London, 400, 407.

Pershing, Gen. John, at Military Conference on Russian situation, 92, 93; at Allied Conferences (Nov. 1917), 215; and Conference of Compiègne, 230, 231; complains of slowness of American preparations, 407–409; alarmed at deficiencies of American troops, 409; his cable from Baker, 412; interviews Haig, 412, 413; his conference with Robertson, 413–416; his lack of coöperation with French and British, 416; confers with Allies about American Army situation, 418–420; comments on American strength, 421, 447; fighting for corporate unity of American forces, 421, 422; receives wire

Pershing, Gen. John, (*Continued*) from Baker, 423, 424; upset at Military Representatives' resolution, 425; gives Pétain four American divisions, 428; to decide on disposal of troops, 431; his angry protests, 433, 434, 438; his stubborn intransigence, 439; meets Foch in Paris, 439, 440; British resentment at, 441–444; another compromise with, 444–446; delays American aeroplanes, 452.

Pétain, Gen. Henri, 218, 219; his plan of campaign for 1918–19, 4; his view of American Army, 16; at Military Conference on Russian situation, 92, 93; estimates his losses, 149; his disagreements with Haig, 209–214, 222; his comments on Foch Memorandum, 225–227; his conflict with Foch, 227, 228, 230–233; meets with Supreme Council at Versailles, 240, 243, 246, 247; and extension of British line, 270, 273–275, 277–282; opposes Foch's command of reserves, 287; misled by Germans, 327; his attitude toward General Reserve plan, 344–359; failure of his arrangement with Haig, 369, 372; constant manœuvring with Haig, 375, 376, 380, 382, 384; confers with Milner, 385; at Doullens, 387–389; watches America, 396; given four American divisions, 428; wishes to beat enemy on French Front, 442.

Petroff, interned in England, 105, 112, 116.

Petrograd, revolution in, 82–85, 93–98, 104.

Pichon, M., makes peace declaration for France, 42; accepts British memorandum on Russia, 120.

Pierrefeu, Jean de, quoted, 346.

Plumer, Gen., popularity of, 291; declines post of C.I.G.S., 315; Milner confers with, 387.

Poincaré, Raymond, President of France, his dislike of Clemenceau, 196; describes Clemenceau's ambition, 365 and *n*.; conferences on Reserve plan, 358, 359; desires coöperation with British, 386; at Doullens, 387–390.

RABERAU, BARON VON, his report on Austria (Jan. 1918), 12.

Rasputin, 79.

Rawlinson, Gen., his letter to Lloyd George, 353, 354; given remainder of Gough's army, 379.

Reading, Lord, proposes American Mission, 398, 399; exchanges cables with Lloyd George, 426, 427, 429–434; his masterly handling of American difficulties, 435–443.

Reichstag Commission, Report of, quoted, 12, 15.

Repington, Col., on question of extending British lines, 267; treachery of, 289, 293–301; quotes Robertson, 348.

Ribot, Alexandre, found wanting, 195; his stately rhetoric, 215.

Roberts, G. H., at Labour Conference, 182.

Robertson, Sir William, 213, 238; his estimate of British losses, 6; at Military Conference on Russian situation, 92, 93; optimistic regarding Korniloff command, 99; quoted, 143, 144; and the man-power problem, 146; at Allied Conferences in Paris (Nov. 1917), 215, 216; agrees to Foch's conference plans, 228; meets with Supreme Council at Versailles, 240, 242–245; at Boulogne Conference, 269; his hostility to General Reserve plan, 287–312; his letter to Repington, 301, 302; Asquith's eulogy of, 302, 303; his reputation not upheld by his record, 307, 308; refuses Board of Control offer, 309; discussion of his resignation, 309–322; takes Eastern Command, 322; more honourable than Haig, 342; and Versailles decisions, 348, 349; meets with American Mission, 401; his unsatisfactory interview with Pershing, 413–416; takes up issue of American troops, 418, 419; succeeded by Wilson, 438.

Roumania, German occupation of, 3; effect of its overthrow on military outlook, 209.

Rumbold, Sir Horace, receives Austrian overtures, 48, 49, 55, 56.

Russia, its armies demoralized, 3; rumbles of revolution in, 75–91; Knox report on, 100–102; falling to pieces as fighting force, 103, 104; complicated situation in, 104–129; negotiates armistice with Germany, 107, 108, 115–117; peace with Germany, 128, 129; effect of its overthrow on military outlook, 209; its food reserves exploited, 241. *See also* Russian Revolution.

Russian Revolution, its influence on world affairs, 74–76; beginnings of, 75–91; crisis in Petrograd, 93–96; fall of Kerensky Government, 104.

INDEX

St. Quentin, German attack on, 422.
Salisbury, Lord, and Unionist War Committee resolutions, 298, 299.
Savinkoff, 101.
Seidler, Pres. Austrian Ministry, his report on food shortage, 12.
Serbia, in German hands, 3.
Simon, Gen., his Polish Division, 88.
Sixte, Prince, result of his letters, 20.
Skobeleff, 80, 81; influence of, 97.
Skrzynski, M. de, and the peace declarations, 48, 49, 51–53.
Smith, Capt., and Trotsky, 116.
Smuts, Gen. J. C., his report on Mensdorff conversations quoted, 21–35, 55, 56; meets Austrians at Berne, 50–53; on Man-Power Committee, 156, 157.
Sonnino, Baron, at Allied Conferences (Nov. 1917), 215; at War Council meeting (Feb. 1918), 277.
Stinnes, Hugo, and Lloyd George, 14.
Stresemann, Herr, 200.

Talat Pasha, expects a *paix blanche*, 36, 37, 56, 59.
Taylor, Dr. Alonzo R., with American Mission in London, 400, 407.
Tchernoff, Minister of Agriculture, arrested, 95; his socialist projects, 97.
Terestchenko, 82–84; in Petrograd crisis, 93, 94, 97.
Third Army. *See* British Third Army.
Thomas, Albert, and Clemenceau, 197.
Tournès, Gen. René, describes ambition of Clemenceau, 357.
Trade Unions, British, deadlock with, 38, 39; Lloyd George's address to, 39–41; General Conference to discuss recruiting, 181–187.
Trotsky, Leon, 76; ruthless methods of, 97; and downfall of Kerensky, 104, 105; his revolutionary appeal, 105; his proposal for general armistice, 106, 107; his interview with Smith, 116; his peace terms, 116, 117; his statement of Bolshevik policy quoted, 130–132.
Tseretelli, Minister of Interior, 97, 98.
Tudor, Gen., forced to retreat, 383.
Turkey, routed by British, 8; angered by German arrogance, 9, 10; makes tentative peace offer to England, 19, 36, 37, 56–62; Versailles Staff recommendations regarding, 255–260.

Unionist War Committee, resolutions of, 298, 299.
United States, not feared by Germany, 15, 16; could not influence situation before summer of 1918, 214; its representatives at Allied Conferences (Nov. 1917), 215; Haig's pessimism regarding American forces, 241–243; estimate of its assistance to Allies, 394–397; report of its Mission in London, 405–408; bungling and delay in war preparations, 407; question of transporting troops to France, 409–420; enthusiasm of the troops, 420, 421; strength in Feb. 1918, 421, 422; its difficulty in appreciating gravity of situation, 427, 428; its troops untrained, 443, 444; sends steady flow of men to Europe, 447, 448; indecision and incompetency in equipping army, 448–453; bravery of its soldiers, 453.

Venizelos, Eleutherios, at Allied Conferences (Nov. 1917), 215, 220.
Versailles Staff (Military Representatives), proposals of, 234–239, 249, 250; their Note 12 quoted, 251–260; consider extension of British line, 275, 276; their resolution on American policy, 424, 425.
Viviani, René, a great orator, 195.
Von Kuhl, Gen. Von, reports on American troops, 15 and *n*.

Wagstaff, Gen., reports enthusiasm of American troops, 420, 421.
War Cabinet, British, in ignorance of Balkan and Austrian situation, 10–13; suspicious of Austrian overtures, 49; considers Russian situation, 100–102, 107, 110–114; and the Bolshevist government, 124–128; asks Geddes to prepare recruiting bill, 188; criticisms of, 208; Haig reports to, 275; efforts to overthrow, 287; and General Reserve plan, 288, 289; and *Morning Post* treachery, 299–301; and problem of Robertson resignation, 311, 315; approves Wilson's appointment, 316; notified of Haig's disobedience, 351–354; receives reports of conditions on Western Front, 367–369; asks figures of strength on Western Front, 368; considers the emergency, 372–374; orders Gough home, 392; considers strength of American Army, 417, 434, 435.
War Council, Supreme, reviews peace declarations, 47; considers military situation, 240–250; Clemenceau's address to, quoted, 261–264; considers extension of British line, 276–281; its resolution on danger of Press revela-

War Council, Supreme (*Continued*) tions, 301; accepts failure of General Reserve, 359, 360; receives Haig's report on American situation, 420; unable to budge Pershing, 440, 441.

War Office, British, its shifting figures of man-power requirements, 145–151, 171; official figures of, 179–181.

Wetzell, Col., on Allied communications systems, 153; advises attack on French Front, 329, 330, 340.

Weygand, Gen., at Allied Conferences (Nov. 1917), 216; his note to Versailles Military Representatives, 228; suggests a Generalissimo, 232; member of Versailles Staff, 260; ability of, 295; receives memorandum from Haig, 387, 388; meets Pershing in Paris, 439.

Whigham, Gen., confers with Pershing, 433; outlines position of American Army, 434.

William II, Kaiser, 183; aware of food shortage, 13; and the Allied peace declarations, 42–44.

Wilson, Sir Henry, 292; urges Irish conscription, 192, 193; at Allied Conferences (Nov. 1917), 216; rejects Weygand's suggestion of Generalissimo, 232; member of Versailles Staff, 260; his General Reserve project, 288; disliked by Robertson, 310; estimate of, 312–315; his appointment as C.I.G.S., 316; his ingratitude, 322; agrees on size of General Reserve, 349; delays despatch to Haig, 349, 350; his letter regarding Haig's disobedience, 352, 353; not aware of Pétain's change of mind, 354; reports from Western Front, 368; fails to deliver Haig report, 372; at Doullens, 387; attends Versailles Conference, 418; succeeds Robertson, 438.

Wilson, Pres. Woodrow, 183, 184; his Fourteen Points, 42, 44; expresses sympathy with Russian people, 128; has passage of arms with Clemenceau, 201, 202; slow to start preparations, 394, 395; sends American Mission to London, 399, 400; receives Balfour's cable, 424; approves proposals of Military Representatives, 425; results of his psychology, 427, 428; Lloyd George appeals to, 428–434; British discontent with, 435–439; unable to control Pershing, 439; thanked by Council, 445, 446; not cut out for a War Minister, 450; contrasted with Lincoln, 450, 451.

Wiseman, Sir William, proposes American Mission to Col. House, 398, 399.

World War, superiority of Allies on Western Front, 7, 8; Germany prepares great offensive, 325–331; progress of offensive on Western Front, 369, 377–386, 392, 393. *See also* British Fifth Army; British Third Army.

Wright, Capt., his abstract of agreement between Haig and Pétain, 346, 347.

Wright, Peter E., his "At the Supreme War Council" quoted, 288, 338, 339, 346, 347.

YOUSOUPOFF, FELIX, and Buchanan, 79.

ZINOVIEFF, his influence in Petrograd, 80.

A000011832157

PSYCHOLOGY

AN INTRODUCTORY STUDY OF THE STRUCTURE AND
FUNCTION OF HUMAN CONSCIOUSNESS

BY

JAMES ROWLAND ANGELL

*Head of the Department of Psychology in the University
of Chicago*

THIRD EDITION, REVISED

NEW YORK
HENRY HOLT AND COMPANY
1906

Copyright, 1904,
BY
HENRY HOLT AND COMPANY

PREFACE

PSYCHOLOGISTS have hitherto devoted the larger part of their energy to investigating the *structure* of the mind. Of late, however, there has been manifest a disposition to deal more fully with its functional and genetic phases. To determine how consciousness develops and how it operates is felt to be quite as important as the discovery of its constituent elements. This book attempts to set forth in an elementary way the generally accepted facts and principles bearing upon these adjacent fields of psychological inquiry, so far as they pertain to the mind of man.

Inasmuch as it is mental activity, rather than mental structure, which has immediate significance for thought and conduct, it is hoped that students of philosophy, as well as students of education, may find the book especially useful. The author has had the interests of such students constantly in mind.

The differing conditions under which introductory courses in psychology are offered at various institutions render it desirable that a text-book should be adaptable to more than one set of circumstances. The present text has accordingly been arranged with the purpose of permitting considerable flexibility in the emphasis laid upon the several portions of the subject. This fact accounts for an amount of repetition and cross-reference which otherwise would have been regarded as unnecessary.

To my teachers, Professor John Dewey and Professor William James, I owe much of what may be found good in these pages. Were not the list too long to recount, I should gladly express my obligations to the many other psychologists by whom I have been influenced in the formation of my views. I am much indebted for advice and suggestion to a number of my colleagues in the University of Chicago, especially to Professor H. H. Donaldson, Professor A. W. Moore, and Dr. J. B. Watson. My wife has given me great assistance in the preparation of my manuscript.

For the use of a number of illustrations acknowledgments are due to the following authors and publishers: William James; D. Appleton & Co., publishers of Barker's "The Nervous System"; W. B. Saunders & Co., publishers of "The American Text-Book of Physiology"; Walter Scott, Ltd., publishers of Donaldson's "Growth of the Brain"; John Murray, publisher of McKendrick and Snodgrass' "Physiology of the Sense Organs"; and G. P. Putnam's Sons, publishers of Loeb's "Physiology of the Brain."

PREFACE TO THE THIRD EDITION

A few purely verbal changes have been introduced into the present edition. Typographical errors have been corrected wherever detected. Otherwise the text remains unaltered.

J. R. A.

CHICAGO, *August* 15, 1905

CONTENTS

CHAPTER I
THE PROBLEMS AND METHODS OF PSYCHOLOGY . . 1

CHAPTER II
THE PSYCHOPHYSICAL ORGANISM AND THE NERVOUS SYSTEM 11

CHAPTER III
A SKETCH OF THE GENERAL RELATIONS OF CONSCIOUSNESS TO NEURAL ACTION 47

CHAPTER IV
ATTENTION, DISCRIMINATION, AND ASSOCIATION . . 64

CHAPTER V
SENSATION 91

CHAPTER VI
PERCEPTION 122

CHAPTER VII
THE PERCEPTION OF SPATIAL AND TEMPORAL RELATIONS 141

CHAPTER VIII
IMAGINATION 161

CHAPTER IX

MEMORY 184

CHAPTER X

THE CONSCIOUSNESS OF MEANING AND THE FORMATION OF CONCEPTS 203

CHAPTER XI

JUDGMENT AND THE ELEMENTS OF REASONING . . 223

CHAPTER XII

THE FORMS AND FUNCTIONS OF REASONING 235

CHAPTER XIII

THE AFFECTIVE ELEMENTS OF CONSCIOUSNESS . . . 256

CHAPTER XIV

FEELING AND THE GENERAL PRINCIPLES OF AFFECTIVE CONSCIOUSNESS 270

CHAPTER XV

REFLEX ACTION AND INSTINCT 283

CHAPTER XVI

THE IMPORTANT HUMAN INSTINCTS 294

CHAPTER XVII

NATURE OF IMPULSE 310

CHAPTER XVIII

THE NATURE OF EMOTION 315

CONTENTS

CHAPTER XIX
GENERAL THEORY OF EMOTION 325

CHAPTER XX
ELEMENTARY FEATURES OF VOLITION 340

CHAPTER XXI
RELATION OF VOLITION TO INTEREST, EFFORT, AND DESIRE 362

CHAPTER XXII
CHARACTER AND THE WILL 376

CHAPTER XXIII
THE SELF 382

PSYCHOLOGY

CHAPTER I

PROBLEMS AND METHODS OF PSYCHOLOGY

Definition of Psychology.—Psychology is commonly defined as the science of consciousness. It is the business of a science systematically to describe and explain the phenomena with which it is engaged. Chemistry, physics, and the various branches of biology all attempt to deal in this manner with some special portion of the facts or processes of nature. Mental facts, or facts of consciousness, constitute the field of psychology.

The Nature of Consciousness.—*Consciousness* we can only define in terms of itself. Sensations, ideas, pains, pleasures, acts of memory, imagination, and will—these may serve to illustrate the experiences we mean to indicate by the term; and our best endeavour to construct a successful definition results in some such list, of which we can only say: "These taken together are what I mean by consciousness." A psychological treatise is really an attempt to furnish the essentials for such a catalogue.

It is generally maintained that despite our difficulty in framing a satisfactory definition of consciousness, we can at least detect one or two of its radical differences from the physical objects which make up the rest of our cosmos.

These latter always possess position and extension, *i. e.*, they occupy space. Psychical facts, or events, never do; on the other hand they possess one characteristic which, so far as we know, is wholly wanting to physical facts, in that they *exist for themselves.* A man not only has sensations and ideas, he knows that he has them. A stone or other physical object has no such knowledge of its own existence or of its own experiences. Yet, whatever may be the value of these distinctions, we need entertain no real fear of encountering any serious misapprehension of the inner nature of consciousness, for each one of us experiences it every day for himself and each is thus fitted to discuss it with some measure of accuracy.

Former Definitions of Psychology.—Formerly psychology was often defined as the science of the soul. But the word *soul* generally implies something above and beyond the thoughts and feelings of which we are immediately conscious; and as it is these latter phenomena with which psychology is primarily engaged, this definition is now rarely used by careful writers. Psychology is also defined at times as the science of mind. The objection to this definition is that the word *mind* ordinarily implies a certain continuity, unity, and personality, which is, indeed, characteristic of normal human beings; but which may, for all we can see, be wholly lacking in certain unusual psychical experiences like those of insanity, or those of dream states, and may be wanting at times in animals. All consciousness everywhere, normal or abnormal, human or animal, is the subject matter which the psychologist attempts to describe and explain; and no definition of his science is wholly acceptable which designates more or less than just this.

The Procedure of the Psychologist.—In his description of conscious processes the psychologist attempts to point out the characteristic features of each distinguishable group of facts and of each member of such groups, and to show how they differ from one another. Thus, for example, the general group known as "sensations" would be described and marked off from the groups known as "feelings"; and the peculiarities of each form of sensation, such as the visual and tactile forms, would be described and distinguished from one another and from those belonging to the auditory form. The psychologist's explanations consist chiefly in showing (1) how complex psychical conditions are made up of simpler ones, (2) how the various psychical groups which he has analysed grow and develop, and finally (3a) how these various conscious processes are connected with physiological activities, and (3b) with objects or events in the social and physical world constituting the environment.

The Fields of Psychology.—In this book we shall be primarily concerned with the facts of normal human consciousness, its constitution, its modes of operation, and its development. But we shall avail ourselves, wherever possible, of useful material from the allied fields of child psychology, abnormal psychology, social psychology, and animal psychology.

Child psychology is occupied with the study of the mental processes of infants and young children, with special reference to the facts of growth. Abnormal psychology has to do (1) with the study of the unusual phases of conscious process, such as are met with in trance, hallucinations, hypnotism, etc.; and is concerned (2) with the more definitely diseased forms of mentality, such as characterise insanity. Social psychology, in its broadest sense, has to do mainly with the psychological principles involved in those expressions of mental life which take form in social relations, organisations, and practices, *e. g.*, the mental attributes of crowds and mobs as contrasted with the mental characteristics of the individuals constituting them. A branch of social psychology, often known as folk psychology, or race psychology, is concerned with the psychical attributes of peoples, especially those of primitive groups as contrasted with civilised nations. Animal psychology is engaged with the study of consciousness, wherever, apart from man, its presence can be detected throughout the range of organic life. The four last-mentioned branches of psychology taken together are sometimes spoken of as comparative psychology, in distinction from the psychology which describes facts concerning normal adult human beings. Those phases of psychology which touch particularly upon the phenomena of development, whether racial or individual, are sometimes spoken of as genetic psychology.

The Methods of Psychology. (1) Introspection.—The fundamental psychological method is introspection. Introspection means looking inward, as its derivation indicates. As a psychological method it consists simply in the direct examination of one's own mental processes. Much mystery has been made of the fact that the mind can thus stand off and observe its own operations, and criticism has been lavishly devoted to proving the impossibility of securing scientific knowledge in any such fashion as this. But it is an undeniable fact that by means of memory we are made aware of our mental acts, and we can trace in this manner by careful and systematic observation many of the rudimentary facts and principles peculiar to human consciousness. When a number of us coöperate in such introspective observation, we greatly augment the exactness and the breadth of our results, and the accepted doctrines of psychology have actually been established by the successive observations of many investigators in much this manner.

(2) Direct Objective Observation.—Moreover, we are able to supplement introspection by immediate objective observation of other individuals. It is thus possible, for example, to detect much which is most characteristic of the emotions, such as anger and fear, by watching the actions of persons about us and noting their expressions, their gestures, etc.

The facts which we thus obtain must of course be interpreted in terms of our direct knowledge of our own experience, gained introspectively. But such observation of others often makes us sensitive to psychological processes in ourselves, which we should otherwise overlook. Finally, it is clear that our psychological facts, whether gained from observation of ourselves, or of others, before they can become of scientific value, must be made the subject of careful reflection and systematic arrangement; otherwise they would be purely haphazard, disconnected fragments, with no more meaning than any other collection of odds and ends. The need of such orderly reasoned arrangement is no more and no less true of the psychological facts gained by observations of others, or by introspection, than it is of physical facts discovered in any realm of science. The facts of gravity had been noticed again and again, but it required the ordering mind of a Newton to set them in intelligent array. Whenever we speak of direct observation, or of introspection, as methods, we shall understand, therefore, this systematic and scientific use of the terms. All the other psychological methods which we shall mention are simply developments of introspection, either in the direction of systematising and perfecting its employment, or of applying its results interpretatively in fields not open to its immediate application; for example, the field of animal consciousness.

(3) **Experiment.**—Experimental psychology, sometimes spoken of as "the new psychology," or the "laboratory psychology," is perhaps the most vigorous and characteristic psychological method of the present day. It is simply an ingenious system for bringing introspection under control, so that its results can be verified by different observers, just as the result of a chemical experiment may be verified by anyone who will repeat the conditions. In every branch of science an experiment consists in making observations of phenomena under conditions of control, so that one may know just what

causes are at work in producing the results observed. A psychological experiment is based on precisely the same principle.

(4) Physiological Psychology and (5) Psychophysics.—Physiological psychology and psychophysics, which are both closely connected, in spirit and in fact, with experimental psychology, are especially devoted to investigating the relations between consciousness on the one hand, and the nervous system and the physical world on the other. Much of physiological psychology, and all of psychophysics, is experimental so far as concerns the methods employed. They both furnish information supplementary to that gathered by ordinary introspection.

The Psychologist's Standpoint.—In our study of mental processes we shall adopt the biological point of view just now dominant in psychology, and regard consciousness, not as a metaphysical entity to be investigated apart from other things, but rather as one among many manifestations of organic life, to be understood properly only when regarded in connection with life phenomena. We shall discover, as we go on, abundant reason for the belief that conscious processes and certain nervous processes are indissolubly bound up with one another in the human being. But at this point, without attempting to justify the assertion, we may lay it down as a basal postulate that the real human organism is a psychophysical organism, and that the mental portion of it is not to be completely or correctly apprehended without reference to the physiological portion. The psychophysical organism is, moreover, a real unit. The separation of the mind from the body which we commonly make in thinking about them is a separation made in behalf of some one of our theoretical or practical interests, and as such, the separation is often serviceable. In actual life experience, however, the two things are never separated. Therefore, although our primary task is to analyse and explain mental facts, we shall attempt to do this in closest possible connection with their accompanying physiological processes.

Our adoption of the biological point of view, while it implies no disrespect for metaphysics, will mean not only that we shall study consciousness in connection with physiological processes wherever possible, but it will also mean that we shall regard all the operations of consciousness—all our sensations, all our emotions, and all our acts of will—as so many expressions of organic adaptations to our environment, an environment which we must remember is social as well as physical. To the biologist an organism represents a device for executing movements in response to the stimulations and demands of the environment. In the main these movements are of an organically beneficial character, otherwise the creature would perish. Mind seems to be the master device by means of which these adaptive operations of organic life may be made most perfect. We shall consequently attempt to see in what particulars the various features of consciousness contribute to this adaptive process. Let it not be supposed that such a point of view will render us oblivious, or insensitive, to the higher and more spiritual implications of consciousness. On the contrary, we shall learn to see these higher implications with their complete background, rather than in detachment and isolation.

Psychology and Natural Science.—In one important particular the method of psychology follows the procedure of the natural sciences, such as physics, botany, and geology. Psychology takes for itself a certain definite domain, *i. e.*, consciousness as a life process. Moreover, it starts out with certain assumptions, or postulates, as they are called, about its subject matter, which it refuses to challenge. The chemist, for example, never stops to inquire whether matter really exists or is simply an illusion. He assumes its reality without question, and forthwith goes about his business. So the psychologist assumes in a common-sense way the reality of mind and the reality of matter. Nor does he question that mind can know matter. These assumptions prevent the necessity of his untangling the metaphysical puzzles which are involved at these points, and leave him free to investigate his field in a purely empirical way. He also attempts, wherever possible, to emulate the natural scientist's use of the idea of causation. Our most reliable forms of knowledge about nature are based upon our knowledge of cause and effect relations. A great deal of our chemical knowledge is in this way exceedingly precise and exact; whereas the lack of such knowledge renders much of our acquaintance with disease extremely superficial and unreliable.

The subject matter of psychology evidently brings it into a distinctly universal relation to all the other sciences, for these sciences are severally engaged in the development of knowledge, and the knowledge-process is itself one of the subjects in which psychology is most interested.

Psychology and Biology.—Inasmuch as psychology is occupied with life phenomena, it is clearly most nearly related to the biological sciences. Indeed, as a natural science it obviously belongs to the biological group. This relationship is as close in fact as it is in theory. The modern psychologist makes frequent use of material furnished him by the anatomist, the physiologist, the zoölogist, and the alienist, and he gives them in return, when he can, such psychological facts as they find it necessary to employ.

Psychology and Philosophy.—Psychology has developed historically out of philosophy, and although it is now in many ways practically independent, its relations with philosophy are necessarily very intimate. The connection is particularly close with those branches of philosophy commonly called normative, *i. e.*, ethics, logic, and æsthetics. These inquiries are primarily concerned with questions of right and wrong, truth and error, beauty and ugliness. It is evident that the profitable discussion of such problems must involve a knowledge of the mental operations employed when we make a right or wrong choice, when we reason falsely or truly, when we experience pleasure in listening to music, etc. In a sense, therefore, psychology furnishes the indispensable introduction to these several philosophical disciplines. It affords an acquaintance with the mental processes which lead respectively to conduct, to knowledge, and to the creation and appreciation of art. It thus enables an intelligent apprehension of the problems which arise in these spheres, and furnishes much of the material essential for their solution. A similar thing is true, though in a less conspicuous and obvious way, of the relation of psychology to metaphysics, and to that form of metaphysical inquiry which formerly was known as rational psychology.

By rational psychology was commonly understood the inquiry into the conditions rendering the existence of consciousness possible. Evidently these inquiries, *i. e.*, rational psychology and metaphysics, together with what is known as epistemology, or the theory of knowledge, are engaged with just such problems as underlie the assumptions of psychology and the natural sciences, *e. g.*, the reality of matter, its independence of mind, etc. It is on this account that metaphysics —which fundamentally represents an effort to solve the problem of the ultimate nature of matter and mind and their relation to one another—is said to be the science of sciences. Although metaphysics is in this sense more fundamental than psychology, and logically antecedent to it, it is so extensively concerned with mental processes that a knowledge of psychology is commonly recognised as practically indispensable for its effective conduct or apprehension. All these branches of philosophy clearly involve, as does psychology, the study of consciousness in a certain sense. But whereas these distinctly philosophical disciplines are primarily interested in some one or another of the implications and products of thought processes, psychology is interested primarily in the constitution and operation of consciousness itself. We may question whether ultimately there are any hard and fast lines severing these philosophical inquiries from one another and from psychology. The distinctions are perhaps rather practical than ultimate. One inquiry inevitably shades off into the others.

Psychology and Education.—Psychology is related to educational theory in much the way that it is to ethics. It may be said to be related to actual educational procedure as theory is to practice. Education has as its function the symmetrical development of the powers of the individual. What the natural relation may be among these faculties, what are the laws of their unfolding, what the judicious methods for their cultivation or repression—these and a thousand similar practical questions can be answered by the assistance of psychological observation, or else not at all. The result which we desire to attain in our educational system must be, in a considerable measure, determined by the social and ethical ideals we have in view. But the securing of the results, the realising of the ideals which we have set up, through our educational machinery—this must be accomplished, if we would work with true insight and not by blind experiment, through a real knowledge of human mental processes. We shall keep constantly before us in this book the facts of growth and the facts of adaptation to the demands of the environment. Clearly these are the facts of practical significance for educational procedure.

CHAPTER II

THE PSYCHOPHYSICAL ORGANISM AND THE NERVOUS SYSTEM

The Union of the Psychical and the Physical in the Organism.—We shall now examine some of the evidence confirmatory of our assertion in the last chapter, that conscious processes and physiological processes are intimately connected in the organism. We shall in this way discover some of the reasons why it is desirable for us at the outset of our study of mental life to learn something about the nervous system, to which subject we shall then devote the remaining portion of the chapter.

Common observation informs us of at least two fundamental types of fact concerning these mind-body relations. We know in this manner (1) that our consciousness or knowledge of the world about us depends primarily upon the use of our senses. A person born blind and deaf has neither visual nor auditory sensations or ideas, and never can have so long as he remains destitute of eyes and ears. By means of the other senses he may be taught much about colours and sounds, as Helen Keller has been; but he never can have the experience which you or I have, when we see a colour or hear a sound, or when we permit a melody "to run through our heads," as we say, or when we call into our minds the appearance of a friend's face. Indeed, if a child becomes blind before he is five years old he commonly loses all his visual ideas and memories just as completely as though he had been born blind. There is every reason to believe that if we were deprived of all our senses from birth, we could never possess knowledge of any kind. The senses thus hold the keys which unlock the doors of intelligence to the mind, and the senses are physical, not mental, things. Apparently, therefore, the most simple and fundamental operations of consciousness are bound up with the existence and activity of certain bodily organs.

Common observation also informs us (2) that the *expressions* of mind ordinarily take the form of muscular movements which we call acts. We hear a bell and our consciousness of the sound results in our going to open the door. We consider a course of action, and the outcome of our deliberation issues in the form of words or deeds, all of which consist primarily in muscular movements. Strange as it may appear, even keeping still involves muscular activity. It would accordingly seem as though the mind were hemmed in between the sense organs on the one hand and the muscles on the other. It would be a truer expression of the facts, however, to say that these are the tools with which the mind works. Through the sense organs it receives its raw material, and by its own operations this material is worked up and organised into the coherent product which we call intelligence. This intelligence is then made effective in practical ways through the rationally controlled action of the voluntary muscles.

There are other facts of a well-known kind whose precise purport is, perhaps, less evident, but whose general implication of intimate connections between mind and body is identical with that of the considerations which we have just mentioned. We know, for example, that blows and wounds may seriously disturb consciousness, or even destroy it. The similar effects of many drugs, such as alcohol, ether, and hashish, are matters of common knowledge. Even coffee and tea exercise a mild influence upon our psychical mood, and the change in general disposition which frequently follows indulgence in a satisfactory meal is a phenomenon familiar to every family circle. Bodily disease often produces a most marked effect upon the mind, and conversely the different effect upon disease, of a cheerful or a depressed mental attitude, is a subject of frequent remark.

When we examine the less familiar evidence offered us by certain branches of modern science, we find our previous impressions strongly confirmed. Thus we learn from pathology, the science of disease, that disordered conditions of particular portions of the brain tissue are accompanied by disturbances of definite kinds in consciousness. In this way we learn, for example, that the destruction or disintegration of the tissue of one region in the brain is followed by the loss of one's visual memories, so that one cannot recall the appearance of familiar objects. A similar disorder in another region costs one the control of certain muscles in the hand, etc. The science of anatomy is able to demonstrate structural connections of nerves between these diseased parts of the brain and the sense organs and muscles over which consciousness has lost control, thus supporting the implication of the pathological evidence already cited. Experimental physiology shows us, that by stimulating (either mechanically or electrically) certain brain areas in animals, we can produce movements of definite muscles, whereas by extirpating these regions we can at least temporarily cripple the muscles and render the will powerless over them. By similar excisions of other brain areas we can cripple definite sense organs. Thus pathology, anatomy, and physiology all point to the same intimate relation of mind and body and indicate more specifically than the observations of every-day experience could do a fixed and positive relation between definite parts of the nervous system and such special phases of consciousness as the visual, the auditory, etc.

Moreover, comparative anatomy, comparative physiology, and comparative psychology all converge upon another cognate principle, *i. e.*, that the development of consciousness among various genera and species of the organic world has run parallel with the development of the nervous system.

Taking all these considerations into account, the deliverances of common sense as well as the teachings of science, it is easy to understand why the modern psychologist finds it judicious in his study of consciousness to learn all that he can about the nervous system, the sense organs, and the motor mechanism.

The Nervous System.—It will assist us in gaining a working idea of the nervous system to bear in mind the fact that its fundamental function consists in "the conversion of incoming sensations into outgoing movements of a kind tending to preserve the creature." Creatures destitute of some form of nervous system are practically incapable of prompt and appropriate adaptation to their surroundings. Plants are thus in large measure the passive victims of their environments. Injury to one part commonly produces little or no immediate effect upon the rest of the plant. But by means of its nervous system every part of an animal organism is brought into vital connection with every other part. Coöperation becomes the controlling principle in the life activities. This coöperation, or coördination, takes the form of movements made in response to sensory stimulations, and the most highly evolved form of nervous system, such as that of the human being, differs from the very rudimentary forms, like that of the jelly fish, only in the complexity of the devices by which these stimulations and movements are connected. When we are studying the structure of this system, we should, then, always remember this fact about the coördination of sensations and movements, as the clue by which to interpret even its most intricate arrangements.

The Elementary Structures.—The nervous system is made up of nerve cells, with their filamentous elongations which are called fibres. A sketch of certain common forms of nerve cells is shown in figures 1, 2, and 3. It will be seen that they are accumulations of granular protoplasmic masses containing a nucleus, and often within this nucleus smaller nucleoli, while from their edges are given off filaments of various forms and sizes. These filaments are outgrowths of the cell-body and constitute an organic part of the structure. The whole structure, including both fibre and cell-body, is nowadays called a neurone. The neurone is, therefore, the

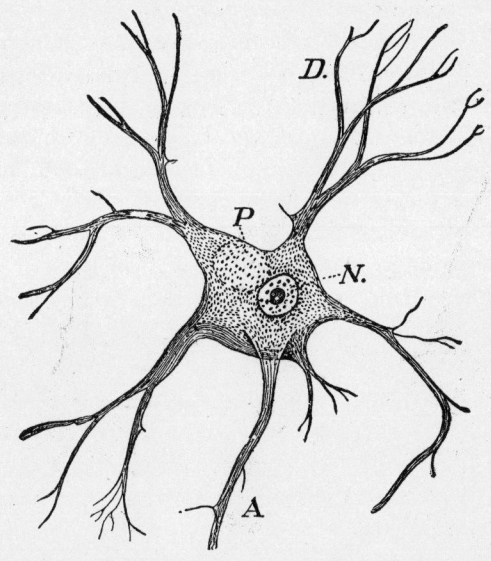

FIG. 1. Isolated body of a large cell from the ventral horn of the spinal cord of man. Multiplied 200 diameters (Donaldson after Obersteiner). *A*, axone (each cell has but one); *D*, dendrites; *N*, nucleus with enclosures; *P*, pigment spot.

real element of the nervous system. It has been estimated that in the nervous system of the adult human being there are about 11,000 millions of these neurones in various stages of development. Their average volume is probably about .00009 of a cubic millimetre.*

* We follow in this statement the conception of the nervous system and the terminology at present generally prevalent among neurologists. It must be remembered, however, that the science of neurology is growing with astonishing rapidity, and radical changes of doctrine are consequently possible at any time.

Certain of the fibrous protuberances are called axones or neurites, others are known as dendrites. The axones, as may be seen from figure 3, are generally smooth in their contours, and when they branch, the divisions commonly occur at right angles. Within the central system the dendrites are rougher and branch more gradually from one another, somewhat like the sticks of a fan. The fully developed axones have a peculiar structure, shown in figure 4. The central strand is known as the axis cylinder. This is a transparent mass

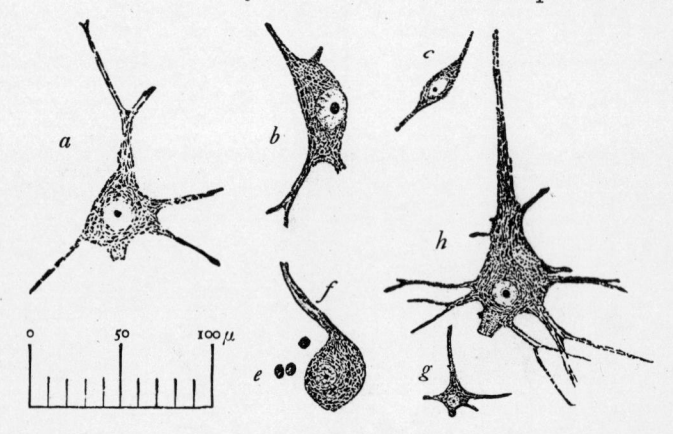

FIG. 2. A group of human nerve cells, all drawn to the same scale: *a*, small motor cell from ventral horn of the spinal cord in the cervical region; *b*, cell from the dorsal part of the thoracic region; *c*, small cell from the top of the dorsal horn of the cord, thoracic region; *e*, small granules from the cerebellum; *f*, Purkinje's cell from same region; *g* and *h*, pyramidal cells from central regions of the cerebral cortex. (Donaldson after Meyer, in the "American Text-book of Physiology.")

which apparently constitutes the true nerve, and conducts nervous impulses from sense organ to nerve centre, and back again from nerve centre to muscle. Outside the axis cylinder is a relatively thick covering known as the medullary sheath. This sheath generally disappears near the cell-bodies and also wherever the fibre terminus approaches other fibre terminals. Outside of this again there is a thin membraneous sheath known as the neurilemma.

Although the cell-bodies and fibres are really parts of single organic cells—the neurones—their notable difference in appearance is accompanied by a distinct difference in function. Both cell-bodies and fibres are sensitive to stimulation,

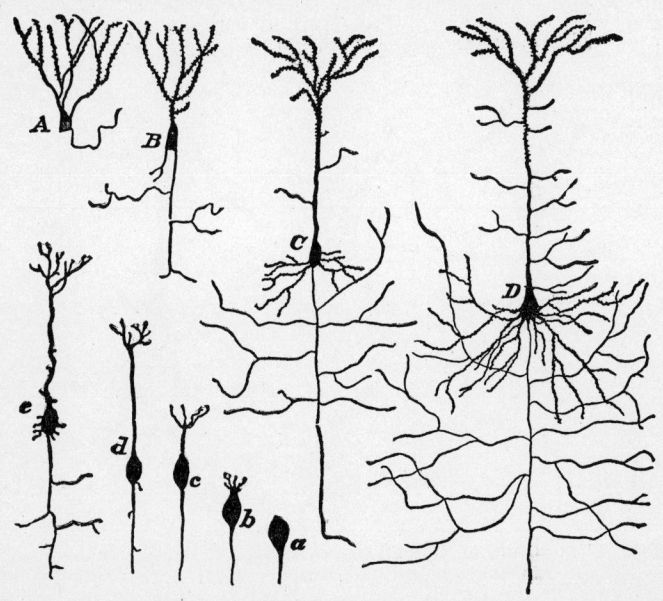

FIG. 3. *A-D*, showing the *phylogenetic* development in a series of vertebrates; *a-e*, the *ontogenetic* development of growing cells in a typical mammal; in both cases only pyramidal cells from the cerebrum are shown; *A*, frog; *B*, lizard; *C*, rat; *D*, man; *a*, neuroblast, or young cell, without dendrites; *b*, commencing dendrites; *c*, dendrites further developed; *d*, first appearance of collateral branches; *e*, further development of collateral and dendrites. (Donaldson after Ramón y Cajal.)

are *irritable*, as the physiologists say, and both possess conductivity. But whereas this exhausts the fundamental functions of the fibres, the cell-bodies are ordinarily supposed to possess the further capacities of reinforcing or inhibiting the impulses sent to them. Moreover, the cell-bodies seem at times to send out nervous excitation along the fibres automatically, without any detectable external stimulation. It will be seen, therefore, that the cell-bodies are in a sense the

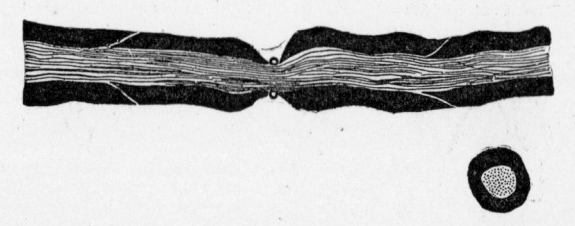

FIG. 4. Longitudinal and transverse section of medullated nerve fibres from the sciatic nerve of the frog. The central fibrillar portion is the axis cylinder. The constriction in the covering sheath represents a "node of Ranvier"; such constrictions occur at intervals along the course of the fibre. (Barker after Biedermann.)

power centres of the nervous system, while the fibres are in the main merely interconnecting mechanisms, putting the several sense organs into relation (1) with the various centres and (2) through these with the muscles.

It is supposed that inside the central nervous system the axones are ordinarily employed to carry impulses away from the cell-bodies, whereas the dendrites probably carry impulses toward them. Outside the central system the afferent fibres leading to the spinal ganglia resemble axones in structure, and so offer apparent exceptions to this rule. In any event the whole nervous system is nothing but an aggregation of neurones with the supporting tissue, called neuroglia, which holds them in place. A nervous impulse originating in the sensory surface of the body, for example in the retina, may be transmitted from one group of neurones to another, until finally it issues, perhaps, from the nerves of the spinal cord, and produces a movement of the foot. This is what would occur if one should step aside upon seeing a heavy object about to fall. In this process of transmitting the impulse through the nervous system, it is not necessary that the groups of neurones should be actually in contact with one another, although this may occur. But they must at least be close together. Contiguity, if not anatomical continuity of groups of neurones, seems to be a *sine qua non* of neural conductivity.

The exact physical nature of neural excitement is not known. Various theories have been propounded in the effort to identify it with recognised forms of chemical or electrical activity, but thus far no hypothesis has been suggested which accords satisfactorily with all the facts. Meantime, we speak of the nervous current, the neural disturbance or excitement, in a purely metaphorical way, to cover the facts which we do know, *i. e.*, that physiological activity of a certain kind occurs in the nervous structures, and is transmitted very rapidly from one point to another. In man the rate of this transmission is about 100 feet per second.

Various Forms of Nervous System.—When we turn to the zoölogist and the comparative anatomist, we are able to obtain certain interesting facts about the development of the nervous system throughout the organic kingdom. From such sources we learn that the simplest types of animal organism, *e. g.*, such protozoans as the amœba, possess no nervous system at all. Every part of the surface of the unicellular amœba (figure 5) is capable of movement, of assimilating food and excreting the waste products. This animal's behaviour suggests that other forms

FIG. 5. Diagram of an amœba. The irregularly shaped mass of protoplasm is shown with N, its nucleus, and CV, a contractile vacuole, which expands and contracts.

of tissue besides nervous tissue are sensitive and capable of conducting impulses. Undoubtedly this is a fact, and we must accordingly think of the nerves as simply specialised forms of protoplasm in which these functions are more highly developed than elsewhere. In certain of the lower metazoans nerve cells appear with fibres extending toward the periphery of the body and possessing sensitive terminations. Among the cœlenterates a very simple nervous system comes to light. In hydroids this is merely a kind of tissue of nerve cells. In echinoderms we meet with a structure like that shown in figure 6. But it is not till we get to such forms as the worms that we find a definite organised centre of control, like the brain or spinal cord. In the annulates of the worm forms there is not only a centre corresponding to a very rudimentary brain, but also one roughly corresponding to the spinal cord. (Figures 7 and 8.) In the molluscs the development is made more complex by the appearance of these groups of central cells clustered together in several directions about the brain. (Figure 9.) Even in the lowest forms of vertebrates, *e. g.*, the acranial amphioxus, we find both a brain and cord. Passing from the lowest to the highest vertebrates up, for example, through the fishes, reptiles, and amphibians to the birds and mammals, we meet with every shade of variation in the development of the several parts of the nervous system. Everywhere, however, from the most primitive metazoan up to man, the general principle is one and the same— a mechanism for connecting sensitive surface organs with muscles.

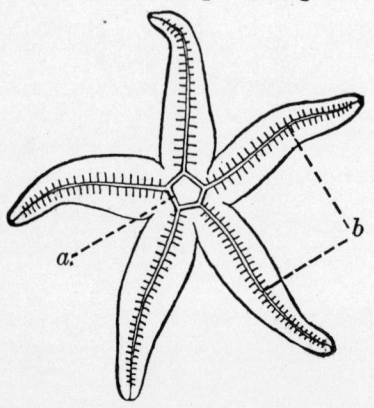

FIG. 6. Nervous system of a starfish; *a*, central nerve ring that surrounds the mouth; *b*, peripheral nerves of the arms. (After Loeb.)

The Gross Structures of the Human Nervous System.—If

we were to examine the human nervous system at one period of its development, we should find it a crude structure of tubular form, with one end enlarged, and slightly constricted at two zones, as shown in figures 10, 11, and 12. The walls of this enlarged portion thicken and spread out as they grow, and in one place dwindle away to a mere membrane. In this manner the various parts of the adult brain are formed, retaining to the end the old tubular contours. The remnant of the cavities in the embryonic brain and cord become respectively the ventricles of the developed brain and the canal of the spinal cord. These cavities remain connected with one another and are filled with the cerebrospinal fluid. The surfaces of the brain and cord are closely invested with a membrane, the pia mater, carrying blood-vessels. This membrane is bathed on its outer surfaces by fluids. A tough, thick membrane, the dura mater, separates the pia mater from the bones of the skull and vertebræ.

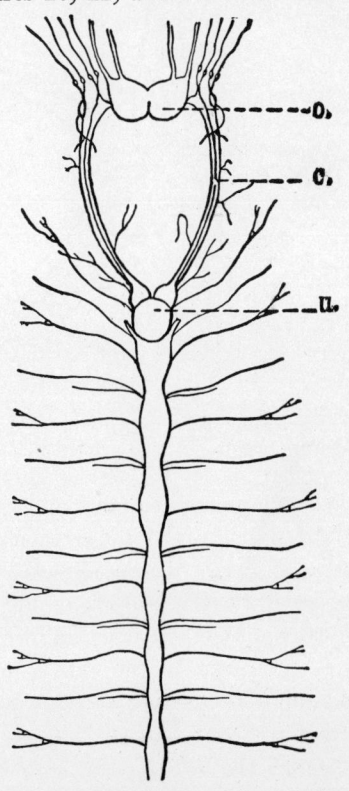

FIG. 7. The brain and a series of segmental ganglia of an annelid (Nereis): *o*, supraœsophageal ganglion, or brain; *c*, commissure; *u*, subœsophageal ganglion. (Loeb after Claparède).

The portion of the embryonic brain known as the fore-brain finally develops into the great masses of the cerebrum. The optic thalami, which are large collections of nerve cells with their fibrous connections, also belonged originally to this general region of the brain. The primitive mid-brain changes less in mass during growth than does the fore-brain, and becomes on its under or ventral surface the crura or peduncles of the brain, while on its upper or dorsal surface it becomes the corpora quadrigemina. The hind-brain develops in its foremost part, dorsally into the cerebellum, and ventrally into the pons. In its lower portions it becomes the medulla oblongata, upon the dorsal surface of which appears the fourth ventricle, with its non-nervous membraneous covering. The spinal cord undergoes the least profound change, as regards its external contours, of any of the embryonic parts of the central system.

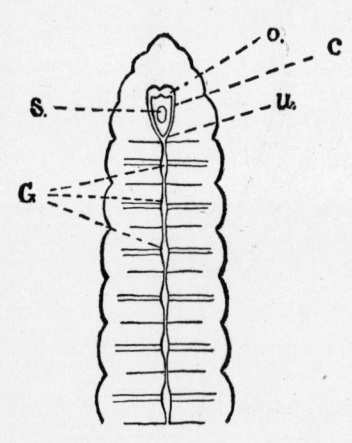

FIG. 8. Dorsal view of central nervous system of an earthworm; *o*, supraœsophageal ganglion; *c*, commissure; *u*, subœsophageal ganglion; *S*, pharynx; *G*, ganglia of the ventral cord. (After Loeb.)

When we take the facts of development into account, therefore, it becomes evident that the various portions of the brain, which seem at first glance so hopelessly confused in their relations to one another, are nevertheless all outgrowths of a single relatively simple structure—the tubular embryonic nervous system, whose walls are everywhere made up of neurones and their supporting tissues, the neuroglia. The general form of the brain is complete some time before birth.

The number of neurones, the nervous element, is also complete at birth. But the maturity of the brain in point of external size is not reached until about seven years of age, and development in the size and interconnections of the neurones goes on indefinitely, certainly with most persons up to forty years of age.

Following Ebbinghaus and others we may classify the neurones of the central nervous system in three general groups, (1) the peripheral neurones, (2) the subcortical neurones, and (3) the cortical neurones.

Peripheral Neurones.— The peripheral neurones, whose *cell-bodies lie outside* the central system, consist of sensory cells and their fibrous prolongations of which a part extend inward toward the centres, and a part outward toward the sensory end-organs, such as the rods and cones of the retina, the hair cells of the cochlea in the internal ear, the touch corpuscles in the skin, etc. (See cuts in Chapter V.) The cell-bodies of these

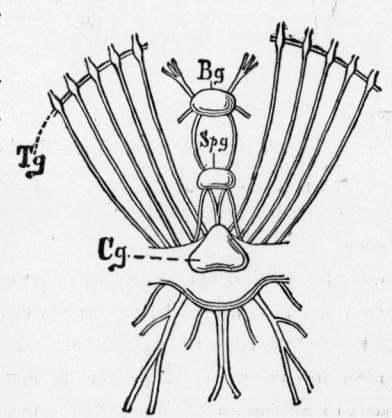

FIG. 9. Brain of a mollusc (Sepia); *Cg*, cerebral ganglion; *Spg*, supraœsophageal ganglion; *Bg*, buccal ganglion; *Tg*, ganglia of the tentacles. (Loeb after Claus.)

neurones are sometimes situated near the central structures, as in the case of the cells in the ganglia of the posterior roots of the spinal cord. These cells distribute their fibres to the skin, muscles, tendons, etc. Sometimes, however, they are in the neighbourhood of the sense organ, as in the case of the auditory nerve, which arises from a cell in the internal ear; the optic nerve, which has its cell-body in the retina, etc. The function of the peripheral neurones is evidently that of transmitting impulses from the sense organs in to the nervous centres, and we need discuss them no further at this point.

Subcortical Neurones.—The subcortical group involves all the gross structures in the central system lying between the

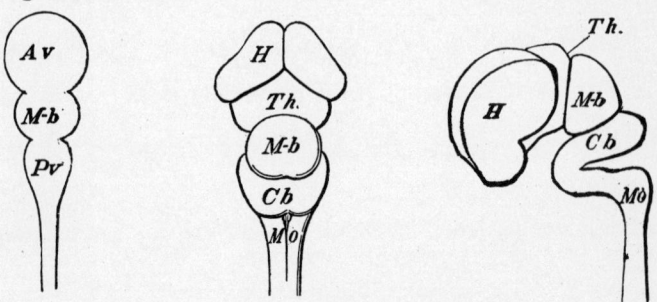

FIGS. 10, 11, and 12. Diagrams illustrating embryological changes in the brain. *Av*, anterior vesicle, or fore-brain; *M-b*, middle vesicle, or mid-brain; *Pv*, posterior vesicle, or hind-brain; *H*, cerebral hemispheres; *Th*, thalamus; *Cb*, cerebellum; *Mo*, medulla oblongata. (James after Hugenin.)

cortices of the cerebrum and the cerebellum on the one hand and the peripheral neurones on the other. Their function is in general that of furnishing neural mechanisms for reflex acts and for connecting the various parts of the central system with one another. This can be best brought out by examining separately some of the more conspicuous gross structures of this group. After we have done this, we shall turn to the cortical groups, whose functions as general control centres we shall then discuss.

We may first consider the spinal cord (figure 13). If we take a cross section of this organ, cutting through at right angles to its long axis, we find a structure such as is shown in figures 14 and 15. In the central portion, grouped about the spinal canal in the general shape of the letter H, is a great mass of cell-bodies giving a peculiar greyish colour to the region. Outside of this is a thick layer of white nerve fibres. Close examination of the grey matter reveals fibres running out laterally to penetrate the white masses. The

THE PSYCHOPHYSICAL ORGANISM

fibres from the cell-bodies in the ventral or anterior region of the grey mass pass out from the spinal cord in bundles, at the general level of the several spinal vertebræ. Thence they may be traced principally to the voluntary muscles of the limbs and trunk. The fibres issuing from the dorsal or posterior region of the grey matter pass out in similar bundles from the posterior sides of the cord, and thence, after uniting with the bundles from the motor region, are distributed chiefly to the sense organs of the skin, joints, muscles, tendons, etc. It may be remarked at this point that the voluntary muscles, such as control the movements of the hand, are commonly striped muscles, whereas the involuntary muscles, *e. g.*, those of the alimentary and circulatory systems, are generally unstriped. The unstriped muscles are mainly connected with the sympathetic nervous system, of which we shall speak briefly a little later. The striped muscles contract and relax more rapidly than the unstriped.

Fig. 13. Showing the ventral surface of the spinal axis, as far up as the pons. The spinal nerves appear on both sides, and on the left the sympathetic ganglia are still in connection with them. C^1, first cervical root; D^1, first thoracic root; D^{12}, twelfth thoracic root; L^1, first lumbar root; S^1, first sacral root; a, b, c, superior, middle, and inferior cervical sympathetic ganglia; d, first thoracic; d^1, eleventh thoracic. (Donaldson after Thomson, in Quain's Anatomy.)

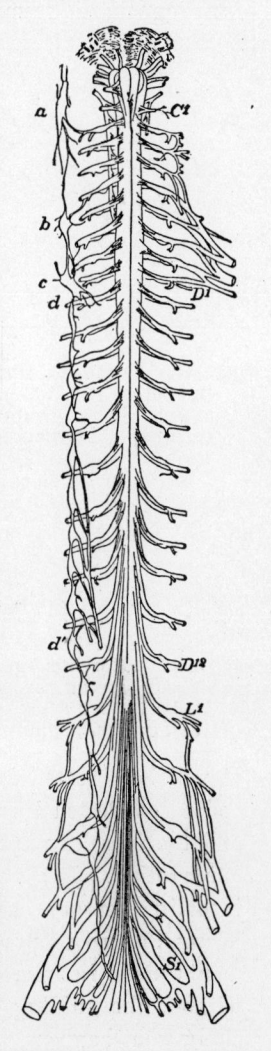

The arrangement of the elements in the spinal cord suggests at once two of its principal functions, and is so typical of the facts generally characterising nervous structure and function that it seems judicious to comment upon it briefly.

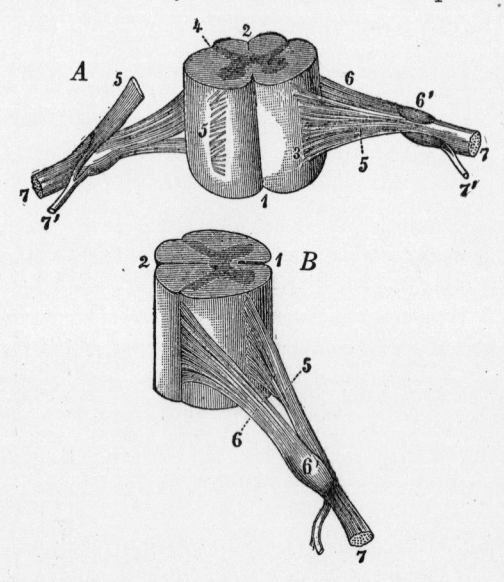

FIG. 14. Portion of cervical region of spinal cord. *A*, cord seen from anterior surface. *B*, cord seen from the lateral surface. *1*, ventral median fissure; *2*, dorsal fissure; *5*, ventral fibres leaving the cord; *6*, dorsal fibres entering the cord; *7*, spinal nerve after the union of the dorsal and ventral bundles of fibres; *7¹*, sympathetic fibres. (After Barker and Rauber.)

It will be observed in the first place, that in the cord cell-bodies, connected through their fibres with the sense organs and the muscles respectively, are in very close proximity to one another. It should be relatively easy, therefore, for an incoming sensory impulse to find its way out over motor nerves and so to produce reflex movements, that is, movements made in immediate response to sensory stimulations, without the guiding action of consciousness. This is precisely what happens, and it is as a reflex mechanism that the spinal cord exercises one of its important functions. As instances of such reflexes we may mention the jerking of the foot when the sole is tickled, and the knee-jerk exhibited when one leg is crossed over the other and the region just below the knee-cap is smartly struck. Furthermore, we should find upon examination that the white fibrous tracts along the external surfaces of the cord connect it with both the higher and the lower parts of the system. (Figures 16 and 17.) It should thus be easy for impulses to pass upward and downward, between the brain on the one hand and the sense organs and muscles on the other. Such ready transmission actually occurs, and it is in this fact that we find the second great function of this organ. The spinal cord is accordingly typical of the central structures in general, in that

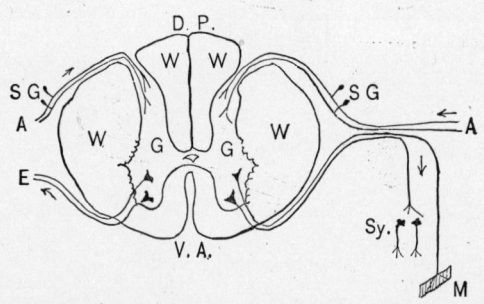

FIG. 15. Diagrammatic cross-section of the spinal cord. *W W*, white fibrous matter; *G G*, grey cellular matter; *A*, afferent sensory fibres passing through *SG*, the spinal ganglion into the posterior horn of the grey matter; *E*, efferent motor fibres, most of which lead to muscles like *M*, many of which connect with the sympathetic ganglia, like *Sy*. *D. P.*, dorsal or posterior, surface of the cord; *V. A.*, ventral, or anterior, surface.

it provides (1) means for the immediate connection of sense organs and muscles and (2) devices for connecting various parts of its own and other nervous structures with one another.

If we were to examine the other subcortical masses lying between the cerebrum and the spinal cord, we should find that, in general, they consist of aggregations of neurones much like those in the cord, but on the whole less simply and regularly disposed. Thus, the medulla, the corpora, and the thalami all display ganglion groups with sensory and motor

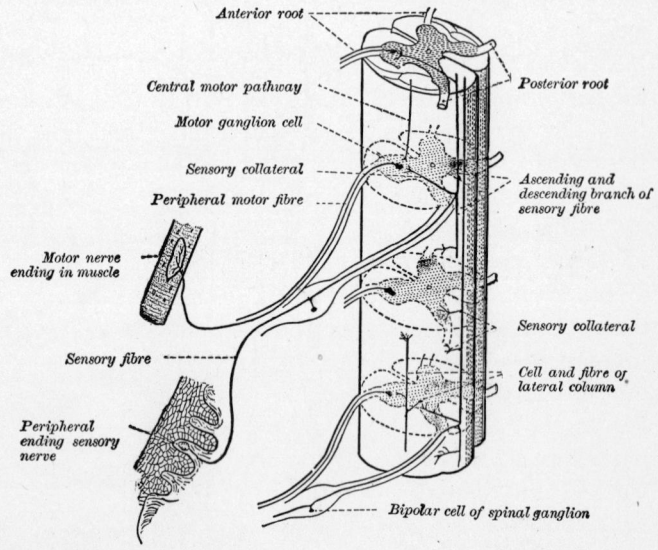

FIG. 16. Schematic representation of sensory and motor pathways in the cord. (After Toldt.)

connections. When we come to speak of their specific functions, we are obliged to indulge largely in speculation, because the facts are evidently extremely complex, and our knowledge of the details involved is notoriously incomplete. Moreover, the specialised functions which are sometimes attributed to them in the case of the lower animals are probably in the human being largely usurped by the cerebral cortex. In any event we must always remember that the nervous system is an organic unit, and no part of it ever acts wholly independently of the other parts, nor is any influence exercised upon one part entirely without significance for the other parts. Any mention of specific functions of different regions must always be made with this reservation in mind.

THE PSYCHOPHYSICAL ORGANISM

Thus, the spinal cord undoubtedly contains the neurones whose innervation is immediately responsible for movements of the hand. But this innervation itself may originate almost anywhere throughout the rest of the nervous system, so that any portion of this system may in a particular case contribute to the production of the special motor consequences. To say that a region of the nervous system presides over any special function is, therefore, simply to say that it is the portion most immediately and most invariably responsible for it.

FIG. 17. Longitudinal section of the cord to show the branching of incoming root fibres in dorsal columns. Above are three (R) root fibres, each of which forms two principal branches. These give off at right angles other branches, collaterals, CC, which terminate in brushes. Z, central cells, whose neurones give off similar collaterals. (Donaldson after Ramón y Cajal.)

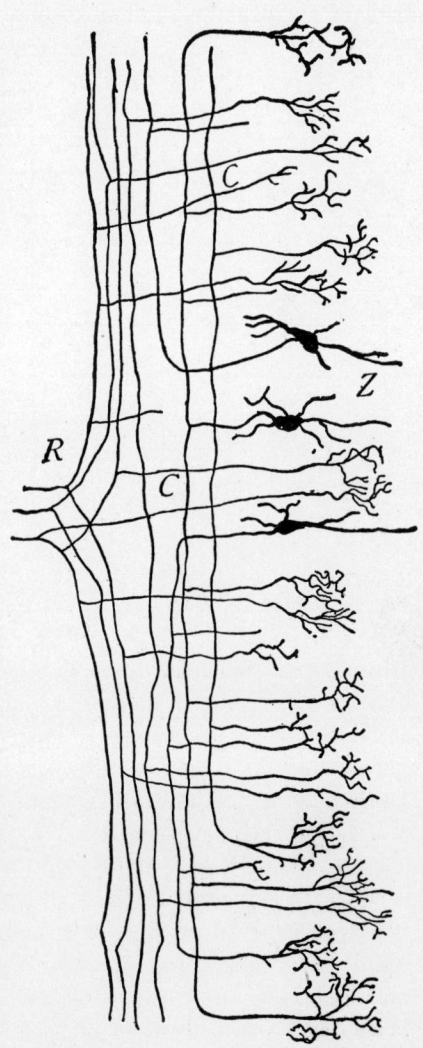

Speaking within such limitations, we may say that there

are two functions of centres lying in the medullic region, about which considerable unanimity of opinion exists. The control of the automatic respiratory movements, and the control of the vaso-motor nerves which govern the calibre of the

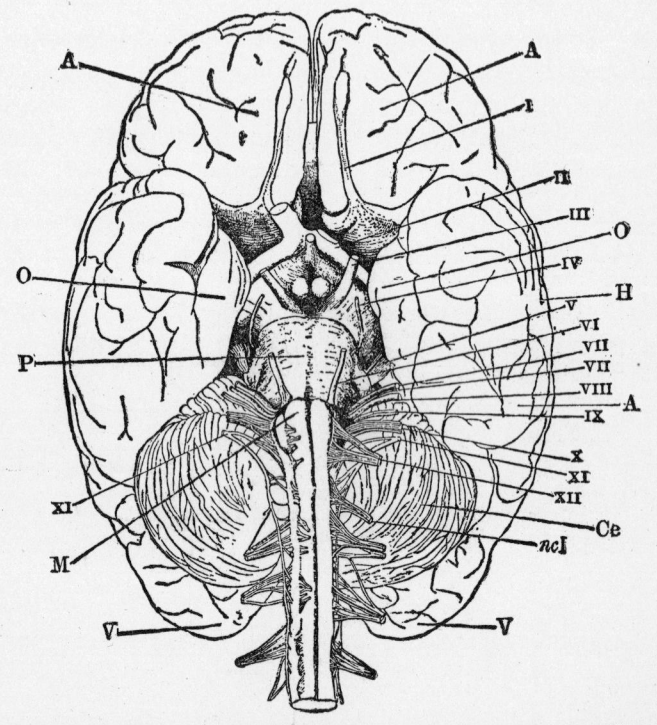

FIG. 18. The human brain from below, with its nerves numbered. (Modified from James after Henle.) *I*, olfactory; *II*, optic; *III*, oculomotorius; *IV*, trochlearis; *V*, trifacial; *VI*, abducens oculi; *VII*, facial; *VIII*, auditory; *IX*, glosso-pharyngeal; *X*, pneumogastric; *XI*, spinal accessory; *XII*, hypoglossal; *ncl*, first cervical, etc. *A*, association centres; *O*, olfactory centres; *V*, visual centres; *M*, medulla oblongata; *Ce*, cerebellum; *P*, pons Varolii.

arteries, are apparently the immediate possessions of neurones belonging in this neighbourhood. Needless to say, all these regions are like the spinal cord in containing pathways for

THE PSYCHOPHYSICAL ORGANISM 31

neural excitation to pass upward and downward, between the cerebrum on the one hand and the sense organs and muscles on the other.

It is in this region of the brain, too, that the cranial nerves are given off, *e. g.*, the nerves of special sense, like the olfactory, the auditory, the optic, the gustatory and trigeminus; such motor nerves as those controlling the eyes, the tongue, the lips, etc. (Figure 18.) It is commonly maintained that the phylogenetic pattern from which the human nervous system has been developed is of a segmental character, each

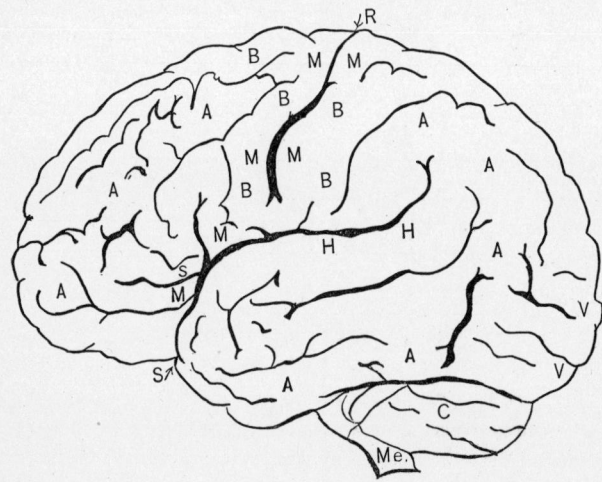

FIG. 19. The left side of the brain. *Me.*, the medulla oblongata cut off just above the point of junction with the spinal cord. *C*, the cerebellum. *R*, the fissure of Rolando. *S*, the fissure of Sylvius. *VV*, region of the occipital lobe where neurones from the optic tract terminate; *MM*, motor cellular centres; *SM*, motor centres controlling muscles used in speech; *HH*, centres where auditory neurones terminate; *BB*, region receiving neurones from the organs of bodily sensations, such as pressure, temperature, movement, etc.; *AA*, association centres.

part of it receiving sensory and motor nerves from relatively distinct regions, or segments, over which they exercise a definite and sometimes exclusive control. In the human being the motor nerves can, indeed, be classified in this segmental way in accordance with the special muscles which they innervate, *e. g.*, those of the head, the upper trunk, the lower trunk, etc. But the connections of the sensory neurones in man make any such segmental divisions of them very hazardous, so that the application of the segmental idea to the interpretation of our human nervous action is somewhat uncertain.

The Cortical Neurones.—The Cerebellum.—So little is known about the operations of the cortex of the cerebellum, that it will not be profitable to discuss it. Suffice it to say that the cerebellum has a very rich connection, by means of both sensory and motor neurones, with the cerebrum and the lower brain centres.

The Cerebrum.—For the psychologist the cerebral hemispheres are the most interesting and most important portions of the nervous system. From the various lines of evidence mentioned earlier in the chapter, we know that consciousness is connected with this part of the brain in an exceedingly intimate way, and we shall consequently devote some little space to its consideration.

The surface of the hemispheres, called the cortex, and shown in figures 19 to 22, is made up of layers of cell-bodies, with their delicate protoplasmic processes. The extraordinary richness of the dendritic development in the cortical neurones furnishes one of the most marked peculiarities of the human cerebrum, as contrasted with those of animals. This intricate dendritic structure apparently represents the bodily counterpart of those elaborate interrelations among ideational processes, which characterise in general the higher forms of intelligence.

Certain of the cortical areas are known to be in functional connection with sense organs from which they receive stimuli. Thus, the region marked H is in connection with the ear, and receives auditory impressions. (Compare figures 18 to 21.) The region marked V is similarly connected with the retina,

THE PSYCHOPHYSICAL ORGANISM

and receives visual impressions. It is reasonably certain that the areas marked *O* receive olfactory stimuli, while the region marked *B* is probably that immediately concerned with the reception of tactual and thermal stimuli. The centres for taste are not clearly made out. It seems probable, however, that they are in the neighbourhood of the olfactory terminals. There is reason to believe that ordinarily the peripheral sensory neurones are in connection with the side of the cortex opposite to that from which they originate. For example, the touch nerves of the left hand find their cortical terminations in the right side of the hemispheres. The optic nerve, however, affords a curious modification of this plan. The neurones from the right side of each retina are connected with the right side of the brain, those from the left side, with the left hemisphere. (See figure 23.) In this particular, as in some others, the optic tract is peculiar. The retina itself differs from all the other sense organs in being a part of the brain, which has in the course of development been dislocated from its original position.

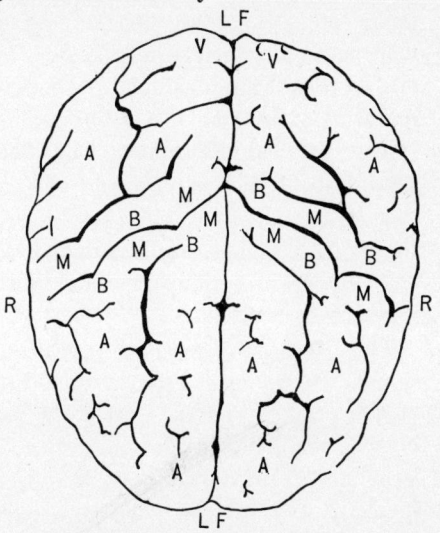

FIG. 20. Diagram showing cerebral hemispheres as seen from above. *LF*, longitudinal fissure separating the hemispheres; *RR*, fissure of Rolando. *VV*, visual regions of the occipital lobes; *AA*, association centres; *MM*, motor centres; *BB*, centres for bodily senses of touch, temperature, etc.

Another great group of these cortical cells in the region

marked *M*, generally known as the region of Rolando, from its proximity to the fissure of that name, is well recognised as being in connection with voluntary muscles, which are controlled from this centre. The voluntary muscles of each half of the body appear as a rule to be controlled by cells situated in the opposite side of the brain. (See figure 24.) In view of such facts as we have just been rehearsing, the cerebral cortex has been described as a projection system, representing every sensitive point and every voluntary muscle

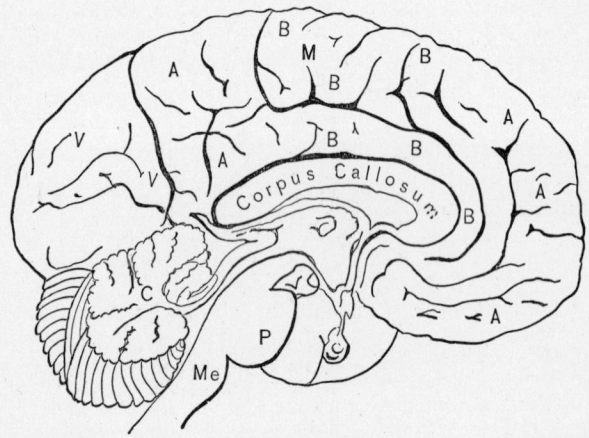

FIG. 21. Mesial surface of the left half of the brain severed along the great longitudinal fissure from the right half. *Me*, medulla oblongata; *P*, pons Varolii; *AA*, association centres; *M*, motor centres; *BB*, centres for bodily sensations, such as touch, temperature, etc.; *VV*, visual centres; *C*, cerebellum.

in the body. There are, however, other large areas in the cortex which are not in immediate control of muscles, nor do they represent the emergence point for neurones in connection with the sense organs.* These centres marked *A* are called by Flechsig, who has studied them most carefully, association centres. One of these centres, lying beneath the fissure of Sylvius, is not shown by our cuts. Their business seems to be that of uniting the several sensory regions, such as *H* and *V*, with one another and with the motor region.

* Certain authorities question this assertion, especially the latter portion of it.

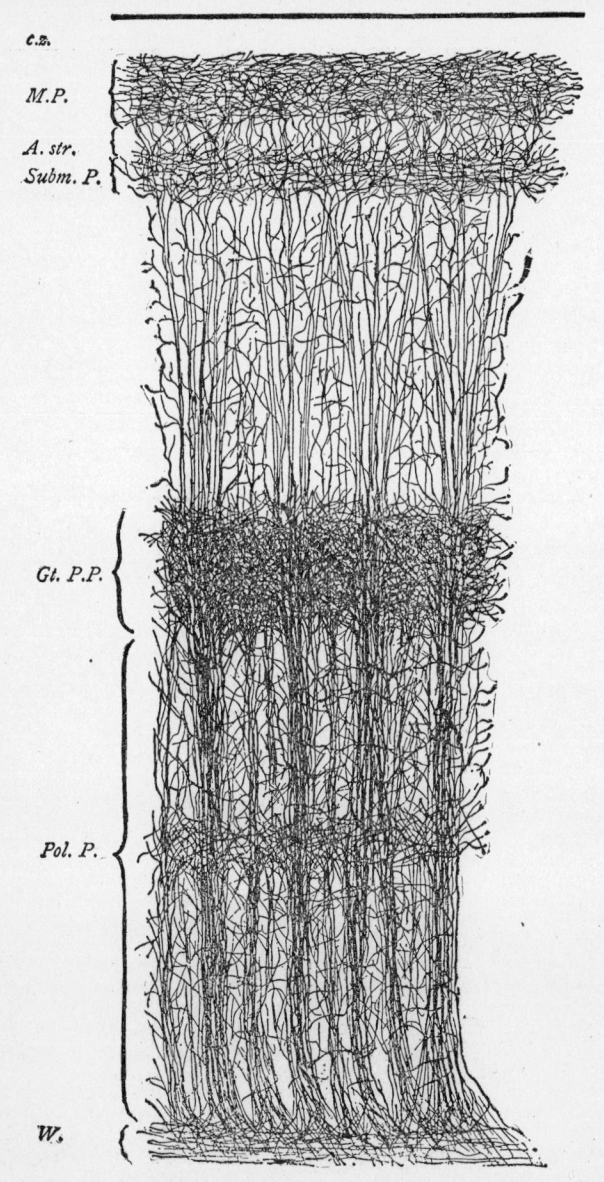

FIG. 22. Cortex of human cerebrum illustrating systems of fibres; *c.z.*, clear zone free from fibres; *M.P.*, plexus in the "molecular" layer; *Gt. P.P.*, great pyramidal plexus; *Pol. P.*, polymorphic plexus; *W.*, white matter. (Barker after Andriezen.)

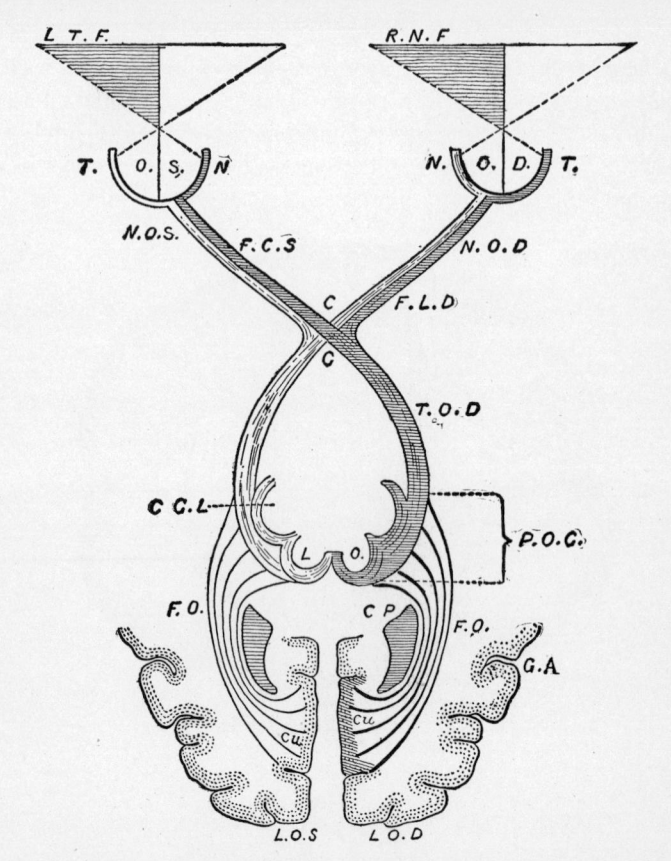

FIG. 23. Scheme of the mechanism of vision. (James after Seguin.) The cuneus convolution (*Cu*) of the right occipital lobe is supposed to be injured, and all the parts which lead to it are darkly shaded to show that they fail to exert their function. *F.O.* are the intra-hemispheric optical fibres. *P.O.C.* is the region of the lower optic centres (corpora geniculata and quadrigemina). *T.O.D.* is the right optic tract; *C*, the chiasma; *F.L.D.* are the fibres going to the lateral or temporal half *T* of the right retina, and *F.C.S.* are those going to the central or nasal half of the left retina. *O.D.* is the right, and *O.S.* the left, eyeball. The rightward half of each is therefore blind; in other words, the right nasal field, *R.N.F.*, and the left temporal field, *L.T.F.*, have become invisible to the subject with the lesion at *Cu*.

THE PSYCHOPHYSICAL ORGANISM

(Compare figure 25.) It appears to be true in a general way that these association centres are relatively larger and more highly developed in those animals possessing most intelligence. There is another extremely important connecting mechanism, made up, however, exclusively of fibres, and

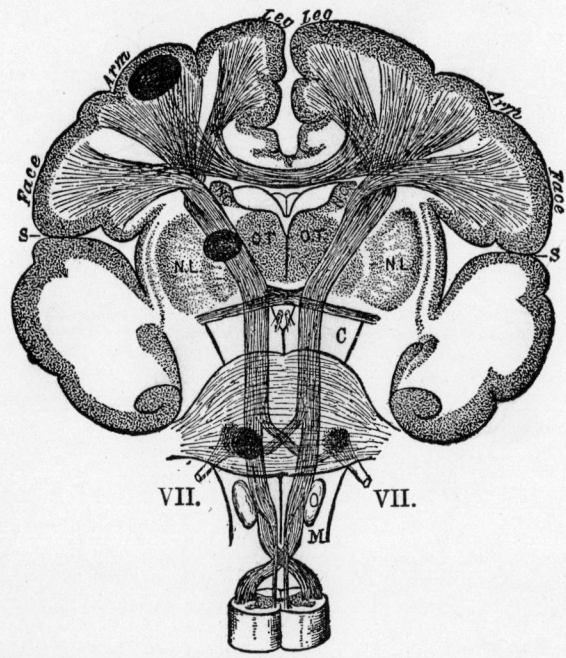

FIG. 24. Schematic transverse section of the human brain to show the crossing of motor fibres in the neighbourhood of the medulla, through the Rolandic region. *S*, fissure of Sylvius; *N. C.*, nucleus caudatus, and *N.L.*, nucleus lenticularis of the corpus striatum; *O.T.*, thalamus; *C*, crus; *M*, medulla oblongata; *VII.*, the facial nerves passing out from their nucleus in the region of the pons. The fibres passing between *O.T.* and *N.L.* constitute the so-called internal capsule.

known as the corpus callosum (figures 21, 25, and 26), by means of which the two sides of the hemispheres are brought into connection with one another. These various devices make it possible for cortical nervous impulses originating in

38 PSYCHOLOGY

the stimulation of some sense organ, like the ear, to pass into other cortical regions like that belonging to vision, and thence out through the Rolandic zone to some muscle, producing, perhaps, a voluntary movement. This is probably

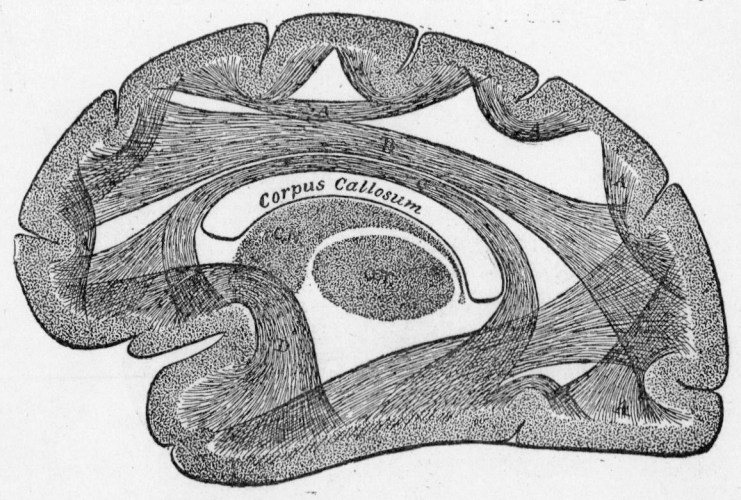

FIG. 25. Fibres associating the cortical centres with one another.
(Schematic, James after Starr.)

what would occur, for example, were we to hear the words "Draw a horse," then to think how a horse looks, and then finally to make the appropriate movements of our hands. This and similar relations are suggested by figure 27.

The Cerebral Cortex and Memory.—When we contrast the cerebral cortex with the other parts of the nervous system, with reference to its significance for consciousness, we find that it is in the memory processes that the most conspicuous differences first come to light. If one suffers the destruction of the retinæ by accident or disease, or if the pathways be interrupted anywhere between the retinæ and the cortex, one becomes blind, but that may be all. When, however, as occasionally happens, one loses the use of the occipital regions, one may not only become blind, but one's visual *memory* also is lost. It is not possible to remember how familiar objects look, and even if seen they may not be recognized. So-called word-blindness, or visual aphasia, is caused in this way, the patient being unable to recognise or understand written words. If the injury is confined to one side of the brain the common result is hemianopsia in more or less serious form, *i. e.*, blindness to one-half of the field of view, owing to the destruction of the cortical centres receiving the fibres from the lateral half of each retina. Similarly, when the auditory region is injured, one loses the memory of auditory experiences. If in this case, as frequently happens, the disorder be confined to one side of the brain, and this be the side most highly developed (the left side in right-handed people), one cannot understand what is heard. This disease is known as sensory, or auditory, aphasia. The patient is not deaf, for the less developed and uninjured half of the cortex may serve for the production of vague auditory consciousness, but the associations which words and familiar sounds ordinarily evoke are wholly gone, because these were possessions of the now diseased side. The mental condition is not unlike that of a person hearing an unknown foreign language. He is not deaf to the words, but they mean nothing to him, for they have no associations.

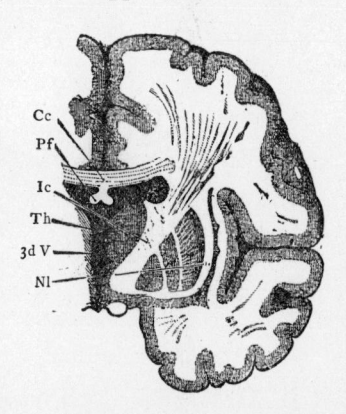

FIG. 26. Transverse section through right hemisphere. (James after Gegenbaur.) *Cc*, corpus callosum; *Pf*, pillars of fornix; *Ic*, internal capsule; *3d V*, third ventricle; *Nl*, nucleus lenticularis.

A closely comparable condition is that of motor aphasia, a disease in which one cannot articulate coherently. One is not necessarily dumb, and there may be no true paralysis of the articulatory muscles. But one simply cannot make the enunciatory movements in their correct order. This disorder is often found connected in right-handed persons with disease of the left side of the motor region of the cerebral cortex, which is in control of these muscles. (Compare figure 19.) But it may be brought about— and often is—as a secondary consequence of auditory or sensory aphasia. If, when we speak, we are in the habit of having in our minds just prior to enunciation the auditory image or thought of how the words are going to sound, any difficulty which prevents our securing these auditory images will effectually prevent our utterance. Now sensory aphasia involves precisely this difficulty in commanding auditory images. As most of us do actually employ auditory thoughts to innervate our speech muscles, for we learn to speak as children by imitating sounds, it is surely not unnatural that sensory aphasia should so often be accompanied by motor aphasia. Cases are on record of persons who employed visual instead of auditory imagery to innervate the speech muscles, and who, upon suffering from lesions in the visual regions of the brain, were seized with

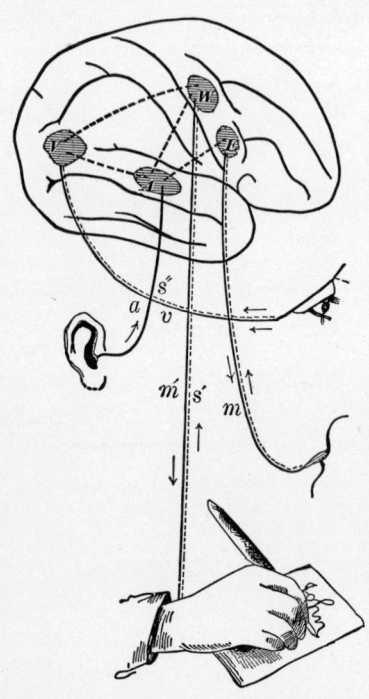

FIG. 27. *A* is the auditory centre, *V* the visual, *W* the writing, and *E* that for speech. (After James.)

THE PSYCHOPHYSICAL ORGANISM

motor aphasia. The sensory-motor arc, or circuit, as we have previously remarked, represents the unit of action, finding no exception in the activity of the complex cortical centres, and any stoppage of it in the sensory portion may be as fatal to its proper operation as a defect in the muscles themselves. This is brought out in the accompanying diagram, figure 28.

Such facts as these we have been describing show us that our memory is in a peculiar way dependent upon the integrity

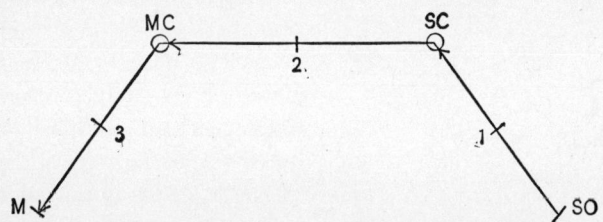

FIG. 28. *SO*, a sense organ; *SC*, a sensory cortical centre; *MC*, a cortical motor centre; *M*, a muscle. If *M* has become accustomed to contracting in response to a stimulus from *SO*, any interruption of the neural pathway joining the two, whether at *1*, or *2*, or *3*, may destroy the coördination and render *M* temporarily useless.

of the cortex. Visual ideas, tactual ideas, auditory ideas, and the like can apparently be recalled only when the several parts of the cortex with which these functions are connected are intact. In the first instance a visual consciousness involves not only a visual cortex, but also a retina, and more or less of the intermediate organs between the two. A similar thing is true of the relation of all the other sense organs to the various elementary forms of sensory experience, such as touch, sound, taste, etc. But once the sensory experience has occurred, the cortex instantly takes up the impress and memory becomes possible. Destroy any part of the nervous system save this, and conscious memory may escape destruction. Destroy any specific sensory region in this cerebral cortex, and the corresponding sensory memories are obliterated or seriously deranged. Destroy a region in the motor zone, and the voluntary control of some muscle, or group of muscles, is affected. Destroy or injure the association centres, and our intelligent conjoining of ideas, impressions, and movements is likely to be impaired. The gravity and permanency of these psychical disorders brought about in the way suggested, *i.e.*, by destruction of certain areas, varies very greatly under different conditions, so that the statements as made must be understood as attempting to convey only the broad general facts.

When one remembers that our most important and significant acts of will are based upon hopes and fears and beliefs which involve our calling upon the memory of our past experience, one begins to appreciate how immensely important for all our life history this memory function of the cortex must be. Thus we choose, for example, one course of action rather than another, because we remember that somebody will be benefited if we act in this way, or injured if we do not. Memory always operates whenever we deliberate, and anything which would deprive us of our memory would effectually destroy the will. The cortex of the cerebrum as the physiological substrate of our conscious memory is thus the unquestioned peer among the various gross structures in the nervous system.

In concluding this statement, two things should be emphasised. (1) The cortex is nowhere in direct connection with a sense organ, but receives all its sensory stimulations through the intermediation of the peripheral neurones and of some of the subcortical groups, like the medulla, and it is similarly in direct connection with no voluntary muscles, but communicates with them by means of the subcortical neurones. The shortest possible pathways which could, so far as is now known, be employed in the transmission of an auditory or visual stimulus to the cortex, and back from the cortex to voluntary muscles, is shown in figures 29 and 30. The anatomical arrangements peculiar to these illustrative cases may be regarded as typical for all sense organs and voluntary muscles, but undoubtedly the pathways generally traversed by nervous impulses are much more complicated and indirect.

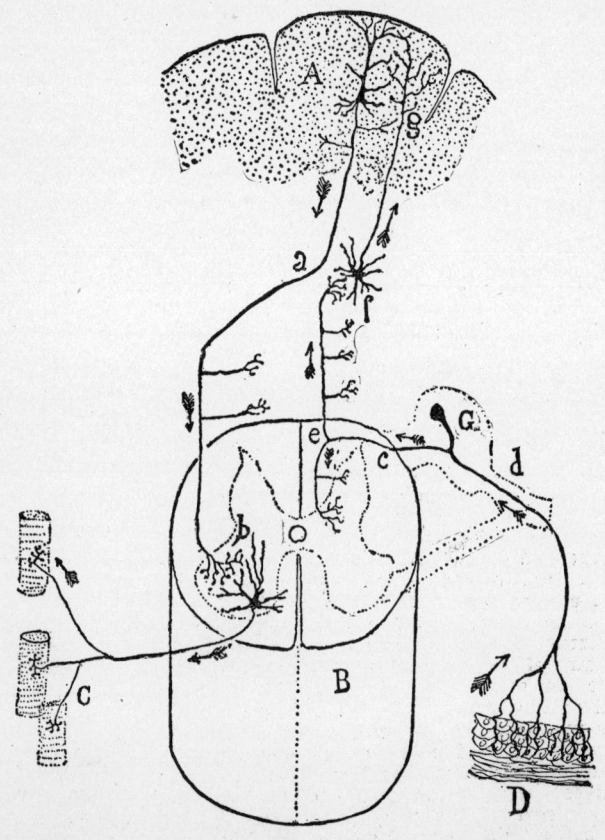

FIG. 29. *D*, periphery of the body; *G*, cell of the posterior sensory ganglion of the cord, sending its fibre *d* to the surface of the body; *c*, a central process of *G* coming into connection with *f*, a cell in the region of the medulla; *f* is shown terminating with branches in the cortex *g*. It is probable, however, that another cell in the medullic region is always employed in the transmission of sensory impulses from *D* to *g*. *A*, a cell of the motor cortex, sending a long process *a* down to the cell *b* in the ventral horn of the cord; *b* sends out a fibre to the muscle *C*.

(2) The cortex seems always to act in an essentially unitary way. Consciousness is, then, the counterpart of the total mass of shifting tensions going on all over the cortex at any given moment. When this tension is greatest in the occipital region, we are aware of visual qualities. When the temporal convolutions are under greatest strain, consciousness is auditory, etc. Moreover, in this picture of consciousness as the counterpart of a unified series of physiological tensions all over the cortex, we must not forget that the whole nervous system is in a measure involved. These tensions are of such a character as to require a constant escapement through the motor pathways, with a momentary establishment of equilibrium as a consequence of such escapement, and a fresh disturbance of equilibrium as a secondary consequence; this latter disturbance being brought about

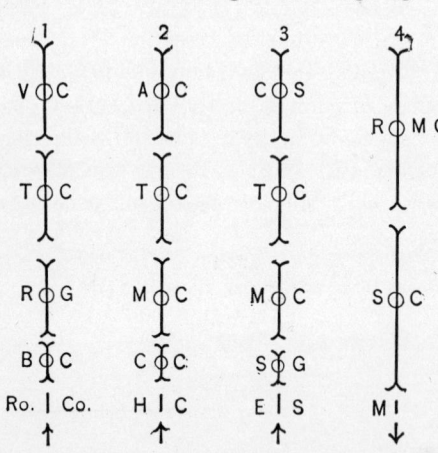

FIG. 30. Diagram to illustrate the shortest pathways from sense organs to cortex, and from cortex to muscles. *1*, the visual tract; *2*, the auditory tract; *3*, a cutaneous tract; *4*, a motor tract. *Ro.* and *Co.*, rods and cones; *BC*, bipolar retinal cell; *RG*, large retinal ganglion; *TC*, cell body in the thalamic region; *VC*, cell in the visual cortex of the occipital region. *HC*, hair cell of the cochlea; *CC*, ganglion cell of the cochlea; *MC* and *TC* as in the visual tract; *AC*, cell in the auditory cortex of the upper temporal region. *ES*, end-organ in the skin; *SG*, cell of the spinal ganglion on the posterior root of the cord; *MC* and *TC* as before; *CS*, sensory cell in the cortex of the Rolandic region. *RMC*, motor cell of the Rolandic region; *SC*, motor cell of the ventral horn of the cord, sending down a process to *M*, a muscle.

through movements actually executed. Such a recurrent series of movements and sensations, illustrated by the accompanying diagram, is involved in every coherent, consecutive occupation of which we are capable. (Figure 31.) Sleep affords practically the only instance of cessation from these coördinated series of stimulations and movements. Ideational processes are often, of course, interpolated between the sensation and the movement, as is suggested by the diagram.

The Autonomic System.—In addition to the central nervous system of which we have thus far spoken must be men-

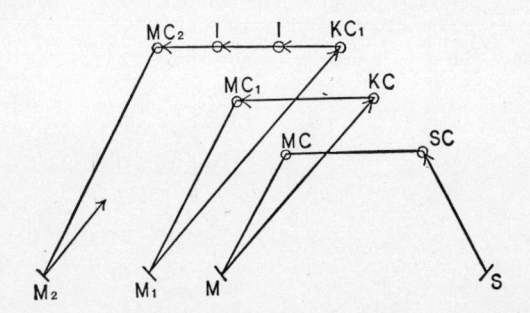

FIG. 31. Diagram to illustrate the progress of a series of coördinated movements. S, a sense organ being stimulated; SC, the cortical centre for this special sense; MC, a motor centre controlling the muscle, M; KC, a sensory centre for the kinæsthetic sensation produced by the contraction of M. MC_1, another motor centre innervating M_1, which in turn produces the kinæsthetic sensation reported at KC_1, etc.; II, ideas or images, whose brain processes may be interpolated anywhere throughout such a series, discharging into the motor centre MC_2, thus originating a fresh series of movements and kinæsthetic sensations.

tioned the autonomic system commonly known as the sympathetic system, and of which the true sympathetic is a highly important part. The autonomic system, about which our exact knowledge is lamentably defective, is apparently an outgrowth of the central system, and the two are intimately connected, both as regards their structure and their action. The striking peculiarity about the autonomic system is, as its name indicates, its relatively self-directing or automatic activity.

The autonomic system of neurones may be conveniently, though roughly, described as made up of three great groups. One of these groups consists of a series of ganglia gathered into two long strands extending up and down each side of the spinal cord. This contains the sympathetic system in the narrower and more precise sense of the term. The second group consists of the great plexuses of ganglia found respectively in the thoracic, abdominal, and pelvic cavities. The third group consists of isolated ganglia scattered miscellaneously through the body, *e. g.*, in the heart, in the walls of the arteries, in the eye cavity, etc. These neurone groups are made up of cell-bodies and fibres for the most part unmedullated. A portion of the impulses which affect their action apparently come from the central system. They certainly discharge impulses into the glands, the unstriped muscles, and, in the case of the heart, into striped muscle. Thus, for example, when an embarrassing announcement is made in our presence a sensory impulse passes over the auditory tract of the central system and thence, among other consequences, impulses are sent to the region in the medulla which controls the sympathetic ganglia connected with the muscular tissue of the blood-vessels, and straightway we find ourselves blushing. The sweat glands may also become active, causing us to perspire.

All the important vegetative and life sustaining processes, such as respiration, circulation, digestion, etc., are under the guidance, partial or entire, of the autonomic nerves. It is consequently to the activity of these parts that we owe our general sense of bodily well-being, as well as our feelings of distress and pain when any of these great life functions go astray. Our consciousness is undoubtedly toned, as it were, all the time, by the condition and activity of the autonomic system. This fact will become very evident when we come to study instinct and emotion. The entire nervous system, therefore, and not simply the central system, is concerned in the modifications of our consciousness.

CHAPTER III

A SKETCH OF THE GENERAL RELATIONS OF CONSCIOUSNESS TO NEURAL ACTION

It will greatly facilitate our subsequent understanding of the operations of consciousness if we pause to examine at this point some of the things which the nervous system is able to accomplish without the direct assistance of the mind, together with certain general relations of consciousness to neural action. Such an examination will bring us face to face with one or two of the fundamental principles, or laws, which control neural action.

A Matter of Terminology.—Let it be understood once and for all that wherever we speak, as occasionally we do, as though the mind might in a wholly unique manner step in and bring about changes in the action of the nervous system, we are employing a convenient abbreviation of expression which harmonises with the ordinary everyday methods of thinking and speaking about these relations. The real fact appears to be, as we observed in the previous chapter, that whenever we have mental activity, we have also neural activity in the cerebral cortex. The basal distinction in the two kinds of nervous action to which we are referring in this chapter is, therefore, not primarily between a form in which the mind suddenly produces changes in the nerves as against one in which it does not, but rather a distinction between certain kinds of neural activity involving consciousness, *e. g.*, cortical activity of the cerebrum, and certain other kinds not involving it, *e. g.*, spinal cord reflexes. To use on every occasion the long modifying phrases necessary to precise accuracy on this matter would evidently be unduly cumbrous, and so we shall employ the commoner modes of expression, but the fundamental facts which lie behind these convenient metaphors must not be forgotten.

Automatic and Reflex Acts.—If we take up the general character of neural action from the genetic point of view, we shall have our attention at once called to the fact that the new-born babe does not come into the world so completely helpless as is sometimes implied. There is a small group of acts which the little stranger is at once able to perform. Respiration, circulation, and digestion are three physiological functions which are carried on from the first. They all involve muscular movements, and constitute what are commonly known as automatic acts. The nervous stimulus for such activities is wholly, or in part, within the organism itself. Thus, the chemical condition of the blood may be responsible for changes in circulation and respiration, the presence of food in the stomach incites its digestive processes, etc. We are as a rule under normal conditions entirely unconscious of those automatic activities whose effects terminate inside the organism, although if anything goes wrong with them they ordinarily cause us pain and in this way we become cognisant of them.

Other motions can be excited by stimuli outside the organism. Thus the sucking movements necessary for the child to obtain its food are capable of being aroused by touching the lips. The fingers will clasp firmly any object put into them, an act said to be reminiscent of the days when our ancestors lived in trees, and the young had to cling to the branches. Acts of this kind are called reflex. A reflex act, as we remarked in the previous chapter, is definable as an act in which a movement is made in direct response to a stimulus outside the organism, without the interposition of consciousness. Of course consciousness sometimes takes cognisance of reflex acts, but it does not produce them. We may be conscious that we have winked, and still the closure of the eyelids be due to a reflex. We are very unlikely not to remark that we have sneezed. Oftentimes, however, reflex acts escape our notice altogether, just as the automatic acts do.

Now such acts as these, few in number and simple as they are, evidently furnish the child with a nucleus of coördinations by means of which to begin the conquering of his world. They are evidently hereditary and, as every normal child possesses them, we may regard them unhesitatingly as racial, or phylogenetic, in nature. The animals generally possess at birth a larger equipment of such inherited coördinations than does man, and certain ones we commonly call instincts. These instincts we shall have occasion to examine with greater detail at a later point in the book, so we may pass them by here with the single remark that they are, as regards their origin, undoubtedly akin to the reflexes and the automatic acts. They represent thus the outcropping of the universal racial characteristics in the individual.

Development of Reflexes.—Were we to observe closely the growth of any child, we should find that from time to time new reflexes were added to his original stock. Thus, winking and sneezing would after a time put in an appearance, and finally at about twelve or fourteen years of age the full store of these reflexes as displayed by the adult would be complete. This course of development undoubtedly runs parallel to the development of the several nerve centres and the intercommunicating pathways.

Continuous Nature of Organic Activity.—In the light of the foregoing statements it may, perhaps, arouse no special surprise, although it is certainly a striking thing, that from the moment of birth until death there is never complete quiet throughout the organism. Always do we find muscular movements, always something is being done, always activity of some kind is going forward. In sleep itself, which we commonly associate with complete repose, respiration and circulation are occurring, and although each specific muscular contraction is followed by a period of recuperation for that particular muscle, viewing the organism as a whole there is never entire quiet. When awake, these automatic activities are augmented in the new-born child by such reflexes as we have mentioned. The reflexes naturally occur but infrequently and as for consciousness, it appears during the first weeks of a child's life only for brief periods, most of the time being devoted to deep sleep. Nevertheless, the points at which it does appear are of fundamental importance for our correct apprehension of its function, and we must examine them with care.

The Appearance of Consciousness.—Evidently the equipment of coördinations with which we have found the new-born infant supplied cannot carry him very far in his adjustment to the complex surroundings amid which he finds himself placed. Why he should have been limited by nature to just the special group of inherited coördinations which we observe in him, is a question for the biologist to answer. We cannot at present go behind the facts. But it is clear at once, that in our list of muscular activities over which the babe has control, there is no mention of means for responding very effectively to auditory or visual stimuli, to mention no others. A closer inspection of the situation will suggest to us the generalisation, which is undoubtedly correct, that we shall find consciousness appearing at those points where there is incapacity on the part of the purely physiological mechanism to cope with the demands of the surroundings. If the reflexes and the automatic acts were wholly competent to steer the organism throughout its course, there is no reason to suppose consciousness would ever put in an appearance. Certainly we never find it intruding itself where these conditions are observed, except in pathological instances.

Let us examine as a typical case what happens when the consciousness of sound first occurs. We know that many children are unable to hear for several days after birth, partly because the middle-ear is filled with mucus. When the time comes, however, that the ear is able to receive the auditory stimulus, we have at once an excitation of the organism for which there is no definite preformed muscular response. Some children, to be sure, early display a tendency to move the head, as does an adult in localising a sound, and this may possibly be a partially hereditary propensity. But it is problematic whether this ever occurs immediately after birth, and certainly it is quite rare. The usual thing under such conditions is unquestionably the appearance of vague consciousness dominantly of the auditory kind; the stimulation having the tendency, if it be intense, to discharge itself according to the law of "diffusion" (of which more anon) throughout many motor channels, involving movements of the muscles in various parts of the body.

Now these movements require coördination. If they are ever to be turned to account they must be controlled and ordered. The new stimulus has broken rudely in upon the coördinated reflex and automatic activities already going on. It has probably affected the circulation and the respiration. If the child were feeding, it may have shocked him into cessation and, in place of the sucking, set up the unwelcome wailing. Such a case is typical of the occasions where consciousness comes to light. The organism has end-organs sensitive to sound stimulations, but no ready-made physiological arrangements for *responding* effectively to such stimuli. Consequently, when a stimulus of sound bursts in upon its activities, some of which, as we have seen, are always in progress, it finds itself helpless and unable to act in any save a random and disordered way. Straightway appears consciousness with its accompanying cortical activities, taking note of the nature of the stimulus and of the various kinds of muscular response which it called forth. From this point on, the development is steady and uninterrupted toward the attainment of those fixed and intelligent modes of reaction, which we call habits.

Were we to examine in the same way the appearance of visual consciousness, we should find a precisely similar state of things, save that in this case the fully developed process involves certain reflexes which are not perfectly matured at birth, like the accommodation of the lens of the eye. But the essential point is the same. Consciousness appears in response to the needs of an organism sensitive to certain kinds of physical stimuli, *i. e.*, in this case light. These stimuli breaking in upon the operations of the organism find it incompetent to cope with them immediately. It has the power of making movements in response, but none of those which are inborn meet the case, and among all the other potential ones there must be intelligent adaptive selection. This is the field of conscious action, and we should find, were we to take time for a thorough exploration of all the sensory forms of consciousness, *e. g.*, taste, smell, touch, etc., that they are all called forth, under the same conditions of inadequacy on the part of the purely hereditary physiological mechanisms of movement, to meet the demand of the physical and social environment.

It shall be our next business to trace in outline the process by which consciousness brings order out of this threatened chaos and leaves the organism a group of habits to which additions are continually made and by means of which the organism becomes increasingly master of the situation. This account will be only a sketch, however, for all the rest of our study will really be devoted to filling in the details. In the chapters upon volition we shall return specifically to these very points.

The Formation of Habits.—It will be remembered that in the previous chapter, when we were studying the nervous system, we observed that in its simplest forms the nervous organism appeared to be little more than a device to connect

CONSCIOUSNESS AND NEURAL ACTION 53

a sense organ with a muscle and so to enable the discharge of movements in response to stimulation. When we examined complex systems, like that of man, where memory processes are clearly in evidence, we noticed that this same principle was everywhere in evidence, although it gained its expression through the most elaborate arrangements in the nervous tissues. We remarked, also, that the normal fate of every incoming sensory stimulus was to find its way out again sooner or later in the form of muscular movements and glandular activities. This tendency is in no way modified by the complexity of the neural structure, except as regards the ease with which we detect such reappearance of the stimulus in the form of motion. If we bear these facts in mind, a considerable part of the mystery seemingly surrounding the processes we are now to investigate will fall away at the outset.

The Beginning of Motor Control.—Let us take as a typical instance of the development of motor control the series of events which occur when a baby first learns to connect a visual impression with a movement of his hand and arm. Suppose a bright, coloured ball is held before his eyes. This stimulus sends strong sensory currents over the optic tracts to the brain centres and somehow or other, as we have seen, these currents must get out again in the form of movements. But we have also seen that there are few or no preformed reflex pathways over which such neural excitement may be discharged. Consequently, instead of some single relatively simple movement like that of reaching, what we observe is precisely what the principle of "diffusion" postulates as normal, *i. e.*, a mass of aimless, uncoördinated movements in a large number of muscles. The face is wrinkled in a frown or a smile, as the case may be, the fingers open and shut, the arms jerk about, the body and legs move spasmodically and possibly the child cries out. This does not seem a very promising beginning for the development of intelligent control, and yet in point of fact it contains just the features most essential for progress. Speaking generally, we may say that such stimulations call out an *excess reaction,* a motor response in which are contained, almost without fail, the special small group of useful and important movements which subsequently become isolated from the general miscellaneous motor matrix in which they at first appear. The manner in which this result is attained we can detect by observing our illustrative baby still further in the light of our knowledge of how we, as adults, acquire new coördinations.

Presently, if the stimulus be made more exciting by moving it to and fro, some of these excess movements of the arms will result in the child's hand coming into contact with the ball. We have already noted the hereditary clasping reflex, and we shall not be surprised, then, to find that the tactual stimulus to the skin of the hand results in the closing of the fingers. Now undoubtedly this first successful grasping of the seen object may be wholly accidental, in the sense that it is wholly unforeseen by the child. He is much more surprised by the occurrence than any of his interested observers, who accredit him with a wealth of conscious purpose and intention of which he is completely innocent. But let us observe what fundamental consequences are bound up with this success.

In the first place, the mere shock of surprise and (generally) pleasure makes the connection of the tactual-motor sensations from his hand with the visual sensations from his eye extremely vivid. As he moves his hand, he finds his visual impressions change. When his hand comes to rest, his visual object also remains quiet. There is no reason to suppose that the child is in any definitely reflective way aware of these things. He does not say to himself: "When I see my hand move, I see the ball move; therefore, the two things are connected in some way." Indeed, it is probably impossible for us in adult life to portray accurately to ourselves the simple immediacy of such experiences as these in infant life. But the important point, after all, is this, that of all the sensations which his whole acquaintance with the ball has brought the child up to this point, the ones connected with his seeing it when he grasps it, and his seeing it change when his arm-and-hand-feeling changed, are the ones most intensely connected in his consciousness.

If we read backward into his mind, then, what we all know about our own adult experiences, we may be sure that the child's memory is extremely likely to retain the highly vivid connection of the visual sensations of the ball with these tactual-motor feelings which accompanied the successful grasping of it. Moreover, the genuineness of this connection is indicated by the evident tendency to make the successful kind of arm movement, rather than any of the dozens of other movements with which he started his response to the ball, provided we give him at once an opportunity to get again the same visual impression from which he set out. To be sure, many of the irrelevant movements persist for a time, but they rapidly become less frequent and finally disappear. The perfect result is of course rarely attained without many trials. In this way, however, the child speedily does for himself what nature did in the case of the reflexes, *i. e.*, gives himself a neural pathway through which sensory impulses may flow out over motor channels for the production of effective coördinated muscular movements. In this case we have observed the establishing of a control connection between eye and hand. The sight of the ball will henceforth tend to call out the appropriate reaching and grasping movement.

The more firmly this connection becomes established, and the more deeply the pathway is cut between the visual sensory centres and the hand-arm motor centres, the more do the irrelevant movements of face, legs, and body tend to drop away. They are inhibited, as we say. Probably this inhibition is in largest measure due to the fact that the newly formed channel is increasingly able to carry off all the neural excitation, and in consequence less remains to overflow into other channels. But the result is certainly beyond question, whatever the means by which it is attained. Moreover, just in proportion as any such coördination becomes perfect, consciousness tends to drop out of the supervision altogether, and to turn the process over to the purely physiological mechanisms of the organism. Figure 32 illustrates certain of the relations which have been described.

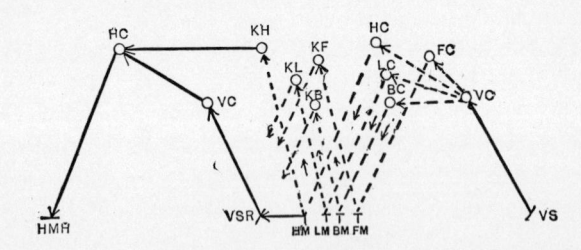

FIG. 32. Diagram to illustrate the establishment of motor control through the principle of "excess discharge." VS, visual stimulus setting up excitation in the retina, which transmits it to VC, visual centre in the occipital cortex. Thence the neural excitement overflows into FC, motor cells controlling muscles of the face, BC, motor cells controlling muscles of the body, LC, motor cells controlling the legs, and HC, motor cells governing the hand and arm. FC, BC, LC, and HC all discharge into their connected muscles, FM, BM, LM, and HM, and each muscular contraction sets up a kinæsthetic sensation, KF, KB, KL, and KH. Of all the movements made HM alone affects the stimulus VS. VSR represents the stimulus reinforced by being moved by the hand. This intensifying of the factors VC, HC, HM, and the connected factor KH, renders the pathway from VS through VC, HC, to HM more pervious than any of the other possible pathways. Consequently the tendency gets fixed for VS, or its connected cortical processes VC and KH, to discharge into the appropriate grasping movement, HMH.

Characteristics of Habit.—The nervous system is not only sensitive to the various forms of stimulation which we call light, sound, temperature, etc., it also manages in some way or other, as we have already observed, to store up the modifications which the stimulations produce in it. These modifications which are thus preserved manifest themselves in the disposition of nervous impulses to run in the same channel which predecessors have cut out. If the nervous system were an inanimate mass, we might liken that which occurs to the process by which a path is made across a meadow. The first wayfarer may have selected his special route for any cause whatsoever, and his course may have been devious, like those of the cows which are said to have laid out the streets of Boston. But he has left a mark in the downtrodden grass, which the next person to cross the field is likely to follow. Presently the grass is wholly worn away, and thereafter everyone follows the beaten path.

The action of nervous impulses is often spoken of as though this kind of thing were precisely what happened. But the moment we recall the fact that the nervous system is part of a living organism, in which processes of nutrition and repair are constantly going forward, and within which many intra-organic changes are producing from moment to moment relatively new conditions, we see that the metaphor of the pathway in the meadow must be abandoned in favour of some idea in which the vital processes of the organism are recognised and the living tissues treated as something other than so much static, plastic clay, which the accidents of the external world can mould to their own exclusive purposes. It is undoubtedly true that when avenues, or channels, of nervous activity become once established, they tend ever after to remain and be employed. But the point which we must emphasise is, that the organism itself largely decides which pathways shall in the first instance become thus established. When one recalls the large number of sense organs on the one hand, and the large number of muscles on the other, between which the central nervous system affords connections, it will at once be appreciated that, if the establishment of dominant connections in the new-born child were left to the accidents of the first external stimulations and to the vagaries of merely passive nervous centres, the chances would favour the acquirement of insane and harmful habits of reaction. Objects which burn would be just as likely to produce movements of grasping as movements of retreat.

We may summarise the general purport of habit as a fundamental principle of nervous action in two propositions. (1) Nervous currents tend to employ those pathways which have been previously employed. (2) The organism itself plays a governing part in determining what pathways shall become thus fixed.

Results of Habit.—The advantages which accrue from habit are almost self-evident. When we compare such habitual coördinations as are involved in writing the familiar English script with those employed in writing the German characters with which most of us are far less familiar, we note that the former letters are much more rapidly executed, that they are much more accurately made, and that they produce far less fatigue. It is evident, therefore, that habit is a most valuable contributor to efficiency in action. Any process which increases speed and accuracy, while at the same time it diminishes the fatigue of labour, is a possession to be cherished.

But more important, if possible, than any of these results is the fact that through the mediation of habits the physiological organism is enabled to cope almost unaided with situations which originally required the assistance of conscious processes, and consciousness is thus left free to go about further attainments, which will in their turn become habits and be handed over to certain of the relatively non-conscious processes of the nervous system. Consciousness is thus ever going on in advance and building up coördinations, which are necessary to the most effective reactions upon the environment. The whole course of mental development could truly enough be described as made up of this process of acquiring habits, which once imbedded in the tissues of the nervous system become the permanent possession of the individual, ready, when need arises, to step in and deal with the necessities of any particular situation.

Acquired and Hereditary Habits.—If we now look back over the ground covered in this chapter, we shall see that consciousness occupies a curious middle-ground between hereditary reflex and automatic activities upon the one hand and acquired habitual activities upon the other. The organism comes into the world with a small capital of these hereditary coördinations. These suffice to meet the most immediate and pressing needs in the conservation of life, but they are hopelessly defective for the attainment of anything beyond these immediate necessities. Now and again the world of light and sound and contact breaks in upon the coördinations which our hereditary neural mechanisms are executing, because the adaptive responses made by these mechanisms are inadequate to the organic necessities of the situation, and at such points we find consciousness appearing. Consciousness immediately enters upon its characteristic cycle. At first of course its activities are vague and crude. But presently it has selected from out the masses of motor responses created by the sensory stimulations to which the sense organs are sensitive, those particular ones which issue in effective muscular control over the environment, and straightway we are confronted with habits. As soon as these habits are firmly established, consciousness betakes itself elsewhere to points where habitual accommodatory movements are as yet wanting and needed.

Thus the progress of events is marked by the emergence of consciousness from a matrix of movements which are apparently unconscious and hereditary, and its disappearance again after a period of activity in the creation of the quasi-reflexes, which we call habits. It is an interesting fact incidental to this development, that when we attempt to inject consciousness into a process which is either reflex or habitual, we upset the accuracy of the coördination and mutilate its efficiency. Thus, to direct attention to the act of swallowing, which is a reflex, is to render it for many persons all but impossible of performance. Witness the common difficulty in taking pills. Similarly, to direct attention to one's mode of walking often results in producing a thoroughly artificial gait quite unlike one's normal manner. The early experiences of appearance before the public, as on the stage, also illustrate this point.

Habit and Will.—Although we do not commonly think of it in this way, a moment's reflection will show us that all expression of the will depends upon our ability to command habitual muscular coördinations. For example, I decide after careful consideration that duty bids me refuse a friend's request. Now note, that if I speak to my friend, I must fall back upon habits of articulation, which cost me much labour as a child to attain, but which now largely take care of themselves. If I decide to write my decision, again I must employ habitual activities, and I cannot by any device communicate intelligibly with my friend without employing these or other similar muscular movements which are essentially habits. Neural habit, therefore, is not only the great emancipator of consciousness from the necessities of endless control over the same trivial round of acts, it is the great tool by which that feature of consciousness which we call the will executes its behests and renders our mental decisions and choices effective in the world of action. Without habits, consciousness could never get beyond the borders of the inevitable daily routine. With habit, however, it is able to pass from victory to victory, leaving behind in captivity the special coördinations it needs.

Intellectual Habits.—We cannot linger to develop the matter, but it may be helpful simply to point out that the mastery of any subject matter, such as mathematics, for instance, involves a precisely similar establishment of habits, which, as the material is thoroughly mastered, are left behind for use when required. We do not ordinarily regard such attainments as concerned in any fundamental manner with muscular movements, although we all recognise readily enough that the sole manner of assuring ourselves a reliable command over a subject matter is to use it, to *do* something with it. We sometimes think of such *doing* as purely mental. In reality, however, movements are involved in all cases, and, even were this not true, the general principle of habit, so far as this stands for a law governing the transmission of nervous currents, would still be valid. The gain in rapidity, efficiency, and lessened fatigue would remain, not to mention the freeing of consciousness for further achievements.

Apart from such command over special departments of information, what are known as "habits of thought," which we are often vaguely told we ought to cultivate, are in reality largely habits of exercising our attention. We are assured, for instance, that the pursuit of certain studies is valuable because it will teach us desirable habits of thought. Now when this assurance means anything more than the expression of a pious hope, it refers either to the attainment of a familiarity bordering on habit, with a useful field of information, or to the securing of general modes of approaching a new subject matter; habits of alert attention, habits of logical division and persistent search for relations, etc. Whether any special studies are preëminently valuable in the production of this second class of results is a question which can be answered more judiciously, if at all, at the end of this book. Meantime, we shall not err seriously if we assert that a wholly fallacious value has often been placed upon so-called formal disciplines, which are supposed to teach us how to do things in general, without any special reference to accomplishing particular results.

Ethical Aspects of Habit.—The moment one gets clearly in mind the physiological nature of habit and its basis in the nervous tissues, its ominous significance for morality becomes evident. To break up a bad habit means not only to secure a penitent, reformatory attitude of mind,—this is often easy to achieve,—it means a complete change in certain parts of the nervous system, and this is frequently a thing of utmost difficulty of attainment. No amount of good resolution can possibly wipe out at once the influences of nervous habits of long standing, and if these habits are pernicious, the slavery of the victim is sure to be pitiable and likely to be permanent. On the other hand, the momentous significance for the individual and society of deeply imbedded habits of a moral kind cannot be overestimated. The existence of such habits means stability, reliability, and the promise of the utmost possible confidence. It is all but impossible for one to break over the moral habits of a lifetime. One may at times be mildly tempted by the possibilities such breaches hold out, but actual violation in overt action is essentially impossible. The man who has been vicious all his life is hardly free to become virtuous, and the virtuous man is in a kind of bondage to righteousness. What one of us could go out upon the street and murder the first person he met? Such action is literally impossible for us so long as we retain our sanity.

In view of these considerations, no one can over-estimate the ethical importance of habit. To make the body, in which our habits are conserved, one's friend and ally and not one's enemy is an ideal which should be strenuously and intelligently held out to every young person. One never can say at what precise moment it may become literally impossible to shake off a bad habit. But we know with perfect certainty that our nervous tissues are storing up every day the results of our actions, and the time is, therefore, sure to come when no amount of merely pious intention can redeem us from the penalty of our folly. Meantime, for one who has fallen under the sway of a habit he wishes to escape from, this general advice can be given: begin the new regime at once, do not wait for a convenient season. If the result is not likely to be physically disastrous, stop wholly, do not taper off. Give yourself surroundings which will offer the least possible temptation. Do not try merely to suppress the bad habit. If possible, put something else which is good in place of it. See to it that you are always occupied in some proper way until you feel sure that the grip of the bad habit is loosened.

On the other hand, it is to be frankly admitted that viewed in a broad way the benefits of habit have their limitation. If the world always did things just as they have been done in the past our civilisation would approach that of the Chinese. But the changes which by the consensus of intelligent persons are beneficial to mankind, the alterations of habit which are progressive, are rarely such as have to do with those purely personal forms of action whose perversion constitutes the most flagrant form of vice.

Moral progress always consists in a harmonised action of wider and wider interests, the securing of broader and truer visions of life. Such progress, while it may change old and accepted habits of life, does not for a moment involve any departure from those rules of personal honesty, sobriety, and chastity which the world's history has demonstrated again and again as the foundations of all sane, happy human life.

CHAPTER IV

ATTENTION, DISCRIMINATION, AND ASSOCIATION

Consciousness and Attention.—We announced our purpose at the outset to adopt a biological point of view in our psychological study, and to attempt at every step to see just how the mind aids in the adjustment of the psychophysical human organism to its environment. If we turn from the merely general statement that the fundamental function of consciousness is to better such adaptive activities, and observe any specific instances of the process of adaptation itself, we shall always find that the actual work of accommodation is going on at the point which we call the point of attention. Attention, we shall accordingly discover, represents the very heart of consciousness, its most important centre of vitality. It therefore deserves our careful notice.

In a vague fashion we all recognise this rudimentary significance of attention. Thus we speak of the awakening of the new-born infant's mind when we first see signs that the child is attending to something. Moreover, we roughly measure the growth of children in intellectual maturity and power by their increasing ability to give prolonged attention to definite trains of thought. Alienists and specialists in nervous disorders inform us that mental disease is commonly accompanied by disturbance in the power of attention. In some forms of neurasthenia the attention is extremely unstable and irritable, flitting from one subject to another with feverish haste. In mania there is often a similar, but much exaggerated, attention to the flow of disconnected ideas. In melancholia, on the other hand, as in the milder types of neurasthenic hypochondria, attention is morbidly fascinated by some single idea, or group of ideas, and cannot be long lured away to the normal business of life.

Definition of Attention.—When we attempt a definition of attention we experience the same sort of difficulty which we met in defining consciousness, and for a similar reason. So long as we are conscious at all, attention in some degree is present. We therefore find it difficult to define it without employing the thing itself in the definition. Because of this fact, attention has been commonly referred to as a "general, or universal, characteristic of consciousness." In default of a wholly satisfactory definition of attention, we may at least illustrate what we mean by the term. When we look at a printed page there is always some one portion of it, perhaps a word, which we see more clearly than we do the rest; and out beyond the margin of the page we are still conscious of objects which we see only in a very imperfect way. The field of consciousness is apparently like this visual field. There is always a central point of which we are momentarily more vividly conscious than of anything else. Fading gradually away from this point into vaguer and vaguer consciousness, is a margin of objects, or ideas, of which we are aware in a sort of mental indirect vision. This fact that consciousness always has a focal point, which reveals the momentary activity of the mind, is what is meant by the fact of attention, so far as it can be described in terms of the *content* of consciousness. Baldwin has suggested the accompanying diagrammatic presentation of the facts we are speaking of, in connection with certain others. (Figure 33.) The margin of mental processes, outside the focal point of attention, constitutes what James calls the "fringe of consciousness." Whether we are attending to objects in the world about us, or to ideas in our own minds, there is always such a fringe, partly made up of sensations, partly of ideas. No matter what we are especially attending to, we are never completely oblivious to all other sensory and ideational processes.

The direction of attention to any part of the field of consciousness is commonly accompanied by a certain increase in duration, together with a certain clarifying and intensifying of this part, as compared with the remainder of the field, which is thus inhibited from further entrance into the mental region. Thus, if we give our definite attention to a musical note we remark its exact quality much more perfectly than when we simply listen to it in a casual way. It is apt to seem more intense, and it certainly tends to linger longer in the mind. Statements of this kind bring out the fact that we use the term attention at times as virtually synonymous with mental activity. To turn the attention to an object is simply to direct one's mental activity toward it. Now, our mental activity, considered as directive, is commonly called conation, and we must accordingly conclude that attention is a rudimentary form of conation, or will. This is unquestionably true. We see, then, that attention is capable of being considered in two different ways. We may emphasise the mere fact of mental activity, illustrated by all attending; or we may dwell upon the *structure* of any moment of such attentive consciousness, and note the fact of its containing a focal point, with a fading margin. But our emphasis upon one or other of these phases of attention does not alter the fact that the mental process, which we describe in these two ways, is one and the same. In the remainder of the chapter we shall therefore make no attempt rigidly to dissever these aspects of every act of attention, although we shall be frankly most

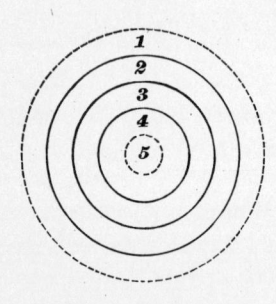

FIG. 33. Graphic representation of the field of consciousness. *1*, the unconscious (physiological); *2*, the subconscious; *3*, diffused, vague consciousness; *4*, active consciousness; *5*, the focal point of attention. (After Baldwin.)

interested in attention as an instance of mental activity. Meantime, the best practical definition of attention is afforded by such an analysis and description of it as is contained in the remainder of this chapter.

The Selective Character of Attention.—Probably the most striking characteristic of attention is its selective nature, and the significance of this function will grow more conspicuous as we examine the facts. We have seen that the nervous system is so constituted that by means of its sense organs it is capable of being affected by various forms of motion in the physical world, *e. g.*, light, heat, sound, etc. This fact has itself sometimes been regarded as a form of cosmic, or organic, selection. Thus, of all the rates of vibration in the physical world, the retina responds only to those between the limits of approximately 440 billions and 790 billions per second. In a similar way the ear selects a certain group of sound vibrations, and so on for the other senses. Undoubtedly there are many forms of vibrations in the physical world to which we are wholly insensitive, because we have no sense organs appropriately attuned to their special rates, and are thus incapable of receiving them.

However all this may be, it is easy to convince oneself that innumerable stimulations of the kind to which we *are* sensitive are always falling upon the sense organs; and were we conscious of all of them at once our minds would present a curious conglomerate. As a matter of fact, only a few of these stimuli ever succeed in producing simultaneously that form of cortical reaction which accompanies consciousness, and consequently we are never at any one moment aware of more than a small part of them. Apparently the psychophysical organism selects from the wide range of potential objects those special ones which shall receive attention and so come to consciousness. Thus, when reading an entertaining book we may become altogether oblivious to the rattling of carts in the street, to the odour of the smoking lamp, to the contact sensations from our clothing, etc. Similarly, when we are preoccupied with some train of thought our attention dwells upon this idea, and turns away from that, according as the one or the other appears to the mind to be relevant and useful for the business in hand. Indeed, were it not for the selective activity of attention exercised in the form of reasoning, it is clear that we could never make any consistent mental advance, but that we should always be at the mercy of our sporadic ideas. We can, perhaps, examine this selective function of attention to best advantage by analysing the principal forms in which attention is found to operate.

Forms of Attention.—Probably the most fundamental division of attentive processes, and certainly one of the oldest, is that into active and passive, or, as they are better termed, voluntary and involuntary attention. A more satisfactory division, which we shall adopt, adds one more class, and recognises (1) voluntary, (2) non-voluntary, or spontaneous, and (3) involuntary attention.

Voluntary Attention.—Active, or voluntary, attention is precisely what the name implies, attention as the result of definitely self-initiated activity. In its clearest and most unambiguous form it always involves mental strain and effort. Whenever we attend to anything because we explicitly will to, we are exercising active attention. It matters not what the object may be to which our minds are thus directed. It may be a sound or an odour, an object which we see, or an object which we touch; a thought in the mind itself, a memory, an emotion, or anything one pleases. So long as it is attended to, as the result of our definite purpose to give it attention, it must be regarded as involving a case of active attention.

That we are capable, within certain limits, of thus directing our mental activity wherever we will is one of the easiest of facts to verify introspectively. Probably the reader has found repeated occasion, before reaching the present point in this book, to make just such voluntary efforts of attention to prevent his mind from wandering off to more attractive by-paths. Obviously the selective nature of attention, upon which we have already insisted so strongly, is conspicuously in evidence in active attention. Moreover, it seems probable that this type of attention, involving, as it does, the purposeful direction of our thoughts, would in its fully developed form be a somewhat later achievement than the other forms, which require for their existence far less of experience. To *direct* one's thought involves the possession of purposes and plans, however rudimentary, and these are the outgrowth of experience and relative maturity. Young infants are hardly capable of voluntary attention in any proper sense, although they may achieve both non-voluntary and involuntary attention from the beginning.

Non-Voluntary Attention.—It requires no extended reflection upon our everyday experience to reveal to us the fact that in the course of every twenty-four hours we attend in an effortless way to a great many things to which we have no explicit purpose to direct our thought, to which we cannot, therefore, be said to attend voluntarily in the full sense of the word; but to which we certainly are not attending *against* our will and in *spite* of ourselves. Such cases constitute what is meant by non-voluntary, or spontaneous, attention. A few illustrations may make the distinction clearer.

It happens not infrequently, for example, that we suddenly arouse to consciousness of the fact that for several minutes our minds have been running off on subjects quite disconnected from the special occupation with which we may at the moment be engaged. We have "lost ourselves," as we say, in some day dream, perhaps. Our prolonged attention to a subject which sincerely interests us is often of this same character. Our attention is not given as the result of any effort on our part. Rather should we find that it required effort to direct our attention elsewhere. It necessitates no strenuous act of will for the boy interested in athletics to give his attention to a newspaper account of a football game. On the contrary, his attention can only be obtained for less exciting themes by some artifice on your part, or by a self-sacrificing effort of volition upon his.

So far as these cases of non-voluntary attention reflect the actual nature of our interests, they must be regarded as affording peculiarly intimate information of the real character of our minds, and so of our wills. They are thus, in this particular, closely related to voluntary attention. After all, what I am interested in, is a very close synonym for what mentally and morally I am. Moreover, it is frequently, and probably with right, maintained that this non-voluntary, or spontaneous, form of attention is the primitive germ, out of which voluntary attention in the full meaning of the term has developed. Certainly something like this, combined at times with involuntary attention, appears to form the beginnings of infant attention. In any event it is clear that however sharply we may be able to mark off at times those instances in which we attend as the result of a definite purpose so to do from those instances in which we find the allurements of an interesting subject have drawn off our attention almost unnoticed, both cases reflect very accurately the texture and character of our minds. To the relationship of these two forms of attentive activity we shall return in a moment with greater fulness.

Involuntary Attention.—However genuinely voluntary and non-voluntary attention may differ from one another, they neither of them involve attention given *against* the will. But there are numerous cases in which, at first sight, anyhow, this form of attention apparently occurs; and it is to this that the name "involuntary attention" has been given. Thus, for example, if the door slams while I am writing this sentence I am seemingly obliged to hear the sound, however much I might prefer not to do so. To be sure, if I am sufficiently preoccupied a very loud noise may in this way escape my notice; and the obliviousness to ordinary sounds, such as the ringing of the dinner-bell, the striking of the clock, etc., of persons thus engrossed in some interesting occupation is too familiar to require comment. Archimedes, absorbed in his studies and unconscious of the sacking of Syracuse, is the classical illustration of this kind of thing.

But despite the fact that when one is thoroughly immersed in some congenial undertaking one becomes relatively insensitive to sensory stimuli, which otherwise would be noticed, the further fact obstinately remains that even under such conditions stimuli of sufficient intensity *will* force themselves into consciousness. Certainly we should all agree that in this way bright flashes of light, loud sounds, unpleasant odours, etc., repeatedly intrude themselves upon our attention distinctly against our wills. Moreover, there are experiences in which ideas, instead of sense impressions, thus force themselves in upon our attention against our wills. What are known as insistent ideas are of this character. The hypochondriac, for instance, is unable long to keep his attention away from his own bodily ailments, real or fancied. He may make a sincere effort to divert his mind, but in spite of himself the unwelcome idea presently shows its face at the door and claims his recognition.

Less definitely morbid than such cases, and still illustrative of the imperious command exercised at times over our attention by certain ideas, are the intense experiences of the emotional kind. Great joy, great grief, great anxiety, brook no prolonged opposition. We may attempt to force our attention on to the lines of the day's work and for a moment succeed, only to find ourselves in the next moment once more mastered by the idea we had attempted to put behind us. Certain psychologists would prefer not to give the name involuntary attention to these cases of attention against the will to ideas. But they are clearly more closely related to this form of attention, as illustrated by our forced attention to intense sensory excitation, than they are to the other classes we have distinguished; and we shall accordingly designate them as cases of involuntary attention.

Interrelations of the Forms of Attention.—We have already intimated that involuntary and non-voluntary, or spontaneous, attention are genetically prior to voluntary attention. Undoubtedly the earliest experiences of a baby involve in largest measure spontaneous attention to sensory stimuli. The rude power with which some of these stimulations force themselves on the child's notice might give ground for the postulation of involuntary attention also. But if we confine the term "involuntary attention" strictly to such cases as those in which we attend against our wills, it is doubtful whether we ought often to apply the designation to a young child's attention; for we can hardly speak with confidence of the newborn child's possessing any resolution *not* to attend to a given stimulus. Spontaneous attention, then, working in the main upon the sensory material supplied by the physical surroundings, constitutes probably the earliest and most fundamental type of attention process.

Voluntary attention is apparently a derivative form of spontaneous attention, which may arise as soon as, and whenever, there is a tendency to the splitting of attention, a felt tendency to opposition against the direction our attentive energies are taking. Evidently this can only occur when we have developed intellectually to a sufficient degree to set over against some momentary disposition, or action, a more or less definitely formed plan involving interests and purposes opposed to the present activities. When we say that in voluntary attention we force ourselves to attend to some particular object or idea, what we evidently mean is, that the mind in its entirety is brought to bear in suppressing certain disturbing objects or ideas, and in bringing to the front the chosen ones. The act of voluntary attention is, in short, an expression of

ATTENTION

the sovereignty of the whole mind over its lesser parts, *i. e.*, over the disturbing or alluring ideas and sensations.

Now, spontaneous, or non-voluntary, attention is likewise in reality just such an expression of our total mental organisation at the moment. Those things to which we spontaneously attend are the things to which our minds, by virtue of their temporary condition, inevitably go out. And if we took into account the entirety of these spontaneous acts of our attention for any considerable period of time, we should undoubtedly secure an extremely accurate portrait of the real constitution of our minds. In the sense, therefore, upon which we commented briefly in an earlier paragraph of the chapter, non-voluntary attention is itself an expression of the individuality of the mind, and thus an expression of the true source of our volitional acts. It is a sort of voluntary attention, in which there is no internal, mental opposition to be overcome, and from which we are consequently apt to feel one characteristic fact of complete volition has been subtracted. But this does not detract from the fact that such spontaneous attention is in reality an expression of the mental organisation, quite as truly, if not so completely, as voluntary attention. It appears, then, that the distinction between voluntary and non-voluntary attention is not absolute, in the sense that we can always determine without question to which class a specific case of attention belongs. Quite the contrary. It appears that there is a gradual transition from one class to the other, through cases which partake of the characteristics of both forms.

Thus, for example, we should have to admit the existence of many cases in which it would be all but impossible to say whether we were attending to certain subjects as the result of a definite purpose and an explicit effort to attend, or as the result of more or less unconscious mental drifting. What shall one say, for instance, of the attention which is given to the routine duties of daily life? Some of them undoubtedly require definite, purposeful attention. Others enlist our spontaneous interest, require no effort and reveal little or no antecedent purpose to attend. Many others are surely on the border line, where it is not easy to say whether our attention is altogether due to spontaneous interest or to preconceived purpose. Meantime, we must admit that it is in voluntary attention that consciousness raises the human being into the greatest freedom from mere routine, with the greatest independence from mere temporary surroundings.

The Psychophysical Organism and the Forms of Attention. —The true relation of involuntary attention to voluntary and non-voluntary attention can hardly be understood without reference to the psychophysical organism as a whole. But fortunately we have all along taken this into account, and our present mention of it will mark no change in our point of view.

So far as concerns such instances as those in which we are forced against our will, or at all events without our mental consent, to notice intense sensations, it would seem that involuntary attention must be fundamentally opposed to voluntary attention at least, whatever might prove to be the case as regards non-voluntary attention. The one form of attention expresses the will, the other either defies, or disregards, the will. Such differences certainly appear to be fundamental; but we shall see reason to modify this view, when we consider that both forms of attention are vital functions which are brought out and developed in the general adaptive reaction of the organism to its social and physical surroundings. If we remember that those objects which are harmful to us commonly stimulate the nerves very violently, we shall begin to see how in the general economy of the organism it may be useful to have our senses so constructed that they shall call our attention to such possible sources of danger as are represented by these intense stimuli, even when we do not consciously desire to have our quiet thus invaded. We shall

ATTENTION

begin to see that in the interests of the continuation of life and health it may be desirable that loud sounds and extreme temperatures, intense lights and violent odours, should have the power to elicit the attentive reaction from us. In a sense, therefore, such reactions are instances of a kind of *organic* selection from among various movements of just those which shall result in our making momentary accommodation to the invading stimulus. If it prove really menacing, we may then take to flight, or adopt such other precautionary measures as the situation demands. If it be, in point of fact, innocuous or insignificant, our minds are left free to revert to the interrupted occupation. Involuntary attention of this kind represents, accordingly, the protest of the primarily physiological portion of the organism against a too complete subserviency to merely intellectual conscious processes.

Involuntary attention is only involuntary when the mind is viewed in isolation from the body. It is a kind of spontaneous bodily attention, and it is undoubtedly selective in a true enough sense. Moreover, even when viewed from the mental side alone, such attention could only properly be called involuntary, never passive. The term passive is quite misleading. Involuntary attention, once it is aroused, is just as genuinely a form of mental activity as is voluntary attention. Its antecedents, both mental and physical, are in part different and often its consequences are different too. But both operations are mental acts, and neither of them can properly be designated in terms of pure passivity.

In all forms of attention, then, we find selective activity going on. Selection always implies a purposive, forward-looking type of action, and this is precisely what attention is in all its forms. It stands for the fact that the organism is teleological in its very constitution. That is to say, the organism contains within itself certain *ends* to be attained in course of development by adjustive activities. In part these ends exist imbedded in the physiological mechanisms, where they come to light as reflex, automatic, and instinctive acts, sometimes accompanied by consciousness; and in part they exist as conscious purposes, in which case they appear as recognised intentions.

In spontaneous attention the selection seems to be psychically originated and directed, but it occurs without effort, even though the end to be achieved is clearly recognised and elaborately planned for. Voluntary attention also appears to involve a distinctly *mental origin* for selection, and we have no new factors here, save the presence of psychical conflict and the feeling of effort. We have seen that in voluntary attention this effort is always *internal* and *mental*—an effort to conquer our own impulses, or thoughts, in the interests of the end to which we are attempting to attend. It is thus sharply distinguishable from the effort to overcome merely external obstacles—a type of effort that often characterises spontaneous attention. Finally, in involuntary attention the selective activity is still clearly present, but its locus appears now to have been transferred from the distinctly mental to the more definitely physiological side of the organism. Of course, in our speaking of voluntary and non-voluntary attention as being primarily psychical in their nature, it must not be understood that we mean to deny the presence of *neural* processes accompanying these activities. All we mean is, that the selective action shows itself to us in these instances *primarily* as a mental event. In involuntary attention it appears primarily as a physiological event. Both groups of attentive activity, however, have the double psychophysical characteristic.

Duration of Attention.—It is extremely difficult to secure reliable information as to the length of time we can and do attend to objects in non-voluntary and involuntary attention; for the conditions in these forms of attention are necessarily very unfavourable to accurate introspection. But having discovered that the differences among the several forms of atten-

ATTENTION

tion are relative and not absolute, we may, perhaps, safely assume that the facts which we find in voluntary attention are fairly representative of the other forms, and these facts are fortunately rather easy to make out. All voluntary attention displays a more or less rhythmic pulse, the duration of which varies considerably under different conditions. If we attempt to attend to a letter on this page, we shall find that we can only do this for a moment or two, unless we constantly observe something new about it. Otherwise we invariably find, either that the eye has moved away to something else, or that the mind has wandered off on to an entirely different subject. However constant the physical object may remain, to which we thus attend, we can only continue our attention to it provided we continually see it in some fresh fashion; provided, that is to say, that the *mental object* keeps changing. This seems to be a fundamental law of our mental life, and did space permit we might profitably enlarge at some length upon its implication. A few consequences we may properly pause to mention.

Consequences of Shifting Attention.—Evidently change is the primal law of mental life, as well as of bodily life. Thought processes which cease to move, cease to exist. They simply go out. To keep a thought alive we must keep turning it over, keep *doing* something with it. Mental paralysis is mental death. It is a familiar experience with all of us, especially with students, that occasionally when a question is asked us our minds either become perfectly blank, or remain for a moment stupidly confronting the mere sound of the words addressed to us. In such a case the only salvation lies in *doing* something, doing almost *anything* is better than such quiescence. Often to begin speaking is sufficient to break the spell, however pointless our remarks may be. The act of speech starts up the cerebral machinery and presently, if we keep our composure, we get our thought once more in movement. Similarly, the boy told to *think* about what he is studying finds himself, in the effort to execute the injunction laid upon him, simply surveying the page before him with an apathetic gaze. He is merely exposing himself innocuously to the light waves proceeding from the page. Mentally he is either in a condition of partial asphyxiation, or his mind is off engaged upon something really of interest to him. He is not in any proper sense *attending* to the subject matter of his work at all. For such a youth the sole possibility of progress consists in taking the topic and forcing his attention to turn it over, ask questions of it, examine it from new sides. Presently, even though such questions and inspections be very foolishly conceived, the subject will start into life, will begin to connect itself with things he already knows, will take its place in the general furniture of his mind; and, if he takes the next and all but indispensable step, and actually puts his rudimentary information to some use, applies it to some practical problem, incorporates it, perhaps, in an essay, or even talks about it with others, he will find he has acquired a real mental tool which he can use, and not simply a dead load which must be carried on his already aching back. What we call *attending* to a *topic* for a considerable period of time will, therefore, always be found to consist in attending to *changing phases* of the subject. Thus, to fix one's mind upon history for an hour or two will involve attending to hundreds of thoughts about the special historical subject, or problem, with which we are concerned. Accordingly, these instances of the practical continuation of attention to a single subject strongly confirm our position, instead of contradicting it, as might seem at first sight to be the case.

Why Attention Shifts.—It has been suggested that the rapid changes of attention are due primarily to fatigue in the delicate cortical cells which are connected with conscious processes. Whether this statement be accepted or not, we gain a very significant suggestion in explanation of these changes, when we remember what the essential function of attention appears to be. We remarked at the outset that attention is simply a name for the operation of the central, and most active, portion of the field of consciousness. We have all along maintained that consciousness is an organic function whose intrinsic occupation consists in furthering the adaptive responses of the organism to its life conditions. We have also pointed out that, if this conception be true at all, it is at the point of attention that we shall find the most obvious and important part of the adjusting activity in progress. Now, in the nature of the case, each particular act of adjustment must be of relatively brief duration. In the case of common objects in the world of sensations it consists as a rule merely in the recognition of the stimulus (*e. g.*, as a colour, as a sound, as a book, or a word, etc.), with a motor response, which consists, perhaps, in some movement of the eyes or head, calculated either to bring to notice some new and useful phase of the stimulus, or to divert further attention altogether away from it. Thus we look, for instance, at a book, recognise it as the one for which we are searching, pick it up and proceed to examine it; in this way continuing the activity of attending to the book, but, as a matter of fact, continuing it in the form of attention to ever new features. The same sort of thing is true when our attention is occupied with ideas, instead of with sensations. In short, so far as attention is really an activity of the relating, adjusting kind, its work is done when the relation between the mind and the thing attended to is once established. This *is* the *mental*, as distinct from the physiological, part of the adjustment; and attention must go elsewhere, because it is intrinsically the adjusting act itself, and other things are demanding of the organism the same energies of adjustment. To retain our attention for any considerable period an object must, therefore, by changing its aspect, present itself as a new object, to which fresh responses can be made.

Range, or Scope, of Attention.—The question is often

asked: How many things can we attend to at once? Various answers have been given, some authorities maintaining that we can attend only to one object at a time, others insisting that we may attend to an indefinite number. We must sharply distinguish between the question in the form in which we have given it, and the question often, but erroneously, treated as synonymous with it, *i. e.*, How many things can we *do* at one time? We have seen in the preceding chapter that there is literally no limit to the number of things we can learn to do at once. It is, in this latter case, simply a question of how elaborate we can make our habitual motor activities. A skilled pianist, or a trained acrobat, may do dozens of things simultaneously. But the question of how many things we can attend to is much more puzzling.

The differences of opinion upon the matter are, however, apparently due in the main to a failure to define with precision the underlying mental conditions. It is the view here adopted, that we never have more than one *mental object* before the mind at any one moment. This object may be complex, or simple, but if it is really present in its entirety to consciousness, it is cognised mentally as a single thing. To illustrate, we may take the case of perceiving a table. If we examine introspectively the manner in which we are conscious of such an object, when we allow the eyes to rest momentarily upon it, we find that we perceive it as a complex *single* object; not as four legs, plus a top, plus a colour, plus a particular shape, etc. Now, these characteristics of a table which we have mentioned all correspond to distinguishable parts of it, and we might speak in a certain sense of having attended to all these circumstances at once. But this would be an injudicious mode of expression, tending to confuse our ability to analyse the physical object, or our own consciousness of the object, with the fact of the manner in which we *actually perceived* it *in* our momentary glance. However many things, therefore, may be present to us at one moment, it seems probable that our consciousness is of all of them as a single mental object, which we may, nevertheless, immediately recognise as being complex in its constitution, meaning, and references. Indeed, we may go further, and say that in order to perceive an object as one, there *must* be some complexity in it, which we thus synthesise into a unit. A pure, undifferentiated conscious quality never does, and apparently never can, constitute the object of a cognising consciousness. Plurality is, in short, just as necessary for an object of attention as unity; but our mental activity always gives the stamp of unification to these plural particulars. How many such particulars can be brought together in any one act of consciousness is a practical problem for experimental psychology.

The various interesting experiments which have been performed to test the so-called *scope* of momentary consciousness must all be interpreted in the light of the foregoing considerations. Thus, we find that with momentary exposure we can cognise four or five letters, under proper conditions. When the letters make words the number which we can cognise in this instantaneous fashion quickly rises. To these facts we shall revert in another chapter.

Some sensations, which have become thoroughly dissociated from one another, seemingly refuse to come together at all into simultaneous objects. Thus, it seems altogether problematic whether we can attend to a sound and a colour simultaneously. We hear the sound and then the attention oscillates to the colour, or vice versa. The same thing is true of sensations of contact, when conjoined with either sound or colour. On the other hand, fusions of two kinds of sensations, like those of taste and smell, are of course always attended to as simultaneous. They are not sensed as two.

Inattention and Scattered, or Dispersed, Attention.—Inattention is often spoken of as though it were a positive mental condition, just like attention. As a matter of fact inattention to any subject simply means attention to some other subject. In school-children of various ages this condition is often exasperating to the last degree. Its cause, however, is not the absolute loss of attention, but the direction of it into some forbidden but attractive channel. Wandering, or sporadic, attention also is never, properly speaking, the negative of attention. It is simply the unstable, flitting, inefficient form of it. This condition is sometimes spoken of as scattered attention, and, when not due to actual mental disease, is certainly attributable, if long continued, to bad mental surroundings, *i. e.*, surroundings which neither encourage nor give scope for the expression of native and normal interests. *Dispersed attention* is another much abused term. To have one's attention completely dispersed would be to become unconscious. The conditions properly describable by this term are illustrated in the general lowering of our mental alertness when we become drowsy. Mental distinctions of all kinds tend, under such circumstances, to become blurred and indefinite. The state is one of fading attention. Nevertheless, as long as we are conscious at all, we are always more clearly aware of some part of the field of thought than we are of the remainder. Our attention is never distributed evenly over the whole of the conscious field. If it ever were thus distributed, completely dispersed attention would, indeed, be realised.

Motor Accompaniments of Attention.—In our description of attention thus far, we have made occasional reference to the part played by sense organs and brain; but this has been somewhat incidental, and we have hardly noticed at all the conspicuous position of muscular activities. To bring out the significant facts bearing on these matters it will be convenient to avail ourselves temporarily of another common classification of attentive processes, differing from that which we have employed. This is the division of attention as **sensory, or ideational**; a division which certain of our illustrations have involved. All attention to objects stimulating the sense organs, every process, therefore, of sensation and perception, involves sensory attention. All attention to ideas, images, thoughts, etc., is ideational attention. The first type of activity involves both sense organ and brain, whereas the second type involves immediately only the brain.

In normal sensory attention muscular movements seem always to be concerned. These movements are accommodatory, and are calculated to put the sense organs in the best attitude to receive distinct impressions from the objects stimulating them. In vision, for example, if we see to best advantage, the eyes must converge upon the objects at which we are looking, the lenses must be accommodated to the distance of the object, and oftentimes the head must be turned, in order to permit the most effective visual operation. In hearing, we similarly tend to turn the head toward the source of the sound, or at all events, to turn in that direction the more sensitive of our ears. In taste, we press against the substance in the mouth with the tongue in order to detect most fully its flavour. In smelling, we inhale in order to bring the odorous particles against the olfactory membrane at the upper part of the nasal cavity. In touch, we explore the object with the hand, if we desire accurate information of its tactual characteristics. We find a similar state of things true, as regards all our sensations, when we make them the object of direct attention.

Each of these cases illustrates the function of the sensory-motor circuit. The light rays falling upon the retina set up currents in sensory nerves, which are transmitted to cells in control of the muscles of the eyes; and these in turn send out impulses, which result in convergence and accommodation. In some cases the sensory impulse may originate in a cortical centre, or in a sense organ other than that which experiences the modifications of the accommodatory movement. Thus, the hand may be moved in response to an idea, or in response to a stimulus from the eye, and not from the skin of the hand itself.

Psychologists have observed a similar kind of muscular accommodation when our attention is directed to intellectual processes. Thus, if we close our eyes and attempt to get a visual mental picture of some particular place, it will generally be found that the eyes tend to turn in the supposed direction of the imagined locality. In attempting to recall an odour we almost inevitably make slight movements of inhalation. In calling up images of taste the tongue moves and salivation is stimulated. Furthermore, the effort to fix our attention firmly upon any train of thought is generally accompanied by a strong tendency to assume some specific bodily attitude, in which we somewhat unconsciously seek to prevent the distraction of our attention by outside disturbances. In this effort the brows are often wrinkled, the breathing impeded, the body bent over and held rigid, the hands clenched, the head tilted in this way or that, etc. The attitudes which we thus assume evidently share with the sense organ accommodations already mentioned, the function of putting the organism in the most advantageous position for meeting the special demand momentarily laid upon it. The psychophysical effort at concentration overflows in movements calculated to assist in reaching the desired end. The actual value of these movements probably varies greatly, and depends (1) upon their success in eliminating, or neutralising, the effect of the disturbing stimuli from without; and (2) in their contribution, through their cortical effects, toward the continuation of the ongoing activity.

Thus, if more nervous energy is being liberated than can be properly disposed of by the pathways of discharge involved in the special matter in hand, these overflow motor pathways may be called in to take care of the excess of neural activity, and so indirectly further the ongoing occupation. The involuntary muscular processes, such as those of respiration and circulation, also reflect the changes in attention. When attention is much perturbed, they display rapid and relatively violent oscillations. When, on the other hand, attention moves along smoothly, these motor reactions are also stable.

The motor activities which accompany processes of attention necessarily, at least in the case of the voluntary muscles, send back to the cortex sensory impulses, which then enter into the general field of consciousness to modify its complexion and tone. These are sometimes spoken of as the "strain sensations" of attention. It seems probable that there is a small group which characterises in some measure all attention, and that the use of any special sense, or any special form of ideational process, involves another specific and relatively constant group. The intensity of these sensations necessarily varies widely from time to time, and is commonly greatest in cases of intense voluntary attention. The muscles most regularly and most obviously affected are those of the face, throat, and chest, although the hand and other parts of the body may be involved. The breathing movements are almost sure to be involved in cases of vigorous attention.

Dr. Gordon has suggested another interesting explanation of the function of these strain sensations. It is possible that in attempting, for example, to force our attention along some mentally difficult path, we primarily crave *more* nervous excitement and stimulation, more *push a tergo;* and these muscular activities setting up definite sensory impulses, which return to the cortex, may possibly furnish this needed help. It may well be that all these accounts of the motor aspects of attention are correct. After what has been said it is, perhaps, unnecessary to insist that motor processes are bound up in an inextricable way with the movements of attention, both as leading up to its effective activity and as secondary consequences of its operation. The idea of the sensory-motor circuit proves to be radically implicated, therefore, in every form of conscious action.

Genetic Features of Attention.—All the evidence which we can command, coming in part from the examination of our own mental operations as adults, and in part from observing how children deal with the objects about them, points to the notion that attention is from the very first engaged in the double process of pulling apart and putting together the various elements of conscious experience. These two processes are commonly known as dissociation and association. It seems to be fairly certain that at the outset of life consciousness is extremely vague and crude in its organisation. To begin with, there is, perhaps, no definite distinction felt between the various kinds of sensations, visual, auditory, tactual, etc. Certainly the process of distinguishing the various kinds of sensory qualities within the range of any given sense series—like the spectral colours in the field of vision—is quite slow in developing. The various colours are undoubtedly distinguished from one another very imperfectly even up to a late period in childhood. Nevertheless, after the first moment of consciousness attention is constantly at work, splitting up experiences which previously were felt as simple, and bringing about an increasingly definite awareness of the several distinguishable qualities within them. The analytical activity of attention is what we called above dissociation, or discrimination. Although we shall have a great deal to say about it under other titles further on in the book, we must glance at some of its more conspicuous features here.

Analytic Activity of Attention.—Discrimination.—When the different distinguishable elements of any state of consciousness blend with one another, so that they lose their individuality, we speak of the resulting condition as a case of *fusion*. Thus, the partial tones in a piano note are generally lost to us as separate sounds, and we seem to hear only a single musical tone. Similarly, when we grasp a book we seldom distinguish the sensations of pressure from those of temperature and tendinous strain. These sensations fuse. Again, the sensations which we get when eating onions, or when drinking coffee, we commonly speak of as being tastes. In point of fact, they largely depend for their characteristic quality upon smell sensations, which fuse with the tastes and in consequence are entirely overlooked by us. Now, it seems probable that the original tendencies of all sensory stimuli, which impinge upon our sense organs simultaneously, is to fuse in just this same fashion; so that were it not for this discriminative action of attention which we are describing, we might remain oblivious to much of the complexity of the objective world. Meantime, it must not be overlooked that once attention has succeeded in analysing some of these originally fusing qualities, we may find their distinctness and separateness enhanced by being experienced simultaneously. Colours, like black and white, red and green, may gain in definiteness and individuality by the contrast effects of juxtaposition.

However it may be in later life, there can be no question that during the first year or two the great agent in furthering discrimination is the change in the objective stimuli, which affect the sense organs from moment to moment. Thus, sounds sometimes occur simultaneously with stimulations of colour, and sometimes they do not. Stimulations of red sometimes occur together with stimulations of blue, and sometimes with white. These changes in the mode of sensory stimulation necessarily produce different forms of cortical reaction; and, as consciousness is conditioned by these cortical activities, we have thus a basis for different states of consciousness. That we are able to recognise the fact that one state of consciousness differs from a second, and is like a third, is an ultimate fact which we cannot further explain. All psychologists agree that this is a fundamental attribute

of consciousness, and, so far as concerns the conditions
under which we actually come in the first instance to attain
this awareness of differences, the description we have just
given seems to represent the undoubted facts. We can put
the matter diagrammatically, as in figure 34. So long as a
certain taste sensation T, and a certain smell sensation S,
are always given us together, we fail to note the complexity
of the sensation, and we experience a fusion possessing a

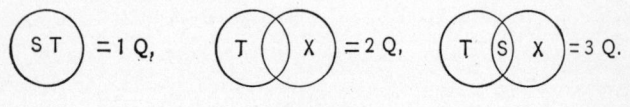

$$(S\ T) = 1\ Q, \qquad (T \cap X) = 2\ Q, \qquad (T\ (S)\ X) = 3\ Q.$$

FIG. 34.

single quality, 1 Q. When, however, the taste sensation happens to be combined with some sensation X other than the
previous smell, we can then note the fact that TX contains
two qualities—2 Q; and if S happens to be combined also
with this X we may immediately note the three qualities S,
X and T. In each case we have, by varying the concomitants, produced a new psychical condition, different from its
predecessors, and in this way we have provided the prerequisites of discrimination.

Evidently, if these are the preconditions of our original
capacity for the dissociating activity of attention, any device
which facilitates the arousal of different nervous conditions
will assist us in making our discriminations. Submitting objects to successive, instead of simultaneous, inspection produces a maximum of nervous difference; and we find accordingly that if we wish, for example, to detect the heavier of
two objects of nearly equal weight, we judge most accurately
when we lift them immediately in succession. If we wish to
tell whether or no two colours match, we let the eye pass
rapidly from one to the other, etc. Of course, when the
objects stimulate different sense organs there is already
considerable difference in the nervous processes resulting, and

to discriminate among them it is only necessary to let either sense be stimulated independently. The kind of discrimination, or comparison, which occurs among ideas in the higher processes of reflection, reasoning, etc., we shall consider at a later point. The form of dissociation which we have described clearly underlies the higher form, because it is concerned with our primary analysis into its rudimentary features of the world as we first know it.

Synthetic Features of Attention.—Simultaneous Association.—Hand in hand with these dissociative, analytical activities of attention is to be found a synthetic process, which serves to unite the various dissevered elements, and to which the name association is commonly given. In a logical sense, one phase of this associative process really precedes and underlies the dissociative activity; for it is evident that if we are to differentiate the two qualities A and B from one another, they must already be together in the mind; that is, they must be associated in some kind of fusion such as we have just been describing. Thus, to distinguish the colour white from the colour black upon this printed page involves not only that the black and the white objects shall be side by side in the space before me, but also that they shall in a way be together in my mind.

It is clear that every act of attention must involve in some degree both discrimination and this form of "simultaneous association." We may, for example, remark that the colours upon a postage stamp are red and white. Such an act is evidently one of discrimination. But it is also quite as truly one of association, for the qualities must be experienced together, must be mentally synthesised, that this special kind of discrimination may occur at all.

Successive Association.—There is another form of association, known as successive association, a term which is commonly restricted to the *sequence* of our *ideas* as they pass through the mind, and is not primarily and properly applied to our sensory and perceptual processes. We shall discuss it in connection with imagery and the higher cognitive functions. Even this kind of association of ideas, however, evidently involves discrimination; for the ideas must be noticed as different, in order that they may be separate ideas at all. And conversely, so far as we remark differences in successive moments of consciousness, we must admit the presence of associative factors of some kind or other, uniting the several temporally distinct contents of consciousness with one another.

Generalising, then, we may say that attention is both a synthetic and an analytic activity. Sometimes our primary purpose and interest in attending is to analyse and discriminate, but we cannot accomplish this without simultaneously employing association. And similarly, although we may be ostensibly engaged in connecting, or associating, the various items of our experience with one another, the execution of our task inevitably involves us in discrimination.

CHAPTER V

SENSATION

Rudimentary Forms of Knowledge.—We now take up in detail the several forms of *cognitive* process through which we attain knowledge. This undertaking will necessarily involve our examining various aspects of consciousness one at a time, and we must unavoidably turn our backs temporarily on most of the processes, apart from the special one we are for the moment engaged in studying. We must bear constantly in mind, therefore, this partial and tentative mode of procedure, remembering that the mind, which we thus analyse piecemeal, is in point of fact a real unit.

The first step in the activity of the sensory-motor circuit, which represents, as we have seen, the unit of action in the nervous system, is the sensory stimulation. This is reported in consciousness as a sensation, at which point we shall accordingly begin our detailed study of the various portions of our psychological processes. Some psychologists regard the feelings of pleasure and pain as even more primordial than sensation in this primitive sensory-motor activity of the organism. Be this as it may, we shall find it practically more convenient to examine the cognitive functions of the organism first; that is to say, those which *inform* us most definitely of an *external world*.

The Evolution of Sense Organs.—That it may be put into the most delicate and complete accord with the world in which it is placed, the organism must be capable of responding to the various objects found therein. To this end we find the sense organs so devised that they may give information about the most widely differing kinds of physical existence.

There seems to be no doubt that even very simple forms of organism are sensitive in a rude way to most, if not all, of the types of sensory stimuli to which human beings respond, *e. g.*, light, sound, mechanical impact, etc. This is simply another way of saying that protoplasm itself is sensitive to these modes of stimulation. But so far as concerns the development of definitely differentiated sense organs, specially devised to receive particular modes of sensory stimuli, the facts seem to indicate great irregularity and wide variation among different organic forms. The kinds of sensitivity which are most certainly and regularly present in the lower orders correspond most nearly to the human cutaneous sensations of touch, pain, and temperature. But beyond such a statement as this, we are hardly in a position to offer any definite outline of sensory development. Not a few animal forms well up in the scale of organisms seem to possess sense organs unknown to man, the nature of whose functions we can, therefore, only speculate about. Moreover, when we come to animals on the level of the birds and quadrupeds, we come upon astonishing anomalies. For example, it seems probable that some birds are essentialy destitute of the sense of smell. This is said to be true of vultures. On the other hand, dogs seem to live in a mental world in which smell probably plays a predominant part. Speaking generally, advance to any high level of intelligence is accompanied by an increasing prominence of vision and hearing, and a decreasing prominence for the rest of the sensations. This fact seems to be largely due to the superior richness and flexibility of the material supplied by these two senses for elaboration into ideational processes. Moreover, these senses are the ones which afford most detailed and accurate information of objects at a distance—an important consideration in developing organisms. Smell is their only rival in this particular, and for

SENSATION

purposes of general orientation, as regards prey, or dangerous animal foes, is made large use of by wild creatures.

Neural Basis of Sensation in Man. (1) Cutaneous Sensations.*—Each form of sensation which we possess is apparently connected with the activity of a specially constituted end-organ. Thus, the sensations of touch or contact probably come from the stimulation of minute structures in the dermis (figure 35), and from nerves ending about the roots of the hair. It is fairly certain that children have a more delicate and accurate sense of touch than adults. There is probably an anatomical reason for this fact. The skin of the child contains practically the same nervous innervation as does that of the adult, but the area thus innervated is much smaller. The difference is most marked on surfaces which are not commonly used for touching. The touch, pain, and temperature apparatus in the nervous system is fairly complete at birth. Sensations of cold probably originate from organs in the skin, such as are shown in figure 36. It is possible, though not wholly certain, that sensations of warmth come from special structures, shown in figure 37; and in the epidermis are found the so-called free nerve endings, *i. e.* nerve fibres which become much attenuated and terminate without contact with any special end-organ. Their stimulation is believed to produce the cutting, smarting, burning sensations of physical pain, which must not be confused with the experience of mere disagreeableness. It will be seen, therefore, that the skin, which affords a covering for all these structures, is in reality

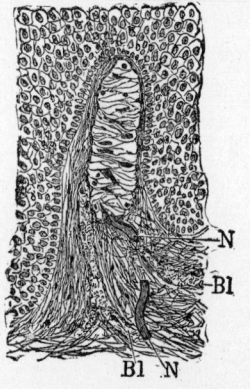

FIG. 35. Tactile corpuscle of Meissner from the skin of the human toe. *Bl*, blood-vessel; *N*, medullated nerve fibre. (Barker after P. Schiefferdecker.)

---

* The anatomical statements of this paragraph must be regarded as tentative and provisional.

a delicate mosaic of sensitive and insensitive spots. Certain spots will respond to stimulations with a sensation of cold, as may be noticed by passing a pencil point gently over the skin of the forearm; other spots with a sensation of pain, or pressure, and others with a sensation of warmth. Moreover, these temperature sensations can be produced by electrical stimulation, and by tapping upon the skin with an object which is thermally indifferent. This fact would evidently seem to indicate the existence of some special organ for these particular sensations. Naturally, the spots are very close together, so that it is often possible to secure several kinds of sensations from what is apparently one and the same spot. Figure 38 shows a rude map of these temperature spots, which are less numerous than the pressure spots, and much less numerous than those responding to pain sensations.

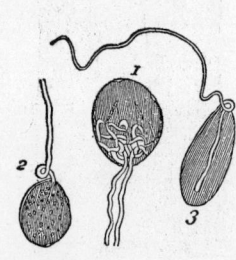

FIG. 36. Various forms of end-bulbs. The axis cylinder of the nerve is seen terminating in little sac-like structures. (McKendrick and Snodgrass after Krause.)

(2) **Kinaesthetic Sensations.**—The insertions of the tendons and ligaments are supplied, as are the muscles, with sensory nerves, by means of which we are made aware of the rotation of the joints when we move any part of the body. The sensations produced in this way are called kinæsthetic. Of their condition at birth we cannot speak with confidence. They are evidently present, but how perfectly developed we do not know. We occasionally have sensations arising in the viscera, and these probably originate either in the pain nerves before mentioned or in nerves of the general tactile variety.

(3) **Olfactory Sensations.**—The olfactory nerves terminate about the olfactory cells of the mucous membrane lining the upper portion of the nasal cavity. (Figures 39 and 40.)

SENSATION 95

The most acute perceptions of smell are probably not obtained before seven years of age, because of mechanical difficulties in the form of the nostril. The abundance of mucus

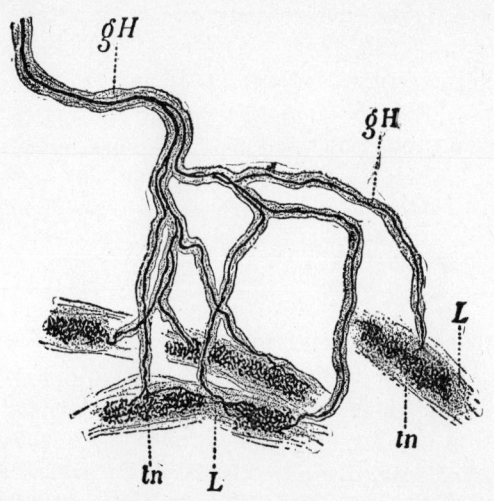

FIG. 37. Ruffini's nerve endings. Cylindrically shaped bodies formed of finely divided nerve fibrils. *gH*, sheath of the nerve; *L*, connective tissue covering; *tn*, terminal interlacings of the axis cylinder. (Barker after Ruffini.)

in infancy has a similar effect, producing obtuse smell sensitivities.

(4) Gustatory Sensations.—The cells in the taste buds, found as a rule only on certain papillæ of the tongue (though occasionally elsewhere in the mouth), furnish us with our taste sensations. (Figure 41.) This sense is well developed at birth, a fact which, perhaps, has a certain evolutionary significance. The sense is often defective in the feeble-minded. It seems probable that there is still further differentiation of the forms of this end-organ; for certain regions, like the base of the tongue, are often especially sensitive to some one taste, in this case bitter. The sides of the tongue are particularly responsive to sour, the tip to sweet and to salt. The centre of the tongue is generally altogether insensitive to taste. The leaves of the plant called *gymnema sylvestre* will, if they be chewed, paralyse the sensitivity for bitter and sweet without affecting the other tastes. Cocaine, if applied to the tongue, causes first a loss of the ability to distinguish bitter, then sweet, and finally salt and sour. Furthermore, some substances, *e. g.*, saccharine, produce one taste in one part of the mouth, and another taste in another part of the mouth. Saccharine is sweet to the tip, and bitter to the base, of the tongue. All these facts are easy to explain, provided there are taste cells, which always respond, however they are stimulated, with some one taste quality. But the facts are not all as yet definitely determined, and we must consequently eschew dogmatic statements.

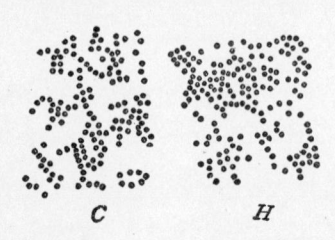

FIG. 38. *C*, cold spots; *H*, hot spots. (McKendrick and Snodgrass after Goldsheider.)

(5) Auditory Sensations.—The auditory nerves terminate at the base of hair cells in the internal ear, such as appear in figure 42. There are many thousands of these cells, and the precise mode of their stimulation by vibrations of the air is extremely interesting, but too complex and too problematic for detailed explanation here. Suffice it to say, that the hair cells are immersed in the liquids contained by the sac-like membranes of the inner ear, and that the external ear and the middle-ear contain physical devices (membranes joined by min-

FIG. 39. Isolated cells from the olfactory region of a rabbit, magnified 560 diameters. *st*, supporting cells; *s*, short, stiff cilia, or, according to some, cones of mucus resembling cilia; *r, r*, olfactory cells. The nerve process has been torn off the lower cell marked *r*. (McKendrick and Snodgrass after Stöhr.)

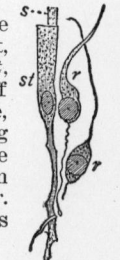

SENSATION 97

ute bones) by means of which the air waves outside the ear are gathered up and multiplied in power, so that they may cause the liquids of the internal ear to vibrate, and thus indirectly stimulate the hair cells. Figure 43 shows the essential parts of the ear. The ear can respond with sensations of sound to vibrations of the air ranging from 16 per second up to 50,000. The great majority of musical experiences arise from tones whose vibration rates fall between 64 and 5,000 per second. We have once before called attention to the fact that, owing to the presence of mucus in the middle and external ear, the new-born child is generally insensitive to ordinary sounds. The position of the drum membrane also contributes to this insensitivity. About four days after birth most children will show response to loud sounds by expressions of fright.

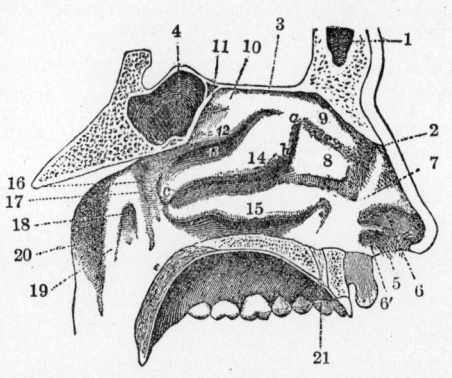

FIG. 40. Outer side of left nostril; *3*, perforated plate of ethmoid bone, through which pass the twigs of the olfactory nerve on their way to olfactory cells of the mucous membrane lining the upper nasal cavity; *6*, vestibule of the nose; *8*, entrance to middle meatus, or passage; *13*, upper meatus leading into the throat; *18*, entrance to Eustachian tube. (McKendrick and Snodgrass after Schwalbe.)

The sensitivity to high-pitched sounds seems to develop sooner than that to low sounds. Localisation of sounds seems to begin with many children at about four months of age. Children a year and more of age often seems extremely sensitive to very weak sounds which older persons cannot hear at all.

The semicircular canals of the internal ear (figure 44)

also contain sensory nerves, which terminate, like the true auditory nerves, about the bases of hair cells. We are said to owe in part to these organs our sense of total bodily translocation, our awareness of our equilibrium, etc., matters to which we shall return in a later paragraph. The fluid in the canals contains little calcareous particles called otoliths. When the body moves in any given direction some of these otoliths are supposed to lag behind, because of their inertia, thus striking the hair cell filaments and setting up a sensory disturbance. As the canals are at right angles to one another, the fluids of some one or two of them would always be most affected by any single movement, and the sensations arising from them could thus by experience come to be connected with specific kinds of movements, e. g., forward, backward, upward, etc. We shall speak at a later point of the alleged sensations arising from these organs.

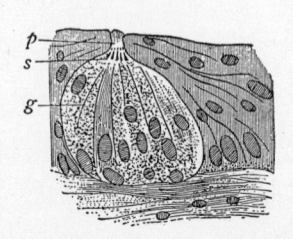

FIG. 41. Taste bud seen in the papilla foliata of a rabbit × 560 d. g, Taste bud, showing outer supporting cells; s, fine ends of taste cells; p, taste pore. (McKendrick and Snodgrass after Stöhr.)

(6) **Visual Sensations.**—The retina, which differs from all the other sense organs in being in reality a part of the brain removed by growth from its original location, contains a most elaborate series of structures. These are shown in figure 45. As in the case of the ear, we shall unfortunately be obliged to content ourselves with the most cursory account of this interesting organ. The optic nerves enter from the back of each eyeball, and the nerve fibres are then distributed radially all over the spherical surfaces of the eyes, as far forward as the lens. (Figure 46.) The fibres turn backward, away from the centre of the eye, and lose themselves among the basal cells of the retinal structure. The light waves make

SENSATION 99

their way in through the dioptric media of the eye, *i. e.*, the cornea, the aqueous humour, the lens, and the vitreous humour, and finally, after passing through the transparent optic fibres, come to the retinal end-organs, the rods and cones. (Figure 47.) At this point the physical ether vibrations which we call light set up physiological changes in the nerve, and the nervous current runs backward along the nerve fibres, and so to the brain.

The rods and cones respond to vibration rates of the ether between 440,000,000,000 and 790,000,000,000 per second.

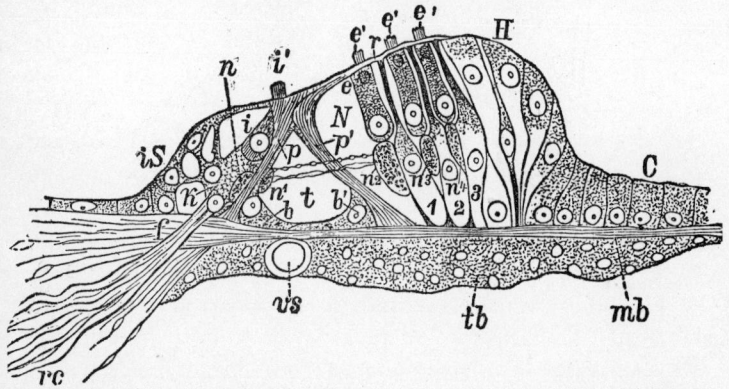

FIG. 42. Cross section of the organ of Corti; *p* and *p*¹, internal and external rods of Corti; *i* and *i*¹, internal hair cells; *e*¹, external hair cells; *mb*, basilar membrane; *rc*, nerve fibres leading from the hair cells inward to the central nervous system. (Barker after Retgius and Rauber.)

These are the rates of the light waves of the spectrum of the sun. By means of the six muscles which are attached to the external surfaces of each eye we are enabled so to move the eyes as to bring the rays of light from the object at which we are looking directly upon the central point of each retina, the so-called *fovea centralis*, the place of clearest vision. This process is convergence. By means of the lens in each eye, which can be made more or less convex, the rays of light from the object at which we are looking are brought to a focus upon this foveal spot, and thus we secure a clear, well-defined image upon each retina. This act is called accommodation.

The retina is fully developed at birth, and some children apparently have a slight control over the movements of fixa-

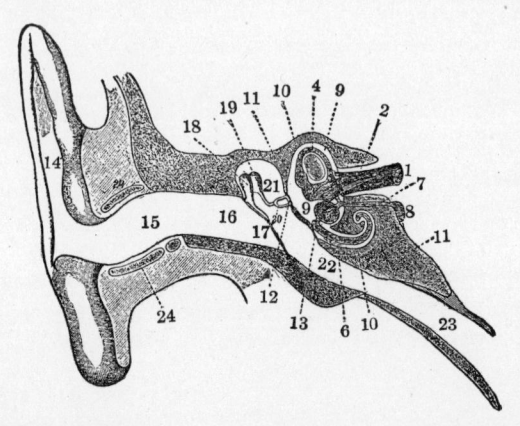

FIG. 43. Diagram of the ear; natural size. *1*, auditory nerve; *2*, internal auditory meatus closed by the cribriform plate of bone through the perforations of which the branches of the auditory nerve pass to the ear; *3-8*, membranous labyrinth composed of *3*, utricle, *4*, semicircular canals, *5*, saccule, *6*, duct of the cochlea (the coils not entirely shown), *7*, endolymphatic duct with, *8*, its saccule lying inside of the cranial cavity; *9*, lymphatic space surrounding the membranous labyrinth; *10*, osseous labyrinth of compact bone lying in the more spongy substance of the petrous bone, *11; 12*, the oval window, filled by the foot-plate of the stirrup-bone; *13*, the round window, across which is stretched the internal tympanic membrane; *14*, auricle; *15, 16*, external auditory meatus; *15*, its cartilaginous, and, *16*, its bony part; *17*, tympanic membrane; *18-20*, auditory ossicles; *18*, hammer; *19*, anvil; *20*, stirrup; *21*, middle ear; *22*, osseous, and, *23*, cartilaginous portion of the Eustachian tube; *24*, cartilages of external auditory meatus. (McKendrick and Snodgrass after Schwalbe.)

tion at birth. This is, however, rare, and such control generally does not come until the third week. But there is much variation. Older children surpass adults in their ability to see in a dim light, and to see small objects at a distance.

This is probably because the optical media, *e. g.*, the humours of the eye, etc., are with them more transparent. The colour sense is often apparently defective in children. But this probably means simply a lack of *experience* in distinguishing colours. The brighter colours are generally preferred. Genuine colour blindness is extremely rare among girls, whereas perhaps one in every twenty-five or thirty boys is defective.

The Elementary Qualities of Sensation.—At this point the question naturally arises as to the number and nature of the elementary sense qualities which the several sense organs mediate. We must next address ourselves to the answering of this question, by scrutinising each department of sensory activity. We may profitably remark, however, at the outset of this undertaking, that these sensory qualities, such as redness and blueness, warmth and cold, etc., with which we shall come into contact, are highly abstract affairs, isolated by us for our psychological purposes from the larger matrix of *actual conscious experience* of which they properly form part. Thus, for example, we are never conscious merely and simply of the colour yellow. It is always a yellow *object* of which we are aware, with some sort of contours, felt against a background of other conscious processes, many of which are not even visual at all. But by turning our analytical processes of attention upon the yellow part of the whole experience, we can practically abstract it for our examination, and study it as though it actually occurred singly and alone. Throughout the next few pages, therefore, we shall be engaged in this process of abstracting pure sensory qualities

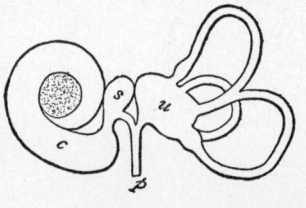

FIG. 44. Membranous labyrinth (diagrammatic). *c*, cochlea; *s*, saccule united by *p*, the ductus endolymphaticus, with *u*, the utricle, arising from which are seen the three semicircular canals. (After McKendrick and Snodgrass.)

102   PSYCHOLOGY

for separate study. Indeed, in a certain sense, as we have already emphatically remarked, all our psychological analysis proceeds by abstracting now this and now that phase of con-

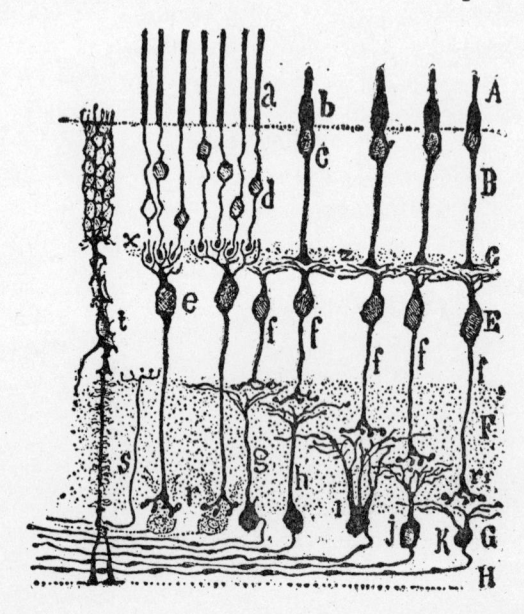

FIG. 45. Scheme of the structure of the retina. *A*, layer of rods and cones; *a*, rods; *b*, cones; *E*, layer of bipolar cells; *G*, layer of large ganglion cells; *H*, layer of nerve fibres; *s*, centrifugal nerve fibre. (Barker after Ramón y Cajal.)

sciousness for detailed inspection. But the fact requires especial notice in the case of sensations, which we are apt to think of as mentally independent and isolated facts. They are only independent and isolated in a thorough-going way, in so far as our reflective manipulation makes them so temporarily. We may add, by way of definition, that it is the consciousness of the *qualities* of *objects stimulating* the sense organs which most psychologists mean to designate by the term *sensation*.

Qualities of Dermal Sensation.—From the skin we obtain

SENSATION

as the rudimentary qualities of sensation, cold, warmth, pain, and pressure; and some psychologists would add heat, a sensation said to differ from warmth, and to be caused by the simultaneous stimulation of cold and warmth. The evidence for this statement, as to the elementary qualities of the cutaneous sensations, consists in the careful examination of every kind of psychical experience which we can obtain from the stimulation of the skin. At first, it may seem that we have many other elementary qualities peculiar to cutaneous reactions. Thus, it is common in the older text-books to see such asserted sensations as hardness, softness, wetness, dryness, active and passive touch, sharpness, smoothness, roughness, etc., referred to the skin. It is true, of course, that these several impressions originate in the skin. But they are quite certainly either compounds of pressure with some of the other sensations already mentioned, or else mere modifications of pressure itself. Thus, if one heat a drop of water to the exact temperature of the skin, and then place it on the hand, it will

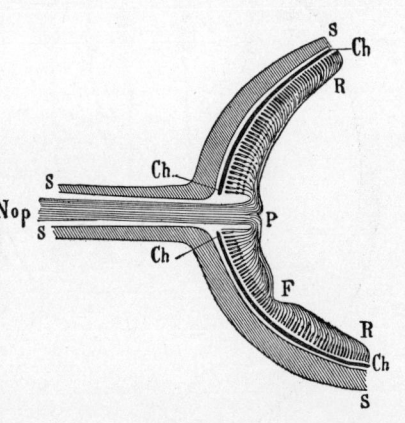

FIG. 46. Scheme of retinal fibres. (James after Küss.) *Nop*, optic nerve; *S*, sclerotic; *Ch*, choroid; *R*, retina; *P*, papilla (blind spot, where no retinal structure is found); *F*, fovea.

prove very difficult to imagine any sensation caused by it other than pressure. Similarly, if a hard and a soft object be made thermally indifferent, and both be laid very gently against the skin, pressure will be the only sensation confidently felt. As the intensity of the pressure increases, the difference will be remarked. But hardness simply means more intense pressure, plus, on most occasions, certain sensations of effort, resistance, or strain, which comes from muscles, or tendons, and not from the skin. And so with the other experiences suggested above. When carefully examined, they

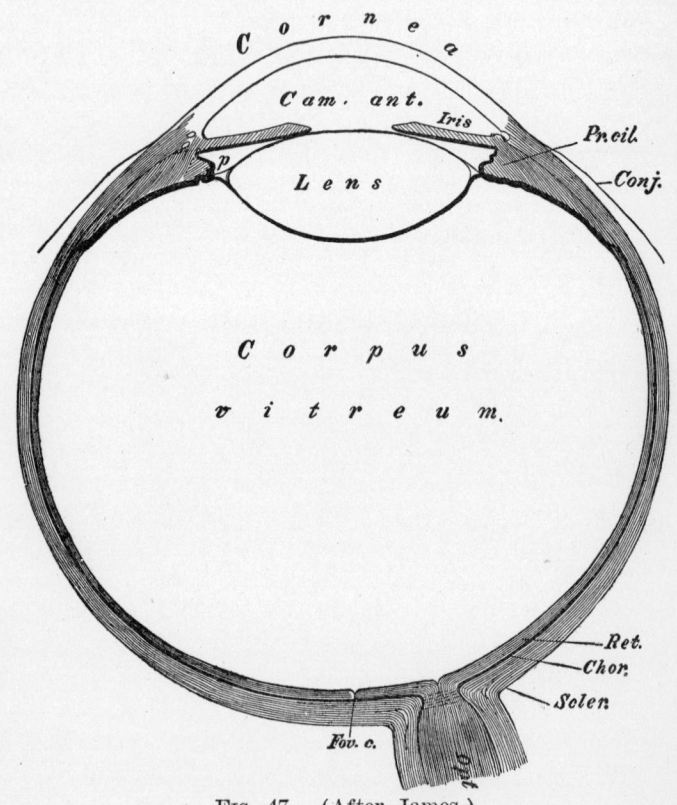

FIG. 47. (After James.)

will all be found capable of resolution into pressure, or pressure and some other sensation, like that of temperature, or tendinous strain. Itching, tickling, and creepy sensations of the skin probably originate at times from the effects upon the dermal end-organs of circulatory changes. Occasionally, however, they are due to very light pressure stimulations. The

SENSATION

creepy feeling is often a complex of the prickly pain sensations with cold sensations, etc. There seems no reason to postulate any new elementary forms of sense experience because of these reactions.

Kinaesthetic Sensation Qualities.—Closely connected with the skin sensations are the kinæsthetic, or organic, sensations. When one lifts a heavy weight there is quickly noticeable, over and above the pressure sensation in the hand, a feeling of strain in the arm. When the hand is firmly clasped this strain is also detectable. This sensation without doubt is largely referable to the sensory nerves about the tendons. The muscles, also, have sensory nerves, as we have noted in a previous paragraph, and there is undoubtedly a muscle sensation. But it is hardly possible introspectively to isolate the sensation without experimental appliances, except in the case of moderate muscular fatigue. The feeling which arises under such conditions of fatigue is, then, the specific sensation concerned. The joints, also, are probably indirect contributors to this group of sensations, through their effect upon the tendons. Certainly we are extremely sensitive to their movements. The sensation which is experienced when we attempt to isolate the joint activity is strikingly like ordinary pressure. This isolation can be accomplished with sufficient accuracy by attaching a heavy weight to a cord, and then, while holding the cord, allowing the weight to sink rapidly to the ground. At the moment when it strikes, one feels a sort of "snap-back" sensation in the joints.

Sensations From the Semicircular Canals.—Many authors are inclined to ascribe a pair of specific sensations intimately connected with the above (provided they are genuine sensations) to the semicircular canals of the internal ear. These canals, upon the basis of this view, are supposed to produce the sensation of dizziness, and the sensation of change of rate of movement, when the whole body is being moved, as occurs when one is on a railroad train. It should be said of these dizziness sensations, that the eyes play a very large part in them, and also that various muscles may be engaged in their production. There is, thus, in no case any conscious reference by us of the sensations to the semicircular canal region. We simply feel our balance disturbed, and note the misbehaviour of the visual field.

Organic Sensations.—The respiratory and circulatory processes produce certain sensory experiences closely akin to the cutaneous ones, *e. g.*, the sensation of "closeness" in the air, perhaps, comes from a genuine intra-thoracic sensation. The sexual organs have a specific sensory quality, and the alimentary tract gives rise to the experiences of nausea, thirst, and hunger. It may, perhaps, be questioned whether these last experiences are not resolvable into other simpler constituent sensation qualities, in which pressure and pain, for example, possibly play a part, and with which the affective factors of pleasantness and unpleasantness are markedly connected. But the disposition among psychologists seems on the whole to be in favour of regarding them as real sensations, with probably some specific end-organ, although the case is far from clear.

Olfactory Qualities.—It is impossible at the present time to say anything definite about the elementary sense qualities of smell. The evidence at present available would make it seem probable that the number is large. We seldom make any attempt at classifying odours by their sense qualities, probably because practical exigencies do not require it. Our only common classification is based upon the affective consequences of the odour stimuli, which we divide into the two great classes, agreeable and disagreeable. We designate odours by the objects from which they come, *e. g.*, violet, orange, leather, etc., adding occasionally to these terms metaphors borrowed from taste, *e. g.*, sour, sweet, terms which are not always applied unambiguously to the mere sense quality, but often involve reference to affective processes, and to other concomitant activities, both muscular and sensory. For example, a sour smell is often one which stirs up unpleasant gustatory sensations, with choking contractions of the throat. The classification most used in a practical way at the present time is Zwaardemaker's modification of Linnæus' table:

1—Ethereal smells, including fruit odours.

2—Aromatic smells, *e. g.*, camphor, spice.

3—Fragrant smells, *e. g.*, many flowers, violets, sweet peas, etc.

4—Ambrosiac smells, *e. g.*, musk.

5—Alliaceous smells, *e. g.* garlic, chlorine.

6—Empyreumatic smells, *e. g.*, burning tobacco, burnt toast, coffee.

7—Hircine smells, *e. g.*, cheese.

8—Virulent smells, *e. g.*, opium.

9—Nauseous smells, *e. g.*, decaying animal matter.

This classification of the table has a purely practical value, however, and cannot be in any way accepted as representing the irreducible sense qualities.

The Qualities of Taste Sensations.—There are, without much question, four and only four elementary qualities of taste sensation, *i. e.*, sour, salt, sweet, and bitter. What we commonly call tastes are generally compounds, or fusions, of taste with temperature, pressure, and smell. Thus, as we have remarked at an earlier point, the characteristic taste of onions will be found astonishingly altered, if one close the nostrils firmly before taking the onion into the mouth. Some authorities incline to add two other elementary tastes to the list of gustatory qualities, *i. e.*, alkaline and metallic. But on the whole, it seems probable that these are compounds of the others already mentioned. Certainly it is remarkable to see how completely these four suffice to describe the true taste sensations, when we are given a large number of substances to test by taste alone, without knowing in advance what they are to be. To make this experiment satisfactorily, one must see to it that smell is absolutely ruled out, that the temperature of the substances is that of the mouth itself; and one must be careful not to confuse the pricking, puckering effects of certain substances, which are not taste sensations at all, with the true taste quality. Furthermore, one must employ solutions to make the test, for many food substances produce characteristic contact sensations which we instantly recognise. Finally, there is a striking difference in the sensitiveness of various parts of the tongue, as was pointed out in an earlier paragraph, to these four kinds of taste stimuli. No other tastes show this local peculiarity.

Auditory Qualities.—Our auditory sensations fall naturally into two great groups—noises and tones. But each of these can be subdivided again into a very large number of distinguishable qualities. We get the sensation qualities which we call noise when less than two complete vibrations of a sound wave are allowed to reach the ear; or, what is perhaps, owing to the reflection of the sound, the same thing, when the waves which do reach the ear are irregular and non-periodic in their mode of vibration. These irregularities may evidently be indefinite in number, and so we get such differences in the sounds as distinguish, for example, the noise of a train from the noise of a drum. These last mentioned cases, however, are what are called complex noises, and are conceived as made up of aggregations of the simple noises first mentioned, of which we can detect some 550 or more. The sensation of tone comes from bodies which vibrate periodically and regularly, like the pendulum. Such bodies are represented best by tuning-forks. In this case we can distinguish some 11,000 qualities. The differences among these qualities are primarily what we call differences in pitch. These arise from differences in the vibration rates of the sounds, and, as we have already learned, we can hear tones ranging in vibration rate from 16 to 50,000 per second. It must be remembered that the musical tones which we commonly hear are not simple, but complex, being constituted of a number of tones —the fundamental and its overtones. The nature, number, and relative intensity of these partial tones determines the timbre of a sound. The characteristic differences in the tone quality of different instruments has this fact as its basis. In the piano, for instance, there is a rich and well-balanced set of the lower partial tones. In the clarinet the odd overtones are predominant; in the flute these overtones are few and weak, etc. The evidence for these facts is not easily obtained without the use of apparatus. But the rough acoustic difference between noise and tone is fortunately familiar to us all, and the other points which we have noted we shall have to accept on authority.

Visual Qualities.—Like the auditory sensations, our visual sensations fall into two general classes—sensations of brightness and sensations of colour. The brightness sensations are caused by the impingement upon the retina of mixed light waves of various lengths; thus, what we call white light is made up of light waves of all lengths. Pure colour sensations are produced by homogeneous light waves, or waves of practically equal length. As a matter of fact, we never experience colours without getting a measure of brightness sensation also. Although it is convenient to distinguish the two forms of sensation from one another, this concomitance must not be forgotten. If we gradually decrease the intensity of white light, we pass first through a series of shades, to which we should ordinarily apply the name grey, and come finally to black. Black and white are thus the extremes of the brightness series of sensations, and between them occur the various shades of grey. We are able to distinguish some 700 different brightness qualities between the deepest black and the most brilliant white.

We are in the habit of referring to the spectral colours, or qualities, as being seven in number, *i. e.*, red, orange, yellow, green, blue, indigo-blue, and violet. This is, however, a merely practical and somewhat arbitrary division. These names apply to distinctions in colour tone which we promptly and easily remark when looking at a sunlight spectrum. But in reality the colour between pure green and pure blue is just as truly entitled to a separate name as is orange, a colour which distinctly suggests both red and yellow. Purple, too, which can be formed by mixing red and violet, the colours at the ends of the spectrum, is a perfectly genuine colour quality, deserving to rank in this respect with the spectrum colours themselves. When we are given proper experimental conditions we find we can distinguish some 150 spectral qualities. This includes the purple.

Elementary Colour Relations. (1) Mixtures and Complementaries.—If we now apply to vision the mode of analysis we have employed heretofore in the case of other sensations, and attempt to reduce the visual spectral qualities, apart from brightness, to those which seem really elementary, we shall find four such colours remaining, *i. e.*, red, yellow, green, and blue. All the others, when closely inspected, appear to us to be compounds. Orange, we have already remarked, appears both reddish and yellowish. Violet has traces both of blue and red, and so with all the transitional hues leading from one of these elementary colours to another. Moreover, if we be given these four colours, we can, as we should naturally expect, produce all the other spectral hues by mixing these elements in proper proportions. Among the mixtures which we can make in this way are certain very peculiar ones, which result when we take two such colours as yellow and blue, or red and blue-green. These pairs of colours, when mixed together, give us, instead of a new spectral hue, simply grey. Colours whose mixture results thus in grey are called complementary colours, and every colour has some complementary in the spectral series, except green, whose complementary is purple, a mixture of red and blue. (Figure 48 shows these relations.)

SENSATION

(2) After-Images.—Our visual sensations are in one particular very remarkable, as compared with our sensations of other kinds. The after-effects of sensory stimulation last longer and are more peculiar than is apparently the case else-

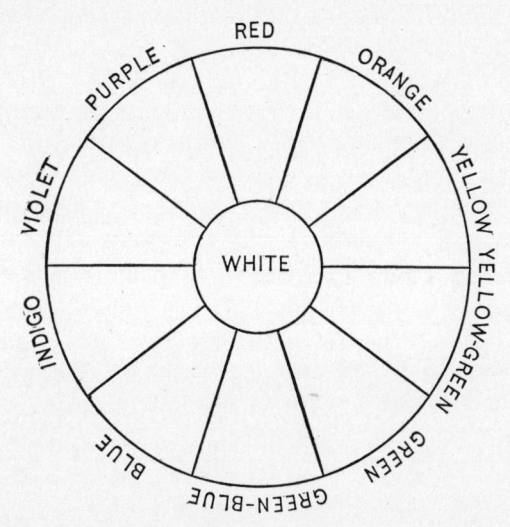

FIG. 48. The colours at opposite ends of any diameter of the circle produce white, if mixed with one another. Purple, which is the complementary colour to green, is not found in the spectrum, but is produced by a mixture of the end-colours of the spectrum, red and violet.

where. There are two principal forms of after-images, as they are called, *i. e.*, positive and negative. After-sensations would, perhaps, be the better term for them. If one suddenly looks at a very bright light, and then closes the eyes, the light continues to be seen for some seconds in its proper intensity and hue. This phenomenon is a positive after-image. If one looks for a few seconds fixedly at a bit of blue paper, and then closes the eyes, or turns them upon some neutral grey back-ground, one sees a yellow patch corresponding in shape to the blue stimulus. This is a negative image. Negative images invert the relations of brightness in the stimulus, so that what was white in the object appears black in the afterimage, and vice versa. They also convert all spectral colours and their compounds into their several complementaries. While all the senses display after-effects similar to the positive visual after-image, none of them has anything *precisely* comparable with the negative image.

(3) Colour Contrast.—The phenomena of contrast also, although characterising in a measure all sense domains, and for that matter all conscious processes, are especially striking in vision. Yellow and blue appear respectively yellower and bluer, when seen side by side, than when seen apart. This seems to be largely because of the fact that the eye moves slightly from one to the other; and the eye fatigued for blue already has a disposition to react with the yellow afterimage. If the part of the retina containing this yellow afterimage process is then exposed to the real *objective* yellow, the power of the stimulus is much enhanced, and we see a deeper, more intense yellow than we otherwise should. This phenomenon is called successive contrast. Simultaneous contrast is an even more interesting phenomenon, and may be illustrated by putting a small bit of grey paper upon any coloured field, and then covering the whole with thin white tissue paper. The grey patch will, under such conditions, always appear as of a colour complementary to that of the field, *i. e.*, it will appear blue, when the field is yellow; yellow, when it is blue; reddish when it is green, etc. The explanations offered for this phenomenon would take us too far into physiological psychology, and we must rest content with the general conclusion that our colour sensations are dependent, not only upon the colour of the objects immediately fixated, but also upon the colours surrounding it, and upon the immediately preceding stimulation.

(4) Defects in Colour Vision.—Finally, we may remark, that the peripheral portions of the retina are seriously defective in their colour reactions. Accurate colour vision belongs only to the central portion of the retina around the fovea. According to most observers, red and green are only seen accurately for a short distance outside this region. Yellow and blue are lost next, and in the extreme periphery only white and grey can be sensed. This condition suggests the pathological colour-blindness from which many persons suffer even at the fovea.

Compound Qualities.—In addition to these colour sensations of which we have been speaking, large numbers exist formed by combining the several spectral qualities (150) with the brightness qualities (700). Some 30,000 distinguishable qualities can be produced in this way. Thus red, for example, can be mixed with white to produce various tints, which we call pink; or with black to produce various shades, which we designate brown. Figure 49 displays in a general way these relations.

Summary of Sensation Qualities.—Reverting now in conclusion to the matter from which we started, and taking all these sensations into account, which we have found originating in the various sense organs, we shall find that, even disregarding smell, of which we cannot speak confidently, we are supplied with more than 42,000 distinguishable sensory qualities. On the other hand, if we consider only the irreducible sense qualities, like redness and sweetness, and call these the sensation elements, we have probably not more than 20 or 25 when smell and sound are left out of the count. The problem of reduction to simple sense forms is, in the case of these last two groups of sensations, fraught with great difficulty and uncertainty.

The Intensity of Sensations.—We have remarked incidentally a number of times in this chapter, that our sensations originate from the stimulation of a specific sense-organ by some form of motion in the physical world about us, such, for example, as the air waves, the ether waves, the heat waves, etc. But it is not only necessary that these various forms of stimuli should fall upon the sense organs. It is also necessary that they should possess sufficient intensity, if we are to become conscious of them. A very faint light, a very faint sound, a very faint odour, may fail altogether to produce a sensation in us. The point at which such a stimulus becomes intense enough to produce a sensation is called the limen, or the threshold. It is also a matter of frequent observation that when sensory stimuli become very intense they cease to be felt as they were before, and we experience pain instead. A very bright and blinding light may cause acute pain. A loud, shrill sound, extreme heat, and extreme cold are all painful. The point at which the various stimuli are thus felt as painful is known as the *upper limit* of sensation. Between the limen and the upper limit fall an indefinite number of gradations of sensory intensities. It should be noted in passing, that certain olfactory and gustatory stimuli can hardly be obtained in sufficient intensity to be called painful; and also that many very weak sensations are unpleasant, *e. g.* weak sounds and faint lights, the tickling from delicate contact, etc.

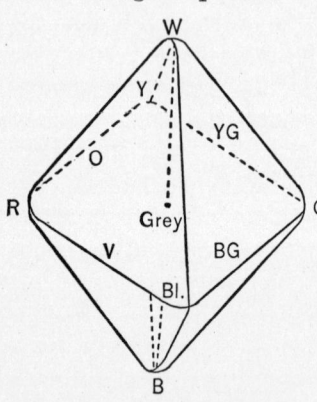

FIG. 49. The colour pyramid. The line *WB* corresponds to the white-black series of colours; the plane *Bl. YG* represents the most saturated spectral colours—*e. g.*, blue, red, green. The lines joining *W* and *B* with the letters representing the several spectral colours, *e. g.*, *Bl.* and *G*, illustrate the transitional tints and shades. (After Ebbinghaus.)

Weber's Law.—Exhaustive experiments have revealed a very interesting law, known after its first careful investigator as "Weber's Law," which obtains among the relations of these sensation intensities, as we experience them. When we

SENSATION

place a weight of 20 grams upon the hand, we find that we observe no change in the pressure sensation until a whole gram has been added to the 20. If we take 100 grams we must add 5 grams before we can observe the change in intensity; and, speaking generally, whatever absolute weight we start with, we find always that we must add the same fraction of its own weight, that is, 1-20, in order to feel that the pressure has changed. A similar thing holds true of the intensity of sounds, but in this case the fraction is approximately 1-3. In sensations of brightness the change must be 1-100, etc. In all these cases the formula is most nearly true in the medium ranges of intensity. When we approach the limen or the upper limit, the relations seem to become irregular, and in the case of certain senses, like smell, the application of the law is somewhat dubious.

Duration of Sensations.—We have seen that every stimulus must possess a definite intensity before it can give rise to a sensation; and it is even more obvious that every such stimulus must also possess a certain duration, if it is to be felt. Moreover, many sensations are very profoundly altered by prolonged duration. Thus, colour sensations will be found to grow dim and to fade, if long continued. Some sensations of sound, on the other hand, seem to become more intense, if continued, and finally occasion pain. The detailed facts about the influence of duration upon sensory processes cannot at present be both accurately and briefly set forth, and we shall therefore pass them by.

Extensity in Sensations.—Certain sensations, like those of vision and touch, always possess, in addition to the previously mentioned characteristics of duration and intensity, a definite *spatial* quality. Some distinguished psychological authorities insist that all sensations are thus spatial, sensations of sound and smell and taste, as well as those of touch and sight. This is not, however, the prevalent view, and we shall not discuss the matter here. Suffice it to say, that a colour sensation cannot exist at all without being experienced as possessing extensity. The same thing is true of pressure; and, in general, all sensations which *ever* possess the quality of extensity *always* possess it, just as they possess duration and intensity. The kinæsthetic sensations are admitted by all psychologists to belong, with pressure, temperature, and vision, to the spatial senses.

If we bring together the points we have gone over in discussing the quality, extensity, duration, and intensity of sensations, we shall see that quality is, in a definite sense, the most fundamental thing about a sensation, and that the other characteristics can fairly be regarded, for our psychological purposes, as subordinate attributes of quality. Thus, a given musical tone may last one second, or three, without essential change of the pitch, which is its quality, psychologically speaking. It may be louder, or softer, without changing its pitch. Furthermore, it may change its timbre, which seems to be a sort of secondary quality, by changing its overtones, and still retain its pitch, or primary quality, unaltered. Similarly, a sensation of red may come from an object one inch square, or from one two inches square, without noticeably changing the hue of the colour.

General Characteristic of the Sensation Quality.—The fundamental characteristic common to all the sensations is a certain something which they occasion in us, for which *shock* is possibly the most appropriate name. This characterises all *transitior* in consciousness, and especially consciousness of immediate sense activities.

Primary Function of Sensation.—A consideration of the sensory-motor circuit makes it evident that the primary organic function of the sensory element in consciousness must be that of instigating movements. Moreover, in Chapter III. we examined certain typical instances, in which we found sensation processes operating to produce movements, and then further operating to report the results of those movements, thus assisting in the establishment of useful coördinations. Although we shall be analysing in the next few chapters the details in the process of acquiring control over the movements which sensations thus bring about, it only remains, so far as concerns the *rudiments* of this process, to add one thing. When we say that sensory stimulation instigates movements, we must not make too sharp a distinction between the stimulation, as sensed, and the movement, when a response is made without deliberation. The nervous process is practically a *continuous* forward movement of impulses from the sense organs clear around to the muscles. There is nowhere any essential break in this feature of the activity. The *act* is literally a unit.

Similarly, if we examine the facts closely, we shall see that the sensory reaction is simply the registration in consciousness of a certain kind of act, and that it varies markedly with the kind of response that is executed by the muscles. What we should commonly call a *sensation* of a disagreeable odour consists not only in the consciousness of a certain kind of olfactory quality; it consists also in the consciousness of tendencies to movement, *e. g.*, choking movements in the throat, violent expiratory movements, movements of the head away from the source of the odour, etc. The sensation of the odour is instantly merged with other sensations which these movements call out, and is markedly modified by them. Furthermore, the kind of sensation which we get from an odour in the first instance will be definitely determined by the kind of movement in progress at the moment when we come into contact with the stimulus. If we are not expecting the odour, our breathing may be free and deep. In consequence, we obtain a deep inhalation of the noxious fumes, and from the blending of this impression with the ongoing mental activity, one kind of sensation results. If we are expecting the odour, or if our breathing happens momentarily to be superficial, the sensation is much modified and weakened. So we see that our consciousness of sensory stimuli is qualified on both sides by movements, *i. e.*, by those movements which lead up to it, and by those which follow it. The sensation-movement process is, therefore, essentially a continuous thing, and our analysis of it into parts is simply for the readier apprehension of its characteristics, and does not at all imply any such actual severance of the various stages of it.

Secondary Function of Sensation.—When our attention is called to the fact, we readily notice, as was intimated earlier in the chapter, that if our sense organs are stimulated, we are commonly made conscious of *objects*, rather than of mere *qualities*, such as we have been describing in this chapter. Thus, if our eyes are exposed to stimulations of light, we ordinarily see such things as people, or trees, or houses, and we do not think of such objects as being merely so much colour. We can, of course, note and recall the colours which belong to these objects, but as our eyes rest upon them we are certainly in adult life infrequently conscious of them as mere aggregates of colour qualities. Similarly, when we hear familiar words, it is very rare that the simple quality of the vocal sounds monopolises our attention. Instead of this, we are instantly absorbed in the *meaning* of the words. On the other hand, a single musical tone, an unfamiliar fragrance, a feeling of warmth, may enter our consciousness almost as pure qualities, to the objective character of which we are practically oblivious. Now, the difference between these two classes of experience marks the difference between sensation and the next of the cognitive processes which we shall study, *i. e.*, perception; and before we can understand satisfactorily the function of sensation, we must attempt to make the distinction clear.

Sensation and Perception.—In the previous chapter we remarked upon the manner in which attention succeeds by dissociation in breaking up the conscious continuum of infancy into distinguishable portions. The infant consciousness, so far as concerns its cognitive features, must be at the outset almost wholly a consciousness of the vague sensation kind, a consciousness of undifferentiated fusions of sensory qualities, plus pleasantness and unpleasantness, which are here temporarily disregarded. Little by little, through the discriminative and associative activities of attention, these qualities become disintegrated and attached to certain recurrent experiences. A visual quality becomes in this fashion extradited, and connected with a kinæsthetic quality from the movement of the hand and arm. Presently in this process the visual consciousness loses its former disconnected vagueness, and becomes an explicitly recognised sign, or symbol, of the hand movement, and, perhaps, of the further agreeable experiences connected with the allaying of hunger. In this way comes to pass the baby's consciousness of his bottle, as an *object* external to himself. The process is evidently one which involves the extrusion, from a vague mass of sensory consciousness, of the several fusions of sensations concerned; and then, the further process of *relating* these sensory groups to one another. Now, so far as we ever approximate the obtaining of a sense quality, severed in all respects, save that of time, from the rest of our consciousness, so far do we tend to become aware merely of quality; but the moment the *relating activity* becomes vitally operative, at that moment do we tend to lose the experience as a mere quality, and begin to give it *objective* character. Speaking in an absolutely literal way, this relating activity is of course never wholly absent; and consequently, save for the hypothetical first moment of consciousness, we are never able to get a really pure sensation. Sensation is in this sense, therefore, an abstraction, as we have already insisted. But, speaking relatively, such illustrations as those from which we started bring out the very striking differences in the degree to which we retain the primary ability to cognise mere quality, as distinguished from the tendency to react upon the sensory stimulations as objects.

James has hit off the point, in one of his happy inspirations, in saying that sensation gives us mere "acquaintance with objects," whereas perception gives us "knowledge about" them. As a matter of fact, it is clear that our sensory experiences which involve simply becoming acquainted with objects are few and far between. The all but universal reaction is one in which we place, or classify, or recognise, the stimulus in some way, thus relating it vitally to our past knowledge. It should be added, too, that this assignment of objective character to our sense experiences is especially prompt and convincing in those senses which most definitely contribute to our awareness of extension, resistance, and externality to the organism, *i. e.*, touch and vision.

Limitations of Sensation.—In general, we may say that the function of sensation is to furnish us with the elementary symbols of the various things in the world about us which stimulate our sensory-motor activities, *e. g.*, odours, colours, sounds, etc. Moreover, it must not be forgotten that, despite the elaborations which it undergoes, this sensuous raw material continues throughout our lives to furnish the body, the content, of all our sensory consciousness; and as our minds pass from one sense element to another, the fact is, as we have already observed, reported by a sort of delicate shock, which is therefore a factor common to all sensation processes. So far as a mere simple symbol is all we need, so far we tend to rest content with the mere awareness of the sensory quality; but there are many kinds of things with which we must come into daily contact for which such symbols are inadequate, because they do not reflect with sufficient accuracy and detail the complexity of the object or stimulus. Consciousness of odours occasionally approximates the condition of sensation, by rendering us aware of specific qualities which relate themselves only in the vaguest way to our past experience, and which we do not think of as objects. Such stimuli are for us essentially simple. But our visual consciousness of the external world is always more or less complex; it always involves more or less of different colours, each of which has its own qualities; and we must consequently become aware of a group of these sensory qualities experienced simultaneously. Such fusions of sensation elements, with their wealth of suggested reactions and relations, we think of as objects.

Similarly, if a very small point be brought in contact with the skin we feel what we call a sensation of touch; and such a sensation, if very light, may fail to suggest definitely any object whatsoever. But if a large area is stimulated by contact we instantly recognise such a complex of sensory qualities as being an *object*, whose nature we generally appreciate with some accuracy. The consciousness of relatively isolated simple qualities is, accordingly, when produced by stimulating the sense organ, what we mean by primary, or peripherally aroused, sensation. When the qualities cease to be simple, and take on definite relations to one another, and to us, especially that of externality, we have the consciousness of objects, which is commonly called perception. Clearly, then, sensation as the consciousness of isolated qualities is a product of mature abstraction. Sensation, as giving the qualitative determinant to all sensory experience, is not only the first stage in the perceptual process, furnishing the vague undifferentiated matrix out of which the richness of qualitative variety is later extradited by analysis, but it is also the constant accompaniment of sensory activities, giving the stuff, the material, out of which perception is elaborated. To a fuller account of the perceptual stage in the cognitive function we must next proceed.

CHAPTER VI

PERCEPTION

Definition of Perception.—Perception has sometimes been defined as "the consciousness of particular material things present to sense." Perception is as a matter of fact always a larger thing than this definition would immediately imply; because we are always aware in the "fringe," in the background of consciousness, of sense activities other than those we speak of as being perceived, especially those connected with the internal operations of our own organism. Perception as psychologists describe it, is therefore, like sensation, something of an abstraction.*

Our definition, however, marks off perception from sensation in its emphasis upon the consciousness of *objects*, or things. Sensation, as we saw in the last chapter, is more appropriately conceived as concerned with the consciousness of qualities. The two processes have this in common, that both are produced by the stimulation of a sense organ. This circumstance serves to mark both of them off from such mental conditions as memory and imagination, in which our consciousness may equally well be engaged with objects. Nevertheless, as we shall see more fully in later chapters, the sen-

*It will be seen from this definition that the psychologist uses the term *perception* in a somewhat narrower sense than that recognised in ordinary usage. We speak in common parlance of perceiving the meaning of a theory, when we refer to our appreciation, or apprehension, of it. In such cases we may be engaged in reflection upon the theory, and our thought may thus be quite independent of any immediate stimulation of sense organs.

suous material of perception and imagination and memory is qualitatively one and the same. Visual mental stuff, for example, whether perceptually or ideationally produced, is *sui generis*, and totally unlike any other kind of mental stuff, such as auditory or olfactory.

It will be seen that the distinction mentioned between the perceptual consciousness of objects and such consciousness of them as we may have in memory and imagination rests upon a physiological basis, *i. e.*, the presence or absence of sense organ activity. The only difference on the *mental* side is commonly to be found in the intensity and objectivity of the two. Perceptions are commonly more intense, and feel more as though *given* to us, than do our memories or imaginings. In hallucination, however, it seems as though mere mental images assumed the vividness and externality of percepts; and in the case of very faint stimulations, *e. g.*, of sound or colour, we cannot always be confident whether we have really perceived something, or merely imagined it. This principle of distinguishing the two is, therefore, not always to be depended upon. Fortunately for our practical interests, the distinction is generally valid and we do not often confuse what we really perceive with what we imagine.

We pointed out the fact in the last chapter that, save for the earliest experiences of infancy, sensation, as a total mental state distinguishable from perception, probably does not occur. The great masses of our sensory experiences are, accordingly, perceptions, and it obviously behooves us to examine them with care.

Analysis of Perception.—We may evidently have perceptions which originate from the stimulation of any sense organ, and we might select an example from any sense department for analysis. Because of their importance for everyday life we may, however, profitably choose a case from visual perceptions for our examination. Let us take the instance of our perception of a chair. When our eyes fall upon such an object we instantly react to it as a *single* object. Although the chair has four legs and a seat, we do not see each of the legs as separate things, and then somehow put them together with the seat, and so *mentally manufacture* a chair for ourselves. On the contrary, our immediate response is the consciousness of a single object. We know of course that the chair possesses these various parts, just as we know that it has various colours, and in a sense we notice these features when we perceive it. But the striking thing is, that despite the great number of sensory nerves which are being stimulated by such an object, we perceive it, not as an aggregate of qualities $a+b+c$, but as a *unit*, a whole, which we can, if necessary, analyse into its parts. The same thing is true as to our perception of words. We naturally see them, not as so many separate letters, but as wholes, or at most as groups of syllables; a fact which modern education wisely takes advantage of in teaching children to recognise *entire words* at a glance.

Evidently this is another phase of the fact which we noted at the time we were studying attention, when we remarked the selective and synthesising nature of attention in its operation upon sensory stimuli. We also came across the same fact in our description of the action of the cortex of the cerebrum. We observed there, that the cortex has its activity determined, now from this sensory source, and now from that, but the response is always of a unifying, synthesising character. This seems to be the reason, too, that our perceptions are so regularly definite, instead of vague, as they apparently might be. The cortical reaction tends toward the systematised orderly form. We note first, then, in our analysis of visual perception, that we commonly perceive objects as single and distinct, not as vague, confused, and aggregated compounds.

If we describe for ourselves just what we perceive in such a case, we should add to our consciousness of the colour of the chair our sense of its size and its shape. We say, for example, that the seat is square, that it looks square. Now it requires only a moment's reflection to convince us that, as we stand at a little distance from the chair, the image of its seat, which is reflected upon the retina, is not square at all, but is a kind of rhomboid, with two acute and two obtuse angles. We become more clearly aware of this fact when we attempt to draw the chair as it appears. We are obliged under these conditions to draw just such a rhomboid as the seat presents to the eye. If we draw a *real* square on the paper, we cannot make it serve acceptably for a chair seat, seen as we now see the chair of our illustration, which is supposed to be at a little distance from us.

Now, how does it come about that we can perceive a rhomboid as a square, which is what we unquestionably do in this case? The reply contains the secret of the fundamental fact about all perceptions. We see it as a square, because we see it, not as it actually is to our vision at this moment, but as our past experience has taught us it must be. Were it not for the influence of this past experience, this *habitual* reaction upon objects like the present chair seat, undoubtedly we should not see it as square. The same thing is true as regards our perception of the height and size of the chair, and the material of its construction. Had we no previous experiences that resembled the present one, we should be hopelessly uncertain as to the element of size. To judge of this with any accuracy we must, to mention only a single circumstance, know with considerable exactness the distance of the chair from us; for the nearer an object is, the larger our visual image of it. Experience has taught us the common size of chairs and tables, and has taught us to allow correctly for the effects of distance, etc. We come at once, then, upon this striking fact, that in some manner or other perception involves a rudimentary *reproductive* process. Somehow, our former perceptions are taken up and incorporated into our present perceptions, modifying them and moulding them into accord with the past.

Moreover, if we interrogate our consciousness carefully, we shall find that in visual perceptions we often, perhaps generally, get an immediate impression of the contact values of the seen object. We get instantly something of the cool-smooth-feeling when we look upon highly polished marble. Velvet seen near at hand gives us similarly a feeling of softness. It is not simply that we know the marble to be cool and smooth, or the velvet to be soft. That would be merely a matter of associating certain ideas with the percept. We mean to designate a phase of the actual perceptual synthesis. Certain bizarre forms of a similar process, known as synæsthesia, illustrate the point. For example, certain persons when they hear music always experience colour sensations accompanying it. We may regard it as certain, therefore, that sensory stimuli affecting only *one* sense organ *may* set up perceptual reactions involving directly more than one sensory area in the cortex, so that the percept resulting may be regarded as a coalescence of several different sense qualities.

Auditory perceptions show just the same influence of experience as do the visual perceptions which we have analysed. When we first hear a foreign language spoken, it is a mere babel of sounds. Presently, as we come to learn the language, the sounds become words with meanings intelligible to us, and our perception of what we hear thus manifests, as in the case of vision, unmistakable dependence upon our past experience. So also with touch. We learn that certain kinds of contact experiences mean door-knobs, or pencils, or books, etc. We might run through the whole list of sense organs and find the same thing true in varying degree.

We may conclude then, that a second important factor in perceptual processes, in addition to the tendency to perceive objects as definite wholes, is the striking combination of the present with the past, of novelty with familarity. Were it not for the fact that the perceived object connects itself in some way with our foregoing experience, it would be entirely meaningless and strange to us. This is the way the words of an unknown language impress us when we hear them. On the other hand, the perceived thing is in some particulars different from these previous experiences, otherwise we could not distinguish the past from the present. Perception is, then, evidently a synthetic experience, and the combination of the new and the old is the essential part of the synthesis. This process of combining the new and the old is often called apperception. In perception, therefore, the raw material supplied by the several senses is taken up into the psychophysical organism, and there, under the process of apperception, given form and meaning by its vital and significant union with the old psychophysical activities. Material taken up in this way becomes as truly a part of the organism as does the food which enters the alimentary tract.

Genesis of Perception.—It is evident from the facts we have examined in the immediately preceding paragraphs, that the development of perception depends upon the degree to which our past experience enters into the results of each new sensory excitation. In the discussion of habit and of attention, we observed that attention undoubtedly does make itself felt, first in *splitting up* the undifferentiated, vague continuum of consciousness into parts; then in connecting these parts with one another; and finally in endowing the organism with habits whereby it may the more promptly and efficiently cope with the conditions it has to meet. Clearly, a fully developed perception is itself simply a kind of habit. That I should be able, when looking at a plane surface limited by four lines making two acute and two obtuse angles, to *see* a square table-top is only explicable by remarking that this perception has been acquired just as most other habits have been, *i. e.*, slowly and by dint of many repetitions.

So far as we can determine, experience begins to operate

upon our sensory excitations at the very outset of life, and the process of perception accordingly begins, but in a very rudimentary manner, immediately after the hypothetical "first moment" of sensation which we described in the previous chapter. Nevertheless, we must suppose that for many weeks the perceptual process is on a very low level of advancement. In the first place, as we pointed out, a perception involves our having some knowledge, however simple, *about* the object. But such knowledge about objects depends upon our ability to connect *various* sensory experiences with the *same* object, and this in turn depends largely upon our ability to control our movements. We mentioned in an earlier chapter that such control is a relatively late acquirement, and accordingly our perceptual processes get no available opportunity for development in early infancy. An illustration will make this clearer.

Let us take the possible course of events involved in a baby's acquiring the perception of a bell. Obviously the visual factors involved cannot be satisfactorily employed, until some control has been attained over the eye muscles, so that the child's eyes are able to converge and follow an object. This attainment is commonly achieved about the third or fourth week of life, although there is great variation here. If the child never touched the bell and never heard it, he might still learn to recognise it when he saw it, as something he had seen before; but he evidently would have no such perception of it as you and I have. As a matter of fact, the bell will be put into his hand, and during the random movements of the hand his eye will sometimes fall upon it. The occasional repetition of this experience will soon serve to fix the association of the touch-hand-movement feelings with the visual consciousness of the bell, so that the thing seen will inevitably suggest the thing felt and moved, and vice versa. Moreover, all the time this has been going on there have been sensory stimulations of sound from the bell. This group of elements, therefore, becomes annexed to the rest of the group, and straightway we have the rudiments of the process by which, when we see or touch or hear a certain kind of object, we promptly perceive it as a bell, *i. e.*, as a something to which a certain total mass of familiar experience belongs.

Such a case as this is typical, and despite certain omissions of detail, may serve to represent the kind of activities which always accompany the acquiring of perceptions. It will be remembered that we connected the perceptual process with the establishment of relations. In the case which we have used for our illustration these relations show clearly in the connecting of one group of sensory experiences with another. The auditory group comes to *mean* the eye group, and both of these come to mean the hand-movement group. Moreover, the definite establishment of these relations is practically dependent upon the motor factors by which the hand and eye come to control the object. When such relations as these are once set up, we have a definite perception of an object *about* which we know something, *i. e.*, that it is an object from which we can get certain kinds of familiar experiences.

It will be seen at once that in this series of events by which the perception becomes definite, the several steps involved are brought about on the strictly mental side by the action of attention, which we have previously sketched. First, there is the dissociative process, throwing out into the foreground of consciousness the visual characteristics of the bell, as distinguished from other things in the visual field. This is followed by the associative, or relating process, which connects this visual bell with the auditory and tactual-motor experiences. It remains, then, to inquire what further development takes place after the accomplishment of this synthesis of the different sensory activities of sound, sight, and touch into the consciousness of a single object.

Development of Perception.—We spoke of fully developed perceptions a moment ago as habits. If this metaphor were entirely appropriate, it might seem that perceptions would come to a certain point of development and then stop. Clearly, our reference to habit was in one particular misleading. Our most perfect habits are all but unconscious. A perception, on the other hand, is distinctly a *conscious* process. The truth of our statement lies in this fact, *i. e.*, that just in the degree in which our necessities permit us to perceive and react upon objects in *literally* the same manner, time after time, do we tend to become unconscious of them and to react to them in accordance with the principle of mere habit. We thus become almost wholly oblivious to the exact appearance of a doorknob which we have occasion to turn very often. Our eyes may rest upon it momentarily, but only long enough to guide the hand in its movement, and often without registering any visual impression of which we could immediately afterward give an exact account. There are also certain features of the neural process in perception which warrant our comparison with habit, and to these we shall come in a moment. The great mass of our perceptions, however, are of objects whose relations to us change sufficiently from time to time to make any complete subsidence of our consciousness of them incompatible with their effective manipulation; consequently we continue to be definitely aware of them.

The development of perception, which goes on in a certain sense more or less all our lives, and in a very definite sense up to the period of mental maturity, is plainly not a development involving simply a more automatic response to objects. Quite the contrary. The process which we commonly think of as growth in the powers of perception consists in the further elaboration of the discriminative and associative activities of attention. We learn to see new things in the old objects, new charactertistics, which before escaped our knowledge. We also learn more about the objects, and thus, when we perceive them, perceive them in a modified and more intelligent way. Speaking literally, it therefore appears that development in perception really involves perceiving *new objects* in the old.

A moment's reflection will show the similarity of this fact to one which we noted when analysing attention, *i. e.*, that to continue our attention to an object for more than a moment we must notice something new about it, see it in a new way. We might of course substitute the word perception for the word attention, inasmuch as attention is an attribute of all consciousness, and then the proposition would read: we cannot continue to *perceive an object* beyond a moment or two, unless we perceive it in a new manner. Perceptions which we do not execute in a new way we have already seen do actually tend to lapse from consciousness, passing over into habits of response which we make to certain physical stimuli.

When a child is taught to observe the arrangement of the petals in a flower, he thenceforth perceives the flower in a new way. To him it really is a new object. All development in perception is of this kind, and constitutes a sort of transformation by the unfolding of the old object into the new and richer one. The larger part of this perceptual development occurs during childhood and adolescence. Nevertheless, there is a continuation of the process in an inconspicuous way far into old age. Thus, we come in childhood to recognise the salient characteristics of the common things about us in every day life. During adolescence we enrich this material by observing more accurately the details of these things, and by increasing our knowledge of their general purport and relations. After attaining maturity our further advance is almost wholly connected with the affairs of our professional, or business, life. The musician becomes more sensitive to the niceties of harmonic accord and the nuances of melodic sequence. The business man becomes more observant of the things which pass under his eye, so far as they are related to his specialty. The elementary school teacher learns how to keep the corner of her eye sensitive to iniquity upon the back seat while apparently absorbed in listening to the recitation of virtue upon the front bench. The mother learns to watch her children with an increasingly intelligent discrimination between acts which indicate illness and those which indicate fatigue, excitement, and transitory irritation. Everywhere development is primarily shown by fresh skill in the detection of new features in old things.

Illusions.—Certain instances of illusion furnish a striking confirmation of the general idea of perception which we have been explaining. An illusion is a false, or erroneous, perception, which is often spoken of as a deception of the senses. But this is misleading, as we shall presently see, for the senses ordinarily operate properly enough. The difficulty is with our reaction upon the sensory material furnished to us. Among the most frequent of such illusions is the misreading of printed words. We sometimes read the words put before us as we have reason to suppose they ought to be, not as they are. Thus, if we come across the word mispirnt, many of us will read it in all good faith as misprint and never see the difference. We react to the general visual impression and its suggestion, and see what really is not before us. If the sentence in which the word occurs is such as to give us a definite anticipation of the word, the probability of our overlooking the typographical error is much increased. Similarly when we come into a darkened room where sits a spectral form—an experience which as children most of us have had— we see a person with startling clearness; and the subsequent discovery, that the supposed person consists of clothing hanging upon a chair, is hard to accept as true. Illusions of sound are very common. We fancy we hear our names called, when in point of fact the sound we thus interpret may have been anything from a summons to some other person of similar name, to the barking of a dog, or the whistle of a locomotive. Tactual illusions are also easy to produce. The so-called "illusion of Aristotle" is a good specimen. (Figure

PERCEPTION

50.) Children often achieve it by crossing the first and second fingers, and then moving to and fro upon the bridge of the nose with the crotch thus formed between the fingers. Presently one becomes distressingly impressed with the fact that one possesses two noses.

This last instance is typical of many illusions, in that it is caused by stimulating with a single object the sides of the two fingers which are not ordinarily in contact with one another, and for the stimulation of which, accordingly, two objects are commonly necessary. We react in the familiar, the habitual, way to the simultaneous stimulation of these areas of the skin. This has invariably been accomplished hitherto by the pressure of two objects, and two objects we therefore feel. It is clear that in such a case the sense organ is in no way at fault. It sends in the impulses communicated to it just as it has always done before; but the reaction which we make upon the impression also follows the usual course, and in this special case happens consequently to be wrong. The same explanation applies to our reading of incorrectly spelled words. Many illusions of movement, *e. g.*, such as we obtain in railroad trains, are of this character. The same general principle holds, but applied in a slightly different manner, when we see, or hear, or otherwise perceive, some object not actually present, because we are expecting to perceive it. Thus, if we are listening for expected footsteps, we find ourselves time after time interpreting other sounds as those of the awaited step. At night the nervous housewife wakens to hear the burglars passing from room to room along the corridor. Step follows step in stealthy but unmistakable rhythm, though the whole impression has no other objective basis than the occasional cracking of floors

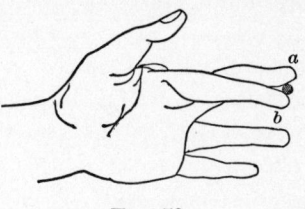

FIG. 50.

and partitions, phenomena which are the constant accompaniments of changing temperature. There are many kinds of illusions, be it said, which do not come immediately under the headings we have discussed. For example, such illusions as that in figure 51 are much too complex in their basis to be properly included, without modification, under the explanatory rubrics we have considered.

It is clear that a consideration of illusion affords new and striking confirmation of the part played in perception by previous experience. The cortical reaction suggested by the

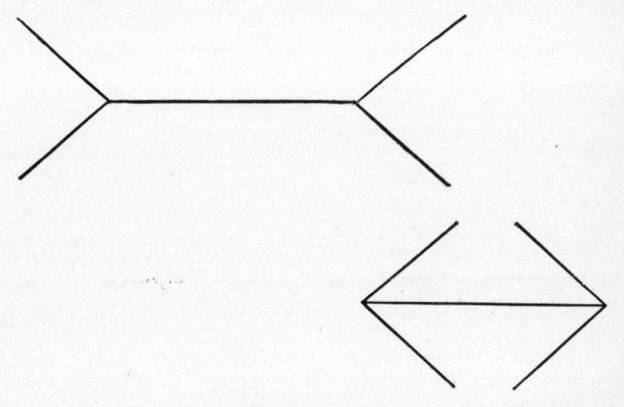

FIG. 51. Despite their contrary appearance, the two horizontal lines will be found of equal length.

stimulus does not happen to correspond to the object actually present. But this cortical reaction is evidently determined by the impress of old perceptual experiences whose traces have been preserved. The same point is admirably illustrated by such drawings as the accompanying, figures 52 and 53. We can see the stairs, either as they appear from above, or from below. In one case the surface a seems nearer to us; in the other case b seems nearer. We can see in the other figure a big picture frame, the frustrum of a pyramid, or the entrance to a square tunnel. Yet one and the same object is presented to the retina in each case. The eye can

PERCEPTION 135

hardly be accused of responsibility for the shifting results. But lines like these have actually been connected in our former perceptions with the several objects named, and in consequence the cortical reaction appropriate to either of them *may* be called out. It would seem abundantly certain, therefore, that while a portion of what we perceive is always supplied from without, another portion, and often the dominant portion, is supplied from within ourselves.

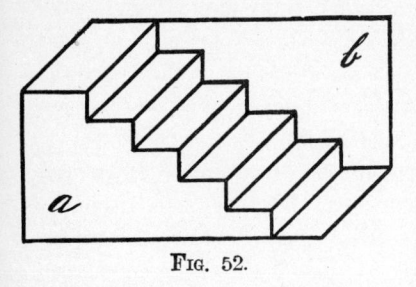

FIG. 52.

Hallucination.—In distinction from illusion, which is essentially perception, (*i. e.*, a consciousness of particular material things present to sense—though other things than those really perceived happen to be present), hallucination is the name given to the consciousness of objects felt to be physically present, when as a matter of fact no object of any kind is at hand. Illusions are every day experiences familiar to all of us. Hallucinations, while by no means infrequent, are much less common and consequently more difficult to describe satisfactorily. Many of the alleged telepathic phenomena involve hallucinations. Thus, for instance, one is sitting alone in a room and suddenly sees another person, known to be thousands of miles distant, come in and sit down. Again, when alone in the same way, one suddenly hears some sentence clearly spoken. In neither case, needless to say, is anyone actually present, save the owner of the hallucination; and

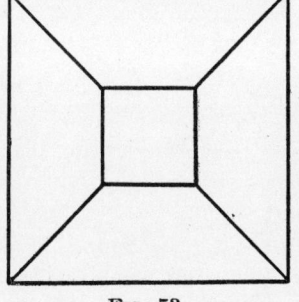

FIG. 53.

there are no obvious external phenomena which could be held accountable for the experience. All the senses seem to be represented from time to time in the hallucinatory perceptions, although hearing and vision are, perhaps, the ones most frequently involved.

An interesting distinction has been made between true hallucination and what is called pseudo-hallucination. In the first case the perceived object not only seems external and real, but there is in the mind of the person experiencing the hallucination no suspicion at the time that the object seen, or heard, is not actually real and present. In the second form there is a sort of background consciousness, such as we sometimes note in dreams, which assures the victim that the phenomenon is after all imaginary and unreal, despite its genuinely objective appearance.

It has been suggested that hallucinations are really extreme forms of illusions, extreme cases of misinterpretation of sensory stimuli, resting upon highly disintegrated cortical forms of reaction. The sensory source of the stimulation has been sought at times in pathological conditions of the sense organs, *e. g.*, congestion of circulation in the eye, or ear, etc.

There are many facts which tend to confirm this view, which is advocated by certain of the most competent judges; and some others which are very difficult of reconciliation with it. A discussion of the point at issue would take us too far afield for present purposes, and readers who are interested in such matters must consult some of the more extended and specialised treatises. Meantime, we must admit that unless this last suggestion is correct, hallucination furnishes an exception to the general rule that cortically initiated conscious processes are less vivid and less definitely externalised than those which originate in sense organs. If hallucination is not peripherally initiated, it belongs to the group of phenomena which we shall examine in the chapter upon imagination, and we may defer further discussion of it until we reach that point.

Neural Process in Perception.—The nervous pathways involved in perception are probably identical with those which we have described in connection with sensation processes. In vision, for example, the occipital regions in the cortex are unquestionably employed, in cases of auditory perception the temporal region is active, etc. But there is this highly important fact to be taken more explicitly into account, *i. e.*, that in perception the cortical activity, which is in part decided by the *kind* of neural stimulus sent into it, is in large measure determined by the *modifications* which *previous experiences* have impressed upon the structure of the hemispheres. Evidently this is but a statement in physiological terms of the doctrine which we have already enunciated in psychological form. As we observed in our discussion of habit, every nervous current which passes through the central system seems to leave its impress behind it, and this impress modifies the nature of the neural excitations which follow it. The case of perception is, accordingly, only a special instance of this general principle, albeit a peculiarly important and conspicuous one. It is on this account, *i. e.*, because of the fundamental importance of the accumulating modifications of the cortex, that we compared perception, earlier in the chapter, to the case of habit. From the side of neural action, therefore, perception cannot be referred simply to the employment of a certain pathway throughout the sensory-motor tracts; it must be referred to a certain *kind* of action, in which the result in consciousness appears to be a product of two neural factors—sensory stimulus into cortex modified by previous experience.

General Function of Perception.—In order to give perceptual processes their proper setting among the psychophysical activities of adjustment, we must revert once again to our notion of the sensory-motor circuit. We have already observed that in this device the sense organs represent so many telephonic receivers ready to transmit inward messages from the external world to the organism. We have also described in a general way the method by which certain kinds of motor reactions to these sensory stimulations are brought to pass. But in the higher brain centres the pathways connecting sense organs with muscles are often extremely complex, and a stimulus transmitted inward by the afferent nerves may lead to innumerable intermediary brain activities before it issues again in movements of the voluntary muscles. Now perception is the conscious concomitant of certain of these brain processes. Memory, imagination, reasoning, etc., are others. Bearing these facts in mind, and observing closely what actually occurs when we are engaged in perceiving objects, we readily detect the main function of perception.

Perception represents the direct, organised, and systematised *internal* reaction of the individual upon his environment. The process is sometimes called presentation, and this is a good name for it. In it the world is presented as a system of relations—not merely reflected as a disorganised mass of atoms and molecules, but constructed by the various activities of attention into definite objects. If sensation is properly described, after a common fashion, as the process in which the mind and the world of matter first come together, perception may be described as the point in which the past and the present come together for the creation of a new object. The perceived thing is not simply the physically present vibrations of atoms and molecules which we call light, or sound, or what not; it is these vibrations, as they are *interpreted* by a psychophysical organism which exposes to them a nervous system already affected by past experiences, that enable it to get only certain specific kinds of results from the present synthesis. Evidently we make far more constant use of our past experience than common-sense observation would lead us to suppose. It is not only when we reflect upon our past life that we shape our action in accordance with its instructions and admonitions; every time we open our eyes to see, or our ears to hear, what *we can* see and hear is in a true sense and in large measure determined for us by what we have *previously learned* to see and hear. It is a moralistic truism that only the good can really love and appreciate virtue. But this principle is not simply, nor primarily, a moral tenet. It is based on irrefutable and unavoidable psychological foundations. It states a law of the mind which we might wish at times to change, but cannot. We can only perceive those things which our experience allows us to perceive. The things may be there before us in all their beauty and purity. But we cannot see them if our minds have been wholly unschooled in such perceptions. The first and basic function of perception, then, is to afford us our primary knowledge of a world of objects amid which we have to live. It is the first actual, definite, and complete step in the process of knowledge whose further and more complex features we have next to examine.

The second great function of perception grows out of the first. Indeed, it might be regarded as in a measure simply a corrolary of the first. All the sensory and afferent processes have their ultimate value, as we saw must be the case in Chapter II., because of the more efficient movements of adjustment to which they lead. Perception is no exception to this rule. Now in order that sensory stimulations may not lead *at once* to motor responses, but may be interpreted and correlated with other sensory impulses, it is evidently necessary that there should be some provision for halting them momentarily, and identifying them, when they come again and again. Perception is the process by which this identification is made possible; and so it comes to pass that perception is the first, both logically and genetically, of the conscious operations by which the life of control is inaugurated.

We have repeatedly seen that perception involves immediately within itself the effects of antecedent experience, and a secondary result of this complication with memory processes is that when we perceive an object which is in any way familiar we instantly *recognise* it. If the object thus recognised be one about which our previous experience is unambiguous, we respond almost instantly with appropriate movements—those of aversion, if it be repulsive or harmful, those of approbation, when the contrary sentiments are aroused. If the object have no such definite antecedent reactions connected with it, we straightway fall to deliberating as to our course of action; or if the impression be wholly fleeting, we pass to some more stimulating enticement.

Perception is thus the gateway through which the mass of sensory excitations (save those already grown purely habitual) must pass before they can be permitted to set up motor responses of the volitional kind. Often the perceptual activity is sufficient to decide this volition. The clock strikes and we rise to leave the room. When mere perception is not felt to be adequate to the case, the matter is handed over to reflective deliberation. In either event, voluntary response is safeguarded. The formation of the elements of the process of knowledge and the inauguration of the control over movements in accordance with the mandates of experience—these are the two great functions of perception. This statement applies without modification to the special phases of perception, to which we shall next advert.

CHAPTER VII

PERCEPTION OF SPATIAL AND TEMPORAL RELATIONS

I. SPACE

The objects which we have mentioned in our analysis of sensory consciousness are all objects perceived by us as parts of a spatial and temporal order; and it is evident that our account of them would be extremely defective if we altogether omitted a study of these time and space relations. We shall consider space first.

Two Fundamental Problems.—Psychologists are divided in opinion upon two fundamental problems concerning our space perceptions. It is maintained in the first place by some of them, the nativists, that space perception is primarily an innate hereditary attainment possessed by us in a rude form prior to, and independent of, all experience. Others, the empiricists, maintain that spatial judgments are as much the results of experience, are as truly acquired, as piano playing or the liking for caviar. We shall not discuss the question, for this would require more time than we can give it. But we may register the dogmatic opinion that both parties to the controversy are in a measure correct. We hold that the crude, vague feeling of extension, of volume, is a genuinely innate experience, unlike any other experience, and underived by mere experience from non-spatial psychical elements. So far we are nativists. On the other hand, we are confident that all accurate knowledge of the meaning of the space relations in our space world, all practically precise perception of direction, position, contour, size, etc., is a result of experience, and could never be gained without it. So far we are empiricists, holding to a *genetic* point of view regarding the development of our adult space consciousness. The analyses and discussions which follow will serve to furnish some of the evidence upon which this view rests.

Sensory Basis of Spatial Perception.—The second main point upon which psychologists are unable to agree concerns the sensory sources from which we gain our spatial judgments, a matter to which we made cursory reference in Chapter V. The majority of psychologists maintain that vision and touch are the only real avenues of spatial perception; whereas certain others, like James, boldly maintain that all forms of sensory consciousness are " voluminous,"—smell and taste and audition, as well as sight and touch. The doctrine maintained in this book is that all forms of sensations are immediately *suggestive* of spatial attributes, *e. g.*, position, size, distance, etc.; but that only sight and touch possess intrinsically and completely the full spatial characteristics. We include in touch, when thus mentioned, all the cutaneous sensations and the motor, or kinæsthetic, sensations. As a matter of fact, however, the temperature and pain sensations, considered apart from pressure and sensations of movement, are ordinarily negligible elements. When involved in conjunction with pressure, they often modify our perceptions materially.

Doubtful Cases.—Taste and smell and hearing are really the debatable sensations. Taste we throw out of court at once, because taste stimuli practically involve invariably the stimulation of cutaneous sensations of contact and temperature. We cannot, therefore, submit the matter to unambiguous introspective analysis. Smells we undoubtedly classify at times in ways suggesting spatial attributes. The smell of illuminating gas seems somehow a more massive, extensive sort of thing than the odour of lemon peel. But if one lessens the disparity in the *intensity* of the two odours, by getting just the merest whiff of the gas and inhaling freely and deeply of the lemon odour, the spatial difference between the two begins to evaporate. There can be no question but that we tend to think of the more intense and more widely diffused odour as the larger. Nor is this remarkable, since we find it actually occupying more of the atmospheric space about us. But when we note that with mild intensities of odours their spatial suggestiveness wanes; when we further note that we have no definite impressions of size, much less of shape, under any conditions; and finally when we remark that even our ability to localise odours is extremely imperfect, we may well question whether smell has itself any properly space quality.

The case of auditory space is similar to that of smell. We are told, for instance, that the tones of the lowest organ pipes are far larger, far more voluminous, than those of the high shrill pipes. A base drum sounds bigger than a pennywhistle, a lion's roar than the squeaking of a mouse, etc. Such illustrations, when adduced as evidence of the spatial character of sounds, evidently contain three possible sources of error. In the first place, we often *know* something about the causes of these sounds, and we tend to transfer the known size of the producing object to the supposed size of the sound. Secondly, and of far more consequence, sounds affect other organs than those of the internal ear, especially when they are loud or of deep pitch. Powerful tones thus jar the whole body, and are felt all over. Moreover, vibrations of the drum membrane of the middle-ear undoubtedly set up crude sensations of pressure, or strain, to which we may come to attach a spatial significance associated with the sound. Add to this, thirdly, the fact that we readily convert judgments based upon the intensity of sounds into judgments about their extensity, just as in the case of smell, and one has a large mass of considerations leading to scepticism concerning the genuineness of intrinsic auditory space relations. Of course, no one doubts that we localise sounds, and of the factors involved in this process we shall have more to say presently. But the fact that certain sounds are located within the head (*e. g.*, when two telephone receivers are placed against the ears and an induction shock sent through them) has been cited to prove the native possession of a true auditory space; for here apparently experience from the other senses, such as vision, would give no direct assistance. But these cases are certainly capable of explanation by means of the intra-cranial sensations set up in pressure nerves by bone vibrations, and by the effect of the imagination, visual and otherwise. Taken alone, such evidence could hardly be conclusive. If we come back, then, to ordinary introspection, we find that all which the most ardent partisans of an auditory space can claim is a much emaciated form of the visual and tactual article. A vague sense of volume, or mass, much vaguer even than that given by mere temperature, with some crude sense of position, would seem to be the utmost capacity. Any sense of contour or shape or exact size, any ability to measure, is lacking. Clearly such a space, even if genuine, which we doubt, would ill deserve to be ranked beside the space of sight and touch. The manner in which we localise sound may best be described after we have analysed visual and tactual space.

Growth of Space Perception.—Our adult cognition of space relations is generally so immediate and unreflective, the feeling for space values so compelling and seemingly inevitable, that we find it difficult to believe that these reactions are the results of a slow process of growth and learning. Nevertheless, this is unquestionably the fact. Babies evidently have no precise perceptions of space until they have acquired a considerable degree of motor control; and even then their appreciation of large expanses and distances is often ludicrously inexact. The child reaching in good faith for the moon is the stock illustration of this sort of thing.

That we have no precise appreciation of visual space relations until experience has brought it to us is abundantly proven by the cases of persons born blind and successfully operated upon for the restoration of sight. Immediately after the operation such persons are almost wholly at a loss for impressions of size, shape, or distance. After the hands have explored the objects seen, and the eyes have been allowed to pass freely to and fro over them, these spatial impressions gradually begin to emerge and take on definiteness. By the use of properly arranged lenses and prisms experiments of various kinds have been made on normal persons, showing that we can speedily accommodate ourselves to the most unusual inversions and distortions of our visual space. We can thus learn to react properly, although all the objects, as we see them, are upside down and turned about as regards their right and left relations. The new relations soon come to have the natural feeling of ordinary perceptions.

These observations show very strikingly that there is nothing rigidly fixed and innate about the form of our space perceiving; that it is a function of experience and can be changed by changing the conditions of the experience. Moreover, it is easy to demonstrate that the space relations, as we perceive them by different senses, are far from homogeneous. Indeed, the impressions which we gain from the same sense are often far from being in agreement. Nevertheless, we feel our space relations to be objectively homogeneous, a result which could hardly come about under such circumstances of sensory disparity without the harmonising effects of experience. To illustrate—the edge of a card pressed gently upon the forearm will feel to the skin shorter than it looks. The same card, if the finger tip is allowed to run slowly along it, will feel longer than it looks. The disappointing disparity between the cavity of a tooth, as it feels to the tongue and appears to the eye, or feels to the finger-tip, is a notorious instance of the same thing. The tongue and the finger-tip both give us *pressure* sensations. Yet they give a very different report of the same object. Similarly, objects seen upon the periphery of the retina appear smaller than when seen by the fovea; and often they undergo a certain distortion in form. That we should perceive, amid all these possible sources of confusion, a fairly stable and well-ordered space world betokens unmistakably the systematising effects of experience, controlled no doubt by the exigencies of our practical interests in effective orientation.

Part Played by Movement.—Even though we recognise the fact that experience brings order and precision and effectiveness into our space perceptions, the general manner by which these results are achieved is not yet clear; much less what factors are chiefly employed in their attainment. It requires only the most cursory examination to convince oneself that the all-important element in the building up and correlating with one another of our various spatial sensations is *movement*. In acquiring accurate touch perceptions, for instance, the finger-tips and hands move over the object, grasp it now in this way and now in that, until a complex set of tactual impressions has been gained from it. Without such movement our touch perceptions are vague in the extreme. If we close our eyes and allow another person to put a series of small objects upon our outstretched hands we receive only the most indefinite impressions of form and size and texture. But allow us to manipulate the same objects in our fingers, and we can give a highly accurate account of them. Similarly, if we wish to compare visually the magnitude and contours of two objects we must allow our eyes to move freely from one to the other. Indeed, reflection must assure us that the *vital meaning* of all space relations is simply a given amount and direction of movement. To pass toward the right means to make a certain kind of movement; to pass upward means to make another kind, etc. To be sure, we assign arbitrary measures to these relations, and we say an object is a *mile* away, or is a *foot* thick and six *inches* high. But the meaning to us of the mile, the foot, and the inch must always remain ultimately expressible in movement.

Were it possible to get at the exact stages in the process by which the child acquires its control over space relations, we should thus secure the most penetrating possible insight into our adult space perceptions. But as this is at present impracticable, we must content ourselves with an analysis of the factors which seem clearly involved in these adult conditions, without regard to their genetic features.

Touch and Vision.—It is certain that touch and vision practically coöperate from the beginning, and we shall isolate them from one another only to point out their respective peculiarities, and not because their operation is independent. The most important, and for practical purposes the most accurate, part of our touch perceptions comes from the hands and finger-tips. By moving the hands over the various parts of the body we come to have a fairly accurate notion of their touch characteristics in terms of the hand as a standard. Moreover, each hand touches the other, and we thus get a kind of check from touch on the tactual standard itself. Generally speaking, when two parts of our body touch each other we *feel* the *one* which is quiet with the one which is moving. Thus, if we stroke the forehead with the fingers we feel the forehead; but if we hold the hand steady and move the head, we feel the fingers. Now in order that we should be able to learn in these ways that a certain amount of sensation in the finger-tips *means* a certain area on the forehead, and, much more, that we should be able to tell with so much accuracy when we are touched what part of the body the sensation comes from, seems to depend upon what Lotze calls the "local sign."

Local Signs.—If one is touched upon the palm and upon the back of the hand, one obtains from both stimulations sensations of pressure; but however much alike they may be as regards duration, intensity, and extensity, we promptly feel a difference in them, which leads us to refer each to its appropriate region. Now this something about touch sensations which permits us to recognise them as locally distinct, although we recognise all of them as being cases of contact, is what is meant by the local sign. These local signs, then, are the relatively *fixed elements* in our space-perceiving processes. It is by learning to correlate one group of them with another group that we can develop by experience the accuracy of our perceptions. Thus, for example, we come to learn that the stimulation of one series of local signs in the order *a-b-c* means a special movement of one hand over the other, say the downward movement of the right hand over the left. The same series stimulated in the order *c-b-a* means the reverse movement. It must be remembered very explicitly at this point that we are including the kinæsthetic sensations of movement under the general heading of touch: since we doubtless have local signs of movement distinct from those of the cutaneous pressure sense, and they doubtless play a very important part here. But they are commonly fused in an inextricable way with the pressure sensations, so that a separate treatment of them seems hardly necessary in a sketch of this kind.

A Caution.—A warning must be held out at this point against the fallacy of supposing that in learning his space world a child uses these local signs in any very reflective way. He does not say to himself: "That movement of localisation was inaccurate because I used the wrong local sign to control it." He generally employs the "try, try again method," until he hits the mark. But his success carries with it a recollection of the total feeling of the successful experience, and in this total feeling the local sign element is an indispensable part, even though the child is not himself definitely cognisant of the fact.

The simultaneous stimulation of a group of these local signs gives us the extensity feeling of touch, and when the impressions come from three-dimensional objects we get, through our motor reactions upon them, experiences of change of motion in three cardinal directions. This seems to be the basis of our tactual tridimensionality.

Delicacy of Touch.—In normal persons touch falls far behind vision in its spatial nicety of function, and far behind its possible capacities, as is shown by the astonishing accuracy of blind persons, who do not, however, seem to be notably more accurate than seeing persons as regards the parts of the body which are not used for tactual exploration, *e. g.*, the forearms and the back. But despite its lesser delicacy, touch-movement undoubtedly plays an important rôle during childhood in furnishing interpretative checks upon our visual estimates of large areas and great distances. The visual perception of a mile, for instance, gets a practical meaning for us largely through our walking over the distance. Moreover, although vision so largely displaces touch in our actual spatial judgments, touch always retains a sort of refereeship. When we doubt the accuracy of our visual perceptions we are likely, whenever possible, to refer the case to touch, and the verdict of this sense we commonly accept uncritically.

Peculiarities of Vision.—Vision resembles the non-spatial senses of smell and hearing in one particular which marks it off characteristically from touch. Touch sensations we commonly refer to the surface of the body itself, although when we tap with a cane, or a pencil, we seem to have a curious kind of projection of part of our sensations out to the farther tip of the object. Visual objects we always place outside ourselves. Even our after-images gotten with closed eyes often seem to float in a space vaguely external to ourselves.

It seems necessary to assume a system of local signs for vision, comparable to those of touch-movement, although doubtless more complex. It must be admitted, however, that introspection is much more uncertain in its deliverances here, than in the case of touch, and we shall be on somewhat speculative ground in assuming the nature of this visual local signature. It seems probable that this attribute of sensations from the periphery of the retina consists primarily in reflex impulses, or tendencies, to movement toward the fovea, the fovea itself furnishing a peculiar feeling which serves more or less as a fixed point of reference. Certain it is that stimulation of any part of the retina tends to release movements turning the fovea toward the stimulus. The incessant and complicated movements of the eyes over the visual field must speedily render the relation of the various retinal points, as conjoined by movements, intricate in the highest degree. But such relations as exist must pretty clearly rest on the intermediation of movements with their motor and retinal effects upon consciousness; and it seems probable, therefore, that the space value of any retinal point comes to be determined by the position it occupies in such a system of movements. Thus, a point 20° to the right of the fovea in the visual field comes to mean to us a definite kind of motor impulse. One 20° to the left, another kind of impulse, etc. Whether the visual local sign is actually this sort of a fused retinal-kinæsthetic affair or not, there can be no doubt that, as adults, we have a remarkably accurate sense of the general space relations of the objects in the field of view, and that we can turn our eyes with unhesitating accuracy to any part of this field.

The Third Dimension.—Psychologists have always been especially interested in the problem of the visual perception of distance, or the third dimension. Bishop Berkeley maintained in his celebrated work entitled "Essay Toward a New Theory of Vision" (1709), that the eye cannot give us any *direct* evidence of distance, because any point in the visual field must affect one point and one only in the retina, and it can affect this no differently when it is two feet away from what it does when four feet away. Therefore, Berkeley concluded that our perception of visual distance is dependent upon our tactual-motor experiences. This view overlooks several important facts, including its plain contradiction of our common feeling about the matter. In the first place, we have two eyes, and each eye sees a part of solid objects varying slightly from that seen by the other. The psychical percept of such objects appears to be a fusion of the factors supplied by the two eyes, and we get from this source the visual feeling of solidity. The stereoscope employs this principle, and by giving us pictures which exaggerate somewhat the disparity in the point of view of the right and left eye affords us a most startling impression of distance and volume. Furthermore, we converge our eyes more upon near points than upon far, and the muscular strain thus brought about may serve to inform us of differences in distance. Similarly, the muscles controlling the lenses contract with varying degrees of intensity in the effort properly to focus rays of light from objects at different distances. How far our consciousness of these focussing movements is significant for our judgments of distance it is difficult to say. But it is at least clear that there are factors operative other than those Berkeley had in mind, and the genuineness of the optical sense of distance can hardly be seriously questioned. The eye is, in short, not merely a *retina*, it is a *binocular* motor organ as well. Normally, therefore, visual perceptions are always fused stereoscopic binocular-motor experiences.

We use in actual practice other forms of criteria for distance. Thus, the apparent size of the object is used as a clue to its distance. By the apparent size of a man we may judge whether he be a mile or a hundred yards away. Conversely, when we know the distance, we can employ it to form an estimate of the size of an object at that distance. Thus, if we know the approximate distance, we can be fairly sure whether the person we see is a man or a boy.

The seeming size of objects runs roughly, but not percisely, parallel with the size of the retinal image. We make a certain compensation for objects at considerable distances.*

The distinctness of the perceptual image is another criterion. Things seen dimly, other things equal, are judged to be far away. Objects near at hand seen dimly in this way, as during a fog, seem much magnified in size. We have dimness, the sign of distance, conjoined with a large image, and we consequently judge the object to be much larger than it is, because of its seeming distance. The contrary form of this confusion is experienced by persons going into the mountains for the first time. The unaccustomed atmospheric clearness renders distant objects unwontedly distinct, and so they are misjudged as much nearer and much smaller than they really are. Our judgments of distance are seriously disturbed, also, when deprived of the assistance of familiar intermediary objects. Persons unacquainted with the sea are wholly unable to guess accurately the distance of vessels or other objects across the water. Light and shadow give us many trustworthy indications of contour, and even the absolute brightness of the light seems to affect our judgment, bright objects seeming to be nearer than those which are less bright.

Inaccuracies of Space Perception.—Despite its general accuracy, our visual perception is subject to sundry eccentric-

* Much mystery has been made of the fact that the image on the retina is upside down, and still we see things right side up. This irrelevant wonder is like marvelling how we can see a sphere, when the cortical cells responsible for our seeing are arranged in a shapeless mass. The fact is, we have no direct personal consciousness of either retina or brain cells. The *psychical* image is a thing entirely distinct from the retinal image. To speak of this psychical image as having one position rather than another is simply equivalent to saying that a certain set of motions are necessary to pass from one part of it to another. To pass from what we call the bottom to the top means a certain series of eye movements, 'or hand movements, and so on.

ities, the precise causes of which we cannot pause to discuss. In many cases, indeed, the reasons for them are far from certain. Thus vertical lines are commonly judged longer than objectively equal horizontal lines. The upper portions of vertically symmetrical figures look larger than the lower portions. The printed letter S and the figure 8 illustrate the supplementary principle, that to make the top and bottom parts appear of equal size the bottom one must be made larger. The seeming size of objects is affected by their surroundings, a kind of spatial contrast evidently existing. Figure 54 illustrates this. We might mention many other instances, but space forbids.

In the establishment of effective correlations among our

FIG. 54. The middle lines of the two figures are of equal length. To most observers the lower one seems shorter. This result is attributed to the contrast effect of the surrounding lines.

several sources of space perception, there can be no question, as we have previously insisted, that movement is the great factor. Objects touched are, by the movement of the eyes, at the same time seen. The superposition of one object upon another, and the successive passing of one hand after the other over the things we touch, must rapidly serve to build up elaborate space perceptions upon the foundation of local signs, some of which are visual and some tactual. Our space, as we know it in adult consciousness, is, then, a distinctly synthetic affair, developed from two or three distinct sensory sources, through the intermediation of localising and exploring movements.

Space Limen.—We may add for those who are interested in the quantitative aspect of these matters, that the limen for space perception in vision has generally been given at 60″, this being the angular distance at which two lines can just be distinguished as two. Recent experimenters report a far smaller angle, one observer finding the limen at 15″, another at 2.5″. In touch, the threshold for the detecting of two points as two is, for the finger-tips, roughly, 2 mm. The tongue is even more sensitive. But this can hardly be called the space limen with propriety, for *single points* are felt as having some extension. Apart from the tongue, the finger-tips are the most delicate tactual surfaces. Speaking generally, the delicacy of tactual space perception seems to be a function, first, of the richness of nervous innervation (those places which are most richly innervated being generally most sensitive), and second, of practice, or use.

Localisation of Sound.—Although we may not admit that auditory sensations are themselves spatial, we cannot question that we localise sounds with considerable accuracy. In our view, however, this localisation occurs in the space world of vision-touch-movement. The two most important factors in the localisation of sound are, first, the relative amplitude of the sound waves distributed to the two ears, and, second, the acoustic complexity of the sound waves. If the right ear is more violently stimulated than the left, we locate the stimulus on the right side of the body. If the two ears are stimulated equally, we judge the sound to be somewhere in the median vertical plane, at right angles to the line joining the ears. But of the precise point in this plane we are very uncertain.

With sounds that have many partial tones, these tones, especially the higher ones, are so affected by the bones of the head and by the external ear, that they reach the two ears in distinctly different condition, save when they occur in the median plane. In consequence the timbre of complex sounds differs with their direction; and it seems quite certain that we employ these differences in our auditory localisation of direction, and possibly also of distance. Our auditory estimates of distance, however, are highly inexact. To put it graphically, a sound on the right side may be heard as a fusion of tones a-b-c-d-e-f by the right ear, whereas by the left ear it could only be heard as a fusion of a-b-c. Now if the sound be moved to a point a little to the right of straight back, the right ear gets a-b-c-d-e, the left ear a-b-c-d. Our perception of the sound is of course always a fusion of the increment coming from the two ears. But our illustration may serve to show how these differences in timbre may act as local indices. Most persons seem to make their localisation of sounds either in the form of visual imagery, or in the form of quasi-reflex localising movements of head and eye. It is possible that cutaneous sensations from the drum membrane are of some consequence in certain localisations, but the evidence for this is hardly conclusive.

II. TIME

Space and Time.—Although certain of our sensations may not, perhaps, contribute directly to our consciousness of space, all of them participate in furnishing us our sense of time. We are probably never wholly oblivious to the feeling of passing time, and now and then it monopolises our entire attention. Unlike our perception of space, however, our direct perception of time is a very limited, cramped sort of an affair. The eye permits us to range over the vast distances of interstellar space, but our perception of time, so far as it is an immediate sensory process, never gets far beyond the present moment. It seems to be based upon our awareness of the changes occurring in consciousness itself.

Primary Characteristics of Time Perception —We may perceive the passing of time, either in the form of a mere vague *duration*, or as an *interval*, depending upon whether we give our attention to the *filling* of the period, or to its *limiting stimuli*. In either case what we become aware of is never a mere *point* of time, sharply marked off from that which has gone before and that which follows. It is always a consciousness of an *extent* of time which confronts us, however limited this extent may be.

The Specious Present.—This consciousness of the sensibly present moment is often referred to as the " specious present " —a phrase suggested by E. R. Clay. This specious present seems to owe its extended nature to the fact that objects which have once been in consciousness do not drop out instantaneously, but fade out often somewhat slowly. We are at any given moment, therefore, aware in the fringe of consciousness not only of that which a moment ago engaged our attention but also of that which a moment hence is more fully to occupy us. This period of waning which our thoughts display before passing entirely out of the field of consciousness is often entitled the period of " primary memory." In any case our direct perception of the passing of time is simply this process in which from moment to moment we become aware of the coming and going among our conscious activities. Evidently the scope of such a perceptual process must be very circumscribed. As a matter of fact our *direct*, as distinguished from our indirect and inferred, consciousness of time never exceeds a few seconds. Under favourable conditions it may mount up to twelve seconds or thereabouts, but ordinarily it is much shorter.

Factors in Direct Perception of Time.—Although all the senses may be employed for this purpose, hearing is the sense from which we gain our most accurate direct perception of time relations. Touch and the motor sensations rank next, and in actual practice generally operate with hearing. If we are attempting to judge accurately the length of two time intervals we tend strongly to tap, or make other rhythmical movements, and our judgment is much assisted by these movements. The shortest interval which we can feel as a time period between two sounds is about 1-50 to 1-80 of a second. Sounds succeeding one another more rapidly than this we may distinguish as qualitatively different from absolutely simultaneous sounds, but we hardly recognise them as temporally separate. Furthermore, we may feel as successive two stimuli which are objectively simultaneous. This is said to be true of the combination of a noise and a light sensation.

When the auditory stimuli follow each other at the rate of less than 1-2 second, we seem to sense the sequence in one way. When they come at intervals of 1-2 second to 3 seconds, we have a different mode of reaction. These latter cases we feel distinctly as durations. Probably the sensory content of these durations is largely made up of kinæsthetic sensations, especially from the respiratory muscles. The shorter intervals first mentioned we sense more as "moments," although they may vary considerably in actual length. They are in no true sense, therefore, felt as mere points in time. If we compare intervals longer than three seconds we find ourselves beginning to employ our consciousness of the number of sensations, or ideas, which come into the mind. We tend to overestimate very small intervals and to underestimate long intervals. The region of relatively correct judgment may be called the indifference zone. This is about 6-10 to 7-10 of a second.

Much as in the case of space perception, we judge richly filled intervals as longer than relatively vacant intervals. "Empty time" is a myth. We always have some consciousness of change, so long as we are conscious at all. We are also subject to illusions and to the effect of contrast, as in spatial processes. An interval seems shorter when preceded by a long interval than when preceded by a short one, and vice versa. An interval bounded by intense stimuli seems shorter than one with more moderate limiting stimuli. If our attention is very much engaged upon some expected event we may perceive it as coming before another event which it actually follows.

Generally speaking, our consciousness of time, as such, is proportional to our interest and absorption in the occupation of the moment. When we are bored, as in waiting for a train, or when ill, time drags outrageously. We may be conscious of every loathsome increment in it. When, on the other hand, we are thoroughly interested, long intervals may pass as in a flash. Certain drugs, such as hashish, have a curious effect upon our time perception, lending a vastly magnified perspective to it, so that events of a moment since seem ages remote. Dreams often display a similar distortion.

Indirect Time Perception.—Clearly our practical use of time relations depends largely on other processes than those of direct perception. For our consciousness of the hour, the day, and the year we resort to the sun and moon, to clocks, watches, calendars and other indirect means of information. Despite the fact that the subject does not bear immediately upon *perception*, it will be convenient to add a few words at this point upon one or two general features of our time consciousness.

General Characteristics of the Apprehension of Time Relations.—When we recall intervals of time which belong to the more or less remote past, we immediately remark a seeming paradox. Intervals which actually passed very slowly for us appear retrospectively to have been very brief. Thus, a tedious illness, when time palled upon us almost beyond endurance, may in recollection seem very short, although we actually know it occupied weeks. Conversely, intervals which passed in a twinkling appear to us in memory as long drawn out. The reason for the paradox is obvious. Our feeling for the length of these remembered intervals depends upon the amount of content, the number of events, which we can read back into them. The interesting intervals are full of such things, whereas the tedious periods are characterised by a depressing sameness, which affords our memory little or nothing to lay hold upon.

The change which comes over our feeling for the various intervals of time as we grow older is an interesting and familiar phenomenon. In childhood the year seems interminable, the month majestic, the week momentous, and even the day important, to say nothing of the hour. In adult years all these periods shrink, the longest ones most markedly. Our feelings for very short intervals, like the second and the minute, undergo no change of which we can speak confidently.

Our notion of very remote times, whether thought of as past or future, is gotten in an almost wholly symbolic way, like our notion of vast numbers. The difference between 2000 B. C. and 6000 B. C. is a thing for which we have a cold intellectual apprehension, quite distinct from our feeling for the difference between 1776 and 1860.

Neural Basis of Time Perception.—We can say very little about the neural basis of time perception, and that little is largely of an inferential and speculative character. If the awareness of passing time rests, as we have maintained, upon our consciousness of the waxing and waning of the thought processes, there should be some fairly constant phase of the cortical activity corresponding to this conscious metabolism. We may suppose this to exist in the rising and falling of the pulses of neural activity throughout the various regions of the cortex. Time consciousness would depend, therefore, upon the overlapping of the activity of various groups of neurones. Beyond some such vague formulation as this we cannot go. Let it be remarked, however, that the conception, though vague, is wholly intelligible.

Physiological Time Sense.—In closing this subject, we may mention two striking and perplexing peculiarities which many persons possess. One of these is the capacity for telling with great accuracy the precise hour, whether by day or by night, without any recourse to watch or clock, and without any deliberate computation or estimate. The other is the ability to awaken exactly at any given hour, without any preliminary disturbance of the soundness of sleep. Both of these performances probably rest upon some sort of recognition by the cortical centres of the rhythm of physiological activities constantly in progress in the body. But after all is said, the matter remains something of a mystery, a mystery which is enhanced, rather than removed, by the familiar attempt to find an explanation in "subconscious" activities. It suggests certain of the experiences met with in post-hypnotic suggestion. Of hypnotism itself we shall have something to say in the final chapter of this book.

CHAPTER VIII

IMAGINATION

General Psychophysical Account of Re-presentation.—In the last chapter we saw that even in those psychophysical processes where the sense organs were most obviously engaged, the effects of past experience were very conspicuous. This fact will suggest at once the probable difficulty of establishing any absolute line of demarcation between processes of perception and those which, in common untechnical language, we call memory and imagination. We shall find as we go on that this difficulty is greater rather than less than our first impressions would indicate, and it will be well to come to the matter with the understanding that we are examining *various stages* in the development of a common process, rather than with any idea of meeting entirely separate and distinct kinds of mental activity. We called attention to this same point at the outset of our analysis of the cognitive functions.

Our study of habit brought out clearly the strong tendency of the nervous system to repeat again and again any action with which it has once successfully responded to a stimulus. This tendency is peculiarly prominent in the action of the brain as distinguished from the lower nervous centres and the peripheral nerves. The undoubted retention by the nervous organism of the modifications impressed upon it by the impact of the physical world, in what we call experience, is commonly designated "organic memory," and forms beyond question the physiological basis of conscious memory. Thus, in perception, as we have just seen, the sensory nerves may bring in excitations of as novel a character as you please, but the brain insists on responding to these stimulations in ways suggested by its previous experience. That is to say, it repeats in part some previous cerebral action. Similarly, we observe that from time to time thoughts flit through our minds which we have had before. This we may feel confident, from the facts we examined in Chapter II., means a repetition in some fashion of the cortical activities belonging to an earlier experience. Sometimes these thoughts are what we would commonly call memories, *i. e.*, they are thoughts of events in our past lives which we recognise as definitely portraying specific experiences. Sometimes they are what we call creations of fancy and imagination. But even in this case we shall find it difficult to convince ourselves that the materials of which such thoughts are constituted have not come to us, like those of clearly recognised memories, from the store-house of our past lives.

Although we shall postpone the detailed examination of memory until the next chapter, and must therefore anticipate somewhat the full proof of our assertion, we may lay down the general principle at once, that all psychophysical activity involves a reinstatement, in part at least, of previous psychophysical processes. Stated in terms of mental life alone, and reading the principle forward instead of backward, it would stand thus: all the conscious processes of an individual enter as factors into the determination of his subsequent conscious activities. With this general conception in mind, we have now to analyse the special form of representation known as imagination.

General Definition of Imagination.—The term imagination, in its ordinary use, is apt to suggest the fanciful and the unreal, the poetic and the purely æsthetic. We speak in this way of great poems as "works of imagination." We describe certain persons as of imaginative temperament when they are subject to romantic flights of fancy, etc. These implications are of course properly a part of the meaning of the word, when employed in its usual untechnical sense. But the psychologist uses the term in a broader way than this. In the preceding chapter we discussed the consciousness of objects present to the senses. Imagination, in the psychologist's meaning, might be called the consciousness of objects not present to sense. Thus, we can imagine a star which we do not see; we can imagine a melody which we do not hear, an odour which we do not actually smell, etc. Stated in the more usual way, imagination consists in the reinstatement of previous sensory excitations. Speaking broadly, both perception and imagination would evidently involve the consciousness of objects, and their primary distinction from one another would be found in the physiological fact that one arises immediately from a sense organ stimulation, while the other does not. The principal psychical difference we pointed out in a previous chapter. The perceptual consciousness, which is peripherally originated, is almost invariably more vivid, enduring, and distinct than the centrally initiated process of imagination, and seems to us somehow more definitely "given" to us, to be more coercive. But the similarity of the one process to the other is quite as obvious, and quite as important, as their difference. The stuff, so to speak, out of which visual *imagination* is made is qualitatively the same kind of material as that out of which visual *perception* is made. Indeed, when we describe imagination as a consciousness of objects, we have already suggested that which is really the fact, *i. e.*, that all imagination is based in one way or another upon *previous perceptual* activities, and consequently the psychical material which we meet in imagination is all of a piece with the material which perception brings to us, and altogether like it, save that in imagination the fabric is often much faded and sometimes much cut up and pieced. So far as we approximate pure sensations in sense experience so far do we have images reinstating approximately pure qualities as distinct from objects. Images of warmth, for instance, may have in them relatively little suggestion of objective character.

Analysis of Imagination. (A) Content.—If we were to ask a dozen persons to think of a rose for a few moments, and then relate for us the ideas which had passed through their minds, we should find that some of them had at once secured a mental picture of the rose in which the colour and the form were represented with considerable accuracy and detail. These persons evidently got visual images of the rose. Others would have found that the word "rose" came at once into mind, followed by other words such as "American Beauty," "red," "bud," etc. These words would, perhaps, have been *heard* mentally, and together with this mental hearing the more acute observers would report for us a similar consciousness of the sensations of movement which arise from the throat and lips when one is enunciating the words. This group of persons would have experienced auditory and motor imagery. Still others would report a faint consciousness of the odour of the rose, which involves olfactory imagery; and a few might tell us that they fancied they got tactual images, such as would arise from the thought of touching the soft petals. It might occur, although we should find this result rare, that some individual would report *all* of these images as passing through his mind in sequence.

It has been asserted that we have no genuine motor, or kinæsthetic, images, because every attempt to think of a movement results in our actually making the movement in a rudimentary way; so that we get a kinæsthetic *sensation* instead of a kinæsthetic *image*. There can be no doubt that this is often the case; *e. g.*, the effort to think how the word "back" sounds will by most persons be found to be accompanied by a definite feeling in the tongue and throat. Moreover, there can be no doubt that the normal procedure is for every kinæsthetic ideational excitement to produce movement. This is only *less immediately* true of ideational excitement of other kinds. Meantime, there seems to be no reason in the nature of the case why we may not have kinæsthetic images in a form definitely distinguishable from the kinæsthetic sensations to which they may lead; and many observers insist that their introspection verifies the reality of these images.

According to the commonly accepted doctrine there are, theoretically at least, as many kinds of images as there are sense organs. If our experiment be amplified and a large number of persons be submitted to it, we shall find that it is much easier for most persons to secure with confidence accurate and reliable images of the visual, auditory, and motor varieties than it is to secure those of the gustatory, thermal, tactual, and olfactory types. Later on we shall inquire into the probable reason for this difference. Moreover, we should find in the same way, if we gathered statistics upon the subject as others have done, that many persons, even though they can with sufficient effort command various forms of images, actually have their imagination in its ordinary use dominated by some one or two forms. From this observation has arisen the recognition of mental " types," and currency has been given to the division into " audiles," " tactiles," " motiles," etc.

These types are, as we have just pointed out, seldom or never absolutely exclusive of one another. But they indicate the prevalent form of mental material. With most of us there appears to be a relatively good representation of several forms, especially the visual, auditory, tactual, and motor. In any event we find that specific images of one kind or another always constitute the content, the material, of imagination.

Image and Idea.—It may serve to clarify the terminology employed from this point on, if we pause to distinguish tentatively between the terms *image* and *idea*. So far as we have in mind the *sensuous content* of a thought, *e. g.*, its visual or auditory character, we use the term image. So far as we wish to emphasise in addition to, or in distinction from, this fact of sensuous constitution the purport, significance, or *meaning* of the image, we use the term idea. Images and ideas do not refer to two different states of consciousness, but to one and the same state, looked at now from the side of sensory character and antecedents, now from the side of meaning. The matter will be discussed more fully in our analysis of the concept.

It should also be reiterated that in speaking of images as though they were distinct mental events, we do not mean to imply that the image constitutes the whole of consciousness at any given moment; nor that thought is made up of disconnected bits of stuff called images. We are simply indulging the kind of abstraction in which we frankly announced our purpose to indulge. Images merely represent, on the cognitive side, the more *substantive* moments in the onward flow of consciousness. They rise by indiscernible gradations out of antecedent conscious processes, and fade away into their successors without a vestige of abrupt separation. Moreover, any given image is merged in a setting of sensory processes representing the momentary bodily conditions, attitude, etc., of which we made mention in discussing the physiological accompaniments of attention.

(B) Mode of Operation of Imagination.—If we watch the play of our images under different conditions, we observe, regardless of the sense department to which they belong, certain marked peculiarities which evidently call for separate classification of some kind. In dreams, for example, there often appears to be the utmost chaos in the fashion in which the images succeed one another; and when we have regard to their composition and character, they occasionally seem to be utterly novel and bizarre inventions, the like of which we have never known in waking experience. The hobgoblins of nightmares, with their inconsequential torments, are illus-

IMAGINATION

trations of this sort of thing. On the other hand, in revery our minds ocasionally wander off amid trains of images which are coherent in their relations to one another, and which evidently spring from recognisable experiences, of which they are in a measure faithful representations. Thus, the recollections of a journey may pass through our minds, diversified by excursions into connected fields of thought suggested by the various incidents of the trip. Can it be that these two forms of imagination are really identical? Is the process which brings back to mind the recollection of the sound of the multiplication table one and the same in kind with that which leads to the sudden perfection of an invention, or the inspiration of a fine verse? To answer this question in even a provisional way requires a closer examination of these two forms of imagination, to which psychologists have assigned the names "reproductive" and "productive" respectively.

Reproductive Imagination.—Reproductive imagination consists in the representation of perceptions, or images, which have previously appeared in our consciousness. Thus, I may close my eyes and obtain a visual image of the desk at which I am writing. Such an image would illustrate what psychologists mean by reproductive imagery, inasmuch as my imagination would in this case simply repeat, or reinstate, some conscious experience which has previously been present in my mind. Evidently at this rate the great mass of the events which we are able to remember would be recalled by means of reproductive imagination. Our ordinary memory processes would be instances of reproductive imagination, or, as it is sometimes called, re-presentation.

Productive Imagination.—Productive imagination on the other hand involves the appearance in consciousness of images which have never before entered the mind in their present order and form. Thus, the visual image of an eight-legged dog might be called up, although it is reasonably certain that most of us have never seen such an animal, nor even a picture of it. Such an image would illustrate, in a rough way, what is meant by productive, or constructive, imagination.

Now it is a favourite conceit of the untutored mind to suppose that it is possible mentally to create absolutely new materials for ideas, that it is possible to burst over the bounds of one's past experience and beget thoughts which are wholly novel. This is a flattering delusion which a little reflection will effectually dispel, although there is a distorted truth underlying the vanity of the belief.

In the case of the eight-legged dog it is clear that, although we may never have encountered just such a creature in any of our adventures, the superfluous legs with which we have endowed him, which constitute his sole claim to novelty, are merely as legs familiar items in every experience with the canine breed.

The productivity of our imagination consists, therefore, in the modest feat of putting together in a new way materials of a thoroughly familiar kind. There is, and can be, no question of our having originated *de novo* fresh elements of the psychical imagery. We shall find a similar thing true of any instance we might examine in which a genius has created a new poem, a new statue, a new melody or symphony, a new machine, or a new commercial process. In each and every case, startling as is the result, and novel as may be the combination in its entirety, the elements which have been thus ingeniously juxtaposed are all of them drawn in one way or another from the richness of the individual's previous experience. Productive imagination is productive, therefore, only within the limits set by the possibility of combining in new ways the materials of past states of consciousness. But such limitations, be it said, afford scope for an amount of originality and creative fertility which far surpass any human accomplishment thus far recorded.

Relation of Productive to Reproductive Imagination.— It appears at once from the foregoing statement that in one sense all productive imagination is really reproductive; and that in consequence we have in the last analysis only one form of relation obtaining between our present imagery and our previous consciousness. Strictly speaking this is undoubtedly true. The differences which attract our attention to the seemingly distinct modes of imagination are primarily differences in the degree to which any given image, or any sequence of images, actually correspond *to the entirety* of some antecedent conscious event in our lives. When the correspondence is obvious, we think of the imagery as reproductive. When it is not, we are likely to credit it with creative characteristics, and justly so, within the limits which we have designated. It only remains to notice one peculiarity about reproductive imagery which serves to modify somewhat the purport of our conclusion.

It is altogether problematical whether any image is ever in a thorough-going way a *mere* reinstatement, or repetition, of a previous perception or image. I may to-day, for example, think by means of an auditory-motor image of the word psychology; I may do exactly the same thing to-morrow, and I shall then speak of having had the same image on two occasions. But it is clear in the first place that I cannot *prove* the two images to be really alike; for I can never get them side by side in my mind for comparison. When one is there, the other has gone, or has not yet arrived, as the case may be. Furthermore, if we turn to the considerations which we canvassed when we discussed the operations of the cerebral cortex, we shall find reason for thinking that no two images ever can be quite alike. For we saw that our consciousness, in which these images appear, and of which they are a part, apparently runs parallel with the brain activities; and it is quite certain that the brain, through its constant change of structure and tension, is never twice in precisely the same condition; and consequently is never in a position to lead twice to the same excitation of consciousness.

On the whole, then, it is perhaps nearer the truth to say that all imagination is productive, rather than reproductive. When we speak of having had the same image on several occasions, what we really mean is that we have had in this way images which we *employed to refer* to the same object. They have thus served our purpose quite as efficiently as they could have done by being actual copies, the one of the other.

The same thing is more obviously true as regards any image which purports to represent a perception. Functionally, as regards what it does for us, what it symbolises, it really does reinstate the perception; but it is not on this account necessarily an exact copy of the perception. The distinction between reproductive and productive imagination must not, therefore, be conceived of as resting on ultimate differences. It marks a practical distinction, which is useful in enabling us to indicate significant variations in the operations of our imagery.

Successive Association of Images.—This is a convenient point at which to consider the principles controlling the sequence of our images, as they pass through the mind. The so-called law of association, which has played historically so important a part in psychology, undertakes to formulate the facts under a single general principle, *i. e.*, the principle of habit. We have mentioned in an earlier chapter the phenomenon known as simultaneous association. The process which we are to examine at this juncture is designated successive association.

The law of association asserts that whenever two images, or ideas, have been at any time juxtaposed in the mind, there is a tendency, if the first of them recurs, for the other to come with it. Furthermore, the law asserts that so far as concerns the sequence of ideationally aroused imagery, no

IMAGINATION

image ever comes into the foreground of consciousness unless it has been in some way connected with its immediate predecessor. The *order* of our thoughts is, in short, determined by our antecedent experience.

It is clear to the most casual reflection that this principle, if true, must operate under a number of definite limitations. We know, for example, that a given idea comes into the mind on one day with a certain set of accompaniments, and on another occasion presents itself with a wholly different escort.

How is such a variation to be accounted for? If we follow James in formulating the relation in brain terms, we may say that the liability of any special cortical activity, such as x, connected with the thought x^1, to arouse any other cortical activity, such as y, connected with the thought y^1, is proportional to the *permeability* of the pathway joining the brain areas involved in the production of x and y, as compared with the permeability of all the other pathways leading from the brain area involved in x to other regions of the cortex. (Figure 55.) Now this permeability must be largely a function of previous use; that is to say, pathways which have by repeated employment become deep-cut in the brain tissues will, other things equal, be most pervious. Stated in purely psychological terms, this will mean that the oftener any two ideas have actually been associated with one another, the more chance there will be that if the first one appears in consciousness the second one will accompany it.

Among the many factors which must affect this permeability of the brain paths, three important ones are easily discernible. These are the frequency, intensity, and recency of associative connection. Images which have been *frequently* associated evidently must be connected with neural activities which will tend, if once aroused, to react in the regular *habitual* way. Images which have been connected with one another in some vivid experience will be connected with intense neural activities, whose modifications of the brain tissues will therefore tend to be relatively deep and permanent. In this case, again, we may look, under the general operation of the principle of habit, for practically the whole of the particular psychophysical activity to be called out, provided anything starts up the first step in the process. Similarly, if two images have been recently associated, the pathways joining the brain tracts responsible for their accompanying cortical activities are likely to be open; and the recurrence of the first image may readily bring with it the reinstatement of the second. When we take into account the enormous number of our perceptual experiences and the varied richness which they present, we see at once that the number of possible associates which the idea of any one of these experiences may possess is extremely large.

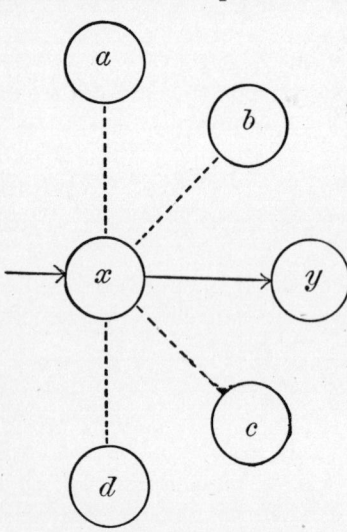

FIG. 55. Although pathways exist connecting the brain process x with the brain processes a, b, c, d, and y, if the pathway from x to y is more pervious than the others, the activity of x is likely to be followed by the activity of y.

If the idea 7 times 9 pops into my head, it is promptly followed by the idea 63. If, however, 4 times 9 comes to my mind, the next idea is 36. In both cases the idea 9 is present, but the subsequent associate depends upon the special concomitant with which the idea 9 is combined in the antecedent thought process. In a similar fashion our memory of special words in poetry depends upon the total mass of verbal associates with which they are surrounded. The word "mirth" occurs in two of the following lines, and taken alone might suggest either of the following groups of words. Taken with its predecessors it rarely fails to awaken its correct consequents.

> "And, if I give thee honour due,
> Mirth, admit me of thy crew,

> "These delights if thou canst give,
> Mirth, with thee I mean to live."

Even if no factors were operative in the modification of the general principle of association, other than those we have already mentioned, we should find it practically impossible ever to *predict* with confidence what particular idea would come to our mind at any special moment. The law of association is not, therefore, a principle of *prediction*, but simply a formula for rendering intelligible in a schematic way the nature of the influences which control the order of our thoughts.

It remains to remark one further factor of equal importance with those already mentioned in its effect in determining what associates shall recur with an idea at any given time. This is our momentary interest, the prevailing tendency of our attention. If our minds are dominantly engaged upon any line of thought, as when we are wrapt up in some absorbing problem, or plunged in some profound emotion, the ideas which flood our minds are almost wholly such as sustain intimate relations to the matter in hand. When we are overcome by sorrow all our thoughts centre about our grief. No other thoughts can gain a hearing from us. And the same thing is true in varying degree of any intense mental preoccupation. We see, then, that the principle of association, or cortical habit, is modified, not only by the changing relations among the factors of past experience already mentioned, *e. g.*, such as frequency and recency, but also by the present psychophysical conditions reflected in such things as our attention and interest. This means, so far as concerns the brain, that those pathways are normally most pervious which connect most intimately with the entire mass of ongoing brain processes. The astonishing vagaries of dream consciousness illustrate what may occur when all dominating purpose is removed and the associative machinery is allowed to run wild and uncontrolled.

Psychologists have been interested in various types of association, which they have called association by contiguity, association by similarity, contrast, etc. Association by contiguity is essentially identical with the process of which we have been speaking heretofore. *A* suggests *B*, not because of any *internal* connection, but because the two have often been contiguous to one another. This contiguity is originally perceptual in character. The objects are actually present together to the physical senses. All association is *primarily* dependent upon the contiguity of perceptual objects, as will be readily apprehended when the dependency of images upon perception is recalled.

Ideas apparently follow one another at times, however, which could not have been previously experienced together, and in certain of these cases we remark at once that the two things suggested by the ideas are similar, contain an internal element of connection. We meet a total stranger, perhaps, and instantly observe the similarity to some absent friend. Poetry owes much of its witchery and charm to the delicate and unusual resemblances which the poet detects for us, as when he says:

> "So gladly, from the songs of modern speech
> Men turn, ...
> And through the music of the languid hours,
> They hear, like ocean on a Western beach
> The *surge* and *thunder* of the Odyssey."

All the more conspicuous forms of genius seem highly endowed with this type of association, which is undoubtedly a genuine form of mental activity. We shall err only if we

IMAGINATION

suppose the similarity to be somehow the cause of the association. As a matter of fact we always observe the similarity *after* the association has occurred, not before, as should be the case if it were strictly speaking a cause. James suggests, and this seems as plausible as anything yet proposed, that the brain activities involved in thoughts of two similar things are in part identical, and that consequently we have in their suggestion of one another a further instance of the principle of cortical habit. (Figure 56.) The brain processes x and y, having the similar thoughts x^1 and y^1 as their concomitants,

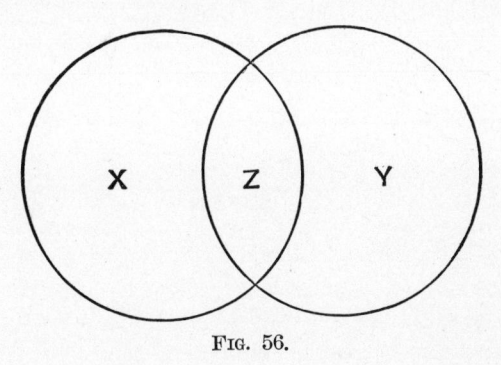

FIG. 56.

possess a common brain activity z. When x is active, there is thus a chance that the excitation of z may stir up y, to which z also belongs. Oftentimes the elements of likeness between two objects are several, as in cases of personal resemblance. On other occasions the resemblance may reduce to a single element. But the principle of explanation is the same in either case.

Association by contrast is really a modification of the contiguity and similarity classes. Things are not felt as contrasting unless they have some element of likeness, and to feel this likeness and difference commonly involves experiencing them together, as when we come to remark the contrast of black with white.

Miss Calkins has pointed out that in certain associative sequences the image which comes into the mind entirely displaces the one which previously held sway. She calls this type of case desistent association. In other cases, however, a part only of the departing image is lost, the rest being taken up into the new image which succeeds it. This she calls persistent association. This analysis seems to touch upon a real distinction, but it clearly introduces no basal alteration into the general nature of the principle controlling the ideational sequences.

Genesis and Function of Imagery.—The best clue to a correct understanding of the function of the image is to be gained, as in the case of all organic activities, when possible, by examining the conditions of its genesis, its appearance upon the field of psychophysical processes.

In several of the preceding chapters we have examined the evidence underlying our thesis, that consciousness appears at those points where the purely physiological mechanisms of the organism prove inadequate to cope with the requirements of its life. We have seen how the organism is endowed at birth with certain established sensory-motor neural pathways, by means of which it is enabled to respond with appropriate movements to certain primitive kinds of stimuli. We have also seen how, at the places where these responses are found insufficient, sensory consciousness appears; and we find, first, vague sensation processes, and then crude perception. We have also noticed how attention, working upon this crude perceptual matrix, succeeds in differentiating it into the multitude of qualities and objects which constitute the world of the adult. In seeking to detect the appearance and the function of imagery, we must remember, then, that from the outset of life organic activities are in progress and the sensory-motor activities in particular are in full swing. Each sensory stimulus is producing movements, which in turn are productive of fresh sensations. It is out from such a

IMAGINATION

cycle of onward moving coördinations as these, therefore, that the image emerges; and if our previous hypothesis is really adequate to all the facts, it must be that the image is called forth by some need of the organism which the processes that we have already described are incompetent to satisfy. This is undoubtedly the case, and we have only to observe the evident limitations in the capacities of the perceptual processes, taken by themselves, to discern certain of the functions which our images subserve.

Perception enables its possessor to register in consciousness the particular object momentarily presented to the senses. But if consciousness never advanced beyond the merely perceptual stage, it is not apparent that it could serve to develop systematised and intelligent movements of response to environmental demands and opportunities. We should always live in the immediate present, and our minds could consciously look neither backward nor forward. Now it is in the image that we find the psychical mechanism for accomplishing both these highly important functions.

If an organism is to be in the fullest possible measure master of its own fate, it must be able to bring to bear upon the incitations of any particular stimulus all the information which its total experience will permit. Its response must thus represent, not only the intrinsic tendency to overt action, which belongs to the stimulus itself, but it must also represent and express all the tendencies to movement which remain as the result of yielding to previous incitations. Unless there be some organic arrangement of this kind, by means of which each act may represent with some adequacy the product of all related experiences in the past, one's actions would be as purely reflex, or as purely haphazard, as those of the least developed creatures. It is obvious that mere perception—although, as we have noticed, it does embody in a certain way the outcome of antecedent consciousness—does not in any sufficient manner provide for such a focussing of one's past experiences upon the selection of specific acts, as is demanded by the best accommodatory responses. Without the image we might make many appropriate reactions, but we should also make many more inappropriate ones than we now do; and any development of intelligence, in the proper sense of the word, would be impossible.*

The image is, then, the primary psychical process by means of which we bring into mind at need the experiences of the past. It is also the means by which we forecast the future. If I wish to remember what I read yesterday, I accomplish it by summoning images which represent the experience at issue. If I wish to decide which of several lines of conduct I had best pursue, or which of several possible acts my enemy is likely to hit upon, I do it in either case by the use of images, which serve me in my tentative prognostication. These images may of course be of any variety, but in my own case they are likely to be largely visual—images of objects, or scenes—and auditory-motor images of words, for my own thinking goes on largely in these terms. The image thus affords us the method by which we shake off the shackles of the world of objects immediately present to sense, and secure the freedom to overstep the limits of space and time as our fancy, or our necessity, may dictate.

If we have correctly diagnosed the chief function of our imagery we may be certain that it makes its first appearance at a very early stage in the conscious life of the human being. For obvious reasons it is not possible to designate the precise

* It is not certain that in animals the effects of pleasure and pain may not at times operate to produce the semblance of reflective intelligence, by discouraging some acts and encouraging others, without the interposition of any definite imagery. On the whole, however, it is difficult to believe that some vague counterpart of the image is not present, provided the action be not really dependent upon veiled reflexes. The impossibility of inspecting directly the animal consciousness renders all dogmatism upon such questions unwarrantable.

moment in the unfolding of the life of the mind at which the image is clearly and distinctly differentiated from the vague matrix of sensory-motor activities which we have seen characterising the first experiences of the child. But we may be confident that it is beginning to emerge in some sense departments, whenever we see unmistakable signs of volition, say at about the twelfth week in most children; and there is no reason why it may not be present, in a crude, indefinite way, from the beginning of extra-uterine life.

The Training of Imagery.—The development of imagery in the main runs parallel with that of perception, with which, as we saw in the previous chapter, it is very intimately connected. It holds to reason, without any elaborate justification, that if any sense organ is allowed to go unused, or is used infrequently, the imagery belonging to that special sense cannot develop freely. In confirmation of this general assertion we have but to notice that the imagery which most of us find we can command with greatest accuracy and flexibility is that belonging to the perceptual processes with which we are most intimately familiar, *i. e.*, vision, hearing, movement, and touch. Compared with these, our images of temperature, smell, and taste are relatively impoverished. Moreover, children who lose their sight before they are five years old commonly lose all their visual images, thus exhibiting further evidence of the connection of the image with sense organ activity. Nevertheless, we have to admit that we display individual peculiarities and preferences in the kind of imagery which we employ that cannot be satisfactorily explained in terms of sense organ activities. The eye and the ear may be used with indifferent frequency and effectiveness, and still the imagery be dominantly of either the visual or auditory kind. Differences of this sort probably rest upon unassignable structural variations, such as those which determine the colour of our eyes.

If we examine the type of development which characterises

the growth of any special form of imagery, such, for example, as the visual, we shall find that two distinct tendencies are discernible. We find (1) that the number of objects which can be simultaneously visualised increases, and (2) that the vividness, detail, and definiteness of the image increases. It is astonishing to observe how rapidly this capacity for visualising unfolds in response to a little systematic effort and practice. By devoting to the task a few minutes each day for a week, one may learn to visualise with great detail and remarkable accuracy the form, size, colour, etc., of even large and complex objects, such, for example, as great buildings. Generally at the outset we find that our images are relatively faint, meagre, and unstable; they lack vividness and veracity in colour, detail in form, and appropriate dimensions in size. Images of other varieties, auditory, for instance, are similarly defective at times, and yield as a rule to discipline, with a corresponding form of development.

But after all, the important development of our imagery is not to be found by inquiring for such changes as we thus detect, when we consider it of and by itself apart from its place in the totality of psychophysical activity. The essential thing is the increase in the dexterity with which we employ it, and the growth in the efficiency with which it serves its special purpose in the economy of the organism. We have already commented upon its principal function. It is the psychical device by which we are enabled consciously to focalise upon our acts the lessons of our previous relevant experiences, and through which we forecast the future in the light of the past.

To perform this function with the greatest ease, promptness, and efficiency is the goal toward which the development of our imagery tends, both in those cases where we, as psychologists, purposely bend our efforts in that direction, and also in those cases characterising ordinary practical life, in which our attention is concentrated upon, and absorbed in, the execution of some act, and for the moment is oblivious to the means employed.

We have already, in an earlier chapter, outlined the general nature of this development, and we need hardly do more here than refer to the significant facts, and cite an instance or two of the process involved. If I wish to express some proposition with the greatest possible force and clearness, I go about it by calling into my mind auditory-motor word images. Clearly I might use other kinds of imagery without affecting the relations which we are now examining. As a matter of fact I generally use, as do most persons under these conditions, auditory and kinæsthetic imagery. From among these word images I select that combination which appeals to my judgment as most appropriate and effective. Evidently the success which I achieve will be in part conditioned by the extent and richness of the images which I am actually able to summon. We speak sometimes of persons possessing a rich vocabulary. In the case of our illustration, my possession of a good vocabulary means, when stated in strictly psychological terms, that I can command a large and effective group of auditory word images.

As a child my imagery of the verbal kind is necessarily circumscribed in amount and phlegmatic in operation. When adult years are reached the amount of the available imagery is ordinarily much augmented, but unless there be discipline in its actual *use*, it is commonly found that much investment of time and effort is needed in order to secure the best and most expressive terms. The only real and infallible means of training one's imagery for such actual operations is found in the definite use of it, either by writing or speaking. Practice is here, as elsewhere, the one invariable clue to the highest attainable success. The business of such imagery is always to be found in some *act*, and the only way to develop it and make it reliable and efficient is by *working* it. For various reasons, which we need not pause to discuss, the possession of a good vocabulary for writing purposes does not necessarily carry with it a rich vocabulary for speaking; and in less degree the converse is true. One commonly requires separate training for each form of activity, if the best results are to be attained.

When we were discussing the principle of habit we observed that all such coördinations as those which we have just mentioned tend, under the influence of practice, to become essentially automatic; and that consciousness consequently tends to disappear from their control. If this be always the case, the idea is at once suggested that in such a process as is involved in our illustration, *i. e.*, the process of linguistic expression, the same tendency should be in evidence. I believe this to be actually the fact, and I think a little observation will confirm the position. We shall have occasion to examine the question more at length when we discuss later on the relation of language to reasoning, but a word or two may properly be inserted here.

Just in the degree to which our linguistic expression involves thoroughly familiar ideas, and deals with familiar situations, do we find our consciousness of definite imagery vague and indistinct. A student inquires: "What did you mention as the date of the battle of Waterloo?" Instantly, almost without any definite consciousness of what I am about to say, I find I have replied—"1815." But when the expression is of some relatively unfamiliar idea, when the thought presents the possibility of several discrepant modes of utterance, I promptly become aware of imagery. Not always verbal imagery of course. That consideration is wholly secondary. But imagery of one kind or another I always find when the coördination required cannot be executed in the purely—or almost purely—habitual manner. If the situations with which we have to cope by means of speech were more widely fixed, instead of being, as they are in fact, relatively unstable and fluid, relatively changeable, I see no reason to doubt that

IMAGINATION

speech, like walking, might become essentially automatic—as I believe it to be in part already.

Summarising, then, we may say that all imagery arises out of perceptual activities, upon which its appearance is, therefore, most immediately dependent; it develops by use in the actual processes of controlling action, and develops its real functions in no other way. This accounts for its appearance in greatest profusion in connection with those sense processes which are most significant for human life. It tends to drop away after it has served, in the general congeries of consciousness, to establish effective habits. It only remains to add, that while it arises from perception, it also reacts upon perception; for we perceive with fresh vitality those objects, qualities, and relations for which we possess distinct images.

CHAPTER IX

MEMORY

Memory and Imagination.—A considerable portion of the mental events which we examined in the last chapter as instances of imagination, might with propriety have been described as phases of memory. In our common use of the term "memory," we mean to indicate such processes as involve recollection in any fashion whatever. We say in this way that our memory informs us that Napoleon was imprisoned at St. Helena; that $8 \times 7 = 56$; that yesterday was rainy, etc. We also speak of remembering that on a certain occasion we made a certain remark to a certain individual. Evidently these illustrations might all be described as cases of reproductive imagination, for they all involve reproductive imagery. We may be reasonably sure at once, then, that memory and imagination have one point at least in common, *i. e.*, the image.

But there is one important difference between memory, in the more precise meaning of the word, and mere imagination, which makes it desirable to devote a separate chapter to its study. We might go on indefinitely having similar, or even identical, images pass through our minds, and, if we did not recognise them as having been previously portions of our experience, we should never in any strict sense be able to speak of our having a memory process. In memory, our consciousness not only re-presents old experiences to us, but we are aware of the images thus brought to us as actually standing for items of our previous states of consciousness. If I am turning over in my mind the wisdom of making a

MEMORY

journey to India, the thoughts which come into my mind are brought there by some form of reinstatement of knowledge which I have gained on some earlier occasion. Productive, or reproductive, processes of imagery are at work. But my attention may be wholly monopolised with the reference of these thoughts to the future. They may not at any point in my thinking present themselves as mere exponents of my antecedent experiences. I think of India as an interesting country, and my attitude is of course determined by things which I have previously learned about it. But this fact of my having gotten my information in some moment of my earlier life may drop wholly out of sight in my enthusiasm over the knowledge itself. Clearly, then, there is a distinction between the mere reappearance of ideas in consciousness, and the fact of memory, as involving *recognition* of these ideas as elements in my *own past* history.

Definition of Memory.—We may define memory, then, with more preciseness than we have before attempted, by quoting James' words. "Memory proper—*is the knowledge of an event or fact,* of which meantime we have not been thinking with the additional consciousness that *we have thought, or experienced it before.*"

Analysis of Memory.—Let us take a specific instance of memory as thus defined and examine it. Suppose we attempt to recall where we were and what we were doing at 10 o'clock on the fifteenth day of last month. Ordinarily we shall be obliged to begin by remembering upon what day of the week that month began, and this in turn may require our remembering upon what day the present month came in. Let us suppose that we find in this way that the fifteenth of the preceding month fell upon a Tuesday. If our life is subject to a fixed routine, this will generally suffice to give us the clue to our whereabouts and doings at the hour suggested. After a moment's reflection we remember, perhaps, that we were in the library reading American history, and upon a little more reflection we may recall what other persons were in the room, and what portions of the text we were reading.

Memory and Association, or Cerebral Habit.—This analysis at once reveals what we shall find true in any case we may select, *i. e.*, that we call back our memory ideas, or images, by means of ideas which are associated with them. In order to solve the problem set us by the question in our illustration, we began by calling into mind ideas which we knew to be connected with the solution. In this way, little by little, we obtain the clue to our occupation at the time suggested. Memory depends, then, for its operation upon the principle of association, and this principle is in the last analysis identical with the law of habit in the cortical processes of the cerebrum, as was shown in the previous chapter.

Memory and Imagery.—If we inquire into the nature of the mental content which has passed through our consciousness in any such case of memory, we find that it is made up of images—visual, auditory, motor, etc. When we reach the goal of our endeavour, and succeed in recalling our presence in the library, we discover that the content of our thought is not only made up of images, but that over and above this fact is to be remarked the peculiar character of the imagery. Just in the measure in which our recollection is detailed and confident, we shall ordinarily find the imagery profuse and exact in its representation of the temporal and spatial order of the events and objects present to consciousness in the original experience. This consideration affords us, therefore, a practical distinction between the imagery involved in mere reproductive imagination and that employed in memory. We can symbolise the matter as in the accompanying diagram (figure 57). In reproductive imagination the image X brings with it only the images Y and Z, and these are insufficient to give it a specific setting in time and space. In memory, the image a brings with it the extensive cluster of images b, c, d, etc., which serve to reinstate with some approach to completeness the experience which they purport to represent. There is commonly a difference, then, both in the quantity and the character of the imagery found in memory as distinct from reproductive imagination. All memory is reproductive imagination. But not all reproductive imagination is memory, as we have defined it.

Memory and Recognition.—One still more important peculiarity is noticeable in this case of memory which we are analysing. After we have, by means of associated images, gotten into mind our whereabouts and acts at the time named,

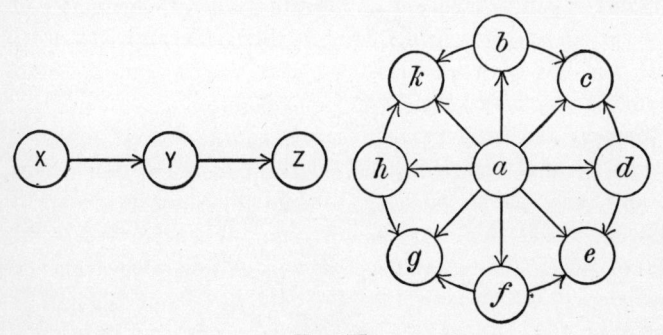

Fig. 57.

and after the imagery portraying our situation has been developed in consciousness, it is still necessary, if this is not all to be futile, that we should *recognise, identify*, and assent to the images thus brought before our notice, as indicating the actual experience to be recalled. This fact of recognition we have previously emphasised as a distinguishing mark of memory when compared with imagination. It seems to be an ultimate and unanalysable property of consciousness. But however much it may baffle our attempts to dissect it, there can be no question of its fundamental import, and we must accordingly take account of it.

Memory an Outgrowth of Recognition.—It seems on the whole probable that memory, in the meaning of our definition, has grown out of a cruder process of recognition which, although it is now no longer sole proprietor of the activity, still accompanies the memory act in its elaborate forms as a basal and indispensable characteristic. If we examine, for example, the actions of an infant, we very early observe evidences of the recognition of objects. Thus, the mother's face, the sounds of preparing food, the contact sensations occasioned when clothing is put on or off, are all of them recognised at a period when it would be hazardous to assume that any independent memory imagery has as yet become disengaged from the general sensory continuum of consciousness. Clearly then, the recognition process may begin with conscious events which are dominantly of the sensory and perceptual kind; whereas our contact with it thus far in our study has been primarily in connection with representational activities of the centrally initiated character.

Psychophysical Conditions of Sensory Recognition.—When we consider the neural conditions under which sensory recognition arises in the young babe, it is immediately suggested to us that recognition depends primarily upon the reëxcitation of pathways in the nervous system over which nervous impulses have previously travelled. The psychical thrill which such stimulation sets up finds an echo in the organism, which is probably the beginning of recognition. If we take this fact of recognition, in connection with the other facts we noticed when describing the beginnings of habit, we shall secure a deeper insight into the mode of development peculiar to the process here at issue.

Take the case of a child learning to recognise its mother. At first, when the mother takes the child up to be fed, the visual, tactual, and gustatory stimulations set up miscellaneous movements which are in the main uncoördinated and utterly variable. Little by little, however, as these sense impressions are repeated, and their agreeable consequences are experienced, the movements tend, after the manner we have already described, to settle down into the relatively coördinated groups which the experience encourages. Smiling, gurgling, jerking the limbs in movements anticipatory of being taken up rapidly appear and become fixed as habits.

Very quickly, then, these repeated sense impressions set up sensory-motor coördinations, of which the conscious process of recognition is the psychical accompaniment. These impressions promptly come to mean certain movements. Indeed, the movements are actually initiated by the impressions, and recognition is the mental state which observes, assents to, and in a sense guides, these physiological responses. The psychophysical activity in recognition does not involve merely a *repetition* of these sense stimulations; it involves a reinstatement of a sensory-motor cycle, and the recognition factor, as we isolate this on the psychological side, is simply the peculiar *quale* which belongs to this cycle. As these responses become more and more automatic, the psychical part of the activity tends to evaporate, as we have so often pointed out. In just the measure in which this occurs do we cease to feel any clear, definite, vital sense of familiarity, any tingling thrill of recognition. This is illustrated in adult life by the "matter of course" manner in which we respond to the thousand and one objects which we see every day—the books, papers, inkstand and pens on our desks, the tables, chairs, windows and lamps in our rooms, the trees on our familiar streets, the shape and colour of our own houses, etc. We recognise all these things of course, but it is with a relatively automatic, dim kind of consciousness, which contrasts sharply with the vivacity and distinctness of the feeling which we get upon first seeing these same objects after prolonged absence. We may feel moderately confident, therefore, that recognition of the sensory variety rests upon the reinstatement of acquired sensory-motor coördinations; *i. e.*, on the genetic side it displays a period of conflict of impulses and movements with maladjustment, a period of increasingly efficient adaptation, and a final period in which the conscious factor tends to drop out, sometimes apparently doing this, sometimes stopping just short of disappearance.

Psychophysical Conditions of Ideational Recognition.—When we recognise ideas, or images, in distinction from perceptions, as having previously occupied our consciousness, the strictly mental features of the case do not differ materially from those we have just described. We are ordinarily, perhaps, more definitely aware of the fringe of suggested images with which an idea that we recognise promptly surrounds itself, although this is apparently not an invariable feature of recognition. But the production of an emotional reaction, or mood, which we may name the familiarity feeling, is common to both the sensory and the ideational forms of recognition. Generally, but not always, the act of recognition is agreeable, and this, too, is true whether the act be of the sensory or the ideational kind. Probably the mere act of recognition is, as such, always agreeable, although the object, or content of the thought recognised, is of course sometimes quite otherwise. Moreover, both kinds of recognition, sensory and ideational, may vary almost indefinitely as regards the distinctness and the degree of elaboration belonging to the various parts of the process. We may thus find that an idea which comes into our mind—for example, the visual image of some person's face—calls up the vague feeling "familiar," "seen before," and nothing more. Or it may surround itself with a number of other images and we may at once recognise it as the face of a speaker whom we heard last week. In both cases, and in all instances of recognition, however, it must be remembered that the *mental act* of explicit recognition is something unique; something which is not simply synonymous with these accompanying conditions which we are describing. When we get these accompanying conditions we get the act too, and when they are all absent, the act is apparently absent. But the mental relating of the remembered idea, or the remembered perception, to the past is something distinctly additional to and beyond these concomitants.

On the physiological side it seems probable that ideational recognition is much like sensory recognition, save as regards the neural processes which initiate it. The sense organ activity is clearly not the immediate predecessor of the cortical action underlying recognition in the case of its ideational form. But the motor response is essentially identical, and its cortical basis is, for all we can see, of a similar character. The matter can be put diagrammatically, as in the accompanying figure (58). In the case of sensory recogni-

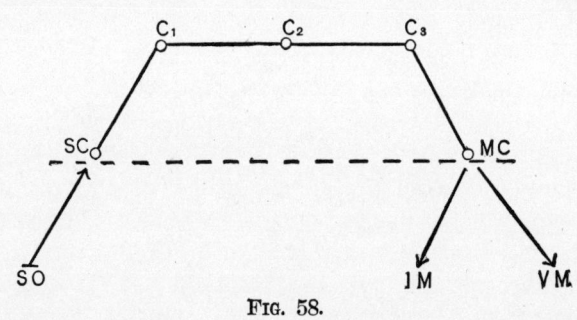

FIG. 58.

tion the process starts in the sense organ (SO) and is transmitted to the sensory regions of the cortex (SC), arousing perception. Thence it is transmitted to other cortical centres (C_1, C_2, etc.), resulting in the arousal of supplementary ideas, which serve to give the perception its place in past experience, and the process is then carried over to the motor regions (MC), and thus out into the voluntary and involuntary muscles, producing the habitual response in completion of the sensory-motor cycle. In ideational recognition the process is of the same character, save that now the sense organ origin of the cortical excitation is lacking. The process starts, so far as we can discern, in some cortical centre like C_1. At all events, if a sensory process is really responsible for the result, it lies so far back in the series of cortical activities that we cannot confidently connect it with the result. It ought not to be necessary to point out that the actual motor reactions characterising these processes of recognition may be of an extremely rudimentary and fragmentary kind. But the tendency to make the movements, with its indication of a degree of innervation in the mortor cortex, seems to be a genuine part of the act.

Remembering and Forgetting.—It has already been abundantly emphasised that memory (using the term from this point on to the end of the chapter in the broader sense of common parlance, as equivalent to *recollection* in its various forms) depends in the last analysis upon the retentiveness of the nervous tissues. When we are not occupied with a thought, or an image, so far as we know, the thought, or image, simply goes out, ceases to exist. Certain psychologists prefer to think of these psychological facts as stored up in the mind in the form of what they call " psychical dispositions," or tendencies. But however it may fare with this last mentioned theory, the modifications of the cortical tissues which our experiences bring about are certainly relatively durable; and when the cortex is called upon to resuscitate a previous experience, it summons the appropriate centres, with their imbedded modifications, to perform again the action previously executed. This is apparently the physical basis of imagination and memory. In one sense, therefore, it is probable that no item of our lives is ever literally and entirely forgotten. Even if we find it impossible, as we sometimes do, voluntarily to recall a certain idea, we must believe that the experience in which we originally encountered it has left its indelible impress upon the substance of the brain, whose action will in consequence be somewhat different from that which it might have manifested had the experience in question never befallen us.

Despite this belief, forgetfulness is a constant and often exasperating characteristic of daily life. It also has a useful function, which we do not always recognise. From the psychophysical point of view we obtained the most important explanation of the value of forgetting when we were examining the facts about attention. In the chapter devoted to attention we found that consciousness is seemingly never impartial in its response to the objects presented to it. It is always primarily concerned with some particular portion of the objective field. It neglects this and attends to that, it is dimly aware of this and keenly cognisant of that. Now, if memory is dependent upon the modifications which neural stimulations impress upon the cerebral cortex, and if consciousness and cortical action run parallel with one another, as we have seen is apparently the case, it holds to reason that those items in any experience which procure our undivided and concentrated attention must succeed in leaving deeper and more permanent traces in the cortical tissues than do those to which we attend in the margin of consciousness, or than those over which we pass uninterestedly. Although the undoubted tendency of the brain is to register and store up all the impressions which are imposed upon it, the gradual change of organic structures must inevitably bring it about that some of the less deeply engraved modifications should gradually become so faint and so disused as to render them practically inert and incompetent to participate vitally in the operations of memory. Temporary functional disconnections of brain centres that normally are connected are familiar to all of us. I know my friend's middle name perfectly well, and yet when asked for it a moment ago I could not command it. Some momentary stoppage of the associated pathways in the cortex checked the attempt at recall. Many of the most serious disorders of insanity involve this kind of disconnection and disintegration among ideas, of course much exaggerated.

One primary reason for our forgetfulness, therefore, is found in the process of attention. We must expect to forget a goodly part of all those items of experience to which we do not lend a vigorous and forceful attention. The only compensation for the lack of such concentration is found in the tedious process of repetition, by means of which we may, with even indifferent attention, grind gradually into our brain tissues any material which we desire to retain.

Forgetting has its use, however, in freeing us from the incubus of much utterly valueless experience. On the whole we remember fairly well those things which are of practical importance to us. Were our minds so organised as to retain with impartial accuracy all the events in our experience, and were their total capacity to remain unchanged, we should find our intellectual possibilities immensely curtailed by the obtrusion of the insignificant and irrelevant. While we are occasionally incommoded by forgetting, it is undoubtedly on the whole an added source of efficiency in our mental operations, that we find the unimportant elements of our knowledge so frequently dropping out of our memories.

Defects in Recollection.—We obtain an interesting sidelight upon normal memory processes by observing some of the common defects and abnormalities to which it is subject. These are in the main exaggerations of common and familiar deficiencies. Thus, in one form of mental disorder everything is forgotten the moment it passes out of the range of perception. We observe in ourselves the counterpart of this case, when after reading a sentence, for instance, we find, as occasionally occurs to all of us, that for a few moments we are absolutely unable to remember anything about it, and often must ignominiously read it again. The opposite type of abnormality is met with in the form of vastly heightened sensitivity to impressions, which can then be recalled with marvellous accuracy and detail. The mathematical prodigies who can recall lists of a hundred or more figures after a single glance are cases in point. With most of us the only phenomenon closely corresponding to this is found in our ability to recall experiences which have been characterised by intense emotional disturbance. The details of some episode in which we have been greatly terrified may linger in our memories with a vividness which rivals the distinctness of the original experience. Again, the memory of events during a severe illness may be almost wholly lost. A similar obliviscence as to the occurrences preceding a severe accident is very frequent.

An interesting disease of memory which furnishes striking confirmation of our conclusions concerning the dependence of memory and imagination upon the image consists in the loss of memory for specific forms of sensory material. Thus, the visual memory may be entirely lost, so that one cannot recall how objects look. Or the auditory images of words may be obliterated. If the imagery which is lost be of the variety chiefly employed by the patient in his thinking, the result is inevitably most disastrous, reducing the victim to a condition bordering upon imbecility.

Another curious disturbance of memory, with which most of us are familiar, is found in the experience of a feeling that we have previously been in the place where we are at the moment, or a feeling that we have previously said the words we are now saying, while as a matter as fact we know that we cannot possibly have been in the given situation, nor have spoken the words. Many explanations have been advanced for this phenomenon, which still remains, however, obscure as to its origin. It probably arises from different causes at different times, and is, perhaps, most often to be regarded as primarily a disturbance of emotional processes connected with the " familiarity feeling."

Lastly there are numerous abnormalities in which the order of remembered events and the time of their occurrence is distorted; things are persistently " remembered," which never occurred, and imaginary events are interpolated among real events, in a manner which baffles analysis. The counterparts of these last named defects in our own every-day life will suggest themselves at once.

When memory begins to decay under the advance of age there is a remarkable uniformity in the order in which certain kinds of knowledge disappear, and in many cases of insanity a similar order of disintegration is observed. Thus, the memory of proper names is among the earliest of the losses, and the more concrete are our ideas, the earlier do we lose the memory of the words for them. Abstract ideas which depend very largely for their existence in our thought upon the words which we use to designate them are by virtue of the law of habit much more persistent; because the word is in this case bound up much more widely and intimately with our use of the idea. So it comes about that the memory of adjectives and verbs, conjunctions and prepositions, outlives that of most nouns and proper names. The objects for which nouns are our verbal symbols we can, and frequently do, think of in terms of imagery other than that of words, *e. g.*, visual, tactual, etc. Consequently the memory of these words is less deeply imbedded in the brain tissues, and when this tissue decays such memories are the first to suffer extinction.

Training and Development of Memory Processes.—It is evident that any effort to train the memory must, if it is to succeed, be based upon the employment of such principles as are natural and inherent in the memory process itself.

Now the first of these principles involves factors which are largely mechanical in their nature. If the cortical basis of recollection is resident in the modifications of nervous tissue, brought about by the impressions which pour in upon us, it is clear that anything which will augment the permanency of these modifications, or increase their number, will in so far make towards the preservation of the accompanying psychical processes and the establishment of an efficient memory. Experience certainly justifies this statement, for we find that any impressions which we can make extremely vivid are likely to be retained in memory for a longer time than would be the case if the impressions were less intense. Such vivid experiences are always productive of deep-seated neural excitement, and we may reasonably suppose that their ready retention and recall is a sign of the depth of the nervous modification produced by them. Similarly, the mere repetition of an impression must serve sooner or later to set up relatively permanent modifications in the brain tissue, and so indirectly accomplish permanency of retention in the mind. These points we have already touched upon in our account of association in the previous chapter.

It is not often easy in a practical way to enhance the effectiveness of our memories through rendering *emotionally* vivid the impressions we wish to preserve. But so far as we can succeed in focalising our attention exclusively upon the matter in hand, so far we do make gains in vividness, and the importance for efficient memory processes of concentrated attention is based upon precisely this fact. Speaking from an empirical point of view, it seems probable that the immense variation in the memory processes of different people is largely connected with this difference in ability to concentrate attention. The habit of giving oneself with complete abandon to the undertaking immediately in hand is one of the most significant clues to the securing of an alert and accurate memory.

Obviously it is simple enough to make use of repetition. We may either do this by giving ourselves over and over again the same sense stimulation, as when we repeat a name which we wish to remember; or we may, after the manner of the modern elementary schools, present the same object to a number of different senses, as when we listen to the sound of the name, then speak it, then write it and look at the written word. In such ways we can increase the depth of the cortical modifications, corresponding to some single sense department, or we can increase the number of cortical areas affected by the stimulus. In either case we evidently increase the total amount of cortical modifications, and so better the chances, not only for the permanent retention, but also for easy and ready recall. The more pathways there are in the brain leading to the stimulation of any special activity, the more likely is it that the given activity can be promptly aroused. The more ideas there are in the mind connected with any given idea, the more chances there are for the latter to be expeditiously produced when needed.

As a matter of fact all memory processes depend in some measure upon this mechanical factor, but it becomes relatively less important as the general level of intellectual development rises. There are many things which children must necessarily get at first in a largely mechanical fashion. Learning to spell, for example, is in English largely a mechanical accomplishment, the available rational elements being chiefly conspicuous by their absence. But for adult undertakings it is a poor memory which responds only to mechanical incitements. Nevertheless, our modern education, with its extensive desertion of all verbatim methods of memorising, is undoubtedly in danger of pouring the baby out with the bath, of discarding a method useful in its place, even though not useful in all places.

Logical Method of Memorising.—The most important factor in assisting the establishment of broad and sound memory processes is of a practical and logical character. If we can once knit up a fact to be remembered with a group of other already known facts with which it is intimately related, we often come to see the entire group as mutually dependent upon, or explanatory of, one another. And thus we find we can retain in memory the total mass more efficiently than we could a much smaller number of items, so long as they remain unrelated. Such an interrelating of the facts has in a sense the effect of reducing the mass to a *single mental* fact. A child being taught the method of long division in arithmetic, or the method of determining the square root of a number, finds the successive steps in the process extremely difficult to keep straight, so long as the procedure is based simply upon the memory of the rule, which states dogmatically the order of the various operations to be performed. But as soon as the relation of the several steps to one another is clearly apprehended, as soon as the real nature of the process is understood, the verbatim memory of the rule becomes a superfluity, which may be forgotten with entire impunity. The several facts represented by the separate arithmetical operations all flow together as integral parts of a larger whole, to which they are seen to be essential. Thereafter, the nightmare of a forgotten rule is banished. In a certain sense, however, the rule can hardly be forgotten as long as the clear apprehension of the relations involved remains. For the rule is simply the verbal formulation of these relations. But under such conditions one's action is free, intelligent, and independent, instead of blind, and slavish to a mere rule-of-thumb.

If we are asked how to go about the creation of these logical relations among the facts with which we wish to equip our memories, the answer will turn upon two points. We must first reflect upon the thing to be remembered, and attempt to give it a setting among the things with which it is most closely connected. No fact ever comes to us wholly isolated from the rest of our knowledge, and most facts bear upon their faces evidence of their most intimate relations. We should at once, then, scrutinise each new fact that comes, and inquire what there is in the series of events or relations to which it belongs that has occasioned its existence. We should ask for the causes which have produced it, and the consequences to which it leads. If we can succeed in setting up relationships of this kind, we find that the new fact becomes a real part of our minds, just as in the case of the arithmetical rules of which we spoke a moment ago. In studying history, for example, such a procedure will mean that we shall try to see any given fact, like a battle, a cession of territory, or a piece of legislation, in the light of all the facts, political, social, economic, geographical, etc., which may bear upon it in any significant way. All the important episodes in a historical period will thus be welded together, each throwing light upon the other in a way which makes it natural and easy to recall them.

An ideally perfect mind would involve, among other things, a complete working out of all the relations sustained by a given fact to all other known facts. In actual experience, however, we find that our information is largely stored away on the compartment principle. Our knowledge of history seldom gets any very intimate articulation with our knowledge of astronomy. The events with which each deals do not appeal to us as intrinsically germane. Similarly, our knowledge of exact science seldom interferes in either a theoretical or a practical way with our knowledge of politics; and it is notorious that, for certain persons at least, religious knowledge and belief is kept quite distinct from every other intellectual and practical interest.

In the second place, we should always, when possible, proceed at once to make some actual use of the information we are seeking to impress upon our memories. In a certain way the process of reflection, which we have just been describing, necessitates our using the facts we are trying to memorise. But we have in mind here a more overt activity. We saw in the previous chapter that the fundamental function of our memory and imagination is the control which they afford over experience, both past and future. These activities are, moreover, only a sort of half-way house between the sensory stimulus and the motor reaction, of which we have heard so much. The relevant motor expression ought, therefore, to be allowed to occur. If all this be true, we shall have some theoretical foundation for the precept we have just formulated, a precept which is abundantly justified by experience. The sooner and oftener we can apply to some practical undertaking a fact we wish to remember, the better the chance of its remaining in our minds. Talking about it, writing about it, incorporating it into some manual constructive activity, if it is a fact which will permit such treatment, are all methods of accomplishing the desired result. A mind trained to concentrated logical reflection upon facts, and then further trained to make the earliest feasible application of them in practical ways, is a mind which will achieve the maximal efficiency in its memory processes.

Mnemonic Systems.—Evidently these methods of training the powers of retention and recall suggest no easy royal road to success. They mean hard work. But they are the only methods which have any large and general significance for the development of the mind. Many catch-penny devices have been hit upon to simplify memorising, and within certain narrow limits such systems have a value. The mnemonic schemes of many so-called "memory systems" illustrate the point. Suppose one has occasion to remember a great many unrelated numbers, like the street addresses of a large group of people. One may greatly facilitate such a feat by first memorising a "form," in which each digit is connected with a consonant, *e. g.*, the 1 with t, 2 with l, 3 with d, etc. The next step is to make a word easily suggested by the person whose name is to be remembered, in which these letters shall occur in proper order. For example, Mr. Smith's number is 122, Mr. Smith is tall. The word tall in the number form means 122, for the vowels are neglected. For special purposes, such as that of our illustration, such methods can be made very useful. But as applied to the acquirement and retention of miscellaneous information they are failures. It requires more time and effort to learn the forms, or frames, and then make the applications, than is required to acccomplish the same result in the ways we have already pointed out.

Idiosyncracies in Form of Recall.—Many persons have curious individual peculiarities in their methods of recalling specific kinds of material. Thus, certain people always think of the numerals by means of a kind of visual framework, known as a number form. These number forms are most various in their shape and size and general character, some of them being seen as coloured in many hues. An example of one of the simpler types is given in the accompanying sketch. (Figure 59.) A person possessing one of these forms always

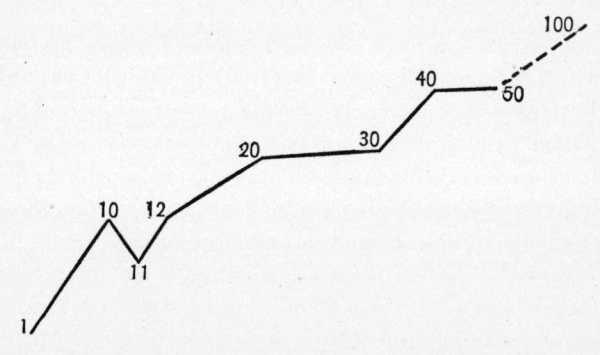

FIG. 59. In this form the numbers are seen extending upward and to the right from about the level of the shoulders.

sees the numbers about which he is thinking appearing in their appropriate place in the framework. Other persons always think of the months of the year, the days of the week, and even the hours of the day, in similar visual frameworks. All these devices seem to represent the effort of the mind to give a concrete basis to abstract relations. But they are for the most part acquired in early childhood in a perfectly naïve way, and apparently indicate native differences in the way different minds get hold of material to be remembered. "Coloured hearing," or chromæsthesia, of which mention was made in the analysis of perception, belongs to the same range of individual idiosyncracy.

CHAPTER X

THE CONSCIOUSNESS OF MEANING AND THE FORMATION OF CONCEPTS

In the actual execution of the functions hitherto described another mental operation is involved in addition to those which we have thus far analysed. This operation is contained in a latent fashion in each of these conscious activities with which we have been dealing; but it comes repeatedly to light as a relatively distinct mental process, and we must accordingly submit it to examination. Indeed, many of the acts which we have used as illustrations throughout our previous study could hardly result as they do were it not for the presence of this mental factor, which is known in its most developed form as *conception*. The mental product which results from it is called a concept. In its more rudimentary form we may call it the consciousness of meaning, and we shall discuss the simpler phase first.

The Consciousness of Meaning.—On the side of function, the most fundamental property of intelligence is, perhaps, the ability to recognise and employ *meanings*. Perception could never lead to the establishment of efficient habitual coördinations were we not able to apprehend the meaning of that which we see and hear and touch. Memory would be an abortive resuscitation of the past could we not recognise the meaning of that which we recall. Imagination in all its forms would be a mere mental logomachy were it not for our ability to understand the meaning of the images which occupy our minds. From beginning to end, therefore, of our mental activities the presence of meaning is absolutely indispensable.

That a thing means something to us is equivalent to saying that it symbolises something for us, that we are aware of some of the relations which it sustains to other things. Now, the mind shows itself from the very outset as a relating activity. We have previously analysed one of the most elementary forms of this relating process in our account of recognition. On the level of perceptual and sensory activities the crude, vague identifying of one experience with an antecedent one must represent in the infant consciousness the first outcropping in an explicit way of the relational factor, the first appearance of the awareness of meaning. An experience which is recognised, no matter how vaguely, is thereby in our very manner of feeling it connected by us symbolically with something else not present.

The fundamental activities of attention—*i. e.*, the manipulation of the sensuous material of experience, now in an analytical, discriminative way, and now in a synthesising, associative way—result inevitably from the very first in the disclosure of innumerable relations involved among masses previously sensed in a rude, inchoate manner. Certain typical forms under which this analytic-synthetic development of relations occurs, we have already described in the chapter on attention, so that we need not repeat the matter at this point. We are emphasising here, however, as we did not do at that juncture, the fact that our noticing of differences and likenesses in the material presented to our senses rests upon our ability to note and employ the relations which these processes of attention throw into relief. It is, in short, because the elements which we thus break out from the total mass of unanalysed sense experience possess meaning for us, symbolise relations of one and another kind, that we can employ them coherently and efficiently. Without this element of apprehended meaning they would remain disconnected, wholly irrational and inert bits of mentality; curious perhaps, but certainly useless. The element of meaning joins them to one

CONSCIOUSNESS OF MEANING

another in a vital organic union. Probably the most fundamental form of this consciousness of meaning and relation is our previously mentioned awareness of sameness and difference. We know at once without tutelage of any kind when two experiences seem to us the same, and when they seem different. Evidently, the process of recognition is closely related to this sense of sameness, if it be not, indeed, found practically identical.

All that we have said, thus far, about sense perception and the analytic-synthetic play of attention upon such material is true in even more obvious fashion, when we come to speak of images and ideas. The idea is, as such, clearly a symbolic affair, finding its *raison d'être* not in itself, but in that which it does, that for which it stands. Evidently *meaning* is the very essence of the idea. Moreover, we develop the meanings and relations among our ideas by means of just the same kind of attention processes as characterised our manipulation of sensory activities. By focussing our attention now upon one feature of a thought, and now upon another, by " abstracting," as it is sometimes called, one phase or another, we analyse our ideas, compare them with one another, and so come to the discernment of unsuspected relations, of unrealised likenesses and differences.

Psychologists are by no means agreed as to the precise nature of the mental activity by means of which we apprehend relations. Certain writers make the whole achievement a function of attention, and disclaim the necessity for any further explanation. Attention is declared to be in its very essence a relating activity, and consequently, so far as we attend, we always attend in a relational way. Other writers maintain that just as certain moments of consciousness are cognisant of percepts or images, so certain other moments are cognisant of relations. Thus James speaks of our having " feelings of relation," *e. g.*, a feeling of " and," a feeling of " if," and a feeling of " for." Certain psychologists of this way of thinking recognise what they call "relational elements" of consciousness comparable with sensation elements.

A complete consideration of this matter would take us too far afield into unsettled principles, and the reader must temporarily countenance the author's dogmatic general statement that the consciousness of relation is a basal factor in all activities of attention; that our attention is sometimes more, and sometimes less, directed toward the extant *relations* than toward the *things* related; but that no moment of cognitive consciousness is wholly lacking in the awareness either of relations or objects. The distinction between objects and relations simply names two features, the static and the dynamic, of a common phenomenon. We come next to consider conception, which constitutes the most overt and elaborate form assumed by our consciousness of meaning, a form in which psychologists and philosophers have always been specially interested.

Definition of Conception.—In our illustrations of the manner in which we consciously avail ourselves of the lessons taught us by experience, we have implied that memory and imagination operate by summoning specific events which apply to the problem immediately confronting us. This is often the case. Thus, I find myself puzzled as to the best method for getting to some very remote country town. I attempt to recall what railroads I employed to get there a year ago, and I solve my problem by applying the recollection which comes to me of this particular achievement. I remember that I took the A and B to junction D, waited two hours and got a train on the X and Y to my destination. But many cases in which we apply the fruits of past experience are of a different order from this. Thus, if I am purchasing scientific instruments from a French firm, I must convert the prices in their catalogue from francs into dollars. This I accomplish by first bringing to mind my idea of a franc, as being approximately a fifth of a dollar, and then performing the appropriate arithmetical operation. In this case I obviously employ my memory in meeting my necessities; but it is memory in the form of reproductive imagination upon which I fall back, and not necessarily the memory of any *single* event or experience, as in the preceding instance. Again, I am interested in certain philanthropic efforts at social reform, and I find that the programme which I am invited to support involves belief in the hereditary nature of acquired characteristics. The theory at issue maintains that vicious traits are acquired and transmitted from parents to children, and my contribution is solicited in the furtherance of a project to prevent the possibility of such acquirement and transmission. Immediately I find my mind busying itself with the idea of heredity, and my final action is, perhaps, determined by the conclusion which I am able to reach upon this point.

Now in these last two cases my use of the idea of a franc or my idea of heredity clearly does not necessarily involve an immediate reference to any single and specific experience of francs or heredity. I might, of course, make the application in this way, if I chose. I might allow my mind to dwell on the last occasion upon which I saw a franc, and on the last book in which I had read of heredity. But this is by no means essential, and often would not occur under such circumstances as we have supposed. Accordingly, these ideas, to wit, franc and heredity, are mental devices by which we succeed in symbolising for ourselves in the one case a number of objects, and in the other case a number of relations, without the necessity of calling to mind any particular occasion upon which we have come in contact with them. We use these ideas fearlessly in our reasoning, and when we have reached our conclusions we make the application to the concrete instance in hand, with entire confidence that the event will justify our action—and generally it does. Such ideas as these are what are usually called concepts, and taking such cases for the moment as reliable illustrations, we may say, following the common usage, that conception is that mental operation by means of which we bring together the common points of our various experiences and mentally consolidate them into ideas; ideas which we are then able to use as symbols, or representatives, of these manifold items.

It should, perhaps, be remarked at this point that the scientific and logical concept is generally credited with a higher degree of exactness and precision than our definition suggests. The concepts of science, such as "metal," are gotten by a process of abstraction and comparison, the result of which is then expressed in the most rigorously exact verbal definition. Evidently, however, these are not the concepts of practical life. The derivation of the word concept (from *concipere*, to take in) may assist us to bear the facts in mind. Conception is thus, as we shall presently see in more detail, the great simplifier of our knowledge, the great labour-saving device by means of which a single idea may do the work of hundreds of other ideas. We apply the term "concept" to this idea, the term "conception" to the mental operation in which the idea is produced.

Analysis of Conception.—If concepts are general ideas of the kind we have indicated it is evident that we must possess them in large numbers. Concepts of men and horses, houses and trees, hats and tables, with others of like ilk, must constitute a large part of our mental furniture. We must also have concepts of such things as colour, odour, and sound; concepts of physical relations, like position, order, and time; concepts of moral attributes, such as good and evil, and dozens of other forms too numerous to mention. We shall probably get ahead most rapidly in our analysis if we take some special instance of conception and examine the mental processes involved in it. Take in this way one's general idea of horse.

Concept and Image.

—If I say to a group of persons, "Fix your attention firmly upon your idea of horse," a certain number of them are certain to find a visual image of a horse arising in their minds. Another group will find that the auditory-motor word-image "horse" is present in their consciousness. Now, according to our definition, the concept of horse must not apply to any special horse, but it must represent all horses. How can the persons who are confronted with a visual image of some particular Bucephalus, or Rosinante, be said to have any concept of horses in general? The correct answer to this question is at once suggested by a reference to the imagery of the second group of persons.

The word-image "horse" evidently does not pretend to refer to one specimen of the class more than to another. It is purely symbolic. When it comes into our consciousness to serve as a concept, it is as though we had agreed mentally with ourselves to accept it as a representative of the physical equine genus. Just as in algebra we allow the early letters of the alphabet to stand for certain quantities in our problems and the later letters for certain others, making the appropriate practical substitutions at the completion of our computation, so here we symbolise certain objects to ourselves by means of auditory word-images. We mentally manipulate these images, draw certain inferences and then execute the substitutions, which in these cases are commonly overt acts. Having, for example, reflected by means of such concepts upon the shortcomings of horses, we decide to purchase an automobile. The concept, which is primarily *mental*, is eventually converted into movements which are physical.

Now, the case of the persons who use visual images is in no respect fundamentally different from that of these users of word imagery. The visual image is, to be sure, for better or for worse, a kind of *copy* of an *individual* in the class which it is supposed to represent. At least it is often a recognisable copy of one of our perceptions of such an individual. But provided that, in our use of an image, we recognise it as *really* symbolising the *class*, and not an individual, and use it, *intending* it to accomplish this purpose for us, it is a matter of essential indifference what special kind of imagery we happen to employ, whether visual, or auditory, or motor.

Two important points emerge from the examination of of this case. (1) The concept apparently involves an image; and, (2) whatever image we use, it is the specific meaning which we attach to it that constitutes it a concept. These two considerations make clear how it comes about that our thought processes seem often so different on different occasions, even when we have been thinking about the same subject. Of course, the order of our thoughts might easily vary at different times, and our conclusions might vary. But how is it that we can think about the *same* things when the *content* of our thought is so different? The content of our thought is, so far at least as concerns the knowledge process, always made up of imagery. To-day this may be largely auditory and verbal, to-morrow largely visual. But provided I use the different images to stand for the same meanings on the two days, I shall come out perfectly well and my thought will unquestionably have been about the *same* object and its relations. Thus it comes to pass that, although we never have literally the same image present twice in our consciousness, we nevertheless can think the same meanings again and again.

The Generic Idea.—This seems the appropriate place to refer to a theory which certain eminent psychologists have espoused, *i. e.*, the theory of generic ideas. The hypothesis upon which the theory rests is that our repeated visual perceptual experiences of tables, for example, result in producing a kind of composite mental photograph of tables. Such a composite photograph would evidently serve us whenever we wished to think of tables in general; that is to say, it would serve as a concept. We might use other images for the same purpose, conspicuously our word-images; but we might equally well use this composite visual image.

We shall make only two comments upon this theory. In the first place it is extremely difficult to determine whether or not we really have such composite images. It would obviously be very difficult to say with entire confidence whether an image possessing the indefiniteness of outline and the indistinctness of detail which a true composite would undoubtedly possess were actually a representative of innumerable individual perceptions; or simply a blurred, vague, imperfectly reinstated image of some single perception. Introspectively, that is to say, the evidence can hardly be made conclusive in support of the theory. Moreover, the brain processes involved in the production of such an image are somewhat difficult to understand when brought into connection with our supposed ability to call up images of specific objects belonging to a given class, of which we might also have a generic image.

In the second place, so far as concerns the function of conception, it appears at once that such a generic image would belong to the class of images which we may call "copy-images," in distinction from images which purport to be *merely* symbols. All images are, of course, symbolic, so far as they stand for something not themselves, and all images are copy-images so far as they serve to reinstate special forms of sense perception. An auditory image may be in this way a copy, good, bad, or indifferent, of an acoustical perception. A visual image may likewise simulate some visual perception. But the auditory image may, on the other hand, serve to symbolise some visual experience, and the visual image, *e. g.*, the visual image of a word, may also symbolise something of a non-visual character. Evidently, copy-images may be hopelessly inadequate, *as copies*, to stand for generalised relations. So, to revert to our original illustration, a visual image of a table would, as a mere copy, be an unsatisfactory representative of the class "table," for no single image could embody all the peculiarities of all tables. This limitation would be as true of the composite image, supposing it to exist, as of any other. It is only as such an image is employed symbolically that it serves satisfactorily as a concept of the class "table." But an image of any table whatever would serve this purpose well enough, provided only that in our thinking we used it with this recognised intention. Furthermore, the word-image, which commonly has no resemblance whatever to the objects symbolised, is always available. So that taking account of these considerations—the doubt as to the actuality of the generic image, and the absence of any special fitness in it for service as the basis of a concept—we may safely omit further discussion of it.

Conception and Language.—Our analysis of conception has brought out the fact that it is by means of this mental process that we are able to make our thoughts the vehicles of definite meanings. It is a familiar fact that language has a precisely similar function. The inference at once suggests itself that language may be nothing but an elaborate conceptual system, and this inference is essentially correct. When we communicate with others we give our ideas outward expression in spoken words, which serve as concepts to the hearer. When we are engaged in reflective thought, we shall often find that we are thinking in terms of word-images, and these word-images in such cases serve as our concepts. Language is thus not only the great *social* medium of thought exchange, it is also in large measure the medium of subjective thought processes.

Some psychologists maintain that all concepts are of the language variety, and philosophers formerly contended that no reasoning would be possible without language. Both of these views are undoubtedly too extreme. We do sometimes reason, and we may have a considerable number of concepts, without resorting to language. Nevertheless, the supplementary statement must be made that language is the great conceptual mechanism, and that we depend upon it far more than upon any other mental material for conveying our meaning, not only when we commune with others, but also in our own private thinking.

In the use of spoken language, as well as in the use of verbal images when we are reflecting, the thought process is often so rapid that we have no distinct consciousness of the words as such. The stress of our interest and attention is upon the meaning which we are seeking, and this seems often to attach to the verbal activity in its entirety as a sentence, or a series of sentences, rather than to the isolated words. This fact does not, however, prejudice the truth of our general assertion that words serve as our most important conceptual symbols.

The use of words as concepts brings readily to our notice certain facts which bear significantly upon our present topic. We defined conception as a process of forming general ideas, and this seems to be the most striking feature in the process. But if all words are essentially concepts, we must have concepts of individual objects as well as of classes; or at all events our method of thinking individual objects must be the same as our method of thinking classes. This is, indeed, the fact. We really have a concept of Jupiter, as well as of gods; a concept of earth, as well as a concept of planets; a concept of this particular book, as well as of books in general. We have only to remember that conception is after all at bottom simply a mental process of designating meanings, to see that we can in this way indicate any meaning we wish; *e. g.*, the meaning of a single object or a dozen; the meaning of a mathematical relation, or of an historical relation; the meaning of a familiar object, or of an impossible one. In each and every case we shall have a concept, and in most cases a word, or a word-image, will be a very convenient device by means of which to think it.

We may easily connect the process by means of which we gain concepts of single objects with the process by means of which we obtain general ideas of classes of objects, if we observe that in both cases we have simply set a boundary line about certain things; in the one case the boundary contains one object, in the other it contains an indefinite number. But in both cases our mental act has been the distinguishing of one kind of meaning from all other kinds of meaning. That form of the process in which our idea refers to some common property, or properties, of a number of experiences has commonly been regarded as the true type of conception, because we appear in such cases to have *abstracted* the common qualities of a number of events, then *generalised* upon these, and so obtained the concept, or general idea. But the process by which we reach a concept of a single object involves abstraction just as truly, if not so extensively, as the previous form of operation. To obtain a concept of London involves setting the idea of London off against all other ideas; involves abstracting it in a perfectly definite way. In a sense, too, our concept of London is just as complete, just as universal, as is the concept city. It applies to *all* of its object, as truly as does the concept city, and it is in a measure an accident, an irrelevant incident, that the total object referred to is singular and not plural.

The process by which we actually come into possession of some of our more abstract general ideas is, perhaps, more complicated than that by which we gain our concepts of particulars. But the fundamental distinction between the two kinds of concepts, after we have attained them, resides in the fact that the one emphasises points of identity and sameness among the various elements of our experience, the other emphasises primarily points of difference. Strictly speaking, then, we may be sure that we have concepts of single objects, as well as of classes of objects. We have, also, concepts of abstract attributes, concepts of relations of all kinds. There is no meaning of any sort accessible to our intelligence for which we may not have a concept. Indeed, in the broad sense of the term, every idea is a concept.

On the whole it is, perhaps, easier to follow the older usage and to retain our original provisional definition of the concept as a generalising idea, and then to remember that such ideas sometimes generalise, so to speak, upon single objects, qualities, or relations, rather than to recast our definition, which would then vary somewhat ambiguously from that traditionally employed. After all, the fundamental points about concepts are those we have already mentioned, which evidently remain untouched by these questions of the number and character of the objects to which the concepts refer: that is, (1) the existence of the concept as a concrete thought, which we call an image; and (2) the use of this image to convey to ourselves, or to others, some definite, recognised, and intended meaning.

The General Function of Conception.—The general function and value of conception in the economy of the psychophysical organism is probably so obvious as to require no further elaboration. It has already been described as the great simplifier of mental operations, the labour-saving device by means of which we are enabled to accomplish with single ideas the work which otherwise might require the coöperation of many. It only remains to call attention afresh to the fact that the mental capacity which permits this condensation of the meaning of many experiences into the meaning of a single image is generically one and the same with that apprehension of meaning which renders perception intelligible, imagination significant, and memory coherent.

Neural Process and Conception.—So far as conception involves imagery, it necessarily follows that it depends upon the reaction of those areas in the cerebral cortex with which the several sense organs are most immediately connected. Beyond this we can say very little, save that there seems some reason to believe that all the more reflective and ratiocinative forms of thought process involve in an important way the action of the Flechsig association centres. It must be frankly admitted that at the present moment the neural counterparts of these higher and more recondite phases of psychical activity are practically unknown. It seems clear that they must in large measure involve the action of the same areas that are concerned in perception and in simple acts of memory. But the nature of the differences in the form of the nervous action, when the psychical act is one of prolonged reasoning with the use of elaborate concepts, as contrasted with the mere accidental calling to consciousness of some familiar visual image, for example, is still altogether a matter of speculation and hypothesis.

Development of Conception.—We have repeatedly seen reason to believe that mental life is in all essential respects like other life phenomena, manifesting periods of growth, maturity, and decay. This view leads us to expect a gradual unfolding of the typical phases of consciousness, which are at the outset latent in the infant mind, rather than the sudden appearance at different times of totally new kinds of mental operation. The development of conception is no exception to this rule.

The appearance of a rude type of recognition, which we have discovered to be the prototype of the developed act of conception, may be detected very early in infant consciousness. But it is exceedingly difficult, not to say impossible, confidently to designate the precise moment at which the first general idea is elaborated. The facts suggest that babies generalise in a rough way upon their experiences at a very early date. Or, if they do not positively generalise, they accomplish the same result negatively, by failing adequately to distinguish and analyse. Infants a few days old, if given some distasteful medicine, will often refuse utterly for hours afterward to take anything into their mouths, and for indefinite periods will reject the medicine itself. It would probably be absurd, however, to suppose that the baby has at this time a general idea of medicine, although one might with propriety speak of a generalised motor reaction. Nor would such a description detract from the genuinely conceptional nature of the reaction, for the concepts of adults may also be considered as forms of generalised motor activity. As soon as language appears, from the fourteenth to the twenty-eighth month, the formation and growth of general ideas is immensely augmented. But our previous assertion about the connection of concepts and language holds true here, and it is certainly reasonable to suppose that crude general ideas antedate the use of adult language forms. In this connection one must not forget that gestures—for example, smiling, scowling, clenching the hands, etc.—are often vehicles for conveying conceptual relations, and that the inarticulate cries and vocalisations of various kinds which precede the intelligent use of words may also be regarded as primitive linguistic concepts. Thus, a certain sound means water, another means milk, and so on. The sign language of deaf-mutes affords admirable illustrations of the same type of expression for concepts.

Formation of New Concepts.—Turning to the development of our concepts after the period of infancy, we find that their transformation proceeds along two main lines, which we can best discuss separately: first, by the creation of essentially new concepts; and second, by the enrichment of old concepts with new material. An important factor in the formation of our concepts, *i. e.*, the process of judgment, cannot be discussed until the next chapter, where we shall, however, revert briefly to the conceptual activity.

We have already seen that concepts are primarily based

upon perceptual processes, just as memory and imagination are. We have also observed the way in which every perception, even the freshest and most novel, involves past experience. We shall, therefore, be safe in assuming that what we call new concepts are only partially new, and really contain a measure of familiar material. For example, when a boy first studies algebra he is introduced to the concept of the equation, to the concept of symbolism in quantitative procedure, to the concept of negative numbers, etc. Now, we speak of such concepts as being new to the boy, and so in a sense they are. But we must also recognise the fact that they are not wholly new, and that if they were they would be entirely unintelligible to him. The significance of the equation as a mathematical tool could never be grasped were the boy's previous experience incapable of furnishing him the notion of equality as a starting point. So, too, the concept of negative numbers could never be mastered were there not the foundation of knowledge about positive numbers to build upon. Granted the rudimentary idea, or concept, of equality, and the concept of the equation becomes a possible intellectual possession. Moreover, once it is gained it takes its place as a perfectly distinct concept, related to the concept of equality and to many other concepts, but still mentally an independent idea.

What the boy really does in getting hold of such a new concept as that of negative numbers is to *compare* the new notion with his old idea of number, to remark their likenesses and differences, and to throw into the foreground, by this process of discrimination, the most practically important features of the new case. The result of this procedure is the boy's first concept of negative numbers. These abstracting, discriminating, and comparing activities of attention are present in varying degree in all self-directed attainments of new concepts.

This form of development of ideas displays in an unmistakable manner the essentially organic nature of our knowl-

CONSCIOUSNESS OF MEANING

edge. Each idea springs out of other ideas, which have gone before, and in turn gives birth to new successors. The connection is not merely one of sequence in time; it is a connection of the genuinely developmental type, in which one idea is, as it were, unfolded from, and given off by, another. Ultimately, therefore, each of our ideas is related, however remotely, to all the others, a fact which constitutes one illustration of the so-called doctrine of the total relativity of knowledge. Speaking metaphorically, but within the bounds of literal fact, we may say that the great tree of knowledge springs from the seed of that vague consciousness with which the infant's life begins. Differentiation followed by fresh synthesis, old experiences blended with new ones, each modifying the other—such is the course of progress.

The natural incentive to the development of these new concepts is to be found in the needs of the individual. We find ourselves confronted with a situation in which our old ideas are inadequate and unsatisfactory. We cannot get ahead. We are thwarted, and find ourselves obliged to set about the securing of new notions to meet the case. The child whose toy refuses to go resorts first to the familiar idea of assistance from parent or nurse. Some day this assistance fails and the child, thrown back upon his own resources, may hit upon the idea of helping himself. The same sort of thing characterises adult procedure. Thus, the frequent disaster arising from surgical operations under the old ideas of clinical cleanliness led to the examination of tissues affected by such operations, and in the light of the modern knowledge of bacterial life a wholly new and more drastic concept of surgical cleanliness has arisen, resulting in an astonishing diminution in the fatal consequences of operative surgery.

When we seek illustrations in the range of our formal educational procedure it is not always so clear that the new concepts are gained in response to felt deficiencies in our existing stock of ideas. The boy confronted with the concepts peculiar to the study of Greek and Latin and mathematics would often forego the attainment of them with definite complacency, not to say enthusiasm. It is evident that if he is to master these subjects he must first secure these concepts; but it would sometimes be a sad perversion of the facts to say that the concepts are obtained as the result of a need *felt* by the boy. A child caught thus in the educational machinery is often whirled about among needs, for which the ideas held out do indeed afford relief, but they are not always needs which the child himself feels. One has, however, only to glance at the history of any specific educational system to recognise that in its inception each system was intended to fit its pupils for some special form of life, and in this vocation the studies offered really had a place. The adult has here attempted to anticipate in the most effectual way the needs which at some time the child is sure to feel. Fortunate the child who is brought up in a system which affords him ideas fitted to his own day and generation, instead of those appropriate to the times and conditions of his great-grandparents.

The concepts which we get in the educational system may not always, then, reflect needs and difficulties of which we personally are as yet cognisant. But the system itself is an effort to epitomise the satisfaction of just those needs which in the human experience of the leaders of our race have been felt to be most imperative. Our general statement remains, therefore, essentially true, *i. e.*, that our new concepts arise out of the inadequacy of those already on hand to cope with the conditions in which we find ourselves.

The Petrifying of Concepts.—This doctrine gets a depressing confirmation by observation of persons who have once settled down into a fixed and narrow vocation in which radically *new demands* are rarely encountered, and when encountered, are found hopelessly baffling. In a degree this condition overtakes everybody as middle age passes by. The result is too often the pathetic person of inflexible sympathies, circumscribed and dogmatic ideas—the person who is sure the world is going to the bow-wows, and who knows it was all much better in his own day. Such persons have ceased to get new concepts, and the old ones are inadequate.

Enrichment of Old Concepts.—Hand in hand with this appearance of relatively new concepts goes the development of our old ideas. This development might be described as having two directions, but in reality the two are one. Our concepts seem sometimes to widen and sometimes to grow more narrow. Thus, we learn more every day about men and women, and so we may truly enough say that our concept of humanity broadens as our experience becomes richer. On the other hand our concept of science may, as our knowledge increases, become more and more restricted in its scope. Many branches of inquiry which would originally have found place under this heading may, in our maturer judgment, belong elsewhere. Both these processes are, however, simply different modes of reaching an identical result, *i. e.*, the clarification of the precise meaning of our concepts.

Every concept is in a sense a working hypothesis, a tentative manner of thinking about things, and is subject at need to revision. Our idea of right is gained in childhood from parental precepts. If we do not stagnate morally, a time must come when we are obliged to reconstruct and modify this childish concept. As our knowledge becomes broader this process of reconstruction may go on indefinitely. This does not mean that we necessarily discard wholly the idea of right which we received from our parents. Far from it! It means that this idea was necessarily a child's idea, and so inadequate to certain adult experiences; and it becomes necessary to develop it in accordance with the new needs. The incentive to this form of growth in our concepts is, then, precisely identical with that which led to our getting what we call new concepts. It is clear that in a certain sense the process we have just described really gives us new concepts. But practically we think of the new idea as a modification of the old one.

The doctrine is sometimes held that our concepts are unchangeable. The difference between this view and the one we have been presenting is largely verbal. In a certain sense our concepts are unalterable. To use our last illustration again, I can remember what I meant by my childish idea of right, and can recall the idea when I will. In this sense the concept does remain a permanent part of my mental equipment, undergoing only such changes as may be due to failing memory. But practically my adult concept which I call my idea of right is, as has just been shown, very different from this childish one out of which it has grown.

CHAPTER XI

JUDGMENT AND THE ELEMENTS OF REASONING

The mental operations which we have thus far described find the culmination of their development in the process which we know as reasoning. This does not mean that reasoning is a totally new form of psychical activity, to which the others are subordinate. It means that in the process of reasoning the full implication and significance of these other conscious processes come clearly to light, while in it they reach their completed evolution. Moreover, it does not mean that reasoning is a form of process which appears only after the other processes which we have studied have been developed. Rudimentary reasoning is present from the beginning of conscious life in the human being, and is clearly involved in each of the processes we have thus far analysed. But in the gradual unfolding of consciousness, by means of which it comes to maturity, we meet more and more complex instances of reasoning, and at each stage we find it involving perception and memory and imagination and conception. At each stage it affords the best index of the real value of these other processes, and in its most elaborate forms it brings out in the clearest possible way their real function. We shall revert to these points more fully later in the chapter. A technical definition of reasoning may well await our examination of certain of the facts upon which such a definition must be based. Meantime, we may define it broadly and provisionally as *purposive thinking*, that is to say, thinking carried on in the interests of some plan which we wish to execute, some problem which we wish to solve, some difficulty which we wish to surmount.

Analysis of Reasoning.—We are often told that the great educational value of mathematics lies in teaching us to reason correctly. Some hardy iconoclasts have ventured to question the extent of the value to be gained from the subject on this score, but at least it seems to be universally admitted that mathematics involves reasoning, and we may, therefore, judiciously seek from it an illustration of the reasoning process for our examination. Take the following arithmetical problem, reminiscent of the perplexities of the days of our academic youth. If thirteen melons cost a dollar and forty-three cents, how much should twenty melons cost? Most of us would solve this problem by finding the cost of one melon through the division of one hundred and forty-three by thirteen; and then the cost of twenty melons by multiplying this quotient by twenty. When the problem is distinctly understood, there instantly comes into our minds, through our memory habits, the idea "cost of one melon"; and straightway we find ourselves executing the relatively habitual process of division. This accomplished, our minds immediately turn—again by virtue of our mental habits—to the multiplication of our quotient by twenty. The reasoning in a case of this kind, therefore, seems to involve the selection of certain ideas out of all those supplied us by the problem, the manipulation of these ideas in accordance with previously acquired habits, and the attainment of the solution by a proper combination of these two processes. So far as there is any originality in such a procedure, we must look for it in the skill and expedition with which we hit upon the right idea to work with, and the accuracy and promptness with which we apply to it the fruits of our previously acquired knowledge.

Should we examine a little more closely the nature of these ideas which we employ we should find that they are clearly concepts. Thus, melon is a concept, cost is a concept, cent is a concept, etc. Were we to give verbal form to the several steps in the process, which we do not always do, we should find that we had such expressions before us as this: one melon eleven cents—eleven times twenty is two hundred and twenty, is two dollars and twenty cents. In other words, we put the concepts together in a form which the psychologists call a judgment. A judgment, when put into words, is what logicians call a proposition, and what grammarians call a sentence. It accordingly appears that a process of reasoning, such as that of our illustration, contains concepts combined in the form of judgments. We have already examined the nature of the concept, but judgment is a new mental operation to which we must now devote our attention.

Analysis of Judgment.—It will facilitate our investigation to begin with those cases of judgment to which we give verbal expression, for they can readily be secured in a concrete form, stripped of the introspective difficulties which beset the analysis of other varieties. It will suggest itself at once that, if the judgment is in any measure equivalent to a proposition or a sentence, we ought to gain assistance, in the distinguishing of its principal forms, from the classifications of the grammarians and logicians. Although the exact meaning of mental judgments and linguistic propositions are not always identical, even where they have the same verbal form, nevertheless many of these classifications are undoubtedly available; and we may expect to find assertative judgments, hypothetical judgments, disjunctive judgments, and so on. In the judgment, "the book is heavy," we have the concept heavy united to the concept book. On the other hand, in the judgment, "the book is not heavy," we have the concepts apparently sundered from one another. Even in this case, however, it is obvious that in the mental state, of which the judgment is the expression, the two *ideas* were together, as truly as in the first case. It is only so far as the ideas refer to objects distinct from themselves that their separation is asserted. In the judgment, "if the storm is severe, the ship will be imperilled," we have two pairs of concepts united to one another, *i. e.*, "storm" and "severe," "ship" and "imperilled." Like the preceding cases, the ideas are brought together mentally, but the *objective* union of one pair is made dependent upon the objective union of the other. The judgment, "Mr. Smith is either a democrat or a populist," gives us a typical instance of disjunction. The concept "Smith" is conjoined mentally with the two concepts "democrat" and "populist," and the *objective* union is asserted of one *or* the other.* In all these verbal precipitates of judgment we seem then to have two or more ideas mentally united in meanings which may imply either the postulated union or severance of the objects to which they refer.

Analytic-Synthetic Judgments.—Availing ourselves of a further classification which the logicians employ, we may speak of analytic or of synthetic judgments. "This wood is white," is an instance of the analytic judgment. It exhibits a property of the wood which is inherent in it, and may, therefore, be said to involve an analysis of the concept, "this wood." "Wood is a combustible" is a synthetic judgment, because it adds to the idea of wood the idea of combustibility, which is not immediately, nor obviously, implied in it. We shall presently see reason to believe that synthetic and analytic judgments are psychologically really one, and for our present purpose we can at least see that they involve, like all the other cases which we have examined, the mental synthesis of concepts, whose objective union, or separateness, we mentally predicate.

* The so-called "impersonal judgment" has caused logicians much controversy. "It rains" is an instance of it. At first sight it appears as though such a judgment could hardly be said to involve a synthesis of two ideas, or concepts, at all. On the whole it seems probable that this form of judgment represents a primitive type of the judging activity, out of which possibly our more elaborate forms have developed. If this be true, the nature of the impersonal judgment will become evident as we go on with our analysis.

Genetic Relation of Concept and Judgment.—Having discovered in these verbal judgments the constant presence of concepts, it will be well to revert to our account of their development, and detect, if possible, the relation of the judgment to this process.

We observed, when studying the origin of concepts, that they spring out of the mind's effort to mark off, and render distinct, the various meanings with which it has to deal. We saw that in the course of experience these meanings grow in definiteness and scope, so that a concept which meets the demands of childhood often needs for the purposes of the adult either to be reconstructed or else discarded in favour of some more adequate notion. If we examine once again some specific instances of the attainment and development of a concept, we shall come upon an instructive fact concerning the relation between conception and judgment. If we consider in this way our concept badness, we find that it has its origin in our very early childish experiences in connection with certain acts for which we were reproved or punished. The notion of parental disapproval quickly became attached to such acts, and, as soon as language could be comprehended at all, we remarked that they received the common appellation, " bad." Unless our account of the memory processes be fundamentally defective, the thought of such deeds should call to mind, in however vague a way, the undesirable consequences which had previously accompanied them. At this early stage, then, we must in a nebulous sort of fashion have brought together in our minds the idea of the act and the idea of its effects in the nature of punishment.

Such a mental act obviously has implicit in it the beginnings of judgment, *i. e., the assertion of a relation between two mental elements*. When, with increasing age, language finally comes to our assistance, we are easily able to apprehend the usage of our elders, and we straightway apply the term " bad " to all acts of a certain character. At this point the idea of badness is for us synonymous with a certain list of acts with which various kinds of adult disapproval are connected. When we are inspired to perform such an act, we promptly execute mentally the judging process quivalent to labelling the act bad. Were we to put our thought into words, we should undoubtedly have a verbal judgment. All of which seems to indicate with no great uncertainty that the origin of such a concept as "badness" is to be found in mental processes which are in their nascent stages crude, vague, undeveloped judgments, involving a rudimentary recognition of relations between certain more or less distinct portions of our experience. We get at these elements of experience mentally by means of rudely distinguished ideas—in the case of our illustration the idea of the act and the idea of its consequences. Such concepts as this, *i. e.*, badness, owe their creation, then, to elaborations of already attained ideas in a primitive form of judgment.

Moreover, if we turn our attention to the subsequent history of such a concept as badness, we find unmistakably, as was pointed out in the last chapter, that its develpoment is accomplished by means of new judgments which are brought to bear upon it from time to time. In childhood, for example, badness may for a long time mean, among other things, disobedience. There comes a time, however, when possibly disobedience seems in some crisis the only alternative to lying. We have also identified lying with badness. What shall we do? Well, whatever we do, we have at least laid the foundation for the reconstructive development of our concept of badness, by noting that disobedience may sometimes be necessary to the attainment of the maximal possible good. We necessarily make judgments about badness in such a case, and the transformation, whether shrinkage or enlargement, which the concept undergoes, is a direct expression of the effect of judgment. The development as well as the origin of such concepts is, accordingly, most intimately bound up with the judging operation.

Before generalising upon this single case, it would, of course, be desirable to examine every variety of concept in order to see if any of them originate independently of such judgments. This is, however, evidently impracticable, and we shall have to fall back upon the consideration that inasmuch as the concept is always a mental recognition, or designation, of specific meaning, there must, in the nature of the case, sooner or later be a judging process involved in it; for judgment is neither more nor less than the overt recognition and expression of just such relations as are embodied in the concept. The concept "gravity," for example, implies certain definite relations which we can only express in detail by means of judgments, and so with all other concepts. We shall accept this account of the relation between the two processes, then, with a large measure of confidence in its correctness.

Order of Development of the Cognitive Processes.—This analysis inevitably raises the question as to what is the most primitive and fundamental mode of conscious operation to which we have thus far given attention. We have shown that the conceptual element is present in perception, and we had already explained that in a genetic sense perception evidently antedates memory and imagination. Now we seem to find judgment as a precursor of the concept. What is the real order of development among these activities?

To secure a correct impression regarding the genetic relations among these processes, we must resort to an analogy which we have employed on a number of previous occasions. The development of an organism of any kind is accomplished by means of the gradual unfolding of structures, and the gradual evolution of functions, out of undifferentiated matrices. The fertilised ovum contains in a way, implicit within itself, all the potentialities of the fully developed organism which may subsequently grow out of it. But no inspection which we could make of the ovum would enable us to detect these invisible members. Step by step the homogeneity of the ovum gives way to more and more complex conditions, until finally the process of assimilation and differentiation issues in the full-grown organism. At each step in the progress toward maturity the several anatomical organs and the various physiological functions are moving together toward completion. At one stage one group of these elements may seem further advanced than others, but there is nevertheless mutual dependence of each of the factors upon the other, and each member of the several groups is from the beginning represented by some forerunner, however crude.

So it is with the psychical operations which we have been studying. Judgment, conception, memory, imagination, perception, and still other processes, which we have not as yet examined, are in one form or another present in consciousness from the very first; and each process, which we have described and analysed under one or another of these names, really involves each of the other processes. At certain moments consciousness presents itself as dominantly engaged in the way we call *perception*, sometimes in the way we call *imagination*. But each operation involves the other, and it would hardly be possible to point to a stage in development where one was obviously present and the other obviously and altogether absent.

Judging is in a precisely similar situation as regards its primary or secondary nature, its early or late appearance, in the history of the individual consciousness. We may, perhaps, make this point clear most easily by examining the case of perception which we have seen to be present past all reasonable question from the earliest moments of waking life. When we perceive a familiar object, say a chair, the mental operation of cognising the object is essentially equivalent to the assertion, "this is a chair," or "this is a thing to sit

JUDGMENT; ELEMENTS OF REASONING

upon." True, we rarely put the conclusion in this explicit form to ourselves. Nevertheless, the mental process is precisely akin to the proposition, and in our first *intelligent* application of names to objects it is exactly of this character. Indeed, the first childish exclamations, which represent in however amorphous a fashion the precursors of language, are of this type. The whole mass of feelings which such early infantile vocalisation may serve to indicate is often extremely complex and extended. One sound may designate an experience, which as adults we should describe as "this-is-the-sound-of-the-coming-to-take-me-up-and-feed-me-which-is-a-delightful-experience." Another sound may represent judgments in the form of a command, such as "I-am-hot-and-I-wish-you-would-take-the-blanket-off."

Let it not be supposed that we mean to credit the half-inarticulate infant with the mental recognition of all the differentiated elements in these cases to which we as adults are sensitive. Quite the contrary. It seems probable, as we saw, when we discussed attention and discrimination, that the early experiences of the baby are extremely vague, not in the sense of being *positively* confused, as adults sometimes are when embarrassed, but in the negative sense, in which vagueness means absence of distinct, well-recognised mental control. These primitive judgments are rudimentary expressions *of just such reactions* upon those indefinite, undifferentiated features of infant consciousness as we find appearing in ourselves when we make judgments about our more highly elaborated and more definitely discriminated ideas. The earliest rudimentary processes of judgment consequently involve the manipulation of unanalysed masses of experience, which we subsequently discover, through processes of dissociation, comparison, and judgment, to be extremely complex. It is quite possible, as has been already suggested, that the impersonal judgments, such as "it thunders," represent survivals of assertions of just this primitive kind about total experiences whose elements are only vaguely and imperfectly analysed.

Judgment as the Primitive Cognitive Activity.—It seems highly probable from the foregoing that in its original form all judgment is essentially a reaction upon immediately present perceptual experiences. Undoubtedly, rude judgments in which memory and imagination play leading rôles may occur at a very early period. But it seems quite certain that their most important functions must come somewhat later than the periods during which *perceptual* judgments are first clearly in evidence. Moreover, inasmuch as these rudimentary forms of judgment appear to involve as their most characteristic features, like the highly developed ideational judgments, the recognition, or assertion, of relations, it seems impossible to deny that the simplest case of perception, with its connection of a first sensory stimulation with something already familiar, is also implicitly, at least, of the same genus as the judgment.

When we ask, then, which of the several mental processes we have described is most fundamental, we must reply that if the question applies to the *order* of appearance in consciousness no single one enjoys this preëminence. They develop together, and are all, in one way or another, present from the outset of conscious life. If the question means, however, which process exhibits most conspicuously the whole scope of cognitive conscious capacities, then we must probably reply, judgment; because in this activity the detection and manipulation of relations is possibly most obvious, and this undoubtedly is the great mental achievement in the building up of knowledge and the controlling of conduct, to which ultimately all these processes revert for their final significance. In this sense, therefore, judgment is the most fundamental operation of consciousness on the cognitive side.

Before leaving this account of judgment and passing on to consider reasoning, a further word should be said of the fact

JUDGMENT; ELEMENTS OF REASONING

which came to our notice a moment ago in speaking of the judging process in the primitive consciousness of infant life. Judgment undoubtedly begins with a process of disentangling the various constituents of some large and relatively vague experience. The operation which we described in an earlier chapter as discrimination is commonly identical with these rudimentary judging processes. Now in so far as judgment does really deal in this way with the analysis of ideational (or perceptual) experiences, which are to start with undifferentiated wholes, it would seem to be necessary to regard it as a process in which relatively vague ideas are resolved into their definite constituents, rather than as a process in which already distinct and separate ideas are brought together. It will be remembered that our previous description of it is more closely allied to the second of these views about it. As a matter of fact both views are correct in the conception which they emphasise, and the disparity between them is only apparent.

Just as we saw was the case in the differentiation of the various sensations out of the relatively homogeneous conscious continuum with which life probably begins, so the materials upon which our judgments are based and with which they deal are all necessarily elements of our own personal experience. So far as we predicate anything of an object,—for example, "iron is a metal,"—it may be said that we have simply *dissected the idea* of iron (our concept), which was already present to our minds, instead of adding to it some *new* idea, *i. e.*, metal. Taken literally, this is a true statement of the facts. It is only false by virtue of that which it fails to add. The concept of iron is a concept distinguished from that of metal. We not only *may* bring these two concepts together mentally, but we frequently *do* unite just such concepts in the form of judgments, which are practically valuable to us in enabling us to emphasise such phases of our thoughts as are momentarily important for us. Judgment is, then, in its most explicit forms, undoubtedly a process in which we synthesise concepts in the course of noting and asserting relations. Yet the concepts which we thus unite are with equal certainty already elements of our stock of knowledge, and so we may seem to have made no gain by the judgment, much less to have added a *new* idea to some old idea. But the gain is often very real, because the synthesis may bring out relations of which previously we were not clearly cognisant. From this point of view judgment is not so much a matter of creating wholly new mental material as it is a matter of *ordering* our mental equipment in the most efficient possible manner.

CHAPTER XII

THE FORMS AND FUNCTIONS OF REASONING

Judgment and Reasoning.—From the illustration with which we set out in the last chapter in our first rough analysis of reasoning, we observed that the solution of the problem with which we were hypothetically engaged involved a series of judgments. We therefore turned aside to examine more closely into the nature of judgment; and we have discovered that this is an analytic-synthetic process, in which concepts are employed and elaborated. As the great majority of our important concepts have a linguistic basis, it goes without saying that reasoning makes almost constant use of language. It now remains to survey somewhat more fully the manner in which our judgments are combined to form the various types of reasoning. We proposed as a provisional definition of reasoning, at the beginning of the last chapter, the phrase "purposive thinking," meaning by this to designate any thought process in which we were thinking toward some end, attempting to overcome some difficulty, or solve some problem. If we turn to certain familiar instances of this sort of thing in every-day life, we shall at once obtain an impression of the fashion in which we make use of our judging activities.

Practical Reasoning.—Suppose that we are about to make a long journey which necessitates a choice from among a number of possible routes. This is a case of the genuinely problematic kind. It requires reflection, a weighing of pros and cons, and the giving of a final decision in favour of one or another of the several alternatives. In such a case the procedure of most of us is after this order. We think of one route as being picturesque and wholly novel, but also as being expensive. We think of another as less interesting, but also as less expensive. A third is, we discover, the most expeditious, but also the most costly of the three. We find ourselves confronted, then, with the necessity of choosing with regard to the relative merits of cheapness, beauty, and speed. We proceed to consider these points in the light of all our interests, and the decision more or less makes itself. We find, for instance, that we must, under the circumstances, select the cheapest route.

Now, this process is evidently made up of a number of judgments, in which we have employed various conceptions of the routes and the consequences connected with their choice. Obviously, also, we have made constant use of the machinery of *association* by means of which the various connected ideas have called one another into the mind. Our conclusion is seemingly the outcome of a series of judgments, whose number may be wholly indeterminate, and whose order is far from systematic. Nevertheless, the process results in a solution of the problem, the conclusion is essentially a reasoned one, and the operation is altogether typical of the fashion in which we actually deal with the practical problems of common experience.

When we look at the successive steps a little more closely, we see that such judgments brought into the foreground some *aspect* of the *general problem* which assisted us in viewing the situation in its entirety. Thus, the idea of cost as less by one route than by the others proved in our final estimate to be of fundamental significance. But we could not isolate this element of the problem and conceive it aright until we had compared the routes with one another, and considered all the expenses involved in each. Only then were we in a position to assert which route was cheapest. This crucial judgment issued *immediately* from our comparison of the several routes with one another, but the process of *comparison* was itself an indispensable step in reaching our final choice. We considered speed in a similar manner, and found that all the routes were satisfactory enough in this particular.

Finally, the consideration of beauty and the pleasure of the journey is canvassed in like manner, and we find from the ideas which come into our minds that one route is markedly preferable. This factor of beauty remains, then, to settle accounts with the item of economy. The ultimate decision involves our taking stock of our financial status, past, present, and future, and the issue is settled on the basis of the story told by this set of facts. Each step in the process has been relatively simple, and entirely intelligible. We have allowed certain ideas, which we have *abstracted* in our *mode of conceiving the problem*, to take up by association other ideas related to them in ways which bear upon the case in hand; and from the judgments which we pass upon the meanings of these ideas our choice is made and our volition determined. Our effectiveness as practical reasoners (or theoretical reasoners, either, for that matter) will depend then, first, upon the skill with which we succeed in *conceiving* the problem correctly, and second, upon the *speed* and *accuracy* with which this conception suggests to our reasoning processes the recall of the special ideas appropriate to the case at hand.

The whole series of judgments employed could finally be reduced to two or three (or possibly to one), which, as the outcome of our tentative weighing of now this claim and now that, have proved to be finally significant. In a sense the judgments have all been connected and related. They have all arisen in response to our persistent dwelling upon the problem before us. But a few of them depend upon one another in an even more intimate way, and these are the permanently significant ones. For example: "Two routes cost more than $1000; I cannot afford to pay more than $800; I must therefore patronize the third route."

Value of Association by Similarity.—In so far as reasoning involves associative processes, it is clear that association by similarity will be of highest importance, especially in the more abstruse forms of thinking. The more complex types of problem with which we have to cope often require for their successful solution the application of facts and principles which have no connection with the matter in hand, save some fragile bond of *similarity*. The detection of these delicate links of relation is an achievement which characterises in high degree only the most remarkable minds, the geniuses. The rest of us find, to be sure, that we outstrip the brutes enormously in our capacity to employ this form of associative nexus. But the great revoluntionary achievements in human reason have to wait upon the man and the hour, and when they are compassed they generally reveal a marvellous manifestation of the capacity for discerning similarity. Newton's formulation of the law of gravity may serve to illustrate the point.

Reasoning and the Syllogism.—Now, to many persons the process of selecting a route for a journey will seem a misleading illustration of reasoning, because it will not appear to be sufficiently abstruse, nor sufficiently orderly and inevitable. It will represent what they may prefer to call "practical thinking," as we have done, although we have not meant by the use of the term to deny to the process the essential character of reasoning. We shall be told that when we really reason we perform such mental deeds as the following syllogism exhibits:

> All men are mortal;
> Socrates is a man,
> Therefore
> Socrates is mortal.

Here we are assured we have new facts attained by reason, here is perfect order and symmetry, instead of miscellaneous groping for correct conclusions, which may, or may not, be attained. Here are judgments arrayed in serried ranks, each

FORMS AND FUNCTIONS OF REASONING

supported by its neighbour, and the final judgment an irrefutable consequence of its companions, from which our thinking set out.

In response to this suggestion we have only to inquire whether or no our *original* thinking *really* goes on in this way, or whether this example illustrates the arrangement of which certain of our thought processes are susceptible *after* they have been pruned of excrescences. Our own view about this question is doubtless indicated by the mode in which we have approached it. There can be no doubt that the celebrated syllogism which we have just proposed reveals an extremely fundamental fact about the relations of certain of our judgments to one another. That the syllogism also represents the actual mode in which we commonly reach conclusions is altogether another proposition, and one to which assent certainly cannot be given. The question here at issue is purely one of fact, and each one must determine for himself whether in his reasoning processes he finds himself proceeding in the syllogistic manner.

When we examine our thinking, with this question in mind, most of us find that neither as regards the order of the several steps, nor as regards their number, does our common reasoning comply with the pattern of the syllogism. In instances like that of our illustration we should rarely have any recourse to the second proposition, or the minor premise, as logicians call it, even provided we found it necessary to consider the truth of the conclusion. Moreover, it would as a rule be only in case we found it necessary to verify the truth of the concluding proposition that we should revert to either of the other propositions; and then the order of our thought would be—first, the conclusion; second, the major premise. So that neither order nor number of judgments is as the syllogism with which we started requires.

As a device for exhibiting the source of our confidence in the truth of the conclusion, the syllogism undoubtedly possesses a value; for it makes explicit and clear in the fewest possible words the fundamentally important relations among the ideas involved. It is, however, as a method of exposition, demonstration, and proof, rather than as a type of actual constructive thinking, that it gets its chief significance. Nevertheless, it possesses one characteristic which is peculiar to many reflective processes, and to this we must briefly refer.

Deduction.—The major premise—" all men are mortal "—contains an assertion of a general principle which we have observed that we may use as a principle of verification for such an assertion as that of the conclusion—" Socrates is mortal." Now, general principles play essentially the same rôle in our thinking as do the general ideas which we discussed in the chapter on conception. They summarise, just as concepts do, large masses of human experience, and in our purposive thinking we repeatedly have occasion to employ them. We might call them complex concepts.

These general principles represent the counterparts in our conscious operations of the principle of habit in our motor coördinations. Just in so far as we regard them as really stable and well established, we use them almost reflexly in our thinking, and apply them without more ado to the determination of conclusions about such facts as they may concern. Thus, having assured ourselves that a certain act is really stealing, we instantly class it as despicable and wrong; having learned that a substance of peculiar appearance is wood, we are immediately prepared to find that it will burn; if we hear of the discovery of a new planet, we assume without question that it will possess an elliptical orbit. These reactions consist in applying to appropriate things the habitual accompaniments of specific objects, or events, in the form of general ideas, or principles, concerning *similar* objects and events. Such a process lends perspective to the special subject to which the principle is applied, by bringing it into overt connection with the experience to which it may be most immediately germane, while it enriches and fortifies the general principle itself by adding to its scope a new and definite instance. It demands no argument, beyond the mention of the facts just described, to demonstrate that we make a constant use of general principles in some such fashion as this.

The problem is at once suggested by the foregoing discussion of deduction, as to how we obtain the general principles therein at issue. This brings us to the complementary process which logicians designate induction.

Induction.—According to the familiar accounts of it induction is the operation by means of which we come to generalise upon individual events. For example, having observed numbers of specific instances of the phenomenon, we come to the conclusion that all paper is combustible. In a similar way we come to assert that all mammals have lungs, that masses attract one another, etc., etc.

Criticism of Induction.—Now, logicians have argued at great length upon the question whether we really succeed by inductive inference in going beyond the particular facts which have actually been examined. They have also considered at great length the criterion, or warrant, upon which inductive principles proceed, supposing that they ever do transcend the facts from which they set out. Sometimes it has been maintained, for example, that the inductive generalisation, "All men are mortal," which is based upon our examination of a finite number of cases of human mortality, obtains its ultimate significance for knowledge simply by virtue of the assumed uniformity of nature. What has happened a number of times will always happen under like conditions, is the meaning of this view. Or, stated more rigidly, whatever has happened under given conditions will always happen under the same conditions. Many other views of the matter have been defended, but we can hardly enter upon them. Suffice it for our purposes to observe that whatever may be the final merit and reliability of inductive inferences, we do in our actual thinking make constant use of such generalisations, and on the whole with practical success.

Indeed, after our account of habit and association and our account of the formation and development of concepts, we should be ill-prepared for any other conclusion. Having found a certain characteristic common to a large number of events, it could not well be otherwise than that we should be predisposed by the principle of habit to connect this character with all other events which we judged to be of like kind. This would tend to occur on the level of mere trains of associative ideas, as in revery, where it might, however, often escape attention; it would also come out clearly in the recognition of points in common among such occurrences as we found ourselves obliged to reason about in the course of overcoming difficulties, whether practical or theoretical. Thus, in revery our thoughts might run upon the planets, and as the ideas of them passed through our minds we should probably think of them all as spherical, and yet this common property might escape our definite notice. In reasoning, however, we should often find it indispensable to emphasise common qualities of this kind. So, for instance, in attempting to predict weather conditions we should speedily find it necessary to proceed on the generalisation that all low barometric phenomena were indicative of storm formation. The same exigencies, therefore, which lead us to form general ideas, also lead us to that special type of idea which we more often call a general principle and express in a proposition.

Deduction and Induction Compared.—In comparing deduction and induction it is often said that induction necessarily precedes deduction, because we obviously cannot apply our general principles until we possess them, and it is by means of induction that we obtain them. It is also said that in deduction our thought proceeds from the more general to the less general, from the universal to the particular; whereas in induction the order of procedure is reversed. There is an element of truth in both assertions, but this form of expressing it is certainly misleading.

The truth in the first contention consists in the fact that all *general principles* are based upon *particular experiences*. But this does not mean that inductive processes occur first, and then at a later step deduction appears. Both kinds of process go on together, as we shall see in a moment. Indeed, strictly speaking, they are in the last analysis simply two phases of one and the same process. The truth in the second assertion resides in the fact that some portions of our thinking proceed under relatively more *habitual* forms than others. The deductive process represents the application of a mental habit, or principle, to a practical case, under just such conditions as we have already described. The inductive process represents more distinctly the *formation* of *these habits* of thought. In both cases, however, so far as concerns the progress of the successive thoughts, we always find that the advance is from particular to particular. Moreover, the advance is not so much an advance from the particular idea x to the independent and particular y, now shown to be related in some way to x, as it is a development of the idea x, hitherto undifferentiated in this special fashion, into the idea x containing a y relation. Thus, the generalisation about low barometric conditions and storm formation is not a mental process in which two wholly disconnected ideas are brought together. It is simply a process in which the hitherto unspecified experience " low-barometer-storm-formation " is resolved into its fuller significance for practical use. Similarly, in subsequent deductive operations with this principle, *i. e.*, all low barometric conditions indicate storms imminent, we proceed from the particular idea " low barometer," to the particular idea " storm forming." However convenient, therefore, it may at times prove to speak of passing from the general to the particular, and vice versa, we must remember that in our actual thought processes we always juxtapose particulars; or more precisely, we deal with discriminable features of a single mental particular. Of course it will be understood from our study of the development of concepts that these particulars are under this treatment modified incessantly, both by expansion and contraction.

We have seen from time to time throughout our work that each mental process which we have examined contains some old features and some new features, that it reflects the principle of habit and the principle of fresh adjustment to novel conditions. Induction and deduction are further illustrations of this same fact. Just as in perception we observed the new element in the sensory stimulus, and the old element in the reaction by a modified cortex, so we have seen that induction represents that function of our purposive thinking in which the new adjustment is uppermost; whereas deduction represents more conspicuously the application of acquired habits. If the parallel is really genuine, we should expect to find, as we have at each previous step, that the two attributes of novelty and familiarity in the elements employed are never entirely dissevered from one another, and so we should expect to find substantial warrant for our remarks a few lines above, that induction and deduction are but phases of a common process. That they are actually conjoined in this way does not mean that they always are met with in a condition of perfect balance. It may much more naturally be expected that sometimes one and sometimes the other will present itself as more immediately important and more properly conspicuous. We have seen an analogous case in the instance of memory when compared with some kinds of perception. In the one case the obvious emphasis falls upon the new, in the other upon the old. So it is in reality with the relation between deduction and induction.

In reaching the induction, "all low barometer = storm formation," we may suppose a number of instances to have been examined before the generalisation is made. Now, the intelligent apprehension of the terms concerned in the judgments, that is, low barometer and storms, evidently involves a reference back to past experience, to past factors of knowledge, which is, as we have seen, the essential feature of deduction. Moreover, the actual procedure by which we assure ourselves of the tenability of such an induction consists in comparing mentally each new instance with previous similar instances. In this operation the old experiences practically occupy the place of general principles, under which we array the new case. So that the deductive characteristics are evidently present in an unmistakable way in inductive forms of reasoning.

Conversely, when we apply a general principle, or infer that a special consequence will follow an event, because of the general class to which it belongs, we inevitably avail ourselves of inductive methods, in so far as we label the new fact. When we predict a storm because we observe a fall in the barometer we are in reality dealing with a *new specific instance*, which we generalise in an essential inductive way. We may call it a case of deduction, because we have already convinced ourselves of the invariability of the connection between the storm phenomena and the particular barometric conditions. Nevertheless, the actual mental process by means of which we make the prediction is quite as truly characterised by induction. We may feel reasonably confident, therefore, that the reasoning processes do not constitute any exception to the rule which we have previously enunciated, that all cognitive mental operations involve both old and new factors.

Reasoning and Purposive Thinking.—It ought now to be fairly clear that the precise significance which we attach to the term reasoning is largely a matter of arbitrary terminology. Undoubtedly some of our purposive thinking takes a highly abstract and systematised form. Undoubtedly, also, most of it goes on in a much more concrete, miscellaneous, hit-and-miss fashion. But it is essentially impossible to draw any sharp line marking off the more orderly and exact procedure from the more promiscuous form; and as the presence of a dominating purpose, plan, or interest seems to control the ideational processes in both cases, it has seemed the simpler and more natural thing to call all purposive thinking reasoning. We are then entirely able to recognise stages of abstraction and complexity in the execution of such thinking without any sacrifice of regard for the facts.

General Function of Reasoning.—In reasoning, with its employment of concepts in judgments, we meet with the most highly evolved of all the psychical devices for assisting the adaptive activities of the organism, and this notion of its general significance is so familiar that it requires no detailed justification. Certain features of its practical operation may, however, profitably be described, especially in connection with our general notion of the relation between conscious and neuro-muscular processes.

In the original sensory stimulations of early infant life we have seen that there is a general overflow of the nervous energy into miscellaneous motor channels, occasioning heterogeneous and uncoördinated movements of various parts of the body. We have also traced in outline the process of the development by means of which the motor escapement becomes confined to certain limited and definite channels, and thus succeeds in establishing coördinated habitual movements. We have seen that these coördinations become more and more elaborate as growth proceeds, and we have noted that in this development the psychical processes which we have analysed as perception, imagination, and memory play an amazingly important part. Now, so far as we mean to cover by the term reasoning all purposive thinking, it is clear that these various mental operations just referred to can only contribute in a significant way to the modification of motor reactions in the measure in which they enter into processes of reasoning.

It must be remembered again, that our purposive thinking is sometimes very rudimentary, simple, and abrupt; and at other times highly complicated, prolonged, and abstract. In reasoning we really find brought together and focalised all the important characteristics of the various mental modes which we have thus far studied.

This may be shown in the case of memory, as an illustration, but it is no truer to the facts here than it would be in the case of perception or imagination. If memory operated so as to bring into our consciousness ideas of our past experiences, but without any special reference to some present need, it would possess a certain intellectual interest comparable with that of a geyser, or other irregular natural phenomenon. But it would be an almost wholly useless adornment of our mental life. It is because memory enables us to recall experiences when we *need* to bring to bear upon some *present perplexity* the *significance* of our *past experience* that it assists us in getting ahead in the world. It is, in short, the part which it plays in purposive thinking which gives it its value. Moreover, this *significance* of the *past experience* is a thing which concretely brings with it tendencies to certain modes of *action*. It is not a mere reinstatement of *ideas* with which we are dealing in such a case. It is a reinstatement of ideas connected with which are certain quasi-habitual actions. For example, we come back to a city which we have not visited for a number of years, and go in search of a friend. We finally reach the street upon which his dwelling stands, but to our surprise we are at once in doubt whether to turn to the right or to the left. We think a moment and succeed in recalling his house number. A moment's inspection of the street numbers suffices to determine our action, and we immediately turn in the correct direction. The memory image, in connection with our perceptual process, instantly resulted in a movement in the appropriate direction.

Similarly, though not always so obviously, with perceptual

activities. If I am engaged in writing, *what* I perceive (my hand, the words, etc.) is certainly in part determined by my mental operations at the moment. Not only so, but my perceiving of the pen and paper are processes directly contributory to the expression of my purposes in my writing. The perception is taken up into the purposive thinking of the moment; or, expressing the facts more accurately, it is itself an integral part of the onward movement of my general purposive thought activities. I cannot execute efficiently that type of purposes which gets expression in writing without the assistance of the perceptual act. Always somewhere imbedded in the general matrix of our conduct, whether lying near the surface or deeply hidden in the recesses of our inner consciousness, we come upon purposes, plans, intentions, which explain our whereabouts and our action; and upon these basal factors rest our particular perceptions, as well as our other mental acts.

Neural Counterpart of Reasoning.—In a diagrammatic manner, but only in such manner, we can indicate the general neural counterpart of our purposive thinking, whether in its simpler, or in its more elaborate forms. In the case of our more distinctly habitual coördinations we long since observed how with a minimum of *conscious* accompaniments a sensory stimulus may make its way in the form of neural excitation from a sense organ directly through the (lower?) centres to appropriate muscular groups. This case is illustrated in the movement of the hand to throw the latch of a familiar door. In the case of stimulations which require a conscious reaction, whether simple or complex, the motor discharge is postponed, sometimes only for an instant, sometimes indefinitely. A typical instance which brings out the more important features of cases where persistent perplexities are involved is the following:

A man sleeping in a strange building is awakened by an alarm of fire. He hastily rises, throws on some clothing, and

FORMS AND FUNCTIONS OF REASONING 249

starts for the stairway. Up to this point the course of the successive neural events has been—auditory stimulus, memory activity, motor response with habitual coördinations, involved in dressing and running toward the remembered stairway. He finds the stairway already filled with smoke. Escape in this way is cut off and he turns back. Again sensory stimulus—this time partly visual, partly olfactory and auditory—and motor response of the habitual variety. His next thought is of a fire-escape, but none is to be discovered. He tries other rooms, but also without success. In these movements we have successive expressions of sensory stimuli, with memory intermediaries suggesting fire-escapes, each group of stimulations discharging into movements carrying him from place to place. Terror has rapidly been overcoming him, and his motions become violent and ill-controlled. Suddenly it occurs to him to make a rope of the bed-clothing. Before he can complete this the fire has made such progress that on looking from the windows he sees he cannot pass through the flames and live. His terror now turns to complete panic, his excitement bursts over into aimless rushing about, and he is on the point of hurling himself from the window when he comes upon another stairway, bounds to the roof, and finally escapes to another building.

In this case we have essentially all the stages of practical reasoning process involved. We have a problem, or a difficulty, reported in the form of a stimulus, which cannot be dealt with in a purely habitual, non-conscious fashion. The first effort to meet this obstacle consists in cortical excitations of relevant memory processes, and the expression of these in the forms of acquired coördinated movements. In many instances the first or second effort would, of course, have achieved success and cut short the remainder of the process. In some more distinctly intellectual forms of problem the memory process would not necessarily express its bearings in the form of actual movements executed at the moment. But the excitation of the cortical activities is of precisely the same kind, and has precisely the same significance, as in the hypothetical case we are considering. Whenever the coördinations employed at the summons of the memory process, in the way we have described, prove inadequate to meet the difficulties in hand, there is always this same progress from one reaction to another, until patience, or the available store of one's experience, has been exhausted.

If the problem constitutes an insignificant stimulus, one or two failures to solve it may result in the abandonment of the effort in favour of some more pressing interest which enlists our more vivid feeling. But when, as in the case of our illustration, the significance of the problem is compelling, we meet, after the failure of all the reactions suggested by memory and executed by habitual coördinations, the remarkable phenomenon we last described. The stimuli apparently continue gathering power, which can no longer be drained off in coherent motor responses, and presently we see very much what we observed with babies, *i. e.*, the breaking over of the neural excitement into almost every motor channel. This diffusion in the case of infants is wholly uncoördinated, whereas with the adult it is coördinated in a measure, but incoherently, and with reference to no single purpose. Nevertheless, such mal-coördinations, which at least serve to bring the organism into new conditions, are sometimes, as in our illustrative case, successful in providing escape from difficulties. Animals make large use of such violent and random movements whenever they are confronted by strange and terrifying conditions. If, after memory has done its work, there still be need for other forms of reaction, this sort of general motor explosion is really all that there is left to fall back upon. Our supposititious man might have thrown himself out of the window, as many others have done under the intellectually stupefying effects of extreme fear, but even so, the neural process would have been highly similar to that which we have described, and it represents the consequences of a practical breakdown in the coördinated movements suggested by memory as competent to meet the case at hand. The neural process in the more abstruse forms of reasoning is probably quite like that which we have now described, save as regards the delicacy and infrequency of the associative links by means of which we pass from idea to idea in our effort to overcome mental difficulties. Sensory discrimination, intellectual abstraction, memory processes, judgments of comparison, habitual coördinations—in varying degree and in shifting combinations these factors are present in all types of reasoning, from the most concrete and simple to the most complicated and abstract.

Genesis of Reason in Human Beings.—The precise moment at which a child passes out of the stage of mere perceptual thinking and succeeds in creating concepts detached from particular events is not one that we can exactly determine, nor is it important that we should do so. It certainly comes in a rudimentary way with the voluntary control of his muscles, and it grows rapidly as soon as he gets control of language. In general, it may be said that its appearance is largely dependent upon the demands which the child's environment makes upon him. So long as he is a mere vegetable, fed and watered at definite intervals, conceptual thinking is of no great consequence. As he comes to attain more complex social relations, and as he finds himself surrounded with increasingly complex situations to deal with, conceptual thinking, with its classifying, simplifying characteristics, becomes essential to effective adaptation. Moreover, when such thinking does appear, we know that the child is beginning the evolution of that special part of his mental life which marks him off most definitely from the higher brutes.

The Reasoning of Animals.—We gain an interesting sidelight upon the reasoning processes of human beings, and especially upon the development of reasoning in children, by observing certain of the mental operations of animals. Two extreme views have been popularly entertained concerning the reasoning powers of animals. One of them is represented by the disposition to apostrophise man as the sole possessor of reason, the lord of creation, ruling over creatures of blind instinct. The other view has found expression in marvelling at the astounding intellectual feats of occasional domestic animals, or at the shrewdness and cunning of their brethren of the wild. Both kinds of animals have been forthwith accredited with the possession of reasoning powers of no mean pretensions. Of recent years rapid advances have been made in the scientific observation of animals, and it seems probable that at no remote day we may possess a fairly accurate impression of the scope and nature of their psychical lives. Meantime we must speak somewhat conservatively and tentatively.

Many of the acts of animals which have enlisted the most unbounded admiration are undoubtedly purely instinctive. And not only so, but it seems probable that many of these instincts are unconscious and just as truly reflex as the most uncontrollable of human reflexes, such as the patellar. Thus, the remarkable actions of ants, whose astonishing system of coöperative government has furnished so many fine rhetorical figures, are apparently due to reflex reactions, to stimulations chiefly of an olfactory kind, to which they are probably obedient in much the same fashion as are the iron filings to the magnet which they seek.

Many acts of animals, which are at least effective expressions of mind, seem upon close examination to consist simply in associating certain acts with certain objects or situations. The original associating of the correct elements may have come about more or less accidentally, and is certainly often the result of many random trials. Thus, a young rat, in attempting to get into a box containing cheese, the entrance to which requires his digging away an amount of sawdust at one particular spot, will often scamper many times around and over the box before starting to dig. If after digging and finding the correct spot he be removed and the sawdust replaced, the same sort of operation generally goes on as did at first, only now he succeeds much more rapidly than before. After a few trials he goes almost instantly to the correct spot, makes few or no useless movements, and promptly gets his reward.

In cases of this kind we see an animal endowed with a large number of motor impulses, which enable him by virtue of his sheer restlessness to achieve his original success in getting food. Little by little the association between the food and the *efficacious* impulse becomes ingrained, all the others fall out, and to the observer, who is innocent of the previous stages of the process, his act appears highly intelligent. As the creature grows older an interesting change comes over his performances. If he be given a problem to solve similar to the one we have just described, he begins in a much calmer and more circumspect way than does his younger protégé. His first success may consequently be less quickly achieved. But in subsequent trials he becomes much more rapidly proficient, and one or two trials may be all that he requires to attain practical perfection in the act. In the mature rat the *memory process* is evidently much more active and reliable.

Reasoning processes of this kind—if one wishes so to label them—are much in evidence in little children. The small boy, striving to repair his toy, turns it this way and that, hammers it, and pulls it about. Sometimes success unexpectedly crowns his labours, and he may then be able to bring about the desired result again. He has a general wish to set his toy aright, much as the rat has his ambition in the matter of the cheese. Neither of them has any clear recognition of the means appropriate to the end, but both of them, by trying one move after another, finally come upon the correct combination, after which memory often enables them to repeat the achievement. In the light of our present knowledge it seems probable that the great mass of seemingly intelligent acts which animals perform, apart from instinctive acts, are of this variety, and therefore involve nothing more elaborate than the association of certain types of situation with certain motor impulses.

Just how far such acts may at times involve the perception of coherent *relations* in the manner characteristic of adult human intelligence, it is essentially impossible to say. One of the vigorously controverted points about animal intelligence comes to light here. Do animals form concepts of any kind? If they do not, they evidently cannot execute the intellectual processes peculiar to the more abstruse forms of human reasoning. Do animals ever employ association of similars in their psychical operations? If not, again we must deny to them one of the most significant features of human thinking. Do their gestures and attitudes, by means of which they seem to communicate with one another, ever rise to the level of real language, furnishing a social medium for definitely recognised meanings? On these points competent observers are not at present altogether agreed. It seems, however, probable that animals rarely, if ever, achieve the distinct separation of ideas and perceptions which human beings attain; and that they do not, therefore, employ the concept in the form in which developed language permits the human to do. The acts of certain of the apes, however, and occasional performances of some of the higher mammals, indicate a very considerable degree of *original* and intelligent reaction to sensory stimulations. The animal consciousness is probably much more exclusively and continuously monopolised by mere awareness of bodily conditions than the human consciousness, and much more rarely invaded in any definite manner by independent images of past experience. Meantime, we have to remember that the nervous system of the higher animals seems to afford all the necessary basis for the appearance and development of the simpler forms of rational consciousness, and the only difference in these processes, as compared with those of man, of which we can speak dogmatically and with entire confidence, is the difference in complexity and elaboration.

CHAPTER XIII

THE AFFECTIVE ELEMENTS OF CONSCIOUSNESS

Feeling and Cognition.—In the foregoing chapters our attention has been chiefly directed to those phases of our consciousness by means of which we come into the possession of knowledge. We have examined the several stages in cognition from its appearance in sensation up through the various steps to reasoning. We have noted the increasing complexity and the increasing definiteness which seems to characterise the development of this aspect of our minds, and we have traced so far as we could the neural basis of the several processes at issue. We have seen that the elements of our knowledge ultimately reduce to sensory activities, for which the immediate preconditions are specialised sense organs and a central nervous system. We have seen how the whole significance of the different stages in the cognitive operation is found in the devices which they represent to further the efficiency of the motor responses which the organism is constantly obliged to make to its environment. We have seen that memory, imagination, and reasoning are thus simply half-way houses between stimuli and reactions which serve to permit the summoning of just those movements which the present situation demands, when interpreted in the light of the individual's past experience.

We stated explicitly at the outset of our analysis of these cognitive operations that we should be obliged temporarily to overlook certain other factors of our consciousness. We come now to take up one of these neglected processes which has as a matter of fact contributed to produce the results in many of our illustrations. This process is commonly known to psychologists as *feeling*. The word *feeling* has many other well-recognised meanings, and the function which it is made to subserve in this present connection is somewhat arbitrarily imposed upon it. Moreover, certain psychologists refuse to use it in this limited fashion. But we shall employ the term to designate in a general way those processes which represent and express the tone of our consciousness. A rough distinction is sometimes made between cognition and feeling by saying that cognition furnishes us the nouns and adjectives, the "whats" of our states of consciousness, while feeling affords the adverbial "how." What are you conscious of? An object, a picture. How does it affect you? Agreeably. The first question and answer bring out the cognitive factors, the second emphasise the feelings. Another line of demarcation which is sometimes proposed is based on the assertion that cognition informs us of objects and relations external to ourselves, whereas feeling informs us of our own internal mental condition. The general character of the distinction will become more evident as we examine more carefully certain specific types of conscious experience.

Elementary Forms of Feeling, or Affection.—If we hold a prism up in the sunlight and throw the spectral colours upon a wall, we not only experience the various sensory qualities of the several colours, we also commonly experience pleasure. If we now turn and look at the sun, we not only see the orb, we also experience discomfort. Similarly, when we strike three tuning forks which harmonise with one another we hear the qualities of the component sounds and we also find them agreeable. Instances of disagreeable sounds will readily suggest themselves. We might examine our sensation of pressure, movement, temperature, smell, and taste, and find the same thing true, *i. e.*, that they are accompanied sometimes by pleasure and sometimes by discomfort. Moreover, we shall find the same kind of sensation, for example, the sensation of sweetness, at one time felt as agreeable, at another time as disagreeable. The converse case is represented by acquired tastes, such as the fondness for olives, where ordinarily the taste is originally unpleasant, but subsequently becomes highly agreeable. Finally, there are many sensations which seem to be essentially neutral and indifferent. We cannot say with confidence that they are clearly and positively either pleasant or unpleasant. Many colours and many sounds are in this manner all but impossible to classify as agreeable or disagreeable. Ideas also, as well as sensations, display escorts of agreeable or disagreeable character. It would, therefore, appear that pleasantness and unpleasantness are attributes of consciousness which, although they may accompany sensory and ideational activities, are distinguishable from sensations. Apparently sensory forms of consciousness may occur without any, or at all events without any unmistakable, accompanying process of agreeableness and disagreeableness. On the other hand, it does not seem possible to point out any case in which the consciousness of pleasantness and unpleasantness occurs independently of sensations or ideas. The agreeable-disagreeable *element* or *phase* of our states of consciousness is often spoken of as " affection," the total complex state in which it occurs being then called " feeling." This seems a convenient usage, even if somewhat arbitrary, and we shall therefore adopt it.

Theories of Wundt and Royce.—Wundt and Royce have recently maintained that there are other dimensions of feeling in addition to those of pleasantness and unpleasantness. Both of these writers speak of feelings of excitement and calm, and Wundt adds a third group, *i. e.*, feelings of strain and relaxation. It is contended that the individual members of these several groups may, theoretically at least, be combined in any manner whatever. Thus, pleasantness may be accompanied by strain and excitement, or by excitement alone, or by increasing quiet alone.

A detailed criticism of these views is not to be thought of

at this time. The author can only indicate the general grounds of his disagreement with these theories, and remark that their enunciation has not as yet called forth very extended assent from psychologists. That our general condition is sometimes one of strain and sometimes one of relaxation naturally admits of no doubt. But our awareness of this condition of strain or relaxation is due primarily to the peculiar kinæsthetic sensations which accompany such states and report the tension of our muscular system. This feature in consciousness is of a sensory nature therefore, and does not warrant a classification with the affective elements. Strain and relaxation may be at times general characteristics of the total attitude of consciousness towards its object. But they belong to the cognitive order of conscious processes.

Again, excitement and its opposite are characteristics which apply beyond question to the general activity of consciousness. But after we have subtracted the effects already mentioned under strain-relaxation, it is not clear that we have anything left to designate as the consciousness of excitement, except our awareness of the general vividness and rate of flow in our conscious states. When we are much excited, commonly our muscles are (some or all of them) tense, our respiration is abnormal, etc. When there is muscular quiet with absence of acute kinæsthetic sensations, only our consciousness of the intensity and rapidity of change in the conscious processes remains. Although we acknowledge, therefore, the appositeness of these new categories as applied to certain general modifications of our consciousness, we maintain that we become aware of these modifications through cognitive channels already recognised and described. We consequently prefer at present to abide by the older analysis of pleasantness and unpleasantness as the two modes of affection fundamentally distinct from sensation.

Pain Sensations and Affection.—It will be judicious before going further to forestall one fertile source of confusion in the description of affection. It will be remembered that in our account of sensations we noted pain, which, we saw reason to believe, probably had a definite nervous organ like other sensations. The characteristic conscious quality arising from this organ is the cutting-pricking sensation. If pain is like other sensations, it should sometimes prove agreeable and sometimes disagreeable, and again neutral. It may possibly seem to strain veracity somewhat to speak of this sensation as ever being neutral, much less agreeable. And yet slight sensations of this character are at least interesting, and many persons secure a certain thrill of pleasurable gratification in gently touching a wound, in approaching with the tongue a sore or loose tooth, etc. That these sensations quickly take on when intense an all but unbearable character is notorious. This disagreeableness constitutes the affective phase of these sensations just as it does with those of sound or vision. When we speak of pain, we shall try to mean such states of consciousness as depend upon the operation of the pain nerves, in connection with which it must be remembered we most often obtain on the side of intensity our maximal experiences of the disagreeable. It is not possible at the present moment to indicate precisely how far pain nerves may be involved in the operation of the other sensory tracts, such as the visual, and therefore how far many of our unpleasant sensory experiences, such as occasionally arise from audition, vision, etc., may be referable to this source. Meantime, we shall follow the indication of the facts best established to-day, with a mental willingness to rehabilitate our conception whenever it may become conclusively inadequate.

Affection and Sensation.—In our study of sensation we discovered that intensity, duration, and extensity were fundamentally significant features in its constitution. If affection is connected with sensory activities, it is highly probable that it will be found related to changes in these basal sensory characteristics.

Relation of Affection to the Duration of Sensory Processes.

—The case of duration is relatively simple and obvious. Sensory stimuli of extremely brief duration may, if we are attempting to attend to them, be somewhat unpleasant. Stimuli which are agreeable at first, such as certain tones, often become positively disagreeable if long continued, and always under such conditions become at least tedious. It must be remembered that in some instances, for example, cases of olfactory and thermal stimulation, the sense organ becomes either exhausted or adapted, as the case may be, and that for this reason the stimuli practically cease to be felt— cease properly to be stimuli. Such cases furnish exceptions to the statement above, which are exceptions in appearance only. Disagreeable stimuli when long continued become increasingly unpleasant until exhaustion sets in to relieve, often by unconsciousness, the strain upon the organism. There is, therefore, for any particular pleasure-giving stimulus a definite duration at which its possible agreeableness is at a maximum. Briefer stimulations are at least less agreeable, and longer ones become rather rapidly neutral or even unpleasant. Disagreeable stimuli probably have also a maximum unpleasantness at a definite period, but the limitations of these periods are much more difficult to determine with any approach to precision. All sensory experiences, if continued long enough, or repeated frequently enough, tend accordingly to lose their affective characteristics and become relatively neutral. As familiar instances of this, one may cite the gradual subsidence of our interest and pleasure in the beauties of nature when year after year we live in their presence; or the gradual disappearance of our annoyance and discomfort at the noise of a great city after a few days of exposure to it. Certain objects of a purely æsthetic character, such as statues, may, however, retain their value for feeling throughout long periods.

Affection and the Intensity of Sensations.—The relations

of affection to the intensity of sensation processes is extremely complex; among other reasons, because the intensity of a sensation is not wholly dependent upon the vigour of the stimulus, but upon the relations momentarily existing between the stimulus and the organism. When one has a headache the sound which otherwise might hardly be noticed seems extremely loud. Commonly, however, sensations of very weak intensity are either indifferent or slightly exasperating and unpleasant; those of moderate intensity are ordinarily agreeable, and those of high intensity are usually unpleasant. Owing to the obvious connection of the sensory attributes of duration and intensity, we shall expect that affection will show variations in keeping with the relation between these two. A very brief stimulus of moderate intensity may affect the nervous system in a very slight degree. A moderate stimulus on the other hand, if long continued, may result in very intense neural activity, and so be accompanied finally by unpleasant affective tone, rather than by the agreeableness which generally belongs to moderate stimulation.

Affection and Extensity of Sensations.—We shall find that the extensity of sensation processes, when regarded alone, possesses no significance for the production of affective phenomena which has not already been exhibited under the head of intensity. A colour which seems to us beautiful, when a sufficient amount of it is presented to us, may become indifferent when its extent is very much diminished. This consists, practically, however, in substituting a moderate intensity of visual stimulation for one of very restricted intensity. On the side of extensity the variations in affective reactions are most important in connection with the perception of form, and to this feature we shall refer at a later point.

Comparison of Affection With Sensation.—It may be remarked before we proceed to another phase of the matter in hand, that affection agrees with sensation in possessing degrees of intensity and duration, although it never displays extensity. It apparently possesses only two fundamental qualities, agreeableness and disagreeableness, which shade through an imaginary zero point into one another. On both sides of this zero point there are ranges of conscious experience whose affective character we cannot introspectively verify with confidence, and we may call this zone the region of neutral affective tone. But we must not suppose that this involves a genuine third elementary quality of affection. Apart from these two qualities, it seems probable that the only variations in affection itself are those which arise from differences in its intensity and duration. The more intimate phases of the changes dependent upon the shifting relations among these attributes we cannot at present enter upon. Wundt, however, maintains that an indefinite number of qualities of agreeableness and disagreeableness exist. Conclusive introspective proof bearing upon the matter is obviously difficult to obtain.

Affection and Ideational Processes.—We have spoken first of affection in dependence upon sensory activities, in part because it is in this connection that it first appears, and in part because the fundamental facts are here more obvious and less complex in their surroundings. But affection is of course a frequent companion of ideational processes, and it is, indeed, in this sphere that it gains its greatest value for the highest types of human beings. We must, therefore, attempt to discover the main conditions under which it comes to light among ideas. We may conveniently take as the basis of our examination the processes which we analysed under the several headings of memory, imagination, and reasoning. Fortunately we shall find that the principles governing affection in these different cases are essentially identical. That our memories are sometimes agreeable and sometimes disagreeable needs only to be mentioned to be recognised as true. Oddly enough, as was long ago remarked, the memory of sorrow is often a joy to us, and the converse is equally true. It does not follow, therefore, that the affective colouring of an act of memory will be like that of the circumstances recalled. It may, or it may not, be similar. Moreover, either the original event or the recalling of it may be affectively neutral. What then determines the affective accompaniment of any specific act of memory? In a general way we may reply, the special conditions at the moment of recall. In a more detailed way we may say whatever furthers conscious activity at the moment in progress will be felt as agreeable, whatever impedes such activities will be felt as disagreeable. An illustration or two may help to make this clearer.

Affection a Concomitant of the Furthering, or Impeding, of Ideational Activities.—Suppose a man goes out to make a number of purchases. At the first shop he gives an order, and upon putting his hand into his pocket to get his purse and pay his bill he finds that the purse is gone. The purse contained a considerable sum of money, and a search through the outlying and generally unused pockets of the owner fails to disclose it. The immediate effect of this discovery is distinctly and unmistakably disagreeable. The matter in hand is evidently checked and broken up. Furthermore, the execution of various other cherished plans is instantly felt to be endangered. Thereupon, the victim turns his attention to the possible whereabouts of the purse. Suddenly it occurs to him that just before leaving home he changed his coat, and instantly the fate of the purse is clear to him. It is serenely resting in the pocket of the coat he previously had on, which is now in his closet. The result of this memory process is one of vivid pleasure. The business in hand can now go on. It may involve a trip home again, but at all events the money is still available, and the whole experience promptly becomes one of agreeable relief.

Suppose that in this same case, instead of being able to recall the circumstances assuring him of the safety of the purse, our illustrative individual had failed to find any such reassuring clue, and did on the other hand distinctly recall being roughly jostled by a group of suspicious-looking characters on the platform of the street car while on the way from his home. In this case the memory process would augment the unpleasantness of the original discovery of the loss. The activity which he had planned for himself would appear more than ever thwarted, and the disagreeableness of the experience might be so intense as to impress itself on his mind for many days to come.

Affection and Memory.—We shall find upon examination that the paradox referred to a few lines above finds its explanation in a manner altogether similar to that of this case just described. The remembrance of a previous success or of a former prosperity may be accompanied by the most disagreeable exasperation, because it jars upon the experiences of the present moment, from which everything but disaster may seem to have fled. Many persons in straitened circumstances often seek a pale and disappointing solace in the memory of better days. Pride makes in this way a vain effort to efface the brute reality of the present, but the effort is generally a melancholy failure. Happiness lies not in the contemplation of such a past, but in the earnest and absorbed performance of the task just at hand. On the other hand, the memory of privation and struggle, once success is achieved, may be pleasurable, because in this case the thought not only does nothing to thwart our present purposes and interests, but even augments our progress by a conviction of our own strength and capacity.

From these brief considerations it is evident that memory processes may contain very intense affective elements, and that apparently these will be painful, or at least unpleasant, when the thought which comes to mind serves to impede our immediate purposes and desires, especially if the impeding is sufficiently serious to arouse emotion; whereas they will be pleasurable when the suggested ideas contribute vigorously to the onward flow of our interests and intentions. Many memory processes stand midway between these extremes, and are neutrally toned. It is not so evident, but it is nevertheless the general opinion of psychologists, that the affective feature in such ideational feelings is qualitatively identical with the affective element in sensory feelings. Sometimes the sensory, peripherally initiated feeling is more intense, sometimes the ideational or centrally initiated feeling. But, so far as concerns the affective elements proper, the two are probably qualitatively alike, and the differences in the total states of consciousness in which they appear are, intensity apart, primarily due to differences in the cognitive and motor elements accompanying them.

Is There an Affective Memory?—An interesting question suggests itself at this point, upon which we may profitably dwell a moment. Do we have memories of our feelings in the same sense in which we have memories of ideas and perceptions? Before we essay an answer we must be sure that we understand exactly what the question means. When we remember events we find that at times the visual image, perhaps, of the surroundings comes into our minds. Sometimes words or motor images may flash upon us. Or again, we may in reply to a question say, " Yes, I remember the circumstances," when in point of fact what we mean is that we are certain we could remember them if necessary, although we do not at the moment make any effort actually to recall them. The last form of memory for feelings we undoubtedly have. We can often say with confidence whether at a definite time we were experiencing pleasure, or displeasure, or neither. But if we actually attempt to recall the event, we find then, as we just remarked, that sometimes the recollection itself is affectively colourless, sometimes it has the affective character of the original event, and sometimes an opposite character. In a practical way, therefore, we have a memory of affective experiences as genuinely as we have in the case of ideas. We can tell what affective tone belonged to vivid experiences. But our ability to reinstate the original affective tone with the cognitive memory of an event is extremely defective. The reasons for this will be clearer after we have examined the neural basis of affection.

Affection and Imagination.—The case of imagination we may readily suppose will prove to be much like that of memory, for we discovered earlier in our work how closely related these two forms of conscious process are. This supposition we find to be correct, and the only important addition which we shall need to make to our previous account of the operation of affection in connection with memory will become manifest in our examination of reasoning, which we shall employ in its broadest meaning to apply to all grades of purposive thinking.

Affection and Reasoning.—In our analysis of reasoning we found that in its most rudimentary forms it seemed to reduce to the ability to apprehend relations and employ them constructively. Recognition we saw was, therefore, in a measure an elementary expression of the reasoning power akin to the crude forms of conception. It has sometimes been maintained by psychologists that all recognition, whether of object or relation, is as such agreeable. The objects or relations which we apprehend are, of course, often unpleasant. But whenever the content of our apprehension is itself indifferent, the act of identifying is said to be agreeable; hence the theory. The agreeableness is admitted to be inconsiderable in such cases as would be illustrated by a person's perception of a familiar book when his eyes chance to fall upon it in an accidental excursion about the room. But it is nevertheless said to be discernible even in instances of this kind, while in all cases of mental struggle with some baffling problem, the detection of a relevant relation, or the appearance of an appropriate idea, is welcomed with a thrill of unmistakable pleasure. Total states of consciousness of this kind, together with such antithetic cases as are mentioned a few lines below, are by certain psychologists designated as "intellectual feelings." Wholly strange surroundings, on the other hand, in which we find nothing familiar to recognise, are said to produce in us at times uneasiness and discomfort. Moreover, we are all familiar with the unpleasantness of an abortive effort to recall a name or a number, and the fruitless effort to solve a problem is often mentally most distressing. Evidently such a formula as that cited above contains a quota of truth, but it is also evident that exceptions are easy to find. In order to reach consistency we must look for the principle lying beneath these formulations. By examining the conditions under which we execute these relatings of conscious processes to one another, we may come upon the law governing their affective consequences.

It will clearly be judicious to follow the clue which we secured in our description of the affective aspect of memory. It is at least possible that this may prove to afford us a basal principle. If so, we shall expect that in so far as any apprehension of relations, or objects, furthers an enterprise at the moment dominating our consciousness, it will be agreeable; whereas in so far as it thwarts or checks such an interest it will be unpleasant. This certainly seems to hold true wherever it is possible to apply it to concrete facts. For example, strange things are not disagreeable, but quite the contrary, provided we are travelling for amusement. If we are in haste to reach some destination in a city, and find that we have accidentally left the street car at the wrong point and are in strange streets surrounded by totally unfamiliar houses, the experience may be momentarily very uncanny and disagreeable, after which it may strike us as amusing, or as exasperating, depending on the circumstances involved. The agreeableness or disagreeableness in the perception of such objects and such relations is, therefore, in no true sense primarily determined by their strangeness or their familiarity. It is determined by the manner in which the perception affects our purposes and interests.

On the other hand, the perception of a familiar object like one's own home may arouse either ennui, tedium, and a sense of unrest, or the keenest pleasure, depending not at all upon the familiarity of the object, but solely upon the mental condition in which we chance to be, and upon the relation which the object bears to this condition. If we are eager to see our parents to communicate some piece of good news we may find the sight of home most delightful. If, on the other hand, we desire, in the midst of a hot summer, to get away to the sea, the very bricks of the house cry out and mock us in our discomfort.

On the whole it appears probable that the principle which obtains in these cases holds good throughout all the purposive thought processes of our mental life. In trains of thought where we almost lose ourselves in complete revery, as well as in those prolonged and strenuous mental operations by means of which we solve the more serious problems, practical or theoretical, with which our pathway is beset, in these and in all the intermediary transitional forms agreeable feeling is the accompaniment of such ideas as further our momentary interests; disagreeableness, on the other hand, is the mark of those which obstruct or thwart those interests.

CHAPTER XIV

FEELING AND THE GENERAL PRINCIPLES OF AFFECTIVE CONSCIOUSNESS

Classifications of Feeling.—We are now in a position to recognise the fact that all forms of the cognitive activities are characterised at times by marked affective qualities. Our feelings may, therefore, be brought for classification under any of the several main forms of the knowledge process. In point of fact the usual classifications of feeling are actually based upon these cognitive factors, and we may profitably examine some of the principal divisions which are secured in this way, although we must remember that they are very misleading groupings if they are understood as arising primarily from peculiarities of the affective element in such complex feelings.

Sensuous and Intellectual Feeling.—Feelings are thus divided into sensuous and intellectual, depending upon whether they originate in, and chiefly terminate in, sense organ activities, or in central processes, like imagination. We have already seen that the affective part of such feelings, the agreeableness or disagreeableness, is probably one and the same, whatever their immediate occasion. It is, however, undoubtedly true, as our discussion in the early part of the previous chapter implied, that many feelings which belong to sensory processes are relatively confined in their significance to these immediate activities, whereas the intellectual feelings commonly run out into a bearing on larger and more remote portions of our mental life. The agreeableness of the taste of candy, for instance, or the delight in the fragrance of violets, commonly exhausts itself in the moment of enjoyment; whereas the pleasure of a fine picture pervades one's life long after the picture itself has passed from one's view. This distinction must not, however, be unduly magnified if the basis for it be laid in the mere part played by the sense organ, for it must be remembered that the picture also is seen by means of a sense organ. Moreover, the feeling which the picture calls out would commonly be designated æsthetic, rather than intellectual. More often, perhaps, the term "intellectual feeling" is employed to cover such cases as wonder, surprise, curiosity, and interest, the apprehension of relations, the feeling of ignorance, and the like. The real distinction, which is hinted at in this old division of feelings, is one that can only be stated correctly when we observe what functions various feelings subserve in the life of the organism. And to this we shall return shortly.

Aesthetic, Ethical, Social, and Religious Feeling.—Other suggested divisions of feeling are the following: æsthetic, ethical, social, and religious. These divisions, like the immediately preceding one, are evidently based upon differences in the objects which call out the feeling, and result in different *cognitive* and *emotional* activities, rather than upon any differences among the affective elements of the feeling itself. Such classifications are undoubtedly suggestive and valuable in their indication of the great avenues along which our feelings are approached. But we must once more carefully guard ourselves against the misapprehension that the affective factor (which ostensibly constitutes, in the theory of many psychologists, the differentia of feeling from other forms of conscious process) is in any true sense the basis of the distinction from one another of the several types of so-called feeling. These classifications are really based upon the possibility of viewing all consciousness as *internal* in its reference, rather than on the presence of affective processes, a view to which we shall return briefly in the final chapter of this book. The specific forms of psychical experience which are peculiar to the various classes that have been mentioned can be examined more profitably in connection with our study of emotions, and we shall, therefore, postpone their further consideration until that time.

Neural Basis of the Affective Element in Feeling.—In our discussion of sensation we observed that the various sensory qualities depend upon the action of specific end-organs. We have now seen that the affective processes may occur in connection with any of the sensational or ideational activities. And the question naturally arises as to their neural basis. Unfortunately our positive and detailed knowledge about the matter is lamentably incomplete. The theory, however, which enjoys widest currency at the present time maintains that the two antithetical forms of affection represent the fundamental modes in which any neural activity may go on. They do not depend, therefore, as sensations and ideas primarily do, upon the action of specific segments of the nervous system; they are rather the counterparts of the manner in which the whole nervous system is affected by the activity initiated in any segment at a particular time. From this point of view pleasure is correlated with physiologically useful and wholesome activities; pain and disagreeableness with the physiologically harmful. Thus, the theory would find the neural explanation for the unpleasant character of dazzling lights and loud, shrill sounds in the manner in which the nervous system as a whole is affected by the reaction from these violent stimulations of the optic and the auditory tracts respectively. The nervous action is conceived as being of a definite form, which is qualitatively similar for all disagreeable or injurious stimuli, but quantitatively different for stimuli of varying intensity or varying harmfulness. As these peripheral sensory tracts, when they are active, always influence more or less directly the whole nervous system, the affective reaction represents in reality the effect of the particular stimuli upon the whole organism. The agreeableness of a musical chord or a sweet odour would, on the basis of this theory, be referable to a normal and efficient reaction of the nerves; the disagreeableness of a discord or a nauseous odour would, on the other hand, find its explanation neurally in an excessive or internally mal-adapted reaction of the organism.

We shall accept the validity of the general conception underlying this theory, although we have to admit that its precise meaning is often found to be vague when we insist upon detailed facts confirmatory of its contention. Moreover, there are some facts which lend themselves to incorporation in the theory only with extreme difficulty. We can best get an insight into the more important considerations by reverting to our fundamental conception of the purpose and significance of consciousness in organic life—a conception which we have stated so often as to render repetition superfluous.

General Significance of Affective Consciousness.—Agreeableness and disagreeableness are the immediate indices of the significance for the organism of the various stimuli and responses which enter its experience. Evidently some such marks, or signs, in consciousness of the value of particular objects or movements are indispensable to the execution by mental processes of the part we have assigned to them. The sign in consciousness of the organically advantageous might very well have been something different from the experience we now name pleasure, and the sign of harmfulness might have been other than that which we now recognise as pain and disagreeableness. But some such symbols there must be, if consciousness is to steer successfully among new sourroundings and in strange environments. If it were necessary to await the loss of one's eyesight before discovering that dazzling lights were injurious, consciousness would certainly be little more than a pernicious aggravation. As a matter of fact such stimulations are instantly felt as disagreeable, and the mind without further information has forthwith a guide to the kind of action appropriate to the occasion. Similarly as regards agreeable experiences. When one is tired and hungry after fatigue and exposure to cold, any food may seem welcome, but warm and well-flavoured food tastes best and will be preferred when choice is possible. In such cases one needs no further experience than is afforded by a specimen of the cold and the warm food to recognise which is more agreeable.

So fundamental is this significance of the affective processes in all those activities immediately connected with the maintenance of life in the individual and the race, that several psychologists of repute have defended the thesis that pleasure and displeasure are the primordial forms of consciousness, the other processes connected with the special senses being of later origin. It is interesting in this connection to note that one writer has assigned displeasure as the original form of consciousness; another, pleasure; while a third has advocated the hypothesis that the two appeared together in advance of other modes of consciousness.

If space permitted, we might examine the evidence for these several points of view, but as this is out of the question, we may remark provisionally that if our analysis of the affective features of consciousness has been thus far correct, we cannot assent to any of the theories just mentioned. It may well be that with the more rudimentary types of mind the affective factors of consciousness dominate over the distinctly sensory and ideational. It may be, too, that the first appearance of consciousness is in connection with the operation of the pain nerves, though this is wholly problematical. But affection, as we know it (and we have no right to go afield from such knowledge) is apparently not a form of consciousness independent of sensations and ideas. Quite the contrary; it invariably appears clearly *in connection* with them; whereas the sensations and ideas are occasionally wholly, or all but wholly, destitute of affective tone. Meantime, it should be reasonably certain that agreeableness and disagreeableness—as signs of the immediate import for the organism of particular moments of experience—are indispensable elements in the successful functioning of consciousness. As Bain puts it, pleasure represents a heightening, and pain a lowering, of some or all of the vital processes, and consciousness is in this way given immediate information of the nature of the situation. We may accept Bain's formula in a general way, although it is far from clear that a raising of vitality is always the immediate outcome of pleasure, and a lowering of it an immediate consequence of discomfort.

Marshall has put the matter somewhat differently, in a manner which certainly fits many of the facts most admirably. He connects pleasurable experience with the use of stored-up nervous energy in amounts less than that actually available, whereas unpleasant experience he connects with the use of nervous energy beyond the limits of the normal modes of functioning. We shall revert to this again. Münsterberg connects pleasantness and unpleasantness, respectively, with movements of extensor and flexor muscles, with expansion and contraction of the organism, a view which certainly has, despite its suggestiveness, only a very general and indefinite basis.

Physiological Expressions of Feeling-Tone.—In connection with this general theory of agreeableness and disagreeableness as expressions respectively of the increase or decrease in organic vigour, certain investigators have reported constant and definite physiological changes accompanying the antitheses of affective tone. Pleasurable experiences are thus said to cause dilation of the peripheral blood-vessels, decreased rate in the heart beat, increased depth of breathing, and heightened tonus of all the voluntary muscles. Disagreeable experiences on the other hand are said to produce constriction of the peripheral blood-vessels, and in general a set of physiological phenomena exactly opposite to those just mentioned as arising from pleasure. Several competent experimentalists have failed to confirm these observations, and the phenomena are apparently verifiable only under certain very definite and normally infrequent conditions. Meantime, there can be no question that all the vital processes, including those of assimilation, secretion, and excretion, are profoundly influenced by intense affective conditions. The only question is whether they are always affected in the same way by the same conscious tone. We shall have occasion to emphasise certain of these phenomena when we examine the emotions.

Genesis of the Affective Elements of Consciousness.—Following our method in previous cases we may ask, first, under what conditions affection makes its earliest appearance. So far as concerns the life history of any given individual, we may say that affection is undoubtedly coincident in its manifestations with the dawn of consciousness. The cry with which the child draws its first breath has led to the assertion that life begins, as well as ends, in pain. However this may be, there is every reason to think that the mental life of the new-born babe is for many days one of vague sensory consciousness, dominated by relatively vivid antitheses of agreeableness and disagreeableness. Certainly the earliest expressions of infants suggest nothing so strongly as pleasure and pain.

If we inquire more closely into the conditions under which expressions of satisfaction and dissatisfaction arise, we find that they align themselves very suggestively with the doctrine which we have repeatedly formulated regarding the origin of consciousness in general. When the child is cold or hungry consciousness is called into play, for the organism does not possess, in its inherited mechanism of reflexes and automatic movements, any device adequate to cope with these difficulties. But the materials of voluntary muscular control have not as yet been acquired, and so the intense dammed-up nervous currents break over into the few pervious pathways of the quasi-reflex type. The crying muscles are liberally represented here, and the child's lamentation, which summons parental assistance, is the outcome of this motor escapement. If there were no damming up of the nervous currents, if the stimulus represented by the cold immediately resulted in releasing efficient motor reactions, there is no reason to suppose consciousness would be aroused. This, however, is not the case. The stimulations are there, and they become more and more insistent. The conditions for the appearance of consciousness are, therefore, at hand, and if we may judge by external expressions it promptly comes to life. But it is confronted with a situation with which it cannot immediately deal. It is reduced to the condition of a spectator conscious of an unnamed, yet imperious need, but almost powerless to render assistance. Now, whenever we encounter such circumstances as these, we shall always find that the affective tone is one of unpleasantness.

In very young babes instances of definite pleasure are somewhat more difficult to secure. The child spends most of its time in relatively deep sleep, and the expressions of gratification which it manifests are, for several days at least, ambiguous. When such expressions do appear, they are apt to be in connection with the satisfaction of hunger. They seem to represent a kind of ratification on the part of consciousness of the activities which have been indulged to relieve hunger. Indeed, if we may judge by external appearances, supported by our knowledge of the conditions in adult life, the whole of this process of allaying hunger, as well as the final stage of satiety, is agreeable. The case is extremely interesting in the apparent contrast which it offers to the conditions of maturity. Prior to the securing of control over the voluntary muscles, the function of consciousness is necessarily in large measure that of an approving or disapproving onlooker, who has little power to make his opinions felt in action.

We have noted the conditions under which painfully toned

consciousness is produced. It would seem at first sight as though these must be synonymous with all those circumstances in which obstacles were to be overcome, and therefore synonymous with *all* those cases where consciousness would be required. This position is, however, only tenable provided we disregard the obvious fact that the organism is in course of development, and that at this early stage, when voluntary movements are not yet under control, the total significance of the various factors in its life is not superficially obvious. Disagreeableness is undoubtedly the counterpart of *continued inability* to cope with a demand laid upon the organism, and the degree of unpleasantness is roughly paralleled by the insistence and the poignancy of the demand. Agreeableness, on the other hand, is the psychical counterpart of effective modes of reaction to a situation. When the situation is being adequately met, therefore, we may expect to find pleasure appearing, whether the successful response has come as a result of definite voluntary acts, as it may in adult life, or as a result in part of outside assistance, as it does in the early days of infancy.

Why Consciousness Is So Often Neutrally Toned.—The question then suggests itself as to why we are not more vividly aware of agreeableness in the normal activities of every-day life. These activities involve more or less of voluntary coördinations, which for the most part go on efficiently, and should consequently, from the point of view we have adopted, produce pleasurable results in consciousness. We have intimated that as a matter of fact a large part of our mental life is neutrally toned. The reply to this query is, therefore, that in so far as we are provided with healthy bodily processes, and in so far as we are engaged in the effective solution of problems which confront us, our consciousness *is* agreeable in tone. But large parts of our daily undertakings are of a routine character which verges upon habit, and in consequence require little vigorous conscious attention, and therefore call out little affective reaction. Moreover, it frequently happens that although our mental operations are efficiently executed from the standpoint of practical results, some of our intra-organic processes are slightly indisposed, and inasmuch as our consciousness reflects the totality of our organic condition, we find ourselves either experiencing very little pleasure, or else feeling positive discomfort.

General Theory of Affective Processes.—It is evidently impossible, therefore, to state the conditions under which agreeableness or disagreeableness is produced, by reference to any *single* set of activities with which our cognitive and volitional processes may be engaged. Consciousness always reflects more than a single group of such activities, and its affective character is always dependent upon the whole gamut of physiological operations going on at any given moment. Under conditions of perfect health we may often predict with much accuracy what the affective results of a given stimulus may be, because we know that ordinarily it will stimulate moderately a well-nourished nerve tract. But unusual neural conditions in any part of the organism may lead to the falsifying of our predictions at any time. The melody which charmed us to-day may irritate us to-morrow, and this, not because the melody, or the auditory nerve, has either of them changed in the meantime, but simply because the digestive processes which yesterday were orderly are to-day chaotic. We see, therefore, that our provisional formulations in the previous chapter were too simple to account for all the facts.

The evidence thus far examined points to the belief that disagreeableness always appears in infancy, as well as in adult life, in connection either with (1) diseased conditions of the organism, or (2) with excessive neural stimulation, or (3) with the checking and impeding of consciousness in its efforts to guide action. The third point may prove to be identical with the second. It is certainly identical in some instances. The function of the unpleasant in consciousness is, then, evidently to furnish an immediate and unambiguous index of conditions which menace the welfare of the organism. Agreeableness appears in connection with (1) healthful organic conditions, (2) the stimulation of nerves inside the limits of their ability to respond with maximal vigour, and (3) the free and unobstructed flow of consciousness, whatever its object. The obvious function of agreeableness is consequently found in the furnishing of immediate exponents of organic welfare. Neither agreeableness nor disagreeableness are unambiguously prophetic. Their important function is in the present. Their meaning for the future requires the light of intelligence and experience. The frenzied delights of a Bacchanalian orgy are certainly no reliable harbingers of health, nor are the pangs of the morrow necessarily indicative of inevitable future disaster. We may now advantageously examine a few typical instances of affective consciousness, in order to test the adequacy of our principle.

The agreeableness and disagreeableness which arise respectively from healthful or diseased conditions of the organism hardly require comment. The organic feelings of a strong, well-fed organism are distinctly buoyant and pleasant; whereas the depression of dyspepsia, the tedious discomfort of a severe cold, etc., are almost unmitigatedly disagreeable. The moderate stimulation of the sense organs by simple stimuli is normally agreeable, and their excessive stimulation normally disagreeable. The pleasure of exercise and the unpleasantness of extreme fatigue, the agreeableness of moderately intense simple colours and tones, and the disagreeableness of those which are very intense, afford instances which we might multiply indefinitely.*

* Acquired tastes and the correlative loss of liking for certain objects constitute interesting instances of the development which goes on in the organism in connection with affective phenomena. It seems probable as regards the acquirement of tastes, that in the case of gustatory sensations at least, certain organic changes in the neutral activities take place, by means of which stimuli,

The intellectual processes involved in grappling with a problem in which we are interested are normally agreeable so long as we seem to be making progress. They speedily become exasperating if we seem to be getting nowhere; and if our minds, by reason of fatigue, distraction, or any other cause, refuse to bring to our aid the ideas which we feel are needed, the operation may become intolerable.

When our emotions are vigorously enlisted in such reflective processes the agreeableness or disagreeableness may be extremely intense. Thus to many persons reflections upon immortality, upon the mercy of God, and other religious ideas may be profoundly uplifting and deeply gratifying so long as the mind meets with no obstacle in working out its conceptions. On the other hand, the mental agony experienced in reaching the belief that immortality is unreal is to many minds all but unbearable. In æsthetic pleasures the situation is ordinarily complicated by the presence of both sensory and intellectual factors. A beautiful picture not only appeals through its richness of colouring and its grace of line to the immediately sensory activities, it also suggests to us ideas which take hold of our sentiments, our emotions, and our intelligence, setting up in us strong tendencies to motor reactions of one or another kind.

Application of the Principles to Aesthetic Experience.— It seems fairly certain that those æsthetic objects which we adjudge agreeable comply with the second of our principles in the moderate stimulation of neural processes which are more than adequate to the demands laid upon them. It seems also to be true that in such cases the third of our principles is justified. An object which we feel to be beautiful

which originally produced excessive reaction, are subsequently adjusted to. The loss of liking for certain flavours may be due to a similar adaptation by means of which the agreeableness of the stimulation passes away, or to an excessive stimulation, which finally overflows into other neural tracts, producing reflexes of the nausea type.

sets up ideational reactions which are unimpeded, focalised, and definite. The picture, if it be a picture, means something fairly definite and real to us. On the other hand, pictures which displease or fail to interest us are either unpleasant as regards their colour,—in which case we probably have either inadequate or excessive optical stimulation of some kind,—or they are faulty in drawing, or confused in meaning, so that our minds either feel a discrepancy between what is portrayed and what is suggested, or else are left thwarted and baffled.

The case of music is one in which to most of us, did we but acknowledge the truth, the sensory element, with its immediate motor effects, is at a maximum, and the ideational at a minimum. But it seems difficult to find an instance of æsthetic experience which does not readily enough conform to our principles. On the whole, then, we may accept these principles, provisionally at least, as indicative of the general facts about the conditions for the appearance of affective reactions, and as suggesting their fundamental significance. We shall now go on to see, in connection with our study of instinct, emotion, and volition, how these affective phases of our consciousness actually enter into the determination of our acts and our character. We can in that way make out most clearly the manner in which they enter into the cognitive operations which we have previously discussed.

CHAPTER XV

REFLEX ACTION AND INSTINCT

Motor Aspect of Conscious Processes.—We come now to study the group of motor powers by means of which the psychophysical organism is enabled to guide its own movements, and so to control in a measure its own fate. In many of the discussions which have gone before it has been necessary to assume that these muscular reactions were occurring, but their intimate nature we have been obliged to overlook. As a matter of fact all the mental operations which we have analysed have their ultimate significance and their final outcome in precisely these motor activities. In reality, therefore, all our previous study has been upon these reactions, for it has all had to do with their immediate psychophysical antecedents, which are functionally a part of them. Nevertheless, it is essential that we should examine the motor phenomena in and of themselves, and much more exhaustively than hitherto. We shall turn, first, to the earliest forms of muscular activity which we find in the human being, and then proceed to study the more highly developed forms which characterise a later period.

Primitive Motor Capacities.—A survey of the motor equipment of a new-born babe discloses the fact, as we have previously seen, that a certain number of automatic and reflex coördinations are already provided for at birth. The automatic activities of respiration, circulation, and digestion are carried on from the first. The reflexes involved in sucking, crying, and clasping the fingers about objects placed in them also take place. But aside from these, the child's motor capacities are potential, rather than actual. This slender store of motor accomplishments finds its explanation in the undeveloped condition of the nervous system at birth.

Meagre as is this array of hereditary motor coördinations to which we have referred, it suffices, with parental assistance, to keep the child alive until the appearance of more adequate adjustments. Moreover, it bears striking evidence to the fact, were any demonstration of it necessary, that the human organism is exactly like that of the lower animals, whose instinctive activities are often sources of so much wonder, in that it possesses at birth preformed pathways in the nervous system, by means of which sensory stimulations may discharge in effective movements of accommodation. The primordial form of motor control over the environment is, then, so far as concerns the human infant, to be found in hereditary reflexes.

Early Motor Development.—Development goes forward at such a tremendous rate that it is difficult to follow with entire confidence the course of motor events during the first year or two of a child's life. But certain of the most important transitions from the conditions we have just described occur commonly during the first three or four months, and we may in passing profitably remark upon the general nature of this change. Afterward we shall go back to look for the appearance of other forms of automatic, reflex, and instinctive acts, which we have seen to be the primitive types of motor activity. We shall find evidences of their development at periods covering a considerable portion of the time of organic growth. Furthermore, we shall find that, in a modified form, the instincts remain throughout life as fundamentally important factors in the evolution of volition and in the foundation of character.

The point to which we wish to call attention for a moment is illustrated by the growth of the hand and eye control. At the outset the eyes are generally destitute of all orderliness of movement. They move independently of one another, and with no special reference to objects in the field of view. In the course of the first few weeks, however, they begin to move together, to converge, and gradually to show a tendency to follow moving objects. At this time the child loses its original blank stare, and from time to time fixates objects with a totally new expression of countenance. About the time that this accomplishment is achieved the hand begins to show a definite development. It explores objects with which it is in contact. The thumb, which at the beginning took little or no part in clasping, is now brought into operation, and the things grasped are moved about in a fairly well coördinated manner. The next step in advance is characteristic of all development in motor control, and consists in the conjoining of the two previously independent coördinations of hand and eye. The eye is now able to follow the hand, and the hand is able to give the eye objects for inspection.

We shall come back with more of detail to this type of intercoördination of acquired forms of control in our analysis of voluntary action. Meantime, it will be helpful to bear in mind that once a coördination, like the eye-coördination, is gotten under command, it is promptly incorporated as a member of a larger coördination, such as the eye-hand coördination, which is in its turn destined to a similar fate in the course of evolving conduct.

Turning back now to a fuller study of the instinctive and reflex types of action, we shall find the general trend of events to be somewhat as follows: The development of the nervous system goes on with astonishing rapidity during the first three years, so that the child has, with the exception of the sexual processes, practically a full store of reflexes established by the end of that time. Contemporaneous with this acquirement of the reflexes occurs the gradual unfolding of the life of impulse, and the upbuilding of this into the elaborate forms of voluntary action, which promptly tend to become habitual. We must now analyse more carefully the details of this process.

Reflex Action.—A reflex act, as has been earlier remarked, is one in which a muscular movement occurs in immediate response to a sensory stimulation without the interposition of consciousness. Consciousness is often aroused by reflex actions, but the motor reaction is not executed in response to conscious motives, and in the more deeply imbedded reflexes consciousness is quite powerless to suppress the movement. Thus, in winking we may be conscious that the eyelid has closed, and at times the movement may be executed voluntarily. But if a cinder or other irritating substance enter the eye we may be wholly unable to resist the tendency to shut the lids. On the other hand, when we are absorbed in reading our eyelids may close dozens of times in the reflex way, without our becoming in any definite manner aware of the fact.

Variability of Reflexes.—We have already referred many times to the (racially) hereditary nature of these reflexes. It remains to point out certain other striking facts about them. In the first place, they are subject, like all organic activities, to the general principles of development. They appear from time to time, as the nervous centres ripen, and are not all given complete at birth. The more rudimentary of them appear within the first few months. Sneezing, coughing, and hiccoughing come within the first few days, as a rule. Winking comes somewhat later, generally from the seventh to the eleventh week. Walking, which is primarily based upon reflexes, does not ordinarily begin until the twelfth to the eighteenth month or thereabouts, and is generally preceded by the creeping movements, which are probably partially reflex. Moreover, no one of the reflex acts is, at the outset, so well coördinated as it speedily becomes. It is clear that the nervous machinery, like other machinery, requires to be used somewhat before its maximum efficiency is available.

Furthermore, the reflexes vary at times in response to the general conditions of the organism. They are not wholly dependent in their operation upon the presence of a stimulus. The child, for example, when sated, stops sucking. When one is nervously wrought up, a slight noise, if unexpected, may result in a violent movement; whereas, if one had been agreeably absorbed in some occupation, no movement of any noticeable kind would have occurred. On the other hand, the essentially mechanical nature of the reflex is rendered obvious by the impartial way in which such responses are often executed, regardless of the desirability of the act at the moment. A man wishes his presence to be unobserved when in a dangerous situation, and he must needs select that occasion to be seized with an irrepressible paroxysm of sneezing. Again, although one is behind a strong screen, one still finds it impossible to avoid winking when any threatening object is seen approaching close to the eyes. It appears, therefore, that whereas the reflexes represent hereditary modifications in the connections of sensory-motor activities,—which are undoubtedly indispensable for the maintenance of organically useful reactions,—they may at times, by virtue of their mechanical nature, react in injudicious ways; and on the other hand, certain of them are unquestionably open to modification, either through the direct control of consciousness, as when one succeeds in suppressing a tendency to wink, or through the indirect effect of general organic conditions. It is evident, therefore, that reflexes represent various degrees of plasticity, but this does not invalidate the doctrine that all of them are hereditary in nature, and that on the whole they contribute distinctly to the general efficiency of those adaptive reactions which the organism makes upon its surroundings.

Instincts.—Instincts have an origin unquestionably similar to that of reflexes. They represent structurally preformed pathways in the nervous system, and stand functionally for effective inherited coördinations made in response to environmental demands. It is, perhaps, impossible to draw any absolutely sharp line between instincts and reflexes, although many principles of demarcation have been proposed. On the whole, the most fertile and suggestive working distinction seems to be found in the presence or absence of some relatively definite end dominating a series of acts. If the motor activity is simple, and is discharged in response to some objectively present stimulus without conscious guidance, it will be safe to call the act a reflex. Moreover, some reflex acts are essentially unconscious, whereas instincts, in the higher animals at all events, appear always to involve consciousness. Instincts accordingly depend more largely than reflexes upon the operations of the higher brain centres. If the activity involves a number of acts, each one of which, considered singly and alone, is relatively useless, but all of which taken together lead up to some adaptive consequence, such as the building of a nest, the feeding of young, etc., it will be safe to call the action instinctive. The difference thus pointed out is founded theoretically upon the nature of the functions subserved by the two types of action, their relative immediacy, generality, etc. It sometimes reduces in practice to a mere difference apparently of degree, or complexity, and will be found on further examination to involve, generally at all events, a difference in the intra-organic conditions leading to the two forms of reaction. It must be frankly confessed, however, that many cases are discoverable in which all distinctions seem arbitrary and fictitious. Too much stress should not be laid, therefore, upon the matter of ultimate differences. It is rather upon the identity of service to the organism that the emphasis should fall, with the added recognition that such service may be rendered in thousands of ways, whose interrelations may well baffle our clumsy and ill-informed attempts at classification.

Modifications of Instincts.—Instincts resemble reflexes in their susceptibility to modifications through experience, and also in their appearance in connection with definite stages in the development of the nervous system. Experience operates in two opposite directions. If the first expression of an instinct chances to be disastrous, and results in pain or fright, the instinct may be either temporarily, or permanently, inhibited. Thus, chicks, which possess the instinctive tendency to peck at food, are said to suppress this tendency when bad-tasting food is given them. On the other hand, if the instinctive action is successful and produces agreeable organic results, it tends at once to become ingrained as a habit. In all creatures which possess even rudimentary forms of conscious memory instincts must, therefore, speedily lose their original and wholly blind character. The tendencies to instinctive reactions must, in such creatures, very early set up organic reminiscences of the previous consequences of their indulgence; and these reminiscent traces must lead either to inhibitory movements or to responses of the habit type, in which the outcome must be in some vague way forecast.

Suppression of Instincts.—Instincts not only appear at definite points in the growth of the nervous system, but certain of them may also atrophy and disappear, provided that at the crucial period the appropriate conditions are not at hand to call them out and fix them as habits. Illustrations of the periodic nature of development in instincts are familiar to everyone. The puppy cannot swim, the older dog can, and he does it instinctively. The bird displays no tendency to nest-building until a certain maturity is attained, and instances of a similar kind might be multiplied indefinitely. The abolition of an instinct by failure to secure expression at the correct time is shown in the case of chickens, which tend at first to follow any moving object. Ordinarily nature provides, of course, that this object shall be the maternal hen. If the opportunity to translate this instinct into a habit is not afforded, the instinct dies within a few days, and thereafter commonly cannot be reëstablished.

Instinct, Experience, and Reason.—The relatively flexible and plastic nature of instincts which is suggested by the foregoing observations finds additional confirmation in the innumerable instances in which intelligence, or unexpected and unusual environment, come in to exercise modifications. In the earlier views of instinct we always find it contrasted with reason, as though the two were radically distinct. The keener insight of our own time shows us that although reason represents the individual's contribution to his own fate in terms of his own experience, while instinct represents the contribution of racial experience, the actual operation of the two factors often displays most intimate interrelations. This is peculiarly true of all the higher animals, and especially man. Indeed, the great difficulty in studying instinct in human beings is due to the fact that intelligence immediately comes in to transform the native reactions in accordance with the dictates of the individual's personal experience.

Even in the lower animals, however, individual experience exercises a guiding influence over the particular forms of instinctive expression, although in many of these cases we must speak very conservatively as to the manner and measure in which consciousness participates. Whatever the explanation of the *modus operandi*, there can be no doubt that birds and insects such as bees and wasps and ants often modify their instinctive methods of nest-building in a most remarkable manner when the exigencies of local conditions require such modification. On the other hand, instincts are often carried out in a bungling fashion, and in the face of circumstances clearly fatal to their successful issue. The well-known disposition of certain dogs and squirrels to attempt, with elaborate efforts at digging, the burying of their bones or nuts when confined upon hard board floors illustrates the occasional futility of irrepressible instincts. The classical observations of the Peckhams upon bees and wasps afford striking instances of instincts misdirected at some crucial moment. They report, for instance, that wasps frequently prepare a nest carefully for the reception of the food store and then seal it up empty.

The obvious implication of such observations is that we have to do in the phenomena of instinct, as these appear in the several genera and species of the organic kingdom, with an overwhelming variety of reactions, all of which evidently emanate from the same type of ancestral source; but with indefinite and unpredictable susceptibility to modifications from environing conditions, and with an equally uncertain submission to conscious guidance. In so highly evolved a nervous system as that possessed by the human being we may naturally anticipate a very considerable number of these ancestral tendencies, and we must also expect to find them very promptly submerged in motor activities under the control of consciousness. These expectations seem to be fully realised by the actual facts.

Origin of Instincts.—Although everyone is agreed that instincts are racial habits transmitted by heredity to the particular individual, there has been wide difference of opinion regarding the precise manner in which they originally became established. The questions here at issue are clearly in large part biological in nature, and this is, therefore, evidently the reason why we find that the authoritative names connected with the conspicuous theories are chiefly those of great naturalists. Two fundamentally opposing views have until recently held the field. One is commonly known as the theory of lapsed intelligence. The American biologist, Cope, was an eminent defender of this view, which regards instincts as organically fixed habits which were originally intelligent adaptive acts partaking of the general character of volition. Wundt has been a distinguished adherent of this view among psychologists. The second theory is known as the reflex theory, and its basal contention is that instincts are simply accumulated reflex adjustments, explicable in their survival by the general principle of natural selection, which tends to weed out accumulations, however acquired, which are not preservative in their effect. Spencer and Weismann are representative adherents of two sub-forms of this theory.

The first theory has been criticised as making too great demands on our credulity concerning the amount of intelligence displayed by primitive forms of consciousness, and also on the score of defective evidence for the transmission of acquired characteristics. The second theory has been held vulnerable in its inability to explain how groups of reflex movements could have been slowly built up, when only the final step in the process rendered the chain really useful. A recent modification of these views, for which J. M. Baldwin stands sponsor among psychologists, is known as the theory of organic selection.

Theory of Organic Selection.—The crucial point in this theory is the supposition that even tentative and imperfect accommodation, with or without conscious direction, may serve to preserve the life of a species during the critical period when the instinct in its entirety is forming, and thus give it opportunity to become permanently imbedded in the organism as both a structural and functional attribute. Whether this view succeeds in weathering the storms of criticism or not, it is at least a highly ingenious and suggestive modification of the two previously extant views. It seems to contain what was most significant in both, while avoiding the more obvious pitfalls belonging to each. It gives scope for the play of intelligence in assisting in the formation of useful reactions, without going to the indefensible extreme of assuming that all valuable coördinations have had such intelligent origin. On the other hand, it offers a practicable hypothesis as to the manner in which movements of essentially reflex character may have been become chained together in instinctive reactions.

Function of Instinct.—Despite the differences which have characterised the opinions of the most acute biologists as to the origin of instincts, there is no divergence of opinion as to their function. They represent, by common consent, those forms of reaction upon the environment which the race has found most effective in maintaining itself against the rigours of climate and geographical habitat, and against the assaults of various forms of animal life. So far, therefore, as we may find traces of true instincts in human beings, we may know that we are confronted with tendencies which represent racial experiences, with reactions which express the pressure of untold ages of men engaged in the struggle for existence. It should, in the light of such considerations, afford us no astonishment to find that some reactions have been preserved, which are either useless at present or even somewhat positively disadvantageous. Moreover, remembering the complex conditions of our organic structure, we may well expect that certain of these instinctive reactions may possess their chief value and significance in the intra-organic physiological changes which they bring about, rather than in movements primarily affecting objects in the environment. Both these anticipations we shall find fulfilled.

CHAPTER XVI

THE IMPORTANT HUMAN INSTINCTS

The Distinction Between Native and Acquired Forms of Reaction.—We come now to examine the general scope and character of human instincts, and we are at once confronted with the concrete difficulties previously mentioned, *i. e.*, the difficulty of distinguishing the genuinely instinctive and hereditary reactions from the merely habitual, or from the acquired. Fortunately, there are certain great basal instinctive activities which we find appearing in children long before they have had sufficient experience to enable them to execute such reactions on the basis of volition; and, furthermore, there is a considerable group of reactions which all of us manifest that appeal to us when our attention is called to the matter as being native and untutored, as all but wholly devoid of purposeful conscious guidance. With these as a clue we may at least make a beginning in our catalogue, and from their analysis secure hints as to other similar instinctive traits.

In all properly constituted babies anger and fear are in evidence, with their appropriate motor expressions, long before experience has afforded opportunity to observe and copy these reactions in others. They are, therefore, unquestionably native. It may, however, be said, that these are emotional processes, and not instincts. Half of this contention is true and half is false. Anger and fear *are* instincts, and they are *also* emotions. Each involves a series of somewhat elaborate organic activities, and these are all of the unpremeditated hereditary type. They possess, however, in addition to these motor characteristics perfectly definite conscious concomitants, and to the *conscious* part of the whole process we commonly give the name emotion. We shall return to a detailed consideration of emotions in the next chapter. Meantime, we find that in anger the brows are wrinkled, the face ordinarily crimson, the veins gorged and prominent, the nostrils dilated, the lips drawn back and the teeth set, the hands clenched, the body tense, and the voice harsh. In extreme fear we meet with pallor and trembling, spasm of the heart, diarrhœa, the appearance of goose-flesh, cold sweat, bristling of the hair, dryness of the mouth, choking, paralysis of the voice, or hoarse screaming, together with tendencies to flight, coupled with a feeling of weakness. These reactions are called out precisely as the instinctive reactions in animals, *i. e.*, by the presence of appropriate stimuli. So far as consciousness is involved in them, the striking thing is the headlong fashion in which we find ourselves plunged into a vortex of intense impulsive feeling, compelling us to acts the consequences of which, in their first expressions, anyhow, are wholly unforeseen.

Utility of Instinctive Reactions.—The utility of such expressions may well arouse one's curiosity. In the case of anger some of the movements evidently have a "use" value, provided actual combat is necessary or desirable. But the trembling of fear, whatever may be said of the tendencies to flight, is a questionable organic asset for an individual wishing to react most effectively upon menacing surroundings. It must be admitted frankly that some of the motor responses displayed in emotional and instinctive discharges are unintelligible at present from the standpoint of utility. The attempt has often been made to refer the preservation of such acts as have no obvious value for the conquest of the environment, and even, perhaps, a deleterious influence upon this task, to their *physiological* usefulness in restoring disturbed organic conditions. Thus, the gorging of the blood vessels in anger, the secretion of tears in grief, the laughter in response to wit and humour, have sometimes been held to assist in relieving the abnormal circulatory conditions in the brain set up by the several emotional experiences. Of such explanations one can only say that they serve, at least temporarily, decently to cloak our ignorance. Nevertheless, there seems to be in the meantime no hesitation in any important quarter in accepting the general hypothesis already mentioned, that these racial habits which we designate emotions and instincts represent types of reaction which were useful at some time in the past history of the race, however problematical their usefulness may be at present.

Genetic Interrelations of Instincts.—The precise order in which the great mass of instincts make their debut is a difficult problem, and one for which it is, perhaps, not altogether profitable to undertake a solution. It seems probable that rudimentary forms of most of the instincts are encountered at a very early date, whereas the occasion for the expression of the matured reaction may be long postponed. Ribot has made it clear that in general those instinctive activities, such as fear and anger, which have to do most immediately with the maintenance of the physiological organism, and to which he gives the name of "egotistical emotions," are the first to appear in infancy and the last to disappear in old age or before the ravages of mental disease. The more altruistic emotions and instincts are for the most part found in a developed condition much later. Thus, sympathy, in unequivocal form, anyhow, occurs only with some considerable mental development. Indeed, it has sometimes been questioned whether sympathy is truly instinctive at all, whether it does not rather reflect the conclusions of intelligent consideration. But on the whole there seems no good reason to cavil at the evidences of its native character, especially as we can discern its seeming presence in certain animals.

List of Human Instincts.—Waiving, then, the question of the order of appearance, we find the generally recognised instincts in man to be as follows: Fear, anger, shyness, curiosity, affection, sexual love, jealousy and envy, rivalry, sociability, sympathy, modesty (?), play, imitation, constructiveness, secretiveness, and acquisitiveness.

Many authorities would add hunting to this list, and it must be admitted that in many races, and in many individuals of all races, it gives strong indications of a fundamentally instinctive nature. It is, however, so honeycombed with the effects of experience, and so irregular in its appearance, that it may fairly be given a position among the disintegrating instincts. Walking and talking are also included by many writers. Whether they shall be counted in or not is, as we have already observed, simply a question of classification. We may call them either chained reflexes or instincts, according to the criterion which we adopt for our divisions. James has added cleanliness to his list, and there are some facts which point to the correctness of this view, both in its application to men and to animals. But it is at best a very imperfect and erratic trait, as any mother of normal children can testify, and we may omit it in consideration of the necessary brevity of our discussion. We shall similarly forego any description of sympathy and modesty.

A perusal of our list brings at once to notice the union of instinct and emotion. A part of the terms apply primarily to *acts*, and so connect themselves with the common implication of the term instinct; whereas the other part suggests much more immediately the conscious feelings characteristic of the several forms of emotional experience. Imitation, play, and constructiveness are examples of the first kind of term; fear, anger, and jealousy illustrate the second. A few comments upon each of the instincts mentioned may serve to emphasise helpfully the typical conditions under which they appear, and the wholly naïve, untutored nature of the motor reactions which they manifest.

Fear.—We have already sufficiently described the motor phenomena in the case of fear, and it surely requires no additional argument to convince one of their native and unsophisticated character. It only remains to notice that in little children, despite some irregularity in different individuals, the normal provocatives are represented by strange objects, frequently by fur, by strange places, and especially by strange people, by being left alone, by darkness, and even occasionally by black objects; and by noises, particularly if very loud and unfamiliar. In later life, in addition to the fear which arises from the presence of actually dangerous situations, such as the menace of a great conflagration, many persons are seized with dizziness and a more or less acute terror upon finding themselves on a very high place, even though the possibility of falling over is efficiently precluded by railings, etc. Others are frightened by anything which verges upon the supernatural. Even the cold-blooded materialist of polite fiction feels his unsentimental blood curdle just a bit at the rehearsal of a thrilling ghost story, and only the possessor of practiced nerves can be alone on a dark night in a cemetery, or a thick wood, without some "creepiness" of the hair and skin.

All of us are likely to find that in the midst of a violent tempest, whether on land or sea, the howling of the wind is a distinct source of mental anxiety quite disproportionate to our sober, intellectual apprehension of its real danger. All these things take hold of our racial instincts, and however vigorously our individual experience attempts through its cortical machinery to put a veto on such nonsense, our lower brain centres refuse to abandon their world-old habits, and accordingly we find that our hearts are beating wildly, our breathing coming in gulps, our limbs trembling, the while we look on, mortified at the weakness we cannot control.

Anger.—Anger has several different forms and the most varied provocatives. We are irritated by the tireless piano next door, exasperated by the teasing child, hurt and vexed by the social snub, angry at the open insult, and perhaps moved to enduring hatred by the obnoxious and unscrupulous enemy. There is a common emotional vein running through all these conditions however much the particular momentary expression may vary. Possibly resentment is the best name wherewith to label this common factor. The instinctive nature of the motor reactions requires no further demonstration than is furnished by the sight of any little child enjoying a tantrum. The explicitly pugnacious element is, under civilised surroundings, inconspicuous after childhood is passed, despite the tremendous virility it displays if the curb be once slackened. The evolution of the race has been notoriously sanguinary, and we should feel no surprise, however much of disgust and regret we may entertain, that under the excitement of actual combat the old brute should display the cloven hoof. The development of so-called civilised codes of war affords interesting instances of the effort rational man makes to clothe with decency the shame of his own brutishness. According to the code, women and children may not be slaughtered, but it is occasionally lawful to despoil them of their flocks and herds, to lay waste their grain, and even to burn the roofs above their heads.

Shyness and Sociability.—The antagonistic instincts to which we have given the names shyness and sociability, not only appear as genuine hereditary impulses in little children, but they also fight, in the case of many persons, a lifelong battle for supremacy over the individual's habits. Sociability is simply an expression of the essentially gregarious nature of man. Some men seem destined for membership in a very small herd,—two or three at most,—others find their most natural surroundings amid large numbers. But the man or child who in one form or another does not natively crave companionship, sympathy, admiration, and confidence from others is essentially insane. Many turn from life and such companions as they chance to have attracted with horror and disgust, seeking in God or in some ideal of their own imagination a companionship which shall be fit and satisfying. But what is such a turning other than the most pathetic appeal for true comradeship, for a real society conformable with the deepest needs of the soul? No, sociability, under whatever limitations, is an expression of the very essence of humanity, and every little child evinces it by shunning solitude.

What often passes with children for a love of solitude is really more truly referable to the operation of the contrary instinct of shyness. In the very nature of the case the two impulses must always have been in unstable equilibrium so long as the drama of human life has been upon the boards. A certain measure of suspicion toward the action and purposes of others must always have been a condition of avoiding harm and imposition. On the other hand, the race is fundamentally gregarious, and all its greatest achievements have come about through coöperative undertakings in which the solidarity of the social structure has been a *sine qua non*. The tension between these two instincts, which we often find existing in ourselves, is no mere idiosyncrasy of our own purely personal organisation. It is rather a replica in us of a conflict which has been a part of the experience of every sane human being that ever lived.

Sociability finds everywhere its natural expression in smiling and in bodily attitudes, or gestures, which are, perhaps, best described as obviously non-pugnacious. The secondary gestures, apart from smiling and laughing, are through imitation early overlaid with the conventional ceremonials of different races and peoples. But in babies we find general extensor movements of reaching and stretching out of the arms, with eyes wide open and gaze fixed, head erect, and often nodding. In shyness the precise reverse is encountered. The

THE IMPORTANT HUMAN INSTINCTS 301

eyes are averted, the hands and arms held close to the body, the whole attitude being one of retreat. In older children and adults blushing and stammering, or even speechlessness, are common concomitants. Strangers and persons feared or venerated are the normal stimulants to shyness. In both kinds of reaction the movements are observed before there can be any question of conscious imitation. They are accordingly of undoubtedly instinctive nature. The great difficulty many persons experience in inhibiting the expressions of shyness also points to a similar conclusion.

A special form of the generic tendency to sociability is found in childish affection for parent or nurse, and in the tender feelings in general which we cherish toward those of whom we are fond. It finds its overt manifestation in facial expression, in modulation of voice, and in caressing gestures in general. The instinct is speedily veiled by experiential influences, but it gives every internal evidence of resting upon a native impulse, and its motor indices apparently require no artificial training. In childhood its common stimulus is found in persons upon whom we are dependent for our daily care. It may even extend in a somewhat imperious fashion to toys and other possessions intimately associated with childish cosmology. In mature life its stimulus is extremely complex, and baffles brevity of description. In general, it extends to all persons and possessions that we cherish as in some sort a part of ourselves.

Curiosity and Secretiveness.—Curiosity and secretiveness are in a measure antithetic impulses, like shyness and sociability; they vary immensely in different individuals, but bear, whenever met with, unmistakable traces of an instinctive origin. Animals afford us abundant instances of curiosity, and many methods of hunting are designed to take advantage of this tendency. Taken broadly, curiosity is simply another name for interest. In its simplest and most immediate form it is represented in the vertiginous fascination which novelty of any kind at times possesses for us. The child must pry about until he has fathomed the depths of your preoccupation. If asked why he wishes to know what you are about, he could give you no rational answer, even if he would. He simply knows that he *must* find out what you are doing. That is his *feeling*, and to ask for any deeper reason is itself unreasonable. The staid business man who allows himself to be lured across the street of a summer evening by the flaring torch of the street fakir has no reputable account to offer of his procedure. Time out of mind he has yielded to the same fascinating bait, always to find the same old bogus gold watches, the same improbable jewelry, the same nauseous medicines, passing out into the capacious maw of the great gullible public. Curiosity is the racial instinct to which our sedate citizen is yielding, and that is all there is to the matter. In this simple form the motor expression is found in the alert and wide-open eyes, the parted lips, the attentive ear, the general attitude of readiness to react to any lead. In its more intellectual phases we shall consider it under the head of interest in a later chapter.

Secretiveness will by many readers be thought unwarrantedly introduced as an instinct. It is not usually of sufficient consequence to justify any extended defence of its instinctive nature. But as a special form of shyness, at least, it deserves a word. It seems to be a development of those instincts among animals which lead them to render themselves as inconspicuous as possible. Certain insects and birds frequent haunts in which the surroundings, whether vegetation or earth, are of a colour similar to their own. In a corresponding fashion many persons feel an ineradicable impulse to conceal their plans, their actions, and their character behind a screen of non-committal silence and reserve. The impulse has no necessary connection with the preservation of a consciously defined personal dignity. It extends quite as forcefully to the suppression of all publicity touching the trivial as it does to the concealment of the momentous. Taciturnity is its commonest expression—if this formulation be not itself a paradox. Its irrational impulsive character is the mark which stamps it instinctive. Many of us are at times secretive of fixed and consciously recognised design. But the sort of thing of which we are here speaking is temperamental and may be felt in the absence of all explicit justification.

Acquisitiveness.—The instinct which we have called acquisitiveness appears chameleon-wise in many colours and under various conditions. As a primitive expression of the recognition of personal property it is one of the earliest and most tempestuous of innate reactions. It commonly gets a bad name at this time, and is often undiscriminatingly entitled selfishness. Certainly the distinction between *meum* and *tuum* is one for which every child betrays a remarkable precocity, although the precocity is commonly much more evident in the emphasising of meum than in the recognition of tuum. But however perverted the moral perspective, the thing is there in the form of an impulse to get hold of, and keep, and guard, something—anything. The particular objects which call it out are altogether incidental to the momentary surroundings and to the age of the special individual. With boys in the "marble age" "glassies" and "alleys" are the recipients of the passion. A little later it may be ribbons bestowed by, or purloined from, the young ladies of the hour; presently it is stocks and bonds and real estate. Now these things are many of them sought for ulterior ends consciously apprehended. But through the whole drama runs the instinctive thread, the impulse to acquisition, binding the whole together into a vital tale of human impulse striving after gratification. So far as it can be said to possess relatively fixed motor expressions, they are to be found in the elaborations of the infantile reaching and grasping, with the facial expression of alert, tense interest, and the intra-organic disturbances which generally accompany such excitement. The impulse takes its origin, however, from so many forms of stimulations that a perfectly fixed and inflexible motor indication of it is hardly to be expected.

Rivalry.—Closely connected with acquisitiveness is the instinct of rivalry, or emulation. It is intimately allied to play and imitation in its origin, and it easily runs to excess in anger, hate, jealousy, and envy. Its stimulus is apparently found in the successful achievements of anyone coming within our own social circle, by virtue of which we are likely to be relegated to inferior positions. If one happens to be a bank clerk one feels no rivalry instigated by the promotion of the janitor, but the advancement of one's fellow clerk is quite another matter.

The small boy views with unmixed admiration the skill of the professional ball-player, but the performances of his rival for a place on the school nine stir his blood in quite a different way. So far as concerns the voluntary muscles, the expression of this impulse has about it hardly anything fixed save the vigour and energy which go into their use when stung by the prick of rivalry.

As we intimated a few lines above, emulation is readily transformed into anger, and this fact points to a kinship which has undoubtedly in the history of racial evolution been most significant. Among the lower animals fighting is a constant and fundamental factor in life history. Under the ameliorating conditions of civilisation mankind has managed in large measure either to eliminate this element from human life or so to change its complexion as to shade its more brutal features, and to substitute for bloodshed and carnage the starvation and bankruptcy which emanates from unsuccessful competition. In so far, therefore, as rivalry represents the survival in modern life of the old fighting propensities, we must look in it for the vestigial evidences of tumult and excitement, of emotional tension, which have always characterised the struggle for existence. Needless to say, we find them in abundance, and hence it is that emulation so easily leads to the more unworthy instinctive expressions; hence it is that so much of moral dignity attaches to him who can feel and cherish rivalry without sacrificing his highest ethical ideals of integrity and respect for others.

Jealousy and Envy.—Viewed merely as natural impulses, jealousy and envy are sufficiently alike to render a separate mention of each unnecessary. Envy is generally applied to our covetousness of the prosperity or possessions of others. This covetousness is often accompanied, as in jealousy, by more or less malignity. Jealousy we commonly apply to a similar feeling toward persons who are our supposed rivals, whether actually successful or simply feared. Both animals and little children manifest jealousy, and no one can question that the *depth* of the feeling, together with these facts, points to its springing from a racially hereditary source. Its characteristic expressions are similar to those of anger and hatred, but commonly occur in milder form.

Sexual Instincts.—Among the most imperious of our impulses are undoubtedly those connected with sex. The approach to sexual maturity is usually attended by very deep-seated organic changes, and these are reflected in a marked development of the whole emotional nature. It is in this fact that we find an explanation of the definite bent which is often imparted to character at this time, leading in certain instances to a life-long devotion to ideals which are lofty and habits which are pure, and in other instances to perversion and debasement of the entire moral nature. This is *the* great formative period, the storm and stress period, of the moral life. The delineation of the basal facts in the birth and development of love between the sexes has been accomplished so perfectly in the great poems and tales of passion as to render futile and superfluous any such brief outline as would be possible here.

Parental Love.—Parental love is a far stronger impulse in the mother than in the father, as a rule. It is unquestionably instinctive in the mother, is given most lavishly during the infancy and childhood of the offspring, but commonly remains to the end one of the majestic forces in the history of humanity. Its expressions are partly those of caressing tenderness and partly those of protection and prescient regard for the needs of the child.

Play.—We come now to speak of the three instincts remaining upon our list, *i. e.*, play, imitation, and constructiveness. They are by no means synonymous, but their connection is so intimate, and their significance for the development of the child so similar and so important, that we shall consider them together, and at some length.

In little children the impulse to play is practically identical with the impulse to use the voluntary muscles. Indeed, the definition of play which enjoys widest currency at the present moment identifies it with the free, pleasurable, and spontaneous activity of the voluntary muscles. For all periods after those of early childhood, say subsequent to seven years of age, there is an increasing disposition to contrast play with work, and to ascribe to the former a certain lack of seriousness. But with little children this lack of seriousness exists only for the sophisticated onlooker. To the child himself his playing is the "real thing." It has all the seriousness which the child is able to reflect in his activities at the time.

The two most important theories regarding play are, perhaps, those advocated respectively by Spencer and Groos. The former regards play as representing a discharge of surplus organic energy. The latter considers it as an impulsive function serving to call into being those activities which presently are to be required in the strenuous conflicts of life. Play has its biological significance, therefore, in the discipline which it affords. So far from finding it necessary to choose one or the other of these theories, reflection suggests that they are entirely reconcilable and distinctly supplementary to one another. It may be that the impulse to play has its racial significance in the opportunity which it affords for the exercise of those forms of coördinated movement which adult life demands. It may, indeed, owe its preservation in hereditary form to just this circumstance. And it may, nevertheless, be also true that in its expression at any specific time the impulse really represents the tapping of reservoirs of surplus energy. These alternatives seem altogether probable, and they serve to connect the obvious present vitality and utility of the play impulse with adequate genetic and historical causes.

Imitation.—As the play impulse actually is observed in its development, it early takes on certain imitative characteristics, and at a slightly later date, perhaps, gives evidence of deserving the name constructive. As in the case of play, we must distinguish several stages or phases in the imitative reactions. There is without much question a purely instinctive form of imitation in which, without any necessary conscious purpose to imitate, acts of others are repeated as accurately as possible. This is conspicuously true of the earlier speech activities, in which the sensations of the vocal sounds made by others seem to discharge immediately, in an almost reflex manner, in articulatory reactions more or less closely resembling the stimulus. At a later period, however, there is a definitely conscious purpose to repeat sounds, and this kind of conscious imitation characterises a large part of the educational process in young children. Indeed, the only propriety in mentioning it in this chapter, so explicitly volitional is it, arises, first, from its possession of a *compelling fascination* for the minds of all normal children, and, second, from its striking similarity to the genuinely instinctive form mentioned above. The name " suggestive imitation " has been given to such acts as appear imitative to an observer but are not necessarily felt to be so by the imitator. A recrudescence of the more purely instinctive type is exhibited in the loss of individual initiative and inhibition in the case of mob action and the movement of crowds, where one falls in, almost unaware, with the purposes and impulses of the mass. "Plastic imitation" has been suggested as a distinguishing name for this class of cases.

Constructiveness.—In childhood constructiveness is hardly more than a convenient term to specify one of the aspects of play. Children delight in the making of things out of their toys, and this may properly be called constructiveness, even in those cases where a carping parental economy might describe the impulse as one of destructiveness. Pulling a feather-duster to pieces to make a nursery Indian may not commend itself highly to the presiding guardian as an evidence of constructive tendencies, but psychologically it is quite as truly entitled to rank here as the activity by means of which the precocious child converts the paternal cigar-box into the inlaid maternal glove-box. Its shortcomings as a constructive performance are ethical and economic, not psychological. In later adult life constructiveness, so far as it is separable from volitional activities exercised under the stress of fear, pride, or other similar emotions, becomes intimately connected with the impulses of artisanship and craftsmanship, in which a native intellectual interest finds a congenial and appropriate channel of expression by means of native deftness in specific forms of manual manipulation. This later type undoubtedly has in it much that is genuinely impulsive, but it is so overlaid with the effects of experience that it will not be profitable for us to dwell longer upon it.

Relation of Play, Imitation, and Constructiveness.—It surely requires no complicated demonstration to prove that these three last-mentioned impulses—play, imitation, and constructiveness—interlace with one another in almost inextricable ways. Much of the strictly impulsive element in constructiveness, if not, indeed, all of it, is play, pure and simple. Many of the plays of children, commonly so recognised, are of a distinctly constructive character. The child building a house from his blocks is, from his own point of view, much more truly described as engaged in construction than as engaged in play. The conscious "make-believe" of many plays, and the simulation of fictitious situations, is seldom obvious in the *earlier* plays of little children. Imitation is often simply a designation for a specific mode of reaction which the special play calls forth, and many games have their point in feats of imitation. Constructive impulses are more often than not dependent for their expression in the first instance upon patterns which determine the mould in which the child casts his activities. Little children running after larger children, they know not why, the boy trying to use a hammer as he has seen his father do, the girl playing at setting the table as she has seen her mother do—these and a hundred other instances illustrative of these points will immediately come to mind. We shall revert to the development of these native modes of reaction in our account of the growth of volitional control. It must suffice here to have pointed out the native organic nature of these expressions. The occasions for their appearance are evidently found wherever a situation affords opportunity for a vigorous organism to react spontaneously and agreeably with movements indicative of control and power.

CHAPTER XVII

NATURE OF IMPULSE

Throughout the whole of the preceding chapter, so far as we have dealt with facts of consciousness, we have had constantly before our notice impulses of one or another kind. Impulse is, then, from the psychologist's standpoint unquestionably the cardinal fact about instincts. The residuum is a matter of physiology and biology. It is a mere matter of neural mechanisms. But so far as we have impulse we have a definite psychical factor, and we must examine it somewhat more intimately.

Impulse and Movement.—Etymologically considered, an impulse is anything which "pushes along." We have repeatedly observed the tendency of all forms of consciousness to pass over into movements, and there can be no doubt that in this sense at least all states of consciousness are naturally impulsive in character. Left to itself, any mental condition would convert itself at once into some kind of muscular movement. This is peculiarly true of direct sensory impressions, which, as we saw in the chapters on sensation and attention, tend, so far as we give them undivided attention, to set up immediate motor responses. It is, however, equally true of images and other centrally aroused psychoses, so far as we become absorbingly attentive to them. If we have reference, then, primarily to the *consequences* which follow upon mental states, there seems to be no obvious exception to the rule that they all tend toward muscular movements, and are, therefore, all intrinsically impulsive.

This fact must not, however, be interpreted as meaning that all states of mind reveal these motor consequences in equal measure, nor that the impulsive element in them is insusceptible of further analysis. Quite the contrary. The disposition to make certain movements is much more marked in cases of anger than in cases of reluctant choice after deliberation. Moreover, the whole psychosis in anger may be much more intense than in the other case, and we may, therefore, be much more vividly aware of these tendencies. It is evident, consequently, that, viewing the matter introspectively, we have to recognise the existence of very different degrees of impulsiveness in our immediate feelings of disposition to movement. The feeling may be very distinct and acute, or it may be so faint and insignificant as to have hardly any existence save the hypothetical one to which our whole observation of conscious operations has committed us.

Development of Impulse.—Furthermore, we shall at once remark another important distinction if we note the changes accruing from the development of the individual's experience. The first time that one of the strong racial impulses is felt, the individual's consciousness contains little or no anticipation of what is about to occur. He is simply aware of an unusual thrill, a passing unrest, which comes to him disclosed in part by muscular movements—half mechanical in their nature. But the inner meaning of his experience is at the moment, perhaps, wholly problematic to him. He is a stranger to himself. How true to the facts this statement is many persons will readily admit by recalling some of the strange, acute mental disturbances of their own adolescent period. The child screaming with fright for the first time is likely to harbour no little shame over the event afterward because of its startling strangeness to him. The youth smitten with his first infatuation is a constant source of wonder to himself. He has become suddenly aware of a multitude of feelings which before were inexistent for him. But all these impulses, once they have been experienced, are thereby forever changed. They may retain, as many of them do, a prodigious intensity and vitality, but thenceforth they have lost a part of their mystery. We know at least so much of what they mean as to anticipate the acts to which they tend to lead. From this time forth we become increasingly aware of the *objects* which are calling them into being and of the consequences to which they lead. The impulses tend, therefore, to become more and more sophisticated. They become illuminated with a knowledge of their meaning, and the immediacy of our feeling and our unrestrained disposition to reaction are lost forever after the original, unsullied reaction. The conscious portion of the instinctive life is modified by growth and experience quite as truly as the purely motor and physiological parts of it.

Consciousness of Impulse.—We have seen that even though we admit impulse as a feature characterising all forms of mental activity, we have also to acknowledge very different degrees in the intensity of this impulsiveness, and very different conditions surrounding its expression. We may observe a further similar peculiarity belonging to those reactions which we most commonly regard as instinctive. We may call the play impulse definitely instinctive, and so give it rank among those expressions of our motor dispositions of which we are most keenly and unambiguously conscious. But it requires no elaborate demonstration to prove that we are most distinctly cognisant of the impulsive nature of this reaction when for any reason its expression is hampered or checked. Moreover, a little observation would bring the conviction that this is a general principle applicable all along the line. We can hardly be said to be *conscious of* the impulse, as an impulse, if the conditions are all ripe for its immediate translation into movement. Under such conditions we are absorbed in the object of our doing, in the *act*, in the consequences, with their thousand ramifications. But the *im-*

NATURE OF IMPULSE

pulse to act, as such, we are hardly aware of in any genuine sense, unless something impedes the impulsive movement. Then we promptly become aware of tense muscles, of thwarted execution. Then we are really *conscious* of the impulse, and we are made conscious of it by means of the nascent and incipient movements to which it has actually given rise. As a matter of fact, few of our impulsive tendencies ever find the opportunity to run wholly free and unconstrained. But so far as they do, we find we have lost consciousness of the impulse, as such. We encounter no exception at this juncture, then, to the facts which we have in the earlier part of the book so often emphasised, *i. e.*, the fact that consciousness appears at those points where there is friction of one kind or another in the purely physiological mechanisms of adjustment.

Types of Impulse.—It remains to comment upon an extremely important distinction among the various forms of impulse. Certain of these seem to be practically invariable in their appearance in all human beings, and they show themselves in the form of relatively fixed forms of movement. These are the instinctive reactions in the strictest sense of the phrase. In this category belong such activities as fear and anger. Certain other impulses are essentially universal but still somewhat less uniform in their appearance than the preceding class. These impulses have a far more variable form of expression. Here belong the reactions we call play, imitation in certain forms, parental love, etc. Both these classes of impulses give every evidence of a racial origin. But the first type is evidently the more stable and more deeply impressed upon the organism. Over against these two classes of impulsive acts—the first of which are properly called instincts, in which the individual is expressing the pressure of racial experience—are to be set the residual conscious activities, which are all impulsive, as we have seen, in the sense in which this indicates their relation to movement. These latter forms of consciousness are, however, representative of the processes by means of which, on the foundation of his racial patrimony, the individual builds up his own adaptive responses to his environment. The antitheses, then, are on both the physiological and the psychological side to be found between impulse as *hereditary*, and founded on inherited neural structure, and impulse as *individual* and reflective of innate *personal* disposition. The first factor represents the element of conservation and habit, the second the element of variation and progress.

CHAPTER XVIII

THE NATURE OF EMOTION

Distinction Between Emotion and Instinct.—Our previous study has already brought us into contact with emotion, once in our analysis of feeling, and again in our examination of instinct. But it still remains for us to discover more exactly the peculiarities of this form of mental experience, and especially to point out its functional significance in the economy of conscious life.

Although as they appear in human beings instinct and emotion are both psychophysical processes, the term "instinct" refers primarily to physiological phenomena, and the term "emotion" to psychological. This is brought out in James' statement that "an emotion is a tendency to feel, and an instinct is a tendency to act characteristically when in the presence of a certain object in the environment." As psychologists we are accordingly under obligation to describe the salient features of these hereditary feelings which accompany the instinctive activities. In the last chapter we found that impulse is present in all instincts, and we exhibited some of the modifications which the impulsive feelings undergo. We must now scrutinise certain other equally important features of the emotional psychosis.

When we feel ourselves in the grasp of any of the more powerful emotions, such as fear or anger or grief, we immediately refer the experience *in toto* to the object which is, as we say, its cause. We say we are afraid *of* the lightning, we are angry *with* our defamer, we are grief-stricken *at* the death of a beloved friend. In this way we come naturally enough to identify the emotion with our consciousness of its immediate provocative, and this fact has often served to becloud the real psychological constitution of these experiences. Thanks to the acumen of two contemporary psychologists, James and Lange, we can now describe more precisely than formerly certain of the psychical conditions indigenous to these states of consciousness.

Physiological Accompaniments of Emotion.—Let us take the case of a person who is extremely timid about thunderstorms. Such a person may be thrown into a paroxysm of fear by the sight of an ominous cloud approaching. Moreover, after the storm has burst, every flash of lightning and every clap of thunder may serve as a fresh source for the waves of terror which surge over the shrinking soul. Now in such a case the usual description of the mental experience would connect the fear *immediately* with the *perception* of the cloud and with the several perceptions of lightning and thunder. The mere perception itself would be accredited with the instant arousal, without further intermediation, of the emotion of fear. Following the arousal of fear, and serving as expressions of it, would be enumerated the several motor reactions which the individual might manifest, *e. g.*, trembling, paling, palpitation of the heart, etc. Now, it need not be questioned that such perceptions as these suggested are perceptions of terrifying objects recognised forthwith as such. But the authors to whom we have referred have pointed out, with a wealth of illustrative detail, that the motor activities just mentioned occur in an essentially reflex way *immediately* upon the perception of the emotional stimulus. These muscular reactions necessarily initiate at once afferent neural currents, which set up sensory and affective disturbances that are promptly reported in consciousness. The Lange-James view insists, therefore, that all accurate introspective observation of such experiences reveals the *emotion* of fear as a conscious state in which *these motor reactions* are represented as essential and integral parts. We may apprehend an object in a cold-blooded and self-controlled way as terrifying and dangerous. This is a common experience among policemen, firemen, and soldiers of a certain temperament. But we never *feel afraid* unless we have already made certain of the motor reactions which characterise fear. If the heart remains undisturbed in its pulsations, if the distribution of the blood in the various parts of the body is not markedly changed, if the breathing is not affected, if we do not tremble, it matters not how clearly we may appreciate the danger of the situation, nor how dangerous the situation may be, the total complex feeling, the *emotion,* of fear is not ours. These movements, then, which common description accredits with the expression of the emotion, are not *merely* expressions, they are rather indispensable causal factors producing the psychical condition which we all recognise when we experience it as the genuine emotion.

The psychological constitution of the emotion of fear is typical of all the strong emotions which lend themselves readily to introspective observation. In each one the organic reverberation which is produced by the emotional stimulus enters into consciousness to give it its characteristic emotional colouring and to mark it off from other modes of mental activity. In anger we ordinarily find the breathing disturbed, the circulation irregular, and many of the voluntary muscles, *e. g.*, those of the hands and face, tense and rigid. These muscular movements are inevitably reported by distinct modifications in the tone of consciousness. In grief an opposite type of muscular condition is met with, *i. e.*, depression of motor tonicity throughout most of the system, but with an equally inevitable reaction upon the conscious mood.

Emotions are, therefore, extremely complex processes, so far, at least, as regards the organic activities which condition them. In emotions we are not only conscious of the emotional object, as in ordinary perceptual acts, we are also overwhelmed by a mass of sensational and affective elements brought about by the intra-organic activities of our own musculature. The prominence of the affective factors to which we have referred in our account of feeling is in large part referable to the hyper-normal, or subnormal, activity set up in the muscles of the respiratory, circulatory, and digestive systems. It will be remembered that under most conditions we are entirely unconscious of these processes. Only under rather unusual circumstances, involving some vivid form of stimulation, do they intrude themselves. But such circumstances, we have already observed, are precisely those to which affective tone almost inevitably attaches, and we have forthwith an obvious reason for the conspicuously affective character of the emotions.

Reply to a Criticism.—It may be said that however true our account of the organic activities involved in emotional psychoses, it is, nevertheless, a false description of the facts to say that we are *conscious* in any *explicit* way of these functions of our bodily selves. Our consciousness, it is alleged, is absorbed in the *object* of the emotion; we are hypnotised by the impending calamity, transfixed in contemplation of our gaucherie, swept away by the sally of wit, etc. The bodily movements are things of which we have little or no distinct mental report. The emotion, consequently, however much entangled with motor activities it may prove to be, cannot be spoken of as consisting in a consciousness of these movements. The point at issue in this contention rests upon a misapprehension of the principle defended in this chapter. It is not maintained that the emotion of fear is made up of a consciousness of some terrifying object, say a serpent, plus the consciousness of a palpitating heart, plus the consciousness of shaking limbs. The assertion is, that our *consciousness* of the *serpent* is *modified* by all the sensory-motor activities going on in the body at the moment, just as is the case in less noticeable degree with every perception. It is further asserted that the motor activities which do occur at such times are characteristic and relatively fixed, and in consequence lead to *relatively fixed psychical* surroundings for any perceptual acts revealing terrifying objects. To state it in neural terms, we may say that the cerebral cortex is a kind of resonance board for the whole organism, and that emotional stimuli produce *definite* and fairly *constant* motor reactions, which are echoed by the cortex. Our attention may, then, be more or less absorbed in the object of any given emotion, but the total mental state is conditioned quite as truly by the sensory consequences of the hereditary motor disturbances as it is by the special sensory activity reporting the object. These motor disturbances constitute in James' terms a characteristic "fringe" for the emotional stimulus.

Significance of Emotion.—We must next inquire into the special significance of the emotional life, and discover, if possible, the reasons for its peculiarities. In emotion we are apparently confronted with a case in which now and again consciousness takes on an unusual intensity. Can we find in our analysis of its intrinsic characteristics, or in our observation of the circumstances under which it becomes manifest, any explanation of this phenomenon? We may at least make the attempt.

Fear.—If we examine a series of emotional situations, such as we find in grief, anger, fear, embarrassment, and pity, we shall discover that in one particular they all agree. In each and every case conscious activity is thrown backward and inward upon itself instead of going forward in the form of well-adjusted processes of control. This condition may last only a moment, or it may run on indefinitely. In one form or another, however, it is the distinguishing mark of all emotional conditions. For example, I am sitting at my desk writing, oblivious of the storm without. Suddenly a blinding flash and a deafening noise, followed by the sound of falling walls, breaks in upon me. Unquestionably, I am thoroughly frightened. For a moment or two I am all but paralysed mentally. My attitude is one of cowering contemplation. In a vague, terror-stricken way I wonder what is coming next. I may have started to my feet, but that is almost a reflex act, and certainly evinces no special intelligence, for I am perhaps quite as well off, and quite as useful, seated as standing. In a moment the paroxysm has passed off and I start forth to see what damage has been done. So long, however, as the fear was in the ascendency my mental activity was of the most futile, inefficient character. At great conflagrations, where persons become panic-stricken under the continued influence of terror, a similar thing is observed. Either they sit cowering in a half-dazed condition, or they rush madly and aimlessly about. Rational conduct has fled, and consciousness has become almost extinct, or else a mere riot of impulses.

Embarrassment.—In profound embarrassment everyone who is capable of the emotion will recognise the applicability of our description. We find ourselves speechless, not simply because the mouth is dry and the tongue paralysed, but also because our thoughts have fled. We have been suddenly reduced to the mental condition of a vegetable, growing rooted to the spot where we stand, a vital mass destitute of informing intelligence.

Grief and Anger.—The prostrating effect of deep grief is nowhere more flagrant and more distressing than in the total inability of the mind to get away from the source of its sorrow and take up the direction of necessary activities. For a person deeply afflicted, freedom of will and action is a sheer delusion. The mind refuses to operate, save in reiterated contemplation of its loss. In anger, on the other hand, it may be at first supposed that mental and motor activity are alike enhanced, rather than otherwise. But this impression proves erroneous upon a closer inspection of the facts. The immediate and instantaneous effect of anger is precisely like that of the other emotions we have just mentioned, *i. e.*, the temporary checking of directive conscious processes. The checking is often only momentary, and is then frequently followed by a torrential motor discharge of a more or less efficient kind, which readily serves to obscure the preceding and invariable inhibition. In children one often sees this latent period, during which the storm is getting up its destructive forces. Presently the apoplectic silence is broken by an outburst, which harks back in its violence to periods long antecedent to the dawn of civilisation.

Emotion a Phenomenon of Interrupted Conscious Action.— This break in the adaptive movements under the supervision of consciousness, which we should observe in all emotions if we took time to analyse all of them, is reflected in the organic reactions which we have already described. The stimulations to which consciousness is responding from moment to moment must drain off through motor channels of some kind. So long as they do not possess emotional vividness they call forth either simple reflex responses, or habitual coördinations under conscious control. The moment the stimulus takes on an emotional hue, however, as we have just seen, the guidance of consciousness is more or less abridged; the motor channels of acquired coördinated voluntary movements are consequently somewhat obstructed, and the only alternative is an overflow of the nervous currents into the involuntary pathways and the instinctive hereditary pathways of the voluntary system. On the neural side, therefore, the profuse motor reaction in emotion represents the discharge of dammed-up impulses which cannot find egress through the sluice-ways of ordinary voluntary movements.

Meaning of the Interruption and Overflow.—Taken in their entirety, what do these two great bodies of fact point to, regarding the function of emotion, *i. e.*, (1) the temporary suspension of voluntary control in the forward movement of consciousness, and (2) the overflow of motor impulses into channels leading partly to the involuntary muscles and partly through hereditary influences to the voluntary system? Stated differently: what makes a situation emotional and why does it lead to these results which we have designated?

Conditions Upon Which the Appearance of Emotion Depends.—We seem entitled to conclude that any situation is emotional in which an impediment to the ongoing activity is encountered so serious as to break up the progress of the consciously directed coördinations occurring at the moment, and of a character requiring a definitely new adaptive reaction of consciousness in order to surmount it. The case represents in a way the very conditions under which we found consciousness first coming to light. An individual we may suppose is going about his business, doing one thing or another, for which he has already attained accurate coördinated reactions. He is considering, perhaps, the wisdom of a certain purchase while his hand writes out a communication upon the subject. Here we have conscious direction of commercial activities through the motor coördinations of the hand. A telegram is put before him reporting the failure of his bank and the loss of his fortune. Such an event may or may not cause an emotion. It depends on the individual, not on the event. But if it does produce an emotion, there will instantly be a break in his coördinated and consciously directed movements. The writing will cease, he may gasp, and drop back in his chair, his mind may refuse to work for a few moments, and he must accommodate himself to the new situation, represented by the idea of his loss, before he *can* act intelligently. The news contained in the despatch has simply erected a mental barrier across the path of his letter-writing. Consciousness cannot instantly adapt itself to the new situation, and in the meantime the motor energy overflows in what we call the expressions of emotion.

If it be true that consciousness tends to appear where the

reflex and hereditary responses of the organism are inadequate to cope with the demands of the environment, we may say with equal truth that emotions appear whenever there is conflict among the motor impulses called forth by any special situation. Both cases demand fresh adjustments of consciousness for the securing of efficient action. The significance of emotion as a fact of consciousness would seem, therefore, to be resident in this monitory function, represented by its compelling announcement of needed adjustments, its report of unstable equilibrium. At all events this is evidently the part it plays, be its teleology what it may, and obviously this conflict with an impediment in the course of carrying out coördinated activities is the universal occasion of its appearance.

Such a view as this finds its most immediate and striking confirmation in the depressive emotions like fear, grief, and embarrassment, but it is not less true of the more sinister emotions, such as anger and jealousy, and it seems to be obvious enough in certain moral crises, in which we speak of the "pangs of conscience." The period of abortive voluntary control is often brief, and frequently the resumption of coördinated action antedates very much the cessation of the organic emotional disturbances. One suffering the depths of grief may thus take up again the weary round of a blighted life, despite the gnawing pain at the heart and the constant presence of the face that has gone. When we turn to the more mirthful emotions, it may not appear so certain that the same principle maintains, yet careful observation will assure us that it does.

Take the case of a man making out his accounts who suddenly learns that he has fallen heir to a million dollars, to a grandson, to a beautiful estate, or anything else which he may be supposed eagerly to desire. Is his consciousness momentarily disconcerted by anything fairly to be called a barrier? Undoubtedly this is so. If the experience is really unexpected, so that he gets a distinct thrill of joy from it, one may be sure of finding that his condition is for a little time one of genial insanity. Ideas may flow in profuse incoherency. But the nearest approach to coördinated movements are those of laughter (one of the channels of undirected motor overflow) and the inane movements of hands and feet. Not for some moments does it occur to him to telegraph his wife, to "treat" the assembled company, or do any other intelligent thing. So far as concerns the suppression of well-ordered movements and rationally conceived conscious processes, joy is no exception to the other emotions we have described. It traverses our common prejudices to designate the objects of joy as in any true sense barriers or impediments to us. But the "barrier" characteristic of emotions only has reference to the processes going forward at the moment, and, with reference to these, objects of the joy-producing kind are as truly obstacles and interruptions as those which occasion grief or fear.

Our appreciation of wit and humour involves a precisely similar form of readjustment. The joke is *par excellence* the typical stimulus provocative of disorganising tendencies in our coördinations. We listen to the skilful *raconteur*, our minds following step by step the evolution of the epic, and then, presto! the unexpected occurs, our minds react to the shock with an appreciation of the anomalies of the situation. The motor discharge in laughter announces the relief of the energy pent up momentarily by the unforeseen *dénouement*, and the total experience constitutes our feeling of the funny, the odd, or the amusing.

On the whole, then, there seems no reason to question the essential validity of this general view of the function of emotion and the conditions which call it forth. We may, therefore, revert with advantage to certain points in our analysis of instinct which must be brought into connection with our theory of emotion.

CHAPTER XIX

GENERAL THEORY OF EMOTION

Further Relations of Emotion and Instinct.—We noticed in a previous chapter that our instinctive reactions are accompanied by consciousness, and we observed further that the consciousness is of the kind which is commonly designated emotional. We did not, however, point out the further fact that this emotional element varies very greatly in the several kinds of instinctive activities which we discussed. This variation characterises not only the qualitative features of the emotion, but especially and conspicuously the intensity of the mental disturbance. After the considerations of the last chapter, it is unnecessary to elaborate upon the vivid and tumultuous nature of the conscious processes in anger, fear, grief, and the reactions of this type. We observed in the cases cited that much of the stinging intensity of the experience is derived from the afferent nervous impulses originating in muscular disturbances of the digestive, circulatory, and respiratory tracts. On the other hand, in such impulsive operations as imitation and play these intra-organic disturbances may be largely lacking. The mind is, under such conditions, monopolised with the achievement of the objective act, and is affected much less definitely by the sensory stimulations of the systems just mentioned. So far as these systems do contribute to modify the condition of consciousness, it is in the direction of the creation of a feeling of general bodily well-being, emanating from the vigorous normal activities of the vital organs.

We must conclude, therefore, that even though we are obliged to admit a minimum measure of emotional tone in all instinctive or impulsive acts, which we refer forthwith to the bodily resonance aroused by all such acts, nevertheless, some instinctive activities are markedly emotional, whereas others are not. Those which are obviously of the emotional type present instances in which the motor reaction is largely confined, so far at least as concerns its immediate significance, to intra-organic disturbances. The defensive emotion of anger is the only one which regularly reveals any strong tendency to pass over into acts producing changes in the surrounding objects. Such impulses as those of play tend, on the contrary, to pass immediately over into acts affecting one's surroundings. In both the more and the less emotional forms of instinct the motor activities are supposedly determined by racial hereditary influences, but in the emotional form this determination is relatively more definite, and often more elaborate, as in fear; whereas, in the other form it is little more than a disposition or tendency to certain kinds of reaction, which are, however, highly modifiable.

While we possess, then, inherited tendencies to acts which seem to affect primarily either our own organism or the environment, as the case may be, it is the former of these tendencies rather than the latter which is ordinarily called out by obstacles to our progress. Whenever such obstructions (perceptual or ideational) are encountered, the motor discharge is thrown back upon the vital processes of the organism itself, and straightway we have an emotion. It now remains to discover, if possible, the meaning of this situation.

Genesis of Emotion.—We described in Chapter XV. the general theory touching the origin of instincts, but we may profitably consider again, in connection with our analysis of emotion and its variable connection with instincts, the question of the genesis of emotional consciousness.

Our study of the various cognitive processes, such as perception and memory, and our study of affective phenomena, has enabled us to ascribe in every case some specific function, or group of functions, which each process serves in the general economy of mental life. The essential problem now before us is to find the real function of emotion, and to account, if possible, for its specific forms. We have already noted its appearance under conditions of stress and tension requiring new conscious coördinations in order to permit progress, and we have connected this fact with the service of emotion as a general monitor reporting friction and the need of additional intelligent supervision. Can we, however, locate the source of this friction and give it its intelligible setting in the history of organic evolution? Can we, moreover, discover any reason for the differences in the qualities which the emotion of fear manifests when compared with grief? If the monitory character of emotion contained an adequate explanation of its function, it does not appear why these two emotions mentioned should display any such radical differences. From this point of view all that is required is some index in consciousness which shall, with a maximum of certainty, attract attention to the difficulties to be overcome.

The direction to which we may unquestionably look for assistance in answering these questions is that hinted at in the account of the evolution of instinct. The best exposition of this theory, and the one which we shall adopt in a general way, has been given by Dewey. His theory can hardly be called conclusively proven, but it is unquestionably the most plausible and luminous exposition of the Darwinian hypothesis, in connection with the Lange-James theory, which has been as yet attempted, and we shall certainly be wise in accepting it provisionally.

Put briefly, it is this: The peculiar feeling which marks each emotion off from other emotions is primarily due to the different reactions which various objects call forth. These reactions are in turn determined by circumstances, which may lie indefinitely far back in the early history of the race, but in each case they required for their effective manipulation special forms of coördination. The coördinations which served these ends were necessarily useful, and so tended to become fixed as organic heritages. Every emotional reaction represents, therefore, the survival of acts *originally useful,* either in the immediate physiological way or in the indirect biological and social way. Wundt and others also recognise forms of reaction which tend to copy already established responses to stimuli, that arouse " analogous feelings." Thus we raise the nostrils in token of moral disgust, just as we do at a nauseous odour. In the present-day individual these originally valuable reactions are not commonly executed as they once were, for they are no longer unequivocally useful. But they appear now in the form of attitudes, or tendencies to action, which are, however, in part inhibited from expression. This inhibition is due to the fact that, owing to our personal experience and our present complex structure, the emotional stimulus tends to produce *two* or *more* different motor reactions, instead of producing simply the old, instinctive, hereditary one. The emotion itself is in essence our *consciousness* of the *conflict* between the several reactions which the stimulus tends to call forth. The conflict subsides only when the two or more groups of nascently aroused coördinations are in some way unified and brought into a larger and more inclusive coördination. Were there no such tendencies to specific forms of movement originally appropriate to special conditions, undoubtedly emotions would be either all alike, or else utterly irregular and disorderly. One or two illustrations may serve, in connection with our previous analysis, to make this general hypothesis clear.

Illustration of the Principle.—Suppose that in walking across a meadow we are suddenly beset by an irate bull. So far as the bull is an interesting and unfamiliar object the visual impression which we get of him undoubtedly tends to bring about such movements as may permit us to examine him more closely. Such tendencies involve movements of approach. In so far, on the other hand, as he is a roaring, devastating mass, indulging a high momentum in our direction, he equally stimulates motions of defence and retreat. Now, however it may be with the first group, this second group of tendencies is very largely instinctive in origin, and involves movements which unquestionably were originally of practical utility, whatever their present worth, *e. g.*, the breathing temporarily checked, as on all occasions immediately preparatory to severe effort; the increasing rapidity of heart-beat, with its consequent augmentation of the circulatory efficiency, etc.; all making for the maximum chance of successful escape from danger. If either of these groups of impulses were carried over into immediate action it seems improbable that the *emotion* of fear, as we know it, would appear at all. Certainly the expression of the motor tendencies indicative of curious interest would not produce fear, and if the impulses looking toward retreat were absolutely alone in the field, it is altogether likely that we should have conditions akin to those which characterise the free expression of the play impulses in children, *i. e.*, heightened sense of vitality, but no such emotion as fear. Evidently these two groups of impulses called forth by the ominously interesting bull cannot both be expressed simultaneously, and in point of fact they tend to inhibit one another. It is the organic outcome of this conflict of impulses, of which we become so keenly conscious as the " emotion." If the disposition usual in such cases finally conquers, we take to our heels, and at this point an instructive confirmation of our theory occasionally comes to light.

If we succeed in *really* putting our *whole* minds into the running, the emotion of fear is practically at an end. We may still have exhilarating, and even exhausting, mental excitement, but terror has fled with our own whole-hearted fleeing. In reality we often fail to throw ourselves thus completely into the act of flight, and, instead of this, images of the pursuing fate keep rising in our minds. We hear the thunder of footsteps, and the air is rent with savage bellowing. Each one of these sounds may stir in us a fresh emotional paroxysm, and in just the same way as the original reaction was aroused. The impulse may be now strong to turn and see how near the brute has come, and over against this tendency is the impulse to run still faster. In this manner recurrent waves of emotion may overwhelm us, until haply we reach the point where free and unimpeded coördinations may once more fare forth. This is most apt to occur on the other side of the bull's fence. But in any case the emotion evaporates when the mutual antagonism and inhibition of impulses cease, and not until then.

A Difficulty.—It may occur to someone to inquire what becomes, on the basis of this theory, of the emotional outbursts of fear on the part of little children, too young to have *knowledge* of the objects serving as stimuli, and, therefore, too young to have any of the acquired tendencies to reaction of which we have spoken, and to which we have assigned so important a part. We have, for example, previously mentioned the fear which children sometimes manifest of fur. The reply to this query is that such seizures are not, properly speaking, emotional at all in the sense in which adult life experiences emotion. True emotion distinctly implicates an element of knowledge. We are afraid of this, that, or the other thing of which we *know* something which inspires our dread. Such reactions, therefore, on the part of children must be altogether on a par, as conscious processes, with the first consciousness of one's organic sensations. They may be disagreeable, and probably are, but they no more deserve the name emotion, before there is a knowledge (however rudimentary) of the significance of the stimulus, than do the immediate feelings of stomach-ache, of fatigue, or of general vitality.

The Case of Satisfaction.—We may take, as an antithetical illustration to put alongside of our description of fear, the

GENERAL THEORY OF EMOTION

emotion of satisfaction, where it might seem that we have necessarily an essential absence of conflict and inhibition. But if we examine a specific instance of emotional elation, such as that which arises from victory in an athletic contest, we instantly meet evidence confirmatory of our view. Up to the moment of final success there has, we may suppose, been an oscillation between anxiety and exultation, as the tide of victory has ebbed and flowed. On the whole, however, if the contest has been close, anxiety and tension have probably dominated in consciousness. Now that the issue is closed, and the die is cast, a tide of riotous joy surges over us. We shout, laugh, and jump, wave hats, canes, umbrellas, whatever comes to hand; our next neighbour is the recipient of jovial thumps and punches, and our whole nature expands triumphantly in unconstrained complacency.

All these performances we think of as *expressions* of the emotion, and the analysis of the previous chapter implied that our consciousness of these movements constitutes the essential differentia of the emotional psychosis from other states of mind. The point we make here is that we should not become so vividly aware of the movements were there not a tendency to *inhibit* them, exercised by tendencies to make *other* movements. All consciousness, to be sure, seems to be toned more or less by the sensory reactions which arise from the constant overflow of neural excitement into the muscles, and in so far every psychosis has an element of emotion in it. But it is in connection with the conflicts sometimes encountered in the expression of our *racially hereditary* impulses that we get the full, clear case, to which the term "gross emotion" is occasionally applied. In the instance of our illustration the inhibitive tendencies mentioned are primarily those expressive of our anxiety, and careful introspection will unquestionably show that the real feeling of joy and satisfaction is precisely contemporaneous with our mental portrayal of the strife and furor of the contest. When we cease to *live over again* in memory the crucial moments of the game the emotion of joy has given way to some other more negative and quiescent state of bodily lassitude and content. It must, of course, be recognised that much which we commonly think of as mental satisfaction is really an altogether unemotional condition of placid vegetation. We stretch ourselves out after a good meal, and are at peace with the world. We are satisfied. But this condition must not be confused with the thrill and tension of real emotion, however undiscriminating our descriptive language may be in calling both experiences states of satisfaction.

The Case of Joyous Emotion.—A precisely similar situation will be found in every case of joyous emotion, whatever its cause. The lover who has at last carried love's citadel; the business man who has cornered his market; the scientist who has proved his theory—one and all get the thrill and poignancy of joy from the stress and eagerness of conflicting impulses in which the whole nature is enlisted. On the one hand are tendencies expressive of doubt, hesitancy, conservative retreat; on the other the expressions of forceful advance, of success and victory. The two sets of motor reactions are in unstable equilibrium, mutually inhibiting one another. The consciousness of our organic activities involved in this condition gives the mental background for our recognition of success, and the total psychical result is the emotion of joy. Once the victory is clearly recognised as won, and the game felt to be wholly over, our joy promptly begins to pale and fade. Moreover, let it not be supposed that intense joy is wholly unalloyed pleasure. Quite the contrary; such joy has its pain.

> "Our sincerest laughter
> With some pain is fraught."

To be sure, the affective tone of joy is dominantly pleasurable, and the reasons for this condition are not far to seek, as we shall presently see. But the emotion is a state of ten-

GENERAL THEORY OF EMOTION 333

sion, and this fact is all too likely to be submerged from notice in our disposition to emphasise the *objective basis* of our joy, rather than the *mental experience* in which it is apprehended.

Why should these special expressions, however, characterise joy rather than others—say those which characterise grief? What utility have these reactions now, or could they ever have possessed, by virtue of which they appear in us as hereditary attitudes? The typical expression of joy is laughter, but laughter, let it be remembered, is also expressive of many other things, *e. g.*, surprise, derision, contempt, and even the more paroxysmal forms of grief—a circumstance which appears anomalous in the light of any theory other than the one herewith set forth. In all these cases the laugh is the motor activity which inevitably accompanies the explosive release from sustained tension, with its suspended breathing. In our account of the attentive processes in consciousness we remarked the holding of the breath as one among other adaptive motor arrangements, all of which involve muscular tension. In joy, in the appreciation of humour, in surprise after expectation, we meet precisely this suspension of breathing suddenly cut short. The innervation of the vocal, facial, and breathing muscles which this involves is the laugh. Stress has often been laid upon the rhythmic nature of laughter, and undoubtedly this is an essential feature of it. But this does not distinguish it from other effective coördinations which are always rhythmic, and of which we shall have more to say in another chapter. Joy is, then, an emotion which, taken in its entirety, involves a measure of antecedent tension, to which the motor reaction involved in laughter and its accompanying gestures constitutes a necessary relief. The stimulus to these tensions is suddenly transformed, we behold it in a new light; the tension may, therefore, be released, and our consciousness of the process by which the release is progressively procured, as we apprehend the stimulus in a new way, *is* the emotion. The utility of the attitude of joy should accordingly be sufficiently obvious.

Utility of Emotional Attitudes.—If space permitted, and had we not already touched upon essentially the same matter in discussing instinct, we might in a similar manner illustrate the original utilities of the attitudes peculiar to anger, grief, and the other rudimentary emotions. Thus, Darwin has suggested that the rolling up of the upper lip in anger is a vestige of habits which belong to the days when men fought with their teeth. The clenching of the fists has an unmistakable implication. The sigh in grief and the sobbing which also belong to this emotion are explicable along lines resembling those we have described in connection with joy. It would undoubtedly be interesting to canvass the expressions of such familiar emotions as reverence, hope, remorse, gratitude, shame, bashfulness, disgust, etc., but we must forego this. The reader must not forget, however, that the utility of these emotional attitudes is generally most evident in connection with their function in primitive conditions of life. This is certainly true of the reactions which have a definitely biological and social value in distinction from a merely physiological value.

The various acts which we call expressions of emotion are simply acts which are, or once were, useful under the circumstances calling forth the activity. It is, therefore, a genetic fallacy to speak as though the emotion first existed, and then sought an appropriate expression. The *expressiveness* of such acts is primarily a thing which exists only for some observer. The acts are, or at all events originally were, means toward the realisation of some end which the individual has in view. The movements of my hand, as I write, are not to *me* expressions of my thought. They are simply means to the end. No more are the emotional reactions primarily expressive to the person making them. When for any of the various reasons we have remarked, and we have wholly overlooked many, the tendencies toward these movements come into relations of conflict with other motor tendencies, we have emotion. This conflict ultimately gives way to a coördination in which both tendencies are brought together, or one suppresses the other, or both are displaced by a third. In any event, consciousness moves on, and that particular emotion with which we started out is at an end.

Mood and Temperament.—While emotions are called forth by specific objects, we are all familiar with the fact that for considerable periods of time we often find ourselves especially susceptible to certain forms of emotion. After receiving a piece of good news we may find every event for hours afterward tending to take on a bright and humorous colouring. On the other hand, it is an equally common experience to find that a fit of indigestion will cast a saffron hue over the most welcome fortune. This predisposition to special forms of emotion we call mood. It seems to rest upon definite organic conditions, which sometimes appear to be originated purely by intra-organic physiological disturbances, but which sometimes are evidently due to the residual effects of past emotions. In the latter case they are practically recurrent, or continuous, emotions. In either case they afford nothing essentially novel for our inspection. Under certain conditions of intense and relatively permanent emotion we speak of the condition as one of passion. Passion, however, is a term which is used very loosely in several other connections.

When we compare individuals with one another, one of the striking differences which we observe concerns their inherited susceptibilities and predispositions to certain forms of emotional response. This characteristic is one of the most important elements in the constitution of what we call temperament. Whereas mood indicates a relatively transitory disposition toward a certain emotional tone, temperament refers to a permanent tendency, contributing to the very warp and woof of character. In the conception of temperament intellectual and volitional attributes are also included, but the emotional factor is, perhaps, the most significant. The classical division of temperaments into sanguine, choleric, melancholic, and phlegmatic may be recalled.

Sentiment.—Emotions are not dependent upon bodily conditions alone for a soil favourable to their development. Indigestion may, indeed, render us prone to irrational irritation and depression, and blooming health may constitute an auspicious prologue to emotions of joy. But another circumstance must be added, if we are to include all the conditioning factors. This additional consideration is found in the trains of ideas which possess our consciousness at any moment, and particularly in those general habits of thought and reflection which characterise our more distinctly intellectual life. If our customary habit of thought is of an altruistic and optimistic turn, there can be no question but that we shall more readily respond to emotional stimulations of the sympathetic type than if our minds are sicklied o'er with a paler and less human cast. These relatively permanent dispositions are what we designate our sentiments. Love, friendship, enmity, etc., are the names by which we know such characteristics. It will be obvious at once that the relation between sentiment and emotion is in a sense reciprocal. Our sentiments predispose us to certain kinds of emotion,—or put more truly, *are* the predispositions to such emotions,—whereas the cultivation of any emotion tends as a rule still further to fix the disposition which it reflects.

We observe that although emotions are conscious experiences which have their proximate causes in the immediately surrounding objects, they are profoundly modified by ideational processes and by antecedent organic conditions, certain of which may be due to temporary bodily derangements, certain others of which may arise from our peculiar personal constitution, and all of which are ultimately derived from our racial heritage.

GENERAL THEORY OF EMOTION

Relation of Emotion to the Rest of Consciousness.—If we undertake to connect our analysis of emotion with the account we have already given of other mental processes, it will at once be evident that we have been dealing with a very complex psychical condition. Clearly there must always be a cognitive element in emotion. We apprehend some object, some circumstance, which is what we call the cause of the emotion. This apprehension inevitably involves *attention* and the assimilative, or associative, activities which we remarked as invariably accompanying cognition. Furthermore, we have repeatedly emphasised the strong affective tone which emotions display, and many of the emotions to which we have referred had already been mentioned as "feelings." It seems desirable to dwell a moment upon the nature of this identification of certain emotions and feelings. It must be definitely understood at the outset that *all* emotions are feelings in the meaning assigned by us to the term feeling. The question we are now briefly to consider is simply that of the precise implication of certain of these emotions to which we had previously accorded a classification as feelings.

Feeling and Emotion.—When we speak of sympathy we sometimes mean to indicate a definite feeling which has many of the characteristics of emotion, and sometimes we refer simply to a sentiment, to a general attitude of mind. The same ambiguity attaches to our use of the opposite condition, *i. e.*, antipathy, and to many other so-called feelings, *e. g.*, pride, humility, love, and hate. The moral feeling of obligation, or the feeling of conscience, affords a further instance of an emotional psychosis. The feeling of dependence, which plays so essential a part in religious phenomena, the feelings of reverence and of faith, all have at times an emotional colouring which cannot be questioned.

The æsthetic consciousness offers repeated instances of feelings which are tinged with emotion, although it must be frankly confessed that much which masquerades as æsthetic appreciation is, even when sincere, far too cold-blooded, far too strictly intellectual, to lay any claim to an emotional character. The orchestral rendition of a Mendelssohn symphony may fill us with the most genuine and delightful emotion, it may interest us merely as a superlative achievement of technique, or it may, frankly, bore us. Evidently its claim to the production of a positive and unmistakable emotion will depend, in part at least, on such circumstances as our mood and our musical development. But it must not be supposed that intellectual activities are, as such, necessarily devoid of all emotional context. We already know that they may possess marked affective tone. The experience of wonder is often a genuinely emotional one, and it is distinctively an emotion belonging to cognitive processes. Belief, too, is often a distinctly emotional experience. Yet belief is essentially a judging process with a complicated development and an intimate dependence upon volition.

The fact of the matter is that such forms of mental life as these which we have just been mentioning are astoundingly elaborate products of our developing consciousness, and although we find evidences here and there in them of native emotional reactions, they are, in our adult life, anyhow, inextricably intertwined with the results of previous personal experience. This makes it impossible to regard them merely as emotions of the purely hereditary type to which the earlier analysis in this chapter has been mainly devoted. But despite this qualification, we see at once whence it is that they get their astonishing impulsive power over us. However small the seed, there can be no doubt that each of these feelings, for which our language has so complex a system of titles, contains within itself the hereditary racial tendencies which constitute and explain the imperiousness of emotion. The truth of this assertion is confirmed by the essentially social character of the most important of these feelings. The social nature of ethical feeling hangs together with the necessarily social character of righteousness. The religious feelings are not less social, so far as they may be conveniently distinguished from the moral feelings. But they find their application in a social order which transcends in part at least the imperfections of life as we know it here. The æsthetic feelings might appear to be purely personal. But a further study discloses the fact that the social element is fundamental here, too. This is, of course, exactly what we should expect of any conscious process which betrays an emotional cast, for the emotions reflect racial habits, and these must inevitably have a social basis.

CHAPTER XX

ELEMENTARY FEATURES OF VOLITION

All of our study up to this point has been devoted to the several distinguishable features of consciousness by means of which mental operations are carried on. We have discussed the several phases of the cognitive activities, such as memory, imagination, perception, conception, judgment, and reasoning. We have described the salient peculiarities of the affective processes. We have analysed the racial hereditary traces in consciousness as shown by emotion, and we have from time to time exhibited the different forms of motor coördinations with which the organism appears to be endowed, and through which it executes its adjusting movements. It remains for us in the following chapters to bring these various descriptions and analyses into perspective with one another by examining in its entirety, and with much more of detail than was furnished in Chapter III., the development and character of voluntary control.

Method of Study.—Hitherto we have made it a general practice to begin our study of a given mental process by analysing its more conspicuous and characteristic features, and then, with this as a starting point, we have turned back to trace, whenever we could, the genesis and function of the process in the individual or the race. We have always laid great stress on this genetic side of the case, because it is evidently impossible to evaluate and interpret a biological phenomenon intelligently unless one knows its antecedents, and mental facts furnish no exception to this rule. But, on

ELEMENTARY FEATURES OF VOLITION

the other hand, mental facts are so complex and elusive that an effort to trace the unfolding of consciousness can hardly be successful save when one has already some inkling of what to look for. In the investigation of volition we can proceed with a much larger measure of freedom than heretofore, because we have already dealt with the more important elements concerned, *e. g.*, attention, sensation, perception, ideas, and movements. We shall, therefore, after a brief analysis of these elements pass on to considerations of a primarily genetic kind. Subsequently we shall return to consider the more complex relations of voluntary acts.

General Analysis of Volition.—When we direct our attention to the immediately discernible features of voluntary acts in adult life, we note that such acts always involve foresight of some end, that this end is desired or at least consented to, and that certain muscular movements then occur which are meant to attain the end.* We observe, further, that on some occasions the mere presence of an idea carries with it instantly and without deliberation the execution of movement, whereas on other occasions arrival at the stage of mental consent requires long trains of reflective thought, and movements expressive of the decision may be postponed indefinitely. Sometimes the decision seems to be a relatively passive affair which makes itself on the basis of the facts considered. Sometimes, on the other hand, the whole self seems to be projected into the choice, and the consciousness of this mandate of the will is designated by James and others as the "fiat."

---

* Inasmuch as certain decisions seem primarily to concern our trains of thought rather than our muscular activities, as when we resolve to continue a course of reflection, our formulation may appear to emphasise unduly the motor features of volition. But it must be remembered that voluntarily carrying on a process of thinking requires the securing of definite motor attitudes, and furthermore, that all such thinking has as its purpose some future action, however long deferred we may expect this action to be.

Moreover, we observe that ordinarily the attainment of a decision finds the muscles already capable of carrying out the necessary coördinations, but occasionally the will can command no adequate motor agents. We may readily illustrate these cases.

As I sit at my desk I feel a draft. Without a moment's hesitation I rise and close the window. Here is a perceptual process, followed immediately by an appropriate movement of voluntary muscles. Again as I write, a word comes into my mind the spelling of which is uncertain. Instantly I turn it up in the dictionary. Here is an idea followed promptly by a movement of the volitional kind. As I proceed with my writing I come to a point where I must decide whether or not to incorporate a certain subject in my text. The merits of the question require long and careful consideration. Finally I decide to drop the matter from my book, and forthwith my writing goes on upon another topic. In all the cases thus far cited I have been in command of the motor coördinations needed to realise my purposes. But if I suddenly desist from writing and decide to step to the piano in the next room and indulge in a sonata, my willing becomes a mere burlesque, for I cannot play. We may safely start, then, from the assumption that every voluntary act involves the presence in the mind of ideas anticipatory of the act. With this doctrine as a point of departure we must examine more precisely our volitional consciousness and its relation to our movements. So far as the "fiat" represents in the author's opinion a genuine feature of volitional processes, it will be discussed in a later chapter in connection with the consciousness of effort. It will evidently be judicious to select for our present study acts which differ as widely as possible, both as regards the muscles employed in their accomplishment and in the character of the results achieved. Let us first, then, consider a series of voluntary acts in which different muscles are concerned.

ELEMENTARY FEATURES OF VOLITION

The Sensory and Ideational Elements of Control Over Voluntary Acts.—When I wish to sing or whistle a melody, I observe that the appropriate muscular movements follow the presence in my consciousness of auditory and kinæsthetic images. I seem first to hear the melody mentally, and to feel the sensations which come from my throat and lips when I do actually sing or whistle. In writing, on the other hand, I observe, especially in the case of words which are difficult to spell, that my movements are more or less controlled by visual imagery. I get a glimpse at a visual image of the word to be used. In this case, however, I am also often aware of auditory images of the sounds of the sequent letters as they would be heard were the word being spelled aloud. There is, moreover, a rather constant escort of kinæsthetic images arising from the former sensations of the hand movements employed in writing the word. I may even use as cues for the ensuing movement the kinæsthetic sensations originating in the muscular contractions of the hand. In throwing at a mark my attention is almost wholly absorbed in looking at the spot for which I am aiming. The control of the throwing movement in this case is largely from visual sensory currents, dimly reinforced, however, by kinæsthetic impressions from various parts of the body. In jumping from a standing position there is first a visual perception of the distance or height to be cleared, followed almost instantly by a setting of the various muscles of the body involved in the act, with a consequent mass of kinæsthetic sensory impressions aroused by these muscular contractions. When these sensations have reached what is judged to be an adequate quality and intensity, the mind says " go," and the jumping occurs.

These illustrations suggest that sensational or ideational processes may be used indifferently as the immediate precursors of coördinated movements, and they suggest, furthermore, that any kind of sensory or ideational material may be used in this way. Our cases have disclosed auditory, visual, and kinæsthetic qualities, but a further search would have revealed still other forms.

If these cases seem too trivial to be fairly illustrative, we may turn to a case involving some serious practical consequences, *e. g.*, the consideration of a large investment. It will, however, be seen at once that such a case promptly reduces to the form of reasoning, and we may, therefore, without more ado refer back to the evidence which we presented in our discussion of that process, to show that imagery of one kind or another is a conspicuous and constant feature of it. We shall find ourselves on such occasions as that of our illustration passing in mental review ideas which represent the pros and cons of the proposed investment. Little by little one of these groups of ideas begins to displace the other, and to become more firmly organised in our consciousness, until at last the opposite group is altogether vanquished and devitalised. The expression of our decision may take verbal form, or it may result in our writing a check, or making some other equally significant motor response.

Types of Connection Between the Sensory-Ideational Elements and Movements.—Now if we call to mind each of our illustrations we shall notice that in certain cases the idea which apparently controlled the voluntary act was an idea of the movement itself. This is partly true in the case of singing, more largely true in the case of jumping, where peripherally aroused impressions dominate over those centrally aroused. That is to say, in certain instances kinæsthetic sensations and images furnish us the material by means of which we practically anticipate, and so control, the movement we wish to make. In other instances, however, the sensations and images have to do primarily with the results of the movements, or with something connected with these results in a secondary fashion. The auditory images used in the control of singing, whistling, and sometimes writing are cases in point. In controlling vocal movements in this way we are employing images which are copies, in a measure, of sensory impressions made upon the ear by the vocalisations. But when the hand movements of writing are thus controlled, we clearly have a roundabout connection between vocal spelling movements, with their auditory consequences, and hand spelling motions. In the case of our investment decision the ideas may have had to do entirely with the conditions of the markets, the vitality of our own bank account, etc., and the act which expressed the decision, *e. g.*, signing our name to a check, may never once have come to mind until the deed was about to be executed. We must recognise from these observations that the ideas and sensations by means of which we supervise our movements may be of the most various character, and their relations to the movements may be either very close, as in the case where they are kinæsthetic, or indefinitely remote. James employs a useful pair of terms in calling those ideas of movement which originate in the part of the body moved, "resident," designating all other ideas which arise from the consequences of the movement, "remote." It must be added, however, that in practice the severance of the two from one another is in most persons by no means so complete as his description implies. After we have commented upon another important characteristic of these volitional acts we must attempt to discover just how it comes about that the various forms of sensation and imagery which we have noted attain their connection with the relevant movements.

Attention and Volition.—More fundamental, perhaps, in volitional processes than the controlling imagery is the fact of attention. No idea can dominate our movements which does not catch and hold our attention. Indeed, volition as a strictly mental affair is neither more nor less than a matter of attention. When we can keep our attention firmly fixed upon a line of conduct, to the exclusion of all competitors, our decision is already made. In all difficult decisions the stress of the situation exists primarily in the tension between the ideas representing the alternatives. First one and then another of the possibilities forces itself upon us, and our attention will not rest for more than a moment or two upon any single one. The chapter upon attention brought to our notice a number of reasons for believing this process to be a universal feature of consciousness, and we can feel no surprise, therefore, to find it playing a dominant rôle in volition where consciousness displays its most significant characteristics. It is by means of our ideas that we anticipate the future and project for ourselves the lines of our conduct, but it is by means of attention that we actually succeed in making some one of these anticipatory ideas real in the form of action. Attention must have something to work upon, and this something is supplied in the form of sensational and ideational presentations. Attention is the function by means of which mental possibility becomes motor actuality. With this fact in mind our next business must be the tracing of the development by means of which the various kinds of ideas which we find ourselves using to control our movements come to have this peculiar power. This undertaking involves our turning back to the conditions in infancy and early childhood, during which most of our important coördinations are established.

Primitive Motor Consciousness.—The primitive consciousness of the new-born child is confronted not only by the objects of the external world outside the organism, it is also in frequent receipt of impressions from those muscular movements of the organism itself to which we have so often referred. The vague precursors in the child's mind of his subsequent clearly recognised perceptions and ideas of movement are thus primordial. In any event, consciousness with the germ of attention in it is present from the beginning, and the stimulations of which it must immediately become aware, in however vague and inarticulate a manner, are in part, from the very outset, sensory stimulations aroused by muscular movements. So far as consciousness is concerned, then, sensation and movement come into existence together; for consciousness they are really one.

Transition From Random to Controlled Movements.—We have already had occasion in earlier chapters to inventory the capital of motor coördinations with which the new-born babe is endowed, and we have found it confined to a few simple reflex movements, for the most part poorly executed, to a few possibly " spontaneous movements," and to a store of automatic activities concerned with respiration, circulation, and nutrition. Voluntary action in any proper sense is wholly wanting, and this finds its immediate explanation in two considerations: (1) the psychological fact that voluntary action implies action toward some recognised end which the absence of experience necessarily precludes; and (2) the physiological fact that the cortical centres are still too imperfectly developed to afford interconnections between the sense organs and the voluntary muscles. The latter consideration is, of course, fatal to any immediate development of voluntary control, but even were the nervous system functionally mature at birth, the first difficulty would prevent the rapid establishing of such control. In our description of impulsive activities in Chapter III. we noticed that little by little the merely random movements of infancy become coördinated with reference to certain sorts of stimuli, until by the end of the third or fourth week, with most children, the eye movements can be controlled, and by the end of the twenty-fourth month all the more important rudimentary muscular movements can be executed. Now, what are the intermediate steps between this period of merely reflex, or random, impulsive activity with which the child begins life and the period of voluntary motor control?

Elementary Principles of Transition.—We may lay down two general propositions to start with, which must be continually borne in mind in order to avoid misapprehension. These principles, which are sustained by all observation, are: (1) that all voluntary control is built upon a foundation of movements which are already going on in an impulsive way; and (2) that the development of control, although from the beginning it extends in a measure, perhaps, to all the voluntary muscles, proceeds more rapidly, now in one group and now in another. Broadly speaking, the larger muscles are first brought under accurate control, while later on the more delicate movements of the small muscles are acquired; a fact which should be taken into account in the early occupations of children. This law of periodic or rhythmic growth characterises all mental and bodily development. A child may have fairly good control of its eye movements, while the arm movements are still vague and inaccurate; and it may have acquired considerable dexterity with its hands, while still unable to command its feet with much success. Volition must not, then, be thought of as a process in which consciousness somehow brings into life movements which previously did not exist. The problem of the evolution of control is the problem connected with the coördinating, in reference to certain ends, of movements already occurring in an uncoördinated way. We are under no obligation to explain the existence of the movements. They are already in evidence. Our problem is simply concerned with the method of their systematisation, and their organisation, in connection with consciousness.

Law of Excess Discharge.—We may profitably select for examination a case illustrative of one typical form in which control over these unordered movements is secured. Let us suppose that a bright and noisy rattle is presented to the notice of a child who has learned to focus his eyes, but who is as yet unable to reach intelligently for objects. How does the child learn to grasp such an object, which he sees and hears? The rattle stimulates at once both eye and ear. The child's first reaction is, perhaps, one of astonished inspection, as he gazes at this unfamiliar thing. The noise continues and the bright colour catches the attention. The sensory currents from the two sense organs find no adequate drainage channels in the motor attitude involved in watching, consequently they begin to overflow into other channels. Now there are already established, as we have remarked a number of times, pervious pathways leading centrifugally away from the motor regions of the central system. These are the pathways employed in the impulsive, instinctive movements, etc. The overflow from our sensory disturbances naturally tends, therefore, to pass off in these directions, and presently we see that the child is moving his hands and arms and head more or less violently, and often the muscles of the trunk and legs are also much affected.

First Accidental Success.—At first these movements are inevitably spasmodic, vague, and uncoördinated. They simply suggest, as we observe them, some sort of explosion in the motor centres. We say that the child is interested by the rattle, that he wants to get it, and no doubt his consciousness is much agitated by the experience. But we must guard against the fallacious supposition that he wants the rattle in any such conscious intelligent manner as an adult might desire an object. The child may be acting as he does simply because his nerves make him do so, just as one sneezes when sufficient pepper is introduced into the nostrils, not because one necessarily wants to sneeze, but because it is impossible to help it. Whatever may be the outcome of the first exposure to such a stimulus as this, the continued presence of the rattle for a few moments is very likely to result in some movement of the arms adequate for grasping it. It will be remembered that the grasping instinct is among the most primitive of all. This successful grasping may not occur until the rattle has been held out in this way a number of times. But the activities which we have described are those which commonly precede such success, whether it be attained quickly or slowly.

Pleasurable Tone of Accidental Success.—The first step, therefore, in securing voluntary control of the hand and arm under such circumstances is based upon the tendency of the sensory stimulations to produce diffused motor discharges throughout many muscles of the body. Certain of these motor activities result in changing the stimulus in some way. The next problem is, therefore, concerned with the consequences of this fact, which in the case of our illustration consists in the successful grasping of the rattle. Such an act affords a new and generally delightful surprise, and in this fact is found the reason for its importance in furthering the volitional control.

According to the general law of habit which we have so often invoked, the persistent drainage of the sensory impulses set up by the rattle, out through the miscellaneous motor channels of the nervous system, would establish a certain predisposition in these impulses to pour out through these same channels whenever the rattle was observed. This seems, indeed, to be the fact. But when the rattle is actually grasped we have a new stimulus immediately introduced. In place of the rattle seen-and-heard, we have now the rattle felt-and-heard-and-seen-moving-with-the-hand. These distinctions, of course, cannot exist for the baby with any such definiteness as they do for us who are looking on. But they exist as differences *actually felt*, however inadequately they might be described, supposing the child were able to express himself. The mere change of the stimulus visually attended to must, then, under the supposed conditions, serve momentarily at least to intensify the child's attention to the total situation. Furthermore, the grasping of the object, involving as it does a definite motor coördination of an efficient kind, is *per se* agreeable, *i. e.*, it is a normal activity of functions (in this instance instinctive) adequate to the demands laid upon them. The result of success in the reaching and grasping, with its heightened conscious tone, will accordingly accentuate the disposition to fix in the form of habit the total series of reactions which have led up to this outcome. It now remains to observe how the child avails himself of the progress thus far attained to master completely the movements concerned.

Progress After First Success.—In the first place, observation will at once disclose the fact that from this point on progress is generally slow and tentative, differing markedly in this respect from certain features of the process by which adults learn new coördinations. A considerable number of attempts may be necessary before the baby can repeat promptly his first successful movement. When the coördination is actually well matured, two striking characteristics distinguish it from the predecessors out of which it has grown. It is accurate, not hesitant nor vague, and it involves only the muscles actually necessary for its performance, instead of many others in various parts of the body. How have these useless movements been eliminated? We cannot reply to this question with as much definiteness and detail as is desirable, but the general nature of the process seems to be somewhat as follows.

Elimination of Useless Movements.—The baby's consciousness is all the time vividly enlisted in the movements which he is making, but the rattle furnishes the constant focus for these, and for the baby's attention. Of all the movements which are made, those are most likely to get notice which are most intimately connected with the immediate field of attention. Needless to say, these are the movements of the child's own hands and arms, which he must see whenever they chance to approach the rattle, and which he must vaguely feel as often as they move. So far, then, as the rattle is the centre of the baby's attention, those sensations will receive most emphasis in consciousness which are most immediately connected with it, which coalesce most readily with it into a single experience, changing when it changes, remaining unchanged when it is unchanged.

Once again, let it not be supposed that we are for a moment offering such an analysis as the above as an account of anything present reflectively to the child. His naïveté may be as great as possible. We are simply describing the kinds of sensations which must apparently get most conspicuous representation in his consciousness. It would seem, then, that the movements of the hand and arm would get most vivid attention among the various random movements of the body, and that of the several movements which the hand and arms might accidentally execute, those again would receive most emphasis which actually resulted in grasping the object. The situation seems to hinge for the explanation of its development into controlled movement, with lapse of useless movements, upon the pleasurable fixation of attention on the rattle and the consequent emphasis of all sensations caused by movements affecting this centre of attention. Such movements as regularly affect the rattle are thereby necessarily emphasised, so long as the rattle is the object of attention, and the predisposition for the sensory impulses to drain out through them is heightened. The others fall away largely because the neural energy is adequately provided for in these new-formed pathways. But they do not fall away at once, and the effective coördination is not set up at once. The process is slow, and gives every indication of being a real growth.

The Case of Ideational Control.—If this account be accepted, it suggests an explanation of how it might come about that when an interesting object was placed before a child he might be able to reach it. Our explanation thus far has been cast in terms of the law of habit, operating under the intensifying effects of agreeable attention upon motor discharges of an impulsive and excess-discharge type. But what explanation does it afford of the ability voluntarily to control the hand and arm movements of this kind when a stimulating object is wanting? How does it account for the origin of such ideational control as was evidenced in our analysis of adult volition at the beginning of the chapter?

If we have been correct thus far in our account of the manner in which movements of the voluntary muscles become coördinated in response to certain sensory stimulations, it ought not to be difficult to get at the manner in which ideational processes secure the same result. The facts upon which the correct explanation rests were discussed in the chapters beginning with perception, memory, and imagination. All centrally initiated imagery is ultimately derived from antecedent sensory sources, and like its sensory precursors it all tends to be converted sooner or later into motor activity. In asking how ideas come to set up movements, therefore, our only problem is how particular ideas come to be followed by particular appropriate movements. The tendency to produce motor changes of some kind is an innate characteristic of all imagery processes. In this sense all our ideas are motor. Or, as certain psychologists would put it, all consciousness is conative. The real question is, why an idea should ever *fail* to produce a movement, and we anticipate our discussion so far as to say forthwith that such failure is due simply and solely to the inhibiting effect of some other ideational process, which is also struggling for motor expression.

In connection with our first illustration of the attainment of control over an eye-hand coördination, we have traced the process by which needless movements are eliminated and accurate efficient ones become fixed. So far as memory images of these movements have been forming and gaining durability in the course of the development, those images have evidently had most opportunity for emphasis which have been constantly connected with the successful coördinations. They are, therefore, most likely to persist in consciousness.

Neural Habit and Ideational Control.—The explanation of the fact that such ideas are able to call forth the movements desired seems to rest wholly upon the principle of neural habit. The appearance in consciousness of the idea of the movement means in the first instance a re-excitation neurally of a certain central portion of a sensory-motor arc. Granted that such an excitation takes place, whatever its neural antecedents, we can feel sure, from the polar nature of nervous currents, that it will issue in a motor discharge. The ideational process simply reinstates, as we have so often noted heretofore, the latter portion of a previous sensory-motor process. This relation is exhibited graphically, although with extreme simplification of the actual facts, in the accompanying diagram (figure 60), in which $SSSM$ represents

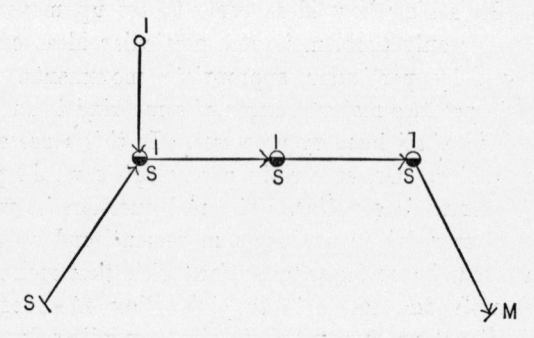

FIG. 60. The pathway from S to M represents the course of a *sensory* stimulus passing from a sense organ to a muscle through cortical centres. The pathway I to M represents the course of an *ideationally*, or *centrally*, aroused neural activity traversing in part the same pathway as the previous sensory stimulus, and issuing in the same muscle.

the course of a sensory impulse forward into a coördinated reaction; and $IIIM$ represents the same reaction, but in this case with its initiation in an image or idea. If it be admitted, then, that we have already discovered the essential steps in the process by which movements become coördinated in reference to certain sensory stimuli, it follows inevitably from the considerations which we have brought forward in earlier chapters that a re-excitement of the central regions connected with these sensory-motor coördinations will, unless inhibited in some definite manner, reproduce the same motor reactions. Imagery is the conscious factor in such central excitations. The idea of a movement is, neurally considered, the beginning of that movement.

The Learning of New Coördinations by Adults.—Having now analysed the primitive establishment of sensory and ideational motor control, it will be profitable to pause a moment and examine certain peculiarities of adult processes. It has sometimes been maintained that adults in learning any new coördination avail themselves, first, of the "resident" imagery, *i. e.*, that which represents the kinæsthetic sensation of the moving part; and that after the coördination has been established they resort to "remote" imagery, *i. e.*, that which represents the sensory effect of the movement upon sense organs other than those in the part of the body moved. There is undoubtedly a measure of truth in this formulation, but it requires some modification before we can accept it. So far as concerns the development of coördinations in babies, it is evidently very difficult, if not impossible, to determine what kinds of imagery are employed; and, anyhow, (as we have seen) the important primary steps in the process are probably based upon the use of sensations, and not images at all. When we turn to adults and examine the facts in the case of acquiring a new series of coördinations, such, for example, as playing the piano, we find very great individual variation, but in general the process is of the following character:

We first employ the visual impression to guide us as to the proper position for our hands. We then attempt to secure a distinct tactual-kinæsthetic impression of the feeling of the hand and fingers when their position is correct for securing certain results, *e. g.*, playing the scale. For a long time the proper playing of the scale requires the control of both the visual and the tactual-kinæsthetic processes, one of which is resident and one remote. Moreover, it is visual and kinæsthetic sensory elements, rather than images or ideas, which are employed at the outset. After the coördination is fairly well established, the sensory control may be disregarded and either kind of imagery may then be employed to discharge the movement. As a matter of fact, when this stage is reached another and more remote form of imagery generally steps in and takes command. Playing commonly is done from a printed score, and always, save upon a few humanely constructed instruments, produces sound. When the control of the finger movements is highly developed, the sight of the score, the visual image of it, or the auditory image of the sound of the composition, may serve entirely well to bring about the movements, which seem to "take care of themselves," as we say.

It appears, therefore, that the change in the form of imagery which we employ in the control of our movements is not to be described merely in terms of a transfer from resident to remote. The sequence of events in the most highly developed cases seems to be of this character, *i. e.*, resident-and-remote-sensations immediately connected with the movements, resident-and-remote-images immediately connected with the movement, remote-sensations-and-images mediately connected with the movement. The clue to the several steps in the onward progress will generally be found in inquiring where one's interest is located at the moment. So long as this is necessarily in the movement itself whose control we desire, the psychological elements will all be found gathered about this. Some of them will be resident, some remote. The moment the movement is mastered, however, interest generally moves forward to the application of the movement in some larger undertaking, and at this stage the mental elements which refer to the movement and bring it into operation may be only remotely connected with it. But the connection is, nevertheless, real, however seemingly remote, and the appropriate muscular activity never follows an idea, unless one's previous experience has in some fashion or other established a nexus of the habit type. The functional organic connection between such ideas and their motor expressions is just as genuine as that displayed by any other kind of ideo-motor fusion. It is only from the standpoint of the outside observer, who either does not know or else neglects the antecedent development, that the two things appear remote and disconnected from one another.

The Disappearance of Consciousness From Controlled Coördinations.—It remains to emphasise once again one of the rudimentary facts about the establishment of motor control before passing on (in the next chapter) to certain of the more complex features of the process. We have repeatedly had occasion to remark that consciousness tends to disappear the moment that physiological conditions are established adequate to the supervision of the various motor adjustments necessary to the organism. The case of volition affords the conspicuous and typical instance of this disposition. When a special form of motor activity is needed, attention steps in and the psychophysical processes which we have just described coöperate to effect a satisfactory coördination. This coördination is then deposited, so to speak, in the nervous system in the form of a habit. When further organic demands arise, this habit is ready at hand and capable of being employed with a minimum of conscious control. In this way consciousness is ever pressing onward, supported by the reserve forces of habitual coördinations, which can at any moment be summoned in the conquest of new realms. Volition has thus no sooner established a habit than it turns about and employs the habit as a tool in the construction of larger, more extensive habits.

In adult life almost all of one's important decisions are carried out in a practically automatic manner by established coördinations of the habit type. Writing, reading, walking, talking—what is there that one does which does not in the last analysis reduce to the use of acquired habits? The ethical and pedagogical importance of this absolutely fundamental nature of habit, upon which we enlarged in Chapter III., must be obvious. When viewed in this way one sees, too, why volitional processes seem at first sight to have so much of the miraculous in them. Why and how should the mere flitting of an idea through my mind lead to such remarkably complex and well-adapted acts as the playing of an aria, the paying of a bill, etc.? The answer is literally impossible, unless we turn back and trace the progress step by step through which the coördinations have become established and come into functional connection with particular ideas. When we have made such an approach to the problem as this, the solution is seen to involve definite and intelligible laws operating in a fixed and definite way.

Conscious Imitation as a Basal Type of Volition.—It will be recalled that we classified one form of imitation among the impulsive types of reaction. Psychologists are at variance with one another as to its instinctive nature. It will appear when we take up the discussion at this point, as it did in the chapter on instinct, that certain varieties of imitation are undoubtedly not instinctive in any demonstrable manner, whereas certain other varieties of it strongly suggest this origin. Moreover, certain forms of reaction which have been called imitative are characterised by the mere repetition of a movement regardless of its immediate provocative. Imitation in the more customary and limited sense applies properly to cases in which the action of some second person is intentionally copied—in purpose, if not in fact. It must also be added that whereas imitation in the common implication of the term applies to acts done consciously and with definite intent, certain imitative reactions are apparently executed without any explicit purpose and with a minimum of conscious supervision. These complexities in the modern meaning ascribed to the term "imitation" need to be borne in mind if one is to avoid confusion. This is especially true when one is referring to such acts for light upon the mode in which voluntary control is attained.

Primary Imitation.—The repetition of monosyllables, such as da-da, which many babies indulge in long before they begin to use vocal sounds intelligently, may serve to illustrate the first type of imitative acts. Sometimes these sounds are closely similar to certain words which the child may have heard. But it seems questionable how far the term imitation can fairly be applied to acts of this character. In any case they belong to the form of activity which Mr. Baldwin has dubbed " circular reactions." The articulatory movements, once they are made, produce auditory and kinæsthetic sensations. These sensory stimulations drain out again through the already pervious pathways leading to the same muscles, and so the process goes on more or less indefinitely. Such employment of the muscles is, within the limits of fatigue, *per se* agreeable, and we must suppose that even though the function of consciousness under these circumstances is largely reduced to that of a spectator, it nevertheless, as spectator, indorses the on-going activity and serves thus in some measure to fix in the habit form the neural-motor groupings which are concerned. Certainly, when one can get the child's attention the movements are commonly checked for the time being, thus suggesting that in some way they are after all in a measure dependent upon the conscious processes.

Characteristics of Conscious Imitation.—Conscious imitation of copies set by other persons and felt by the child to be models, which he strives to duplicate, constitute a later, more complex, and possibly more important form of action. Indeed, Mr. Baldwin will have it that in this condition we meet the real beginning of volition, and to it he assigns the convenient designation " persistent imitation." The term " persistent " emphasises the fact that such imitative movements are made again and again in the face of partial failure, until success is finally achieved.

It must be remembered, however, that many consciously imitative acts are not repeated, or at all events are repeated after long intervals and without any reference to their previous performance. Thus, a child may make a definite effort to repeat a new word that he hears his parents use. His failure may be ludicrous and it may be weeks before another effort is made. In the case of older children and adults persistent imitation is an omnipresent phenomenon. If one boy in a group jumps over a fence, every other boy feels himself under obligation to go and do likewise; and those whose efforts are below the accepted standard of excellence promptly devote themselves to correcting the defect, adopting for their pattern, so far as possible, the achievement of the leader of the group. In social life one large mass of people is always engaged in attempting to follow the pace of the leaders. Each smaller group has its own chief, who again sets the pattern for that group, and in no realm of life, whether æsthetic or religious, practical or theoretical, are we ever wholly free of the disposition to imitate. What is the actual process involved in the more rudimentary expressions of this deep-seated human tendency?

The process may take place under either of two forms, seemingly distinct, but fundamentally alike. The imitation may be directed to repeating certain movements, *e. g.*, the gestures, intonation, or facial expression of some other person, or it may be concerned with the production of a result similar to some standard object set up as a model, *e. g.*, a letter, or a figure, in which case the actual movements employed may vary considerably from time to time without seriously impairing the integrity of the copy. Although this instance of reproducing some visible outline is more highly evolved than certain of the earlier forms of conscious imitation, it will serve satisfactorily to exemplify the basal facts about such activities and their relation to developing volition. It will be seen, moreover, that they are distinguished in one respect only from the type of developing coördination which we first described, *i. e.*, in the presence of an external standard with which their results are compared.

A young child learning to write is commonly given a copy, and then the teacher takes a pen and demonstrates how it should be held, and how the writing movement should be made. When the child essays his imitation the usual result is something of this kind: The pen is grasped with needless severity, the brows are wrinkled, the muscles of the body are tense, the breathing is spasmodic, and often the mouth is open, and the tongue discovered to be making futile movements in secondary imitation of the hand-tracing. Evidently the stimulus has resulted, as in other cases which we have examined, in an overflow of nervous energy into muscles which are largely irrelevant to the success of the immediate enterprise in hand. The product of this effort is compared with the copy, its failure to comply with the original is noted, and another effort is made. Or the repetition may be forthcoming simply because the act itself is agreeable, and with a splendid disregard of any disparity between copy and original. In other cases, candour compels one to admit, the next attempt is made under the influence of some one of the various forms of suasion of which the teacher may be master. When the activity goes forward of the child's own initiative, however, and when he is left more or less to himself, he slowly manages to improve his work both as regards faithfulness of portrayal and as regards the elimination of useless movements. Now this result is achieved in much the same manner as already described in connection with our illustrative baby and rattle, so that however fundamental these conscious imitative processes may be, in putting the child in touch with his social surroundings the method of procedure adds nothing essential to the forms we have already studied.

CHAPTER XXI

RELATION OF VOLITION TO INTEREST, EFFORT, AND DESIRE

The foregoing chapter has brought to our notice certain of the rudimentary features of voluntary action. We have traced the general development by means of which impulsive and other primary forms of movement set up sensory excitation, which is then appropriated by attention and converted either directly or indirectly as imagery into a mechanism of control over the movements. We have also remarked the tendency of attention in volition to produce the semi-conscious, or nonconscious, quasi-automatic acts which we call habits, and its further tendency to pass on, as soon as such habitual coördinations are established, to the formation of yet other habits. In the present chapter we must examine certain of the wider and more general characteristics of volition, and especially its relations to effort, interest, and desire.

Theory of Selective Attention in Volition.—When we described in the last chapter the manner in which choice is accomplished by means of the selective activity of attention, which rejects certain ideas and clings to others, we made no special attempt to explain *why* attention displays these preferences. Indeed, no ultimate explanation can be given for these decisions, any more than an ultimate explanation can be given for the constitution of the sun. But in a proximate way we can get at the reason, and we find it is connected very closely with our whole view of the nature of organic life and the significance of mind for living creatures.

Spontaneous Attention.—In our account of attention, early in the book, we emphasised the basal nature of what we called spontaneous or non-voluntary attention, *i. e.*, attention directed freely and without compulsion in a manner expressive of the mind's inner interests. We have recently been discussing a parallel fact in the motor region under the name of impulse. When we put these two groups of considerations together, we find that the psychophysical organism manifests, both on the psychical and the physiological sides, definite projective tendencies. Certain kinds of movement, certain kinds of objects, appeal to us at once natively and without reflection. We come into the world, so to speak, with a bias already favouring certain experiences at the cost of other possible ones. Moreover, we vary from one another very markedly as regards the special directions of this bias. So far, then, as choice comes down to a question of attention to ideas, we may be sure that by virtue of this spontaneous characteristic of attention certain ideas will from the first be given preference over others.

If we take the situation on the level of our own adult consciousness, we find that we are naturally disposed to attend to those ideas which immediately interest us, rather than to those which do not. But when we ask the further question, *why* they interest us, we can only point again to the spontaneous and impulsive nature of attention. We get back here finally to the admission that both the hereditary and the personal history of each of us has produced differences in our impulsive and spontaneous modes of acting which we all recognise in one another, and for which we can offer no detailed explanation. Fortunately, however, we can point out somewhat more intimately certain of the fundamental features of interest as a mode of consciousness, and this we may briefly undertake.

Interest.—Interest has sometimes been treated by psychologists as one of the intellectual feelings. In the case of mere curiosity the reason for this is fairly obvious. Indeed, we mentioned curiosity as one of these feelings, when we were analysing affective consciousness. But if we consider the type of interest which we feel in an absorbing pursuit, a game, an experiment, or a business venture, then we recognise that such interest, however truly it may display affective characteristics, is a phenomenon which belongs conspicuously among the conative processes of mental life. To bring out the point it is sometimes said that " we may *give* attention, but we always *take* interest." This statement discloses the positively active, self-expressive, self-assertive nature of interest. We have observed that attention is always in point of fact an expression of organic activity, but the subjective difference between listless attention to a tedious subject and the kind of attention we give to things which interest us is unmistakable.

Stimulus to Interest.—Like other psychical experiences, interest always has some stimulus. However completely absorbed we may conceivably become in our own merely subjective feelings, interest always has some *object* to which it refers, and the object is definitely recognised. This gives us at once a point of identity and a point of difference between pure impulse and interest. Both are internally projective, internally expressive, but one has a *recognised* object toward which it is directed, whereas the other at first has not. Spontaneous attention may be a primary mental activity. Interest is always secondary. It is a conscious phenomenon attaching to objects of which we have already had some experience. When we seek to discover what attributes an object must possess in order to be interesting, we are forced back at once upon uninstructive generalities. We may say, for example, that all objects which call out emotion are likely to be interesting—in a broad meaning of the word. But we have instantly to admit that in the main we cannot say in advance of the actual test with each individual whether an object will call out an emotion or not. The peculiarities of personal constitution, the vicissitudes of personal history, the reigning mood, these and a thousand other factors may all enter in to modify the reaction.

In the same general way it is sometimes said that strange things are interesting. But this statement also has limitations of a serious character. Things may be so strange as to be utterly meaningless to us, and in such cases we are essentially oblivious to them. The behaviour of primitive peoples confronted for the first time with the paraphernalia of civilisation is replete with illustrations of this fact. Again, the affairs of our daily routine are said to interest us, *because* we are accustomed to them. If this assertion of interest in routine were always true, which, unfortunately, perhaps, is not the case, the explanation offered for the fact is evidently in flat contradiction with the implication of the previous instance of interest in strange things. Indeed, considered impartially, it is difficult to discern any reason why either strange or familiar things should be *per se* interesting simply by virtue of their familiarity or strangeness.

The moment we accept the view that the individual, as born into the world, has certain predispositions toward spontaneous attention in given directions, just as he has native impulsive movements, we instantly get a standpoint which renders intelligible the different forms of interest which different individuals reveal, even though we may be quite unable to account specifically for the special interests which any particular person evinces.

Attention and Interest as Organising Activities.—When we recall the fact that attention is essentially an organising activity, bringing into relation with one another the various objects toward which it is successively directed, we can readily appreciate how the existence of spontaneous attention should, at a very early date in the life of each of us, serve to establish a positive and systematised predisposition to emphasise certain interests and obliterate others. To the child of strongly artistic bent everything is absorbingly interesting which touches in any way upon art, and all other interests tend to become subservient to this, on pain of absolute suppression. With most of us spontaneous attention runs out to welcome a miscellaneous range of objects and experiences, and the development of a single paramount interest is often slow or altogether wanting.

There is nothing incompatible (*crede experto*) in a boy's being thoroughly interested in both fishing and geometry. The incompatibility arises only when one interest assumes the right to control the other permanently, or at improper seasons. While spontaneous attention is, therefore, primarily responsible for the differentiation of our interests, the subsequent course of development involves the coördination of these interests with one another. In this process we call into play in varying measures our reflective abilities and thus elaborate, each for himself, a certain hierarchy of interests. Not that this undertaking is, perhaps, ever accomplished with a definite recognition of what is in progress. But as adults we can all discern that such a process has actually been going forward in us. In childhood our interests were chaotic, disconnected, unordered. In maturity they are fairly well marked out and related to one another. Many of the adolescent and childish interests have disappeared altogether. The interests in toys and in dancing may have evaporated. In their stead we find interests in the home, in our professions, in certain kinds of amusement, etc.

It may be said that, after all, this elimination and precipitation of interests which we find characterising adult life is again explicable in the last resort only by the action of spontaneous attention. This is probably true in so far as it means that in the last analysis the explanation of what vitally interests us is to be found in our native constitution. But in distinction from the cruder expressions of this spontaneous attention in childhood and infancy, the conditions in later life reveal a much more reflective and rational exercise of the function. Moreover, we have at this point to remember once again that man is from beginning to end a social creature; he is constantly under the pressure of social influences; and a large part of the explanation for the special directions which attention finally does take, in building up the interests of each one of us, will be found to lie in the effects of the social rewards and punishments meted out to us by our companions.

Put a child into a group of religious ascetics to grow up and the chances are that the only interests which will really get opportunity to live and thrive will be those which are conformable to the ideals of such a community. On the other hand, let him be cast among pirates, and a totally different group of interests will blossom forth. This is not because the child is a hypocrite. It is simply because one of the most universal of all objects of spontaneous attention is found in the attitudes and actions toward us of those among whom we live. A certain amount of repression from them may not stifle a vigorous interest. But many a taste which might in a kinder social climate take root and bring forth rich fruit dies ere it is fairly planted, because of the frosts of social disapprobation.

Interest a Dynamic Phase of Consciousness.—Interest evidently represents the spontaneous, dynamic side of our psychical make-up. The self is in a very true sense reflected in one's interests. It would be truer to say that a person's emotional reactions *disclose* his interests than to say, as is occasionally done, that his emotions *call forth* interest. Furthermore, in the light of our preceding analysis, it seems clear that the interest which we are said to feel in strange things finds its basis in the expansion of our *selves*. Not the absolutely strange thing do we find interesting, but the thing familiar enough to be vitally connected with our past experience and still novel enough to be felt as a definite enlargement of this experience. As we saw long since, all such expansive states of consciousness are, other things equal, intrinsically agreeable, and they afford a definite appeal to the accommodatory function of attention. The interest of the customary, the habitual, has a precisely similar basis. It is only as we *find ourselves* and feel the experience as a real *expression* of ourselves that routine is interesting. Whatever is *purely* mechanical in it is simply disregarded in consciousness.

The artist is the man above all others to whom routine is utterly delightful, not because it is easy, not because it fosters the caprices of his indolence, but because it calls into action the very heart of the man himself. Moreover, let it not be overlooked that the artisan or the professional man who thus delights in his work for its own sake is in so far an artist— the carpenter, the engineer, the lawyer, and the teacher. Each is making, or doing, that which gives overt expression to his own inner nature. So far as routine is disagreeable, apart from sheer physical fatigue, it is because it does not call out an expression of the real self, nor of its keener interests. It is executed in spite of those interests, and against their violent and increasing protest. Let it be understood that we are not here discussing the ethics of routine, the righteousness nor unrighteousness of our feelings, either of satisfaction or disgust. We are simply pointing out the conditions under which routine *is* interesting or otherwise, and showing their connection with the sources of interest in the strange and the novel.

Moral Decisions.—To many persons moral decisions which are made with great effort and under the influence of active conscience appear to be the most genuine expressions of the will, the most typical instances of volition. Such experiences are felt to reveal more intimately and deeply than any others the real nature of our personal character and power. The man of strong will is thus the man who can wrestle successfully with temptation, feeling to the uttermost the poignancy of his desire, but still opposing to it the irresistible force of his ideal. It behooves us, in view of this widespread feeling about the significance of decision with effort, to consider the important facts in the case. Are we, indeed, in these decisions made conscious of some inner and unique constituent of the mind which on other occasions is wanting, or at all events lurks so surreptitiously in the background as to defy detection?

Volition and Effort.—Broadly speaking, there are three main forms of voluntary processes involving the consciousness of effort. We neglect for the present, at least, the case of mere physical effort, such as is involved in lifting a heavy weight. We are conscious of effort when we attempt to keep our attention upon some tedious and uninteresting subject. We are also conscious of effort when we must make some momentous decision, where a correct choice evidently involves a large number of complex considerations which we are not certain we have properly in mind, or when we are in doubt as to our possession of the precise facts. Such cases need not implicate our own personal desires on either side. Complicated financial problems often illustrate such situations. In both these cases, however, the feeling of effort does not attach primarily to the fact of *choosing* among the alternatives. It is a feeling of strain and tension which we refer to the whole intellectual process. It partakes more nearly of fatigue than of any other single namable experience of a familiar kind. The third type of case is represented by the moral crisis in which we find ourselves beset by some immoral but alluring project that thrills every fibre in our being with passionate desire. To this tempest of evil inclination there is opposed only the pale, uninteresting sense of duty; and yet, little by little, conscience makes itself felt, and when the moment for decision comes we gather ourselves together and, throwing the whole power of our will into the struggle, we throttle our passion and save unsullied our fidelity to the right. Experiences of this kind have time out of mind been the mainstay of defenders of the freedom of the will. Here, they say, is an obvious and undeniable case where the will comes in to bring about action in the line of the greatest resistance, instead of in the line of least resistance, as the mechanical philosophers insist must always occur. We must decline to enter upon the question of the freedom of the will, which metaphysics has preëmpted, but an analysis of the psychology of effort we may profitably undertake.

Analysis of Effort.—Two antagonistic theories have been maintained about the feeling of effort in such a case as that of our last illustration. Certain psychologists have held that under such circumstances we are immediately and unmistakably aware of our own will. Others insist that accurate introspection discloses to us nothing peculiar to experiences of this character beyond the consciousness of many sensations of muscular strain which originate from the tense condition of the voluntary muscles, especially those connected with respiration. We must distinguish very sharply, in dealing with this disagreement, between the *fact* of *volitional activity* and its *mental representative* which informs us directly of this activity. Undoubtedly crises of the kind mentioned do involve volitional activities of the most basal character. Undoubtedly, too, they do reflect in the most exact manner the real moral nature. But it does not follow from this that we are conscious of a *conative element* in consciousness akin, as an element, to sensation. The issue here is one of introspective accuracy, and on the whole the evidence seems to favour the second of the two theories we have mentioned. Our consciousness of effort is a consciousness of the emotional kind, in which a very large group of sensations of muscular tension is present. Commonly, too, the affective tone of the experience is distinctly unpleasant.

Consciousness of Mental and Moral Effort an Emotional Experience.—If we call to mind what reactions we customarily exhibit under circumstances of the kind suggested by our illustrations, we find that our breathing is checked and spasmodic, our faces set, our brows contracted, our hands clenched, etc. All the muscular attitudes contribute their sensory increments to the total consciousness of the moment, and observation certainly shows that our sense of the effort involved in a moral decision runs essentially parallel with the intensity of these motor reactions. When the muscles are quiescent we have no keen sense of effort; when the *feeling* of effort is strong the muscular tensions are always in evidence. We have asserted that the consciousness of effort, so far as it belongs to ethical decisions, appears when *desires* are opposed to *ideals*. We shall discuss the nature of desire in a moment, and we shall then discover confirmatory facts tending to bear out our contention that ordinarily the feeling of mental effort (disregarding the consciousness of fatigue) is itself essentially emotional. Its general nature can, therefore, be identified with that of the other emotions which we have already discussed. It is a phenomenon connected with the mutual inhibition of competing motor tendencies. Until the moment of decision has arrived these impulses are dammed up in the organism itself, and we meet the consequences in the form of tense motor contractions. When the choice has been made the inhibitions fade away and coördinated movements expressive of the decision are promptly executed. It has already been suggested that ultimately the utility of these muscular rigidities is to be found in the added stimulation which they furnish us, augmenting thus the weakening momentum of our onward moving selective activities. Their function would thus be found, like that of the accommodatory movements in attention, in their contribution to the *amount* of conscious activity available.

After all, it must not be forgotten that however much our

consciousness of effort may depend upon certain sensations of strain and tension, the *psychical import* of the feeling is essentially that which the most spiritualistic psychologists have assumed. Effort means conflict within the self, within consciousness; it means lack of harmony among our ideals and interests and aims; it indicates imperfect systematisation and coördination among the mental processes themselves. The *act* by which the dominant system of interests and ideas manifests its sovereignty and executes its behests is the "fiat" of our last chapter. All this is perfectly compatible with our finding it distinguished by certain peripheral sensory conditions by means of which we come subjectively to know of it.

Volition and Impulse.—Although we readily recognise and admit that the volitional processes in childhood are, in their origin, dependent upon impulses, it is not so obvious that adult conduct is in the same manner bound up with impulse. Nevertheless, this is the fact, as we shall now see. Indeed, the statement is often made that the development of volition is neither more nor less than a process of reducing our impulses to order, and that a mature character is simply one in which the impulses are thus subordinated to some systematised principles. Instead, therefore, of the conception that a developed will or character is one in which all primitive impulses have been extirpated or repressed, we have the conception of these impulses as continuously operative, but operative in a rational and coherent way, rather than in the chaotic fashion characterising childhood and infancy. This view is unquestionably correct in its general implications, and an examination of the nature of desire will assist to exhibit the fact.

Volition, Desire, and Aversion.—Large portions of our daily acts occur with a minimum of conscious supervision and volition. This fact we have had repeated occasion to emphasise, and we have found its explanation in the estab-

RELATION OF VOLITION TO DESIRE

lishment of complicated habits reflecting our customary routine. There is, however, a highly important residuum of acts in which our wills are most vividly enlisted. This group of acts appears whenever we step outside the beaten path of habit, or when habits are threatened with violation. The clerk who is tempted to cut his work in order to see a ball-game, the young man who is considering an advantageous offer to change his occupation, the school-boy whose attention to his books is diverted by the alluring cries of his truant comrades, these afford illustrations of the workings of desire. Now, if we pass in review the various things which we seriously wish for ourselves, we shall find that the vividness of the desire is proportional to the extent to which some one or more of our rudimentary impulses and emotions are enlisted. Objects which do not appeal to any of these primary instinctive reactions do not call forth intense desire. At most, we sporadically "wish" for such things. But the wishing is of a relatively cold-blooded, incidental kind, utterly distinct from the hot, passionate, craving which we feel for objects of the first class. Moreover, along with desire, which is the positive aspect of the phenomenon, must be mentioned aversion, which is like desire in its emotional character, but which discloses to us the negative phase of the process.

The experiences in which we are conscious of the definite yearning of desire, or the positive distaste of aversion, are, therefore, those which directly or indirectly call into activity such impulses as play, love, sympathy, grief, ambition, vanity, pride, jealousy, envy, fear, and hate. Without these or their congeners to colour the occasion we rarely meet with anything which we could justly call either desire or aversion. It hardly needs to be pointed out that in many cases desire and aversion involve several such emotional factors. Pride and love may be thus conjoined, sympathy and grief, fear and envy.

Although the term *desire* is generally applied to the more

intellectualised forms of craving, we must add to the list the so-called appetites. Bain has classified these as the appetites of hunger, thirst, sex, sleep, repose, and exercise. They are all immediately concerned with recurrent organic conditions, but they may readily be developed in such connections as to take on a relatively ideal character. Whether or no they come to occupy a place coördinate with the other forms of desire depends upon the degree to which they chance to secure such an integral connection with our general intellectual life and character.

Desire.—In its most overt and definite manifestations desire appears, therefore, to be a form of consciousness in which the blind, impulsive character of a pure instinct is modified by a knowledge of the object which will satisfy the impulse. There is on this account, however, little or no lessening of the restless disposition or craving to express the impulse. Desire accordingly gains its power and vivacity from its impulsive nature; it gains its rationality from experience. After our emotions and instincts have been once expressed, we know in the future what to expect of them. Desire is the conscious condition which represents this knowledge of what an emotional impulse means. It is the craving unrest for the object which we know will give us pleasurable satisfaction. To be sure we desire some things which we know will cause us pain, but in such cases it may be fairly questioned whether there is not always, save in occasional pathological cases of the insane type, more or less reference to some secondary or ulterior gratification. The tired mother insists on watching by the bedside of her sick child, even when others are ready to take her place and spare her the exhausting ordeal.

Aversion.—Aversion, on the other hand, is the precisely polar condition in which again we realise the significance of the object which is mentally present to us, and recognise, on the basis of our experience, that the realisation of it will be disagreeable. We consequently draw back from it and strive to shun it. Paradoxical as it may seem, both desire and aversion are apt to be dominantly unpleasant; desire, because of the *temporary* thwarting of inclination and impulse; aversion, either because of the dread of permanent thwarting of some one or more cherished and agreeable experiences, or because of some positive menace of pain. To be sure, there is often a certain exquisite delight in this discomfort of desire, as the poets have repeatedly recognised.

Basal Nature of Desire in Formation of Character.—It should be evident from the foregoing discussion that desire occupies an extremely fundamental position in the development of will and the formation of character. In the first place, the actual psychical condition presented by desire affords us a striking instance of the great salient features of the mind with which all our previous study has been concerned. In it we find elaborate thought processes at work; we find conspicuous affective factors and we see the whole onward moving conative character of consciousness brought clearly to light. Moreover, it discloses to us an epitome of the character at any given moment. What one really *desires* is the best possible index of the sort of character one really possesses.

CHAPTER XXII

CHARACTER AND THE WILL

Volition and Character.—Inasmuch as consciousness is a systematising, unifying activity, we find that with increasing maturity our impulses are commonly coördinated with one another more and more perfectly. We thus come to acquire definite and reliable habits of action. Our wills become formed. Such fixation of modes of willing constitutes character. The really good man is not obliged to hesitate about stealing. His moral habits all impel him immediately and irrepressibly *away from* such actions. If he does hesitate, it is in order to be sure that the suggested act *is* stealing, not because his character is unstable. From one point of view the development of character is never complete, because experience is constantly presenting new aspects of life to us, and in consequence of this fact we are always engaged in slight reconstructions of our modes of conduct and our attitude toward life. But in a practical common-sense way most of our important habits of reaction become fixed at a fairly early and definite time in life.

The general manner of speech, the mode of dressing, purely personal manners, etc., are commonly fixed before twenty-one. The general attitude toward moral and religious ideals is likely to be gained sometime during, or just after, adolescence. Professional habits come somewhat later. Speaking broadly, however, for the average individual the dominant *tone* of his habits, social, moral, æsthetic, and intellectual, is set by the time he is thirty. By this time the direction of his desires and his interests is likely to be finally formed, and for the rest of his life he will but elaborate and refine upon this stock of tendencies.

CHARACTER AND THE WILL

When we recall the fact that habit depends ultimately upon the preservation of physical changes in neural tissues, we see how powerful an ally, or how frightful an enemy, one's habits may be. The man who has led a life of kindliness and sobriety not only has a fund of agreeable sentiments upon which his friends and neighbours can rely, he actually *could not* be mean and selfish and sordid without an herculean effort, for his nervous system contains imbedded in its structures the tendency to altruistic deeds.

Moral Development.—When we describe the development of character as a process in which our impulses become coördinated with one another, we have in mind a very specific course of events. Thus, for example, the little child in learning obedience to his parents may be engaged with the impulses of love, of fear, and of anger. We may suppose that the child has been forbidden to do something. This occasions disappointment and anger. Disobedience is threatened. The parents may appeal to the child's affection or to his fear of punishment in the effort to secure the desired action. The competing impulses must be ordered with reference to one another. Anger and obstinacy may carry the day, love may win, or fear may triumph. Now, whatever the actual outcome, the *set* given to character by the result is undoubted and will make itself manifest on the next occasion when obedience is at stake.

At first sight it might seem as though in such a case as that of our illustration the question were not one of *coördinating* two impulses, but rather of allowing one to suppress the other. This is the view which many good persons take of the whole course of moral education. But this theory is based on a fatal misapprehension of both the psychological *facts* and the ethical desirabilities of the situation.

If one judged simply by external appearances, one might assume that when the child yielded to the appeal to his affection the impulse of anger was wholly rooted out. This, however, is not strictly the fact. The impulse has met the obstruction of an opposing impulse, and the act which follows involves a coalescence of the two, an ordering of the two with reference to one another. Obedience given under such conditions is far more than the mere execution of certain muscular movements. It is a mental process in which the self, with its capacities for anger and love and a thousand other emotions, gives expression to its innermost nature. The tendency to react with anger upon any thwarting of desire is a part of the make-up of the self. The disposition to show love and obedience to the parent is also an integral part of it. When the two impulses come in conflict, one is not merely suppressed. Rather is the tendency to action *diverted* into other channels by means of the substitution of the competing impulse. Under such conditions obedience is not the purely mechanical thing it may later become—a thing, like eating or dressing, which concerns sheer muscular dexterity. It is rather a vital outpouring of the self, in which the seeming suppression of the anger is only a suppression as regards certain movements, for the disposition to make the angry response has entered in to colour with a deeper and more lasting hue the beauty of the submission to love's dictates.

All seeming *suppression* of impulses will be found to be based upon the *expression* of *other* impulses, not upon sheer brute repression. To root out a bad impulse we must set some contrary impulse to work. Moreover, in a character built up in this way the control of the morally more dangerous desires becomes a source of increased richness and power in life. Tennyson expressed this truth when he said

> "That men may rise on stepping stones
> Of their dead selves to higher things."

Only one who has really suffered can truly sympathise with grief. Only one who has been really tempted and tried can be morally altogether reliable.

The Will.—When we bring all our considerations together, it becomes obvious that the proposition from which we set out early in our work is true in a very wide and deep sense. Mind we have found to be, indeed, an engine for accomplishing the most remarkable adjustments of the organism to its life conditions. We have seen how the various features of cognitive and affective consciousness contribute each its quota to the general efficiency of the reaction which the organism is able to make upon its surroundings, physical and social. We have seen finally that in the will we have the culmination of all these activities of control. But it must have been observed that we have not found any specific mental element or event to which we could give the name *will*.

No, the term will is simply a convenient appellation for the whole range of mental life viewed from the standpoint of its activity and control over movement. The *whole mind active*, this is the will. To say that there is no such thing as *the* will (a statement which troubles many right-minded persons) is simply the psychologist's perverse way of saying that mentally there is nothing but *will*. There is no specific mental element to be called will, because all states of consciousness are in their entirety the will.

We have seen this doctrine justified in the last two chapters, wherein we have discovered volition concerned with impulses, with pleasure and pain, with emotion, with ideas, with sensations, with memory, with reasoning, and with every form and type of mental operation. We have observed the evolving control beginning with the mere mastery of movements, passing from this to more and more remote ends, for the attainment of which the previously mastered movements now available as habitual coördinations are employed, until finally we find the mind setting up for itself the ideas which we call *ideals*, and by means of these shaping the whole course of a lifetime. What these ideals shall be for any one of us depends upon the operations of interest and desire, and these in turn depend in part upon the sort of tendencies which we have inherited, and in part upon the forces of our social and physical environment. We may prate as much as we please about the freedom of the will, no one of us is wholly free from the effects of these two great influences. Meantime, each one of us has all the freedom any brave, moral nature can wish, *i. e.*, the freedom to do the best he can, firm in the belief that however puny his actual accomplishment there is no better than one's best.

Training of the Will.—A deal of twaddle is sometimes indulged in as to the training of the will. The will is spoken of as though it were a race-horse which once a day requires to be given its paces about the track. What is obviously in the minds of persons who discuss the question in this way is the wisdom of some form of moral calisthenics, *e. g.*, self-denial, constructive and aggressive altruism, etc. Now, it is not necessary to enter into an extended argument upon this special recommendation, although it seems evident that apart from a deep moral interest in the thing done it could only produce moral prigs. If the moral interest is there, the artificial gymnastics will be superfluous. Life is rich in opportunities for larger and more intelligent kindliness. But disregarding this form of moral discipline, the development of volition evidently is not a thing to be hastened by any special form of exercise, because the will we have seen to be simply another name for the whole mental activity. Any purposeful intellectual occupation affords means of developing certain features of control. Play develops certain other features. Art develops volitional processes in one direction, mathematics develops them in another. So far as a well-developed will consists in the ability voluntarily to direct one's attention effectively and for unlimited periods in definite directions (and this certainly is a very basal conception), all thoughtful activity facilitates its attainment.

Healthiness of Will.—The well-trained man is the man whose mind is stored with a fund of varied knowledge which he can promptly command when the necessity for it arises; he is the man who can keep his attention upon the problem in hand as long as necessary, and in the face of distraction; he is, moreover, the man who, having paused long enough to see the situation correctly and to bring to bear upon it all the relevant knowledge he possesses, acts thereupon promptly and forcefully. Defects in any of these requirements may defeat efficient action and proclaim the actor a person of feeble or defective character.

The ignorant person cannot act effectively when nice discrimination and wide knowledge are necessary, as they often are. Even the learned person ordinarily cannot go far, provided his attention is wayward and fitful. His effort is too disconnected ever to accomplish large results. The person who is flighty and precipitate is either a genius or a fool—commonly the latter. On the other hand, the hopelessly careful person, whose life is spent in a morass of doubt and indecision, balancing imponderable considerations and splitting insignificant hairs—he, also, is likely to belong to the incompetents and inefficients. Evidently the attainment of a will which can fill all these requirements for the avoidance of pitfalls requires a training on every side of one's nature, requires a rich experience and a powerful dominant purpose running through it. All life offers us such training, and our success in building up a strong, rich character depends much more on *how* we do our work than upon *what work* we do. There is no calling so humble that it may not afford scope for the expression and development of all the great human interests, if we really put *ourselves* into it, and not our mere labour.

CHAPTER XXIII

THE SELF

Before we can satisfactorily complete our sketch of the structure and function of consciousness, we must turn our attention to the feeling of personality and selfhood. The normal human mind is never a mere string of states of consciousness. It is always a unitary affair in which the past, the present, and even the future are felt to hang together in an intimate personal way. In our previous study we have been obliged to examine now one aspect of the mind and now another, but we have always emphasised this partial, piecemeal character of our method, and we must now attempt to trace in bolder outlines the contours of the whole, the salient features of the concrete, actual self.

The Consciousness of Personal Identity.—Philosophers and psychologists have criticised with relentless vigour the *tenability* of our common-sense notions of personal identity. Undoubtedly the basis of this conviction which we all have that our self continues in some way the same from moment to moment is extremely precarious from a logical and metaphysical point of view. But from the strictly psychological standpoint, so far as concerns the structure and function of consciousness, personal identity is as real as memory or attention. However much our thoughts may vary from time to time, however much our opinions may alter, however much our characters may seem to be transformed as the years go by, we still feel that as a personality we are somehow unchanged. We even feel this to be true, in some degree, of our bodies, which change conspicuously as the days of childhood pass and the period of maturity and old age comes on. It is still *my* body, whether I am a child or an old man, and it has always been mine, and never for a moment capable of confusion with the body of any one else.

When we try to discern the most important psychological contributors to this feeling of identity, we discover two which are evidently of radical significance. The first of these is memory. Were we not able to identify among our various thoughts those which represent former experiences of our own, it is certain that any feeling of personal identity which we might have would differ fundamentally from that which we now possess. Undoubtedly that peculiar use of the memory process which we call *anticipation* plays an important part in this connection. The second factor is a persistent background consciousness of our own organism. When the *bodily* sensations and feelings are seriously deranged we always experience a strange sense of uneasiness and distress which is often wholly out of proportion to any actual pain that we may be suffering. Our general sense of *bodily existence*, then, gives a fairly constant *tone* to our consciousness, and thus furnishes a certain impression of sameness or continuity. Beyond question there are other phases of consciousness which contribute their quota toward the same end. But these two are certainly preëminent.

It is a remarkable fact that our sense of the identity and continuity of our own personality is essentially unaffected by the interruptions which occur in the onflowing of consciousness. In coma, as in sleep, consciousness may, so far as we can discover, be wholly suspended. Yet upon its return it once more claims its own from out of the past, and under such circumstances it ordinarily manifests no disturbance whatever of the feeling of personal identity.

Subject-Object Nature of Consciousness.—If we examine from a more critical and reflective point of view the implications of consciousness for the concept of the self, we come upon certain suggestive facts. To be conscious of an object involves not only some *mental presentation* of the object, but also some *subject* to whom it is presented. Con—sciousness (knowledge over against something, *for* some one) has no other possible meaning than just this. Indeed, so irrefutable does this idea of consciousness appear to be, that it has but rarely been called in question, although many of the inferences which have been founded upon it have been severely, and often justly, attacked.

This fact of the bipolar nature of consciousness has been the basis of many doctrines and has been designated by many different terms. Thus, James speaks of the self as "knower" and "known," of the "I" and the "me." Kant recognises the *empirical self* and the *pure Ego*. There are advantages and disadvantages attaching to each of these terms, and there can hardly be said to be any accepted usage. The reader is, therefore, free to accept that which best pleases him.

Meantime, it must be clear that all of our descriptions and analyses of the foregoing chapters have had primarily to do with the *object half* of consciousness, the *content side* of the mind. Perceptions, images, emotions—the things we are aware of—all belong to this objective phase of consciousness. To be sure, we could not apparently be aware of such experiences were it not for the subject phase of the mind. But once we have admitted the *reality* of this subject factor, we seem to have done all we can with it. It persistently avoids direct observation, because, forsooth, it is itself the observer.

If we regard the self as characterised by these two indissoluble aspects, and inquire what then becomes of personal identity, we have to admit at once that there can be no unchanging nature in the *object* side of consciousness. The contents of consciousness are constantly undergoing alteration, and we noticed in an earlier chapter that we probably never have exactly the same thought twice. Identity of any thorough-going kind is thus out of the question here. Of the subject side of consciousness it seems impossible to predicate anything save its existence. Its *function*, to be sure, must apparently remain fixed. It must always be the *knower annealing* the various elements of our experience into some sort of unity. But beyond this *functional* identity, which we can *infer* with some confidence, we have little evidence as to any of its possible attributes. Clearly, then, the personal identity in which common-sense believes rests on the evidence of some of the more unreflective and immediate influences such as we mentioned a few lines above.

We may remark in passing that this necessity for a subject of our states of consciousness has constituted one of the strongest rational considerations adducible in support of the belief in the soul. But it is to be said, on the other hand, that there are logically possible alternatives to this identification of the knower with the soul, so that we cannot defensibly be dogmatic even here.

Consciousness as Internal and External.—Before leaving this general topic one more distinction must be mentioned. Consciousness, when considered merely in its objective aspect, may be thought of in either of two ways. Thus, a perception of a cart may be thought of as *external*, in so far as it reports to me something outside my mind. But in so far as the perception is *my* experience, it may be thought of as *internal*. It is sometimes said, accordingly, that all consciousness viewed as external is essentially cognitive, knowledge-bringing; whereas, viewed as internal, it is feeling, self-reflecting. Certain of the classifications of feeling to which we referred in earlier chapters are based upon this conception of the *internal* reference discernible in all consciousness. But it should be evident at once that this distinction is by no means synonymous with that between the subject and object aspects of mental life.

Development of the Consciousness of Self.—Despite the extensive study given of late to the subject of this section by Baldwin (to whom the author is indebted for certain views) and others, we cannot as yet be said to have any generally accepted theory, and the description which follows is offered tentatively as the author's present conception.

It seems reasonably certain that the distinction which the *child* at an early age makes between his own personality and that of others is as completely submerged in the vague conscious continuum of *infancy* as is the distinction between different sensations. When it begins definitely to differentiate, it seems not unlikely that the first step consists in remarking the differences which characterise the behaviour of persons and the behaviour of things. Things and persons thus get set over against one another. Things are relatively stable and fixed in their actions. Persons, on the other hand, are highly irregular and unpredictable. Of course, the child's consciousness of both things and persons is from the beginning his own private personal experience. But it may safely be asserted that there is no awareness of the self in a "self-conscious" way until the vague apprehension is attained of *other* persons as distinct from things.

As the child gradually attains control over his movements, things tend in certain particulars to obey his impulses in a more immediate way than do persons. They can be seen, reached, touched, and moved more confidently and more regularly than persons. On the other hand, they show themselves altogether more imperturbable than persons to indirect modes of control. If the child cries, parent or nurse promptly responds. *Things* remain just where they were. Furthermore, persons show themselves able to furnish many comforting and agreeable experiences in the way of caresses, food, and clothing, which things of their own initiative rarely or never afford. The moment imitation becomes possible, persons offer the most satisfactory stimuli. What they do, can, by virtue of the similarity of structure in various organisms, often be approximated by the child. We might mention other distinctions which the child must feel, but these will suffice to suggest the lines along which the development takes place.

When this resolution of the objective world into persons and things is once achieved, there is every reason to think that the precipitation of self-consciousness follows close at hand, if it be not, indeed, synchronous with it. The whole process must in the nature of the case be extremely inchoate and protoplasmic in character. Nevertheless, it must contain within it the essential elements for the more elaborate differentiations of adult life. Moreover, if this be in any way a true account of the genesis of self-consciousness, it is evident that such consciousness will, from the outset, be *social* in its constitution. The child remarks certain objects which behave in a manner altogether distinct from other objects. These he comes to recognise as individuals, which he later calls persons. Something like their independence of action he comes to feel in himself. He naturally identifies himself with them, and thus gives to his first dimly recognised consciousness *of* self the *social hall-mark*. Needless to add, after what has gone before in this book, the actual *content* of his consciousness is always in larger or smaller measure social. The relations in which he finds himself are social. The criteria for the reality of many of the things which he is called upon to accept are social. Language is social. By imitation he is plunged at once into social usages, and did space permit, and were it necessary, we might trace out the whole gamut of social influences which bound his self-hood on every side. But our primary point here is that the first definite self-consciousness of the child is a consciousness in which he identifies himself in some sort with others, defines himself in terms of agreement or disagreement with others.

The fact should be emphasised, however, that the element

of disagreement is quite as important, both for the child and for society, as the element of agreement or imitation. Every individual is in some sense a variant from the human norm, and in so far he is a contributor to the richness of human life and achievement. This variation may take the form of trivial peculiarities of manner and speech, of inventions of a scientific and practical character, of reforms in morals or art; or it may be embodied in the harmless enthusiasms of a crank, or in the dangerous prepossessions of a lunatic. In each and every case the individual is making his addition to the store of social possessions. In finding that his consciousness of self necessitates his projecting himself against society, we must not, then, for a moment suppose that this means that he *merely imitates* others, and so arrives at the knowledge of his own Ego. It is in the character of variant from the norm that the genius gets his paramount significance for the social organism. Society sometimes progresses by the slow accretion of incremental changes originating from the conduct of large numbers of commonplace individuals. But the great changes which lend themselves to confident detection and identification are commonly traceable to the towering personality of some genius.

Doubtless in the earlier periods of childhood (after the consciousness of self as such has once become established) the actual *content* of such consciousness is largely personal and bodily—an awareness of impulses, of pleasures, pains, and the like. But as the mind develops and a broader appreciation is reached of the general integration of human life and the physical cosmos, this self-feeling spreads out to embrace larger and larger interests. The social factor unfolds into a vivid apprehension of the picture of ourselves which we may imagine to be entertained by various persons and groups of persons. Furthermore, we come increasingly to read into the motives and characters of others the peculiarities which introspection reveals within ourselves. In a certain sense the vagueness which marks the beginning of self-feeling is never entirely lost. We come to include in our *practical* conception of ourselves so many things which lie outside of us, that the lines which separate the self from the not-self inevitably become hazy. Thus, our bodies, our clothing, our family, our friends, our fortune, our club, our church, our country—these, and a thousand similar things, get identified in a more or less intimate way with our self, which unfolds more and more to take in these widening interests. Meantime, there is always a residuum whose status is neither clearly within nor without the self.

The question may be raised whether a child growing up alone on a desert island would fail to develop self-consciousness because of his inability to follow the course of events which we have described, with its emphasis on the distinguishing between persons and things, and its further emphasis on the social nature of self-feeling. The reply—resting on speculative probability—is that undoubtedly something corresponding to self-consciousness might develop under such conditions through the operations of imagination. But the *content* of such a self-consciousness, and the order and nature of the steps in its unfolding, would certainly differ radically from anything with which we have personal acquaintance.

Ethical and Religious Aspects of the Self.—Although in a general way the consciousness of self is from the first social in its nature, it speedily takes on two *explicitly* social aspects, the moral and the religious, which warrant a few moments' consideration. Among the very earliest of our social experiences are those of praise and criticism, reward and punishment for our deeds. Parents, guardians, and associates of all kinds unite in thus furthering or hindering our enterprises. The vivid feeling for the distinction between right and wrong is thus aroused in us at a very tender age. As we come to have a definite consciousness of our own personality, we inevitably tend to array ourselves for or against the usages which have been thus imposed upon us. We come to appreciate something of the ground upon which they rest, something of the advantages and drawbacks which attend their observance. We take as regards these matters a definite conscious attitude toward society at large and our immediate associates in particular. We evolve a distinctly ethical self, recognising certain obligations on our own part toward our fellows, and postulating a similar obligation for them in their treatment of us.

As we grow older this conception of ourselves as moral persons with duties and obligations takes on a broader and more enlightened character. We extend our sense of responsible interest from our immediate family and acquaintances to our town, state, and country, and often (among the more humanitarianly minded of us) we manage in a fairly definite way to include the interests of all mankind. Coincident with this expansion in the *range* of our moral selfhood is often to be remarked a growth in the *intelligence* of our *appreciation* of the real ethical situation. We come to detect more justly and more sympathetically both the grounds of our neighbour's moral ideals and the reasons for his occasional moral lapses, and we may become in consequence more helpful to him, as well as more valuable in furthering the general cause of moral progress in the world. Our moral self thus expands both by *intension* and *extension*.

The religious consciousness cannot ordinarily be severed altogether from the moral consciousness, yet the two mark quite distinct differences of stress which deserve separate treatment. The religious sentiments, in distinction from those of a merely moral sort, seem to involve a definite sense of *personal relationship* to a supreme, or at least superior, being. In the higher forms of religious faith this being is conceived as the incarnation of all holiness, righteousness, and truth. He is thus the one perfect companion for the highest ideal self, the one object worthy of complete reverence. Belief in such a being constitutes the essence of the most developed forms of religious faith, and around such a belief cluster all the distinctly religious emotions, such as reverence, awe, love, gratitude, and the feeling of personal confidence which we call faith.

The full mental vision of such a being, with an accompanying sense of our own unworthiness, is often the immediate forerunner of the cataclysmic experiences characterising certain forms of conversion. The whole moral and religious perspective of life is suddenly altered. We see ourselves and others in a different light, and the world takes on a new form. The frequency with which this special phenomenon is encountered during adolescence has led certain psychologists to connect the experience with the deep-seated physiological changes which mark that period. But, however much of truth there may be in this contention,—and undoubtedly there is much,—we must still recognise the fact that sudden conversion, profound and genuine reformation, is a thing met with at all ages and under the most various conditions.

Disturbances of the Self.—The consciousness of self is subject to certain striking disturbances which merit a few words. The phenomena of alternating personality are among the most interesting of these. In the "successive" form of this disorder a person may suddenly lose his memory of his past life, forget his name, his home, and his friends, and start afresh with a new name, a new occupation, etc. Often his temperament and character change simultaneously with this loss of memory. Whereas originally he may have been honest, cheerful, and vigorous, he now shows himself unreliable, pessimistic, and lazy. A few weeks or months later on he suddenly reverts to his former personality and recovers all his memories of his earlier life, although he has no vestige of recollection as to the events which occurred during the period of his altered selfhood. Cases are on record where several characters have been assumed in this way, one after the other.

In the case of "simultaneous" personalities we have a more complex and much more ambiguous condition. Here there seems to be in addition to the normal consciousness which superintends the ordinary business of life, a sort of "split-off" consciousness, which is independent of the first and can be gotten at only in indirect ways. Moreover, as in the case of *successive* personalities, the temperament and character of these two selves are often very different. The one may be gentle and pious, the other riotous and profane. Sometimes this secondary self can be tapped by whispering to the patient while he is engaged in conversation with some one else, and then the responses may be written, apparently without any cognisance on the part of the normal consciousness of what has taken place. The memories of the two selves seem to be often distinct. Sometimes, as in alternating personality of the successive type, the secondary self may know all about the primary self, without the converse appearing to be true.

These quaint modifications of self-consciousness are difficult to reconcile with many of our prepossessions as to personality and the connection of mind and body. But they at least serve one purpose of positive value. They contain an impressive warning against our natural disposition to assume that our own personal type of self-consciousness is necessarily the only type. Evidently the consciousness of self is susceptible of mutations like other forms of consciousness, and no generalisation about it should be accepted without a survey of *all* the facts. For instance, the disintegrations of personality which are met with in the various forms of insanity must be taken into account.

Minor Variations of Self-Consciousness.—Less profound and less prolonged than the disturbances already mentioned are the changes in personality which characterise certain forms of trance. In the genuine cases of so-called mediumistic trance the medium becomes more or less oblivious to ordinary sense impressions, and often appears to be half unconscious. Under these circumstances he assumes the personality of some other individual, usually some one who is dead, and his utterances purport to be expressions of the knowledge and the sentiments of the " control," as the person is called who ostensibly speaks through the medium. Many of these cases of mediumship have been carefully examined. Most of them have proved fraudulent. A few appear to be perfectly genuine, so far as concerns the psychophysiological conditions manifested. But the *interpretation* of the phenomena is a matter upon which there exists the widest divergence of expert opinion. Most scientifically trained psychologists refuse to give these cases any serious consideration, beyond admitting the possibility of their representing a genuine abnormality like insanity. A few insist that we have here fairly convincing evidence of relations among minds which transcend all our usual modes of communication with one another.

In hypnotism, also, we may meet with cases of altered personality produced under the influence of suggestion. Changes in sensitivity, in motor control, and memory are not especially difficult to produce. The phlegmatic person may become choleric, the reserved person become flippant and rude, the irreligious become pious, etc. Commonly, if the hypnotic sleep has been deep, there is, upon awakening, little or no memory of what has occurred during the trance. But all the facts can usually be recalled during a subsequent hypnotisation. A curious phenomenon is that of post-hypnotic suggestion. A person told to perform some action after awakening may have no recollection of the injunction upon arousing from the hypnotic slumber, but with few exceptions he will at the time designated faithfully execute the act. Facts of this kind have led to a good deal of needless alarm as to the dangers of hypnotism. In point of fact it is practically impossible to force a person to do anything seriously offensive to his moral or æsthetic sense of the right and the decent. Moreover, persons of normal make-up cannot be hypnotised against their wills—at all events not until the process has been performed so often as to become more or less habitual. A thing much more to be feared in our day is the auto-suggestion of a hypnotic character by virtue of which mobs and great crowds give way to the wildest and most beastly excesses. Although hypnotism undoubtedly has therapeutic value, it should not be indiscriminately cultivated by untrained persons.

Dreams afford a familiar instance of disturbed personality. Sometimes this is manifested simply in the ridiculous judgments which we pass upon dream situations, and the absurd sentiments which they call forth. Occasionally, however, we actually seem to have become some other person. Despite the frequent occurrence of dreams, no wholly satisfactory theory of their causes and conditions is yet at hand. Undoubtedly sensory stimulations, partly from the external senses, partly from the viscera and other intra-organic sources, are largely responsible for the beginning of dreams. Undoubtedly, also, the higher forms of systematised control, the "apperceptive activities" of many authors, are temporarily in abeyance. Although most of us would maintain that we often have dreamless sleep, it has been vigorously urged that we dream all the time during sleep, and that consciousness is consequently never altogether interrupted. Certainly it is true that we frequently forget our dreams with marvellous rapidity, and we ordinarily find that we are dreaming when awakened. But while these considerations afford a measure of presumptive evidence in favour of the hypothesis, they are not conclusive, and the weight of opinion unquestionably regards dreamless sleep as a frequent occurrence.

The Subconscious and the Unconscious.—Many striking and characteristic experiences are connected with regions of our personality which lie distinctly below the level of clear consciousness. Consciousness does not terminate with sharp edges which mark it off definitely and finally from the non-conscious. On the contrary, as was maintained early in our work, there is a gradual fading out from a focal centre of clearest consciousness toward a dimmer region of partial consciousness, which we may designate the zone of the *subconscious*. This subconscious area again gives way to a region of entire non-consciousness.

To the activity of the subconscious we are probably indebted for many of our unreasoned impressions and sentiments, for many of our unexpected ideas, for certain of our unreflective movements, especially those of the habitual variety. Not a few of our personal preferences and prejudices are probably referable to influences originating here. Such phenomena as those of automatic writing with the planchette, where persons may write considerable numbers of words without any clear idea of what is being written, belong to the border-line of influences lying between the subconscious and the unconscious. Taken all in all, subconscious factors must go to make up a very respectable portion of our total personality, and no doubt are accountable for many of the characteristics which sometimes cause us to wonder at ourselves and question whether or no we really have the kind of character we supposed.

The *unconscious* has been made in recent years the great panacea for all psychological and philosophical difficulties. Whatever one cannot explain otherwise may be explained by the action of the unconscious. The asserted facts of telepathy, clairvoyance, crystal-gazing, shell-hearing, hypnotism, and all the phenomena of spiritualism, not less than the metaphysical perplexities of personality, mind, matter, and their interrelations, have been treated by the universal elixir of the unconscious. Needless to say, our modest business at this point is with no such majestic influence as all this suggests. The term unconscious has two proper uses in psychology. It is, first, a limiting concept set over against consciousness of every kind; whatever is not conscious is unconscious. Evidently this use of the term is largely negative in its implication. As a positive concept the unconscious is, in the second place, practically synonymous with the physiological. Thus, to say that an unconscious factor entered in to determine certain of the movements of our voluntary muscles is simply to affirm that certain *neural* activities, whose obvious counterparts we cannot detect in consciousness, have contributed to the total mass of motor excitations. In this sense the unconscious ceases to be a sheer enigma, and becomes a more or less convenient term wherewith to designate those marginal neural actions which evidently modify the reactions we make, without, however, producing noticeable mental changes.

Summary.—If we take stock of the various points which we have canvassed in this chapter, we see that although the self undoubtedly manifests tendencies toward the systematic unification of its own experiences, it is far from being a simple unity. It is highly complex in constitution, and in many particulars highly unstable. It is distinctly and characteristically a life phenomenon, with periods of growth and expansion, periods of maturity, and periods of decay and disintegration. But after all, the feeling of selfhood is the very core of our psychical being. About it are gathered all the joys and all the miseries of life. However much a critical philosophy may shake our confidence in the implication of the feeling, the fact of its existence is for each of us the one absolutely indubitable fact.

INDEX

Abnormal, consciousness, 391; psychology, 3.
Abstract ideas, 214.
Abstraction, 214.
Accommodation, motor, in attention, 82; of lens, 99.
Acquaintance, 120.
Acquisitiveness, 303.
Action, muscular, varieties of, 48, 283.
Æsthetic feelings, 271, 281, 337*f*.
Affection, as elementary phase of feeling, 257.
After-images, 111.
After-sensations, *see* after-images.
Agreeableness as affection, 257-259.
Alimentary sensations, *see* sensations, organic.
Alternating personality, 391.
Altruistic emotions, 296.
Amœba, 19.
Analysis, sensory and intellectual, 86-89.
Anger, 299, 320.
Annelids, nervous system of, 20, 21.
Animals, reasoning of, 252.
Aphasia, auditory, 39; motor, 39; visual, 39.
Apperception, 127.
Aristotle's illusion, 132.
Association, simultaneous, 89; successive, 89, 170*ff.*; cerebral basis of, 171; important factors in, 171*ff.*; by contiguity, 174; by singularity, 174*f.*; by contrast, 175; desistent and persistent, 176.
Association centres in cortex, 34.

Attention, and adaptation of sense organ, 82; change necessary to, 76; and field of consciousness, 64*ff.*; motor factors in, 82; relation to interest, 362*ff.*; attention and will, 345; varieties of, 68; involuntary, 70, non-voluntary, or spontaneous, 69; voluntary, 68; simultaneous to different objects, 79; selective character of, 67; as mental activity, 66.
Audition, *see* hearing.
Auditory centre, 32.
Auditory image, 164.
Auditory ossicles, *fig.* 43.
Automatic acts, 48, 283.
Automatic writing, 395.
Autonomic system, 45.
Axis cylinder, 16, *fig.* 4.
Axone, 16, 18.

BAIN, 275, 374.
BALDWIN, 65, 292, 358, 386.
Belief, 338.
BERKELEY, 150.
Biology and psychology, 8.
Black, *see* colour.
Blind-spot, *fig.* 46.
Bodily expression and emotion 316, 334.
Brain, structure and functions of, and connection with consciousness, 21-45.
Brightness sensations, 109.

CALKINS, 175.
Calmness, as affective element, 258.
Canals, semicircular, 98, 105.
Cell-body, 15*ff.*

INDEX

Cerebral laws and association, 171.
Cerebrum, 32.
Cerebellum, 32.
Change in Consciousness, 76.
Character, Chapter XXII.
Child psychology, 3.
Chromæsthesia, 202.
Choice, *see* volition.
Circulatory sensations, *see* sensations, organic.
CLAY, 156.
Clearness in attention, 66.
Coalescence of sensations, 126.
Cochlea, *figs.* 43, 44.
Cognition, *see* Chapters V. to XII. inclusive.
Cold, sensations of, 103; neural basis of, 93*f.*
Colour blindness, normal peripheral, 112; abnormal, 101.
Colour, complementaries and mixtures, 110; sensations of, 109.
Comparative psychology, 4.
Comparison, process of, 86, 218.
Complex tone, 109.
Conation and attention, 66; and will, 353.
Concept, nature of, 208, 215; and image, 209; function of, 215; change and growth of, 216*ff.*; and meaning, 203; and judgment, 227.
Conscience, feeling of, 337.
Consciousness, appearance of, 50; definition of, 1; relation of to the nervous system, Chapter III.; motor aspects of, 283, 346.
Contiguity, association by, 174*ff.*
Contrast, in colour, 112; in space perception, 153; in association, 174*f.*
Convergence of eyes, 99.
Coördinations, **primary,** 283; acquired, 294; establishment of control over, 53*ff.*, Chapter XX.
COPE, 291.
Corpora quadrigemina, 22, 28.

Corpus callosum, 37, *figs.* 21, 25, 26.
Cortex, cerebral, 32-45, *figs.* 18-22.
Corti, organ of, *fig.* 42.
Cranial nerves, 31, *fig.* 18.
Curiosity, 301.
Currents in nerves, *see* nerve currents.
Cutaneous sensations, *see* sensations.

DARWIN, 327.
Deaf-mutes, 217.
Deduction, 240.
Dendrite, 16, 18.
Desire, analysis of, and relation to volition, 374*ff.*
DEWEY, 327.
Difference, feeling of, 87.
Difference limen, *see* Weber's law.
Diffusion, law of, 53.
Disagreeableness as affection, 257.
Discrimination, as analytic attention, 86; relation to association, 89.
Dispersed attention, 81.
Dissociation, *see* discrimination.
Distance, perception of, 150.
Dizziness, and relation to semicircular canals, 105.
Double personality, *see* alternating personality.
Dreams, 394.
Dura mater, 21.
Duration, perception of, 156; of sensations, 115; of sensations in relation to feelings, 261.

Ear, *figs.* 42-44.
Earthworm, nervous system of, *fig.* 8.
EBBINGHAUS, 23.
Effort, feeling of, 369.
Ego, *see* self.
Embarrassment, 320.
Emotion, Chapters XVIII., XIX.; bodily factors in, 316;

origin of, 326; relation to instincts, 315.
Emulation, *see* rivalry.
End-organs, 91-101.
Envy, 305.
Epistemology, 9.
Ethical feelings, 271, 337.
Excess discharge, law of, 348*ff*.
Excitement, as affective element, 258.
Experimental psychology, 5.
Extensity, in sensation, 115; in space perception, 142.

Faith, 391.
Familiarity, feeling of, 188, 195.
Fear, 298, 319.
Feeling, Chapters XIII. and XIV.; elements of, 257; classifications of, 270; relation to emotion, 337.
Folk psychology, 3.
Forgetting, 192.
Fovea, 99, *fig.* 46.
Freedom of will, 380.
Fringe of consciousness, 66.
Fusion, or coalescence, 126.

General idea, 208.
Generic idea, 210.
Genetic psychology, 4.
Genius, and association, 174.
GORDON, 85.
Grey, sensations of, *ee* brightness.
Grief, 320.
GROOS, 306.
Gustatory sensations, *see* taste.

Habit, formation of, 52*ff*.; results of, 58; ethical significance of, 61; relation to volition, 60; in thought, 61.
Hallucinations, 135.
Hardness, consciousness of, 103.
Hatred, 299.
Hearing, sensations of, 108; cortical centre for, 32; end-organ of, 96, *figs.* 42-44.
Heat, sensations of, 103.
Hemianopsia, 39, *fig.* 23.
Hemispheres, connection with volition and memory, 38; structure of, 32.
Humour, feeling of, 324.
Hunger sensations, 106.
Hypnotic states, 393.

Ideas, connection with images, 165; and concepts, 208; motor, 353.
Identity, personal, 382; modifications of, 391*ff*.
Illusion, 132.
Images, distinction from sensation and perception, 163; types of, 165; function of, 176; relation to idea, 165; to volition, 352-354.
Imagination, Chapter VIII.
Imitation, as instinctive, 307; as volitional, 358.
Impulse, Chapter XVII.
Inattention, 81.
Induction, 241.
Inhibition, and volition, 55, 352.
Instinct, Chapters XV. to XVII. inclusive; origin of, 291; value of, 293; relation to emotion, 315; variability of, 289; human, Chapter XVI.
Intellectual feeling, 270.
Intensity of sensation, 113; relation to affective consciousness, 261; and Weber's law, 114.
Interest, nature of, 363; relation to attention, 365; to volition, 362-368.
Introspection, 4.

JAMES, 66, 120, 142, 171, 175, 185, 205, 297, 315, 316, 345.
Jealousy, 305.
Judgment, analysis and forms of, 225*f*.; relation to conception, 227*ff*.; to reasoning, 236*ff*.; genesis of, 229*ff*.

Kinæsthetic, sensation, 94, 105; image, 164; function in establishment of motor control, 344, 354.

INDEX

Knowledge, development of, 218*ff*., 232*ff*.; theory of, 9.

Labyrinth, *figs*. 43, 44.
LANGE, 316.
Lapsed intelligence, theory of, 291.
Laughter, significance of, 333.
Limen, 114.
Local sign, nature of, 147.
Localisation, of functions in the hemispheres, 32*ff*.
LOTZE, 147.
Love, 305.

MARSHALL, 275.
Meaning, apprehension of, 203*ff*.
Mediums, 392*f*.
Medullary sheath, 16.
Medulla oblongata, 22, 30, *fig*. 18.
Memory, Chapter IX., affective, 265; analysis of, 185: defects of, 194; and forgetting, 192; physical basis of, 186; distinction between memory and imagination, 184; relation to recognition, 187*ff*.; improvement of, 196*ff*.; idiosyncracies of, 202.
Mental activity, *see* attention and effort.
Mental blindness, *see* aphasia, visual.
Metaphysics, 9.
Mind, meaning of the word, 2.
Modesty, 297.
Molluscs, nervous system of, 20, *fig*. 9.
Mood, 335.
Morbid psychology, 3.
Motion, sensations of, images of, *see* kinæsthetic.
Motor aphasia, 39.
Motor region of cortex, 34.
MUENSTERBERG, 275.
Muscular sensations, *see* kinæsthetic.

Nerve-currents, nature of, and rate of conduction, 19.
Nerve-endings, *see* end-organs.

Nerves, structure of, 14*ff*.; functions of, 14.
Nervous system, central, 21*ff*.; autonomic, 45.
Neurilemma, 17.
Neuroglia, 18.
Neurone, definition of, 15.
Neurones, peripheral, 23; cortical, 32; subcortical, 24.
Noise, 108.

Object, perception of, 80, 119, 122; fixation of attention and change of, 76.
Occipital cortex and vision, 33.
Odour, *see* smell.
Olfactory end-organ, 94-95, *figs*. 39, 40.
Olfactory region of cortex, 33.
Optic end-organ, *see* retina.
Organic selection, theory of, 292.
Organic sensations, *see* sensations.
Otoliths, 98.
Overtones, 109.

Pain, as sensation, 93; its relation to affection, 259.
Partial tone, 109.
Passion, 335.
Passive consciousness, 75.
Peckhams, 291.
Perception, Chapter VI.; and sensation, 118; and ideational activities, 163; neural basis of, 137; of space and time, Chapter VII.
Personal identity, *see* identity.
Philosophy and psychology, 8.
Physiological psychology, 6.
Pia mater, 21.
Pitch, 108.
Play, 306.
Pleasure, as affective element, 257.
Practical reasoning, 235.
Present, the specious, 156.
Pressure, sensations of, *see* touch.
Productive imagination, 167; relation to reproductive imagination, 169.

INDEX

Psychical dispositions, 192.
Psychology, definition of, 1; methods of, 4; fields of, 3; relation to philosophy, 8; to the natural sciences, 7; to education, 10.
Psychophysics, 6; and character of human organism, 11*ff*.

Quality, of sensations, 101; consciousness of, as sensation, 118.

Race psychology, 3.
Reasoning, Chapters XI., XII.; elements of, 224; forms of, Chapter XII.; in brutes, 252.
Recognition, sensory, 188; ideational, 190; relation to memory, 187.
Reflex action, definition of, 286; relation to instincts, 288; variability of, 286.
Relations, between objects, feelings of, 205.
Relativity of knowledge, 219.
Relaxation, as affective element, 258.
Religious feeling, 271, 389.
Representation, general nature of, 161.
Reproductive imagination, 167; relation to productive imagination, 169.
Resistance, consciousness of, 104.
Respiratory sensations, *see* sensations, organic.
Retention of material in memory, 192.
Retina, 98*ff*., *figs*. 45-47.
RIBOT, 296.
Rivalry, 304.
Rhythm, of attention, 77; in judgments of time, 157.
ROYCE, 258.

Sameness, feeling of, as element in apprehension of meaning, 87, 204*f*.
Satisfaction, feeling of, 331.
Selection, in attention, 67.

Self, Chapter XXIII.; development of feeling of, 385; disturbance of, 391; ethical and religious aspects of the, 389; identity of the, 382; social nature of, 387.
Semicircular canals, 98, *figs*. 43, 44; sensations from, 105.
Sensation, Chapter V.; and perception, 118; functions of, 116; qualities of, 101*ff*.; intensity of, 113; duration of, 115; extensity in, 115; common characteristics, 116.
Sensations, of sound, 108; of sight, 109; of smell, 106; of taste, 107; of temperature, 103; of touch, 103; organic, 106; of movement, 105.
Sense organs, structure of, 93*ff*.
Sensory c res in cortex, 32*ff*., *figs*. 18-21.
Sentiment 336.
Shyness, 299.
Sight, *see* vision.
Similarity, association by, 174*ff*.
Simple tone, 108.
Size, apparent of objects, 147, 152.
Skin-senses, *see* sensations.
Smell, sensations of, 106; end-organ, 94, *fig*. 39; cortical basis, 33.
Sociability, 299.
Social feeling, 271, 387.
Social psychology, 3.
Softness, consciousness of, 103.
Soul, in psychology, 2; relation to the self, 385.
Space, *see* perception of space.
Span, or scope, of consciousness, 79.
Speech, centres of, in cortex, 40, *fig*. 19; as instinctive, 307.
SPENCER, 292, 306.
Spinal cord, structure and functions of, 24*ff*.; *figs*. 13-17.
Spontaneous attention, 69; relation to interest, 362.
Starfish, nervous system of, *fig*. 6.
Strain, as affective element, 258.

Strain sensations, 85, 370.
Subconscious, the, 66, 394.
Substantive states of mind, 166.
Symbolic nature of presentational consciousness, 204.
Sympathetic system, 45.
Sympathy, 296*f.*
Synæsthesia, 126.

Tactile centre in cortex, 33.
Tactile image, 164*f.*
Taste, sensations of, 107; end-organ for, 95, *fig.* 41; centres in cortex, 33.
Telepathy, 395.
Temperament, 335.
Temperature, sensations of, 103; end-organs for 93*ff.*, *figs.* 36-38; centres in cortex, 33.
Tendons, sensations from, *see* sensations of movement.
Third dimension of space, perception of, 149*ff.*
Thirst, sensation of, 106.
Thought, order of, 170*ff.*
Threshold, *see* limen.
Tickling, 104.
Timbre, 109.
Time, judgment of intervals of, 156; memory of, 158.

Tone, as auditory element 108.
Touch, sensations of, 103; end-organs of, 93; cortical centres for, 33; images of, 164*f.*; in space perception, 147-149, 154.
Tympanum, *fig.* 43.

Unconscious, the, 66, 394.
Unity of thought, 79*ff.*

Vision, sensations of, 109; end-organ of, 98, *figs.* 45-47; centre in cortex, 33; mental images of, 164.
Volition, Chapters XX.-XXII.; relation to attention, 345; to imagery, 343, 352; to impulse, 347; to character, Chapter XXII.
Voluminousness of sensations, 142.

Walking, 286.
Warmth, sensations of, 103.
Weber's law, 114.
WEISSMANN, 292.
Will, *see* volition.
WUNDT, 258, 292, 328.

WORKS IN PHILOSOPHY AND PSYCHOLOGY

Aikins's Principles of Logic.
By Herbert Austin Aikins, Professor of Philosophy in Western Reserve University. x + 489 pp. 12mo. $1.50.

Angell's Psychology.
By James Rowland Angell, Professor of Pyschology in the University of Chicago. 12mo. $1.50.

Baldwin's Elements of Psychology.
By James Mark Baldwin, Professor in Johns Hopkins University. xv + 372 pp. 12mo. $1.50.

Baldwin's Handbook of Psychology.
By James Mark Baldwin, Professor in the Johns Hopkins University.
SENSES AND INTELLECT. xiv + 343 pp. 8vo. Revised Edition. $1.80.
FEELING AND WILL. xii + 394 pp. 8vo. $2.00.

Colegrove's Memory.
An Inductive Study. By F. W. Colegrove. With an Introduction by G. Stanley Hall, LL.D. 369 pp. 12mo. $1.50.

Dewey & Tufts's Ethics.
By John Dewey, Professor in Columbia University, and James H. Tufts, Professor in the University of Chicago. (American Science Series.) [In preparation.]

Falckenberg's History of Modern Philosophy.
Nicolas of Cusa to the Present Time. By Richard Falckenberg, Professor in the University of Erlangen. Translated, with the author's co-operation, by A. C. Armstrong, Jr., Professor of Philosophy in Wesleyan University. xvi + 655 pp. 8vo. $3.50.

Hyde's Practical Ethics.
By William De Witt Hyde, President of Bowdoin College. xi + 208 pp. 16mo. 80 cents.

James's Principles of Psychology. ADVANCED COURSE.
By William James, Professor of Psychology in Harvard University. Two volumes. 8vo. (American Science Series.) $4.80.

James's Psychology. BRIEFER COURSE.
By William James, Professor in Harvard University. xiii + 478 pp. 12mo. (American Science Series.) $1.60.

James's Talks to Teachers on Psychology.
By William James, Professor in Harvard University, author of "Principles of Psychology." xii + 301 pp. 12mo. $1.50.

Jastrow's Chapters in Modern Psychology.
By Joseph Jastrow, Professor in the University of Wisconsin. [In preparation.]

Works in Philosophy and Psychology.

Paulsen's Introduction to Philosophy.

By Friedrich Paulsen, Professor in the University of Berlin. Translated, with the author's sanction, by Frank Thilly, Professor in the University of Missouri. First American from the Third German Edition. xxiv + 437 pp. 8vo. $3.00.

Wenley's Outlines of Kant's Critique.

Outline Introductory to Kant's Critique of Pure Reason. By R. M. Wenley, Professor in the University of Michigan. iv + 66 pp. 16mo. 75 cents.

Zeller's History of Greek Philosophy.

By Dr. Edward Zeller. Translated, with the author's sanction, by Sarah F. Alleyne and Evelyn Abbott. xiv + 363 pp. 12mo. $1.40.

Modern Philosophers

Edited by Professor E. HERSHEY SNEATH

Descartes: The Philosophy of Descartes.

Selected and translated by H. A. P. Torrey, Professor in the University of Vermont. xii + 345 pp. 12mo. $1.50.

Hegel: The Philosophy of Hegel.

Translated extracts from Hegel's works, with an introduction by Josiah Royce, Professor in Harvard College. [In preparation.]

Hume: The Philosophy of Hume.

Selected, with an introduction, by Herbert A. Aikins, Professor in Western Reserve University. 176 pp. 12mo. $1.00.

Locke: The Philosophy of Locke.

By John E. Russell, A.M., Professor of Philosophy in Williams College. 160 pp. 12mo. $1.00.

Reid: The Philosophy of Reid.

With introduction and notes by E. Hershey Sneath, Ph.D., Instructor in Philosophy in Yale University. viii + 368 pp. 12mo. $1.50.

Spinoza: The Philosophy of Spinoza.

Translated from the Latin, and edited with notes by George Stuart Fullerton, Professor of Philosophy in the University of Pennsylvania. Second Edition, Enlarged. vi + 358 pp. 12mo. $1.50.

HENRY HOLT AND COMPANY
NEW YORK